VW Golf
Owners Workshop Manual

Peter T Gill

Models covered

(5633 - 400)

Golf ('Mk VI') Hatchback & Estate

Petrol: 1.4 litre (1390cc), inc. turbo
Turbo-diesel: 1.6 litre (1599cc) & 2.0 litre (1968cc)

*Does NOT cover models with 1.2 litre, 1.6 litre or 2.0 litre petrol engines or
1.4 litre TSi supercharged/turbo ('Twincharger') petrol engine*
Does NOT cover GTI or R versions, or Golf Plus, Golf Cabriolet or Jetta

© Haynes Publishing 2014

A book in the **Haynes Owners Workshop Manual Series**

ABCDE
FGHIJ
KLMNO
PQRST

ISBN **978 0 85733 633 0**

British Library Cataloguing in Publication Data
A catalogue record for this book is available from the British Library.

Printed in the USA

Haynes Publishing
Sparkford, Yeovil, Somerset BA22 7JJ, England

Haynes North America, Inc
861 Lawrence Drive, Newbury Park, California 91320, USA

Haynes Publishing Nordiska AB
Box 1504, 751 45 UPPSALA, Sverige

Contents

Contents

REPAIRS AND OVERHAUL

Engine and associated systems

Transmission

Brakes and Suspension

Body equipment

REFERENCE

Index

The Mk 6 Golf models covered by this manual date from January 2009 to October 2012 and are available in 3- and 5-door Hatchback body styles and 5-door estate models.

Models have been produced with a wide range of engines, including 1.2, 1.4, 1.6 and 2.0 litre petrol turbo and non-turbo versions, as well as normally-aspirated and turbocharged 1.6 and 2.0 litre diesel engines. All engines use either 'indirect' or 'direct' fuel injection, and are fitted with a wide range of emission control systems. All the engines are of a well-proven design and, provided regular maintenance is carried out, are unlikely to give trouble. The engines covered in this manual are 1.4-litre petrol (turbo and non-turbo engines) and 1.6 litre & 2.0 litre turbo diesel engines.

Fully-independent front and rear suspension is fitted, with the components attached to a subframe assembly; the rear suspension uses trailing arms together with multi-link transverse arms.

A five- or six-speed manual gearbox is fitted, with a six- or seven-speed DSG semi-automatic transmission available for petrol and diesel models.

A wide range of standard and optional equipment is available within the model range to suit most tastes, including an anti-lock braking system and air conditioning.

For the home mechanic, Golf models are straightforward vehicles to maintain, and most of the items requiring frequent attention are easily accessible.

Your Golf Manual

The aim of this manual is to help you get the best value from your vehicle. It can do so in several ways. It can help you decide what work must be done (even should you choose to get it done by a garage). It will also provide information on routine maintenance and servicing, and give a logical course of action and diagnosis when random faults occur. However, it is hoped that you will use the manual by tackling the work yourself. On simpler jobs it may even be quicker than booking the car into a garage and going there twice, to leave and collect it. Perhaps most important, a lot of money can be saved by avoiding the costs a garage must charge to cover its labour and overheads.

The manual has drawings and descriptions to show the function of the various components so that their layout can be understood. Tasks are described and photographed in a clear step-by-step sequence.

References to the 'left' and 'right' of the vehicle are in the sense of a person in the driver's seat facing forward.

Acknowledgements

Thanks are due to Draper Tools Limited, who provided some of the workshop tools, and to all those people at Sparkford who helped in the production of this manual.

This manual is not a direct reproduction of the vehicle manufacturer's data, and its publication should not be taken as implying any technical approval by the vehicle manufacturers or importers.

We take great pride in the accuracy of information given in this manual, but vehicle manufacturers make alterations and design changes during the production run of a particular vehicle of which they do not inform us. No liability can be accepted by the authors or publishers for loss, damage or injury caused by any errors in, or omissions from, the information given.

Working on your car can be dangerous. This page shows just some of the potential risks and hazards, with the aim of creating a safety-conscious attitude.

General hazards

Scalding

• Don't remove the radiator or expansion tank cap while the engine is hot.
• Engine oil, transmission fluid or power steering fluid may also be dangerously hot if the engine has recently been running.

Burning

• Beware of burns from the exhaust system and from any part of the engine. Brake discs and drums can also be extremely hot immediately after use.

Crushing

• When working under or near a raised vehicle, always supplement the jack with axle stands, or use drive-on ramps.
Never venture under a car which is only supported by a jack.
• Take care if loosening or tightening high-torque nuts when the vehicle is on stands. Initial loosening and final tightening should be done with the wheels on the ground.

Fire

• Fuel is highly flammable; fuel vapour is explosive.
• Don't let fuel spill onto a hot engine.
• Do not smoke or allow naked lights (including pilot lights) anywhere near a vehicle being worked on. Also beware of creating sparks (electrically or by use of tools).
• Fuel vapour is heavier than air, so don't work on the fuel system with the vehicle over an inspection pit.
• Another cause of fire is an electrical overload or short-circuit. Take care when repairing or modifying the vehicle wiring.
• Keep a fire extinguisher handy, of a type suitable for use on fuel and electrical fires.

Electric shock

• Ignition HT and Xenon headlight voltages can be dangerous, especially to people with heart problems or a pacemaker. Don't work on or near these systems with the engine running or the ignition switched on.

• Mains voltage is also dangerous. Make sure that any mains-operated equipment is correctly earthed. Mains power points should be protected by a residual current device (RCD) circuit breaker.

Fume or gas intoxication

• Exhaust fumes are poisonous; they can contain carbon monoxide, which is rapidly fatal if inhaled. Never run the engine in a confined space such as a garage with the doors shut.
• Fuel vapour is also poisonous, as are the vapours from some cleaning solvents and paint thinners.

Poisonous or irritant substances

• Avoid skin contact with battery acid and with any fuel, fluid or lubricant, especially antifreeze, brake hydraulic fluid and Diesel fuel. Don't syphon them by mouth. If such a substance is swallowed or gets into the eyes, seek medical advice.
• Prolonged contact with used engine oil can cause skin cancer. Wear gloves or use a barrier cream if necessary. Change out of oil-soaked clothes and do not keep oily rags in your pocket.
• Air conditioning refrigerant forms a poisonous gas if exposed to a naked flame (including a cigarette). It can also cause skin burns on contact.

Asbestos

• Asbestos dust can cause cancer if inhaled or swallowed. Asbestos may be found in gaskets and in brake and clutch linings. When dealing with such components it is safest to assume that they contain asbestos.

Special hazards

Hydrofluoric acid

• This extremely corrosive acid is formed when certain types of synthetic rubber, found in some O-rings, oil seals, fuel hoses etc, are exposed to temperatures above 4000C. The rubber changes into a charred or sticky substance containing the acid. *Once formed, the acid remains dangerous for years. If it gets onto the skin, it may be necessary to amputate the limb concerned.*
• When dealing with a vehicle which has suffered a fire, or with components salvaged from such a vehicle, wear protective gloves and discard them after use.

The battery

• Batteries contain sulphuric acid, which attacks clothing, eyes and skin. Take care when topping-up or carrying the battery.
• The hydrogen gas given off by the battery is highly explosive. Never cause a spark or allow a naked light nearby. Be careful when connecting and disconnecting battery chargers or jump leads.

Air bags

• Air bags can cause injury if they go off accidentally. Take care when removing the steering wheel and trim panels. Special storage instructions may apply.

Diesel injection equipment

• Diesel injection pumps supply fuel at very high pressure. Take care when working on the fuel injectors and fuel pipes.

Warning: Never expose the hands, face or any other part of the body to injector spray; the fuel can penetrate the skin with potentially fatal results.

Remember...

DO

• Do use eye protection when using power tools, and when working under the vehicle.
• Do wear gloves or use barrier cream to protect your hands when necessary.
• Do get someone to check periodically that all is well when working alone on the vehicle.
• Do keep loose clothing and long hair well out of the way of moving mechanical parts.
• Do remove rings, wristwatch etc, before working on the vehicle – especially the electrical system.
• Do ensure that any lifting or jacking equipment has a safe working load rating adequate for the job.

DON'T

• Don't attempt to lift a heavy component which may be beyond your capability – get assistance.
• Don't rush to finish a job, or take unverified short cuts.
• Don't use ill-fitting tools which may slip and cause injury.
• Don't leave tools or parts lying around where someone can trip over them. Mop up oil and fuel spills at once.
• Don't allow children or pets to play in or near a vehicle being worked on.

The following pages are intended to help in dealing with common roadside emergencies and breakdowns. You will find more detailed fault finding information at the back of the manual, and repair information in the main chapters.

If your car won't start and the starter motor doesn't turn

☐ If it's a model with automatic transmission, make sure the selector is in the P or N position.
☐ Open the bonnet and make sure that the battery terminals are clean and tight.
☐ Switch on the headlights and try to start the engine. If the headlights go very dim when you're trying to start, the battery is probably flat. Try jump starting using another car.

If your car won't start even though the starter motor turns as normal

☐ Is there fuel in the tank?
☐ Is there moisture on electrical components under the bonnet? Switch off the ignition, and then wipe off any obvious dampness with a dry cloth. Spray a water-repellent aerosol product (WD-40 or equivalent) on ignition and fuel system electrical connectors like those shown in the photos. Pay special attention to the ignition coils wiring connector. (Note that diesel engines do not normally suffer from damp.)

A Check the condition and security of the battery connections.

B Check that the fuses in the fusebox located on the left-hand side of the engine compartment.

C Check the wiring to the ignition coils beneath the engine top cover (petrol models only).

Check that electrical connections are secure (with the ignition switched off) and spray them with a water-dispersant spray like WD-40 if you suspect a problem due to damp.

D Check that the starter motor wiring is secure.

Jump starting

1 *The battery has been drained by repeated attempts to start, or by leaving the lights on.*

2 *The charging system is not working properly (alternator drivebelt slack or broken, alternator wiring fault or alternator itself faulty).*

3 *The battery itself is at fault (electrolyte low, or battery worn out).*

When jump-starting a car, observe the following precautions:

✓ Before connecting the booster battery, make sure that the ignition is switched off.

   Caution: Remove the key in case the central locking engages when the jump leads are connected

✓ Ensure that all electrical equipment (lights, heater, wipers, etc) is switched off.

✓ Take note of any special precautions printed on the battery case.

✓ Make sure that the booster battery is the same voltage as the discharged one in the vehicle.

✓ If the battery is being jump-started from the battery in another vehicle, the two vehicles MUST NOT TOUCH each other.

✓ Make sure that the transmission is in neutral (or PARK, in the case of automatic transmission).

1 Connect one end of the red jump lead to the positive (+) terminal of the flat battery.

2 Connect the other end of the red lead to the positive (+) terminal of the booster battery.

3 Connect one end of the black jump lead to the negative (-) terminal of the booster battery.

4 Connect the other end of the black jump lead to a bolt or bracket on the engine block, well away from the battery, on the vehicle to be started.

5 Make sure that the jump leads will not come into contact with the fan, drive-belts or other moving parts of the engine.

6 Start the engine using the booster battery and run it at idle speed. Switch on the lights, rear window demister and heater blower motor, then disconnect the jump leads in the reverse order of connection. Turn off the lights etc.

Wheel changing

⚠ **Warning: Do not change a wheel in a situation where you risk being hit by other traffic. On busy roads, try to stop in a lay-by or a gateway. Be wary of passing traffic while changing the wheel – it is easy to become distracted by the job in hand.**

Preparation

☐ When a puncture occurs, stop as soon as it is safe to do so.

☐ Park on firm level ground, if possible, and well out of the way of other traffic.

☐ Use hazard warning lights if necessary.

☐ If you have one, use a warning triangle to alert other drivers of your presence.

☐ Apply the handbrake and engage first or reverse gear (or Park on models with automatic transmission).

☐ Chock the wheel diagonally opposite the one being removed – a couple of large stones will do for this.

☐ If the ground is soft, use a flat piece of wood to spread the load under the jack.

Changing the wheel

1 The spare wheel and tools are stored in the luggage compartment, lift up the floor panel/carpet. Release the retaining strap (where fitted) and remove the tool kit from the centre of the spare wheel. Unscrew the centre fastener and remove the spare wheel.

2 Use the wire hook to remove the wheel bolt caps. Use the wheel brace to slacken each of the wheel bolts by half a turn.

3 Use the special adapter when slackening the locking wheel bolts.

4 Make sure the jack is located on firm ground, and engage the jack head correctly with the sill. Then raise the jack until the wheel is raised clear of the ground.

5 Unscrew the wheel bolts (using the adapter provided) and remove the wheel. Place the wheel under the vehicle sill in case the jack fails.

6 Fit the spare wheel and screw in the bolts. Lightly tighten the bolts with the wheel brace then lower the car to the ground.

7 Securely tighten the wheel bolts in a diagonal sequence then refit the wheel trim/ hub cap/wheel bolt covers (as applicable). Stow the punctured wheel and tools back in the boot, and secure them in position.

Finally...

☐ Remove the wheel chock.

☐ Check the tyre pressure on the wheel just fitted. If it is low, or if you don't have a pressure gauge with you, drive slowly to the next garage and inflate the tyre to the correct pressure.

☐ The wheel bolts should be slackened and retightened to the specified torque at the earliest possible opportunity (see Chapter 1A or 1B).

☐ Have the damaged tyre or wheel repaired as soon as possible, or another puncture will leave you stranded.

Note: *If a temporary 'space-saver' spare wheel has been fitted. Special conditions apply to its use. This type of spare wheel is only intended for use in an emergency, and should not remain fitted any longer than it takes to get the punctured tyre repaired. While the temporary wheel is in use, ensure it is inflated to the correct pressure, do not exceed 50mph, and avoid harsh acceleration, braking or cornering.*

Identifying leaks

Puddles on the garage floor or drive, or obvious wetness under the bonnet or underneath the car, suggest a leak that needs investigating. It can sometimes be difficult to decide where the leak is coming from, especially if an engine undershield is fitted. Leaking oil or fluid can also be blown rearwards by the passage of air under the car, giving a false impression of where the problem lies.

 Warning: Most automotive oils and fluids are poisonous. Wash them off skin, and change out of contaminated clothing, without delay.

 The smell of a fluid leaking from the car may provide a clue to what's leaking. Some fluids are distinctively coloured. It may help to remove the engine undershield, clean the car carefully and to park it over some clean paper overnight as an aid to locating the source of the leak. Remember that some leaks may only occur while the engine is running.

Sump oil

Engine oil may leak from the drain plug...

Oil from filter

...or from the base of the oil filter.

Gearbox oil

Gearbox oil can leak from the seals at the inboard ends of the driveshafts.

Antifreeze

Leaking antifreeze often leaves a crystalline deposit like this.

Brake fluid

A leak occurring at a wheel is almost certainly brake fluid.

Power steering fluid

Power steering fluid may leak from the pipe connectors on the steering rack.

Towing

When all else fails, you may find yourself having to get a tow home – or of course you may be helping somebody else. Long-distance recovery should only be done by a garage or breakdown service. For shorter distances, DIY towing using another car is easy enough, but observe the following points:

☐ Use a proper tow-rope – they are not expensive. The vehicle being towed must display an ON TOW sign in its rear window.
☐ Always turn the ignition key to the 'on' position when the vehicle is being towed, so that the steering lock is released, and the direction indicator and brake lights work.

☐ The towing eye is kept inside the spare wheel (see *Wheel changing*). To fit the eye, unclip the access cover from the relevant bumper and screw the eye firmly into position
☐ Before being towed, release the handbrake and select neutral on the transmission.
Caution: On models with automatic transmission, do not tow the car at speeds in excess of 30 mph or for a distance greater than 30 miles. If towing speeds/ distances are to exceed these limits, then the car must be towed with its front wheels off the ground.

☐ Note that greater-than-usual pedal pressure will be required to operate the brakes, since the vacuum servo unit is only operational with the engine running.
☐ The driver of the car being towed must keep the tow-rope taut at all times to avoid snatching.
☐ Make sure that both drivers know the route before setting off.
☐ Only drive at moderate speeds and keep the distance towed to a minimum. Drive smoothly and allow plenty of time for slowing down at junctions.

Introduction

There are some very simple checks which need only take a few minutes to carry out, but which could save you a lot of inconvenience and expense.

These checks require no great skill or special tools, and the small amount of time they take to perform could prove to be very well spent, for example:

☐ Keeping an eye on tyre condition and pressures, will not only help to stop them wearing out prematurely, but could also save your life.

☐ Many breakdowns are caused by electrical problems. Battery-related faults are particularly common, and a quick check on a regular basis will often prevent the majority of these.

☐ If your car develops a brake fluid leak, the first time you might know about it is when your brakes don't work properly. Checking the level regularly will give advance warning of this kind of problem.

☐ If the oil or coolant levels run low, the cost of repairing any engine damage will be far greater than fixing the leak, for example.

Underbonnet check points

◄ 1.4 litre petrol engine

A *Engine oil level dipstick*

B *Engine oil filler cap*

C *Coolant expansion tank*

D *Brake (and clutch) fluid reservoir*

E *Screen washer fluid reservoir*

F *Battery*

◄ 1.6 litre diesel engine

A *Engine oil level dipstick*

B *Engine oil filler cap*

C *Coolant expansion tank*

D *Brake (and clutch) fluid reservoir*

E *Screen washer fluid reservoir*

F *Battery*

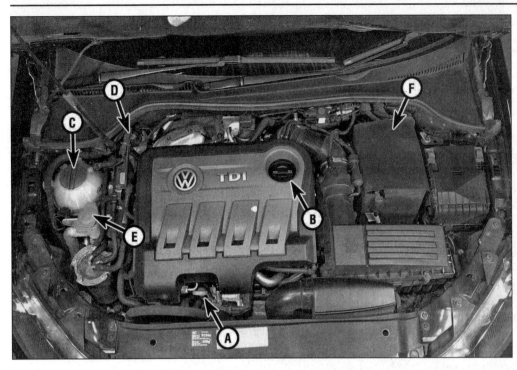

◀ 2.0 litre diesel engine

A *Engine oil level dipstick*

B *Engine oil filler cap*

C *Coolant expansion tank*

D *Brake (and clutch) fluid reservoir*

E *Screen washer fluid reservoir*

F *Battery*

Engine oil level

Before you start

✔ Make sure that the car is on level ground.
✔ Check the oil level before the car is driven, or at least 5 minutes after the engine has been switched off.

> **HAYNES HiNT**
> *If the oil is checked immediately after driving the vehicle, some of the oil will remain in the upper engine components, resulting in an inaccurate reading on the dipstick.*

The correct oil

Modern engines place great demands on their oil. It is very important that the correct oil for your car is used (see *Lubricants and fluids*).

Car care

● If you have to add oil frequently, you should check whether you have any oil leaks. Place some clean paper under the car overnight, and check for stains in the morning. If there are no leaks, then the engine may be burning oil.

● Always maintain the level between the upper and lower dipstick marks (see photo 2). If the level is too low, severe engine damage may occur. Oil seal failure may result if the engine is overfilled by adding too much oil.

1 The dipstick is located at the front of the engine (see *Underbonnet check points*); the dipstick is often brightly coloured or has a picture of an oil-can on the top for identification. Withdraw the dipstick.

3 Oil is added through the filler cap aperture, unscrew the cap.

2 Note the oil level on the end of the dipstick, which should be between the upper (MAX) mark and lower (MIN) mark.

4 Top-up the level; a funnel may help to reduce spillage. Add the oil slowly, checking the level on the dipstick often. Don't overfill (see *Car care*).

Coolant level

Warning: Do not attempt to remove the expansion tank pressure cap when the engine is hot, as there is a very great risk of scalding. Do not leave open containers of coolant about, as it is poisonous.

Car care

● With a sealed-type cooling system, adding coolant should not be necessary on a regular basis. If frequent topping-up is required, it is likely there is a leak. Check the radiator, all hoses and joint faces for signs of staining or wetness, and rectify as necessary.

● It is important that antifreeze is used in the cooling system all year round, not just during the winter months. Don't top up with water alone, as the antifreeze will become diluted.

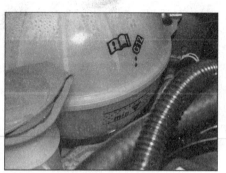

1 The coolant level must be checked with the engine cold; the coolant level should be between the MAX and MIN marks on the expansion tank.

2 If topping-up is necessary, remove the pressure cap (see Warning) from the expansion tank. Slowly unscrew the cap to release any pressure present in the cooling system, and remove the cap.

3 Add a mixture of water and antifreeze to the expansion tank until the coolant level is between the level marks. Once the level is correct, securely refit the cap.

Brake (and clutch) fluid level

Warning: Brake fluid can harm your eyes and damage painted surfaces, so use extreme caution when handling and pouring it.

Warning: Do not use fluid that has been standing open for some time, as it absorbs moisture from the air, which can cause a dangerous loss of braking effectiveness.

Before you start

✔ Make sure that your car is on level ground.

Safety first!

● If the reservoir requires repeated topping-up this is an indication of a fluid leak somewhere in the system, which should be investigated immediately.
● If a leak is suspected, the car should not be driven until the braking system has been checked. Never take any risks where brakes are concerned.

1 The upper (MAX) fluid level marking is on the side of the upper reservoir, which is located at the rear of the engine compartment. First wipe clean the area around the filler cap with a clean cloth.

2 If topping-up is necessary, unscrew the cap and remove it along with the rubber seal.

3 Carefully add fluid, avoiding spilling it on the surrounding paintwork. Use only the specified hydraulic fluid. After filling to the correct level, refit the cap and diaphragm and tighten it securely. Wipe off any spilt fluid.

Screen washer fluid level

● Screenwash additives not only keep the windscreen clean during bad weather, they also prevent the washer system freezing in cold weather – which is when you are likely to need it most. Don't top-up using plain water, as the screenwash will become diluted, and will freeze in cold weather.

 Warning: On no account use engine coolant antifreeze in the screen washer system – this may damage the paintwork.

1 The washer fluid reservoir is located in the right-hand side of the engine compartment. To check the fluid level, open the cap and then look down the clear filler neck.

2 If topping-up is necessary, add water and a screenwash additive in the quantities recommended on the bottle.

Wiper blades

1 Check the condition of the wiper blades: if they are cracked or show signs of deterioration, or if the glass swept area is smeared, renew them. For maximum clarity of vision, wiper blades should be renewed annually.

2 To remove a windscreen wiper blade, turn the ignition on, then turn the ignition off, and press the wiper switch stalk down once. This places the arms in the 'service' position. Lift the wiper from the screen and press the securing clip ...

3 ... slide the blade upwards from the end of the wiper arm, taking care not to allow the wiper arm to spring back and damage the windscreen. When completed, return the blades to the park position by pressing the wiper switch stalk again.

4 To remove the rear wiper blade, tilt the wiper blade, depress the retaining tab and slide the blade out of the hooked end of the arm, taking care not to allow the arm to spring back and damage the rear screen.

Tyre condition and pressure

It is very important that tyres are in good condition, and at the correct pressure - having a tyre failure at any speed is highly dangerous. Tyre wear is influenced by driving style - harsh braking and acceleration, or fast cornering, will all produce more rapid tyre wear. As a general rule, the front tyres wear out faster than the rears. Interchanging the tyres from front to rear ("rotating" the tyres) may result in more even wear. However, if this is completely effective, you may have the expense of replacing all four tyres at once!

Remove any nails or stones embedded in the tread before they penetrate the tyre to cause deflation. If removal of a nail does reveal that the tyre has been punctured, refit the nail so that its point of penetration is marked. Then immediately change the wheel, and have the tyre repaired by a tyre dealer.

Regularly check the tyres for damage in the form of cuts or bulges, especially in the sidewalls. Periodically remove the wheels, and clean any dirt or mud from the inside and outside surfaces. Examine the wheel rims for signs of rusting, corrosion or other damage. Light alloy wheels are easily damaged by "kerbing" whilst parking; steel wheels may also become dented or buckled. A new wheel is very often the only way to overcome severe damage.

New tyres should be balanced when they are fitted, but it may become necessary to re-balance them as they wear, or if the balance weights fitted to the wheel rim should fall off. Unbalanced tyres will wear more quickly, as will the steering and suspension components. Wheel imbalance is normally signified by vibration, particularly at a certain speed (typically around 50 mph). If this vibration is felt only through the steering, then it is likely that just the front wheels need balancing. If, however, the vibration is felt through the whole car, the rear wheels could be out of balance. Wheel balancing should be carried out by a tyre dealer or garage.

1 Tread Depth - visual check
The original tyres have tread wear safety bands (B), which will appear when the tread depth reaches approximately 1.6 mm. The band positions are indicated by a triangular mark on the tyre sidewall (A).

2 Tread Depth - manual check
Alternatively, tread wear can be monitored with a simple, inexpensive device known as a tread depth indicator gauge.

3 Tyre Pressure Check
Check the tyre pressures regularly with the tyres cold. Do not adjust the tyre pressures immediately after the vehicle has been used, or an inaccurate setting will result.

Tyre tread wear patterns

Shoulder Wear

Underinflation (wear on both sides)
Under-inflation will cause overheating of the tyre, because the tyre will flex too much, and the tread will not sit correctly on the road surface. This will cause a loss of grip and excessive wear, not to mention the danger of sudden tyre failure due to heat build-up.
Check and adjust pressures
Incorrect wheel camber (wear on one side)
Repair or renew suspension parts
Hard cornering
Reduce speed!

Centre Wear

Overinflation
Over-inflation will cause rapid wear of the centre part of the tyre tread, coupled with reduced grip, harsher ride, and the danger of shock damage occurring in the tyre casing.
Check and adjust pressures

If you sometimes have to inflate your car's tyres to the higher pressures specified for maximum load or sustained high speed, don't forget to reduce the pressures to normal afterwards.

Uneven Wear

Front tyres may wear unevenly as a result of wheel misalignment. Most tyre dealers and garages can check and adjust the wheel alignment (or "tracking") for a modest charge.
Incorrect camber or castor
Repair or renew suspension parts
Malfunctioning suspension
Repair or renew suspension parts
Unbalanced wheel
Balance tyres
Incorrect toe setting
Adjust front wheel alignment
Note: *The feathered edge of the tread which typifies toe wear is best checked by feel.*

Battery

Caution: Before carrying out any work on the vehicle battery, read the precautions given in 'Safety first!' at the start of this manual.

✔ Make sure that the battery tray is in good condition, and that the clamp is tight. Corrosion on the tray, retaining clamp and the battery itself can be removed with a solution of water and baking soda. Thoroughly rinse all cleaned areas with water. Any metal parts damaged by corrosion should be covered with a zinc-based primer, then painted.

✔ Periodically (approximately every three months), check the charge condition of the battery, as described in Chapter 5A, Section 3.

✔ If the battery is flat, and you need to jump start your vehicle, see *Roadside repairs*.

> **HAYNES HiNT**
> *Battery corrosion can be kept to a minimum by applying a layer of petroleum jelly to the clamps and terminals after they are reconnected.*

1 Lift the plastic cover (or insulation cover) to gain access to the battery positive terminal, which is located on the left-hand side of the engine compartment. The exterior of the battery should be inspected periodically for damage such as a cracked case or cover.

2 Check the battery lead clamps for tightness to ensure good electrical connections, and check the leads for signs of damage.

3 If corrosion (white, fluffy deposits) is evident, remove the cables from the battery terminals, clean them with a small wire brush, then refit them. Automotive stores sell a tool for cleaning the battery post ...

4 ... as well as the battery cable clamps. **Note:** *VW specifically prohibit the use of grease on the battery terminals.*

Electrical systems

✔ Check all external lights and the horn. Refer to Chapter 12 Section 2 for details if any of the circuits are found to be inoperative.

✔ Visually check all accessible wiring connectors, harnesses and retaining clips for security, and for signs of chafing or damage.

> **HAYNES HiNT**
> *If you need to check your brake lights and indicators unaided, back up to a wall or garage door and operate the lights. The reflected light should show if they are working properly.*

1 If a single indicator light, brake light, sidelight or headlight has failed, it is likely that a bulb has blown, and will need to be renewed. Refer to Chapter 12, Section 5 for details. If both brake lights have failed, it is possible that the switch has failed (see Chapter 9, Section 18).

2 If more than one indicator or tail light has failed, it is likely that either a fuse has blown or that there is a fault in the circuit. The main fuses are located behind the facia right-hand end cover. Additional fuses and relays are located in the left-hand side of the engine compartment fusebox.

3 To renew a blown fuse, simply pull it out and fit a new fuse of the correct rating (see *Wiring diagrams*). If the fuse blows again, it is important that you find out why – a complete checking procedure is given in Chapter 12, Section 2.

Lubricants and fluids

Note: *Using lubricants and fluids that do not meet the VW standard may invalidate the warranty*

Petrol engines:

Standard (distance/time) service interval	Multigrade (high-lubricity) engine oil, viscosity SAE 5W/40 to 20W/50 VW engine oil VW 505 01, 502 00 or better
LongLife (variable) service interval	VW LongLife engine oil VW 503 01, 504 00 or better

Diesel engines:

Standard (distance/time) service interval:	Multigrade (high-lubricity) engine oil, viscosity SAE 5W/40 to 20W/50
Engines without particulate filter	VW 505 01, 507 00 or better
Engines with particulate filter	VW 507 00 or better
LongLife (variable) service interval:	VW LongLife engine oil
Engines without particulate filter	VW 506 01, 507 00 or better
Engines with particulate filter	VW 507 00 or better
Cooling system	VW additive G12 plus-plus (TL-VW 774 G) or G12 plus (TL-VW 774 F) - antifreeze and corrosion protection
Manual transmission	Synthetic gear oil, viscosity SAE 75W/90 VW G50
DSG semi-automatic transmissions	G 052 145
Braking system	Hydraulic fluid to SAE J1703F or DOT 4

Tyre pressures

Note: *The recommended tyre pressures for each vehicle are given on a sticker attached to the inside of the fuel filler flap or the drivers side B-pillar. The pressures given are for the original equipment tyres – the recommended pressures may vary if any other make or type of tyre is fitted; check with the tyre manufacturer or supplier for latest recommendations. The following pressures are typical.*

Golf models	Front	Rear
Normal load	2.0 bars (29 psi)	2.0 bars (29 psi)
Full load	2.3 bars (33 psi)	2.8 bars (41 psi)
Emergency spare wheel	4.2 bars (61 psi)	

Chapter 1 Part A:
Routine maintenance and servicing – petrol models

Contents

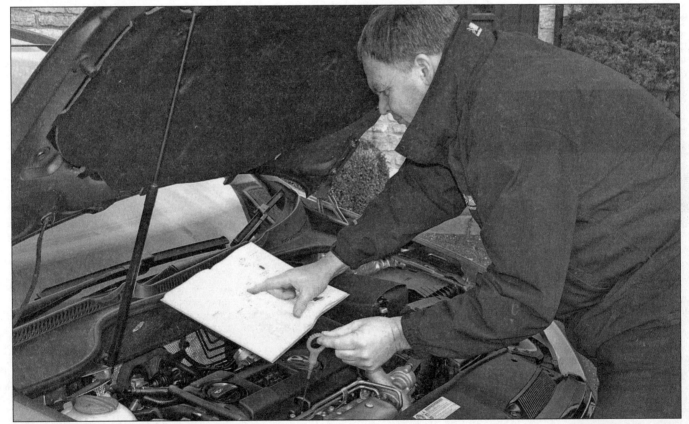

Degrees of difficulty

| Easy, suitable for novice with little experience 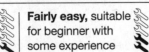 | Fairly easy, suitable for beginner with some experience | Fairly difficult, suitable for competent DIY mechanic 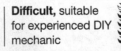 | Difficult, suitable for experienced DIY mechanic 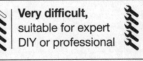 | Very difficult, suitable for expert DIY or professional |

Lubricants and fluids

Refer to *Lubricants, fluids and tyre pressures*

Engine codes*

1.4 litre petrol engines:
Non-turbocharged engines	CGGA & BUD
Turbo-charged engines	CAXA

See 'Vehicle identification' at the end of this manual for the location of engine code markings.

Capacities

Engine oil – including filter (approximate)

1.4 litre engines:
Engine code CGGA & BUD	3.2 litres
Engine code CAXA	3.6 litres

Cooling system (approximate)

1.4 litre engines	5.6 litres

Transmission

Manual transmission*:
Type 0AF	2.0 litres
Type 0AJ	2.2 litres
Type 02S	1.9 litres

* See Chapter 7A for application details

DSG transmission:
Type 0AM (7-speed)	1.7 litres

* See Chapter 7B for application details

Fuel tank (approximate)

All models	55 litres

Washer reservoirs

Models with headlight washers	5.5 litres
Models without headlight washers	3.0 litres

Cooling system

Antifreeze mixture:
40% antifreeze	Protection down to -25°C
50% antifreeze	Protection down to -35°C

Note: *Refer to antifreeze manufacturer for latest recommendations.*

Ignition system

	Type	Electrode gap
Spark plugs:		
1.4 litre engine codes:		
CGGA & BUD	VW 101 905 617 C	1.0 to 1.1 mm
CGGA & BUD	VW 101 905 601 F	1.0 to 1.1 mm
CAXA	VW 101 905 626 B	0.8 to 0.9 mm

Brakes

Brake pad lining minimum thickness:
Front	2.0 mm
Rear	2.0 mm

Torque wrench settings

	Nm	lbf ft
Manual gearbox filler/drain plug:		
0AJ & 0AF transmission:		
Hexagon plug	30	22
Multi-point plug	25	18
02S transmission:		
Drain plug	35	25
Pivot pin bolt	25	18
Oil filter	20	15
Oil filter cap/cover	25	18
Reversing light switch	20	15
Roadwheel bolts	120	89
Spark plugs	25	18
Sump drain plug*	30	22

*Do not re-use

The maintenance intervals in this manual are provided with the assumption that you, not the dealer, will be carrying out the work. These are the minimum intervals recommended by us for vehicles driven daily. If you wish to keep your vehicle in peak condition at all times, you may wish to perform some of these procedures more often. We encourage frequent maintenance, since it enhances the efficiency, performance and resale value of your vehicle.

When the vehicle is new, it should be serviced by a dealer service department (or other workshop recognised by the vehicle manufacturer as providing the same standard of service), in order to preserve the warranty. The vehicle manufacturer may reject warranty claims if you are unable to prove that servicing has been carried out as and when specified, using only original equipment parts or parts certified to be of equivalent quality.

All VW Golf models are equipped with a service interval display indicator in the instrument panel. Every time the engine is started the panel will illuminate for approximately 20 seconds with service information. With the standard non-variable display, the service intervals are in accordance with specific distances and time periods. With the LongLife display, the service interval is variable according to the number of starts, length of journeys, vehicle speeds, brake pad wear, bonnet opening frequency, fuel consumption, oil level and oil temperature, however the vehicle **must** be serviced at least every two years. The service reminder is displayed 20 days before the service is due. Once the service interval has been reached, the display will flash 'Spanner' or 'Service Now'. Note that if the variable (LongLife) service interval is being used, the engine must **only** be filled with the recommended **long-life** engine oil (see *Lubricants and fluids*).

After completing a service, VW technicians use a special instrument to reset the service display to the next service interval, and a print-out is put in the vehicle service record. The display can be reset by the owner as described in Section 5, but note that for models using the 'LongLife' interval, the procedure will automatically reset the display to the 10 000 miles 'distance' interval. To have the display reset to the 'variable' (LongLife) interval, it is necessary to take the vehicle to a VW dealer who will use a special instrument to encode the on-board computer.

Every 250 miles or weekly
☐ Refer to *Weekly checks*

Every 10 000 miles or 12 months, whichever comes first
☐ Renew the engine oil and filter (Section 3)
Note: *Frequent oil and filter changes are good for the engine. We recommend changing the oil at least once a year.*
☐ Check the front and rear brake pad thickness (Section 4)
☐ Reset the service interval display (Section 5)

Every 20 000 miles or 2 years, whichever comes first
In addition to the items listed above, carry out the following:
☐ Check the condition of the exhaust system and its mountings (Section 6)
☐ Check all underbonnet components and hoses for fluid and oil leaks (Section 7)
☐ Check the condition of the auxiliary drivebelt (Section 8)
☐ Check the coolant antifreeze concentration (Section 9)
☐ Check the brake hydraulic circuit for leaks and damage (Section 10)
☐ Check the headlight beam adjustment (Section 11)
☐ Renew the pollen filter element (Section 12)
☐ Check the manual transmission oil level (Section 13)
☐ Check the underbody protection for damage (Section 14)
☐ Check the condition of the driveshaft gaiters (Section 15)
☐ Check the steering and suspension components for condition and security (Section 16)
☐ Check the battery condition, security and electrolyte level (Section 17)
☐ Lubricate all hinges and locks (Section 18)
☐ Check the condition of the airbag unit(s) (Section 19)

Every 20 000 miles or 2 years, whichever comes first (continued)
☐ Check the operation of the windscreen/tailgate/head-light washer system(s) (as applicable) (Section 20)
☐ Check the engine management self-diagnosis memory for faults (Section 21)
☐ Check the operation of the sunroof and lubricate the guide rails (Section 22)
☐ Carry out a road test and check exhaust emissions (Section 23)

Every 40 000 miles or 4 years, whichever comes first
Note: *Many dealers perform these tasks at every second service.*
☐ Renew the air filter element (Section 24)
☐ Renew the spark plugs (Section 25)
☐ Check the condition of the auxiliary drivebelt (Section 26)
☐ Check the automatic transmission fluid level (Section 27)

Every 60 000 miles or 4 years
☐ Renew the timing belt (Section 28)
Note: *VW specify timing belt inspection after the first 60 000 miles and then every 20 000 miles until the renewal interval of 120 000 miles, however, if the vehicle is used mainly for short journeys, we recommend that this shorter renewal interval is adhered to. The belt renewal interval is very much up to the individual owner but, bearing in mind that severe engine damage will result if the belt breaks in use, we recommend the shorter interval.*

Every 2 years
☐ Renew the brake (and clutch) fluid (Section 29)
☐ Renew the coolant (Section 30)*
* Note: *This work is not included in the VW schedule and should not be required if the recommended VW G12 LongLife coolant antifreeze/inhibitor is used.*

Underbonnet view of a 1.4 litre model (engine code CAXA)

1 Engine oil filler cap
2 Engine oil dipstick
3 Coolant expansion tank
4 Windscreen/headlight washer fluid reservoir
5 Throttle housing
6 Brake master cylinder fluid reservoir
7 Inlet manifold
8 High pressure fuel pump
9 Battery
10 Fusebox
11 Turbocharger
12 Alternator
13 Evaporative emission charcoal canister
14 Oil filter

Front underbody view

1 Sump drain plug
2 Oil level/temperature sensor
3 Manual transmission
4 Oxygen sensor
5 Exhaust front pipe
6 Air conditioning compressor
7 Radiator and electric cooling fans
8 Auxiliary drivebelt
9 Driveshafts
10 Front suspension lower arms
11 Steering track rods
12 Crossmember

Rear underbody view

1 Fuel tank
2 Fuel filter
3 Track control rods
4 Rear subframe
5 Rear anti-roll bar
6 Trailing arms
7 Lower transverse links
8 Handbrake cables
9 Exhaust rear silencers and tail pipe

Maintenance procedures

1 Introduction

This Chapter is designed to help the home mechanic maintain his/her vehicle for safety, economy, long life and peak performance.

The Chapter contains a master maintenance schedule, followed by Sections dealing specifically with each task in the schedule. Visual checks, adjustments, component renewal and other helpful items are included. Refer to the accompanying illustrations of the engine compartment and the underside of the vehicle for the locations of the various components.

Servicing your vehicle will provide a planned maintenance programme, which should result in a long and reliable service life. This is a comprehensive plan, so maintaining some items but not others, will not produce the same results.

As you service your vehicle, you will discover that many of the procedures can – and should – be grouped together, because of the particular procedure being performed, or because of the proximity of two otherwise unrelated components to one another. For example, if the vehicle is raised for any reason, the exhaust can be inspected at the same time as the suspension and steering components.

The first step in this maintenance programme is to prepare yourself before the actual work begins. Read through all the Sections relevant to the work to be carried out, then make a list and gather all the parts and tools required. If a problem is encountered, seek advice from a parts specialist, or a dealer service department.

2 Regular maintenance

1 If, from the time the vehicle is new, the routine maintenance schedule is followed closely, and frequent checks are made of fluid levels and high-wear items, as suggested throughout this manual, the engine will be kept in relatively good running condition, and the need for additional work will be minimised.
2 It is possible that there will be times when the engine is running poorly due to the lack of regular maintenance. This is even more likely if a used vehicle, which has not received regular and frequent maintenance checks, is purchased. In such cases, additional work may need to be carried out, outside of the regular maintenance intervals.
3 If engine wear is suspected, a compression test (refer to the relevant Part of Chapter 2) will provide valuable information regarding the overall performance of the main internal components. Such a test can be used as a basis to decide on the extent of the work to be carried out. If, for example, a compression test indicates serious internal engine wear, conventional maintenance as described in this Chapter will not greatly improve the performance of the engine, and may prove a waste of time and money, unless extensive overhaul work is carried out first.
4 The following series of operations are those most often required to improve the performance of a generally poor-running engine:

Primary operations

a) Clean, inspect and test the battery (See 'Weekly checks').
b) Check all the engine-related fluids (See 'Weekly checks').
c) Check the condition and tension of the auxiliary drivebelt (Section 8).
d) Renew the spark plugs (Section 25).
e) Check the condition of the air filter, and renew if necessary (Section 24).
f) Check the condition of all hoses, and check for fluid leaks (Section 7).

5 If the above operations do not prove fully effective, carry out the following secondary operations:

Secondary operations

All items listed under Primary operations, plus the following:
a) Check the charging system (see Chapter 5A).
b) Check the ignition system (see Chapter 5B).
c) Check the fuel system (see Chapter 4A).

3.3a The engine oil drain plug location on the sump

3.3b The seal is integral with the plug

HAYNES
HiNT

Keep the drain plug pressed into the sump while unscrewing it by hand the last couple of turns. As the plug releases, move it away sharply so the stream of oil issuing from the sump runs into the container, not up your sleeve.

Every 10 000 miles or 12 months

3 Engine oil and filter renewal

1 Frequent oil and filter changes are the most important maintenance procedures, which can be undertaken by the DIY owner. As engine oil ages, it becomes diluted and contaminated, which leads to premature engine wear.

2 Before starting this procedure, gather all the necessary tools and materials. Also make sure that you have plenty of clean rags and newspapers handy, to mop-up any spills. Ideally, the engine oil should be warm, as it will drain better, and more built-up sludge will be removed with it. Take care, however, not to touch the exhaust or any other hot

3.6 Engine oil filter location on Turbo models

3.9a Apply a thin film of oil to the canister-type filter sealing ring ...

parts of the engine when working under the vehicle. To avoid any possibility of scalding, and to protect yourself from possible skin irritants and other harmful contaminants in used engine oils, it is advisable to wear gloves when carrying out this work. Access to the underside of the vehicle will be greatly improved if it can be raised on a lift, driven onto ramps, or jacked up and supported on axle stands (see *Jacking and vehicle support*). Whichever method is chosen, make sure that the vehicle remains level, or if it is at an angle, that the drain plug is at the lowest point. Undo the retaining screws and remove the engine undertray(s).

3 Using a socket and wrench or a ring spanner, slacken the drain plug about half a turn **(see illustrations)**. Position the draining container

3.7 Using a filter removal tool to slacken the filter

3.9b ... and then screw the filter onto the housing – CAXA engine code filter shown

under the drain plug, and then remove the plug completely **(see Haynes Hint)**. The seal is integral with the drain plug. Consequently, the drain plug must be renewed.

4 Allow some time for the old oil to drain, noting that it may be necessary to reposition the container as the oil flow slows to a trickle.

5 After all the oil has drained, clean the area around the drain plug opening, and fit the new plug. Tighten the plug to the specified torque.

6 If the filter is also to be renewed, move the container into position under the oil filter.

On 1.4 litre engine codes CGGA and BUD a canister-type filter is located from below on the front of the cylinder block.
On 1.4 litre engine code CAXA, a canister-type filter is located from above on the front right-hand side of the engine **(see illustration)**.

7 To remove the canister-type oil filter, use an oil filter removal tool if necessary, and slacken the filter initially, then unscrew it by hand the rest of the way **(see illustration)**. Empty the oil in the filter into the container.

8 Clean the filter housing and check the old filter to make sure that the rubber sealing ring has not stuck to the engine. If it has, carefully remove it.

9 To fit the canister-type oil filter, apply a light coating of clean engine oil to the sealing ring on the new filter, and then screw it into position on the engine **(see illustrations)**. Tighten the filter firmly by hand only – **do not use any tools**.

10 Remove the old oil and all tools from under the car. Refit the engine undertray(s), tighten the retaining screws securely, and then lower the car to the ground.

11 Remove the dipstick, and then unscrew the oil filler cap from the cylinder head cover. Fill the engine, using the correct grade and type of oil (see *Lubricants and fluids*). An oil can spout or funnel may help to reduce spillage. Pour in half the specified quantity of oil first, and then wait a few minutes for the oil to run to the sump. Continue adding oil a small quantity at a time until the level is up to the maximum mark on the dipstick. Refit the filler cap.

12 Start the engine and run it for a few

4.1 The outer brake pads can be observed through the holes in the wheels

H31925

4.3 The thickness (a) of the brake pad linings must not be less than the specified amount

5.2 Press reset button (A) and then clock setting button (B)

minutes; check for leaks around the oil filter seal and the sump drain plug. Note that there may be a few seconds delay before the oil pressure warning light goes out when the engine is started, as the oil circulates through the engine oil galleries and the new oil filter (where fitted) before the pressure builds-up.

⚠️ *Warning: On turbocharged engines, do not increase the engine speed above idling while the oil pressure light is illuminated, as considerable damage can be caused to the turbocharger.*

13 Switch off the engine, and wait a few minutes for the oil to settle in the sump once more. With the new oil circulated and the filter completely full, recheck the level on the dipstick, and add more oil as necessary.

14 Dispose of the used engine oil safely, with reference to *General repair procedures* in the *Reference* section of this manual.

4 Brake pad check

1 The outer brake pads can be checked without removing the wheels, by observing the brake pads through the holes in the wheels **(see illustration)**. If necessary, remove the wheel trim. The thickness of the pad lining must not be less than the dimension given in the Specifications.

2 If the outer pads are worn near their limits, it is worthwhile checking the inner pads as well. Apply the handbrake then jack up vehicle and support it on axle stands (see *Jacking and vehicle support*). Remove the roadwheels.

3 Use a steel rule to check the thickness of the brake pads, and compare with the minimum thickness given in the Specifications **(see illustration)**.

4 For a comprehensive check, the brake pads should be removed and cleaned. The operation of the caliper can then also be checked, and the condition of the brake disc itself can be fully examined on both sides. Refer to Chapter 9, Section 4 (front) or Chapter 9, Section 8 (rear).

5 If any pad's friction material is worn to the specified minimum thickness or less, *all four pads at the front or rear, as applicable, must be renewed as a set.*

6 On completion of the check, refit the road-wheels and lower the vehicle to the ground.

5 Resetting the service interval display

1 After all necessary maintenance work has been completed; the service interval display must be reset. VW technicians use a special dedicated instrument to do this, and a print-out is then put in the vehicle service record. It is possible for the owner to reset the display as described in the following paragraphs, but note that the procedure will automatically reset the display to a 10 000 mile interval. To continue with the 'variable' intervals which take into

consideration the number of starts, length of journeys, vehicle speeds, brake pad wear, bonnet opening frequency, fuel consumption, oil level and oil temperature, the display must be reset by a VW dealership using the special dedicated instrument.

2 To reset the standard display (vehicles without text message display), follow the procedures below **(see illustration)**:

a) *Switch off the ignition.*
b) *Press and hold down the trip reset button '0.0/SET' beneath the speedometer.*
c) *Switch the ignition on.*
d) *Release the reset button '0.0/SET'.*
e) *Then briefly press the clock setting button beneath the rev counter (within 20 seconds).*
f) *Service interval will then be reset.*

3 To read the service information on this display

a) *Switch the ignition on (engine not running).*
b) *Press the trip reset button '0.0/SET' twice to change menu.*
c) *Then press the clock setting button (beneath the rev counter) four times.*
d) *Service interval display will flash.*
e) *The remaining days/kilometers will be displayed.*

4 On models with multi-function switch on the steering wheel or windscreen wiper lever, to reset the display follow the procedure below.

a) *Select the settings on the menu, using buttons on steering wheel or wiper lever.*
b) *Select the menu option **Reset** in the **Service** sub-menu.*
c) *Confirm the request by pressing **OK**.*
d) *Service interval will then be reset.*

Every 20 000 miles or 2 years

6 Exhaust system check

1 With the engine cold (at least an hour after the vehicle has been driven), check the complete exhaust system from the engine to the end of the tailpipe. The exhaust system is most easily checked with the vehicle raised on

a hoist, or supported on axle stands, so that the exhaust components are readily visible and accessible (see *Jacking and vehicle support*).

2 Check the exhaust pipes and connections for evidence of leaks, severe corrosion and damage. Make sure that all brackets and mountings are in good condition, and that all relevant nuts and bolts are tight. Leakage at any of the joints or in other parts of the system will usually show up as a black sooty stain in the vicinity of the leak.

3 Rattles and other noises can often be traced to the exhaust system, especially the brackets and mountings. Try to move the pipes and silencers. If the components are able to come into contact with the body or suspension parts, secure the system with new mountings. Otherwise separate the joints (if possible) and twist the pipes as necessary to provide additional clearance.

A leak in the cooling system will usually show up as white- or antifreeze-coloured deposits on the area adjoining the leak.

7 Hose and fluid leak check

1 Visually inspect the engine joint faces, gaskets and seals for any signs of water or oil leaks. Pay particular attention to the areas around the camshaft cover, cylinder head, oil filter and sump joint faces. Bear in mind that, over a period of time, some very slight seepage from these areas is to be expected – what you are really looking for is any indication of a serious leak. Should a leak be found, renew the offending gasket or oil seal by referring to the appropriate Chapters in this manual.

2 Also check the security and condition of all the engine-related pipes and hoses. Ensure that all cable-ties or securing clips are in place and in good condition. Clips that are broken or missing can lead to chafing of the hoses, pipes or wiring, which could cause more serious problems in the future.

3 Carefully check the radiator hoses and heater hoses along their entire length. Renew any hose that is cracked, swollen or deteriorated. Cracks will show up better if the hose is squeezed. Pay close attention to the hose clips that secure the hoses to the cooling system components. Hose clips can pinch and puncture hoses, resulting in cooling system leaks.

8.2 Checking the underside of the auxiliary drivebelt with a mirror

4 Inspect all the cooling system components (hoses, joint faces, etc) for leaks **(see Haynes Hint)**. Where any problems of this nature are found on system components, renew the component or gasket with reference to Chapter 3.

5 Where applicable, inspect the automatic transmission fluid cooler hoses for leaks or deterioration.

6 With the vehicle raised, inspect the petrol tank and filler neck for punctures, cracks and other damage. The connection between the filler neck and tank is especially critical. Sometimes a rubber filler neck or connecting hose will leak due to loose retaining clamps or deteriorated rubber.

7 Carefully check all rubber hoses and metal fuel lines leading away from the petrol tank. Check for loose connections, deteriorated hoses, crimped lines, and other damage. Pay particular attention to the vent pipes and hoses, which often loop up around the filler neck and can become blocked or crimped. Follow the lines to the front of the vehicle, carefully inspecting them all the way. Renew damaged sections as necessary.

8 From within the engine compartment, check the security of all fuel hose attachments and pipe unions, and inspect the fuel hoses and vacuum hoses for kinks, chafing and deterioration.

8 Auxiliary drivebelt check

1 Apply the handbrake, then jack up the front of the vehicle and support it on axle stands (see *Jacking and vehicle support*).

2 Using a socket on the crankshaft pulley bolt, turn the engine slowly clockwise so that the full length of the auxiliary drivebelt can be examined. Look for cracks, splitting and fraying on the surface of the belt; check also for signs of glazing (shiny patches) and separation of the belt plies. Use a mirror to check the underside of the drivebelt **(see illustration)**. If damage or wear is visible, or if there are traces of oil or grease on it, the belt should be renewed (see Section 26).

9 Antifreeze check

1 The cooling system should be filled with the recommended G12 antifreeze and corrosion protection fluid – **do not** mix this antifreeze with any other type. Over a period of time, the concentration of fluid may be reduced due to topping-up (this can be avoided by topping-up with the correct antifreeze mixture – see Specifications) or fluid loss. If loss of coolant has been evident, it is important to make the necessary repair before adding fresh fluid.

2 With the engine **cold**, carefully remove the cap from the expansion tank. If the engine is not completely cold, place a cloth rag over the cap before removing it, and remove it slowly to allow any pressure to escape.

3 Antifreeze checkers are available from car accessory shops. Draw some coolant from the expansion tank and observe how many plastic balls are floating in the checker. Usually, 2 or 3 balls must be floating for the correct concentration of antifreeze, but follow the manufacturer's instructions.

4 If the concentration is incorrect, it will be necessary to either withdraw some coolant and add antifreeze, or alternatively drain the old coolant and add fresh coolant of the correct concentration (see Section 30).

10 Brake hydraulic circuit check

1 Check the entire brake hydraulic circuit for leaks and damage. Start by checking the master cylinder in the engine compartment. At the same time, check the vacuum servo unit and ABS units for signs of fluid leakage.

2 Raise the front and rear of the vehicle and support it on axle stands (see *Jacking and vehicle support*). Check the rigid hydraulic brake lines for corrosion and damage. Also check the brake pressure regulator in the same manner.

3 At the front of the vehicle, check that the flexible hydraulic hoses to the calipers are not twisted or chafing on any of the surrounding suspension components. Turn the steering on full lock to make this check. Also check that the hoses are not brittle or cracked.

4 Lower the vehicle to the ground after making the checks.

11 Headlight beam adjustment

1 Accurate adjustment of the headlight beam is only possible using optical beam-setting equipment, and this work should therefore be carried out by a VW dealer or service station with the necessary facilities.

2 Basic adjustments can be carried out in an emergency, and further details are given in Chapter 12, Section 8.

12 Pollen filter element renewal

1 The pollen filter is located in the heater unit and is accessed from inside the car, on the passenger's side.

2 Remove the clips and withdraw the facia lower trim from beneath the glovebox **(see illustration)**.

3 Slide the cover to the left to remove the

access cover **(see illustrations)**. If the cover has been removed previously there may be a screw securing the cover in place.

4 Slide out the pollen filter element downwards from the heater unit **(see illustration)**.

5 Fit the new element then refit the access cover, making sure that the locating lugs are fitted correctly in the housing. If any of the lugs have been broken off, fit a screw into the cover to make sure it is secure.

6 Refit the trim beneath the facia/glovebox.

13 Manual transmission oil level check

1 Park the car on a level surface. For improved access to the filler/level plug, apply the handbrake, then jack up the front of the vehicle and support it on axle stands (see *Jacking and vehicle support*), but note that the rear of the vehicle should also be raised to ensure an accurate level check. The oil level must be checked before the car is driven, or at least 5 minutes after the engine has been switched off. If the oil is checked immediately after driving the car, some of the oil will remain distributed around the transmission components, resulting in an inaccurate level reading.

0AF & 0AJ transmissions

2 Undo the retaining screws and remove the engine undertray. Wipe clean the area around the transmission filler/level plug which is situated on the rear right-hand side of the final drive casing **(see illustration)**.

3 The oil level should reach the lower edge of the filler/level hole. A certain amount of oil will have gathered behind the filler/level plug, and will trickle out when it is removed; this does **not** necessarily indicate that the level is correct. To ensure that a true level is established, wait until the initial trickle has stopped, then add oil as necessary until a trickle of new oil can be seen emerging. The level will be correct when the flow ceases; use only good-quality oil of the specified type.

4 If the transmission has been overfilled so that oil flows out when the filler/level plug is removed, check that the car is completely level

12.2 Remove the facia lower trim from beneath the glovebox

12.3b ... and screw (where fitted) ...

(front-to-rear and side-to-side), and allow the surplus to drain off into a suitable container.

5 When the oil level is correct, refit the filler/level plug and tighten it to the specified torque.

6 Wipe off any spilt oil then refit the engine undertray(s), tighten the retaining screws securely, and lower the car to the ground.

02S transmission

7 Undo the fasteners and remove the engine undertray.

8 On these transmissions, it's impossible to check the level of the oil through the 'filler' plug, due to the engine/transmission installation angle; the level of the fluid is above the lower edge of the filler hole. The only method of ensuring the correct fluid level is to completely drain and refill the transmission.

9 Remove the air cleaner housing as described in Chapter 4A, Section 2.

12.3a Remove the access cover...

12.4 ... then slide out the pollen filter element

10 In order to drain the transmission, the pivot pin must be removed from the underside of the transmission casing. However, to prevent the position of the selector forks being altered, press the selector shaft down, then turn the angled locking rod upwards, and lock the shaft in position **(see illustration)**.

11 Place a container under the transmission casing.

12 Unscrew the drain plug from the base of the differential housing, and allow the oil to drain **(see illustration)**.

13 Then undo the retaining bolt, pull out the pivot pin nearest the passenger's roadwheel and allow the oil to drain **(see illustration 13.12)**. The pivot pin O-ring seal must be renewed.

14 When the oil has finished draining clean the surrounding area, then refit the pivot pin (with a new O-ring seal), and tighten the retaining bolt to the specified torque.

15 When the oil has finished draining, clean

13.2 Oil filler/level plug location - 0AF & 0AJ transmissions

13.10 Press down the selector shaft (2), and rotate the locking rod (1) upwards

13.12 Oil drain pug (A) and pivot pin (B) - 02S transmission

the surrounding area, refit the drain plug and tighten it to the specified torque.
16 Rotate the selector-shaft locking rod to its original position.
17 Unscrew the reversing light switch from the top of the transmission casing.
18 Using a 600 mm length of 10 mm (external) diameter hose, and funnel, add 1.9 litres of new oil to the transmission.
19 Refit the reversing light switch, and tighten it to the specified torque.
20 The remainder of refitting is a reversal of removal.

14 Underbody protection check

Raise and support the vehicle on axle stands (see *Jacking and vehicle support*). Using an electric torch or lead light, inspect the entire underside of the vehicle, paying particular attention to the wheel arches. Look for any damage to the flexible underbody coating, which may crack or flake off with age, leading to corrosion. Also check that the wheel arch liners are securely attached with any clips provided – if they come loose, dirt may get in behind the liners and defeat their purpose. If there is any damage to the under seal, or any corrosion, it should be repaired before the damage gets too serious.

15 Driveshaft gaiter check

1 With the vehicle raised and securely supported on stands, slowly rotate the roadwheel. Inspect the condition of the outer constant velocity (CV) joint rubber gaiters, squeezing the gaiters to open out the folds. Check for signs of cracking, splits or deterioration of the rubber, which may allow the grease to escape, and lead to water and grit entry into the joint. Also check the security and condition of the retaining clips. Repeat these checks on the inner joints **(see**

15.1 Check the condition of the driveshaft gaiters (arrowed)

illustration). If any damage or deterioration is found, the gaiters should be renewed (see Chapter 8, Section 3).
2 At the same time, check the general condition of the CV joints themselves by first holding the driveshaft and attempting to rotate the wheel. Repeat this check by holding the inner joint and attempting to rotate the driveshaft. Any appreciable movement indicates wear in the joints, wear in the driveshaft splines, or a loose driveshaft retaining nut.

16 Steering and suspension check

1 Raise the front and rear of the vehicle, and securely support it on axle stands (see *Jacking and vehicle support*).
2 Visually inspect the track rod end balljoint dust cover, the lower front suspension balljoint dust cover, and the steering rack-and-pinion gaiters for splits, chafing or deterioration. Any wear of these components will cause loss of lubricant, together with dirt and water entry, resulting in rapid deterioration of the balljoints or steering gear.
3 Check the power steering fluid hoses for chafing or deterioration, and the pipe and hose unions for fluid leaks. Also check for signs of fluid leakage under pressure from the steering gear rubber gaiters, which would indicate failed fluid seals within the steering gear.

16.4 Check for wear in the bearings by grasping the wheel top and bottom and trying to rock it

16.5 Check for wear in the bearings and ball joints by grasping the wheel at the sides and trying to rock it

4 Grasp the roadwheel at the 12 o'clock and 6 o'clock positions, and try to rock it **(see illustration)**. Very slight free play may be felt, but if the movement is appreciable, further investigation is necessary to determine the source. Continue rocking the wheel while an assistant depresses the footbrake. If the movement is now eliminated or significantly reduced, it is likely that the hub bearings are at fault. If the free play is still evident with the footbrake depressed, then there is wear in the suspension joints or mountings.
5 Now grasp the wheel at the 9 o'clock and 3 o'clock positions, and try to rock it as before **(see illustration)**. Any movement felt now may again be caused by wear in the hub bearings or the steering track rod balljoints. If the inner or outer balljoint is worn, the visual movement will be obvious.
6 Using a large screwdriver or flat bar, check for wear in the suspension mounting bushes by levering between the relevant suspension component and its attachment point. Some movement is to be expected as the mountings are made of rubber, but excessive wear should be obvious. Also check the condition of any visible rubber bushes, looking for splits, cracks or contamination of the rubber.
7 With the car standing on its wheels, have an assistant turn the steering wheel back-and-forth about an eighth of a turn each way. There should be very little, if any, lost movement between the steering wheel and roadwheels. If this is not the case, closely observe the joints and mountings previously described, but in addition, check the steering column universal joints for wear, and the rack-and-pinion steering gear itself.
8 Check for any signs of fluid leakage around the front suspension struts and rear shock absorber. Should any fluid be noticed, the suspension strut or shock absorber is defective internally, and should be renewed. **Note:** *Suspension struts/shock absorbers should always be renewed in pairs on the same axle to ensure correct vehicle handling.*
9 The efficiency of the suspension strut/shock absorber may be checked by bouncing the vehicle at each corner. Generally speaking, the body will return to its normal position and stop after being depressed. If it rises and returns on a rebound, the suspension strut/shock absorber is probably suspect. Examine also the suspension strut/shock absorber upper and lower mountings for any signs of wear.

17 Battery check

1 The battery is located on the left-hand side of the engine compartment. Where an insulator cover is fitted **(see illustration)**, open the cover to gain access to the battery.
2 Check that both battery terminals and all the

17.1 Pull back the battery insulator cover

17.2 Check that the terminals are secure

17.3 Check that the battery clamp (arrowed) is secure

fuse holder connections are securely attached **(see illustration)** and are free from corrosion. **Note:** *Before disconnecting the terminals from the battery, refer to 'Disconnecting the battery' in the Reference Chapter at the end of this manual.*

3 Check the battery casing for signs of damage or cracking and check the battery retaining clamp bolt is securely tightened **(see illustration)**. If the battery casing is damaged in any way the battery must be renewed (see Chapter 5A, Section 3).

4 If the vehicle is not fitted with a sealed-for-life maintenance-free battery, check the electrolyte level is between the MAX and MIN level markings on the battery casing. If topping-up is necessary, remove the battery from the vehicle then remove the cell caps/cover (as applicable). Using distilled water, top the electrolyte level of each cell up to the MAX level mark then securely refit the cell caps/cover. Ensure the battery has not been overfilled then refit the battery to the vehicle (see Chapter 5A, Section 3).

5 On completion close up the battery insulator cover.

18 Hinge and lock lubrication

1 Lubricate the hinges of the bonnet, doors and tailgate with light general-purpose oil. Similarly, lubricate all latches, locks and lock strikers. At the same time, check the security and operation of all the locks, adjusting them if necessary (see Chapter 11, Section 11).

2 Lightly lubricate the bonnet release mechanism and cable with suitable grease.

19 Airbag unit check

Inspect the exterior condition of the airbag(s) for signs of damage or deterioration. If an airbag shows signs of damage, it must be renewed (see Chapter 12, Section 25 & 26). Note that it is not permissible to attach any stickers to the surface of the airbag, as this may affect the deployment of the unit.

20 Windscreen/tailgate/ headlight washer system check

1 Check that each of the washer jet nozzles are clear and that each nozzle provides a strong jet of washer fluid.

2 The tailgate jet should be aimed to spray at the centre of the screen, using a pin.

3 The windscreen washer nozzles should be aimed slightly above the centre of the screen using a small screwdriver to turn the jet eccentric (see Chapter 12, Section 20).

4 The headlight inner jet should be aimed slightly above the horizontal centreline of the headlight, and the outer jet should be aimed slightly below the centreline. VW technicians use a special tool to adjust the headlight jet after pulling the jet out onto its stop.

5 Especially during the winter months, make sure that the washer fluid frost concentration is sufficient.

21 Engine management self-diagnosis memory fault check

This work should be carried out by a VW dealer or a diagnostic specialist using special equipment. The diagnostic socket is located below the facia, at the right-hand side above the bonnet release handle **(see illustration)**.

21.1 Diagnostic socket – arrowed

22 Sunroof check and lubrication

1 Check the operation of the sunroof, and leave it in the fully open position.

2 Wipe clean the guide rails on each side of the sunroof opening, then apply lubricant to them. VW recommend lubricant spray G 052 778.

23 Road test and exhaust emissions check

Instruments and electrical equipment

1 Check the operation of all instruments and electrical equipment including the air conditioning system.

2 Make sure that all instruments read correctly, and switch on all electrical equipment in turn, to check that it functions properly.

Steering and suspension

3 Check for any abnormalities in the steering, suspension, handling or road 'feel'.

4 Drive the vehicle, and check that there are no unusual vibrations or noises, which may indicate wear in the driveshafts, wheel bearings, etc.

5 Check that the steering feels positive, with no excessive 'sloppiness', or roughness, and check for any suspension noises when cornering and driving over bumps.

Drivetrain

6 Check the performance of the engine, clutch (where applicable), gearbox/transmission and driveshafts.

7 Listen for any unusual noises from the engine, clutch and gearbox/transmission.

8 Make sure the engine runs smoothly at idle, and there is no hesitation on accelerating.

9 Check that, where applicable, the clutch action is smooth and progressive, that the drive is taken up smoothly, and that the pedal travel is not excessive. Also listen for any noises when the clutch pedal is depressed.

10 On manual gearbox models check that all gears can be engaged smoothly without noise, and that the gear lever action is smooth and not abnormally vague or 'notchy'.

11 On automatic transmission models, make sure that all gearchanges occur smoothly, without snatching, and without an increase in engine speed between changes. Check that all the gear positions can be selected with the vehicle at rest. If any problems are found, they should be referred to a VW dealer.

12 Listen for a metallic clicking sound from the front of the vehicle, as the vehicle is driven slowly in a circle with the steering on full-lock. Carry out this check in both directions. If a clicking noise is heard, this indicates wear in a driveshaft joint, in which case renew the joint if necessary.

Braking system

13 Make sure that the vehicle does not pull to one side when braking, and that the wheels do not lock when braking hard.

14 Check that there is no vibration through the steering when braking.

15 Check that the handbrake operates correctly without excessive movement of the lever, and that it holds the vehicle stationary on a slope.

16 Test the operation of the brake servo unit as follows. With the engine off, depress the footbrake four or five times to exhaust the vacuum. Hold the brake pedal depressed, and then start the engine. As the engine starts, there should be a noticeable 'give' in the brake pedal as vacuum builds-up. Allow the engine to run for at least two minutes, and then switch it off.

If the brake pedal is depressed now, it should be possible to detect a hiss from the servo as the pedal is depressed. After about four or five applications, no further hissing should be heard, and the pedal should feel considerably harder.

17 Under controlled emergency braking, the pulsing of the ABS unit must be felt at the footbrake pedal.

Exhaust emissions check

18 Although not part of the manufacturer's maintenance schedule, this check will normally be carried out on a regular basis according to the country the vehicle is operated in. Currently in the UK, exhaust emissions testing is included as part of the annual MOT test after the vehicle is 3 years old. In Germany the test is made when the vehicle is 3 years old, then repeated every 2 years.

Every 40 000 miles or 4 years

24 Air filter element renewal
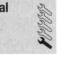

Engine code CGGA and BUD

1 Undo the screws and lift the front edge of the air filter cover, then disengage it from the rear edge **(see illustrations)**.

2 Note its fitted position, then lift the element from the housing **(see illustration)**.

3 Remove any debris and wipe clean the interior of the housing.

4 Fit the new filter element in position.

5 Refit the cover and tighten the screws securely.

Engine code CAXA

6 The air cleaner is located in front of the battery on the left-hand side of the engine compartment. First, remove the engine top cover.

7 Undo the screws and remove the lid from the air cleaner **(see illustrations)**.

8 Undo the screw and slide out the clamp,

24.1a Undo the air filter cover screws (arrowed)...

24.1b ...and lift the cover from place

24.2 Remove the filter element

24.7a Undo the screws...

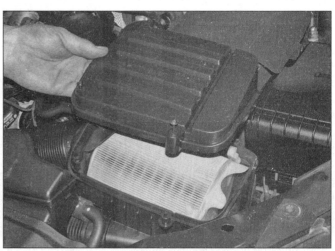

24.7b ... and remove the filter upper cover

24.8a Undo the retaining screw ...

24.8b ... and remove the retaining clamp ...

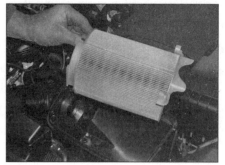

24.8c ...followed by the air filter element

then remove the filter element from the housing **(see illustrations)**.

9 Fit the new filter element using a reversal of the removal procedure.

25 Spark plug renewal

1 The correct functioning of the spark plugs is vital for the correct running and efficiency of the engine. It is essential that the plugs fitted are appropriate for the engine (a suitable type is specified at the beginning of this Chapter). If this type is used and the engine is in good condition, the spark plugs should not need attention between scheduled renewal intervals. Spark plug cleaning is rarely necessary, and should not be attempted unless specialised equipment is available, as damage can easily be caused to the firing ends.

2 Undo the retaining bolts, and remove the cover from the top of the engine **(see illustrations)**, unclip the hoses (where applicable).

3 Disconnect the wiring plug connectors from the top of the coils **(see illustration)**. If required, release the clips to allow the wiring to move from the wiring harness guide.

4 Remove the ignition HT coils from the tops of the spark plugs. VW technicians use special tool T10094A to pull out the coils, however, a hooked tool or length of welding rod bent to hook under the connectors may be used instead **(see illustrations)**.

5 It is advisable to remove the dirt from the spark plug recesses using a clean brush, vacuum

cleaner or compressed air before removing the plugs, to prevent dirt dropping into the cylinders.

6 Unscrew the plugs using a spark plug spanner, suitable box spanner or a deep socket and extension bar **(see illustration)**.

Keep the socket aligned with the spark plug – if it is forcibly moved to one side, the ceramic insulator may be broken off. The use of a universal joint socket will be helpful. As each plug is removed, examine it as follows.

25.2a Undo the screws (arrowed)...

25.2b ...then release the hoses, as the cover is removed

25.3 Disconnect the wiring connector

25.4a Use a hooked tool to pull up the ignition coil...

25.4b ...making sure it is located (arrowed) securely

25.4c A length of welding rod bent as shown, can be used to pull out the coils

25.4d Withdraw the coil from the cylinder head

25.6 Using a deep socket and extension to remove the spark plug

25.11a If single electrode plugs are being fitted, check the electrode gap using a feeler gauge...

25.11b ...or a wire gauge...

25.12 ...and if necessary adjust the gap by bending the electrode

25.13 Use a rubber hose to avoid cross-threading the spark plugs

7 Examination of the spark plugs will give a good indication of the condition of the engine. If the insulator nose of the spark plug is clean and white, with no deposits, this is indicative of a weak mixture or too hot a plug (a hot plug transfers heat away from the electrode slowly, a cold plug transfers heat away quickly).

8 If the tip and insulator nose are covered with hard black-looking deposits, then this is indicative that the mixture is too rich. Should the plug be black and oily, and then it is likely that the engine is fairly worn, as well as the mixture being too rich.

9 If the insulator nose is covered with light tan to greyish-brown deposits, then the mixture is correct and it is likely that the engine is in good condition.

10 The spark plug electrode gap is of considerable importance as, if it is too large or too small, the size of the spark and its efficiency will be seriously impaired. On engines fitted with multi-electrode spark plugs, it is recommended that the plugs are renewed rather than attempting to adjust the gaps. On other spark plugs, the gap should be set to the value given by the manufacturer.

11 To set the gap on single electrode plugs, measure it with a feeler blade and then bend open, or closed, the outer plug electrode until the correct gap is achieved. The centre electrode should never be bent, as this may crack the insulator and cause plug failure, if nothing worse. If using feeler blades, the gap

is correct when the appropriate-size blade is a firm sliding fit **(see illustrations)**.

12 Special spark plug electrode gap adjusting tools are available from most motor accessory shops, or from some spark plug manufacturers **(see illustration)**.

13 Before fitting the spark plugs, check that the threaded connector sleeves are tight, and that the plug exterior surfaces and threads are clean. It's often difficult to screw in new spark plugs without cross-threading them – this can be avoided using a piece of rubber hose. Fit a short length of rubber hose over the end of the spark plug. The flexible hose acts as a universal joint to help align the plug with the plug thread, the hose will slip on the spark plug, preventing thread damage to the aluminium cylinder head **(see illustration)**.

14 Remove the rubber hose (if used), and tighten the plug to the specified torque using the spark plug socket and a torque wrench. Refit the remaining spark plugs in the same manner.

15 Reconnect and refit the HT leads/ignition coils using a reversal of the removal procedure.

26 Auxiliary drivebelt check and renewal

1 The poly-vee drivebelt drives the alternator and where fitted, the air conditioning compressor **(see illustrations)**.

26.1a Auxiliary belt routing – with air-conditioning – CAXA engines

1 Coolant pump
2 Idler roller
3 Alternator pulley
4 Tensioning roller
5 Air-conditioning compressor
6 Crankshaft pulley

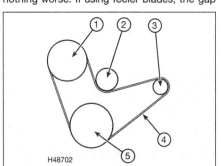

26.1b Auxiliary belt routing – without air-conditioning – CAXA engines

1 Coolant pump
2 Tensioning roller
3 Alternator pulley
4 Auxiliary belt
5 Crankshaft pulley

26.1c Auxiliary belt routing – CGGA and BUD engines

1 Crankshaft pulley
2 Tensioning roller
3 Alternator pulley
4 Auxiliary belt
5 Air-conditioning compressor

2 On all engines, the drivebelt tension is adjusted automatically by a spring-tensioned idler.

Checking

3 See Section 8 for information on checking the condition of the drivebelt. When the belt is removed, check all pulleys are free from any damage and are secure. Also check that the alternator and air-conditioning compressor are mounted securely.

Renewal

4 For improved access, apply the handbrake, and then jack up the front of the vehicle and support it on axle stands (see *Jacking and vehicle support*). Remove the right-hand front roadwheel, and then remove the access panel from the inner wheel arch **(see illustration)**.

5 If the drivebelt is to be re-used, mark it for clockwise direction to ensure it is refitted the same way round.

6 On CGGA and BUD engines, use a spanner to turn the tensioner central bolt clockwise to release the tension on the drivebelt, then insert a suitable drill bit or metal rod (approximately 5.5 mm diameter) through the hole in front of the pulley wheel to hold the tensioner **(see illustration)**.

7 On CAXA engines, use a spanner to turn the tensioner central bolt anti-clockwise to release the tension on the drivebelt, then insert a suitable drill bit or metal rod (approximately 4.0 mm diameter) through the hole beneath the pulley wheel to hold the tensioner **(see illustration)**.

8 Note how the drivebelt is routed, then remove it from the crankshaft pulley **(see illustration)**, alternator pulley and air conditioning compressor pulley (where fitted).

9 Locate the new drivebelt on the pulleys, then by holding the pressure of the tensioner

26.4 Remove the inner wheel arch panel

26.7 Turn the tensioner with a spanner and lock in position (arrowed) - CAXA engines

26.6 Turn the tensioner with a spanner and remove belt - CGGA & BUD engines

26.8 Remove the belt from around the pulleys

with a spanner, remove the locking pin. Slowly release the pressure on the spanner, so that the tensioner takes up the slack in the belt. Check that the belt is located correctly in the multi-grooves in the pulleys.

10 Start the engine and check that the drivebelt runs, as it should over the pulleys. Make sure that all tools and hands are kept clear of the drivebelt with the engine running.

11 With the engine stopped, refit the access panel and roadwheel, and then lower the vehicle to the ground.

27 DSG transmission oil renewal

The DSG transmission fitted to 1.4 litre petrol engines is the 7-speed dual clutch (0AM) transmission. The transmission is filled for life, and does not have an oil level checking procedure. If there has been an oil leak from the transmission, after the leak has been rectified, renew the transmission oil as described in Chapter 7B, Section 6.

Every 60 000 miles or 4 years

28 Timing belt renewal

Note: *This Section only applies to engine codes CGGA and BUD. VW recommend only a* **check** *at this interval, however, we recommend that the timing belt be renewed.*

Inspection

1 Release the clips and remove the upper

timing belt cover (refer to Chapter 2A, Section 5).

2 Using a spanner or socket on the crankshaft pulley bolt, turn the engine slowly in a clockwise direction. **Do not** turn the engine on the camshaft bolt.

3 Check the complete length of the timing belt for signs of cracking, tooth separation, fraying, side glazing, and oil or grease contamination. Use a torch and mirror to check the underside of the belt.

4 If there is any evidence of wear or

damage as described in the last paragraph, the timing belt **must** be renewed. A broken belt will cause major damage to the engine.

5 After making the check, refit the upper timing belt cover and remove the spanner/ socket from the crankshaft pulley bolt.

Renewal

6 Refer to Chapter 2A, Section 5, for removal and refitting procedure.

Every 2 years

29 Brake (and clutch) fluid renewal

⚠ **Warning: Brake hydraulic fluid can harm your eyes and damage painted surfaces, so use extreme caution when handling and pouring it. Do not use fluid that has been standing open for some time, as it absorbs moisture from the air. Excess moisture can cause a dangerous loss of braking effectiveness.**

1 The procedure is similar to that for the bleeding of the hydraulic system as described in Chapter 9, Section 2, except that the brake fluid reservoir should be emptied by syphoning, using an old, clean antifreeze tester or similar before starting, and allowance should be made for the old fluid to be expelled when bleeding a section of the circuit. Since the clutch hydraulic system also uses fluid from the brake system reservoir, it should also be bled at the same time by referring to Chapter 6, Section 2.

2 Working as described in Chapter 9, Section 2, open the first bleed screw in the sequence, and pump the brake pedal gently until nearly all the old fluid has been emptied from the master cylinder reservoir.

3 Top-up to the MAX level with new fluid, and continue pumping until only the new fluid remains in the reservoir, and new fluid can be seen emerging from the bleed screw. Tighten the screw, and top the reservoir level up to the MAX level line.

4 Work through all the remaining bleed screws in the sequence until new fluid can be seen at all of them. Be careful to keep the master cylinder reservoir topped-up to above the MIN level at all times, or air may enter the system and greatly increase the length of the task.

5 When the operation is complete, check that all bleed screws are securely tightened, and that their dust caps are refitted. Wash off all traces of spilt fluid, and recheck the master cylinder reservoir fluid level.

6 On models with manual transmission, once the brake fluid has been changed the clutch fluid should also be renewed. Referring to Chapter 6, Section 2, bleed the clutch until new fluid is seen to be emerging from the slave cylinder bleed screw, keeping the master cylinder fluid level above the MIN level line at all times to prevent air entering the system. Once the new fluid emerges, securely tighten the bleed screw then disconnect and remove the bleeding equipment. Securely refit the dust cap then wash off all traces of spilt fluid.

7 On all models, ensure the master cylinder fluid level is correct (see *Weekly checks*) and thoroughly check the operation of the brakes and (where necessary) clutch before taking the car on the road.

30 Coolant renewal

Note: *This work is not included in the VW schedule and should not be required if the recommended VW G12 LongLife coolant antifreeze/inhibitor is used. However, if standard antifreeze/inhibitor is used, the work should be carried out at the recommended interval.*

 Warning: Wait until the engine is cold before starting this procedure. Do not allow antifreeze to come in contact with your skin, or with the painted surfaces of the vehicle. Rinse off spills immediately with plenty of water. Never leave antifreeze lying around in an open container, or in a puddle in the driveway or on the garage floor. Children and pets are attracted by its sweet smell, but antifreeze can be fatal if ingested.

Cooling system draining

1 With the engine completely cold, unscrew the expansion tank cap.

2 Firmly apply the handbrake then jack up the front of the vehicle and support it on axle stands (see *Jacking and vehicle support*). Undo the retaining screws and remove the engine undertray to gain access to the base of the radiator.

3 Position a suitable container beneath the coolant drain outlet, which is fitted to the coolant bottom hose end fitting. Loosen the drain plug (there is no need to remove it completely) and allow the coolant to drain into the container. If desired, a length of tubing can be fitted to the drain outlet to direct the flow of coolant during draining. Where no drain outlet is fitted to the hose end fitting, remove the retaining clip and disconnect the bottom hose from the radiator to drain the coolant (see Chapter 3, Section 2).

4 On engines with an oil cooler, to fully drain the system also disconnect one of the coolant hoses from the oil cooler which is located at the front of the cylinder block.

5 If the coolant has been drained for a reason other than renewal, then provided it is clean, it can be re-used.

6 Once all the coolant has drained, securely tighten the radiator drain plug or reconnect the bottom hose to the radiator (as applicable). Where necessary, also reconnect the coolant hose to the oil cooler and secure it in position with the retaining clip. Refit the undertray, and tighten the retaining screws securely.

7 Reconnect the auxiliary radiator coolant hoses, when draining has ceased.

Cooling system flushing

8 If the recommended VW coolant has not been used and coolant renewal has been neglected, or if the antifreeze mixture has become diluted, the cooling system may gradually lose efficiency, as the coolant passages become restricted due to rust, scale deposits, and other sediment. The cooling system efficiency can be restored by flushing the system clean.

9 The radiator should be flushed separately from the engine, to avoid excess contamination.

Radiator flushing

10 To flush the radiator, first tighten the radiator drain plug.

11 Disconnect the top and bottom hoses and any other relevant hoses from the radiator (see Chapter 3, Section 2).

12 Insert a garden hose into the radiator top inlet. Direct a flow of clean water through the radiator, and continue flushing until clean water emerges from the radiator bottom outlet.

13 If after a reasonable period, the water still does not run clear, the radiator can be flushed with a good proprietary cleaning agent. It is important that their manufacturer's instructions are followed carefully. If the contamination is particularly bad, insert the hose in the radiator bottom outlet, and reverse-flush the radiator.

Engine flushing

14 To flush the engine, remove the thermostat (see Chapter 3, Section 4).

15 With the bottom hose disconnected from the radiator, insert a garden hose into the coolant housing. Direct a clean flow of water through the engine, and continue flushing until clean water emerges from the radiator bottom hose.

16 When flushing is complete, refit the thermostat and reconnect the hoses.

Cooling system filling

17 Before attempting to fill the cooling system, ensure the drain plug is securely closed and make sure that all hoses are securely connected and their retaining clips are in good condition. If the recommended VW coolant is not being used, ensure that a suitable antifreeze mixture is used all year round, to prevent corrosion of the engine components (see following sub-Section). **Note:** *VW recommend that only distilled water should be used.*

18 Remove the expansion tank filler cap and slowly fill the system with the coolant. Continue to fill the cooling system until bubbles stop appearing in the expansion tank. Help to bleed the air from the system by repeatedly squeezing the radiator bottom hose.

19 When no more bubbles appear, top the coolant level up to the MAX level mark then securely refit the cap to the expansion tank.

20 Run the engine at a fast idle speed until the cooling fan cuts in. Wait for the fan to stop then switch the engine off and allow the engine to cool.

21 When the engine has cooled, check the coolant level with reference to Weekly checks. Top-up the level if necessary, and refit the expansion tank cap.

Antifreeze mixture

22 If the recommended VW coolant is not being used, the antifreeze should always be renewed at the specified intervals. This is necessary not only to maintain the antifreeze properties, but also to prevent corrosion, which would otherwise occur as the corrosion inhibitors become progressively less effective.

23 Always use an ethylene-glycol based antifreeze which is suitable for use in mixed-metal cooling systems. The quantity of antifreeze and levels of protection are indicated in the Specifications.

24 Before adding antifreeze, the cooling system should be completely drained, preferably flushed, and all hoses checked for condition and security.

25 After filling with antifreeze, a label should be attached to the expansion tank, stating the type and concentration of antifreeze used, and the date installed. Any subsequent topping-up should be made with the same type and concentration of antifreeze.

Caution: Do not use engine antifreeze in the windscreen/tailgate washer system, as it will damage the vehicle paintwork. A screenwash additive should be added to the washer system in the quantities stated on the bottle.

Chapter 1 Part B:
Routine maintenance and servicing – diesel models

Contents

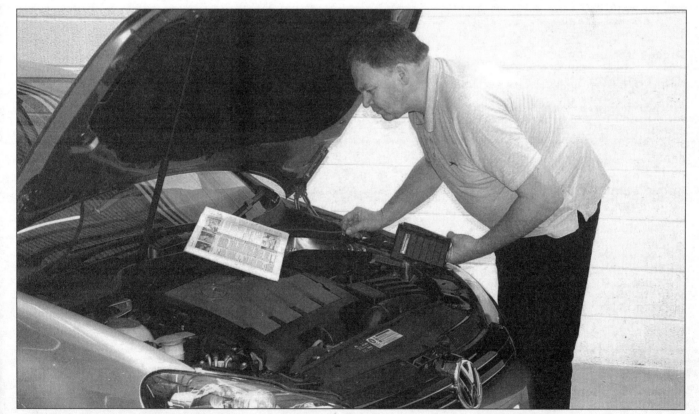

Degrees of difficulty

| Easy, suitable for novice with little experience | Fairly easy, suitable for beginner with some experience | Fairly difficult, suitable for competent DIY mechanic | Difficult, suitable for experienced DIY mechanic | Very difficult, suitable for expert DIY or professional 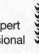 |

Lubricants and fluids

Refer to *Lubricants, fluids and tyre pressures*

Engine codes*

Manufacturer's engine codes*:

1599 cc (1.6 litre), 16-valve, DOHC	CAYB and CAYC
1968 cc (2.0 litre), 16-valve, DOHC	CBAA, CBAB, CBBB, CFFA, CFFB and CFGB

See 'Vehicle identification' at the end of this manual for the location of engine code markings.

Capacities

Engine oil (including filter)
All engines	4.3 litres

Cooling system
All engines	6.2 litres

Transmission*
Manual transmission:
Type 0A4	1.9 litres
Type 02Q	2.3 litres

* See Chapter 7A for application details

DSG transmission:
Type 02E	5.5 litres
Type 0AM	1.7 litres

* See Chapter 7B for application details

Fuel tank (approximate)
All models	55 litres

Washer reservoirs
Models with headlight washers	5.5 litres
Models without headlight washers	3.0 litres

Cooling system

Antifreeze mixture:
40% antifreeze	Protection down to -25°C
50% antifreeze	Protection down to -35°C

Note: *Refer to antifreeze manufacturer for latest recommendations.*

Brakes

Brake pad lining minimum thickness:
Front	2.0 mm
Rear	2.0 mm

Torque wrench settings

	Nm	lbf ft
Manual gearbox filler/drain plug:		
02Q transmission:		
Multi-point socket head	30	22
Hexagon socket head	45	31
0A4 transmission:		
Drain/filler plug	35	25
Oil filter cap	25	18
Roadwheel bolts	120	89
Sump drain plug	30	22

Maintenance schedule

The maintenance intervals in this manual are provided with the assumption that you, not the dealer, will be carrying out the work. These are the minimum intervals recommended by us for vehicles driven daily. If you wish to keep your vehicle in peak condition at all times, you may wish to perform some of these procedures more often. We encourage frequent maintenance, since it enhances the efficiency, performance and resale value of your vehicle.

When the vehicle is new, it should be serviced by a dealer service department (or other workshop recognised by the vehicle manufacturer as providing the same standard of service), in order to preserve the warranty. The vehicle manufacturer may reject warranty claims if you are unable to prove that servicing has been carried out as and when specified, using only original equipment parts or parts certified to be of equivalent quality.

All VW Golf models are equipped with a service interval display indicator in the instrument panel. Every time the engine is started the panel will illuminate for approximately 20 seconds with service information. With the standard non-variable display, the service intervals are in accordance with specific distances and time periods. With the LongLife display, the service interval is variable according to the number of starts, length of journeys, vehicle speeds, brake pad wear, bonnet opening frequency, fuel consumption, oil level and oil temperature, however the vehicle **must** be serviced at least every two years. The service reminder is displayed 20 days before the service is due. Once the service interval has been reached, the display will flash 'Spanner' or 'Service Now'. Note that if the variable (LongLife) service interval is being used, the engine must **only** be filled with the recommended **long-life** engine oil (see *Lubricants and fluids*).

After completing a service, VW technicians use a special instrument to reset the service display to the next service interval, and a print-out is put in the vehicle service record. The display can be reset by the owner as described in Section 5, but note that for models using the 'LongLife' interval, the procedure will automatically reset the display to the 10 000 miles 'distance' interval. To have the display reset to the 'variable' (LongLife) interval, it is necessary to take the vehicle to a VW dealer who will use a special instrument to encode the on-board computer.

Every 250 miles
☐ Refer to *Weekly checks*

Every 10 000 miles or 12 months, whichever comes first
☐ Renew the engine oil and filter (Section 3)
Note: *Frequent oil and filter changes are good for the engine. We recommend changing the oil at least once a year.*
☐ Check the front and rear brake pad thickness (Section 4)
☐ Reset the service interval display (Section 5)

Every 20 000 miles or 2 years, whichever comes first
In addition to the items listed above, carry out the following:
☐ Check the condition of the exhaust system and its mountings (Section 6)
☐ Check all underbonnet components and hoses for fluid and oil leaks (Section 7)
☐ Renew the fuel filter* (Section 8)
☐ Check the condition of the auxiliary drivebelt (Section 9)
☐ Check the coolant antifreeze concentration (Section 10)
☐ Check the brake hydraulic circuit for leaks and damage (Section 11)
☐ Check the headlight beam adjustment (Section 12)
☐ Renew the pollen filter element (Section 13)
☐ Check the manual transmission oil level (Section 14)
☐ Check the underbody protection for damage (Section 15)
☐ Check the condition of the driveshaft gaiters (Section 16)
☐ Check the steering and suspension components for condition and security (Section 17)
☐ Check the battery condition, security and electrolyte level (Section 18)
☐ Lubricate all hinges and locks (Section 19)
☐ Check the condition of the airbag unit(s) (Section 20)
☐ Check the operation of the windscreen/tailgate/headlight washer system(s) (as applicable) (Section 21)
☐ Check the engine management self-diagnosis memory for faults (Section 22)
☐ Check the operation of the sunroof and lubricate the guide rails (Section 23)
☐ Carry out a road test and check exhaust emissions (Section 24)
* Only when using diesel fuel not conforming to DIN EN 590 or when using RME fuel (diester)

Every 40 000 miles or 4 years, whichever comes first
Note: *Many dealers perform these tasks at every second service.*
☐ Renew DSG transmission oil renewal (Section 25)
☐ Renew the air filter element (Section 26)
☐ Renew the fuel filter* (Section 27)
☐ Check the condition of the auxiliary drivebelt (Section 28)
* Only when using diesel fuel conforming to DIN EN 590

Every 60 000 miles or 4 years
☐ Renew the timing belt and tensioner roller (Section 29)
Note: *VW specify a timing belt renewal interval of 112 000 miles for 1.6 litre models, and 75 000 miles for 2.0 litre models up to 2010 and 130 000 miles for 2.0 litre models from 2010. They specify a tensioner roller renewal interval of 200 000 miles for 1.6 litre models, and 130 000 miles for 2.0 litre models. However, if the vehicle is used mainly for short journeys, we recommend that a shorter renewal interval be adhered to. The belt and tensioner renewal interval is very much up to the individual owner but, bearing in mind that severe engine damage will result if the belt breaks in use, we recommend a shorter interval.*

Every 95 000 miles, then every 19 000 miles
☐ Check the particulate filter ash deposit mass (Section 32)

Every 2 years
☐ Renew the brake (and clutch) fluid (Section 30)
☐ Renew the coolant* (Section 31)
** **Note:** This work is not included in the VW schedule and should not be required if the recommended VW G12 LongLife coolant antifreeze/inhibitor is used.*

Underbonnet view of a 1.6 litre model

1 Engine oil filler cap
2 Engine oil dipstick
3 Oil filter
4 Coolant expansion tank
5 Fuel filter
6 Windscreen/headlight/
   rear window washer fluid
   reservoir
7 Common fuel rail
8 Particulate filter
9 High-pressure fuel pump
10 Battery
11 Fusebox
12 Air cleaner housing

Front underbody view

1 Sump drain plug
2 Manual transmission drain
   plug
3 Auxiliary belt
4 Sump insulator cover
5 Air conditioning compressor
6 Radiator and electric cooling
   fans
7 Air duct/hoses to intercooler
8 Starter motor
9 Engine oil level/temperature
   sensor
10 Front anti-roll bar drop-links
11 Front brake calipers
12 Front suspension lower arms
13 Steering track rod arms
14 Driveshafts
15 Front suspension subframe
16 Exhaust pipe

Rear underbody view

1 Exhaust rear silencer
2 Rear track control lower arm
3 Rear anti-roll bar
4 Rear wheel bearing housing
5 Rear suspension transverse links
6 Spare wheel well
7 Rear suspension subframe beam
8 Rear trailing arm and bracket
9 Fuel tank
10 Hydraulic brake lines
11 Handbrake cables

Maintenance procedures

1 Introduction

This Chapter is designed to help the home mechanic maintain his/her vehicle for safety, economy, long life and peak performance.

The Chapter contains a master maintenance schedule, followed by Sections dealing specifically with each task in the schedule. Visual checks, adjustments, component renewal and other helpful items are included. Refer to the accompanying illustrations of the engine compartment and the underside of the vehicle for the locations of the various components.

Servicing your vehicle will provide a planned maintenance programme, which should result in a long and reliable service life. This is a comprehensive plan, so maintaining some items but not others, will not produce the same results.

As you service your vehicle, you will discover that many of the procedures can – and should – be grouped together, because of the particular procedure being performed, or because of the proximity of two otherwise unrelated components to one another. For example, if the vehicle is raised for any reason, the exhaust can be inspected at the same time as the suspension and steering components.

The first step in this maintenance programme is to prepare yourself before the actual work begins. Read through all the Sections relevant to the work to be carried out, then make a list and gather all the parts and tools required. If a problem is encountered, seek advice from a parts specialist, or a dealer service department.

2 Regular maintenance

1 If, from the time the vehicle is new, the routine maintenance schedule is followed closely, and frequent checks are made of fluid levels and high-wear items, as suggested throughout this manual, the engine will be kept in relatively good running condition, and the need for additional work will be minimised.
2 It is possible that there will be times when the engine is running poorly due to the lack of regular maintenance. This is even more likely if a used vehicle, which has not received regular and frequent maintenance checks, is purchased. In such cases, additional work may need to be carried out, outside of the regular maintenance intervals.
3 If engine wear is suspected, a compression test (refer to Chapter 2C or 2D) will provide valuable information regarding the overall performance of the main internal components. Such a test can be used as a basis to decide on the extent of the work to be carried out. If, for example, a compression test indicates serious internal engine wear, conventional maintenance as described in this Chapter will not greatly improve the performance of the engine, and may prove a waste of time and money, unless extensive overhaul work is carried out first.
4 The following series of operations are those most often required to improve the performance of a generally poor-running engine:

Primary operations

a) Clean, inspect and test the battery (See 'Weekly checks').
b) Check all the engine-related fluids (See 'Weekly checks').
c) Drain the water from the fuel filter.
d) Check the condition and tension of the auxiliary drivebelt (Section 9).
e) Check the condition of the air filter, and renew if necessary (Section 26).
f) Check the condition of all hoses, and check for fluid leaks (Section 7).
5 If the above operations do not prove fully effective, carry out the following secondary operations:

Secondary operations

All items listed under Primary operations, plus the following:
a) Check the charging system (see Chapter 5A).
b) Check the preheating system (see Chapter 5C).
c) Renew the fuel filter (Section 8) and check the fuel system (see Chapter 4B).

3.2a The engine undertray is secured by a number of screws

3.2b Pull the plastic cover upwards to release it

3.3 Undo the sump drain plug

Every 10 000 miles or 12 months

3 Engine oil and filter renewal

1 Frequent oil and filter changes are the most important preventative maintenance procedures, which can be undertaken by the DIY owner. As engine oil ages, it becomes diluted and contaminated, which leads to premature engine wear.

2 Before starting this procedure, gather all the necessary tools and materials. Also make sure that you have plenty of clean rags and newspapers handy, to mop-up any spills. Ideally, the engine oil should be warm, as it will drain better, and more built-up sludge will be removed with it. Take care, however, not to touch the exhaust or any other hot parts of the engine when working under the vehicle. To avoid any possibility of scalding, and to protect yourself from possible skin irritants and other harmful contaminants in used engine oils, it is advisable to wear gloves when carrying out this work. Access to the underside of the vehicle will be greatly improved if it can be raised on a lift, driven onto ramps, or jacked up and supported on axle stands (see *Jacking and vehicle support*). Whichever method is chosen, make sure that the vehicle remains level, or if it is at an angle, that the drain plug is at the lowest point. Undo the retaining screws and remove the engine undertray, then also remove the engine top cover **(see illustrations)**.

3 Slacken the sump drain plug about half a turn. Position the draining container under the drain plug, and then remove the plug completely **(see illustration and Haynes Hint)**. To drain all oil from the engine, loosen the cap from the top of the oil filter housing using a socket or spanner - this will allow the oil to drain from the filter housing into the sump.

4 Allow some time for the old oil to drain, noting that it may be necessary to reposition the container as the oil flow slows to a trickle.

5 After all the oil has drained, wipe off the drain plug with a clean rag, and fit a new sealing washer. Clean the area around the drain plug opening, and refit the plug. Tighten the plug securely. **Note:** *On some engines, the sealing washer is integral with the drain plug. On these engines, the drain plug must be renewed.*

6 Place absorbent cloths around the oil filter housing to catch any spilt oil. Where necessary, unbolt the bracket and unclip the solenoid valve from above the oil filter **(see illustration)**.

7 Fully unscrew the cap from the top of the oil filter and remove it together with the filter element. Recover the large sealing ring from the cap, and the small sealing ring from the centre rod. Unclip the filter element from the cap and dispose of it **(see illustrations)**.

8 Using a clean rag, wipe all oil and sludge from the inside of the filter housing and cap.

9 Fit new sealing rings, then refit the assembly and tighten to the specified torque. Make sure the filter element is engaged with the cap and the correct way up **(see illustrations)**. Wipe up any spilt oil before refitting the engine top cover.

Keep the drain plug pressed into the sump while unscrewing it by hand the last couple of turns. As the plug releases, move it away sharply so the stream of oil issuing from the sump runs into the container, not up your sleeve.

3.6 Remove the solenoid valve - arrowed

3.7a Use a 32 mm socket to unscrew the filter cap ...

3.7b ... and withdraw the filter and cap ...

3.7c ... then slide the old filter from the cap

3.9a The new oil filter comes with three O-ring seals

3.9b Fit the three seals to the oil filter cap in the positions shown …

3.9c … then slide the new filter to the cap …

10 Remove the old oil and all tools from under the car then refit the undertray and lower the car to the ground. Also refit the engine top cover.

11 Remove the dipstick, and then unscrew the oil filler cap from the cylinder head cover. Fill the engine, using the correct grade and type of oil (see *Lubricants and fluids*). An oil can spout or funnel may help to reduce spillage. Pour in half the specified quantity of oil first **(see illustration)**, then wait a few minutes for the oil to run to the sump (see *Weekly checks*). Continue adding oil a small quantity at a time until the level is up to the maximum mark on the dipstick. Refit the filler cap.

12 Start the engine and run it for a few minutes; check for leaks around the oil filter cap and the sump drain plug. Note that there may be a few seconds delay before the oil pressure warning light goes out when the engine is started, as the oil circulates through the engine oil galleries and the new oil filter before the pressure builds-up.

⚠️ *Warning: Do not increase the engine speed above idling while the oil pressure light is illuminated, as considerable damage can be caused to the turbocharger.*

13 Switch off the engine, and wait a few minutes for the oil to settle in the sump once more. With the new oil circulated and the filter completely full, recheck the level on the dipstick, and add more oil as necessary.

14 Dispose of the used engine oil safely, with reference to *General repair procedures* in the *Reference* section of this manual.

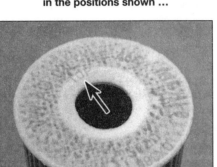

3.9d … noting 'TOP' on the filter for correct fitting

3.9e Lubricate the O-ring seals with clean engine …

3.9f …then refit to the oil filter housing

3.11 Pour in half the specified quantity of oil first, wait, then add the rest

4 Brake pad check

1 The outer brake pads can be checked without removing the wheels, by observing the brake pads through the holes in the wheels **(see illustration)**. If necessary, remove the wheel trim. The thickness of the pad lining must not be less than the dimension given in the Specifications.

2 If the outer pads are worn near their limits, it is worthwhile checking the inner pads as well. Apply the handbrake then jack up vehicle

and support it on axle stands (see *Jacking and vehicle support*). Remove the roadwheels.

3 Use a steel rule to check the thickness of the brake pads, and compare with the minimum thickness given in the Specifications **(see illustration)**.

4.1 The outer brake pads can be observed through the holes in the wheels

4.3 The thickness (a) of the brake pad linings must not be less than the specified amount

5.2 Press reset button (A) and then clock setting button (B)

4 For a comprehensive check, the brake pads should be removed and cleaned. The operation of the caliper can then also be checked, and the condition of the brake disc itself can be fully examined on both sides. Refer to Chapter 9, Section 4 (front) or Chapter 9, Section 8 (rear).

5 If any pad's friction material is worn to the specified minimum thickness or less, *all four pads at the front or rear, as applicable, must be renewed as a set.*

6 On completion of the check, refit the roadwheels and lower the vehicle to the ground.

5 Resetting the service interval display

1 After all necessary maintenance work has been completed; the service interval display must be reset. VW technicians use a special dedicated instrument to do this, and a print-out is then put in the vehicle service record. It is possible for the owner to reset the display as described in the following paragraphs, but note that the procedure will automatically reset the display to a 10 000 mile interval. To continue with the 'variable' intervals which take into consideration the number of starts, length of journeys, vehicle speeds, brake pad wear, bonnet opening frequency, fuel consumption, oil level and oil temperature, the display must be reset by a VW dealership using the special dedicated instrument.

2 To reset the standard display (vehicles without text message display), follow the procedures below **(see illustration)**:
  a) *Switch off the ignition.*
  b) *Press and hold down the trip reset button '0.0/SET' beneath the speedometer.*
  c) *Switch the ignition on.*

  d) *Release the reset button '0.0/SET'.*
  e) *Then briefly press the clock setting button beneath the rev counter (within 20 seconds).*
  f) *Service interval will then be reset.*

3 To read the service information on this display
  a) *Switch the ignition on (engine not running).*
  b) *Press the trip reset button '0.0/SET' twice to change menu.*
  c) *Then press the clock setting button (beneath the rev counter) four times.*
  d) *Service interval display will flash.*
  e) *The remaining days/kilometers will be displayed.*

4 On models with multi-function switch on the steering wheel or windscreen wiper lever, to reset the display follow the procedure below.
  a) *Select the settings on the menu, using buttons on steering wheel or wiper lever.*
  b) *Select the menu option* **Reset** *in the* **Service** *sub-menu.*
  c) *Confirm the request by pressing* **OK**.
  d) *Service interval will then be reset.*

Every 20 000 miles or 2 years

6 Exhaust system check

1 With the engine cold (at least an hour after the vehicle has been driven), check the complete exhaust system from the engine to the end of the tailpipe. The exhaust system is most easily checked with the vehicle raised on a hoist, or suitably supported on axle stands, so that the exhaust components are readily visible and accessible (see *Jacking and vehicle support*).

2 Check the exhaust pipes and connections for evidence of leaks, severe corrosion and damage. Make sure that all brackets and

A leak in the cooling system will usually show up as white- or antifreeze-coloured deposits on the area adjoining the leak.

mountings are in good condition, and that all relevant nuts and bolts are tight. Leakage at any of the joints or in other parts of the system will usually show up as a black sooty stain in the vicinity of the leak.

3 Rattles and other noises can often be traced to the exhaust system, especially the brackets and mountings. Try to move the pipes and silencers. If the components are able to come into contact with the body or suspension parts, secure the system with new mountings. Otherwise separate the joints (if possible) and twist the pipes as necessary to provide additional clearance.

7 Hose and fluid leak check

1 Visually inspect the engine joint faces, gaskets and seals for any signs of water or oil leaks. Pay particular attention to the areas around the camshaft cover, cylinder head, oil filter and sump joint faces. Bear in mind that, over a period of time, some very slight seepage from these areas is to be expected – what you are really looking for is any indication of a serious leak. Should a leak be found, renew the offending gasket or oil seal by referring to the appropriate Chapters in this manual.

2 Also check the security and condition of all the engine-related pipes and hoses. Ensure that all cable-ties or securing clips are in place and in good condition. Clips, which are broken or missing, can lead to chafing of the

hoses, pipes or wiring, which could cause more serious problems in the future.

3 Carefully check the radiator hoses and heater hoses along their entire length. Renew any hose that is cracked, swollen or deteriorated. Cracks will show up better if the hose is squeezed. Pay close attention to the hose clips that secure the hoses to the cooling system components. Hose clips can pinch and puncture hoses, resulting in cooling system leaks.

4 Inspect all the cooling system components (hoses, joint faces, etc) for leaks **(see Haynes Hint)**. Where any problems of this nature are found on system components, renew the component or gasket with reference to Chapter 3.

5 Where applicable, inspect the automatic transmission fluid cooler hoses for leaks or deterioration.

6 With the vehicle raised, inspect the fuel tank and filler neck for punctures, cracks and other damage. The connection between the filler neck and tank is especially critical. Sometimes a rubber filler neck or connecting hose will leak due to loose retaining clamps or deteriorated rubber.

7 Carefully check all rubber hoses and metal fuel lines leading away from the tank. Check for loose connections, deteriorated hoses, crimped lines, and other damage. Pay particular attention to the vent pipes and hoses, which often loop up around the filler neck and can become blocked or crimped. Follow the lines to the front of the vehicle, carefully inspecting them all the way. Renew damaged sections as necessary.

8 From within the engine compartment, check the security of all fuel hose attachments and pipe unions, and inspect the fuel hoses and vacuum hoses for kinks, chafing and deterioration.

8 Fuel filter renewal (vehicles using high sulphur diesel fuel)

Note: *Carry out this procedure at this interval only when using diesel fuel not conforming to DIN EN 590 or when using RME fuel (diester) – this fuel is not available in the UK. There is no longer any requirement to drain water from the filter.*
   Refer to Section 27, for renewal of fuel filter.

9 Auxiliary drivebelt check

1 Apply the handbrake, then jack up the front of the vehicle and support it on axle stands (see *Jacking and vehicle support*).
2 Using a socket on the crankshaft pulley bolt, turn the engine slowly clockwise so that the full length of the auxiliary drivebelt can be examined. Look for cracks, splitting and fraying on the surface of the belt; check also for signs of glazing (shiny patches) and separation of the belt plies. If damage or wear is visible, or if there are traces of oil or grease on it, the belt should be renewed (see Section 28).

10 Antifreeze check

1 The cooling system should be filled with the recommended G12 antifreeze and corrosion protection fluid – **do not** mix this antifreeze with any other type. Over a period of time, the concentration of fluid may be reduced due to topping-up (this can be avoided by topping-up with the correct antifreeze mixture – see Specifications) or fluid loss. If loss of coolant has been evident, it is important to make the necessary repair before adding fresh fluid.
2 With the engine **cold**, carefully remove the cap from the expansion tank. If the engine is not completely cold, place a cloth rag over the cap before removing it, and remove it slowly to allow any pressure to escape.
3 Antifreeze checkers are available from car accessory shops. Draw some coolant from the expansion tank and observe how many plastic balls are floating in the checker. Usually, 2 or 3 balls must be floating for the correct concentration of antifreeze, but follow the manufacturer's instructions.
4 If the concentration is incorrect, it will be necessary to either withdraw some coolant and add antifreeze, or alternatively drain the old coolant and add fresh coolant of the correct concentration (see Section 31).

13.2 Remove the facia lower trim from beneath the glovebox

13.3b ... and screw (where fitted) ...

11 Brake hydraulic circuit check

1 Check the entire brake hydraulic circuit for leaks and damage. Start by checking the master cylinder in the engine compartment. At the same time, check the vacuum servo unit and ABS units for signs of fluid leakage.
2 Raise the front and rear of the vehicle and support it on axle stands (see *Jacking and vehicle support*). Check the rigid hydraulic brake lines for corrosion and damage.
3 At the front of the vehicle, check that the flexible hydraulic hoses to the calipers are not twisted or chafing on any of the surrounding suspension components. Turn the steering on full lock to make this check. Also check that the hoses are not brittle or cracked.
4 Lower the vehicle to the ground after making the checks.

12 Headlight beam adjustment

1 Accurate adjustment of the headlight beam is only possible using optical beam-setting equipment, and this work should therefore be carried out by a VW dealer or service station with the necessary facilities.
2 Basic adjustments can be carried out in an emergency, and further details are given in Chapter 12, Section 8.

13.3a Remove the access cover...

13.4 ... then slide out the pollen filter element

13 Pollen filter element renewal

1 The pollen filter is located in the heater unit and is accessed from inside the car, on the passenger's side.
2 Remove the clips and withdraw the facia lower trim from beneath the glovebox **(see illustration)**.
3 Slide the cover to the left to remove the access cover **(see illustrations)**. If the cover has been removed previously there may be a screw securing the cover in place.
4 Slide out the pollen filter element downwards from the heater unit **(see illustration)**.
5 Fit the new element then refit the access cover, making sure that the locating lugs are fitted correctly in the housing. If any of the lugs have been broken off, fit a screw into the cover to make sure it is secure.
6 Refit the trim beneath the facia/glovebox.

14 Manual transmission oil level check

1 Park the car on a level surface. For improved access to the filler/level plug, apply the handbrake, then jack up the front of the vehicle and support it on axle stands (see *Jacking and vehicle support*), but note that the rear of the vehicle should also be raised to ensure an accurate level check. The oil level must be checked before the car is driven, or

14.3 Removing oil filler/level plug - 02Q transmission

14.10 Press down the selector shaft (2), and rotate the locking rod (1) upwards

14.5 Oil drain plug (A) and filler/level plug (B) - 02Q transmission

14.12 Oil drain pug (A) and pivot pin (B) - 0A4 transmission

at least 5 minutes after the engine has been switched off. If the oil is checked immediately after driving the car, some of the oil will remain distributed around the transmission components, resulting in an inaccurate level reading.

02Q transmission

2 Undo the retaining screws and remove the engine undertray. Wipe clean the area around the transmission filler/level plug, which is situated on the front of the transmission casing.

3 The oil level should reach the lower edge of the filler/level hole. A certain amount of oil will have gathered behind the filler/level plug, and will trickle out when it is removed (**see illustration**); this does **not** necessarily indicate that the level is correct. To ensure that a true level is established, wait until the initial trickle has stopped, then add oil as necessary until a

16.1 Check the condition of the driveshaft gaiters (arrowed)

trickle of new oil can be seen emerging. The level will be correct when the flow ceases; use only good-quality oil of the specified type.

4 If the transmission has been overfilled so that oil flows out when the filler/level plug is removed, check that the car is completely level (front-to-rear and side-to-side), and allow the surplus to drain off into a suitable container.

5 When the oil level is correct, refit the filler/level plug and tighten it to the specified torque (**see illustration**).

6 Wipe off any spilt oil then refit the engine undertray(s), tighten the retaining screws securely, and lower the car to the ground.

0A4 transmission

7 Undo the fasteners and remove the engine undertray.

8 On these transmissions, it's impossible to check the level of the oil through the 'filler' plug, due to the engine/transmission installation angle; the level of the fluid is above the lower edge of the filler hole. The only method of ensuring the correct fluid level is to completely drain and refill the transmission.

9 Remove the air cleaner housing as described in Chapter 4B, Section 2.

10 In order to drain the transmission, the pivot pin must be removed from the underside of the transmission casing. However, to prevent the position of the selector forks being altered, press the selector shaft down, then turn the angled locking rod upwards, and lock the shaft in position (**see illustration**).

11 Place a container under the transmission casing.

12 Unscrew the drain plug from the base of the differential housing, and allow the oil to drain (**see illustration**).

13 Then undo the retaining bolt, pull out the pivot pin nearest the passenger's roadwheel and allow the oil to drain (**see illustration 13.12**). The pivot pin O-ring seal must be renewed.

14 When the oil has finished draining clean the surrounding area, then refit the pivot pin (with a new O-ring seal), and tighten the retaining bolt to the specified torque.

15 When the oil has finished draining, clean the surrounding area, refit the drain plug and tighten it to the specified torque.

16 Rotate the selector-shaft locking rod to its original position.

17 Unscrew the reversing light switch from the top of the transmission casing.

18 Using a 600 mm length of 10 mm (external) diameter hose, and funnel, add 1.9 litres of new oil to the transmission.

19 Refit the reversing light switch, and tighten it to the specified torque.

20 The remainder of refitting is a reversal of removal.

15 Underbody protection check

Raise and support the vehicle on axle stands (see *Jacking and vehicle support*). Using an electric torch or lead light, inspect the entire underside of the vehicle, paying particular attention to the wheel arches. Look for any damage to the flexible underbody coating, which may crack or flake off with age, leading to corrosion. Also check that the wheel arch liners are securely attached with any clips provided – if they come loose, dirt may get in behind the liners and defeat their purpose. If there is any damage to the under seal, or any corrosion, it should be repaired before the damage gets too serious.

16 Driveshaft gaiter check

1 With the vehicle raised and securely supported on stands, slowly rotate the roadwheel. Inspect the condition of the outer constant velocity (CV) joint rubber gaiters, squeezing the gaiters to open out the folds. Check for signs of cracking, splits or deterioration of the rubber, which may allow the grease to escape, and lead to water and grit entry into the joint. Also check the security and condition of the retaining clips. Repeat these checks on the inner joints (**see illustration**). If any damage or deterioration is found, the gaiters should be renewed (see Chapter 8, Section 3).

2 At the same time, check the general condition of the CV joints themselves by first holding the driveshaft and attempting to rotate the wheel. Repeat this check by holding the inner joint and attempting to rotate the driveshaft. Any appreciable movement indicates wear in the joints, wear in the driveshaft splines, or a loose driveshaft retaining nut.

17 Steering and suspension check

1 Raise the front and rear of the vehicle, and securely support it on axle stands (see *Jacking and vehicle support*).
2 Visually inspect the track rod end balljoint dust cover, the lower front suspension balljoint dust cover, and the steering rack-and-pinion gaiters for splits, chafing or deterioration. Any wear of these components will cause loss of lubricant, together with dirt and water entry, resulting in rapid deterioration of the balljoints or steering gear.
3 Check the power steering fluid hoses for chafing or deterioration, and the pipe and hose unions for fluid leaks. Also check for signs of fluid leakage under pressure from the steering gear rubber gaiters, which would indicate failed fluid seals within the steering gear.
4 Grasp the roadwheel at the 12 o'clock and 6 o'clock positions, and try to rock it **(see illustration)**. Very slight free play may be felt, but if the movement is appreciable, further investigation is necessary to determine the source. Continue rocking the wheel while an assistant depresses the footbrake. If the movement is now eliminated or significantly reduced, it is likely that the hub bearings are at fault. If the free play is still evident with the footbrake depressed, then there is wear in the suspension joints or mountings.
5 Now grasp the wheel at the 9 o'clock and 3 o'clock positions, and try to rock it as before **(see illustration)**. Any movement felt now may again be caused by wear in the hub bearings or the steering track rod balljoints. If the inner or outer balljoint is worn, the visual movement will be obvious.
6 Using a large screwdriver or flat bar, check for wear in the suspension mounting bushes

17.4 Check for wear in the bearings by grasping the wheel top and bottom and trying to rock it

by levering between the relevant suspension component and its attachment point. Some movement is to be expected as the mountings are made of rubber, but excessive wear should be obvious. Also check the condition of any visible rubber bushes, looking for splits, cracks or contamination of the rubber.
7 With the car standing on its wheels, have an assistant turn the steering wheel back-and-forth about an eighth of a turn each way. There should be very little, if any, lost movement between the steering wheel and roadwheels. If this is not the case, closely observe the joints and mountings previously described, but in addition, check the steering column universal joints for wear, and the rack-and-pinion steering gear itself.
8 Check for any signs of fluid leakage around the front suspension struts and rear shock absorber. Should any fluid be noticed, the suspension strut or shock absorber is defective internally, and should be renewed. **Note:** *Suspension struts/shock absorbers should always be renewed in pairs on the same axle to ensure correct vehicle handling.*
9 The efficiency of the suspension strut/shock absorber may be checked by bouncing the vehicle at each corner. Generally speaking, the body will return to its normal position and stop after being depressed. If it rises and returns on a rebound, the suspension strut/shock absorber is probably suspect. Examine also the suspension strut/shock absorber upper and lower mountings for any signs of wear.

17.5 Check for wear in the bearings and ball joints by grasping the wheel at the sides and trying to rock it

18 Battery check

1 The battery is located on the left-hand side of the engine compartment. Where an insulator cover is fitted **(see illustration)**, open the cover to gain access to the battery.
2 Check that both battery terminals and all the fuse holder connections are securely attached **(see illustration)** and are free from corrosion. **Note:** *Before disconnecting the terminals from the battery, refer to 'Disconnecting the battery' in the Reference Chapter at the end of this manual.*
3 Check the battery casing for signs of damage or cracking and check the battery retaining clamp bolt is securely tightened **(see illustration)**. If the battery casing is damaged in any way the battery must be renewed (see Chapter 5A, Section 3).
4 If the vehicle is not fitted with a sealed-for-life maintenance-free battery, check the electrolyte level is between the MAX and MIN level markings on the battery casing. If topping-up is necessary, remove the battery from the vehicle then remove the cell caps/cover (as applicable). Using distilled water, top the electrolyte level of each cell up to the MAX level mark then securely refit the cell caps/cover. Ensure the battery has not been overfilled then refit the battery to the vehicle (see Chapter 5A, Section 3).
5 On completion close up the battery insulator cover.

18.1 Pull back the battery insulator cover

18.2 Check that the terminals are secure

18.3 Check that the battery clamp (arrowed) is secure

22.1 Diagnostic socket - arrowed

19 Hinge and lock lubrication

1 Lubricate the hinges of the bonnet, doors and tailgate with light general-purpose oil. Similarly, lubricate all latches, locks and lock strikers. At the same time, check the security and operation of all the locks, adjusting them if necessary (see Chapter 11, Section 11).
2 Lightly lubricate the bonnet release mechanism and cable with suitable grease.

20 Airbag unit check

Inspect the exterior condition of the airbag(s) for signs of damage or deterioration. If an airbag shows signs of damage, it must be renewed (see Chapter 12, Section 25 & 26). Note that it is not permissible to attach any stickers to the surface of the airbag, as this may affect the deployment of the unit.

21 Windscreen/tailgate/ headlight washer system check

1 Check that each of the washer jet nozzles are clear and that each nozzle provides a strong jet of washer fluid.
2 The tailgate jet should be aimed to spray at the centre of the screen, using a pin.
3 The windscreen washer nozzles should be aimed slightly above the centre of the screen using a small screwdriver to turn the jet eccentric (see Chapter 12, Section 20).
4 The headlight inner jet should be aimed slightly above the horizontal centreline of the headlight, and the outer jet should be aimed slightly below the centreline. VW technicians use a special tool to adjust the headlight jet after pulling the jet out onto its stop.

5 Especially during the winter months, make sure that the washer fluid frost concentration is sufficient.

22 Engine management self-diagnosis memory fault check

This work should be carried out by a VW dealer or a diagnostic specialist using special equipment. The diagnostic socket is located below the facia, at the right-hand side above the bonnet release handle (see illustration).

23 Sunroof check and lubrication

1 Check the operation of the sunroof, and leave it in the fully open position.
2 Wipe clean the guide rails on each side of the sunroof opening, then apply lubricant to them. VW recommend lubricant spray G 052 778.

24 Road test and exhaust emissions check

Instruments and electrical equipment

1 Check the operation of all instruments and electrical equipment including the air conditioning system.
2 Make sure that all instruments read correctly, and switch on all electrical equipment in turn, to check that it functions properly.

Steering and suspension

3 Check for any abnormalities in the steering, suspension, handling or road 'feel'.
4 Drive the vehicle, and check that there are no unusual vibrations or noises, which may indicate wear in the driveshafts, wheel bearings, etc.
5 Check that the steering feels positive, with no excessive 'sloppiness', or roughness, and check for any suspension noises when cornering and driving over bumps.

Drivetrain

6 Check the performance of the engine, clutch (where applicable), gearbox/transmission and driveshafts.
7 Listen for any unusual noises from the engine, clutch and gearbox/transmission.
8 Make sure the engine runs smoothly at idle, and there is no hesitation on accelerating.
9 Check that, where applicable, the clutch

action is smooth and progressive, that the drive is taken up smoothly, and that the pedal travel is not excessive. Also listen for any noises when the clutch pedal is depressed.
10 On manual gearbox models check that all gears can be engaged smoothly without noise, and that the gear lever action is smooth and not abnormally vague or 'notchy'.
11 On automatic transmission models, make sure that all gearchanges occur smoothly, without snatching, and without an increase in engine speed between changes. Check that all the gear positions can be selected with the vehicle at rest. If any problems are found, they should be referred to a VW dealer.
12 Listen for a metallic clicking sound from the front of the vehicle, as the vehicle is driven slowly in a circle with the steering on full-lock. Carry out this check in both directions. If a clicking noise is heard, this indicates wear in a driveshaft joint, in which case renew the joint if necessary.

Braking system

13 Make sure that the vehicle does not pull to one side when braking, and that the wheels do not lock when braking hard.
14 Check that there is no vibration through the steering when braking.
15 Check that the handbrake operates correctly without excessive movement of the lever, and that it holds the vehicle stationary on a slope.
16 Test the operation of the brake servo unit as follows. With the engine off, depress the footbrake four or five times to exhaust the vacuum. Hold the brake pedal depressed, and then start the engine. As the engine starts, there should be a noticeable 'give' in the brake pedal as vacuum builds-up. Allow the engine to run for at least two minutes, and then switch it off. If the brake pedal is depressed now, it should be possible to detect a hiss from the servo as the pedal is depressed. After about four or five applications, no further hissing should be heard, and the pedal should feel considerably harder.
17 Under controlled emergency braking, the pulsing of the ABS unit must be felt at the footbrake pedal.

Exhaust emissions check

18 Although not part of the manufacturer's maintenance schedule, this check will normally be carried out on a regular basis according to the country the vehicle is operated in. Currently in the UK, exhaust emissions testing is included as part of the annual MOT test after the vehicle is 3 years old. In Germany the test is made when the vehicle is 3 years old, then repeated every 2 years.

26.2 Undo the retaining screws ...

26.3 ... and lift off the upper cover

27.2a Clean around the top of the fuel filter ...

27.2b ... and place some cloth to catch spilt fuel

27.3a Carefully prise up the top ...

27.3b ... and remove it from the filter housing

Every 40 000 miles or 4 years

25 DSG transmission oil renewal

1 The semi-automatic (DSG) dual shift gearbox is fitted to the following diesel models.
  a) The 1.6 litre diesel engine has the 7-speed dual clutch (0AM) transmission.
  b) The 2.0 litre diesel engine has the 6-speed dual clutch (02E) transmission.
2 Both transmissions are filled for life, and are not part of the service schedule. If there has been an oil leak from the transmission, after the leak has been rectified, renew the transmission oil as described in Chapter 7B, Section 6.

26 Air filter element renewal

1 The air cleaner is located in front of the battery in the left-hand front corner of the engine compartment.
2 Undo the cover retaining screws and lift the air cleaner cover, taking care not to put any strain on the intake ducting and air mass meter **(see illustration)**.
3 With the cover raised, withdraw the air filter element, noting how it is fitted **(see illustration)**.
4 Remove any debris that may have collected inside the air cleaner.

5 Fit a new air filter element in position, ensuring that the edges are securely seated.
6 Refit the lid and tighten the screws, then refit the engine top cover.

27 Fuel filter renewal (vehicles using standard diesel fuel)

Note: *Carry out this procedure at this interval only when using diesel fuel conforming to DIN EN 590 (standard fuel in the UK).*
1 The fuel filter is mounted in the right-hand front corner of the engine compartment. Place rags around the filter to absorb any fuel that may be spilt.

27.4 Remove the old filter element ...

2 Before removing the fuel filter, clean around the fuel pipes on the top of the filter housing to prevent any dirt entering the fuel system **(see illustrations)**. Place some cloth around the filter housing to catch any fuel spillage.
3 Undo the screws and lift the cover complete with fuel hoses from the top of the filter housing and move it to one side **(see illustrations)**. Remove the seal and discard, as a new one must be used on refitting.
4 Withdraw the old filter element out from the housing and discard **(see illustration)**.
5 Use a pipette/syringe to draw out the dirty fuel and water residue from inside the fuel filter lower housing. Then insert the new filter element, pressing it down fully into position **(see illustrations)**.
6 To help the engine start easier (to prevent

27.5a ...then use a pipette to draw out the old fuel ...

27.5b ... and insert the new filter element

27.7a Fit new seal ...

27.7b ... then refit the upper cover

having to bleed the system), top up the lower filter housing with clean diesel, making sure that no dirt or water enters the system.

7 Fit a new seal to the cover, then refit the cover back on the lower filter housing, making sure the top is located in the filter correctly **(see illustrations)**. Press down firmly and evenly, then insert the screws and tighten them in a diagonal sequence.

8 Start and run the engine at idle, then check around the fuel filter for fuel leaks. **Note:** *It may take a few seconds of cranking before the engine starts.*

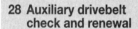

28 Auxiliary drivebelt check and renewal

Check

1 See Section 9, for information on checking the condition of the drivebelt.

2 There are two different types of tensioner fitted to diesel engines; the routing of the belt is the same, although the procedure for belt renewal is different.

3 When the belt is removed, check all pulleys are free from any damage and are secure. Also check that the alternator and air-conditioning compressor are mounted securely.

Renewal

4 For improved access, apply the handbrake, and then jack up the front of the vehicle and support it on axle stands (see *Jacking and vehicle support*).

5 Remove the right-hand front roadwheel, then remove the access panel from the inner wheel arch.

With tensioner spring element

6 Use a spanner on the centre bolt and turn the tensioner clockwise. Lock the tensioner in its released position by inserting a locking pin

(Allen key or similar) through the lug into the tensioner body **(see illustrations)**.

7 Note how the drivebelt is routed, then remove it from the crankshaft pulley **(see illustration)**, alternator pulley, and air conditioning compressor pulley (as applicable).

8 Locate the new drivebelt on the pulleys, then by holding the pressure of the tensioner with a spanner, remove the locking pin. Slowly release the pressure on the spanner **(see illustration)**, so that the tensioner takes up the slack in the belt. Check that the belt is located correctly in the multi-grooves in the pulleys.

9 Start the engine and check that the drivebelt runs, as it should over the pulleys. Make sure that all tools and hands are kept clear of the drivebelt with the engine running.

10 With the engine stopped, refit the access panel and roadwheel, and then lower the vehicle to the ground. Refit the engine top cover if removed.

With tensioner roller

11 Undo the tensioner roller retaining bolt, and remove the tensioner roller from the engine. Note the retaining bolt is below the tensioner roller, and goes up through the mounting bracket in a vertical direction **(see illustration)**. Discard the retaining bolt, as a new one will be required for refitting.

12 Note how the drivebelt is routed, then remove it from the crankshaft pulley, alternator pulley, and air-conditioning compressor pulley (as applicable).

13 Locate the new drivebelt on the pulleys, then fit the tensioner roller, making sure its guide pin is located correctly in the mounting bracket.

14 Fit the new retaining bolt, and then tighten to the following five stages:

a) Tighten bolt by hand at this point.
b) Tighten bolt until it reaches stop.
c) Turn the bolt back through 90°
b) Tighten bolt to 30Nm.
c) Tighten a further 90°

15 When tensioner roller is fitted and the belt is tensioned, check the tensioner retaining bolt. The part of the bolt that has protruded out through the upper end of the mounting bracket (behind the tensioner roller) must not protrude more than 2.5mm higher than the outer surface of the tensioner roller. This ensures that the bolt has been tightened to its end stop.

28.6a Turn the tensioner clockwise ...

28.6b ... and lock the tensioner in position

28.7 Note the fitted position of the belt before removal

28.8 With the locking pin removed, slowly take up the slack in the belt

16 Start the engine and check that the drivebelt runs, as it should over the pulleys. Make sure that all tools and hands are kept clear of the drivebelt with the engine running.
17 With the engine stopped, refit the access panel and roadwheel, and then lower the vehicle to the ground. Refit the engine top cover if removed.

Every 60 000 miles or 4 years

29 Timing belt and tensioner roller renewal

Refer to Chapter 2C, Section 7 (1.6 litre engines) or Chapter 2D, Section 7 (2.0 litre engines) for details of renewing the timing belt and tensioner roller.

28.11 Auxiliary drivebelt with tensioning roller

1	Auxiliary belt	5	Dowel
2	Tensioning roller	6	Mounting bracket
3	Crank pulley/vibration damper	7	Tensioning roller securing bolt
4	Securing bolt		

Every 2 years

30 Brake (and clutch) fluid renewal

⚠️ *Warning: Brake hydraulic fluid can harm your eyes and damage painted surfaces, so use extreme caution when handling and pouring it. Do not use fluid that has been standing open for some time, as it absorbs moisture from the air. Excess moisture can cause a dangerous loss of braking effectiveness.*

1 The procedure is similar to that for the bleeding of the hydraulic system as described in Chapter 9, Section 2, except that the brake fluid reservoir should be emptied by siphoning, using an old, clean antifreeze tester or similar before starting, and allowance should be made for the old fluid to be expelled when bleeding a section of the circuit. Since the clutch hydraulic system also uses fluid from the brake system reservoir, it should also be bled at the same time by referring to Chapter 6, Section 2.
2 Working as described in Chapter 9, Section 2, open the first bleed screw in the sequence, and pump the brake pedal gently until nearly

all the old fluid has been emptied from the master cylinder reservoir.
3 Top-up to the MAX level with new fluid, and continue pumping until only the new fluid remains in the reservoir, and new fluid can be seen emerging from the bleed screw. Tighten the screw, and top the reservoir level up to the MAX level line.
4 Work through all the remaining bleed screws in the sequence until new fluid can be seen at all of them. Be careful to keep the master cylinder reservoir topped-up to above the MIN level at all times, or air may enter the system and greatly increase the length of the task.
5 When the operation is complete, check that all bleed screws are securely tightened, and that their dust caps are refitted. Wash off all traces of spilt fluid, and recheck the master cylinder reservoir fluid level.
6 On models with manual transmission, once the brake fluid has been changed the clutch fluid should also be renewed. Referring to Chapter 6, Section 2, bleed the clutch until new fluid is seen to be emerging from the slave cylinder bleed screw, keeping the master cylinder fluid level above the MIN level line at all times to prevent air entering the system. Once the new fluid emerges, securely tighten

the bleed screw then disconnect and remove the bleeding equipment. Securely refit the dust cap then wash off all traces of spilt fluid.
7 On all models, ensure the master cylinder fluid level is correct (see *Weekly checks*) and thoroughly check the operation of the brakes and (where necessary) clutch before taking the car on the road.

31 Coolant renewal

Note: *This work is not included in the VW schedule and should not be required if the recommended VW G12 LongLife coolant antifreeze/inhibitor is used. However, if standard antifreeze/inhibitor is used, the work should be carried out at the recommended interval.*

⚠️ *Warning: Wait until the engine is cold before starting this procedure. Do not allow antifreeze to come in contact with your skin, or with the painted surfaces of the vehicle. Rinse off spills immediately with plenty of water. Never leave antifreeze lying around in*

31.4 Disconnect hose from the circulation pump

an open container, or in a puddle in the driveway or on the garage floor. Children and pets are attracted by its sweet smell, but antifreeze can be fatal if ingested.

Cooling system draining

1 With the engine completely cold, unscrew the expansion tank cap.

2 Firmly apply the handbrake then jack up the front of the vehicle and support it on axle stands (see *Jacking and vehicle support*). Undo the retaining screws and remove the engine undertray(s) to gain access to the base of the radiator.

3 Position a suitable container beneath the coolant drain outlet, which is fitted to the coolant bottom hose end fitting. Loosen the drain plug (there is no need to remove it completely) and allow the coolant to drain into the container. If desired, a length of tubing can be fitted to the drain outlet to direct the flow of coolant during draining. Where no drain outlet is fitted to the hose end fitting, remove the retaining clip and disconnect the bottom hose from the radiator to drain the coolant (see Chapter 3, Section 2).

4 Release the clamps and disconnect the hoses from the electric coolant circulation pump (see Chapter 3, Section 7), located at the front side of the cylinder block, below the oil cooler **(see illustration)**.

5 To fully drain the system also disconnect one of the coolant hoses from the oil cooler, which is located at the front of the cylinder block.

6 If the coolant has been drained for a reason other than renewal, then provided it is clean, it can be re-used, though this is not recommended.

7 Once all the coolant has drained, securely tighten the radiator drain plug or reconnect the bottom hose to the radiator (as applicable). Also reconnect the coolant hose to the oil cooler and secure it in position with the retaining clip. Refit the undertray(s), tighten the retaining screws securely.

Cooling system flushing

8 If the recommended VW coolant has not been used and coolant renewal has been neglected, or if the antifreeze mixture has become diluted, the cooling system may gradually lose efficiency, as the coolant passages become restricted due to rust, scale deposits, and other sediment. The cooling system efficiency can be restored by flushing the system clean.

9 The radiator should be flushed separately from the engine, to avoid excess contamination.

Radiator flushing

10 To flush the radiator, first tighten the radiator drain plug.

11 Disconnect the top and bottom hoses and any other relevant hoses from the radiator (see Chapter 3, Section 2).

12 Insert a garden hose into the radiator top inlet. Direct a flow of clean water through the radiator, and continue flushing until clean water emerges from the radiator bottom outlet.

13 If after a reasonable period, the water still does not run clear, the radiator can be flushed with a good proprietary cleaning agent. It is important that their manufacturer's instructions are followed carefully. If the contamination is particularly bad, insert the hose in the radiator bottom outlet, and reverse-flush the radiator.

Engine flushing

14 To flush the engine, remove the thermostat (see Chapter 3, Section 4).

15 With the bottom hose disconnected from the radiator, insert a garden hose into the coolant housing. Direct a clean flow of water through the engine, and continue flushing until clean water emerges from the radiator bottom hose.

16 When flushing is complete, refit the thermostat and reconnect the hoses.

Cooling system filling

17 Before attempting to fill the cooling system, ensure the drain plug is securely closed and make sure that all hoses are connected and are securely retained by their clips. If the recommended VW coolant is not being used, ensure that a suitable antifreeze mixture is used all year round, to prevent corrosion of the engine components (see following sub-Section). **Note:** *VW recommend that only distilled water should be used.*

18 Remove the expansion tank filler cap and slowly fill the system with the coolant. Continue to fill the cooling system until bubbles stop appearing in the expansion tank. Help to bleed the air from the system by repeatedly squeezing the radiator bottom hose.

19 When no more bubbles appear, top the coolant level up to the MAX level mark then securely refit the cap to the expansion tank.

20 Run the engine at a fast idle speed until the cooling fan cuts in. Wait for the fan to stop then switch the engine off and allow the engine to cool.

21 When the engine has cooled, check the coolant level with reference to *Weekly checks*. Top-up the level if necessary, and refit the expansion tank cap.

Antifreeze mixture

22 If the recommended VW coolant is not being used, the antifreeze should always be renewed at the specified intervals. This is necessary not only to maintain the antifreeze properties, but also to prevent corrosion, which would otherwise occur as the corrosion inhibitors become progressively less effective.

23 Always use an ethylene-glycol based antifreeze which is suitable for use in mixed-metal cooling systems. The quantity of antifreeze and levels of protection are indicated in the Specifications.

24 Before adding antifreeze, the cooling system should be completely drained, preferably flushed, and all hoses checked for condition and security.

25 After filling with antifreeze, a label should be attached to the expansion tank, stating the type and concentration of antifreeze used, and the date installed. Any subsequent topping-up should be made with the same type and concentration of antifreeze.

Caution: Do not use engine antifreeze in the windscreen/tailgate washer system, as it will damage the vehicle paintwork. A screenwash additive should be added to the washer system in the quantities stated on the bottle.

Every 95 000 miles, then every 19 000 miles

32 Particulate filter ash deposit mass check

Eventually, the amount of ash deposited in the particle filter by the filtration process will cause a blockage, and engine running problems. VW state that the maximum amount of ash is 60g. At this point, the particle filter must be renewed. Unfortunately, the mass of the ash can only be established using dedicated VW diagnostic equipment, connected to the vehicle through the diagnostic plug under the drivers side of the facia. Consequently, we recommend this task is entrusted to a VW dealer or suitably equipped specialist.

Chapter 2 Part A:
1.4 litre indirect injection petrol engine in-car repair procedures

Contents

Degrees of difficulty

Easy, suitable for novice with little experience	Fairly easy, suitable for beginner with some experience	Fairly difficult, suitable for competent DIY mechanic	Difficult, suitable for experienced DIY mechanic	Very difficult, suitable for expert DIY or professional

Specifications

General

Type	Four-cylinder in-line, belt-driven double (DOHC) overhead camshaft, four stroke, liquid-cooled
Manufacturer's engine codes*:	
1390 cc (1.4 litre)	CGGA and BUD
Maximum power output.	59 kW at 5000 rpm
Maximum torque output.	130 Nm at 4200 rpm
Bore	76.5 mm
Stroke.	75.6 mm
Compression ratio	10.5 : 1
Compression pressures:	
Minimum compression pressure	Approximately 7.0 bar
Maximum difference between cylinders.	Approximately 3.0 bar
Firing order.	1 – 3 – 4 – 2
No.1 cylinder location.	Timing belt end

* Note: *See 'Vehicle identification' at the end of this manual for the location of engine code markings.*

Camshafts

Camshaft endfloat	0.40 mm
Camshaft bearing running clearance	N/A
Camshaft run-out.	N/A

Lubrication system

Oil pump type.	Rotor type, driven directly from crankshaft
Oil pressure (oil temperature 80°C):	
At idling.	No figure specified
At 2000 rpm	2.0 bar
In excess of 2000 rpm	7.0 bar maximum

Torque wrench settings

	Nm	lbf ft
Ancillary (alternator, etc) bracket mounting bolts	50	37
Auxiliary drivebelt tensioner securing bolt:		
M8 bolt:		
Stage 1	20	15
Stage 2	Angle-tighten a further 90°	
M10 bolt	45	33
Big-end bearing caps bolt/nuts*:		
Stage 1	30	22
Stage 2	Angle-tighten a further 90°	
Camshaft carrier bolts*:		
Stage 1	10	7
Stage 2	Angle-tighten a further 90°	
Camshaft sealing cap bolts	10	7
Camshaft sprocket bolts*:		
Stage 1	20	15
Stage 2	Angle-tighten a further 90°	
Coolant pump bolts	20	15
Crankcase breather/oil separator bolts	10	7
Crankshaft oil seal housing bolts	10	7
Crankshaft pulley/sprocket bolt*:		
Old type (without drilled head):		
Stage 1	90	66
Stage 2	Angle-tighten a further 90°	
New type (with drilled head):		
Stage 1	150	111
Stage 2	Angle-tighten a further 180°	
Cylinder head bolts*:		
Stage 1	30	22
Stage 2	Angle-tighten a further 90°	
Stage 3	Angle-tighten a further 90°	
Driveplate mounting bolts*:		
Stage 1	60	44
Stage 2	Angle-tighten a further 90°	
Engine mountings:		
Left-hand mounting-to-body bolts:		
Large bolts*:		
Stage 1	40	30
Stage 2	Angle-tighten a further 90°	
Small bolts	25	18
Left-hand mounting-to-engine bracket bolts	100	74
Right-hand mounting-to-body bolts*:		
Stage 1	40	30
Stage 2	Angle-tighten a further 90°	
Right-hand mounting plate bolts (small bolts)	25	18
Right-hand mounting-to-engine bracket bolts	100	74
Right-hand mounting bracket-to-engine bolts	50	37
Rear engine/transmission mounting:		
Bracket-to-subframe bolts*:		
Stage 1	20	15
Stage 2	Angle-tighten a further 90°	
Bracket-to-transmission bolts*:		
Stage 1	40	30
Stage 2	Angle-tighten a further 90°	
Engine-to-automatic transmission bolts:		
M12 bolts	80	59
M10 cylinder block-to-transmission bolts	60	44
M10 sump-to-transmission bolts	25	18
Engine-to-manual transmission bolts:		
M10 bolts	40	30
M12 bolts	80	59
Engine-to-manual transmission cover plate bolts	10	7
Exhaust manifold nuts	25	18
Exhaust pipe-to-manifold nuts	40	30
Flywheel mounting bolts*:		
Stage 1	60	44
Stage 2	Angle-tighten a further 90°	
Oil cooler securing nut	25	18

Torque wrench settings (continued)

	Nm	lbf ft
Oil drain plug	30	22
Oil level/temperature sender-to-sump bolts.	10	7
Oil pick-up pipe securing bolts	10	7
Oil pressure warning light switch	25	18
Oil pump securing bolts*	12	9
Sump:		
Sump-to-cylinder block bolts.	13	10
Sump-to-transmission bolts	45	33
Timing belt idler pulley bolt	50	37
Timing belt outer cover bolts:		
Small bolts	10	7
Large bolts	20	15
Timing belt rear cover bolts:		
Small bolts	10	7
Large bolt (coolant pump bolts)	20	15
Timing belt tensioner:		
Main timing belt tensioner bolt	20	15
Secondary timing belt tensioner bolt	20	15

* Do not re-use

1 General information

How to use this Chapter

This Part of Chapter 2 describes those repair procedures that can reasonably be carried out on the engine while it remains in the vehicle. If the engine has been removed from the vehicle and is being dismantled as described in Part E, any preliminary dismantling procedures can be ignored.

Note that while it may be possible physically to overhaul certain items while the engine is in the vehicle, such tasks are not usually carried out as separate operations, and usually require the execution of several additional procedures (not to mention the cleaning of components and of oilways); for this reason, all such tasks are classed as major overhaul procedures, and are described in Part E of this Chapter. *Caution: The crankshaft must not be removed on these engines – just loosening and retightening the main bearing bolts will render the cylinder block unserviceable. If the crankshaft or bearings are excessively worn or damaged, the complete cylinder block must be renewed.*

Engine description

Throughout this Chapter, engines are identified by the manufacturer's code letters. A listing of all engines covered, together with their code letters, is given in the Specifications.

The engines are water-cooled, double overhead camshaft, in-line four-cylinder units. All engines have an aluminium-alloy cylinder head and block. All engines are mounted transversely at the front of the vehicle, with the transmission bolted to the left-hand end of the engine.

The crankshaft is of five-bearing type, and thrustwashers are fitted to the centre main bearing to control crankshaft endfloat.

The crankshaft and main bearings are matched to the alloy cylinder block, and it is not possible to reassemble the crankshaft and cylinder block once the components have been separated. If the crankshaft or bearings are worn, the complete cylinder block/crankshaft assembly must be renewed.

The inlet camshaft is driven by a toothed belt from the crankshaft sprocket, and the exhaust camshaft is driven from the inlet camshaft by a second toothed belt. The camshafts are located in a camshaft carrier, which is bolted to the top of the cylinder head.

The valves are closed by coil springs, and run in guides pressed into the cylinder head. The camshafts actuate the valves by roller rockers and hydraulic tappets. There are four valves per cylinder, two inlet valves and two exhaust valves.

The oil pump is driven directly from the front of the crankshaft. Oil is drawn from the sump through a strainer, and then forced through an externally mounted, renewable filter. From there, it is distributed to the cylinder head, where it lubricates the camshaft journals and hydraulic tappets, and also to the crankcase, where it lubricates the main bearings, connecting rod big-ends, gudgeon pins and cylinder bores. A coolant-fed oil cooler is fitted to most engines.

On all engines, engine coolant is circulated by a pump, driven by the main timing belt. For details of the cooling system, refer to Chapter 3.

Operations with engine in car

The following operations can be performed without removing the engine:

a) Compression pressure – testing.
b) Camshaft carrier – removal and refitting.
c) Crankshaft pulley – removal and refitting.
d) Timing belt covers – removal and refitting.
e) Timing belt – removal, refitting and adjustment.
f) Timing belt tensioner and sprockets – removal and refitting.
g) Inlet camshaft timing belt, sprockets and tensioner – removal and refitting.
h) Inlet camshaft adjuster mechanism – removal and refitting.
i) Camshaft oil seals – renewal.
j) Camshafts and hydraulic tappets – removal, inspection and refitting.
k) Cylinder head – removal and refitting.
l) Cylinder head and pistons – decarbonising.
m) Sump – removal and refitting.
n) Oil pump – removal, overhaul and refitting.
o) Crankshaft oil seals – renewal.
p) Engine/transmission mountings – inspection and renewal.
q) Flywheel/driveplate – removal, inspection and refitting.

Note: *It is possible to remove the pistons and connecting rods (after removing the cylinder head and sump) without removing the engine. However, this is not recommended. Work of this nature is more easily and thoroughly completed with the engine on the bench, as described in Chapter 2E.*

2 Compression test – description and interpretation

Caution: The following work may insert fault codes in the engine management ECU. These fault codes must be cleared by a VW dealer, with specialist equipment.

Note: *A suitable compression tester will be required for this test.*

1 When engine performance is down, or if misfiring occurs which cannot be attributed to the ignition or fuel systems, a compression test can provide diagnostic clues as to the engine's condition. If the test is performed regularly, it can give warning of trouble before any other symptoms become apparent.

2 The engine must be fully warmed-up to normal operating temperature, the battery must be fully charged and the spark plugs must be removed. The aid of an assistant will be required.

3.4a Crankshaft pulley timing mark aligned with TDC mark on timing belt cover

3.4b Timing mark scribed on inner flange of pulley aligned with TDC mark on timing belt cover

3 Engine assembly and valve timing marks – general information and usage

General information

1 TDC is the highest point in the cylinder that each piston reaches as it travels up-and-down when the crankshaft turns. Each piston reaches TDC at the end of the compression stroke and again at the end of the exhaust stroke, but TDC generally refers to piston position on the compression stroke. No 1 piston is at the timing belt end of the engine.

2 Positioning No 1 piston at TDC is an essential part of many procedures, such as timing belt removal and camshaft removal.

3 The design of the engines covered in this Chapter is such that piston-to-valve contact may occur if the camshaft or crankshaft is turned with the timing belt removed. For this reason, it is important to ensure that the camshaft and crankshaft do not move in relation to each other once the timing belt has been removed from the engine.

4 The crankshaft pulley has a mark which, when aligned with a corresponding reference mark on the timing belt cover, indicates that No 1 piston (and hence also No 4 piston) is at TDC. Note that on some models, the crankshaft pulley timing mark is located on the outer flange of the pulley. In order to make alignment of the timing marks easier, it is advisable to remove the pulley (see Section 4) and, using a set-square, scribe a corresponding mark on the inner flange of the pulley **(see illustrations)**.

5 There is also a timing mark, which can be used with the crankshaft sprocket – this is useful if the crankshaft pulley and timing belt have been removed. When No 1 piston is at TDC, the crankshaft sprocket tooth with the chamfered inner edge aligns with a cast arrow on the oil pump **(see illustration)**.

6 The camshaft sprockets are equipped with

3 Disable the ignition and fuel injectors by removing the relevant fuses, see wiring diagrams in Chapter 12.

4 Fit a compression tester to the No 1 cylinder spark plug hole. The type of tester that screws into the plug thread is preferred.

5 Have the assistant hold the throttle wide open and crank the engine for several seconds on the starter motor. **Note:** *The throttle will not operate until the ignition is switched on.* After one or two revolutions, the compression pressure should build-up to a maximum figure and then stabilise. Record the highest reading obtained.

6 Repeat the test on the remaining cylinders, recording the pressure in each.

7 All cylinders should produce very similar pressures. Any difference greater than that specified indicates the existence of a fault. Note that the compression should build-up quickly in a healthy engine. Low compression on the first stroke, followed by gradually increasing pressure on successive strokes, indicates worn piston rings. A low compression reading on the first stroke, which does not build-up during successive strokes, indicates leaking valves or a blown head gasket (a cracked head could also be the cause). Deposits on the undersides of the valve heads can also cause low compression.

8 If the pressure in any cylinder is reduced to the specified minimum or less, carry out the following test to isolate the cause. Introduce a teaspoonful of clean oil into that cylinder through its spark plug hole and repeat the test.

9 If the addition of oil temporarily improves the compression pressure, this indicates that bore or piston wear is responsible for the pressure loss. No improvement suggests that leaking or burnt valves, or a blown head gasket, may be to blame.

10 A low reading from two adjacent cylinders is almost certainly due to the head gasket having blown between them and the presence of coolant in the engine oil will confirm this.

11 If one cylinder is about 20 percent lower than the others and the engine has a slightly rough idle; a worn camshaft lobe could be the cause.

12 If the compression reading is unusually high, the combustion chambers are probably coated with carbon deposits. If this is the case, the cylinder head should be removed and decarbonised.

13 On completion of the test, refit the spark plugs and the fuses.

14 Have any fault codes cleared by a VW dealer.

3.5 Crankshaft sprocket tooth with chamfered edge aligns with cast arrow on oil pump

3.6 Camshaft sprocket positioning holes aligned with holes in camshaft carrier (No 1 piston at TDC)

TDC positioning holes. When the positioning holes are aligned with the corresponding holes in the camshaft carrier, No 1 piston is at TDC on the compression stroke **(see illustration)**.

7 Additionally, the flywheel/driveplate has a TDC marking, which can be observed by unscrewing a protective plastic cover from the transmission bellhousing. The mark takes the form of a notch in the edge of the flywheel on manual transmission models, or an O marking on automatic transmission models. Note that it is not possible to use these marks on all models due to the limited access available to view the marks.

Setting No 1 cylinder to TDC

Note: *Suitable locking pins will be required to lock the camshaft sprockets in position during this procedure. On some engines, it may be necessary to use a small mirror to view the timing marks from under the wheel arch.*

8 Before starting work, make sure that the ignition and all electrical consumers are switched off.

9 Remove the engine top cover, and remove the air cleaner assembly as described in Chapter 4A.

10 If desired, to make the engine easier to turn, remove all of the spark plugs as described in Chapter 1A.

11 Apply the handbrake, then jack up the front of the vehicle and support on axle stands (see Jacking and vehicle support). Remove the right-hand front roadwheel, then remove the securing screws and/or clips, and remove the appropriate engine undertrays and wheel arch liner to enable access to the crankshaft pulley.

12 Remove the upper timing belt cover as described in Section 5.

13 Turn the engine clockwise, using a spanner on the crankshaft pulley bolt, until the TDC mark on the crankshaft pulley or flywheel/driveplate is aligned with the corresponding mark on the timing belt cover or transmission casing, and the locking pin holes in the camshaft sprockets are aligned with the corresponding holes in the camshaft carrier.

14 If necessary, to give sufficient clearance for the camshaft locking tool to be engaged with the camshaft sprockets, unbolt the air

3.16 Improvised tool used to lock camshaft sprockets in position at TDC (viewed with engine removed, and timing belt removed from engine)

cleaner support bracket from the engine mounting.

15 A suitable tool will now be required to lock the camshaft sprockets in the TDC position. A special VW tool is available for this purpose, but a suitable tool can be improvised using two M8 bolts and nuts, and a short length of steel bar. With the camshaft sprocket positioned as described in paragraph 13, measure the distance between the locking pin hole centres, and drill two corresponding 8 mm clearance holes in the length of steel bar. Slide the M8 bolts through the holes in the bar, and secure them using the nuts.

16 Slide the tool into position in the holes in the camshaft sprockets, ensuring that the pins (or bolts) engage with the holes in the camshaft carrier **(see illustration)**. The engine is now locked in position, with No 1 piston at TDC on the firing stroke.

4   Crankshaft pulley – removal and refitting

Removal

1 Switch off the ignition and all electrical consumers and remove the ignition key.

2 For improved access, jack up the front of the vehicle, and support securely on axle stands (see *Jacking and vehicle support*). Remove the right-hand front roadwheel.

3 Remove the securing screws and/or release the clips, and withdraw the relevant engine

undertray and wheel arch liner to enable access to the crankshaft pulley.

4 If necessary (for any later work to be carried out), turn the crankshaft using a socket or spanner on the crankshaft pulley bolt, until the relevant timing marks align (see Section 3).

5 Remove the auxiliary drivebelt, as described in Chapter 1A, Section 26.

6 To prevent the crankshaft from turning as the pulley bolt is slackened, a suitable tool can be used. Engage the tool with two of the slots in the pulley **(see illustration)**.

7 Counterhold the pulley, and slacken the pulley bolt (take care – the bolt is very tight) using a socket and a suitable extension.

8 Unscrew the bolt, and remove the pulley **(see illustration)**.

9 Refit the crankshaft pulley securing bolt, with a spacer washer positioned under its head, to retain the crankshaft sprocket.

Refitting

10 Unscrew the crankshaft pulley/sprocket bolt used to retain the sprocket, and remove the spacer washer, then refit the pulley to the sprocket. Ensure that the locating pin on the sprocket engages with the corresponding hole in the pulley.

11 Oil the threads of the new crankshaft pulley bolt. Prevent the crankshaft from turning as during removal, then fit the new pulley securing bolt, and tighten it to the specified torque, in the two stages given in the Specifications.

12 Refit and tension the auxiliary drivebelt as described in Chapter 1A, Section 26.

13 Refit the engine undertray and wheel arch liner.

14 Refit the roadwheel and lower the vehicle to the ground.

5   Timing belt covers – removal and refitting

Upper outer cover

1 Remove the air cleaner assembly as described in Chapter 4A, Section 2.

2 Release the two securing clips, and lift the cover from the engine **(see illustration)**.

3 Refitting is a reversal of removal.

4.6 Counterhold the crankshaft pulley using a tool similar to that shown

4.8 Removing the crankshaft pulley

5.2 Removing the upper outer timing belt cover

5.5a Release the two securing clips...

5.5b ...then unscrew the two lower securing bolts...

5.5c ...and the single bolt securing the cover to the engine mounting bracket...

5.5d ...and withdraw the lower timing belt cover

Lower outer cover

4 Remove the crankshaft pulley, as described in Section 4.

5 Release the two cover securing clips, located at the rear of the engine, then unscrew the two lower securing bolts, and the single bolt securing the cover to the engine mounting bracket. Withdraw the cover downwards from the engine **(see illustrations)**.

6 Refitting is a reversal of removal, but refit the crankshaft pulley with reference to Section 4.

Rear timing belt cover

Note: *As the rear timing belt cover securing bolts also secure the coolant pump, it is advisable to drain the cooling system (see Chapter 1A, Section 30) before starting this procedure, and to renew the coolant pump*

seal/gasket (Chapter 3, Section 7) before refitting the cover. Refill the cooling system with reference to Chapter 1A, Section 30.

7 Remove the timing belt as described in Section 6.

8 Unbolt the timing belt idler pulley/bracket assembly **(see illustration)**.

9 Unscrew the rear timing belt cover securing bolt located next to the right-hand engine lifting eye **(see illustration)**.

10 Unscrew the two securing bolts, and remove the rear timing belt cover. Note that the bolts also secure the coolant pump **(see illustration)**.

11 Refitting is a reversal of removal, but tighten the timing belt idler pulley/bracket bolt to the specified torque, and refit the timing belt as described in Section 6.

6 Timing belt(s) – removal and refitting

Main timing belt

Removal

1 The engines in this Chapter have two timing belts; the main timing belt drives the inlet camshaft from the crankshaft, and the secondary timing belt drives the exhaust camshaft from the inlet camshaft.

2 Switch off the ignition and all electrical consumers and remove the ignition key.

3 Remove the air cleaner assembly as described in Chapter 4A, Section 2.

4 Release the two securing clips and remove the upper outer timing belt cover.

5 Turn the crankshaft to position No 1 piston at TDC on the firing stroke, and lock the camshaft sprockets in position, as described in Section 3.

6 Remove the crankshaft pulley as described in Section 4. Refit the crankshaft pulley securing bolt, with a spacer washer positioned under its head, to retain the crankshaft sprocket.

7 Remove the lower outer timing belt cover, as described in Section 5.

8 Where applicable, on models with air conditioning, unscrew the securing bolt, and remove the auxiliary drivebelt idler pulley.

9 Similarly, unscrew the two securing screws, and move the coolant expansion tank clear of the working area **(see illustrations)**.

10 Attach a hoist and lifting tackle to the right-hand (timing belt end) engine lifting bracket, and raise the hoist to just take the weight of the engine.

11 Remove the complete right-hand engine mounting assembly, as described in Section 17.

12 Unscrew the four securing bolts, and remove the right-hand engine mounting bracket from the engine.

13 If either of the timing belts are to be refitted, mark their running directions to ensure correct refitting.

14 Engage a suitable Allen key with the hole in the main timing belt tensioner plate, then

5.8 Removing the idler pulley/bracket assembly (viewed with engine removed)

5.9 Unscrew the rear timing belt cover securing bolt located next to the right-hand engine lifting eye

5.10 Removing the rear timing belt cover (viewed with engine removed)

6.9a Unscrew the securing screws...

6.9b ...and move the coolant expansion tank clear of the working area

6.14 Slacken the tensioner bolt and lever the tensioner anti-clockwise using an Allen key, then retighten the tensioner bolt

slacken the tensioner bolt, lever the tensioner anti-clockwise using the Allen key (to release the tension on the belt), and retighten the tensioner bolt (see illustration).

15 Temporarily remove the camshaft sprocket locking tool, then slide the main timing belt from the sprockets, noting it's routing (see illustration). Refit the camshaft sprocket locking tool once the timing belt has been removed.

16 Turn the crankshaft a quarter-turn (90°) anti-clockwise to position No's 1 and 4 pistons slightly down their bores from the TDC position. This will eliminate any risk of piston-to-valve contact if a camshaft is turned whilst the timing belt is removed.

Refitting

17 Where applicable, reposition the crankshaft at TDC (see paragraph 20) and ensure that the secondary drivebelt has been refitted and tensioned. Temporarily remove the camshaft sprocket locking tool, and fit the main timing belt around the sprockets. Work in an anti-clockwise direction, starting at the coolant pump, followed by the tensioner roller, crankshaft sprocket, idler roller, inlet camshaft sprocket and the second idler roller. If the original belt is being refitted, observe the running direction markings. Once the belt has been refitted, refit the camshaft sprocket locking tool.

18 Ensure that the tensioner bolt is slack, then engage an Allen key with the hole in the tensioner plate, and turn the plate clockwise until the tension indicator pointer is aligned with the centre of the cut-out in the backplate (see illustration). Tighten the tensioner securing bolt to the specified torque.

19 Remove the camshaft sprocket locking tool.

20 Using a spanner or socket on the crankshaft pulley bolt, turn the engine through two complete turns in the normal direction of rotation, until the crankshaft sprocket tooth with the chamfered inner edge is aligned with the corresponding mark on the oil pump housing. Check that the locking tool can again be fitted to lock the camshaft sprockets in position – if not, one or both of the timing belts may have been Incorrectly fitted.

21 With the crankshaft timing marks

aligned, and the camshaft sprockets locked in position, check the tension of the timing belts. The secondary and main tension indicators should be positioned as described in paragraphs 38 and 18 respectively – if not, repeat the appropriate tensioning procedure, then recheck the tension.

22 When the belt tension is correct, refit the right-hand engine mounting bracket, and tighten the securing bolts to the specified torque.

23 Refit the complete right-hand engine mounting assembly, as described in Section 17.

24 Disconnect the hoist and lifting tackle from the engine lifting bracket.

25 Refit the coolant reservoir.

26 Where applicable, refit the auxiliary drivebelt idler pulley.

27 Refit the lower outer timing belt cover, with reference to Section 5, if necessary.

6.15 Removing the main timing belt

6.32a Slacken the secondary timing belt tensioner bolt, and lever the tensioner clockwise using an Allen key...

28 Refit the crankshaft pulley as described in Section 4.

29 Refit the upper outer timing belt cover.

30 Refit the air cleaner assembly then refit the engine top cover.

Inlet camshaft timing belt

Removal

31 Once the main timing belt has been removed, to remove the secondary timing belt, proceed as follows.

32 Engage a suitable Allen key with the hole in the secondary timing belt tensioner plate, then slacken the tensioner bolt, and lever the tensioner clockwise using the Allen key (to release the tension on the belt). Unscrew the securing bolt, and remove the secondary timing belt tensioner (see illustrations).

33 Temporarily remove the camshaft sprocket

6.18 The pointer must align with the centre of the cut-out (arrowed)

6.32b ...then unscrew the securing bolt and remove the tensioner

6.33 Removing the secondary timing belt

6.34 Crankshaft sprocket tooth with chamfered edge aligned with cast arrow on oil pump

6.37 The secondary timing belt tensioner pointer should be positioned on the far right of the tensioner backplate, and the lug on the backplate should be engaged with the core plug hole

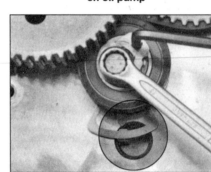

6.38 Turn the tensioner anti-clockwise until the tensioner pointer aligns with the lug on the tensioner backplate, with the lug positioned against the left-hand stop in the core plug hole

locking tool, and slide the secondary timing belt from the sprockets **(see illustration)**. Refit the sprocket locking tool once the belt has been removed.

Refitting

34 Check that the camshaft sprockets are still locked in position by the locking pins, and then turn the crankshaft a quarter-turn (90°) clockwise to reposition No's 1 and 4 pistons at TDC. Ensure that the crankshaft sprocket tooth with the chamfered inner edge is aligned with the corresponding mark on the oil pump housing **(see illustration)**.

7.3 Turn the tensioner anti-clockwise to the position shown before fitting. Note that the cut-out engages with the bolt (A) on the cylinder block when fitting

35 Temporarily remove the camshaft sprocket locking tool, and fit the secondary timing belt around the camshaft sprockets. Make sure that the belt is as tight as possible on its top run between the sprockets (but note that there will be some slack in the belt). If the original belt is being refitted, observe the running direction markings. Refit the camshaft sprocket locking tool once the belt has been fitted to the sprockets.

36 Check that the secondary timing belt tensioner pointer is positioned on the far right of the tensioner backplate.

37 Press the secondary timing belt up using the tensioner, and fit the tensioner securing bolt (if necessary turn the tensioner with an Allen key until the bolt hole in the tensioner aligns with the bolt hole in the cylinder head).

7.8a Removing the smaller...

Make sure that the lug on the tensioner backplate engages with the core plug hole in the cylinder head **(see illustration)**.

38 Use the Allen key to turn the tensioner anti-clockwise until the tensioner pointer aligns with the lug on the tensioner backplate, with the lug positioned against the left-hand stop in the core plug hole **(see illustration)**. Tighten the tensioner bolt to the specified torque.

7 Timing belt tensioner and sprockets – removal and refitting

Main timing belt tensioner

Removal

1 Remove the main timing belt as described in Section 6.

2 Unscrew the main timing belt tensioner bolt, and remove the tensioner from the engine.

3 Engage an Allen key with the hole in the tensioner plate, and turn the tensioner anti-clockwise **(see illustration)**.

Refitting

4 Refit the tensioner to the engine, ensuring that the cut-out in the tensioner backplate engages with the bolt on the cylinder block. Refit the tensioner securing bolt, and tighten by hand.

5 Refit and tension the main timing belt as described in Section 6.

Inlet camshaft timing belt tensioner

6 Removal and refitting of the tensioner is described as part of the timing belt removal procedure in Section 6.

Main timing belt idler pulleys

Removal

7 Remove the timing belt as described in Section 6.

8 Unscrew the securing bolt and remove the relevant idler pulley. Note that the smaller pulley (the idler pulley nearest the inlet manifold side of the engine) can be removed complete with its mounting bracket (unbolt the mounting bracket bolt, leaving the pulley attached to the bracket) **(see illustrations)**.

7.8b ...and larger timing belt idler pulleys

7.13 Refitting the crankshaft sprocket. Pulley locating pin (arrowed) must be outermost

7.18 Refit the sprocket, ensuring that the lug (1) on the sprocket engages with the notch (2) in the end of the camshaft

7.19 Tighten the sprocket securing bolt using a suitable tool to hold the sprocket stationary

Refitting

9 Refit the relevant idler pulley and tighten the securing bolt to the specified torque. Note that if the smaller idler pulley has been removed complete with its bracket; ensure that the bracket locates over the rear timing belt cover bolt on refitting.

10 Refit and tension the main timing belt as described in Section 6.

Crankshaft sprocket

Removal

11 Remove the main timing belt as described in Section 6.

12 Unscrew the crankshaft pulley bolt, and the washer used to retain the sprocket, and withdraw the sprocket from the crankshaft.

Refitting

13 Commence refitting by positioning the sprocket on the end of the crankshaft, noting that the pulley locating pin must be outermost **(see illustration)**. Temporarily refit the pulley securing bolt and washer to retain the sprocket.

14 Refit the main timing belt as described in Section 6.

Camshaft sprockets

Removal

15 Remove the main and secondary timing belts as described in Section 6. Ensure that the crankshaft has been turned a quarter-turn (90°) anti-clockwise to position No's 1 and 4 pistons slightly down their bores from the TDC

position. This will eliminate any risk of piston-to-valve contact if a camshaft is turned whilst the timing belt is removed.

16 The relevant camshaft sprocket bolt must now be slackened. The camshaft must be prevented from turning as the sprocket bolt is unscrewed – **do not** rely solely on the sprocket locking tool for this. To hold the sprocket, make up a tool and use it to hold the sprocket stationary by means of the holes in the sprocket.

17 Unscrew the camshaft sprocket bolt, and withdraw the sprocket from the end of the camshaft, noting which way round it is fitted.

Refitting

18 Commence refitting by offering the sprocket up to the camshaft, ensuring that lug on the sprocket engages with the notch in the end of the camshaft. If both camshaft sprockets have been removed, note that the double sprocket (for the main and secondary timing belts) should be fitted to the inlet camshaft, and note that the exhaust camshaft sprocket must be fitted first **(see illustration)**.

19 Fit a new sprocket securing bolt, then use the tool to hold the sprocket stationary, as during removal, and tighten the bolt to the specified torque, in the two stages given in the Specifications **(see illustration)**.

20 Refit the secondary and main timing belts as described in Section 6.

Coolant pump sprocket

21 The coolant pump sprocket is integral with the coolant pump. Refer to Chapter 3, Section 7, for details of coolant pump removal.

8 Camshaft carrier – removal and refitting

Note: *New camshaft carrier securing bolts must be used on refitting. Suitable sealant (VW AMV 188 003, or equivalent) will be required, and two M6 studs (approximately 80 mm long) will be required ñ see text.*

Removal

1 Switch off the ignition and all electrical consumers and remove the ignition key.

2 Unbolt the cover from the camshaft carrier.

3 Remove the main and secondary timing belts, as described in Section 6.

4 Remove the ignition HT coils as described in Chapter 5B, Section 3. Unbolt the coil wiring earth lead from the top of the camshaft cover, then release the coil wiring from the clips on the camshaft cover, and move the wiring clear of the camshaft cover.

5 Disconnect the breather hose from the rear of the cylinder head.

6 Disconnect the inlet camshaft position sensor wiring connector **(see illustration)**.

7 Disconnect the wiring plug from the oil pressure warning light switch, located at the front left-hand corner of the camshaft carrier. Release the wiring harness from the clip on the end of the camshaft carrier, and move the wiring to one side **(see illustrations)**.

8 Remove the rear timing belt cover securing

8.6 Disconnect the wiring connector from the inlet camshaft position sensor

8.7a Disconnect the oil pressure warning light switch wiring plug...

8.7b ...then release the wiring from the clip on the end of the camshaft carrier

8.8 Remove the rear timing belt cover securing bolt located next to the right-hand engine lifting eye

8.9 Remove the camshaft carrier securing bolts...

8.10 ...then lift the camshaft carrier from the cylinder head

8.14 Apply a thin, even coat of sealant to the cylinder head mating face of the camshaft carrier

8.17 Tightening a camshaft carrier bolt through the specified Stage 2 angle

bolt, located next to the right-hand engine lifting eye **(see illustration)**.
9 Working progressively from the centre out, in a diagonal sequence, slacken and remove the camshaft carrier securing bolts **(see illustration)**.
10 Carefully lift the camshaft carrier from the cylinder head **(see illustration)**. The camshafts can be removed from the carrier, as described in Section 9.

Refitting

11 Commence refitting by thoroughly cleaning all traces of old sealant, and all traces of oil and grease, from the mating faces of the cylinder head and camshaft carrier. Ensure that no debris enters the cylinder head or camshaft carrier.
12 Ensure that the crankshaft is still positioned a quarter-turn (90°) anti-clockwise from the TDC position, and that the camshafts are locked in position with the locking tool, as described in Section 3.
13 Check that the valve rockers are correctly located on the valves, and securely clipped into position on the hydraulic tappets.
14 Apply a thin, even coat of sealant to the cylinder head mating face of the camshaft carrier **(see illustration)**. Do not apply the sealant too thickly, as excess sealant may enter and block the oil ways, causing engine damage.
15 Carefully lower the camshaft carrier onto the cylinder head, until the camshafts rest on the rockers. Note that the camshaft carrier locates on dowels in the cylinder head and if

desired, to make fitting easier, two guide studs can be made up as follows:
a) Cut the heads off two M6 x 80mm bolts, to turn them into threaded studs.
b) Then cut slots in the top of each bolt shaft to enable the bolt to be unscrewed using a flat-bladed screwdriver.
c) Screw one bolt/stud into each of the camshaft carrier bolt locations at opposite corners of the cylinder head.
d) Lower the camshaft carrier over the bolts/studs to guide it into position on the cylinder head.
16 Fit new camshaft carrier securing bolts, and tighten them progressively, working from the centre out, in a diagonal sequence (i.e. tighten all bolts through one turn, then tighten all bolts through a further turn, and so on). Ensure that the camshaft carrier sits squarely on the cylinder head as the bolts are tightened,

9.3 Remove the inlet camshaft position sensor

and make sure that the carrier engages with the cylinder head dowels. Where applicable, once the camshaft carrier contacts the surface of the cylinder head, unscrew the two guide studs, and fit the two remaining new camshaft carrier securing bolts in their place.
17 Tighten the camshaft carrier securing bolts to the specified torque, in the two stages given in the Specifications **(see illustration)**.
18 Leave the camshaft carrier sealant to dry for approximately 30 minutes before carrying out any further work on the cylinder head or camshaft carrier.
19 Once the sealant has been allowed to dry, refit the rear timing belt cover bolt.
20 Reconnect the oil pressure warning light switch wiring plug, and clip the wiring into position on the end of the camshaft carrier.
21 Reconnect the camshaft position sensor wiring connector.
22 Refit the ignition coils with reference to Chapter 5B, Section 3.
23 Refit the secondary and main timing belts, as described in Section 6.
24 Refit the cover to the camshaft carrier and tighten the bolts securely.

9 Camshafts – removal, inspection and refitting

Removal

1 Remove the camshaft carrier as described in Section 8.
2 Remove the camshaft sprockets, with reference to Section 7.
3 If the inlet camshaft is to be removed, unscrew the securing bolt, and remove the inlet camshaft position sensor **(see illustration)**.
4 Remove the relevant camshaft carrier endplate **(see illustration)**.
5 Carefully withdraw the relevant camshaft from the endplate end of the camshaft carrier, taking care not to damage the bearing surfaces of the camshaft and housing as the camshaft is withdrawn **(see illustration)**.

Inspection

6 Visually inspect the camshafts for evidence of wear on the surfaces of the lobes and journals. Normally their surfaces should be smooth and

9.4 Remove the camshaft carrier endplate

9.5 Withdraw the camshaft from the endplate end of the camshaft carrier

9.10 Renew the camshaft carrier endplate O-ring

have a dull shine; look for scoring, erosion or pitting and areas that appear highly polished, indicating excessive wear. Accelerated wear will occur once the hardened exterior of the camshaft has been damaged, so always renew worn items. **Note:** *If these symptoms are visible on the tips of the camshaft lobes, check the corresponding rocker, as it will probably be worn as well.*

7 If the machined surfaces of the camshaft appear discoloured or blued, it is likely that it has been overheated at some point, probably due to inadequate lubrication. This may have distorted the shaft, so check the run-out as follows: place the camshaft between two V-blocks and, using a DTI gauge, measure the run-out at the centre journal. No maximum run-out figure is quoted by the manufacturers, but it should be obvious if the camshaft is excessively distorted.

8 To measure camshaft endfloat, temporarily refit the relevant camshaft to the camshaft carrier, and refit the endplate to the rear of the camshaft carrier. Anchor a DTI gauge to the timing belt end of the camshaft carrier and align the gauge probe with the camshaft axis. Push the camshaft to one end of the camshaft carrier as far as it will travel, then rest the DTI gauge probe on the end of the camshaft, and zero the gauge display. Push the camshaft as far as it will go to the other end of the camshaft carrier, and record the gauge reading. Verify the reading by pushing the camshaft back to its original position and checking that the gauge indicates zero again.

9 Check that the camshaft endfloat measurement is within the limit listed in the Specifications. Wear outside of this limit may be cured by renewing the relevant camshaft carrier endplate, although wear is unlikely to be confined to any one component, so renewal of the camshafts and camshaft carrier must be considered.

Refitting

10 Refitting is a reversal of removal, bearing in mind the following points.
a) *Before refitting the camshaft, renew the camshaft oil seal, with reference to Section 11.*
b) *Lubricate the bearing surfaces in the camshaft carrier, and the camshaft lobes before refitting the camshaft(s).*

c) *Renew the sealing O-ring on each camshaft carrier endplate (see illustration).*
d) *Refit the camshaft sprocket(s) with reference to Section 7, noting that if both sprockets have been removed, the exhaust camshaft sprocket must be fitted first.*
e) *Refit the camshaft carrier as described in Section 8.*

10 Rockers and tappets – removal, inspection and refitting

Removal

1 Remove the camshaft carrier, as described in Section 8.
2 As the components are removed, keep them in strict order, so that they can be refitted in their original locations.
3 Unclip the rockers from the hydraulic tappets, and lift them from the cylinder head **(see illustration)**.
4 Carefully lift the tappets from their bores in the cylinder head. It is advisable to store the tappets (in order) upright in an oil bath whilst they are removed from the engine.

Inspection

5 Check the cylinder head bore contact surfaces of the tappets for signs of scoring or damage. Similarly, check the tappet bores in the cylinder head for signs of scoring or damage. If significant scoring or damage is found, it may be necessary to renew

10.3 Removing a rocker (hydraulic tappets arrowed)

the cylinder head and the complete set of tappets.
6 Inspect the hydraulic tappets for obvious signs of wear or damage, and renew if necessary. Check that the oil holes in the tappets are free from obstructions.
7 Check the valve, tappet, and camshaft contact faces of the rockers for wear or damage, and also check the rockers for any signs of cracking. Renew any worn or damaged rockers.
8 Inspect the camshaft lobes, as described in Section 11.

Refitting

9 Oil the tappet bores in the cylinder head, and the tappets themselves, then carefully slide the tappets into their original bores **(see illustration)**.
10 Oil the rocker contact faces of the tappets, and the tops of the valve stems, then refit the rockers to their original locations, ensuring that the rockers are securely clipped onto the tappets.
11 Check the endfloat of each camshaft, as described in Section 9, then refit the camshaft carrier as described in Section 8.

11 Camshaft oil seals – renewal

Right-hand oil seals

1 Remove the main and secondary timing belts as described in Section 6.

10.9 Oil the tappets before fitting

11.12 Locate the new O-ring in the groove in the endplate

2 Remove the relevant camshaft sprocket as described in Section 7.

3 Drill two small holes into the existing oil seal, diagonally opposite each other. Take great care to avoid drilling through into the seal housing or camshaft sealing surface. Thread two self-tapping screws into the holes and, using a pair of pliers, pull on the heads of the screws to extract the oil seal.

4 Clean out the seal housing and the sealing surface of the camshaft by wiping it with a lint-free cloth. Remove any swarf or burrs that may cause the seal to leak.

5 Lubricate the lip and outer edge of the new oil seal with clean engine oil, and push it over the camshaft until it is positioned above its housing. To prevent damage to the sealing lips, wrap some adhesive tape around the end of the camshaft.

12.4 Disconnect the radiator hoses from the coolant housing

12.9 Unscrew the bolt securing the oil level dipstick tube bracket to the cylinder head

6 Using a hammer and a socket of suitable diameter, drive the seal squarely into its housing. **Note: Select a socket that bears only on the hard outer surface of the seal, not the inner lip that can easily be damaged**.

7 Refit the relevant camshaft sprocket with reference to Section 7.

8 Refit and tension the secondary and main timing belts as described in Section 6.

Left-hand oil seals

9 The camshaft oil seals take the form of O-rings located in the grooves in the camshaft carrier endplates.

10 Unscrew the securing bolts, and remove the relevant camshaft endplate.

11 Prise the old O-ring from the groove in the endplate.

12 Lightly oil the new O-ring, and carefully locate it in the groove in the endplate (**see illustration**).

13 Refit the endplate and tighten the bolts securely.

12 Cylinder head –
removal, inspection
and refitting

Note: *The cylinder head must be removed with the engine cold. New cylinder head bolts, a new cylinder head gasket, new inlet manifold O-rings, and a new exhaust manifold gasket will be required on refitting.*

12.7 A lifting bracket can be bolted to the cylinder block using a long bolt screwed into the hole next to the coolant pump

12.13 Disconnect the coolant temperature sensor wiring plug

Removal

1 Switch off the ignition and all electrical consumers, and remove the ignition key.

2 Drain the cooling system as described in Chapter 1A, Section 30.

3 Remove the air cleaner assembly, complete with the air trunking, as described in Chapter 4A, Section 2.

4 Release the hose clips, and disconnect the two radiator hoses from the coolant housing at the transmission end of the cylinder head (**see illustration**). Similarly, release the hose clips and disconnect the remaining three small coolant hoses from the rear of the coolant housing.

5 Remove the main and secondary timing belts as described in Section 6.

6 As the engine is currently supported using a hoist attached to the engine lifting brackets bolted to the cylinder head, it is now necessary to attach a suitable bracket to the cylinder block, so that the engine can still be supported as the cylinder head is removed.

7 A suitable engine lifting bracket can be bolted to the cylinder block using spacers, and a long bolt screwed into the hole located next to the coolant pump (**see illustration**). Ideally, attach a second set of lifting tackle to the hoist, adjust the lifting tackle to support the engine using the bracket attached to the cylinder block, and then disconnect the lifting tackle attached to the bracket on the cylinder head. Alternatively, temporarily support the engine under the sump using a jack and a block of wood, and then transfer the lifting tackle from the bracket on the cylinder head to the bracket bolted to the cylinder block.

8 Remove the camshaft carrier, rockers and tappets, with reference to Section 8 and Section 10.

9 Unscrew the bolt securing the oil level dipstick tube bracket to the cylinder head, then lift the dipstick tube, and turn it to one side, to clear the working area (**see illustration**). Release the wiring harnesses from the clip on the dipstick tube bracket. Note that the dipstick tube bracket bolt also secures the inlet manifold.

10 Disconnect the fuel supply line located next to the coolant expansion tank. Squeeze the button to do this.

11 Disconnect the hose from the charcoal canister to the inlet manifold.

12 Disconnect the hose from the brake servo to the inlet manifold.

13 Disconnect the wiring from the following:
 a) *Knock sensor on the rear of the engine.*
 b) *Inlet manifold pressure sender and air temperature sender.*
 c) *Engine speed sender.*
 d) *Coolant temperature sender (see illustration).*
 e) *Oil pressure switch.*
 f) *Throttle valve control module.*
 g) *Injectors.*
 h) *Heated vacuum valve on oil separator.*
 i) *Crankcase breather on inlet manifold.*

12.14a Unclip the wiring from the bracket on the exhaust heat shield...

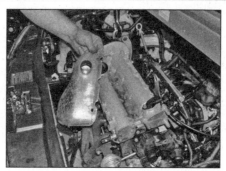

12.14b ...then remove the heat shield

12.18 Lift the inlet manifold back from the engine

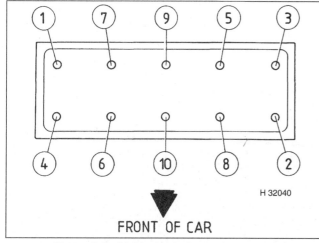

12.19a Cylinder head bolt slackening sequence

12.19b Slackening the cylinder head bolts

14 Unclip the wiring from the bracket attached to the exhaust heat shield, then unscrew the securing bolts (two upper bolts and one lower bolt), and remove the heat shield **(see illustrations)**.

15 Disconnect the exhaust front section from the manifold with reference to Chapter 4C, Section 7. If desired, the exhaust manifold can be removed completely.

16 Unscrew and remove the bolt securing the timing belt inner cover to the cylinder head (located near the right-hand engine lifting eye).

17 Unbolt and remove the timing belt idler bracket.

18 Slacken the securing clamp and release the EGR pipe from the inlet manifold, then unscrew the six securing bolts (three upper and three lower) and lift the inlet manifold back from the engine **(see illustration)**. Ensure that the inlet manifold is adequately supported in the engine compartment, and take care not to strain any wires, cables or hoses. Recover the O-rings if they are loose.

19 Progressively slacken the cylinder head bolts in order, then unscrew and remove the bolts **(see illustrations)**.

20 With all the bolts removed, lift the cylinder head from the block **(see illustration)**. If the cylinder head is stuck, tap it with a soft-faced mallet to break the joint. **Do not** insert a lever into the gasket joint. As the cylinder head is

lifted off, release the coolant pump pipe from the thermostat housing on the cylinder head.

21 Lift the cylinder head gasket from the block.

Inspection

22 Dismantling and inspection of the cylinder head is covered in Part E of this Chapter. Additionally, check the condition of the coolant pump pipe-to-thermostat housing O-ring, and renew if necessary.

Refitting

23 The mating faces of the cylinder head and block must be perfectly clean before refitting

12.20 Removing the cylinder head

the head. Use a scraper to remove all traces of gasket and carbon, also clean the tops of the pistons. Take particular care with the aluminium surfaces, as the soft metal is easily damaged. Make sure that debris is not allowed to enter the oil and water passages – this is particularly important for the oil circuit, as carbon could block the oil supply to the camshaft and crankshaft bearings. Using adhesive tape and paper, seal the water, oil and bolt holes in the cylinder block. To prevent carbon entering the gap between the pistons and bores, smear a little grease in the gap. After cleaning a piston, rotate the crankshaft to that the piston moves down the bore, and then wipe out the grease and carbon with a cloth rag. Clean the other piston crowns in the same way.

24 Check the head and block for nicks, deep scratches and other damage. If slight, they may be removed carefully with a file. More serious damage may be repaired by machining, but this is a specialist job.

25 If warpage of the cylinder head is suspected, use a straight-edge to check it for distortion, as described in Part E of this Chapter.

26 Ensure that the cylinder head bolt holes in the crankcase are clean and free of oil. Syringe or soak up any oil left in the bolt holes. This is most important in order that the correct bolt tightening torque can be applied, and

12.28a Ensure that the dowels are in place in the cylinder block

12.28b Ensure that the part number and OBEN/TOP markings on the cylinder head gasket are uppermost

to prevent the possibility of the block being cracked by hydraulic pressure when the bolts are tightened.

27 Ensure that the crankshaft has been turned to position No's 1 and 4 pistons slightly down their bores from the TDC position (see Section 3). This will eliminate any risk of piston-to-valve contact as the cylinder head is refitted. Also ensure that the camshaft sprockets are locked in the TDC position using the locking tool, as described in Section 3.

28 Ensure that the cylinder head locating dowels are in place in the cylinder block, and then fit a new cylinder head gasket over the dowels, ensuring that the part number is uppermost. Where applicable, the OBEN/TOP marking should also be uppermost **(see illustrations)**. Note that VW recommend that the gasket is only removed from its packaging immediately prior to fitting.

29 Lower the cylinder head into position on the gasket, ensuring that it engages correctly over the dowels. As the cylinder head is lowered into position, ensure that the coolant pump pipe engages with the thermostat housing (use a new O-ring if necessary).

30 Fit the new cylinder head bolts, and screw them in as far as possible by hand.

31 Working progressively, in sequence,

tighten all the cylinder head bolts to the specified Stage 1 torque **(see illustration)**.

32 Again working progressively, in sequence, tighten all the cylinder head bolts through the specified Stage 2 angle.

33 Finally, tighten all the cylinder head bolts, in sequence, to the specified Stage 3 angle.

34 Reconnect the lifting tackle to the right-hand engine lifting bracket on the cylinder head, then adjust the lifting tackle to support the engine. Once the engine is adequately supported using the cylinder head bracket, disconnect the lifting tackle from the bracket bolted to the cylinder block, and unbolt the improvised engine lifting bracket from the cylinder block. Alternatively, remove the trolley jack and block of wood from under the sump.

35 Refit the rockers and tappets, and camshaft carrier as described in Sections 10 and 8.

36 Further refitting is a reversal of removal, bearing in mind the following points.

a) Renew gaskets and O-rings as required.
b) Ensure that all wires, pipes and hoses are correctly reconnected and routed, as noted before removal.
c) Tighten all fixings to the specified torque, where given.
d) On completion, refill the cooling system as described in Chapter 1A, Section 30.

13 Sump – removal and refitting

Note: *VW sealant (D 176 404 A2 or equivalent) will be required to seal the sump on refitting.*

Removal

1 Apply the handbrake, then jack up the front of the vehicle and support securely on axle stands (see *Jacking and vehicle support*).

2 Remove the securing screws and withdraw the engine undertray(s).

3 Detach the exhaust front pipe from the exhaust manifold with reference to Chapter 4C, Section 7, and support to one side. Recover the gasket.

4 Drain the engine oil as described in Chapter 1A, Section 3.

5 Where fitted, disconnect the wiring connector from the oil level/temperature sender in the sump.

6 Unbolt the cover plate from the transmission.

7 Unscrew and remove the bolts securing the sump to the cylinder block, and then withdraw the sump. If necessary, release the sump by tapping with a soft-faced hammer.

Refitting

8 Begin refitting by thoroughly cleaning the mating faces of the sump and cylinder block. Ensure that all traces of old sealant are removed.

9 Ensure that the cylinder block mating face of the sump is free from all traces of old sealant, oil and grease, and then apply a 2.0 to 3.0 mm thick bead of silicone sealant (VW D 176 404 A2 or equivalent) to the sump. Note that the sealant should be run around the inside of the bolt holes in the sump. The sump must be fitted within 5 minutes of applying the sealant.

10 Offer the sump up to the cylinder block, then refit the sump-to-cylinder block bolts, and lightly tighten them by hand, working progressively in a diagonal sequence. **Note:** *If the sump is being refitted with the engine and transmission separated, make sure that the sump is flush with the flywheel/driveplate end of the cylinder block. If necessary, temporarily screw two M6 studs into the block to act as guides.*

11 Refit the sump-to-block bolts, and then tighten them lightly, using a socket.

12 Working in a diagonal sequence, progressively tighten the sump-to-cylinder block bolts to the specified torque.

13 Refit the cover plate to the transmission and tighten the bolts.

14 Refit the exhaust front pipe together with a new gasket with reference to Chapter 4C, Section 7.

15 Refit the wiring connector to the oil level/temperature sender (where fitted), then refit the engine undertray(s), and lower the vehicle to the ground.

16 Allow at least 30 minutes from the time of refitting the sump for the sealant to dry, then refill the engine with oil, with reference to Chapter 1A, Section 3.

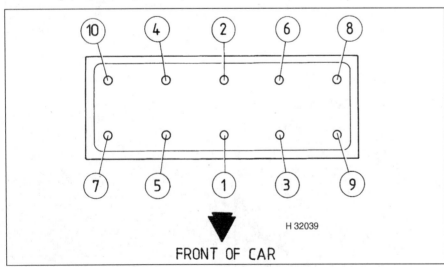

FRONT OF CAR

H 32039

12.31 Cylinder head bolt tightening sequence

14.7 Removing the oil pick-up pipe

14.9 Removing the oil pump

14.11 Lifting off the oil pump rear cover

14 Oil pump –
removal, inspection
and refitting

Removal

1 Remove the main timing belt, as described in Section 6.

2 Refit the crankshaft pulley securing bolt, with a spacer washer positioned under its head, to retain the crankshaft sprocket.

3 Turn the crankshaft a quarter-turn (90°) clockwise to reposition No's 1 and 4 pistons at TDC. Ensure that the crankshaft sprocket tooth with the chamfered inner edge is aligned with the corresponding mark on the oil pump housing (see Section 3).

4 Turn the crankshaft to move the crankshaft sprocket three teeth anti-clockwise away from the TDC position. The third tooth to the right of the tooth with the ground down outer edge must align with the corresponding mark on the oil pump housing. This procedure positions the crankshaft with one of the polygon cams pointing upwards to enable correct oil pump refitting.

5 Remove the main timing belt tensioner, as described in Section 7.

6 Remove the sump as described in Section 13.

7 Unscrew the securing bolts and remove the oil pick-up pipe from the oil pump and cylinder block **(see illustration)**. Recover the gasket.

8 Remove the crankshaft sprocket; noting which way round it is fitted.

9 Unscrew the securing bolts, noting their locations to ensure correct refitting, and remove the oil pump **(see illustration)**. Recover the gasket.

Inspection

10 No spare parts are available for the oil pump, and if worn or faulty, the complete pump must be renewed.

11 To inspect the oil pump rotors, remove the securing screws, and lift off the oil pump rear cover **(see illustration)**.

12 Note that the rotors fit with the punched dots on the edges of the rotors facing the oil pump cover **(see illustration)**.

13 Lift out the rotors, and inspect them

for wear and damage. If there are any signs of wear or damage, the complete oil pump assembly must be renewed.

14 Lubricate the contact faces of the rotors with clean engine oil, then refit the rotors to the pump, ensuring that the punched dots on the edges of the rotors face the pump cover.

15 Refit the pump cover, and tighten the screws securely.

16 Using a flat-bladed screwdriver, prise the crankshaft oil seal from the oil pump, and discard it **(see illustration)**.

17 Thoroughly clean the oil seal seat in the oil pump.

18 Press or drive a new oil seal into position in the oil pump, using a socket or tube of suitable diameter **(see illustration)**. Ensure that the seal seats squarely in the oil pump. Ensure that the socket or tube bears only on the hard outer ring of the seal, and take care not to damage the seal lips. Press or drive

the seal into position until it is seated on the shoulder in the housing. Make sure that the closed end of the seal is facing outwards.

Refitting

19 Commence refitting by cleaning all traces of old gasket and sealant from the mating faces of the cylinder block and oil pump.

20 Wind a length of tape around the front of the crankshaft to protect the oil seal lips as the oil pump is slid into position.

21 Fit a new oil pump gasket over the dowels in the cylinder block **(see illustration)**.

22 Turn the inner oil pump rotor to align one of the drive cut-outs in the edge of the inner rotor with the line on the oil pump rear cover **(see illustration)**.

23 Lightly oil the four tips of the oil pump drive cam on the end of the crankshaft.

24 Coat the lips of the crankshaft oil seal with a thin film of clean engine oil.

14.12 Note that the rotors fit with the punched dots facing the oil pump cover

14.16 Prise the crankshaft oil seal from the oil pump

14.18 Driving a new oil seal into the oil pump using a socket

14.21 Fit a new gasket over the dowels in the cylinder block

14.22 Align one of the drive cut-outs (1) in the edge of the rotor with the line (2) on the oil pump rear cover

25 Slide the oil pump into position over the end of the crankshaft until it engages with the dowels, taking care not to damage the oil seal, and ensuring that the inner rotor engages with the drive cam on the crankshaft **(see illustration)**.
26 Fit new oil pump securing bolts, to the locations noted before removal, and tighten them to the specified torque **(see illustration)**.
27 Remove the tape from the end of the crankshaft, then refit the crankshaft sprocket, noting that the pulley locating pin must be outermost. Temporarily refit the securing bolt and washer to retain the sprocket.
28 Refit the oil pick-up pipe, using a new gasket, and tighten the securing bolts to the specified torque **(see illustration)**.
29 Refit the sump as described in Section 13.
30 Refit the main timing belt tensioner as described in Section 7.
31 Refit the main timing belt as described in Section 6.

15 Flywheel/driveplate – removal, inspection and refitting

Removal

1 On manual transmission models, remove the gearbox (Chapter 7A, Section 3) and clutch (Chapter 6, Section 6).
2 On automatic (DSG) transmission models,

14.26 Fit the new oil pump securing bolts to the locations noted before removal

14.25 Slide the oil pump over the end of the crankshaft. Note the tape used to protect the oil seal

remove the automatic transmission as described in Chapter 7B, Section 2.
3 The flywheel/driveplate bolts are offset to ensure correct fitment. Unscrew the bolts while holding the flywheel/driveplate stationary. Temporarily insert a bolt in the cylinder block, and use a screwdriver to hold the flywheel/driveplate, or make up a holding tool.
4 Lift the flywheel/driveplate from the crankshaft. If removing a driveplate, note the location of the shim (where applicable – between the driveplate and the crankshaft), and the spacer under the securing bolts. Recover the engine-to-transmission plate if it is loose.

Inspection

5 Check the flywheel/driveplate for wear and damage. Examine the starter ring gear for excessive wear to the teeth. If the driveplate or its ring gear is damaged, the complete driveplate must be renewed. The flywheel ring gear, however, may be renewed separately from the flywheel, but the work should be entrusted to a VW dealer. If the clutch friction face is discoloured or scored excessively, it may be possible to regrind it, but this work should also be entrusted to a VW dealer.

Refitting

6 Refitting is a reversal of removal, bearing in mind the following points.
a) *Ensure that the engine-to-transmission plate is in place before fitting the flywheel/ driveplate.*

14.28 Fit a new oil pick-up pipe gasket

b) *Use new bolts when refitting the flywheel or driveplate, and then coat the threads of the bolts with locking fluid before inserting them. Tighten the securing bolts to the specified torque.*
c) *On manual transmission models, follow the procedure Chapter 6, Section 6, for refitting the clutch and Chapter 7A, Section 3, for refitting the transmission.*
d) *On automatic (DSG) transmission models, follow the procedure in Chapter 7B, Section 2, for refitting the transmission.*

16 Crankshaft oil seals – renewal

Timing belt end oil seal

1 Remove the main timing belt as described in Section 6, and the crankshaft sprocket with reference to Section 7.
2 To remove the seal without removing the oil pump, drill two small holes diagonally opposite each other, insert self-tapping screws, and pull on the heads of the screws with pliers.
3 Alternatively, the oil seal can be removed with the oil pump, as described in Section 14.
4 Thoroughly clean the oil seal seating in the oil pump.
5 Wind a length of tape around the end of the crankshaft to protect the oil seal lips as the seal is fitted.
6 Fit a new oil seal to the oil pump, pressing or driving it into position using a socket or tube of suitable diameter. Ensure that the socket or tube bears only on the hard outer ring of the seal, and take care not to damage the seal lips. Press or drive the seal into position until it is seated on the shoulder in the oil pump. Make sure that the closed end of the seal is facing outwards.
7 Refit the crankshaft sprocket with reference to Section 7, and the main timing belt as described in Section 6.

Flywheel/driveplate end oil seal

8 The crankshaft left-hand oil seal is integral with the housing, and must be renewed as an assembly, complete with the crankshaft speed/position sensor wheel. The sensor wheel is attached to the oil seal/housing assembly, and is a press-fit on the crankshaft flange.
9 VW special tool T10134 is required to fit this assembly and, in the workshop, we found that there is no means of accurately aligning the sensor wheel on the crankshaft without the tool (there is no locating key, and there are no alignment marks). If the sensor wheel is not precisely aligned on the crankshaft, the crankshaft speed/position sensor will send incorrect TDC signals to the engine management ECU, and the engine will not run correctly (the engine may not run at all).
10 To renew the crankshaft seal using the VW special tool, follow the procedures, as described in Chapter 2B, Section 13.

17 Engine/transmission mountings – inspection and renewal

Inspection

1 If improved access is required, jack up the front of the vehicle, and support it securely on axle stands (see *Jacking and vehicle support*). Remove the engine top cover that also incorporates the air filter, and then remove the engine undertray(s).
2 Check the mounting rubbers to see if they are cracked, hardened or separated from the metal at any point; renew the mounting if any such damage or deterioration is evident.
3 Check that all the mountings are securely tightened; use a torque wrench to check if possible.
4 Using a large screwdriver or a crowbar, check for wear in the mounting by carefully levering against it to check for free play. Where this is not possible, enlist the aid of an assistant to move the engine/transmission back-and-forth, or from side-to-side, whilst you observe the mounting. While some free play is to be expected, even from new components, excessive wear should be obvious. If excessive free play is found, check first that the fasteners are correctly secured, and then renew any worn components as described in the following paragraphs.

Renewal

Right-hand mounting

5 Attach a hoist and lifting tackle to the engine lifting brackets on the cylinder head, and raise the hoist to just take the weight of the engine. Alternatively the engine can be supported on a trolley jack under the engine. Use a block of wood between the sump and the head of the jack, to prevent any damage to the sump.
6 For improved access, unbolt the coolant reservoir and move it to one side, leaving the coolant hoses connected.
7 Move any wiring harnesses, pipes or hoses to one side to enable removal of the engine mounting.
8 Where applicable, unbolt the bracket for the charcoal canister from the mounting and move it to one side
9 Unscrew the bolts securing the mounting to the engine **(see illustration)**, and then unscrew the bolts securing it to the body. Also, unbolt the movement limiter. Withdraw the mounting from the engine compartment.
10 Refitting is a reversal of removal, bearing in mind the following points.
  a) *Use new securing bolts.*
  b) *Tighten all fixings to the specified torque.*

Left-hand mounting

Note: *New mounting bolts will be required on*

17.9 Right-hand engine mounting

refitting (there is no need to renew the smaller mounting-to-body bolts).
11 Remove the engine top cover, which also incorporates the air filter.
12 Attach a hoist and lifting tackle to the engine lifting brackets on the cylinder head, and raise the hoist to just take the weight of the engine and transmission. Alternatively the engine can be supported on a trolley jack under the transmission. Use a block of wood between the transmission and the head of the jack, to prevent any damage to the transmission.
13 Remove the battery, as described in Chapter 5A, Section 3, and then disconnect the main starter motor feed cable from the positive battery terminal box.
14 Release any relevant wiring or hoses from the clips on the battery tray, then unscrew the four securing bolts and remove the battery tray.
15 Unscrew the bolts securing the mounting to the transmission, and the remaining bolts securing the mounting to the body, then lift the mounting from the engine compartment.
16 Refitting is a reversal of removal, bearing in mind the following points:
  a) *Use new mounting bolts.*
  b) *Tighten all fixings to the specified torque.*

Rear mounting (torque arm)

17 Apply the handbrake, then jack up the front of the vehicle and support securely on axle stands (see *Jacking and vehicle support*). Remove the engine undertray(s) for access to the rear mounting (torque arm).
18 Support the rear of the transmission beneath the final drive housing. To do this, use a trolley jack and block of wood, or alternatively wedge a block of wood between the transmission and the subframe.
19 Working under the vehicle, unscrew and remove the bolt securing the mounting to the subframe.
20 Unscrew the two bolts securing the mounting to the transmission, then withdraw the mounting from under the vehicle **(see illustration)**.
21 Refitting is a reversal of removal, but use new mounting securing bolts, and tighten all fixings to the specified torque.

17.20 Engine/transmission lower rear mounting components

18 Oil pressure relief valve – removal, inspection and refitting

1 The oil pressure relief valve is an integral part of the oil pump. The valve piston and spring are located to the side of the oil pump rotors and can be inspected once the oil pump has been removed from the engine and the rear cover has been removed (see Section 14). If any sign of wear or damage is found the oil pump assembly will have to be renewed; the relief valve piston and spring are not available separately.

19 Oil pressure warning light switch – removal and refitting

Removal

1 The oil pressure warning light switch is fitted to the front of the cylinder head, on its left-hand end. To gain access to the switch, remove the engine top cover.
2 Disconnect the wiring connector and wipe clean the area around the switch **(see illustration)**.
3 Unscrew the switch from the cylinder head and remove it along with its sealing washer. If the switch is to be left removed from the engine for any length of time, plug the hole in the cylinder head.

19.2 Disconnect the oil pressure switch wiring connector

20.1 Oil level/temperature sender

Refitting

4 Examine the sealing washer for signs of damage or deterioration and if necessary renew.

5 Refit the switch, complete with washer, and tighten it to the specified torque.

6 Securely reconnect the wiring connector then refit the engine cover. Check and, if necessary, top-up the engine oil as described in *Weekly checks*.

20 Oil level/temperature sender – removal and refitting

Removal

1 The oil level/temperature sender is fitted to bottom of the sump **(see illustration)**.

2 Drain the engine oil as described in Chapter 1A Section 3.

3 Disconnect the wiring connector and wipe clean the area around the sender.

4 Undo the three retaining bolts and remove the sender.

Refitting

5 Examine the sealing washer for signs of damage or deterioration and if necessary renew.

6 Refit the switch and tighten the retaining bolts to the specified torque.

7 Securely reconnect the wiring connector then refill the engine with oil, with reference to Chapter 1A, Section 3.

8 On completion, check and, if necessary, top-up the engine oil as described in *Weekly checks*.

Chapter 2 Part B:
1.4 litre direct injection petrol engine in-car repair procedures

Contents

Degrees of difficulty

Easy, suitable for novice with little experience 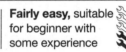	**Fairly easy,** suitable for beginner with some experience	**Fairly difficult,** suitable for competent DIY mechanic	**Difficult,** suitable for experienced DIY mechanic	**Very difficult,** suitable for expert DIY or professional

Specifications

General

Type	Four-cylinder in-line, chain-driven double (DOHC) overhead camshaft, four stroke, liquid-cooled, turbocharged

Manufacturer's engine codes*:

1390 cc (1.4 litre)	CAXA
Maximum power output	90 kW at 5000 rpm
Maximum torque output	200 Nm at 1500 – 4000 rpm
Bore	76.5 mm
Stroke	75.6 mm
Compression ratio	10.0 : 1
Compression pressures:	
Minimum compression pressure	Approximately 11.0 bars
Maximum difference between cylinders	Approximately 3.0 bars
Firing order	1 – 3 – 4 – 2
No.1 cylinder location	Crankshaft pulley end
Direction of crankshaft rotation	Clockwise (when viewed from right-hand side of vehicle)

* Note: *See 'Vehicle identification' at the end of this manual for the location of engine code markings.*

Lubrication system

Oil pump type	Chain-driven from crankshaft
Minimum oil pressure (oil temperature 80°C):	
At 2000 rpm	2.0 bar

Camshaft

Camshaft endfloat (maximum)	0.40 mm

Torque wrench settings

	Nm	lbf ft
Auxiliary drivebelt idler pulley bolt	40	30
Auxiliary drivebelt tensioner:		
Stage 1:		
Non-turbo engines	20	15
Turbo engines	40	30
Stage 2	Angle-tighten a further 90°	
Camshaft housing:		
Stage 1	10	7
Stage 2	Angle-tighten a further 90°	
Camshaft position sensor	10	7
Camshaft sprocket bolt**:		
Exhaust:		
Stage 1	50	37
Stage 2	Angle-tighten a further 90°	
Inlet:		
Stage 1	50	37
Stage 2	Angle-tighten a further 90°	
Coolant pump pulley	20	15
Crankshaft oil seal housing**	12	9
Crankshaft pulley bolt**:		
Stage 1	150	111
Stage 2	Angle-tighten a further 180°	
Cylinder head bolts**:		
Stage 1	30	22
Stage 2	Angle-tighten a further 90°	
Stage 3	Angle-tighten a further 90°	
Crankshaft speed sender	5	4
Driveplate bolts* **:		
Stage 1	60	44
Stage 2	Angle-tighten a further 90°	
Engine mountings**:		
RH engine mounting:		
Limiter:		
Stage 1	20	15
Stage 2	Angle-tighten a further 90°	
Mounting to engine:		
Stage 1	60	44
Stage 2	Angle-tighten a further 90°	
Mounting to body:		
Stage 1	40	30
Stage 2	Angle-tighten a further 90°	
LH engine mounting*:		
Mounting to body:		
Stage 1	60	44
Stage 2	Angle-tighten a further 90°	
Mounting to transmission:		
Stage 1	40	30
Stage 2	Angle-tighten a further 90°	
Rear mounting (torque arm)*:		
To transmission:		
Stage 1:		
Grade 8.8	40	30
Grade 10.9	50	37
Stage 2	Angle-tighten a further 90°	
To subframe:		
Stage 1	100	74
Stage 2	Angle-tighten a further 90°	
Flywheel bolts* **:		
Stage 1	60	44
Stage 2	Angle-tighten a further 90°	
Fuel line:		
Banjo bolt	15	11
Union nut	15	11
Oil filter cap	25	18
Oil level and temperature sender	10	7
Oil pressure switch	25	18
Oil pump	25	18

Torque wrench settings (continued)

	Nm	lbf ft
Oil pump sprocket**:		
Stage 1	20	15
Stage 2	Angle-tighten a further 90°	
Oil pump chain tensioner	15	11
Sump	13	10
Sump oil drain plug	30	22
Thermostat housing	10	7
Timing chain tensioner	9	7
Timing cover:		
M6 bolt	10	7
M10 bolt	50	37

* Use thread-locking compound.
**Do not re-use

1 General information

How to use this Chapter

This Part of Chapter 2 describes those repair procedures that can reasonably be carried out on the engine while it remains in the vehicle. If the engine has been removed from the vehicle and is being dismantled as described in Part E, any preliminary dismantling procedures can be ignored.

Note that while it may be possible physically to overhaul certain items while the engine is in the vehicle, such tasks are not usually carried out as separate operations, and usually require the execution of several additional procedures (not to mention the cleaning of components and of oil ways); for this reason, all such tasks are classed as major overhaul procedures, and are described in Part E of this Chapter. *Caution: The crankshaft must not be removed on these engines – just loosening and retightening the main bearing bolts will render the cylinder block unserviceable. If the crankshaft or bearings are excessively worn or damaged, the complete cylinder block must be renewed.*

Engine description

The engine is a double overhead camshaft (DOHC), in-line four-cylinder unit, which is mounted transversely at the front of the vehicle, with the transmission bolted to the left-hand end of the engine. It has a direct injection fuel system, referred to as TSi (Turbocharged Stratified Injection). Non-turbo versions are referred to as FSi (Fuel Stratified Injection).

The cylinder block, cylinder head and camshaft housing are all cast in aluminium alloy. The cylinder bores are machined in the cylinder block. The crankshaft has five main bearings, and thrustwashers are fitted to number 3 main bearing to control crankshaft endfloat.

Camshaft drive is by chain from the crankshaft, and the chain is tensioned by a hydraulic tensioner. The valves are closed by coil springs and the camshafts actuate the valves by roller rockers and hydraulic tappets. There are 4 valves per cylinder.

The flywheel is located on a flange at the left-hand end of the crankshaft. The main bearings and the big-end bearings are of shell type, whilst the connecting rod small-end bearings are of the bronze bush type, being pressed into the connecting rod and reamed to suit.

The oil pump is chain-driven from the front of the crankshaft. Oil is drawn from the sump through a strainer and circulated through an externally mounted filter to the various engine components.

Operations with engine in car

The following work can be carried out with the engine in the vehicle:

a) Compression pressure – testing.
b) Crankshaft pulley – removal and refitting.
c) Timing cover – removal and refitting.
d) Timing chain – renewal.
e) Timing chain tensioner and sprockets – removal and refitting.
f) Camshaft(s) and hydraulic tappets – removal and refitting.
g) Cylinder head – removal and refitting*.
h) Cylinder head – decarbonising.
i) Sump – removal and refitting.
j) Oil pump – removal, overhaul and refitting.
k) Crankshaft oil seals – renewal.
l) Engine/transmission mountings – inspection and renewal.
m) Flywheel/driveplate – removal, inspection and refitting.

* Cylinder head dismantling procedures are detailed in Chapter 2E.
Note: It is possible to remove the pistons and connecting rods (after removing the cylinder head and sump) without removing the engine from the car, however this is not recommended. Work of this nature is more easily and thoroughly completed with the engine on the bench, as described in Chapter 2E.

2 Compression test – description and interpretation

1 When engine performance is down, or if misfiring occurs which cannot be attributed to the ignition or fuel systems, a compression test can provide diagnostic clues as to the engine's condition. If the test is performed regularly, it can give warning of trouble before any other symptoms become apparent.
2 The engine must be fully warmed-up to normal operating temperature, the battery must be fully charged, and the spark plugs together with their ignition coils must be removed (Chapter 1A, Section 25). The aid of an assistant will also be required.
3 Remove the fuel pump fuse, with reference to wiring diagrams in Chapter 12.
4 Fit a compression tester to the No 1 cylinder spark plug hole – the type of tester which screws into the plug thread is to be preferred.
5 Have the assistant hold the throttle wide open and crank the engine on the starter motor; after one or two revolutions, the compression pressure should build-up to a maximum figure and then stabilise. Record the highest reading obtained.
6 Repeat the test on the remaining cylinders, recording the pressure in each.
7 All cylinders should produce very similar pressures, of the order of 10 to 15 bars. Any one cylinder reading below 7 bars, or a difference of more than 3 bars between cylinders, suggests a fault.
8 Note that the compression should build-up quickly in a healthy engine; low compression on the first stroke, followed by gradually

3.5 Engine top cover retaining bolts (arrowed)

3.6 Coolant pipe retaining bolt and harness earth connection at the left-hand end of the cylinder head (arrowed)

increasing pressure on successive strokes, indicates worn piston rings.

9 A low compression reading on the first stroke, which does not build-up during successive strokes, indicates leaking valves or a blown head gasket (a cracked head could also be the cause).

10 If the pressure in any cylinder is reduced to 10 bars or less, carry out the following test to isolate the cause. Introduce a teaspoonful of clean oil into that cylinder through its spark plug hole and repeat the test.

11 If the addition of oil temporarily improves the compression pressure, this indicates that bore or piston wear is responsible for the

pressure loss. No improvement suggests that leaking or burnt valves, or a blown head gasket, may be to blame.

12 A low reading from two adjacent cylinders is almost certainly due to the head gasket having blown between them; the presence of coolant in the engine oil will confirm this.

13 If one cylinder is about 20 percent lower than the others and the engine has a slightly rough idle; a worn camshaft lobe could be the cause.

14 On completion of the test, refit the spark plugs, ignition coils and refit the fuel pump fuse.

3 Engine assembly and valve timing marks - general information and usage

Note: *A dial gauge and adapter are required to determine the position of No 1 piston, and VW tool T10171 is required to position the camshafts at TDC.*

1 Top dead centre (TDC) is the highest point in its travel up-and-down its cylinder bore that each piston reaches as the crankshaft rotates. While each piston reaches TDC both at the top of the compression stroke and again at the top of the exhaust stroke, for the purpose of timing the engine, TDC refers to the No 1 piston position at the top of its compression stroke.

2 No 1 piston and cylinder are at the right-hand (timing chain) end of the engine. Note that the crankshaft rotates clockwise when viewed from the right-hand side of the vehicle.

3 Switch off the ignition and all electrical consumers, and remove the ignition key. Remove all the spark plugs as described in Chapter 1A, Section 25.

4 Drain the coolant as described in Chapter 1A, Section 30.

5 Undo the bolts securing the engine top cover, unclip the coolant hoses from the right-hand end, and pull the cover upwards **(see illustration)**.

6 Disconnect the hoses, then undo the bolt and remove the coolant pipe from the camshaft housing/cylinder block **(see illustration)**.

7 Unclip the wiring harness, and pull the coolant pipe away from the cylinder head **(see illustration)**.

8 Disconnect the wiring plug, and unscrew the oil pressure switch **(see illustration)**.

9 Undo the bolts and remove the covers for access to the camshafts **(see illustration)**. Discard the O-ring seals – new ones must be fitted.

10 Turn the engine with a socket on the

3.7 Unclip the wiring harness (arrowed)

3.8 Unscrew the oil pressure switch (arrowed)

3.9 Undo the bolts (arrowed) and remove the covers

3.10 Exhaust and inlet camshafts set at TDC

crankshaft pulley bolt until the TDC timing holes in the ends of the exhaust and inlet camshafts are at the 4 o'clock and 8 o'clock positions respectively. The engine is now at TDC on No 1 piston **(see illustration)**.

11 Screw the dial gauge and adapter into No 1 spark plug hole, then determine TDC position by rotating the crankshaft back-and-forth so that the gauge can be zeroed. Now turn the crankshaft anti-clockwise 45°, and then turn it slowly to the TDC position **(see illustration)**. If the crankshaft is turned more than 0.01 mm past TDC, repeat the procedure.

12 With No 1 piston finally at TDC, mark the left-hand ends of the camshafts accurately in relation to the camshaft housing with a felt-tipped pen. Note that VW technicians use tool number T10171 to verify this position **(see illustration)**, however, although the preferable method, the tool is unlikely to be available to the home mechanic.

13 Remove the dial gauge and adapter.

14 The remainder of refitting is a reversal of removal.

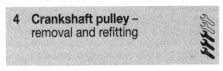

4   Crankshaft pulley – removal and refitting

Note: *The crankshaft pulley bolt must be renewed whenever removed.*

Removal

1 Apply the handbrake, then jack up the front of the vehicle and support it on axle stands (see *Jacking and vehicle support*). Remove the right-hand front roadwheel.

2 Undo the retaining screws and remove the right-hand front wheel arch liner, from under the wing panel.

3 Mark the auxiliary drivebelt for normal rotation to ensure correct refitting, and note it's routing for ease of refitting. Remove the drivebelt as described in Chapter 1A Section 26.

4 Set the engine to its TDC position as described in Section 3.

Caution: Do not turn the engine during the following procedure.

5 The crankshaft pulley must now be held stationary while the bolt is loosened **(see illustration)**. VW technicians use a tool that locates in the pulley cut-outs, and a similar tool can be fabricated out of a length of metal bar with two long bolts attached to one end. If a tool is not available, have an assistant engage 4th gear and apply firm pressure to the footbrake pedal, then loosen the crankshaft pulley bolt.

6 Unscrew and remove the bolt and withdraw the pulley from the nose of the crankshaft **(see illustrations)**. The bolt must be renewed whenever removed, however, on non-turbo engines, it is recommended that the modified sleeve and discs (see Note) are also renewed together with a new oil seal at the same time. Check with your VW dealer to confirm which

3.11 Determining the exact TDC position with a dial gauge

sleeve is fitted, and if necessary remove them from the nose of the crankshaft. Remove the oil seal with reference to Section 13.

Refitting

7 Thoroughly clean the nose of the crankshaft and timing cover.

8 Fit the new bolt. It is important to check that the crankshaft does not turn, especially during the angle tightening. Hold the pulley as for removal and note the TDC markings made in paragraph 4. After fully tightening the bolt in the two stages given in Specifications, the marks must remain aligned with each other. If not, a new bolt must be obtained and the procedure repeated.

9 Refit the auxiliary drivebelt as described in Chapter 1A, Section 26.

10 Refit the wheel arch liner, then refit the roadwheel and lower the vehicle to the ground.

4.5 Crankshaft pulley and bolt

4.6b ...and remove the crankshaft pulley

3.12 Using VW tool T10171 to set the camshafts at TDC

5   Timing cover – removal and refitting

Removal

1 Apply the handbrake, then jack up the front of the vehicle and support it on axle stands (see *Jacking and vehicle support*). Remove the right-hand front roadwheel and the under shield from beneath the engine. For improved access, also remove the right-hand front wheel arch liner.

2 Mark the auxiliary drivebelt for normal rotation to ensure correct refitting, and note it's routing for ease of refitting. Loosen the coolant pump pulley retaining bolts **(see illustration)**, then remove the drivebelt as described in Chapter 1A, Section 26.

4.6a Unscrew the bolt...

5.2 Loosen the coolant pump pulley retaining bolts

5.4 Remove the coolant pump pulley

5.6a Remove the compressor/tensioner mounting bracket...

5.6b ...and the auxiliary drivebelt idler pulley

3 Set the engine to its TDC position as described in Section 3.

4 Fully unscrew the retaining bolts and remove the coolant pump pulley from the drive flange **(see illustration)**.

5 Refer to Chapter 3 and unbolt the air conditioning compressor from its mounting bracket and suspend to one side. **Do not** disconnect the refrigerant lines.

6 Unbolt the compressor/tensioner mounting bracket and the auxiliary drivebelt idler pulley **(see illustrations)**.

7 Remove the alternator as described in Chapter 5A, Section 5.

8 Remove the crankshaft pulley as described in Section 4.

9 Remove the sump as described in Section 9.

10 The right-hand end of the engine must now be supported while the engine mounting is removed, and the engine then held in a safe position in order to carry out the remaining

work. To do this, use a hoist or support bar attached to the engine lifting eyes – this is preferable to using a trolley jack beneath the engine. With the engine supported, remove the right-hand engine mounting with reference to Section 15.

11 Progressively unscrew and remove all of the retaining bolts, noting their locations as they are of different lengths, then remove the timing cover from the engine. Note that most of the bolts require an Allen key to remove them. If necessary, tap the cover lightly to release it, and then withdraw the cover from the location dowels. Remove the gasket and the O-ring seal and discard them, as new ones must be used on refitting **(see illustration)**.

12 As the cover is removed, the bearing sleeve may remain in the oil seal. Leave the sleeve in position if the oil seal is not to be renewed. Alternatively, renew the oil seal with reference to Section 13 **(see illustration)**.

Refitting

13 Thoroughly clean the cover and block/head contact surfaces, and then locate a new gasket on the engine **(see illustration)**.

14 To aid refitting, temporarily fit two studs to the block/head to act as guides. Locate the cover together with the bearing sleeve onto the engine **(see illustration)**, then insert the bolts and tighten them progressively to the specified torques.

15 The remainder of refitting is a reversal of removal.

---

6 Timing chain, tensioner and sprockets – removal, inspection and refitting

Removal

1 Remove the timing cover as described in Section 5.

2 The timing chain tensioner rail must now be released from the chain and the hydraulic tensioner locked. To do this, press the lower end of the rail rearwards so that it forces the piston into the hydraulic tensioner, then insert a suitable 3.0 mm diameter tool through the holes provided to retain the piston **(see illustration)**.

3 Unbolt the tensioner from the cylinder block **(see illustration)**.

4 Mark the timing chain for direction of rotation so that it is refitted the same way round **(see illustration)**.

5 While holding the inlet camshaft sprocket

5.11 Remove the O-ring seal from the inside of the timing cover

5.12 Remove the bearing sleeve from the timing cover

5.13 Fit a new timing cover gasket

5.14 Locate the timing cover on the engine

6.2 Press the timing chain tensioner and insert a 3.0 mm diameter drill bit or rod to lock the tensioner

6.3 Remove the timing chain tensioner

6.4 If the timing chain is to be refitted, mark it with a dab of paint

6.6a Unscrew the bolt...

6.6b ...remove the exhaust camshaft sprocket...

6.6c ...and shaft...

6.6d ...then unhook the timing chain from the inlet camshaft sprocket...

6.6e ...and remove the inlet camshaft sprocket

6.7 Remove the plastic cover...

6.9 ...unbolt the chain tensioner...

stationary, loosen both sprocket retaining bolts, noting that the inlet camshaft adjuster sprocket bolt has a left-hand thread. Use a holding tool made from two lengths of bar, with two bolts located to engage with the sprocket.
6 Unscrew and remove the bolts and remove the timing chain, camshaft sprockets and exhaust camshaft sprocket shaft. Unhook the chain from the crankshaft sprocket **(see illustrations)**.
7 To remove the oil pump sprocket, first remove the plastic cover **(see illustration)**.
8 Hold the sprocket stationary and loosen the retaining bolt.
9 Using a screwdriver, unhook the chain tensioner spring and remove it. Unscrew the mounting bolt and remove the chain tensioner **(see illustration)**.
10 Mark the oil pump chain for direction of rotation so that it can be refitted the same way

round. Remove the retaining bolt and remove the sprocket and chain from the crankshaft sprocket **(see illustration)**. Discard the oil pump sprocket bolt as a new one must be used on refitting.

11 Pull the sprocket from the crankshaft, noting that it has a lug that locates in a groove in the crankshaft journal **(see illustration)**.
12 Remove the timing chain guides from the engine **(see illustration)**.

6.10 ...and remove the sprocket and chain from the crankshaft sprocket

6.11 Remove the crankshaft sprocket

6.12 Remove the timing chain guides

6.15 Mark the crankshaft sprocket in relation to the cylinder block so that its position can be easily checked

6.16 Tighten the oil pump sprocket bolt

Inspection

13 Thoroughly clean all components, and then examine the timing chain and oil pump drive chain for excessive wear. Also check the sprocket teeth for wear. If the engine has covered a high mileage, the chain and sprockets should be renewed as a matter of course.

14 The crankshaft pulley bolt must be renewed whenever removed.

Refitting

15 Check that the crankshaft is still at TDC, then refit the sprocket and engage the lug with the groove. As a precaution against the sprocket moving out of the groove, mark it in relation to the cylinder block so that its position can be easily checked (see illustration).

16 Engage the oil pump sprocket in the chain, making sure the chain is the correct way round, then locate the chain on the crankshaft sprocket. Locate the sprocket on the oil pump (it will only go in one position), insert the new bolt and tighten to the specified torque and angle while holding it as for removal (see illustration).

17 Refit the oil pump chain tensioner and tighten the mounting bolt to the specified torque. Refit the tensioner spring and the plastic cover.

18 Check that the crankshaft sprocket is still aligned with the TDC mark made on the cylinder block.

19 Refit the sprocket to the exhaust camshaft using a new bolt, and hand-tighten it.

20 With the timing chain the correct way round as previously noted, engage it with the crankshaft sprocket, then locate the chain on the front guide and exhaust sprocket. Engage the inlet camshaft sprocket in the chain and refit to the camshaft with a new bolt. Hand-tighten the bolt at this stage.

21 Refit the timing tensioner and tighten the bolts to the specified torque.

22 Remove the locking tool to release the tensioner.

23 Check that the TDC marks on the crankshaft sprocket and cylinder block, and the marks on the ends of the camshafts are still aligned correctly.

24 Tighten the camshaft sprocket bolts to the specified torque and angle while holding them stationary as for removal.

25 Check the TDC timing marks on the crankshaft sprocket and ends of the camshafts for correct alignment.

26 Refit the timing cover with reference to Section 5.

7 Camshaft housing, camshafts and hydraulic tappets – removal, inspection and refitting

Removal

1 Remove the turbocharger as described in Chapter 4C, Section 4.

2 Remove the timing cover as described in Section 5.

3 Remove the timing chain and camshaft sprockets as described in Section 6.

4 For the remaining removal procedure the pistons must be positioned halfway down their bores as a precaution against the valves touching them. Temporarily refit the crankshaft pulley, insert and tighten the pulley bolt, then turn the crankshaft 45° anti-clockwise so that all of the pistons are half-way down their bores.

5 Disconnect the wiring from the fuel low-pressure sender, and from the high-pressure pump.

6 Unbolt the earth cable from the camshaft housing.

7 Remove the ignition coils with reference to Chapter 5B, Section 3, and then remove the wiring harness and cable guide. Note that VW technicians use a special tool (T10094) to remove the coils, however, a length of bent welding rod or similar hooked under the wiring plugs may be used to extract them.

8 Cover the fuel line to the high-pressure pump with cloth then unscrew the banjo and union nut and disconnect it.

⚠ **Warning: The fuel system is under pressure – wear gloves and eye protection to prevent injuries.**

9 Unscrew the bolts and move the fuel lines to one side.

10 Disconnect the wiring from the camshaft position sensor (see illustration).

11 Remove the engine oil dipstick.

12 Remove the inlet manifold with reference to Chapter 4A, Section 8.

13 Unbolt the left-hand engine lifting eye.

14 Progressively unscrew the mounting bolts and remove the camshaft housing complete with camshafts from the top of the cylinder head. If it is tight, use a mallet or rubber hammer to tap the housing in several places in order to release it from the locating dowels and studs.

15 With the camshaft housing on the bench, clean away the sealant from the cylinder head and cover. Remove the small filter and O-ring from the cylinder head (see illustration).

16 Obtain a suitable box with compartments for each of the roller/rocker arms and hydraulic tappets, so that they can be identified for their correct position. Remove the arms and hydraulic tappets from the cylinder head and

7.10 Disconnect the wiring from the camshaft position sensor

7.15 Remove the small filter from the cylinder head

7.16 Place the roller/rocker arms and hydraulic tappets in a box with compartments to keep them identified for position

7.17 Remove the camshafts from the housing

7.19 Clean the camshafts and inspect them for wear and damage

place them in the box, making sure they are identified for location to ensure correct refitting **(see illustration)**.

17 Identify each camshaft for location and position, and then lift them out from the camshaft housing **(see illustration)**. **Note:** *The inlet camshaft has an additional cam to operate the high-pressure pump.*

Inspection

18 Thoroughly clean the camshafts and housing, making sure that all of the sealant is removed from the mating surfaces. Also, clean the cylinder head upper mating surface.

Caution: Make sure that the TDC alignment marks are not removed from the ends of the camshaft and the housing.

19 Visually inspect each camshaft for evidence of wear on the surfaces of the lobes and journals **(see illustration)**. Normally their surfaces should be smooth and have a dull shine; look for scoring, erosion or pitting and areas that appear highly polished, indicating excessive wear. Accelerated wear will occur once the hardened exterior of the camshaft has been damaged, so always renew worn items.

20 If the machined surfaces of the camshaft appear discoloured or blued, it is likely that it has been overheated at some point, probably due to inadequate lubrication.

21 To measure the camshaft endfloat, temporarily locate them in the housing and refit the EGR valve and end cover. Anchor a DTI gauge to the end of the housing and align the gauge probe with the camshaft axis.

7.23a Detach the hydraulic tappets from the roller/rockers to inspect them…

Push one of the camshafts to one end of the housing as far as it will travel, then rest the DTI gauge probe on the end of the camshaft, and zero the gauge display. Push the camshaft as far as it will go to the other end of the housing, and record the gauge reading. Verify the reading by pushing the camshaft back to its original position and checking that the gauge indicates zero again. Repeat the checking procedure for the remaining camshaft.

22 Check that the camshaft endfloat measurement is within the limit given in the Specifications. Wear outside of this limit is unlikely to be confined to any one component, so renewal of the camshafts and housing must be considered.

23 Inspect the hydraulic tappets and roller/rockers for obvious signs of wear or damage, and renew if necessary **(see illustrations)**. Check that the oil holes in the tappets are free from obstructions.

7.23b …then reassemble them

Refitting

24 Lubricate the camshaft journals and bearing surfaces in the camshaft housing, then locate the camshafts in their respective bores.

25 Set the camshafts to their TDC position. If the VW tool is available, fit the special tool to hold the camshafts **(see illustration)**.

26 With the camshaft housing inverted on the bench, apply a thin film of sealant to the mating surfaces **(see illustration)**. Do not apply the sealant too thick otherwise it may enter the lubrication system and cause expensive damage to the engine.

27 Lubricate the roller/rocker arms and hydraulic tappets, and refit them to their correct positions in the cylinder head **(see illustration)**, then refit the small O-ring to the cylinder head. Make sure each arm is correctly clipped to the tappets.

28 As an aid to refitting the camshaft housing,

7.25 Fit the VW tool to hold the camshafts in their TDC position

7.26 Apply a thin film of sealant to the camshaft housing mating surface

7.27 Lubricate the roller/rocker arms and hydraulic tappets before refitting them

fit two temporary studs to two opposite corners of the cylinder head **(see illustration)**. Taking care not to allow any oil to drop onto the sealant, carefully lower the housing onto the cylinder head.

29 Remove the temporary studs and insert the retaining bolts hand-tight. Now progressively tighten the bolts to the Stage 1 specified torque, starting in the centre and working outwards in a spiral fashion.

30 Angle-tighten the bolts by the specified amount.

31 The remainder of refitting is a reversal of removal.

8 Cylinder head – removal, inspection and refitting

Removal

1 Remove the engine and transmission from the vehicle, and remove the transmission from the engine as described in Part E of this Chapter.

2 Remove the inlet manifold(s) as described in Chapter 4A, Section 8.

3 Remove the exhaust manifold as described in Chapter 4C, Section 6.

4 Unbolt the thermostat housing from the left-hand end of the cylinder head, and at the same time release it from the rear engine coolant pipe. Recover the gasket and O-ring **(see illustrations)**.

5 Remove the timing cover as described in Section 5.

8.4a Remove the thermostat housing from the cylinder head and release it from the rear engine coolant pipe...

8.4c ...and O-ring seal from the coolant pipe

7.28 Fit two temporary studs as shown to act as guides for the camshaft housing

6 Remove the camshaft housing, camshafts and hydraulic tappets as described in Section 7.

7 Progressively slacken the cylinder head bolts in the reverse order to that given for tightening in paragraph 21. Remove the cylinder head bolts **(see illustration)**. Note: *The bolts must not be re-used – obtain new ones.*

8 With all the bolts removed, lift the cylinder head from the block (together with the inlet and exhaust manifolds, if not removed). If the cylinder head is stuck, tap it with a soft-faced mallet to break the joint. Do not insert a lever into the gasket joint.

9 Lift the cylinder head gasket from the block.

Inspection

10 Dismantling and inspection of the cylinder head is covered in Part E of this Chapter.

8.4b ...then recover the gasket...

8.7 Remove the cylinder head bolts

11 The mating faces of the cylinder head and block must be perfectly clean before refitting the head.

12 Use a scraper to remove all traces of gasket and carbon, also clean the tops of the pistons. Take particular care with the aluminium surfaces, as the soft metal is easily damaged.

13 Make sure that debris is not allowed to enter the oil and water passages – this is particularly important for the oil circuit, as carbon could block the oil supply to the camshaft and crankshaft bearings. Using adhesive tape and paper, seal the water, oil and bolt holes in the cylinder block. To prevent carbon entering the gap between the pistons and bores, smear a little grease in the gap. After cleaning a piston, rotate the crankshaft so that the piston moves down the bore, and then wipe out the grease and carbon with a cloth rag. Clean the other piston crowns in the same way.

14 Check the head and block for nicks, deep scratches and other damage. If slight, they may be removed carefully with a file. More serious damage may be repaired by machining, but this is a specialist job. If warpage of the cylinder head is suspected, use a straight-edge to check it for distortion, as described in Part E of this Chapter.

Refitting

15 Before refitting the cylinder head, the pistons must be positioned halfway down their bores as a precaution against the valves touching them. To do this, temporarily refit the crankshaft pulley, insert and tighten the pulley bolt, then turn the crankshaft 45° anti-clockwise.

16 Ensure that the cylinder head bolt holes in the cylinder block are clean and free of oil. Syringe or soak up any oil left in the bolt holes. This is most important in order that the correct bolt tightening torque can be applied, and to prevent the possibility of the block being cracked by hydraulic pressure when the bolts are tightened.

17 Ensure that the cylinder head locating dowels are in place in the cylinder block, and then fit a new cylinder head gasket over the dowels, ensuring that the part number is uppermost **(see illustration)**. Where

8.17 Fit the new cylinder head gasket

8.20 Cylinder head bolt tightening sequence

9.6 Remove the sump

applicable, the OBEN/TOP marking should also be uppermost. Note that VW recommend that the gasket is only removed from its packaging immediately prior to fitting.

18 Lower the cylinder head into position on the gasket, ensuring that it engages correctly over the dowels.

19 Insert the new cylinder bolts and tighten them as far as possible by hand.

20 Working in sequence, tighten all the cylinder head bolts to the specified Stage 1 torque **(see illustration)**.

21 Again working in sequence, tighten all the cylinder head bolts through the specified Stage 2 angle.

22 Finally, tighten all the cylinder head bolts, in sequence, through the specified Stage 3 angle.

23 Refit the hydraulic tappets, camshafts and camshaft housing as described in Section 7.

24 Refit the timing cover as described in Section 5.

25 Clean the contact surfaces then refit the thermostat housing to the cylinder head and rear engine coolant pipe, using a new gasket and O-ring. Tighten the bolts to the specified torque.

26 Refit the exhaust manifold (Chapter 4C, Section 6) and inlet manifold (Chapter 4A, Section 8).

27 Refit the transmission to the engine, and refit the assembly to the vehicle as described in Part E of this Chapter.

9 Sump – removal and refitting

Removal

1 Apply the handbrake, then jack up the front of the vehicle and support securely on axle stands (see *Jacking and vehicle support*).

2 Remove the securing screws and withdraw the engine undertray(s).

3 Drain the engine oil as described in Chapter 1A, Section 3.

4 Unbolt the front exhaust pipe from the exhaust manifold with reference to Chapter 4C, Section 7. Release the pipe from its mountings and support to one side away from the sump.

5 Disconnect the wiring connector from the oil level/temperature sender on the base of the sump.

6 Unscrew and remove the bolts securing the sump to the cylinder block, and then withdraw the sump **(see illustration)**. If necessary, release the sump by tapping with a soft-faced mallet.

Refitting

7 Commence refitting by thoroughly cleaning the mating faces of the sump and cylinder block. Ensure that all traces of old sealant are removed.

8 Ensure that the cylinder block mating face of the sump is free from all traces of old sealant, oil and grease, and then apply a 2.0 to 3.0 mm thick bead of silicone sealant (VW D 176 600 A1 or equivalent) to the sump **(see illustration)**. Note that the sealant should be run around the inside of the bolt holes in the sump. The sump must be fitted within 5 minutes of applying the sealant.

9 Offer the sump up to the cylinder block, then refit the retaining bolts, and progressively tighten them in diagonal sequence to the specified torque.

10 Reconnect the wiring to the oil level/temperature sender on the sump.

9.8 Apply sealant to the sump mating surface

11 Refit the front exhaust pipe to the exhaust manifold together with a new gasket with reference to Chapter 4C, Section 7.

12 Refit the engine undertray(s) and lower the vehicle to the ground.

13 Allow at least 30 minutes from the time of refitting the sump for the sealant to dry, then refill the engine with oil, with reference to Chapter 1A, Section 3.

10 Oil pump, drive chain and sprockets – removal, inspection and refitting

Removal

1 Remove the sump as described in Section 9. It is not necessary to remove the timing cover unless renewing the timing chain.

2 Remove the plastic cover from the oil pump, then hold the sprocket stationary and loosen the retaining bolt.

3 Press the chain tensioner outwards with a screwdriver, then unscrew the bolt and remove the sprocket from the oil pump and chain. Note that the sprocket will only fit in one position on the oil pump.

4 Unscrew the mounting bolts and withdraw the oil pump from the dowels in the cylinder block **(see illustration)**.

5 If it is required to remove the oil pump

10.4 Remove the oil pump

12.1 Oil level/temperature sender

chain and tensioner, refer to Section 6 for the removal of the timing cover.

Inspection

6 Thoroughly clean all components, then examine the oil pump drive chain for excessive wear. Also check the sprocket teeth for wear. If the engine has covered a high mileage, the chain and sprockets should be renewed as a matter of course. Note: *The crankshaft pulley bolt must be renewed whenever removed.*

Refitting

7 If removed, refit the oil pump drive chain and tensioner with reference to Section 6.
8 Locate the oil pump on the cylinder block dowels, insert the mounting bolts and tighten them to the specified torque.
9 Engage the sprocket with the chain, then press the tensioner outwards with a screwdriver, locate the sprocket on the oil

pump, and tighten the retaining bolt to the specified torque and angle while holding the sprocket stationary as for removal.
10 Refit the plastic cover.
11 Refit the sump with reference to Section 9.

11 Oil pressure warning light switch – removal and refitting

Removal

1 The oil pressure warning light switch is located on the left-hand end of the cylinder head.
2 Undo the bolt and pull the coolant pipe away from the cylinder head **(see illustration 3.6)**.
3 Disconnect the wiring connector and wipe clean the area around the switch.
4 Unscrew the switch from the cylinder head and remove it, along with its sealing washer **(see illustration 3.8)**. If the switch is to be left removed from the engine for any length of time, plug the cylinder head aperture.

Refitting

5 Examine the sealing washer for signs of damage or deterioration and if necessary renew.
6 Refit the switch, complete with washer, and tighten it to the specified torque.
7 Securely reconnect the wiring connector then check and, if necessary, top-up the engine oil as described in *Weekly checks*.

12 Oil level/temperature sender – removal and refitting

Removal

1 The oil level/temperature sender is fitted to bottom of the sump **(see illustration)**.
2 Drain the engine oil as described in Chapter 1A Section 3.
3 Disconnect the wiring connector and wipe clean the area around the sender.
4 Undo the three retaining bolts and remove the sender.

Refitting

5 Examine the sealing washer for signs of damage or deterioration and if necessary renew.
6 Refit the switch and tighten the retaining bolts to the specified torque.
7 Securely reconnect the wiring connector then refill the engine with oil, with reference to Chapter 1A, Section 3.
8 On completion, check and, if necessary, top-up the engine oil as described in *Weekly checks*.

13 Crankshaft oil seals – renewal

Timing chain end oil seal

1 Remove the crankshaft pulley as described in Section 4, then note the fitted depth of the oil seal in the timing cover.
2 Carefully lever the old seal out of the timing cover using a suitable flat-bladed screwdriver, taking care not to damage the cover or crankshaft intermediate sleeve. Alternatively, punch or drill two small holes opposite each other in the seal, then screw a self-tapping screw into each and pull on the screws with pliers to extract the seal **(see illustration)**.
3 Clean the cover recess and sleeve. Note that the new oil seal must not be oiled or greased, and the contact surfaces of the timing cover and sleeve must be completely dry.
4 New oil seals are provided with a fitting adapter incorporating an oil seal expander. First, make sure the intermediate sleeve is located fully on the crankshaft, then hold the expander on the crankshaft nose and press the oil seal over it onto the sleeve. Using the adapter, drive the oil seal fully into the timing cover **(see illustrations)**. Alternatively, the seal can be tapped into position using a suitable tubular drift, such as a socket, which bears only on the hard outer edge of the seal. Note that the sealing lips must face inwards.
5 Refit the crankshaft pulley as described in Section 4.

Flywheel/driveplate end oil seal

Note: *The flywheel end oil seal is integral*

13.2 Prise out the crankshaft timing chain end oil seal

13.4a Fit the expander on the nose of the crankshaft...

13.4b ...then press the oil seal over it onto the crankshaft sleeve...

13.4c ...and drive it fully into the timing cover

13.9a Remove the engine speed sender...

13.9b ...and recover the rubber grommet

13.10 Unscrew the housing securing bolts...

with the oil seal housing and speed sender, and is supplied with a new timing ring. If the oil seal is faulty, the housing must be renewed, however, a special VW tool (T10134) is required to press the new housing into position. Note that removing the oil seal will also remove the serrated timing ring from the end of the crankshaft, and a special VW tool is required to fit the ring in its exact position.

6 Remove the flywheel/driveplate as described in Section 14. Also, remove the intermediate plate.

7 Set the engine to TDC as described in Section 3.

8 Remove the sump as described in Section 9.

9 Disconnect the wiring from the engine speed sender on the oil seal housing, then unbolt and remove the sender and recover the rubber grommet **(see illustrations)**.

10 Unscrew and remove the housing securing bolts **(see illustration)**. Discard the bolts, as new ones must be used on refitting.

11 The housing must be pressed off using three M6 bolts screwed into the threaded holes provided. Tighten the bolts progressively until the housing is released **(see illustrations)**, then remove the bolts. As the housing is removed, the timing ring will be forced from the end of the crankshaft. If the housing is to be re-used, do not move the timing ring from its TDC position.

12 To fit the new housing, first check that the hole in the timing ring is aligned with the TDC mark on the housing. New housings are supplied with a plastic clip holding the ring in the correct position **(see illustrations)**.

13 Assemble the new housing to the special VW tool, making sure that the TDC pin and

hole are aligned and the lip support ring is located in the oil seal **(see illustrations)**.

14 Wipe clean the crankshaft and check that the engine is still at TDC.

15 Fit the tool and new housing over the crankshaft and onto the cylinder block, using two M6 bolts to guide the housing. By tightening the tool nut to 35 Nm (26 lbf ft), the timing ring is forced onto the end of the crankshaft. The timing ring is in its fully fitted position if there is a distance of 0.5 mm between its outer edges and the outer surface of the crankshaft. After tightening the nut, there must also be a small air gap between the housing and the cylinder block **(see illustrations)**.

16 Remove the guide bolts and fit the new housing securing bolts, tightening them to the specified torque.

17 Insert the crankshaft speed sender

13.11a ...then use three M6 bolts to force the housing from the cylinder block

13.11b Flywheel end oil seal and housing together with the timing ring

13.12a Remove the plastic clip...

13.12b ...and check that the hole in the timing ring is aligned with the TDC mark on the housing

13.13a Assemble the new housing to the VW tool...

13.13b ...making sure that the pin and hole are aligned with each other

13.15a Fit the housing and tool to the end of the crankshaft...

13.15b ...then tighten the centre nut to force the timing ring onto the crankshaft

13.15c Check the clearance between the timing ring and the outer surface of the crankshaft

mounting bolt and tighten to the specified torque.
18 Refit the sump as described in Section 9.
19 Refit the intermediate plate and flywheel with reference to Section 14.

14 Flywheel/driveplate – removal, inspection and refitting

Removal

1 On manual transmission models, remove the gearbox (Chapter 7A, Section 3) and clutch (Chapter 6, Section 6).
2 On automatic (DSG) transmission models, remove the automatic transmission as described in Chapter 7B, Section 2.
3 The flywheel/driveplate bolts are offset to ensure correct fitment. Unscrew the bolts while holding the flywheel/driveplate stationary. Temporarily insert a bolt in the cylinder block, and use a screwdriver to hold the flywheel/driveplate, or make up a holding tool **(see illustration)**. Discard the bolts, as new ones must be used on refitting.
4 Lift the flywheel/driveplate from the crankshaft. Recover the engine-to-transmission intermediate plate if it is loose **(see illustrations)**.

Inspection

5 Check the flywheel/driveplate for wear and damage. Examine the starter ring gear for excessive wear to the teeth. If the driveplate or its ring gear is damaged, the

complete driveplate must be renewed. The flywheel ring gear, however, may be renewed separately from the flywheel, but the work should be entrusted to a VW dealer. If the clutch friction face is discoloured or scored excessively, it may be possible to regrind it, but this work should also be entrusted to a VW dealer.

Refitting

6 Refitting is a reversal of removal, bearing in mind the following points.
a) *Ensure that the engine-to-transmission plate is in place before fitting the flywheel/driveplate.*
b) *Use new bolts when refitting the flywheel or driveplate, and then coat the threads of the bolts with locking fluid before inserting them. Tighten the securing bolts to the specified torque.*
c) *On manual transmission models, follow the procedure Chapter 6, Section 6, for refitting the clutch and Chapter 7A, Section 3, for refitting the transmission.*
d) *On automatic (DSG) transmission models, follow the procedure in Chapter 7B, Section 2, for refitting the transmission.*

15 Engine/transmission mountings – inspection and renewal

Inspection

1 If improved access is required, jack up the front of the vehicle, and support it securely on

axle stands (see *Jacking and vehicle support*). Remove the engine undertray(s).
2 Check the mounting rubbers to see if they are cracked, hardened or separated from the metal at any point; renew the mounting if any such damage or deterioration is evident.
3 Check that all the mountings are securely tightened; use a torque wrench to check if possible.
4 Using a large screwdriver or a crowbar, check for wear in the mounting by carefully levering against it to check for free play. Where this is not possible, enlist the aid of an assistant to move the engine/transmission back-and-forth, or from side-to-side, whilst you observe the mounting. While some free play is to be expected, even from new components, excessive wear should be obvious. If excessive free play is found, check first that the fasteners are correctly secured, and then renew any worn components as described in the following paragraphs.

Renewal

Right-hand mounting

5 Attach a hoist and lifting tackle to the engine lifting brackets on the cylinder head, and raise the hoist to just take the weight of the engine. Alternatively the engine can be supported on a trolley jack under the engine. Use a block of wood between the sump and the head of the jack, to prevent any damage to the sump.
6 For improved access, unbolt the coolant reservoir and move it to one side, leaving the coolant hoses connected.

14.3 Unscrew the flywheel bolts using a home-made holding tool

14.4a Remove the flywheel from the crankshaft...

14.4b ...and remove the intermediate plate

15.7 Undo the canister retaining nut/bolts - arrowed

15.8 Right-hand engine mounting

15.14a Left-hand engine mounting

7 Undo the retaining bolts and move the charcoal canister to one side **(see illustration)**. Where applicable, move any wiring harnesses, pipes or hoses to one side to enable removal of the engine mounting.

8 Unscrew the bolts securing the mounting to the engine **(see illustration)**, and then unscrew the bolts securing it to the body. Also, unbolt the movement limiter. Withdraw the mounting from the engine compartment.

9 Refitting is a reversal of removal, bearing in mind the following points.

a) Use new securing bolts.
b) Tighten all fixings to the specified torque.

Left-hand mounting

10 Remove the engine top cover that also incorporates the air filter.

11 Attach a hoist and lifting tackle to the engine lifting brackets on the cylinder head, and raise the hoist to just take the weight of the engine and transmission. Alternatively the engine can be supported on a trolley jack under the transmission. Use a block of wood between the transmission and the head of the jack, to prevent any damage to the transmission.

12 Remove the battery, as described in Chapter 5A, Section 3, and then disconnect the main starter motor feed cable from the positive battery terminal box.

13 Release any relevant wiring or hoses from the clips on the battery tray, then unscrew the

15.14b Remove the left-hand engine mounting

four securing bolts and remove the battery tray.

14 Unscrew the bolts securing the mounting to the transmission, and the remaining bolts securing the mounting to the body, then lift the mounting from the engine compartment. Note that on some models, the earth cable is located on the mounting **(see illustrations)**.

15 Refitting is a reversal of removal, bearing in mind the following points:

a) Use new mounting bolts.
b) Tighten all fixings to the specified torque.

Rear lower mounting (torque arm)

16 Apply the handbrake, then jack up the front of the vehicle and support securely on axle stands (see *Jacking and vehicle*

15.16 Rear engine mounting/torque arm - arrowed

support). Remove the engine undertray(s) for access to the rear mounting (torque arm) **(see illustration)**.

17 Support the rear of the transmission beneath the final drive housing. To do this, use a trolley jack and block of wood, or alternatively wedge a block of wood between the transmission and the subframe.

18 Working under the vehicle, unscrew and remove the bolt securing the mounting to the subframe.

19 Unscrew the two bolts securing the mounting to the transmission, then withdraw the mounting from under the vehicle.

20 Refitting is a reversal of removal, but use new mounting securing bolts, and tighten all fixings to the specified torque.

Notes

Chapter 2 Part C:
1.6 litre diesel engine in-car repair procedures

Contents

Degrees of difficulty

Easy, suitable for novice with little experience	Fairly easy, suitable for beginner with some experience	Fairly difficult, suitable for competent DIY mechanic	Difficult, suitable for experienced DIY mechanic	Very difficult, suitable for expert DIY or professional 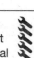

Specifications

General

Manufacturer's engine codes*:
   1599 cc (1.6 litre), 16-valve, DOHC . . . .   CAYB and CAYC

Maximum outputs:	Power	Torque
Engine code:		
CAYB	66 kW @ 4200 rpm	230 Nm @ 1500 to 2500 rpm
CAYC	77 kW @ 4400 rpm	250 Nm @ 1500 to 2500 rpm

Bore . . . .   79.5 mm
Stroke. . . . .   80.5 mm
Compression ratio . . . .   16.5 :1
Firing order. . . . .   1 – 3 – 4 – 2
No.1 cylinder location. . . . .   Timing belt end
* **Note:** See 'Vehicle identification' at the end of this manual for the location of engine code markings.

Lubrication system

Oil pump type. . . . .   Gear type, belt-driven from crankshaft
Oil pressure switch (green) . . . .   0.5 bar
Oil pressure (oil temperature 80°C):
   Minimum @ idling . . . .   0.6 bar
   Minimum @ 2000 rpm. . . . .   1.0 bar
   Maximum @ high rpm. . . . .   5.0 bar

Torque wrench settings	Nm	lbf ft
Ancillary (alternator, etc) bracket mounting bolts*:		
Stage 1 (all six bolts)	40	30
Stage 2 (for two lower bolts)	Angle-tighten a further 45°	
Stage 2 (for four upper bolts)	Angle-tighten a further 90°	
Auxiliary drivebelt tensioner securing bolt:		
Stage 1	20	15
Stage 2	Angle-tighten a further 180°	
Big-end bearing caps bolts*:		
Stage 1	30	22
Stage 2	Angle-tighten a further 90°	
Camshaft retaining frame bolts	10	7
Camshaft cover bolts	10	7
Camshaft sprocket hub centre bolt	100	74
Camshaft sprocket-to-hub bolts*:		
Stage 1	20	15
Stage 2	Angle-tighten a further 45°	
Common rail bolts	22	16
Coolant pump bolts	15	11
Crankshaft oil seal housing bolts	15	11
Crankshaft pulley-to-sprocket bolts*:		
Stage 1	10	7
Stage 2	Angle-tighten a further 90°	
Crankshaft sprocket bolt*:		
Stage 1	120	89
Stage 2	Angle-tighten a further 90°	
Cylinder head bolts*:		
Stage 1	30	22
Stage 2	60	44
Stage 3	Angle-tighten a further 90°	
Stage 4	Angle-tighten a further 90°	
Engine mountings:		
RH engine mounting*:		
Mounting bracket to engine:		
Stage 1	40	30
Stage 2	Angle-tighten a further 180°	
Mounting to body:		
Stage 1	40	30
Stage 2	Angle-tighten a further 90°	
Mounting to bracket:		
Stage 1	60	44
Stage 2	Angle-tighten a further 90°	
LH engine/transmission mounting*:		
Mounting to body:		
Stage 1	40	30
Stage 2	Angle-tighten a further 90°	
Mounting to bracket on transmission:		
Stage 1	60	44
Stage 2	Angle-tighten a further 90°	
Rear mounting link*:		
Link-to-transmission:		
Short (front) bolt:		
Stage 1	40	30
Stage 2	Angle-tighten a further 90°	
Long (rear) bolt:		
Stage 1	60	44
Stage 2	Angle-tighten a further 90°	
Link-to-subframe:		
Stage 1	100	74
Stage 2	Angle-tighten a further 90°	
Flywheel*:		
Stage 1	60	44
Stage 2	Angle-tighten a further 90°	
Fuel pump hub nut	95	70
Fuel pump sprocket bolts*	20	15
Main bearing cap bolts*:		
Stage 1	65	48
Stage 2	Angle-tighten a further 90°	

Torque wrench settings (continued)

	Nm	lbf ft
Oil cooler screws	11	7
Oil drain plug*	30	22
Oil filter housing-to-cylinder block bolts*:		
Stage 1	14	10
Stage 2	Angle-tighten a further 180°	
Oil filter cover	25	18
Oil level/temperature sensor-to-sump bolts	9	7
Oil pick-up pipe securing bolts	9	7
Oil pressure warning light switch	22	16
Oil pump securing bolts	16	11
Piston oil spray jet bolt	27	19
Sump:		
Sump-to-cylinder block bolts	13	9
Sump-to-transmission bolts	40	30
Thermostat housing	15	11
Timing belt outer cover bolts	10	7
Timing belt tensioner roller securing nut:		
Stage 1	20	15
Stage 2	Angle-tighten a further 45°	
Timing belt idler pulleys:		
Lower idler roller nut	20	15
Upper idler roller (small) bolt	15	11
Upper idler roller (large) bolt*:		
Stage 1	50	37
Stage 2	Angle-tighten a further 90°	

*Do not re-use fasteners

1 General information

How to use this Chapter

This Part of Chapter 2 describes those repair procedures that can reasonably be carried out on the engine while it remains in the vehicle. If the engine has been removed from the vehicle and is being dismantled as described in Part E, any preliminary dismantling procedures can be ignored.

Note that while it may be possible physically to overhaul certain items while the engine is in the vehicle, such tasks are not usually carried out as separate operations, and usually require the execution of several additional procedures (not to mention the cleaning of components and of oilways); for this reason, all such tasks are classed as major overhaul procedures, and are described in Part E of this Chapter.

Engine description

Throughout this Chapter, engines are referred to by type, and are identified and referred to by the manufacturer's code letters. A listing of all engines covered, together with their code letters, is given in the Specifications at the start of this Chapter.

The engines are water-cooled, double overhead camshafts (DOHC), in-line four-cylinder units, with cast-iron cylinder blocks and aluminium-silicone alloy cylinder heads. All are mounted transversely at the front of the vehicle, with the transmission bolted to the left-hand end of the engine.

The crankshaft is of five-bearing type, and thrustwashers are fitted to the centre main bearing (No.3) to control crankshaft endfloat.

Drive for the exhaust camshaft is by a toothed timing belt from the crankshaft, with the intake camshaft driven by interlocking gears at the left-hand end of both camshafts. The gears incorporate a toothed backlash compensator element. Each camshaft is mounted at the top of the cylinder head, and is secured by a bearing frame/ladder.

The valves are closed by coil springs, and run in guides pressed into the cylinder head. The valves are operated by roller rocker arms incorporating hydraulic tappets.

The gear-type oil pump is driven by a belt from the right-hand (timing belt) end of the crankshaft. Oil is drawn from the sump through a strainer, and then forced through an externally mounted, renewable filter. From there, it is distributed to the cylinder head, where it lubricates the camshaft journals and hydraulic tappets, and also to the crankcase, where it lubricates the main bearings, connecting rod big-ends, gudgeon pins and cylinder bores. A coolant-fed oil cooler is fitted to the oil filter housing on all engines. Oil jets are fitted to the base of each cylinder – these spray oil onto the underside of the pistons, to improve cooling.

All engines are fitted with a combined brake servo vacuum pump, driven by the camshaft on the transmission end of the cylinder head.

On all engines, engine coolant is circulated by a pump, driven by the timing belt. For details of the cooling system, refer to Chapter 3.

Operations with engine in car

The following operations can be performed without removing the engine:

a) Compression pressure – testing.
b) Camshaft cover – removal and refitting.
c) Crankshaft pulley – removal and refitting.
d) Timing belt covers – removal and refitting.
e) Timing belt – removal, refitting and adjustment.
f) Timing belt tensioner and sprockets – removal and refitting.
g) Camshaft oil seals – renewal.
h) Camshafts and hydraulic tappets – removal, inspection and refitting.
i) Cylinder head – removal and refitting.
j) Cylinder head and pistons – decarbonising.
k) Sump – removal and refitting.
l) Oil pump – removal, overhaul and refitting.
m) Crankshaft oil seals – renewal.
n) Engine/transmission mountings – inspection and renewal.
o) Flywheel/driveplate – removal, inspection and refitting.

Note: It is possible to remove the pistons and connecting rods (after removing the cylinder head and sump) without removing the engine. However, this is not recommended. Work of this nature is more easily and thoroughly completed with the engine on the bench, as described in Chapter 2E.

3.8 The alignment mark (arrowed) on the crankshaft sprocket should be almost vertical

2 Compression and leakdown tests – description and interpretation

Compression test

Note: *A compression tester suitable for use with diesel engines will be required for this test.*

1 When engine performance is down, or if misfiring occurs which cannot be attributed to the ignition or fuel systems, a compression test can provide diagnostic clues as to the engine's condition. If the test is performed regularly, it can give warning of trouble before any other symptoms become apparent.

2 The engine must be fully warmed-up to normal operating temperature, the battery must be fully charged, and you will require the aid of an assistant.

3 Remove the glow plugs as described in Chapter 5C, Section 2, and then fit a compression tester to the No.1 cylinder glow plug hole. The type of tester that screws into the plug thread is preferred. **Note:** *Part of the glow plug removal procedure is to disconnect the fuel injector wiring plugs. As a result of the plugs being disconnected and the engine cranked, faults may be stored in the ECU memory. These must be erased after the compression test.*

4 Have your assistant crank the engine for several seconds on the starter motor. After one or two revolutions, the compression pressure should build-up to a maximum figure and then stabilise. Record the highest reading obtained.

3.9b ...so the marks on the tool and sprocket align (arrowed)

3.9a Fit the tool to the hole in the oil seal housing (arrowed)...

5 Repeat the test on the remaining cylinders, recording the pressure in each.

6 The cause of poor compression is less easy to establish on a diesel engine than on a petrol engine. The effect of introducing oil into the cylinders (wet testing) is not conclusive, because there is a risk that the oil will sit in the recess on the piston crown, instead of passing to the rings. However, the following can be used as a rough guide to diagnosis.

7 All cylinders should produce very similar pressures. Any difference greater than that specified indicates the existence of a fault. Note that the compression should build-up quickly in a healthy engine. Low compression on the first stroke, followed by gradually increasing pressure on successive strokes, indicates worn piston rings. A low compression reading on the first stroke, which does not build-up during successive strokes, indicates leaking valves or a blown head gasket (a cracked head could also be the cause).

8 A low reading from two adjacent cylinders is almost certainly due to the head gasket having blown between them and the presence of coolant in the engine oil will confirm this.

9 On completion, remove the compression tester, and refit the glow plugs, with reference to Chapter 5C, Section 2.

10 Reconnect the wiring to the injector solenoids. Finally, have a VW dealer or suitably equipped specialist erase any fault codes from the ECU memory.

Leakdown test

11 A leakdown test measures the rate at

3.9c Insert a 6 mm locking tool into the camshaft hub ...

which compressed air fed into the cylinder is lost. It is an alternative to a compression test, and in many ways it is better, since the escaping air provides easy identification of where pressure loss is occurring (piston rings, valves or head gasket).

12 The equipment required for leakdown testing is unlikely to be available to the home mechanic. If poor compression is suspected, have the test performed by a suitably equipped garage.

3 Engine assembly and valve timing marks – general information and usage

General information

1 TDC is the highest point in the cylinder that each piston reaches as it travels up-and-down when the crankshaft turns. Each piston reaches TDC at the end of the compression stroke and again at the end of the exhaust stroke, but TDC generally refers to piston position on the compression stroke. No 1 piston is at the timing belt end of the engine.

2 Positioning No 1 piston at TDC is an essential part of many procedures, such as timing belt removal and camshaft removal.

3 The design of the engines covered in this Chapter is such that piston-to-valve contact may occur if the camshaft or crankshaft is turned with the timing belt removed. For this reason, it is important to ensure that the camshaft and crankshaft do not move in relation to each other once the timing belt has been removed from the engine.

Setting TDC on No 1 cylinder

Note: *VAG special tool T10050 is required to lock the crankshaft sprocket in the TDC position. Alternatively obtain a tool from automotive tool specialists. Try asttools.co.uk.*

4 Raise the front of the vehicle and support it securely on axle stands (see *Jacking and vehicle support*). Remove the front right-hand road wheel, then release the fasteners and remove the lower section of the wheelarch liner.

5 Remove the auxiliary drivebelt as described in Chapter 1B, Section 28.

6 Remove the crankshaft pulley/vibration damper as described in Section 5.

7 Remove the timing belt outer covers as described in Section 6.

8 Using a spanner or socket on the crankshaft sprocket bolt, turn the crankshaft in the normal direction of rotation (clockwise) until the alignment mark on the face of the sprocket is almost vertical, and the hole in the camshaft sprocket hub aligns with the hole in the cylinder head **(see illustration)**.

9 While in this position it should be possible to insert the VAG tool T10050 to lock the crankshaft, and a 6 mm diameter rod/drill bit to lock the camshafts **(see illustrations)**.

Note: *The mark on the crankshaft sprocket and the mark on the VAG tool must align, whilst at the same time the shaft of tool must engage in the drilling in the crankshaft oil seal housing.*

10 The engine is now set to TDC on No.1 cylinder.

4 Camshaft cover – removal and refitting

Removal

1 Remove the fuel injectors (Chapter 4B, Section 4) and fuel rail (Chapter 4B, Section 11).
2 Remove the timing belt upper cover as described in Section 6.
3 Note their fitted positions, then disconnect the vacuum hoses from the camshaft cover, and release them, and the wiring loom from the retaining clips at the rear of the cover **(see illustration)**.
4 Squeeze together the sides of the collar, and disconnect the breather hose from the camshaft cover **(see illustration)**.
5 Release the wiring from the clips at the rear of the cover, then unscrew the camshaft cover retaining bolts and lift the cover away. If the cover sticks, do not attempt to lever it off – instead free it by working around the cover and tapping it lightly with a soft-faced mallet **(see illustration)**.
6 Recover the camshaft cover gasket. Inspect the gasket carefully, and renew it if damage or deterioration is evident – note that the retaining bolts and seals must be pushed fully through the cover **(see illustrations)**.
7 Clean the mating surfaces of the cylinder head and camshaft cover thoroughly, removing all traces of oil – take care to avoid damaging the surfaces as you do this.

Refitting

8 Refit the camshaft cover by following the removal procedure in reverse, tightening the cover retaining bolts to the specified torque, starting with the centre bolts and working outwards.

3.9d …with the arrow almost at the 12 o'clock position

4.4 Squeeze together the sides of the collar to disconnect the breather hose

5 Crankshaft pulley – removal and refitting

Removal

1 Switch off the ignition and all electrical consumers and remove the ignition key.
2 Raise the front right-hand side of the vehicle, and support securely on axle stands (see *Jacking and vehicle support*). Remove the roadwheel.
3 Remove the securing fasteners and withdraw the lower section of the front wheel arch liner.
4 Slacken the bolts securing the crankshaft pulley to the sprocket **(see illustration)**. If necessary, the pulley can be prevented from

4.3 Unclip the wiring from the retaining clips

4.5 Undo the bolts and lift away the camshaft cover

turning by counterholding with a spanner or socket on the crankshaft sprocket bolt.
5 Remove the auxiliary drivebelt, as described in Chapter 1B, Section 28.
6 Unscrew the bolts securing the pulley to the sprocket, and remove the pulley. Discard the bolts – new ones must be fitted.

Refitting

7 Refit the pulley over the locating peg on the crankshaft sprocket, then fit the new pulley securing bolts.
8 Refit and tension the auxiliary drivebelt as described in Chapter 1B, Section 28.
9 Prevent the crankshaft from turning as during removal, then fit the pulley securing bolts, and tighten to the specified torque.
10 Refit the wheel arch liner.
11 Refit the roadwheel and lower the vehicle to the ground.

4.6a Renew the cover seal if necessary

4.6b Bolts and seals must be pushed fully through the cover before fitting the gasket

5.4 Undo the pulley bolts, counterholding it with a socket on the centre sprocket bolt

6.1 Pull the plastic cover upwards from the mountings

6.2 Unclip the hoses from the retaining clips

6.3a Disconnect the wiring connector ...

6.3b ...undo the two retaining bolts ...

6.3c ... and withdraw the mounting bracket

6.4 Remove the washer reservoir filler neck

6.5a Undo the filter retaining bolts/nut (arrowed) ...

6.5b ... and release the fuel pipe retaining clip

6.6 Move the coolant reservoir to one side

6 Timing belt covers –
removal and refitting

Upper outer cover

1 Pull the engine top cover upwards to release the mountings **(see illustration)**.

2 Release the hoses from the retaining clips on the right-hand side of the cylinder head and move them to one side **(see illustration)**.

3 Disconnect the wiring plug, undo the retaining bolts, and remove the pressure differential sender (for particulate filter) including bracket from the top of the engine mounting and move it to one side **(see illustrations)**.

4 Undo the retaining bolt, then twist the washer reservoir filler neck to remove it from engine compartment **(see illustration)**.

5 Undo the retaining bolts and nut, then remove the fuel filter from the engine mounting and move it to one side **(see illustrations)**. The fuel hoses do not need to be disconnected from the filter.

6 To make access easier, undo the retaining bolt, disconnect the wiring connector and move the coolant reservoir to one side **(see illustration)**.

6.7 Disconnect the temperature sensor wiring connector

6.8a Release the rear lower clip (arrowed)…

6.8b … the two upper front clips (arrowed) …

6.8c …and manoeuvre the upper cover from place

6.12a Undo the lower cover retaining bolts (arrowed)

6.12b …and manoeuvre the lower cover from place

7 Disconnect the radiator outlet temperature sensor wiring plug **(see illustration)**.
8 Release the 3 clips and remove the timing belt upper cover **(see illustrations)**.
9 Refitting is a reversal of removal, noting that the lower edge of the upper cover engages with the lower cover.

Lower outer cover

10 Remove the upper cover as described previously.
11 If not already done, remove the crankshaft pulley as described in Section 5.
12 Unscrew the five bolts securing the lower cover, and remove it **(see illustrations)**.
13 Refitting is a reversal of removal; noting that the upper edge of the lower cover engages with the upper cover.

Rear cover

14 Remove the timing belt, tensioner and

sprockets as described in Section 7 and Section 8.
15 Undo the retaining bolt and remove the rear hub cover from the end of the camshaft.
16 Slacken and withdraw the retaining bolts and lift the timing belt inner cover from the studs on the end of the engine, and remove it from the engine compartment **(see illustrations)**. It may be required to remove the coolant pump (Chapter 3, Section 7), before the rear cover can be removed.
17 Refitting is a reversal of removal.

7	Timing belt – removal, inspection and refitting

Note: *There are two types of tensioner fitted to this engine and they are not interchangeable* **(see illustration)**. *Check to see which type is*

fitted before removing the timing belt. Type A tensioner requires a locking pin for installation and it tensions the belt by rotating clockwise. Type B tensioner does not require a locking pin for installation and it tensions the belt by rotating anti-clockwise. See text.

Removal

1 The primary function of the toothed timing

H48705

7.0 Two types of tensioner type (A) and (B)

A Roller tensions
clockwise

B Roller tensions
anti-clockwise

16.16a Remove the retaining bolts …

16.16b … and remove the rear cover

7.4 Slacken the sprocket-to-hub bolts (arrowed)

7.6 Insert an Allen key, slacken the nut, and rotate the hub anti-clockwise until a 2 mm rod/drill bit (arrowed) can be inserted to lock the hub to the pulley

belt is to drive the camshaft, but it also drives the coolant pump and high-pressure fuel pump. Should the belt slip or break in service, the valve timing will be disturbed and piston-to-valve contact may occur, resulting in serious engine damage. For this reason, it is important that the timing belt is tensioned correctly, and inspected regularly for signs of wear or deterioration.

2 Switch off the ignition and all electrical consumers and remove the ignition key.

3 Set the engine to TDC on No. 1 cylinder as described in Section 3.

4 Slacken the three bolts securing the sprocket to the camshaft hub by 90° **(see illustration)**.

5 Slacken the three bolts securing the sprocket to the high-pressure fuel pump by 90° **(see illustration)**.

Type A tensioner

6 Insert a suitable Allen key into the tensioner

7.16 Rotate the high-pressure fuel pump clockwise until a 6 mm drill bit/rod can be inserted into the housing and hub (arrowed)

7.5 Slacken the high-pressure fuel pump sprocket bolts (arrowed)

7.7 Rotate the tensioner hub clockwise until it hits the stop

hub, then slacken the retaining nut and rotate the tensioner hub anti-clockwise until it can be locked in place using a 2.0 m pin/drill bit **(see illustration)**.

7 Leaving the pin in place, now rotate the tensioner hub clockwise to the stop, and hand-tighten the retaining nut **(see illustration)**.

Type B tensioner

8 Insert a suitable Allen key into the tensioner hub, then slacken the retaining nut and rotate the tensioner hub clockwise, until the tensioner hub is loosened. When in position hand-tighten the retaining nut.

All engines

9 If the original timing belt is to be refitted, mark the running direction of the belt, to ensure correct refitting.

Caution: If the belt appears to be in good condition and can be re-used, it is essential

7.17a Rotate the sprockets fully clockwise until the fuel pump sprocket...

that it is refitted the same way around, otherwise accelerated wear will result, leading to premature failure.

10 Slide the belt from the sprockets, taking care not to twist or kink the belt excessively if it is to be re-used.

Inspection

11 Examine the belt for evidence of contamination by coolant or lubricant. If this is the case, find the source of the contamination before progressing any further. Check the belt for signs of wear or damage, particularly around the leading edges of the belt teeth. Renew the belt if its condition is in doubt; the cost of belt renewal is negligible compared with potential cost of the engine repairs, should the belt fail in service. The belt must be renewed if it has covered the mileage given in Chapter 1B, however, if it has covered less, it is prudent to renew it regardless of condition, as a precautionary measure.

12 If the timing belt is not going to be refitted for some time, it is a wise precaution to hang a warning label on the steering wheel, to remind yourself (and others) not to attempt to start the engine. Have the battery disconnected to prevent any engine damage.

13 If the tensioner roller is to be renewed, the engine mounting will need to be removed, as described in Section 16. Then the tensioner removed as described in Section 8.

Refitting

14 Ensure that the crankshaft and camshaft are still set to TDC on No 1 cylinder, as described in Section 3. The camshaft sprocket bolts should be renewed, and slackened at this point.

15 Renew the high-pressure fuel pump sprocket bolts one at a time. They should also be slackened.

16 Using a screwdriver on the bolts heads, rotate the high-pressure fuel pump clockwise until a 6.0 mm locking pin/drill bit can be inserted into the housing adjacent to the sprocket, locking the pump in place **(see illustration)**.

17 Rotate the camshaft sprocket and high-pressure fuel pump sprocket fully clockwise so that the securing bolts are at the end of the elongated holes **(see illustrations)**.

18 Loop the timing belt loosely under the

7.17b ...and camshaft sprocket bolts are at the end of the elongated holes

7.20 Timing belt routing

7.21a Rotate the tensioner clockwise ...

7.21b ...until the pointer (arrowed) is just past the gap in the base plate

7.22 Turn the tensioner anti-clockwise and secure the retaining nut (1)

7.23a Counterhold the camshaft sprocket ...

7.23b ... and the pump sprocket, while the bolts are tightened

crankshaft sprocket. **Note:** *Observe any direction of rotation markings on the belt.*
19 Fit the belt around the tensioner pulley, engage the timing belt teeth with the camshaft sprockets, then manoeuvre it into position around the coolant pump sprocket and the fuel pump sprocket. Make sure that the belt teeth seat correctly on the sprockets. **Note:** *Slight adjustment to the position of the camshaft sprocket may be necessary to achieve this. Avoid bending the belt back on itself or twisting it excessively as you do this.*
20 Finally, fit the belt around the idler roller **(see illustration)**. Ensure that any slack in the belt is in the section of belt that passes over the tensioner roller.

Type A tensioner

21 Loosen the timing belt tensioner securing nut, and pull out the tensioner locking pin. Turn the tensioner clockwise with an Allen key until

the pointer is just past the middle of the gap in the tensioner base plate **(see illustrations)**. With the tensioner held in this position, tighten the securing nut to the specified torque and angle.

Type B tensioner

22 Loosen the timing belt tensioner securing nut, and turn the tensioner anti-clockwise with an Allen key until the pointer is just past the middle of the gap in the tensioner base plate **(see illustration)**. With the tensioner held in this position, tighten the securing nut to the specified torque and angle.

All engines

23 Counterhold the camshaft sprocket and fuel pump sprocket with a home made tool to prevent any rotation, and then tighten the camshaft sprocket and fuel pump sprocket bolts to 20 Nm **(see illustrations)**.

24 Remove the sprockets' locking tools and the crankshaft locking tool **(see illustrations)**.
25 Using a spanner or wrench and socket on the crankshaft pulley centre bolt, rotate the crankshaft clockwise through two complete revolutions. Reset the engine to TDC on No.1 cylinder, with reference to Section 3 and refit the crankshaft locking tool.
26 Check that the tensioner roller indicator arm is centred, or within a maximum of 5 mm to the right of the notch in the base plate **(see illustration)**. If not, hold the tensioner hub stationary with an Allen key, slacken the retaining nut and position the arm in the centre of the notch. Tighten the retaining nut to the specified torque. Remove the Allen key.
27 Check that the camshaft sprocket locking pin can still be inserted. **Note:** *It's very difficult to align the locking point of the fuel pump*

7.24a Remove the upper locking pins ...

7.24b ... and crankshaft locking tool

7.26 Check the pointer (arrowed) is centred or within 5mm to the right of the gap in the base plate

7.27 Slight misalignment of the pump sprocket timing hole (arrowed) is acceptable

hub again *(see illustration). However, a slight misalignment of holes will not affect engine performance.*

28 If the camshaft sprocket locking pin cannot be inserted, pull the crankshaft locking tool slight away from the engine, and rotate the crankshaft *anti-clockwise* slightly past TDC. Now slowly rotate the crankshaft clockwise until the camshaft sprocket locking tool can be inserted.

29 If the locating pin of the crankshaft locking tool is to the left of the corresponding hole, slacken the camshaft sprocket bolts, slowly rotate the crankshaft clockwise until the locking tool can be fully inserted. Tighten the camshaft sprocket bolts to 20 Nm.

30 If the locating pin of the crankshaft locking tool is to the right of the corresponding hole, slacken the camshaft sprocket bolts, rotate the crankshaft anti-clockwise slightly until the pin is to the left of the hole, then slowly rotate

it clockwise until the lock tool can be fully inserted. Tighten the camshaft sprocket bolts to 20 Nm.

31 Remove the crankshaft and camshaft locking tools, then rotate the crankshaft 2 complete revolutions clockwise and check the locking tools can be reinserted. If necessary, repeat the adjustment procedure described previously.

32 Tighten the camshaft and fuel pump sprocket bolts to the specified torque.

33 The remainder of refitting is a reversal of removal.

8 Timing belt tensioner and sprockets – removal and refitting

Timing belt tensioner

Removal

1 In order to remove the timing belt tensioner, the engine mounting bracket must first be removed. Either support the engine from above using a crossbeam or an engine hoist or support if from underneath with a trolley jack and block of wood.

2 Remove the timing belt as described in Section 7.

3 Undo the bolts and remove the right-hand engine mounting.

4 Undo the bolt securing the coolant pipe to the mounting bracket **(see illustration)**.

5 Working in the wheelarch area, undo the nut securing the lower end of the coolant pipe.

6 Undo the 3 retaining bolts and remove the engine mounting bracket **(see illustration)**.

7 Unscrew the timing belt tensioner nut, and remove the tensioner from the engine.

Refitting

8 When refitting the tensioner to the engine, ensure that the lug on the tensioner backplate engages with the corresponding cut-out in the rear timing belt cover, then refit the tensioner nut **(see illustration)**.

9 The remainder of refitting is a reversal of removal.

Idler pulleys

Removal

10 Remove the timing belt as described in Section 7.

11 Unscrew the relevant idler pulley/roller securing bolt/nut, and then withdraw the pulley **(see illustration)**.

Refitting

12 Refit the pulley and tighten the securing bolt or nut to the specified torque. **Note:** *Renew the large roller/pulley retaining bolt (where applicable).*

13 Refit and tension the timing belt as described in Section 7.

Crankshaft sprocket

Note: *A new crankshaft sprocket securing bolt must be used on refitting.*

Removal

14 Remove the timing belt as described in Section 7.

15 The sprocket securing bolt must now be slackened, and the crankshaft must be prevented from turning as the sprocket bolt is unscrewed. To hold the sprocket, make up a suitable tool, and screw it to the sprocket using a two bolts screwed into two of the crankshaft pulley bolt holes.

16 Hold the sprocket using the tool, then slacken the sprocket securing bolt. Take care, as the bolt is very tight. Do not allow the crankshaft to turn as the bolt is slackened.

17 Unscrew the bolt, and slide the sprocket from the end of the crankshaft, noting which way round the sprocket's raised boss is fitted. If required, use a puller to withdraw the sprocket from the end of the crankshaft **(see illustration)**.

8.4 Coolant pipe upper mounting bolt and lower mounting nut (arrowed)

8.6 Engine mounting bracket bolts (arrowed)

8.8 Ensure the lug on the backplate engages with the cut-out in the timing belt cover (arrowed)

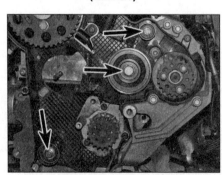

8.11 Timing belt idler pulleys

8.17 Using a puller to remove the crankshaft sprocket

8.27 Fabricate a home made tool to counterhold the hub. Undo the bolt...

8.28 ...and slide the hub from the camshaft

8.29 Ensure the integral key aligns with the keyway in the camshaft (arrowed)

Refitting

18 Commence refitting by positioning the sprocket on the end of the crankshaft.

19 Fit a new sprocket securing bolt, then counterhold the sprocket using the method employed on removal, and tighten the bolt to the specified torque in the two stages given in the Specifications.

20 Refit the timing belt as described in Section 7.

Camshaft sprocket

Removal

21 Remove the timing belt as described in Section 7, then rotate the crankshaft 90° anti-clockwise to prevent any accidental piston-to-valve contact.

22 Unscrew and remove the three retaining bolts and remove the camshaft sprocket from the camshaft hub.

Refitting

23 Refit the sprocket ensuring that it is fitted the correct way round, as noted before removal, then insert the new sprocket bolts, and tighten by hand only at this stage.

24 If the crankshaft has been turned, turn the crankshaft clockwise 90° back to TDC.

25 Refit and tension the timing belt as described in Section 7.

Camshaft hub

Note: *VAG technicians use special tool T10051 to counterhold the hub, however it is possible to fabricate a suitable alternative.*

Removal

26 Remove the camshaft sprocket as described previously in this Section.

27 Engage special tool T10051 with the three locating holes in the face of the hub to prevent the hub from turning. If this tool is not available, fabricate a suitable alternative. Whilst holding the tool, undo the central hub retaining bolt about two turns **(see illustration)**.

28 Slide the hub from the camshaft. If necessary, attach VW tool T10052 (or a similar three-legged puller) to the hub, and evenly tighten the puller until the hub is free of the camshaft taper **(see illustration)**.

Refitting

29 Ensure that the camshaft taper and the

hub centre is clean and dry, locate the hub on the taper, noting that the built-in key in the hub taper must align with the keyway in the camshaft taper **(see illustration)**.

30 Hold the hub in this position with tool T10051 (or similar home-made tool), and tighten the central bolt to the specified torque.

31 Refit the camshaft sprocket as described previously in this Section.

Coolant pump sprocket

32 The coolant pump sprocket is integral with the coolant pump. Refer to Chapter 3 for details of coolant pump removal.

9 Camshaft and hydraulic tappets – removal, inspection and refitting

Note: *A new camshaft oil seal(s) will be required on refitting. VW removal tool T40094 (or similar tool) will be required to refit the camshafts – this is necessary to prevent damage to the retaining frame and cylinder head as the camshafts are refitted.*

Removal

1 With the timing set at TDC, remove the camshaft hub (see Section 8).

2 Remove the camshaft cover (see Section 4).

3 Remove the brake vacuum pump as described in Chapter 9, Section 21.

4 If the camshafts are not going to be renewed, use two flat pieces of metal flat bar

and cable ties and secure the two camshafts to the retaining frame **(see illustrations)**. Progressively unscrew the camshaft retaining frame bolts in the reverse of the sequence shown in illustration 9.27, and carefully remove the retaining frame, complete with camshafts. Remove the oil seal from the end of the camshaft and discard it – a new one will be required for refitting.

5 If the camshafts are going to be renewed, progressively unscrew the camshaft retaining frame bolts in the reverse of the sequence shown in illustration 9.27, and carefully remove the retaining frame. Then carefully lift the camshafts from the cylinder head, keeping them identified for location. Remove the oil seal from the end of the camshaft and discard it – a new one will be required for refitting.

6 Lift the rocker arms and hydraulic tappets from place. Store the rockers and tappets in a container with numbered compartments to ensure they are refitted to their correct locations. It is recommended that the tappets are kept immersed in oil for the period they are removed from the cylinder head.

Inspection

7 If the camshafts are still secured to the retaining frame, mark the two sprockets in relation with each other, then cut the cable ties to remove them from the frame **(see illustration)**. With the camshafts removed, examine the retaining frame and the bearing locations in the cylinder head for signs of

9.4a Using flat metal bar and cable ties to secure the camshafts ...

9.4b ... to the upper ladder frame for removal

9.7 Make alignment marks for the position of the sprockets

9.10 Check the tappets for wear

9.12 VW special tool no. T40094 shown

9.13a Position the inlet camshaft on the tool with the head bolt indent facing outwards ...

9.13b ...then slide the end of the special tool, in to the slot in the end of the camshaft

obvious wear or pitting. If evident, a new cylinder head will probably be required. Also check that the oil supply holes in the cylinder head are free from obstructions.

8 Visually inspect the camshafts for evidence of wear on the surfaces of the lobes and journals. Normally their surfaces should be smooth and have a dull shine; look for

scoring, erosion or pitting and areas that appear highly polished, indicating excessive wear. Accelerated wear will occur once the hardened exterior of the camshaft has been damaged, so always renew worn items. **Note:** *If these symptoms are visible on the tips of the camshaft lobes, check the corresponding rocker arm, as it will probably be worn as well.*
9 If the machined surfaces of the camshaft appear discoloured or blued, it is likely that it has been overheated at some point, probably due to inadequate lubrication. This may have distorted the shaft, so have the camshaft runout and endfloat checked by an automotive engine reconditioning specialist.
10 Inspect the hydraulic tappets for obvious signs of wear or damage **(see illustration)**, and renew if necessary. Check that the oil holes in the tappets are free from obstructions.

Refitting

11 Oil the rocker arms and hydraulic tappets, and then refit them to their original positions.

⚠️ *Warning: After fitting hydraulic tappets, wait a minimum of 30 minutes (or preferably, leave overnight) before starting the engine; to allow the tappets time to settle, otherwise the valve heads will strike the pistons.*

Using VW special tool No.T40094

12 If the camshafts were removed from the retaining frame, use the VW special tool No.T40094, as shown in the following procedures **(see illustration)**.
13 Position the inlet camshaft as shown with the cylinder head bolt indents facing outwards, then slide the end support into the slot in the end of the camshaft **(see illustrations)**.
14 Position the exhaust camshaft on the supports, again with the cylinder head bolt indents facing outwards, and then fit the locating clamp into the slot in the end of the camshaft **(see illustrations)**.
15 Fit the VW clamping tool No.T40096 to the double gear on the exhaust camshaft, tightening the knurled thumb wheel until the faces of the gear teeth are in alignment **(see illustration)**. Note some camshafts only have a single sprocket, so will not require this procedure.
16 Slide the exhaust camshaft towards the inlet camshaft until the gear teeth engage **(see illustration)**.

9.14a Position the exhaust camshaft on the tool with the head bolt indent facing outwards ...

9.14b ... then fit special tool clamp into the slot in the end of the exhaust camshaft

9.15 Tighten the thumbwheel to align the gear teeth. Ensure the clamping jaw with the arrow is seated on the wider gear

9.16 Slide the exhaust camshaft to the inlet camshaft until the teeth are in mesh

9.17a Lubricate the bearing mountings ...

9.17b ...and fit the upper ladder frame to the camshafts

9.18 Secure the camshafts in place in the frame using tool No. T40095

17 Ensure the gasket faces of the retaining frame are clean, then apply a smear of clean engine oil to the bearing surfaces and lower the frame into position over the camshafts (see illustrations). Ensure the bearing surfaces locate correctly on the camshafts.
18 Fit the clamping tool No.T40095 over the camshafts and frame, and tighten the thumbwheels to hold the camshafts in position in the frame (see illustration).
19 Slide out locking clamps from each end of the camshafts (see illustrations), and then lift the camshafts, retaining frame and clamping tool from the VW special tool no. 40094.

Without VW special tool

20 Ensure the gasket faces of the retaining frame are clean, then apply a smear of clean engine oil to the bearing surfaces and turn it upside down on a clean surface.
21 Position the camshafts on the retaining frame with the cylinder head bolt indents facing outwards. Align the marks made on the camshaft sprockets on removal (see illustration 9.7).
22 If a double gear is fitted to the exhaust camshaft, fit the VW clamping tool No.T40096 (or similar) to align the faces of the teeth. If the VW clamping tool is not available use two flat bladed screwdrivers and a pair of pliers, this will need an assistant to keep firm pressure on the camshafts to make sure they locate in the retaining frame correctly (see illustrations). Note some camshafts only have a single sprocket, so will not require this procedure.
23 With the marks on the sprockets aligned and the cylinder head bolt indents facing

9.19a Slide the locking tool out from the end of the inlet camshaft ...

9.19b ... and remove the locking clamp from the end of the exhaust camshaft

outwards, the slot in the end of the inlet camshaft (that drives the vacuum pump) should be horizontal and the slot in the end of the exhaust camshaft (that locates the timing belt sprocket) should be at the top when fitted (see illustrations).

24 With the camshafts correctly in position, ensuring the camshafts locate correctly in the bearing surfaces on the retaining frame, use two flat pieces of metal flat bar and cable ties to secure them in position (see illustration). *Caution: Make sure the camshafts are*

9.22a VW special tool for aligning teeth on sprocket

9.22b Using two flat bladed screwdrivers and a pair of pliers to align teeth

9.23a inlet camshaft slot needs to be horizontal

9.23b Slot in end of exhaust camshaft should be at the 12 o'clock position

9.24 Camshafts are secured to the ladder frame with two pieces of flat bar and cable ties

9.25a Apply a 2.0 mm thick bead of sealant ...

9.25b ... to the area shown by the thick, black line, taking care not to block the oil holes (arrowed)

9.26a Fit a new seal/end cap to the cylinder head

9.26b Check that the locating dowels are in place

9.27 Camshaft retaining frame bolt tightening sequence

located correctly in the bearing surfaces on the retaining frame, otherwise damage can occur, and this could damage the retaining frame when tightening down onto the cylinder head. The retaining frame is

matched to the cylinder head and can only be purchased with a new cylinder head. If there is any doubt, then the VW special tool should be used, see previous refitting procedure.

9.28 Remove the cable ties and flat bar from the top of the ladder frame

10.2 Screw in a self-tapping screw, then pull the screw and seal from place

All

25 Ensure the sealing surfaces of the cylinder head are clean, and then apply a 2.0 mm wide bead of sealant (D 176 501 A1 or equivalent) as shown. Take care not to apply too much sealant, ensuring the oil holes supply holes are not blocked **(see illustrations)**.

26 Fit a new sealing cap to the timing belt end of the cylinder head and make sure the locating dowels are fitted to the cylinder head **(see illustrations)**.

27 Apply a smear of clean engine oil to the bearing surfaces and place the camshafts, frame and clamping tool in place on the cylinder head. Progressively, carefully, hand tighten the frame retaining bolts in the sequence shown **(see illustration)**, until the retaining frame makes contact with the cylinder head over the complete surface, then tighten the bolts to the specified torque, again in the correct sequence.

28 Remove the gear aligning tool (T40096) and the clamping tool (T40095), or the metal flat bars and cable ties from the top of the camshaft retaining frame **(see illustration)**.

29 Renew the camshaft oil seal as described in Section 10.

30 The remainder of refitting is a reversal of removal.

10 Camshaft oil seals – renewal

Right-hand oil seal

1 Remove the camshaft sprocket and hub, as described in Section 8.

2 Drill two small holes into the existing oil seal, diagonally opposite each other. Take great care to avoid drilling through into the seal housing or camshaft sealing surface. Thread two self-tapping screws into the holes, and using a pair of pliers, pull on the heads of the screws to extract the oil seal **(see illustration)**.

3 Clean out the seal housing and the sealing surface of the camshaft by wiping it with a lint-free cloth. Remove any swarf or burrs that may cause the seal to leak.

4 Do not lubricate the lip and outer edge of the new oil seal, push it over the camshaft

until it is positioned in place above its housing. To prevent damage to the sealing lips, wrap some adhesive tape around the end of the camshaft **(see illustration)**.

5 Using a hammer and a socket of suitable diameter, drive the seal squarely into its housing. Make sure the seal is fitted the correct way around, some have 'OUTSIDE' stamped on the seal **(see illustration)**. Note: Select a socket that bears only on the hard outer surface of the seal, not the inner lip that can easily be damaged.

6 Refit the camshaft sprocket and its hub, as described in Section 8.

Left-hand oil seal

7 The left-hand camshaft oil seal is formed by the brake vacuum pump seal. Refer to Chapter 9, Section 21, for details of brake vacuum pump removal and refitting.

11 Cylinder head – removal, inspection and refitting

Note: *The cylinder head must be removed with the engine cold. New cylinder head bolts and a new cylinder head gasket will be required on refitting, and suitable studs will be required to guide the cylinder head into position – see text.*

Removal

1 Remove the battery as described in Chapter 5A, Section 3.

2 Drain the cooling system (Chapter 1B, Section 31) and engine oil (Chapter 1B, Section 3).

3 Pull the plastic cover on the top of the engine upwards to release it from its mountings.

4 Remove the air filter housing as described in Chapter 4B, Section 2.

5 Undo the bolts and remove the battery tray **(see illustration)**.

6 Remove the radiator cooling fan(s) and shroud as described in Chapter 3, Section 5.

7 Undo the bolts and remove the air hose/duct from the intercooler to the turbocharger. Release the wiring looms from the clips as necessary to enable the duct to be manoeuvred from place.

8 Remove the camshaft cover as described in Section 4.

9 Remove the camshaft sprocket and hub as described in Section 8.

10.4 Using a plastic sleeve to slide seal over end of camshaft

10 Remove the inlet manifold as described in Chapter 4B, Section 5.

11 Undo the retaining bolts, and remove the charge air pipe from the turbocharger **(see illustration)**.

12 Remove the EGR pipes from the cylinder head as described in Chapter 4D, Section 3.

13 Remove the exhaust manifold as described in Chapter 4D, Section 5. There is no need to completely remove the particulate filter from the vehicle. Slacken the Allen bolt and release the clamp securing the diesel particulate filter/catalytic converter to the turbocharger, then undo the bolts/nuts securing the brackets to the cylinder block/head and lay the filter/converter to one side.

14 Apply a little lubrication spray to the rubber sleeve, pull up the pipe from the vacuum pump, then undo the 4 retaining bolts and remove the vacuum pump from the left-hand end of the cylinder head **(see illustration)**.

11.5 Battery tray securing bolts (arrowed)

10.5 Note some seals have 'OUTSIDE' (arrowed) to show fitted position

Renew the pump-to-cylinder head seal/gasket (Chapter 9, Section 21).

15 Disconnect the coolant temperature sensor wiring plug at the left-hand end of the cylinder head, and release the wiring loom from any retaining clips.

16 Disconnect the gearchange cables from the levers on the transmission as described in Chapter 7A Section 2 (manual transmission) or Chapter 7B Section 4 (DSG transmission).

17 Undo the bolts/nut, securing the gearchange bracket to the top of the transmission. Move the bracket and cables to one side.

18 Note their fitted locations, then release the clamps and disconnect the various coolant hoses from the cylinder head.

19 Disconnect the wiring connector from the oil pressure switch, undo the bolt securing the pipe bracket at the left-hand end of cylinder head **(see illustrations)**, and the bolt

11.11 Remove the charge air pipe from the turbocharger

11.14 Disconnect the vacuum pipe

11.19a Disconnect the oil pressure switch wiring connector

11.19b Undo the retaining bolt/screw and remove the lifting bracket

11.20 Undo the bolt (arrowed) securing the timing belt guard

11.21 Undo the cylinder head bolts using a M12 multi-splined (12 pointed star) tool

securing the lifting bracket on the rear of the head.

20 Undo the bolt securing the timing belt guard adjacent to the timing belt tensioner, and the bolt securing the camshaft position sensor, then remove the tensioner retaining nut **(see illustration)**.

21 Using an M12 multi-splined tool (12 pointed star), undo the cylinder head bolts, working from the outside-in, evenly and gradually **(see illustration)**. Remove the bolts and recover the washers. Check that nothing remains connected, and starting at the gearbox side, lift the cylinder head from the engine block, sliding the belt tensioner from the mounting stud as the cylinder head is removed. Seek assistance if possible, as it is a heavy assembly, especially as it is being removed complete with the manifolds.

22 Remove the gasket from the top of the block, noting the locating dowels. If the dowels are a loose fit, remove them and store them with the head for safekeeping. Do not discard the gasket yet – it will be needed for identification purposes.

Inspection

23 Dismantling and inspection of the cylinder head is covered in Part Chapter 2E.

Cylinder head gasket selection

Note: *A dial test indicator (DTI) will be required for this operation.*

24 Examine the old cylinder head gasket for manufacturer's identification markings **(see illustration)**. These will be in the form of holes, and a part number on the edge of the

gasket. Unless new pistons have been fitted, the new cylinder head gasket must be of the same type as the old one.

25 If new piston assemblies have been fitted as part of an engine overhaul, or if a new short engine is to be fitted, the projection of the piston crowns above the cylinder head mating face of the cylinder block at TDC must be measured. This measurement is used to determine the thickness of the new cylinder head gasket required.

26 Anchor a dial test indicator (DTI) to the top face (cylinder head gasket mating face) of the cylinder block, and zero the gauge on the gasket mating face.

27 Rest the gauge probe on No 1 piston crown, and turn the crankshaft slowly by hand until the piston reaches TDC. Measure and record the maximum piston projection at TDC **(see illustration)**.

28 Repeat the measurement for the remaining pistons, and record the results.

29 If the measurements differ from piston-to-piston, take the highest figure, and use this to determine the thickness of the head gasket required as follows:

Piston projection	Gasket identification (number of holes)
0.91 to 1.00 mm	1
1.01 to 1.10 mm	2
1.11 to 1.20 mm	3

30 Purchase a new gasket according to the results of the measurements.

Refitting

31 The mating faces of the cylinder head and block must be perfectly clean before refitting

the head. Use a scraper to remove all traces of gasket and carbon, also clean the tops of the pistons. Take particular care with the aluminium surfaces, as the soft metal is easily damaged.

32 Make sure that debris is not allowed to enter the oil and water passages – this is particularly important for the oil circuit, as carbon could block the oil supply to the camshaft and crankshaft bearings. Using adhesive tape and paper, seal the water, oil and bolt holes in the cylinder block.

33 To prevent carbon entering the gap between the pistons and bores, smear a little grease in the gap. After cleaning a piston, rotate the crankshaft to that the piston moves down the bore, and then wipe out the grease and carbon with a cloth rag. Clean the other piston crowns in the same way.

34 Check the head and block for nicks, deep scratches and other damage. If slight, they may be removed carefully with a file. More serious damage may be repaired by machining, but this is a specialist job.

35 If warpage of the cylinder head is suspected, use a straight-edge to check it for distortion, as described in Chapter 2E, Section 7.

36 Ensure that the cylinder head bolt holes in the crankcase are clean and free of oil. Syringe or soak up any oil left in the bolt holes. This is most important in order that the correct bolt tightening torque can be applied, and to prevent the possibility of the block being cracked by hydraulic pressure when the bolts are tightened.

37 Turn the crankshaft anti-clockwise all the pistons at an equal height, approximately half-way down their bores from the TDC position (see Section 3). This will eliminate any risk of piston-to-valve contact as the cylinder head is refitted.

38 Where applicable, refit the manifolds with reference to Chapter 4B, Section 5 and/or Chapter 4D, Section 5.

39 Ensure that the cylinder head locating dowels are in place in the cylinder block, and then fit the new cylinder head gasket over the dowels, ensuring that the part number is uppermost **(see illustration)**. Note that VW recommend that the gasket is only removed from its packaging immediately prior to fitting.

11.24 The holes (arrowed) identify the thickness of the cylinder head gasket

11.27 Measure the piston protrusion using a DTI gauge

11.39 Ensure the dowels are in place, then fit the new gasket with the part number uppermost (arrowed)

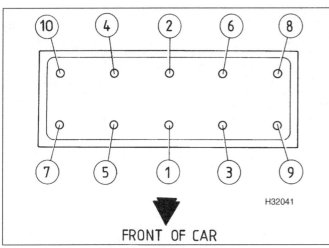

11.42a Cylinder head bolt tightening sequence

11.42b Tighten the cylinder head bolts to the Stage 1 torque

40 Lower the cylinder head into position on the gasket, ensuring that it engages correctly over the dowels. Refit the timing belt tensioner as the cylinder head is refitted.

41 Fit the washers in place then fit the new cylinder head bolts to the locations, and screw them in as far as possible by hand. Do not oil the bolt threads.

42 Working progressively, in sequence, tighten all the cylinder head bolts to the specified Stage 1 torque **(see illustrations)**.

43 Again working progressively, in sequence, tighten all the cylinder head bolts to the specified Stage 2 torque.

44 Tighten all the cylinder head bolts, in sequence, through the specified Stage 3 angle **(see illustration)**.

45 Finally, tighten all the cylinder head bolts, in sequence, through the specified Stage 4 angle.

46 The remainder of the refitting procedure is a reversal of the removal procedure, noting the following points:

a) Tighten all fasteners to their specified torque where given.

b) Renew all seals and gaskets.

c) Refill the cooling system as described, in Chapter 1B, Section 31.

d) Refill the engine oil, as described in Chapter 1B, Section 3.

e) Ensure all wiring is correctly routed.

f) Run the vehicle and make sure the cooling fans operate when the engine gets up to temperature.

12 Sump –
removal and refitting

Removal

1 Apply the handbrake, then jack up the front of the vehicle and support securely on axle stands (see *Jacking and vehicle support*).

2 Remove the securing screws and withdraw the engine undershield(s).

3 Drain the engine oil as described in Chapter 1B, Section 3.

4 Release the retaining clips and remove the air hose from the intercooler outlet to the charge air pipe **(see illustration)**.

5 Undo the retaining bolts, release the clamp and move the charger air pipe from the front of the cylinder block **(see illustrations)**. Disconnect the charger air pressure sensor wiring plug.

6 Disconnect the wiring connector from the oil level/temperature sender in the sump.

7 Release the retaining clips and remove the

11.44 Use an angle-tightening gauge

12.4 Slacken the two retaining clips - arrowed

12.5a Undo the retaining bolt on the end of the sump - arrowed ...

12.5b ...and the bolt on the front of the cylinder block ...

12.5c ...then disconnect the pressure switch wiring connector

12.7a Release the two clips (arrowed) at the rear of the sump

12.7b At the front, prise down the centre pin and pull the clip downwards (arrowed)

12.7c Remove the insulation cover from the around the sump

12.8a Undo the three transmission to sump bolts (arrowed) …

12.8b … and also the four bolts (arrowed), at the transmission end of the sump

12.8c Lower the sump from the cylinder block

sump insulation cover from the sump (see illustrations).

8 Unscrew and remove the bolts securing the sump to the cylinder block, and the bolts securing the sump to the transmission casing,

then withdraw the sump (see illustrations). If necessary, release the sump by tapping with a soft-faced hammer.

Refitting

9 Begin refitting by thoroughly cleaning the mating faces of the sump and cylinder block. Ensure that all traces of old sealant are removed.

10 Ensure that the cylinder block mating face of the sump is free from all traces of old sealant, oil and grease, and then apply a 2.0 to 3.0 mm thick bead of silicone sealant (VW D 176 404 A2 or equivalent) to the sump (see illustration). Note that the sealant should be run around the inside of the bolt holes in the sump. The sump must be fitted within 5 minutes of applying the sealant.

11 Offer the sump up to the cylinder block, then refit the sump-to-cylinder block bolts, and lightly tighten them by hand, working

progressively in a diagonal sequence. Note: *If the sump is being refitted with the engine and transmission separated, make sure that the sump is flush with the flywheel end of the cylinder block.*

12 Refit the sump-to-transmission casing bolts, and tighten them lightly, using a socket.

13 Again working in a diagonal sequence, lightly tighten the sump-to-cylinder block bolts, using a socket.

14 Tighten the sump-to-transmission casing bolts to the specified torque.

15 Working in a diagonal sequence, progressively tighten the sump-to-cylinder block bolts to the specified torque.

16 The remainder of refitting is a reversal of removal, noting to allow at least 30 minutes from the time of refitting the sump for the sealant to dry, then refill the engine with oil, with reference to Chapter 1B, Section 3.

13 Oil pump and drive belt – removal, inspection and refitting

Oil pump removal

1 Remove the sump as described in Section 12.

2 Unscrew the flange bolts and remove the oil pick-up pipe/filter from the oil pump (see illustration). Recover the O-ring seal and discard, as a new one will be required for refitting.

3 Unscrew the securing bolt, and remove the oil baffle from the cylinder block (see illustration).

12.10 Apply a bead of sealant around the inside of the bolt holes

H46180

13.2 Remove the oil pick-up pipe/filter

13.3 Remove the oil baffle plate bolt (which is also one of the oil pump mounting bolts)

13.4 Oil pump mounting bolts - arrowed

13.11 Fit a new seal to the end of the oil pick-up pipe

4 Unscrew and remove the mounting bolts, and release the oil pump from the dowels in the crankcase (see illustration). Unhook the oil pump drive sprocket from the belt and withdraw the oil pump and oil pick-up pipe from the engine. Note, the bolt holding the baffle plate is also one of the pump mounting bolts.

Oil pump inspection

5 Clean the pump thoroughly, and inspect for signs of damage or wear. If evident, renew the oil pump.

Oil pump refitting

6 Prime the pump with oil by pouring oil into the pick-up pipe aperture while turning the driveshaft.
7 If the drive belt and crankshaft sprocket have been removed, delay refitting them until after the oil pump has been mounted on the cylinder block.
8 Engage the oil pump sprocket with the drive belt, and then locate the oil pump on the dowels. Refit and tighten the mounting bolts to the specified torque.
9 Where applicable, refit the drive belt and crankshaft sprocket using a reversal of the removal procedure.
10 Refit the oil baffle plate, and tighten the securing bolt.
11 Refit the pick-up pipe to the oil pump, using a new O-ring seal, and tighten the securing bolts (see illustration).
12 Refit the sump as described in Section 12.

Oil pump drive belt and sprockets

Note: *VW sealant (D 176 404 A2 or equivalent) will be required to seal the crankshaft oil seal housing on refitting, and it is advisable to fit a new crankshaft oil seal.*

Removal

13 Proceed as described in paragraphs 1 and 2.
14 To remove the belt, remove the timing belt as described in Section 7, then unbolt the crankshaft oil seal housing from the cylinder block, as described in Section 15. Unhook the belt from the sprocket on the end of the crankshaft.
15 The oil pump drive sprocket is a press-fit

on the crankshaft, and cannot easily be removed. Consult a VW dealer for advice if the sprocket is worn or damaged.

Inspection

16 It is wise to renew the belt in any case if the engine is to be overhauled, If there is any doubt as to the condition of the belt, renew it.

Refitting

17 If the oil pump has been removed, refit the oil pump as described previously in this Section before refitting the belt and sprocket.
18 Engage the oil pump sprocket with the belt, then engage the belt with the crankshaft sprocket.
19 Fit a new crankshaft oil seal to the housing, and refit the housing as described in Section 15.
20 Where applicable, refit the oil baffle and pick-up pipe, and tighten the securing bolts.
21 Refit the sump as described in Section 12.

14 Flywheel – removal, inspection and refitting

Removal

1 On manual gearbox models, remove the gearbox (see Chapter 7A, Section 3) and clutch (see Chapter 6, Section 6).
2 On semi-automatic (DSG) transmission models, remove the transmission as described in Chapter 7B, Section 2.

14.3 Flywheel bolts are offset and can only be fitted in one position - DSG transmission (0AM) shown

3 The flywheel can only be fitted in one position due to the offset of the flywheel mounting holes in the end of the crankshaft (see illustration). Note, manual models are fitted with a dual-mass flywheel.
4 Rotate the outside of the dual-mass flywheel so that the bolts align with the holes (if necessary).
5 Unscrew the bolts and remove the flywheel. Using a locking tool, counter-hold the flywheel to prevent it from turning (see illustration). Discard the bolts, as new ones must be fitted. **Note:** *In order not to damage the flywheel, do not allow the bolt heads to make contact with the flywheel during the unscrewing procedure.*

Inspection

6 Check the dual-mass flywheel for wear and damage. Examine the starter ring gear for excessive wear to the teeth. If the driveplate or its ring gear are damaged, the complete driveplate must be renewed. The flywheel ring gear, however, may be renewed separately from the flywheel, but the work should be entrusted to a VW dealer. If the clutch friction face is discoloured or scored excessively, it may be possible to regrind it, but this work should also be entrusted to a VW dealer.
7 The following are guidelines only, but should indicate whether professional inspection is necessary. The dual-mass flywheel should be checked as follows:
Warpage: Place a straight edge across the face of the drive surface, and check by trying

14.5 Use a locking tool to counterhold the flywheel

14.7a Flywheel warpage check – see text

14.7b Flywheel free rotational movement check alignment marks – see text

14.7c Flywheel lateral movement check marks – see text

14.8 Use new bolts when refitting

15.2 Pull the screw and seal from place using pliers

15.5 Using a plastic sleeve to slide the seal over the end of the crankshaft

to insert a feeler gauge between the straight edge and the drive surface **(see illustration)**. The flywheel will normally warp like a bowl – ie. Higher on the outer edge. If the warpage is more than 0.40 mm, the flywheel may need replacing.

Free rotational movement: This is the distance the drive surface of the flywheel can be turned independently of the flywheel primary element, using finger effort alone. Move the drive surface in one direction and make a mark where the locating pin aligns with the flywheel edge. Move the drive surface in the other direction (finger pressure only) and make another mark **(see illustration)**. The total of free movement should not exceed 20.0 mm. If it's more, the flywheel may need replacing.

Total rotational movement: This is the total distance the drive surface can be turned

independently of the flywheel primary element. Insert two bolts into the clutch pressure plate/damper unit mounting holes, and with the crankshaft/flywheel held stationary, use a lever/pry bar between the bolts and use some effort to move the drive surface fully in one direction – make a mark where the locating pin aligns with the flywheel edge. Now force the drive surface fully in the opposite direction, and make another mark. The total rotational movement should not exceed 44.00 mm. If it does, have the flywheel professionally inspected.

Lateral movement: The lateral movement (up and down) of the drive surface in relation to the primary element of the flywheel, should not exceed 2.0 mm. If it does, the flywheel may need replacing. This can be checked by pressing the drive surface down on one side into the flywheel (flywheel horizontal) and

making an alignment mark between the drive surface and the inner edge of the primary element. Now press down on the opposite side of the drive surface, and make another mark above the original one. The difference between the two marks is the lateral movement **(see illustration)**.

There should be no cracks in the drive surface of the flywheel. If cracks are evident, the flywheel may need replacing.

Refitting

8 Refitting is a reversal of removal. Use new bolts when refitting the flywheel or driveplate **(see illustration)**, and coat the threads of the bolts (if not already coated with locking compound) with locking fluid before inserting them. Tighten them to the specified torque.

15 Crankshaft oil seals – renewal

Note: *The oil seals are a PTFE (Teflon) type and are fitted dry, without using any grease or oil. These have a wider sealing lip and have been introduced instead of the coil spring type oil seal.*

Timing belt end oil seal

1 Remove the timing belt as described in Section 7, and the crankshaft sprocket with reference to Section 8.
2 To remove the seal without removing the housing, drill two small holes diagonally opposite each other, insert self-tapping screws, and pull on the heads of the screws with pliers **(see illustration)**.
3 Alternatively, to remove the oil seal complete with its housing, proceed as follows.
a) *Remove the sump as described in Section 12. This is necessary to ensure a satisfactory seal between the sump and oil seal housing on refitting.*
b) *Unbolt and remove the oil seal housing.*
c) *Working on the bench, lever the oil seal from the housing using a suitable screwdriver. Take care not to damage the seal seating in the housing.*
4 Thoroughly clean the oil seal seating in the housing.
5 Wind a length of tape around the end of the crankshaft (or a plastic sleeve) to protect the oil seal lips as the seal (and housing, where applicable) is fitted **(see illustration)**.
6 Fit a new oil seal to the housing, pressing or driving it into position using a socket or tube of suitable diameter. Ensure that the socket or tube bears only on the hard outer ring of the seal, and take care not to damage the seal lips. Press or drive the seal into position until it is seated on the shoulder in the housing **(see illustration)**. Make sure that the closed end of the seal is facing outwards.
7 If the oil seal housing has been removed,

15.6 Carefully tap the seal into position

15.12a Remove the intermediate plate from the dowels …

15.12b … and from behind the top of the crankshaft seal housing

proceed as follows, otherwise proceed to paragraph 11.

8 Clean all traces of old sealant from the crankshaft oil seal housing and the cylinder block, then coat the cylinder block mating faces of the oil seal housing with a 2.0 to 3.0 mm thick bead of silicone sealant (VW D 176 404 A2, or equivalent). Note that the seal housing must be refitted within 5 minutes of applying the sealant.

Caution: DO NOT put excessive amounts of sealant onto the housing as it may get into the sump and block the oil pick-up pipe.

9 Refit the oil seal housing, and tighten the bolts progressively to the specified torque.

10 Refit the sump as described in Section 12.

11 Refit the crankshaft sprocket with reference to Section 8, and the timing belt as described in Section 7.

Flywheel end oil seal

Note: *In these engines, the seal, sealing flange and sender wheel are a complete unit. Special tools are required to refit the sealing flange, and press the sender wheel onto the end of the crankshaft. It is not possible to accurately fit these parts without the tools, which may be available from VW (part no. T10134) and are available from aftermarket automotive tool specialists. E.g. Laser tools).*

12 Remove the flywheel as described in Section 14, then prise the intermediate plate from the locating dowels on the cylinder block and unhook it from behind the top of the seal housing **(see illustrations)**.

13 Undo the bolt securing the crankshaft speed sensor and remove it from the seal housing, then undo the bolts securing the sealing flange to the cylinder block **(see illustrations)**.

14 Insert three 6 x 35 mm bolts into the threaded holes in the sealing flange. Tighten the bolts gradually and evenly, and press the sealing flange, and sender wheel from the crankshaft/cylinder block **(see illustrations)**. The seal, sender wheel and sealing flange are supplied as a complete unit.

15 Ensure the mating face of the cylinder block Is clean and free from debris. The new sealing flange/seal/sender wheel assembly is supplied with a sealing lip support ring, which serves as a fitting sleeve, and must not

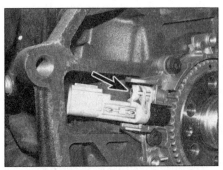
15.13a Undo the crankshaft speed sensor retaining bolt - arrowed

be removed prior to installation. Equally, the sender wheel must not be separated from the assembly.

16 If using the VW tool, proceed as follows. If using an aftermarket tool specialist's product,

15.14a Screw in three 6 x 35 mm bolts …

15.16a Rotate the nut until its level with the end of the flat clamping surface…

15.13b Sealing flange bolts (arrowed)

follow the instructions supplied with the tool. Rotate the large spindle nut until it's level with the end of the clamping surface of the spindle, then clamp the spindle in a vice **(see illustrations)**.

15.14b …and draw the sealing flange and sender wheel from place

15.16b …then clamp it in a vice

15.17a Rotate the nut until the inner part of the tool …

15.17b …is flush with the flat surface of the housing

15.18a Remove the securing clip …

15.18b …the hole in the sender wheel should align with the marking on the flange (arrowed)

17 Press the tool housing downwards until it rests on the nut and washer. Rotate the nut until the inner part of the tool is at the same height as the housing **(see illustration)**.

18 Remove the seal securing clip. The hole on

15.19a Press the assembly downwards on a clean, flat surface…

15.21 With the pin engaged in the hole, tighten the 3 knurled screws to secure the flange to the tool

the sender wheel must align with the marking on the sealing flange **(see illustrations)**.

19 Place the flange outer side down on a clean, flat surface, then press the seal guide fitting sleeve (supplied ready fitted), housing, and sender wheel downwards until all the components are flat on

15.19b …so the upper edge of the sender wheel is level with the edge of the flange

the surface. In this position the upper edge of the sender wheel should be level with the edge of the sealing flange **(see illustrations)**.

20 Place the sealing flange on the assembly tool, so the pin locates in the hole in the sender wheel **(see illustration)**.

21 Push the sealing flange and guide fitting sleeve against the tool whilst tightening the 3 knurled screws. Ensure the pin is still located in the sender wheel **(see illustration)**.

22 Ensure the end of the crankshaft is clean, and is locked at TDC on No. 1 cylinder as described in Section 3.

23 Unscrew the large nut to the end of the spindle threads, then press the spindle inwards as far as possible **(see illustration)**.

24 Align the flat side of the assembly with the sump flange, then secure the tool to the crankshaft using the integral Allen bolts **(see illustration)**. Only hand tighten the bolts.

25 Insert two M7x 35 mm bolts to guide

15.20 Fit the flange to the tool, ensuring the pin locates in the hole (arrowed)

15.23a Unscrew the nut to the end of the thread …

15.23b …and push the spindle in as far as possible

15.24 Hand-tighten the Allen bolts (arrowed), to secure the tool to the crankshaft

15.25 Use two M7 x 35 mm bolts (arrowed) to guide the sealing flange

15.26 Push the black knob into the hole in the crankshaft

15.27a After tightening the spindle nut to 35 Nm ...

15.27b ...there should be an air gap between the sealing flange and the cylinder block (arrowed)

15.28 Remove the tool and seal fitting guide sleeve

15.29 Measure the fitted depth of the sender wheel in relation to the end of the crankshaft

the sealing flange to the cylinder block (see illustration).

26 Using hand pressure alone, push the tool assembly onto the crankshaft until the seal guide fitting sleeve contacts the crankshaft flange, then push the guide pin (black knob) into the hole in the crankshaft. This is to ensure the sender wheel reaches its correct installation position (see illustration).

27 Rotate the large nut until it makes contact with the tool housing, then tighten it to 35 Nm. After tightening this nut, a small air gap must still be present between the sealing flange and cylinder block (see illustrations).

28 Unscrew the large nut; the two M7 x 35 Nm screws, the three knurled screws and the Allen bolts securing the tool to the crankshaft. Remove the tool, and pull the seal guide fitting sleeve from place (if it didn't come out with the tool) (see illustration).

29 Use a vernier caliper or feeler gauge to measure the fitted depth of the sender wheel in relation to the crankshaft flange (see illustration). The correct depth is 0.5 mm.

30 If the gap is correct, fit the sealing flange bolts and tighten them to the specified torque.

31 If the gap is too small, re-attach the tool to the sealing flange and crankshaft, then refit the two M7 x 35 mm guide bolts to the flange. Tighten the large spindle nut to 40 Nm, remove the tool and re-measure the air gap. If the gap is still too small, re-attach the tool and tighten the spindle nut to 45 Nm. Re-measure the gap. When the gap is correct, refit the flange retaining bolts, and tighten them to the specified torque.

32 The remainder of refitting is a reversal of removal.

16 Engine/transmission mountings – inspection and renewal

Inspection

1 If improved access is required, jack up the front of the vehicle, and support it securely on axle stands (see Jacking and vehicle support). Remove the engine top cover that also incorporates the air filter, and then remove the engine undershield(s).

2 Check the mounting rubbers to see if they are cracked, hardened or separated from the metal at any point; renew the mounting if any such damage or deterioration is evident.

3 Check that all the mountings are securely tightened; use a torque wrench to check if possible.

4 Using a large screwdriver or a crowbar,

16.8 Undo the filter retaining bolts/nut - arrowed

check for wear in the mounting by carefully levering against it to check for free play. Where this is not possible, enlist the aid of an assistant to move the engine/transmission back-and-forth, or from side-to-side, whilst you observe the mounting. While some free play is to be expected, even from new components, excessive wear should be obvious. If excessive free play is found, check first that the fasteners are correctly secured, and then renew any worn components as described in the following paragraphs.

Renewal

Right-hand mounting

Note: New mounting securing bolts will be required on refitting.

5 Attach a hoist and lifting tackle to the engine lifting brackets on the cylinder head, and raise the hoist to just take the weight of the engine. Alternatively the engine can be supported on a trolley jack under the engine. Use a block of wood between the sump and the head of the jack, to prevent any damage to the sump.

6 For improved access, unscrew the coolant reservoir and move it to one side, leaving the coolant hoses connected.

7 Disconnect the wiring plug, undo the retaining bolts, and remove the pressure differential sender (for particulate filter) including bracket from the top of the engine mounting and move it to one side (see illustrations 6.3a & 6.3b).

8 Undo the retaining bolts and move the fuel filter to one side (see illustration). Where applicable, move any wiring harnesses, pipes

16.9 Right-hand engine mounting

16.10 There must be at least 10 mm between the bracket and the chassis member (arrowed)

16.14 Left-hand engine/transmission mounting

16.19 Rear mounting arm-to-transmission bolts

or hoses to one side to enable removal of the engine mounting.

9 Unscrew the bolts securing the mounting to the engine bracket, and then unscrew the bolts securing it to the body **(see illustration)**. Withdraw the mounting from the engine compartment.

10 Refitting is a reversal of removal, bearing in mind the following points.

a) Use new securing bolts.

b) There must be at least 10 mm between the engine mounting bracket and the right-hand side chassis member **(see illustration)**.

c) The side of the mounting support arm must be parallel to the side of the engine mounting bracket.

d) Tighten all fixings to the specified torque.

Left-hand mounting

Note: *New mounting bolts will be required on refitting.*

11 Remove the engine top cover.

12 Attach a hoist and lifting tackle to the engine lifting brackets on the cylinder head, and raise the hoist to just take the weight of the engine and transmission. Alternatively the engine can be supported on a trolley jack under the transmission. Use a block of wood between the transmission and the head of the jack, to prevent any damage to the transmission.

13 Remove the battery and battery tray, as described in Chapter 5, Section 3.

14 Unscrew the bolts securing the mounting to the transmission, and the remaining bolts securing the mounting to the body **(see illustration)**, then lift the mounting from the engine compartment.

15 Refitting is a reversal of removal, bearing in mind the following points:

a) Use new mounting bolts.

b) The edges of the mounting support

arm must be parallel to the edge of the mounting.

c) Tighten all fixings to the specified torque.

Rear mounting (torque arm)

Note: *New mounting bolts will be required on refitting.*

16 Apply the handbrake, then jack up the front of the vehicle and support securely on axle stands (see *Jacking and vehicle support*). Remove the engine undershield(s) for access to the rear mounting (torque arm).

17 Support the rear of the transmission beneath the final drive housing. To do this, use a trolley jack and block of wood, or alternatively wedge a block of wood between the transmission and the subframe.

18 Working under the vehicle, unscrew and remove the bolt securing the mounting to the subframe.

19 Unscrew the two bolts securing the mounting to the transmission, then withdraw the mounting from under the vehicle **(see illustration)**.

20 Refitting is a reversal of removal, but use new mounting securing bolts, and tighten all fixings to the specified torque.

17 Engine oil cooler/ filter housing – removal and refitting

Removal

1 The oil cooler is mounted on the lower part of the oil filter housing on the front of the cylinder block.

2 Position a container beneath the oil filter housing to catch escaping oil and coolant.

3 Clamp the oil cooler coolant hoses to minimise coolant spillage, or drain the cooling system as described in Chapter 1B, Section 31.

4 Unscrew the oil cooler retaining screws and remove the oil cooler from the front of the oil filter housing **(see illustrations)**. Recover the O-rings from between the cooler and the oil filter housing, new ones will be required for refitting.

5 If required, disconnect the coolant hose, unclip the dipstick from the side of the housing, then undo the retaining bolts and remove the oil filter housing from the cylinder block **(see illustrations)**.

17.4a Undo the engine oil cooler retaining screws

17.4b Renew the seals/gaskets

17.5a Disconnect the coolant hoses ...

17.5b ...release the oil dipstick guide tube retaining clip (arrowed) ...

17.5c ... and undo the filter housing retaining bolts (arrowed)

17.6 Renew the seals/gaskets

Refitting

6 Refitting is a reversal of removal, bearing in mind the following points:
  a) *Use new oil cooler and housing O-rings* (see illustration).
  b) *Tighten the oil cooler and filter housing bolts to the correct torque.*
  c) *On completion, check and if necessary top-up the oil and coolant levels.*

18 Oil pressure warning light switch – removal and refitting

18.1 Oil pressure warning light switch location - arrowed

18.2 Remove the air intake hose

Removal

1 The oil pressure warning light switch is fitted to the left-hand rear of the cylinder head (see illustration). Remove the engine top cover to gain access to the switch.
2 Slacken the retraining clips and remove the air intake hose from the turbocharger (see illustration).
3 Disconnect the wiring connector and wipe clean the area around the switch.
4 Unscrew the switch and remove it, along with its sealing washer (where fitted). If the switch is to be left removed from the engine for any length of time, plug the aperture in the cylinder head.

Refitting

5 Examine the sealing washer for signs of damage or deterioration and if necessary renew.
6 Refit the switch, complete with washer (where fitted), and tighten it to the specified torque.
7 Securely reconnect the wiring connector, refit the air intake hose and then, if necessary, top-up the engine oil as described in *Weekly checks*. On completion, refit the engine top cover.

19.1 Oil level/temperature sensor location

19 Oil level/temperature sender – removal and refitting

Removal

1 The oil level/temperature sender is fitted to bottom of the sump (see illustration).
2 Drain the engine oil as described in Chapter 1B Section 3.
3 Disconnect the wiring connector from the sender.
4 Release the retaining clips and remove the insulation cover from the sump (see illustration).

19.4 Remove the insulation cover to access the bolts

5 Wipe clean the area around the sender, then undo the three retaining bolts and remove the sender.

Refitting

6 Examine the sealing washer for signs of damage or deterioration and if necessary renew.
7 Refit the switch and tighten the retaining bolts to the specified torque.
8 Refit the insulation cover, then reconnect the wiring connector and refill the engine with oil (refer to Chapter 1B, Section 3).
9 On completion, check and, if necessary, top-up the engine oil as described in *Weekly checks*.

Notes

Chapter 2 Part D:
2.0 litre diesel engine in-car repair procedures

Contents

Degrees of difficulty

Easy, suitable for novice with little experience	**Fairly easy,** suitable for beginner with some experience	**Fairly difficult,** suitable for competent DIY mechanic	**Difficult,** suitable for experienced DIY mechanic	**Very difficult,** suitable for expert DIY or professional

Specifications

General

Manufacturer's engine codes: *	
1968 cc (2.0 litre), 16-valve, DOHC	CBAA, CBAB, CBBB, CFFA, CFFB and CFGB

Maximum outputs:	**Power**	**Torque**
Engine code CBAA & CFFA	100 kW @ 4200 rpm	320 Nm @ 1750 to 2500 rpm
Engine code CBAB & CFFB	103 kW @ 4200 rpm	320 Nm @ 1750 to 2500 rpm
Engine code CBBB & CFGB.	125 kW @ 4200 rpm	350 Nm @ 1750 to 2500 rpm

Bore	81.0 mm
Stroke	95.5 mm
Compression ratio	16.5 :1
Compression pressures:	
Minimum compression pressure	Approximately 19.0 bar
Maximum difference between cylinders.	Approximately 5.0 bar
Firing order.	1 – 3 – 4 – 2
No 1 cylinder location.	Timing belt end

* Note: *See 'Vehicle identification' at the end of this manual for the location of engine code markings.*

Lubrication system

Oil pump type.	Gear type, chain-driven from crankshaft
Oil pressure switch (green cap)	0.5 bar
Oil pressure switch (brown cap)	0.7 bar
Oil pressure (oil temperature 80°C):	
Minimum @ idling	0.6 bar
Minimum @ 2000 rpm:	
CBAA, CBAB & CBBB	2.0 bar
CFFA, CFFB & CFGB	1.0 bar
Maximum @ high rpm:	
CBAA, CBAB & CBBB	7.0 bar
CFFA, CFFB & CFGB	5.0 bar

Torque wrench settings

	Nm	lbf ft
Ancillary (alternator, etc) bracket mounting bolts: *		
Stage 1	40	30
Stage 2	Angle-tighten a further 45°	
Auxiliary drivebelt tensioner securing bolt:		
Stage 1	20	15
Stage 2	Angle-tighten a further 180°	

Torque wrench settings (continued)

	Nm	lbf ft
Balancer shaft drivegear bolts: *		
Stage 1	20	15
Stage 2	Angle-tighten a further 90°	
Balance shaft housing to cylinder block: *		
M7:		
Stage 1	13	10
Stage 2	Angle-tighten a further 90°	
M8:		
Stage 1	20	15
Stage 2	Angle-tighten a further 90°	
Balance shaft idler gear: *		
Stage 1	90	66
Stage 2	Angle-tighten a further 90°	
Big-end bearing caps bolts: *		
Stage 1	30	22
Stage 2	Angle-tighten a further 90°	
Camshaft bearing frame bolts/nut	10	7
Camshaft cover bolts	10	7
Camshaft sprocket hub centre bolt	100	74
Camshaft sprocket-to-hub bolts: *		
Stage 1	20	15
Stage 2	Angle-tighten a further 45°	
Common rail bolts	22	16
Coolant pump bolts	15	11
Crankshaft oil seal housing bolts	15	11
Crankshaft pulley-to-sprocket bolts: *		
Stage 1	10	7
Stage 2	Angle-tighten a further 90°	
Crankshaft sprocket bolt: *		
Stage 1	120	89
Stage 2	Angle-tighten a further 90°	
Cylinder head bolts: *		
Stage 1	30	22
Stage 2	50	37
Stage 3	Angle-tighten a further 90°	
Stage 4	Angle-tighten a further 90°	
Engine mountings: *		
RH engine mounting:		
Mounting bracket to engine:		
Stage 1	40	30
Stage 2	Angle-tighten a further 180°	
Mounting to body:		
Stage 1	40	30
Stage 2	Angle-tighten a further 90°	
Mounting to bracket:		
Stage 1	60	44
Stage 2	Angle-tighten a further 90°	
LH engine/transmission mounting:		
Mounting to body:		
Stage 1	40	30
Stage 2	Angle-tighten a further 90°	
Mounting to bracket on transmission:		
Stage 1	60	44
Stage 2	Angle-tighten a further 90°	
Rear mounting link:		
M10 strength class 8.8:		
Stage 1	40	30
Stage 2	Angle-tighten a further 90°	
M10 strength class 10.9:		
Stage 1	50	37
Stage 2	Angle-tighten a further 90°	
M12:		
Stage 1	60	44
Stage 2	Angle-tighten a further 90°	
Flywheel: *		
Stage 1	60	44
Stage 2	Angle-tighten a further 90°	

Torque wrench settings (continued)

	Nm	lbf ft
Fuel injector:		
Retaining nuts	22	16
Cover bolts	5	4
Fuel pump hub nut	95	70
Fuel pump sprocket bolts: *		
Stage 1	20	15
Stage 2	Angle-tighten a further 90°	
Intermediate gear bolt: *		
Stage 1	90	66
Stage 2	Angle-tighten a further 90°	
Main bearing cap bolts: *		
Stage 1	65	48
Stage 2	Angle-tighten a further 90°	
Oil cooler screws (CFFA, CFFB & CFGB)	11	7
Oil cooler centre bolt (CBAA, CBAB & CBBB)	25	18
Oil drain plug*	30	22
Oil filter housing-to-cylinder block bolts: *		
Stage 1	15	11
Stage 2	Angle-tighten a further 90°	
Oil filter cover	25	18
Oil level/temperature sensor-to-sump bolts	10	7
Oil pick-up pipe securing bolts	10	7
Oil pressure warning light switch	20	15
Oil pump securing bolts:		
M6	10	7
M7: *		
Stage 1	13	10
Stage 2	Angle-tighten a further 90°	
Piston oil spray jet bolt	25	18
Sump:		
Sump-to-cylinder block bolts	15	11
Sump-to-transmission bolts	45	33
Thermostat housing	15	11
Timing belt outer cover bolts	10	7
Timing belt tensioner roller securing nut:		
Stage 1	20	15
Stage 2	Angle-tighten a further 45°	
Timing belt idler pulleys:		
Lower idler roller nut	20	15
Upper idler roller (small) bolt	20	15
Upper idler roller (large) bolt: *		
Stage 1	50	37
Stage 2	Angle-tighten a further 90°	

* Do not re-use fasteners

1 General information

How to use this Chapter

This Part of Chapter 2 describes those repair procedures that can reasonably be carried out on the engine while it remains in the vehicle. If the engine has been removed from the vehicle and is being dismantled as described in Part E, any preliminary dismantling procedures can be ignored.

Note that while it may be possible physically to overhaul certain items while the engine is in the vehicle, such tasks are not usually carried out as separate operations, and usually require the execution of several additional procedures (not to mention the cleaning of components and of oilways); for this reason, all such tasks are classed as major overhaul procedures, and are described in Part E of this Chapter.

Engine description

Throughout this Chapter, engines are referred to by type, and are identified and referred to by the manufacturer's code letters. A listing of all engines covered, together with their code letters, is given in the Specifications at the start of this Chapter.

The engines are water-cooled, double overhead camshafts (DOHC), in-line four-cylinder units, with cast-iron cylinder blocks and aluminium-silicon alloy cylinder heads. All are mounted transversely at the front of the vehicle, with the transmission bolted to the left-hand end of the engine.

The crankshaft is of five-bearing type, and thrustwashers are fitted to the centre main bearing to control crankshaft endfloat.

Drive for the exhaust camshaft is by a toothed timing belt from the crankshaft, with the intake camshaft driven by interlocking gears at the left-hand end of both camshafts. The gears incorporate a toothed backlash compensator element. Each camshaft is mounted at the top of the cylinder head, and is secured by a bearing frame/ladder.

The valves are closed by coil springs, and run in guides pressed into the cylinder head. The valves are operated by roller rocker arms incorporating hydraulic tappets.

A twin, counter-rotating balance shaft assembly is fitted to the base of the cylinder block. The rearmost balance shaft is driven by a gear on the crankshaft, via an intermediate gear bolted to the balance shaft housing. The two balance shafts are geared together.

The gear-type oil pump is driven by the front balance shaft. Oil is drawn from the sump through a strainer, and then forced through an externally-mounted, renewable filter. From there, it is distributed to the cylinder head, where it lubricates the camshaft journals and hydraulic tappets, and also to the crankcase, where it lubricates the main bearings, connecting rod big-ends, gudgeon pins and cylinder bores. A coolant-fed oil cooler is fitted to the oil filter housing on all engines. Oil jets are fitted to the base of each cylinder – these spray oil onto the underside of the pistons, to improve cooling.

All engines are fitted with a brake servo vacuum pump driven by the camshaft on the transmission end of the cylinder head.

On all engines, engine coolant is circulated by a pump, driven by the timing belt. For details of the cooling system, refer to Chapter 3.

Operations with engine in car

The following operations can be performed without removing the engine:
- a) Compression pressure – testing.
- b) Camshaft cover – removal and refitting.
- c) Crankshaft pulley – removal and refitting.
- d) Timing belt covers – removal and refitting.
- e) Timing belt – removal, refitting and adjustment.
- f) Timing belt tensioner and sprockets – removal and refitting.
- g) Camshaft oil seals – renewal.
- h) Camshafts and hydraulic tappets – removal, inspection and refitting.
- i) Cylinder head – removal and refitting.
- j) Cylinder head and pistons – decarbonising.
- k) Sump – removal and refitting.
- l) Oil pump – removal, overhaul and refitting.
- m) Crankshaft oil seals – renewal.
- n) Engine/transmission mountings – inspection and renewal.
- o) Flywheel – removal, inspection and refitting.

Note: It is possible to remove the pistons and connecting rods (after removing the cylinder head and sump) without removing the engine. However, this is not recommended. Work of this nature is more easily and thoroughly completed with the engine on the bench, as described in Chapter 2E.

2 Compression and leakdown tests – description and interpretation

Compression test

Note: A compression tester suitable for use with diesel engines will be required for this test.

1 When engine performance is down, or if misfiring occurs which cannot be attributed to the ignition or fuel systems, a compression test can provide diagnostic clues as to the engine's condition. If the test is performed regularly, it can give warning of trouble before any other symptoms become apparent.

2 The engine must be fully warmed-up to normal operating temperature, the battery must be fully charged, and you will require the aid of an assistant.

3 Remove the glow plugs as described in Chapter 5C, Section 2, and then fit a compression tester to the No 1 cylinder glow plug hole. The type of tester that bolts into the plug thread is preferred. **Note:** Part of the glow plug removal procedure is to disconnect the fuel injector wiring plugs. As a result of the plugs being disconnected and the engine cranked, faults will be stored in the ECM memory. These must be erased after the compression test.

4 Have your assistant crank the engine for several seconds on the starter motor. After one or two revolutions, the compression pressure should build-up to a maximum figure and then stabilise. Record the highest reading obtained.

5 Repeat the test on the remaining cylinders, recording the pressure in each.

6 The cause of poor compression is less easy to establish on a diesel engine than on a petrol engine. The effect of introducing oil into the cylinders (wet testing) is not conclusive, because there is a risk that the oil will sit in the recess on the piston crown, instead of passing to the rings. However, the following can be used as a rough guide to diagnosis.

7 All cylinders should produce very similar pressures. Any difference greater than that specified indicates the existence of a fault. Note that the compression should build-up quickly in a healthy engine. Low compression on the first stroke, followed by gradually increasing pressure on successive strokes, indicates worn piston rings. A low compression reading on the first stroke, which does not build-up during successive strokes, indicates leaking valves or a blown head gasket (a cracked head could also be the cause).

8 A low reading from two adjacent cylinders is almost certainly due to the head gasket having blown between them and the presence of coolant in the engine oil will confirm this.

9 On completion, remove the compression tester, and refit the glow plugs, with reference to Chapter 5C, Section 2.

10 Reconnect the wiring to the injector solenoids. Finally, have a VW dealer or suitably equipped specialist erase the fault codes from the ECM memory.

Leakdown test

11 A leakdown test measures the rate at

3.8 The alignment mark (arrowed) on the crankshaft sprocket should be almost vertical

which compressed air fed into the cylinder is lost. It is an alternative to a compression test, and in many ways it is better, since the escaping air provides easy identification of where pressure loss is occurring (piston rings, valves or head gasket).

12 The equipment required for leakdown testing is unlikely to be available to the home mechanic. If poor compression is suspected, have the test performed by a suitably equipped garage.

3 Engine assembly and valve timing marks – general information and usage
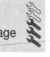

General information

1 TDC is the highest point in the cylinder that each piston reaches as it travels up-and-down when the crankshaft turns. Each piston reaches TDC at the end of the compression stroke and again at the end of the exhaust stroke, but TDC generally refers to piston position on the compression stroke. No 1 piston is at the timing belt end of the engine.

2 Positioning No 1 piston at TDC is an essential part of many procedures, such as timing belt removal and camshaft removal.

3 The design of the engines covered in this Chapter is such that piston-to-valve contact may occur if the camshaft or crankshaft is turned with the timing belt removed. For this reason, it is important to ensure that the camshaft and crankshaft do not move in relation to each other once the timing belt has been removed from the engine.

Setting TDC on No 1 cylinder

Note: VAG special tool T10050 is required to lock the crankshaft sprocket in the TDC position. Alternatively obtain a tool from automotive tool specialists.

4 Raise the front of the vehicle and support it securely on axle stands (see Jacking and vehicle support). Remove the front right-hand roadwheel, then release the fasteners and remove the lower section of the wheel arch liner.

5 Remove the auxiliary drivebelt as described in Chapter 1B, Section 28.

6 Remove the crankshaft pulley/vibration damper as described in Section 5.

7 Remove the timing belt outer covers as described in Section 6.

8 Using a spanner or socket on the crankshaft sprocket bolt, turn the crankshaft in the normal direction of rotation (clockwise) until the alignment mark on the face of the sprocket is almost vertical, and the hole in the camshaft sprocket hub aligns with the hole in the cylinder head **(see illustration)**.

9 While in this position it should be possible to insert the VAG tool T10050 to lock the crankshaft, and a 6 mm diameter rod/drill bit to lock the camshafts **(see illustrations)**. **Note:** The mark on the crankshaft sprocket and the mark on the VAG tool must align,

3.9a Fit the tool to the hole in the oil seal housing (arrowed) . . .

3.9b . . . so the marks on the tool and sprocket align (arrowed)

3.9c Insert a 6 mm drill bit/rod to lock the camshaft hub (arrowed)

4.3 Disconnect the vacuum hoses from the camshaft cover (arrowed)

4.4 Squeeze together the sides of the collar (arrowed) and disconnect the breather hose

4.5 Undo the bolts and lift away the camshaft cover

whilst at the same time the shaft of tool must engage in the drilling in the crankshaft oil seal housing.

10 The engine is now set to TDC on No 1 cylinder.

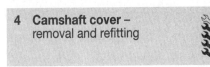

4 Camshaft cover – removal and refitting

Removal

1 Remove the fuel injectors (Chapter 4B, Section 4) and fuel rail (Chapter 4B, Section 11).
2 Remove the timing belt upper cover as described in Section 6.
3 Note their fitted positions, then disconnect the vacuum hoses from the camshaft cover, and release them and the wiring loom from the retaining clips at the left-hand end of the cover **(see illustration)**.
4 Squeeze together the sides of the collar, and disconnect the breather hose from the camshaft cover **(see illustration)**.
5 Release the wiring from the clips at the rear of the cover, then unscrew the camshaft cover retaining bolts and lift the cover away. If the cover sticks, do not attempt to lever it off – instead free it by working around the cover and tapping it lightly with a soft-faced mallet **(see illustration)**.
6 Recover the camshaft cover gasket. Inspect the gasket carefully, and renew it if damage or deterioration is evident – note that the retaining bolts and seals must be pushed fully through the cover **(see illustrations)**.

4.6a Renew the cover seal if necessary

7 Clean the mating surfaces of the cylinder head and camshaft cover thoroughly, removing all traces of oil – take care to avoid damaging the surfaces as you do this.

4.6b Bolts and seals must be pushed fully through the cover before fitting the gasket

Refitting

8 Refit the camshaft cover by following the removal procedure in reverse, tightening the cover retaining bolts to the specified torque in the sequence shown **(see illustration)**.

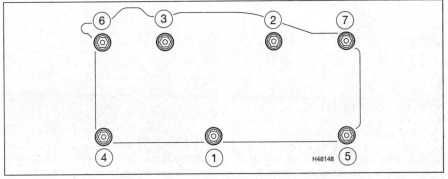

4.8 Cylinder head cover bolt tightening sequence

5.4 Undo the pulley bolts, counterholding it with a socket on the centre sprocket bolt

6.1 Pull the plastic cover upwards from the mountings

6.2 Disconnect the wiring plug and undo the retaining bolt (arrowed)

5 Crankshaft pulley – removal and refitting

Removal

1 Switch off the ignition and all electrical consumers and remove the ignition key.
2 Raise the front right-hand side of the vehicle, and support securely on axle stands (see *Jacking and vehicle support*). Remove the roadwheel.
3 Remove the securing fasteners and withdraw the lower section of the front wheel arch liner.
4 Slacken the bolts securing the crankshaft pulley to the sprocket **(see illustration)**. If necessary, the pulley can be prevented from turning by counterholding with a

spanner or socket on the crankshaft sprocket bolt.
5 Remove the auxiliary drivebelt, as described in Chapter 1B, Section 28.
6 Unscrew the bolts securing the pulley to the sprocket, and remove the pulley. Discard the bolts – new ones must be fitted.

Refitting

7 Refit the pulley over the locating peg on the crankshaft sprocket, then fit the new pulley securing bolts.
8 Refit and tension the auxiliary drivebelt as described in Chapter 1B, Section 28.
9 Prevent the crankshaft from turning as during removal, then fit the pulley securing bolts, and tighten to the specified torque.
10 Refit the wheel arch liner.
11 Refit the roadwheel and lower the vehicle to the ground.

6 Timing belt covers – removal and refitting

Upper outer cover

1 Pull the engine top cover upwards to release the mountings **(see illustration)**.
2 Disconnect the wiring plug, undo the retaining bolt, and remove the exhaust gas pressure sensor bracket by pushing it forwards **(see illustration)**.
3 Disconnect the wiring plug, unclip the fuel hoses, then release the clamps and disconnect the hoses from the filter **(see illustrations)**. Note the fitted locations of the hoses to aid refitting. Plug the openings to prevent contamination.
4 Undo the bolts/nut and remove the fuel filter assembly **(see illustration)**. Release the hose clamp, as the filter assembly is withdrawn.
5 Disconnect the fuel temperature sensor wiring plug, then release the clamp and disconnect the fuel supply pipe from the high-pressure fuel pump **(see illustration)**. Plug the openings to prevent contamination, and place a rag above the alternator to prevent fuel ingress.
6 Slide up the hose retaining clips, then undo the two retaining bolts and remove the supplementary fuel pump **(see illustration)**.
7 Disconnect the radiator outlet temperature sensor wiring plug, then release the three clips and remove the timing belt upper cover **(see illustrations)**.

6.3a Note their positions, then disconnect the hoses from the fuel filter

6.3b Plug the openings to prevent contamination

6.4 Undo the nut/bolts (arrowed) and remove the fuel filter

6.5 Disconnect the fuel supply hose and temperature sensor (arrowed)

6.6 Supplementary fuel pump retaining bolts (arrowed)

6.7a Disconnect the temperature sensor wiring plug (arrowed)

6.7b Release the clips (arrowed) . . .

6.7c . . . and manoeuvre the timing belt upper cover from place

8 Refitting is a reversal of removal, noting that the lower edge of the upper cover engages with the centre cover.

Centre outer cover

9 Remove the crankshaft pulley as described in Section 5. It is assumed that, if the centre cover is being removed, the lower cover will be also – if not, simply remove the components described in Section 5 for access to the crankshaft pulley, and leave the pulley in position.
10 Undo the retaining nuts/bolts and move the coolant pipe that lies across the centre cover, away towards the inner wing.
11 With the upper cover removed (paragraphs 1 to 6), unscrew and remove the three retaining bolts from the centre cover. Withdraw the centre cover from the engine, noting how it fits over the lower cover (see illustration). Note if the auxiliary belt tensioner is in the 'locked' position as described in the belt removal procedure, the locking drill bit/rod must be removed for access to the cover retaining bolt.
12 Refitting is a reversal of the removal procedure, using a little thread-locking compound on the retaining bolts.

Lower outer cover

13 Remove the upper and centre covers as described previously.
14 If not already done, remove the crankshaft pulley as described in Section 5.
15 Unscrew the remaining bolts securing the lower cover, and remove it (see illustration).
16 Refitting is a reversal of removal; locate the centre cover in place before fitting the top two bolts.

6.11 Centre timing belt cover bolts (arrowed)

Rear cover

17 Remove the timing belt, tensioner and sprockets as described in Section 7 and Section 8.
18 Slacken and withdraw the retaining bolts and lift the timing belt inner cover from the studs on the end of the engine, and remove it from the engine compartment.
19 Refitting is a reversal of removal.

---

7 Timing belt – removal, inspection and refitting

Removal

1 The primary function of the toothed timing belt is to drive the camshaft, but it also drives the coolant pump and high-pressure fuel pump. Should the belt slip or break in

6.15 Lower cover retaining bolts (arrowed)

service, the valve timing will be disturbed and piston-to-valve contact may occur, resulting in serious engine damage. For this reason, it is important that the timing belt is tensioned correctly, and inspected regularly for signs of wear or deterioration.
2 Switch off the ignition and all electrical consumers and remove the ignition key.
3 Set the engine to TDC on No1 cylinder as described in Section 3.
4 Slacken the three bolts securing the sprocket to the camshaft hub (see illustration).
5 Slacken the three bolts securing the sprocket to the high-pressure fuel pump (see illustration).
6 Insert a suitable Allen key into the tensioner hub, then slacken the retaining nut and rotate the tensioner hub anti-clockwise until it can be locked in place using a 2.0 mm pin/drill bit (see illustration).

7.4 Slacken the sprocket-to-hub bolts (arrowed)

7.5 Slacken the high-pressure fuel pump sprocket bolts (arrowed)

7.6 Insert and Allen key, slacken the nut, and rotate the hub anti-clockwise until a 2 mm rod/drill bit (arrowed) can be inserted to lock the hub to the pulley

7.14 Rotate the high-pressure fuel pump clockwise until a 6 mm drill bit/rod can be inserted into the housing and hub (arrowed)

7.15b . . . and camshaft sprocket bolts are at the end of the elongated holes

7 Now rotate the tensioner hub clockwise to the stop, and hand-tighten the retaining nut.

8 If the original timing belt is to be refitted, mark the running direction of the belt, to ensure correct refitting.

Caution: If the belt appears to be in good condition and can be re-used, it is essential that it is refitted the same way around, otherwise accelerated wear will result, leading to premature failure.

9 Slide the belt from the sprockets, taking care not to twist or kink the belt excessively if it is to be re-used.

Inspection

10 Examine the belt for evidence of contamination by coolant or lubricant. If this is the case, find the source of the contamination before progressing any further. Check the belt for signs of wear or damage, particularly around the leading edges of the belt teeth.

7.19 Rotate the tensioner clockwise until the pointer (arrowed) is just past the gap in the backplate

7.15a Rotate the sprockets fully clockwise until the fuel pump sprocket . . .

7.18 Timing belt routing

Renew the belt if its condition is in doubt; the cost of belt renewal is negligible compared with potential cost of the engine repairs, should the belt fail in service. The belt must be renewed if it has covered the mileage given in Chapter 1, however, if it has covered less, it is prudent to renew it regardless of condition, as a precautionary measure.

11 If the timing belt is not going to be refitted for some time, it is a wise precaution to hang a warning label on the steering wheel, to remind your self (and others) not to attempt to start the engine.

Refitting

12 Ensure that the crankshaft and camshaft are still set to TDC on No 1 cylinder, as described in Section 3. The camshaft sprocket bolts should be renewed, and slackened at this point.

13 Renew the high-pressure fuel pump

7.22 The pointer should be centred in, or within 5 mm to the right of, the gap in the backplate

sprocket bolts one at a time. They should be kept loose.

14 Using a screwdriver on the bolts heads, rotate the high-pressure fuel pump clockwise until a 6.0 mm locking pin/drill bit can be inserted into the housing adjacent to the sprocket, locking the pump in place **(see illustration)**.

15 Rotate the camshaft sprocket and high-pressure fuel pump sprocket fully clockwise so that the securing bolts are at the end of the elongated holes **(see illustrations)**.

16 Loop the timing belt loosely under the crankshaft sprocket. **Note:** *Observe any direction of rotation markings on the belt.*

17 Fit the belt around the tensioner pulley, engage the timing belt teeth with the camshaft sprockets, then manoeuvre it into position around the coolant pump sprocket and the fuel pump sprocket. Make sure that the belt teeth seat correctly on the sprockets. **Note:** *Slight adjustment to the position of the camshaft sprocket may be necessary to achieve this. Avoid bending the belt back on itself or twisting it excessively as you do this.*

18 Finally, fit the belt around the idler roller **(see illustration)**. Ensure that any slack in the belt is in the section of belt that passes over the tensioner roller.

19 Loosen the timing belt tensioner securing nut, and pull out the tensioner locking pin. Turn the tensioner clockwise with an Allen key until the pointer is just past the middle of the gap in the tensioner backplate **(see illustration)**. With the tensioner held in this position, tighten the securing nut to the specified torque and angle.

20 Counterhold the camshaft sprocket with a homemade tool to prevent any rotation, and then tighten the camshaft sprocket and fuel pump sprocket bolts to 20 Nm (15 lbf ft). Remove the sprockets locking tools and the crankshaft locking tool.

21 Using a spanner or wrench and socket on the crankshaft pulley centre bolt, rotate the crankshaft clockwise through two complete revolutions. Reset the engine to TDC on No1 cylinder, with reference to Section 3 and refit the crankshaft locking tool.

22 Check that the tensioner roller indicator arm is centred, or within a maximum of 5 mm to the right of the notch in the backplate **(see illustration)**. If not, hold the tensioner hub stationary with an Allen key, slacken the retaining nut and position the arm in the centre of the notch. Tighten the retaining nut to the specified torque. Remove the Allen key.

23 Check that the camshaft sprocket locking pin can still be inserted. **Note:** *It's very difficult to align the locking point of the fuel pump hub again. However, a misalignment of holes will not affect engine performance.*

24 If the camshaft sprocket locking pin cannot be inserted, pull the crankshaft locking tool slight away from the engine, and rotate the crankshaft *anti-clockwise* slightly past TDC. Now slowly rotate the crankshaft clockwise until the camshaft sprocket locking tool can be inserted.

25 If the locating pin of the crankshaft locking

8.4 Coolant pipe upper mounting bolt and lower mounting nut (arrowed)

8.6 Engine mounting bracket bolts (arrowed)

8.8 Ensure the lug on the backplate engages with the cut-out in the timing belt cover (arrowed)

tool is to the left of the corresponding hole, slacken the camshaft sprocket bolts, slowly rotate the crankshaft clockwise until the locking tool can be fully inserted. Tighten the camshaft sprocket bolts to 20 Nm (15 lbf ft).

26 If the locating pin of the crankshaft locking tool is to the right of the corresponding hole, slacken the camshaft sprocket bolts, rotate the crankshaft *anti-clockwise* slightly until the pin is to the left of the hole, then slowly rotate it clockwise until the lock tool can be fully inserted. Tighten the camshaft sprocket bolts to 20 Nm (15 lbf ft).

27 Remove the crankshaft and camshaft locking tools, then rotate the crankshaft two complete revolutions clockwise and check the locking tools can be reinserted. If necessary, repeat the adjustment procedure described previously.

28 Tighten the camshaft and fuel pump sprocket bolts to the specified torque.

29 The remainder of refitting is a reversal of removal.

8 Timing belt tensioner and sprockets – removal and refitting

Timing belt tensioner

Removal

1 In order to remove the timing belt tensioner, then engine mounting bracket must first be removed. Either support the engine from above using a crossbeam or an engine hoist, or support if from underneath with a trolley jack and block of wood.

2 Remove the timing belt as described in Section 7.

3 Undo the bolts and remove the right-hand engine mounting.

4 Undo the bolt securing the coolant pipe to the mounting bracket **(see illustration)**.

5 Working in the wheel arch area, undo the nut securing the lower end of the coolant pipe.

6 Undo the 3 retaining bolts and remove the engine mounting bracket **(see illustration)**.

7 Unscrew the timing belt tensioner nut, and remove the tensioner from the engine.

Refitting

8 When refitting the tensioner to the engine,

ensure that the lug on the tensioner backplate engages with the corresponding cut-out in the rear timing belt cover, then refit the tensioner nut **(see illustration)**.

9 The remainder of refitting is a reversal of removal.

Idler pulleys

Removal

10 Remove the timing belt as described in Section 7.

11 Unscrew the relevant idler pulley/roller securing bolt/nut, and then withdraw the pulley.

Refitting

12 Refit the pulley and tighten the securing bolt or nut to the specified torque. **Note:** *Renew the large roller/pulley retaining bolt (where applicable)*.

13 Refit and tension the timing belt as described in Section 7.

Crankshaft sprocket

Note: *A new crankshaft sprocket securing bolt must be used on refitting.*

Removal

14 Remove the timing belt as described in Section 7.

15 The sprocket securing bolt must now be slackened, and the crankshaft must be prevented from turning as the sprocket bolt is unscrewed. To hold the sprocket, make up a suitable tool, and bolt it to the sprocket using two bolts bolted into two of the crankshaft pulley bolt holes.

8.27 Fabricate a home-made tool to counterhold the hub. Undo the bolt . . .

16 Hold the sprocket using the tool, then slacken the sprocket securing bolt. Take care, as the bolt is very tight. Do not allow the crankshaft to turn as the bolt is slackened.

17 Unscrew the bolt, and slide the sprocket from the end of the crankshaft, noting which way round the sprocket's raised boss is fitted.

Refitting

18 Commence refitting by positioning the sprocket on the end of the crankshaft.

19 Fit a new sprocket securing bolt, then counter hold the sprocket using the method employed on removal, and tighten the bolt to the specified torque in the two stages given in the Specifications.

20 Refit the timing belt as described in Section 7.

Camshaft sprocket

Removal

21 Remove the timing belt as described in Section 7, then rotate the crankshaft 90° anti-clockwise to prevent any accidental piston-to-valve contact.

22 Unscrew and remove the three retaining bolts and remove the camshaft sprocket from the camshaft hub.

Refitting

23 Refit the sprocket ensuring that it is fitted the correct way round, as noted before removal, then insert the new sprocket bolts, and tighten by hand only at this stage.

24 If the crankshaft has been turned, turn the crankshaft clockwise 90° back to TDC.

25 Refit and tension the timing belt as described in Section 7.

Camshaft hub

Note: *VAG technicians use special tool T10051 to counter hold the hub, however it is possible to fabricate a suitable alternative.*

Removal

26 Remove the camshaft sprocket as described previously in this Section.

27 Engage special tool T10051 with the three locating holes in the face of the hub to prevent the hub from turning. If this tool is not available, fabricate a suitable alternative. Whilst holding the tool, undo the central hub retaining bolt about two turns **(see illustration)**.

8.28 . . . and slide the hub from the camshaft

8.29 Ensure the integral key aligns with the keyway in the camshaft (arrowed)

28 Slide the hub from the camshaft. If necessary, attach VW tool T10052 (or a similar three-legged puller) to the hub, and evenly tighten the puller until the hub is free of the camshaft taper (see illustration).

Refitting

29 Ensure that the camshaft taper and the hub centre are clean and dry, locate the hub on the taper, noting that the built-in key in the hub taper must align with the keyway in the camshaft taper (see illustration).
30 Hold the hub in this position with tool T10051 (or similar home-made tool), and tighten the central bolt to the specified torque.
31 Refit the camshaft sprocket as described previously in this Section.

Coolant pump sprocket

32 The coolant pump sprocket is integral with the coolant pump. Refer to Chapter 3 for details of coolant pump removal.

9 Camshaft and hydraulic tappets – removal, inspection and refitting

Note: *A new camshaft oil seal(s) will be required on refitting. VW removal tool T40094 (or similar tool) will be required to refit the camshafts – this is necessary to prevent damage to the retaining frame and cylinder head as the camshafts are refitted.*

Removal

1 Remove the camshaft hub as described in Section 8.
2 Remove the camshaft cover as described in Section 4.
3 Remove the brake vacuum pump as described in Chapter 9, Section 21.
4 Progressively unscrew the camshaft retaining frame bolts in the **reverse** of the sequence shown in illustration 9.20, and carefully remove the retaining frame.
5 Carefully lift the camshafts from the cylinder head, keeping them identified for location. Remove the oil seal from the end of the camshaft and discard it – a new one will be required for refitting.
6 Lift the rocker arms and hydraulic tappets from place. Store the rockers and tappets in a container with numbered compartments to ensure they are refitted to their correct locations. It is recommended that the tappets are kept immersed in oil for the period they are removed from the cylinder head.

Inspection

7 With the camshafts removed, examine the retaining frame and the bearing locations in the cylinder head for signs of obvious wear or pitting. If evident, a new cylinder head will probably be required. Also check that the oil supply holes in the cylinder head are free from obstructions.
8 Visually inspect the camshafts for evidence of wear on the surfaces of the lobes and journals. Normally their surfaces should be smooth and have a dull shine; look for scoring, erosion or pitting and areas that appear highly polished, indicating excessive wear. Accelerated wear will occur once the hardened exterior of the camshaft has been damaged, so always renew worn items. **Note:** *If these symptoms are visible on the tips of the camshaft lobes, check the corresponding rocker arm, as it will probably be worn as well.*
9 If the machined surfaces of the camshaft appear discoloured or blued, it is likely that it has been overheated at some point, probably due to inadequate lubrication. This may have distorted the shaft, so have the camshaft runout and endfloat checked by an automotive engine reconditioning specialist.
10 Inspect the hydraulic tappets for obvious signs of wear or damage, and renew if necessary. Check that the oil holes in the tappets are free from obstructions.

Refitting

11 Oil the rocker arms and hydraulic tappets, and then refit them to their original positions.

⚠️ *Warning: After fitting hydraulic tappets, wait a minimum of 30 minutes (or preferably, leave overnight) before starting the engine, to allow the tappets time to settle, otherwise the valve heads will strike the pistons.*

12 To set up the tool, remove the supports number 3, 4 and 5, then install the supports number 1, 2, 9 and 10 as shown (see illustrations).

9.12a The different elements of tool No T40094

9.12b Position tools No 1, 2, 9 and 10 as shown

9.14 Fit tool No 11 into the slot (arrowed)
in the end of the exhaust camshaft

9.13 Position the inlet camshaft on the tool with the bolt indent (arrowed) facing
outwards, then slide tool No 8 in to the slot in the end of the camshaft and use a 0.50 mm
feeler gauge to remove any free play

13 Position the inlet camshaft as shown with the cylinder head bolt indent facing outwards, then slide the support number 8 into the slot in the end of the camshaft and remove any free play with a 0.50 mm feeler gauge (see illustration).

14 Position the exhaust camshaft on supports numbers 9 and 10, and fit the tool No 11 into the slot in the end of the camshaft (see illustration).

15 Fit the clamping tool No T40096 to the gear on the exhaust camshaft, tightening the knurled thumb wheel until the faces of the gear teeth are in alignment. If necessary, use a 13 mm spanner (see illustration).

16 Slide the exhaust camshaft towards the inlet camshaft until the gear teeth engage.

17 Ensure the gasket faces of the retaining frame are clean, then apply a smear of clean engine oil to the bearing surfaces and lower

the frame into position over the camshafts. Ensure the bearing surfaces locate correctly on the camshafts.

18 Fit the clamping tool No T40095 over the camshafts and frame, and tighten the thumbwheels to hold the camshafts in position in the frame (see illustration).

19 Ensure the sealing surfaces of the cylinder head are clean, and then apply a 2.0 mm wide bead of sealant (D 176 501 A1 or equivalent) as shown. Take care not to apply too much sealant, ensuring the oil holes supply holes are not blocked (see illustration).

20 Slide out tool No's 8 and 11, then lift the camshafts, retaining frame and clamping tool from the tool No T40094. Place the camshafts, frame and tool in place on the cylinder head. Progressively and carefully, hand-tighten the frame retaining bolts in the sequence shown, until the retaining frame makes contact with the cylinder head over the complete surface, then

9.15 Tighten the thumbwheel to align the gear teeth. Ensure the
clamping jaw with the arrow in seated on the wider gear

9.18 Secure the camshafts in place in the frame using tool
No T40095 (arrowed)

9.19 Apply a 2.0 mm thick bead of sealant to the area shown by the thick, black line. Take care not to block the oil holes (arrowed)

9.20 Camshaft retaining frame bolt tightening sequence

tighten the bolts to the specified torque, again in the correct sequence **(see illustration)**.

21 Remove the gear aligning tool (T40096) and the clamping tool (T40095).

22 Renew the camshaft oil seal (Section 10), then drive in a new sealing cap.

23 The remainder of refitting is a reversal of removal.

10 Camshaft oil seals –
   renewal

Right-hand oil seal

1 Remove the camshaft sprocket and hub, as described in Section 8.

10.2 Bolt in a self-tapping screw, then pull the bolt and seal from place

2 Drill two small holes into the existing oil seal, diagonally opposite each other. Take great care to avoid drilling through into the seal housing or camshaft sealing surface. Thread two self-tapping screws into the holes, and using a pair of pliers, pull on the heads of the screws to extract the oil seal **(see illustration)**.

3 Clean out the seal housing and the sealing surface of the camshaft by wiping it with a lint-free cloth. Remove any swarf or burrs that may cause the seal to leak.

4 Do not lubricate the lip and outer edge of the new oil seal, push it over the camshaft until it is positioned in place above its housing. To prevent damage to the sealing lips, wrap some adhesive tape around the end of the camshaft.

11.5 Battery tray bolts (arrowed)

5 Using a hammer and a socket of suitable diameter, drive the seal squarely into its housing. **Note:** *Select a socket that bears only on the hard outer surface of the seal, not the inner lip that can easily be damaged.*

6 Refit the camshaft sprocket and its hub, as described in Section 8.

Left-hand oil seal

7 The left-hand camshaft oil seal is formed, by the brake vacuum pump seal, which is fitted to the cylinder head. Refer to Chapter 9, Section 21 for details of brake vacuum pump removal and refitting.

11 Cylinder head –
   removal, inspection
   and refitting

Note: *The cylinder head must be removed with the engine cold. New cylinder head bolts and a new cylinder head gasket will be required on refitting, and suitable studs will be required to guide the cylinder head into position – see text.*

Removal

1 Remove the battery as described in Chapter 5A, Section 3.

2 Drain the cooling system (Chapter 1B, Section 31) and engine oil (Chapter 1B, Section 3).

3 Pull the plastic cover on the top of the engine upwards from its mountings.

4 Remove the air filter housing as described in Chapter 4B, Section 2.

5 Undo the 3 bolts and remove the battery tray **(see illustration)**.

6 Remove the radiator cooling fan(s) and shroud as described in Chapter 3, Section 5.

7 Undo the bolts and remove the air hose/duct from the intercooler to the turbocharger. Release the wiring looms from the clips as necessary to enable the duct to be manoeuvred from place.

8 Remove the camshaft cover as described in Section 4.

9 Remove the camshaft sprocket and hub as described in Section 8.

10 Disconnect the wiring plugs from the EGR valve and throttle body/intake manifold flap.

11 Disconnect the charge air pressure sensor wiring plug, then undo the 2 retaining bolts, release the clamps, and remove the charge air pipe and hose from the front of the engine **(see illustrations)**.

12 Undo the bolt securing the oil level dipstick guide tube to the throttle body/intake manifold flap **(see illustration)**.

13 Undo the 2 bolts securing the connecting pipe to the EGR valve **(see illustration)**.

14 Undo the front retaining bolt, twist the charge air pipe clockwise and disconnect it from the turbocharger. Note their fitted positions, and unclip the vacuum hoses from the charge air pipe **(see illustration)**.

15 Apply a little lubrication spray to the rubber sleeve, pull up the pipe from the vacuum pump, then undo the 4 retaining bolts and

11.11a Disconnect the pressure sensor wiring plug (arrowed) . . .

11.11b . . . then remove the charge air pipe and hose (arrowed)

11.12 Oil level dipstick guide tube bolt (arrowed)

11.13 EGR pipe-to-valve bolts (arrowed)

11.14 Charge air pipe retaining bolt (arrowed). Note the position of the vacuum hoses

11.15 With some lubrication, the hose connection pulls up from the vacuum pump

remove the vacuum pump from the left-hand end of the cylinder head (see illustration). Renew the pump-to-cylinder head seal.

16 Disconnect the coolant temperature sensor wiring plug at the left-hand end of the cylinder head, and release the wiring loom from any retaining clips.

17 Disconnect the gear change cables from the levers on the transmission, as described in Chapter 7A, Section 2 (manual transmission), or Chapter 7B, Section 4 (DSG transmission).

18 Undo the bolts/nut, securing the gear-change bracket to the top of the transmission. Move the bracket and cables to one side.

19 Undo the bolts securing the EGR pipe to the cooler at the left-hand end of the engine, and the nut securing the bracket to the cylinder head, then remove the pipe (see illustration). Recover the gasket at each end.

20 Working underneath the vehicle, slacken the Allen bolt and release the clamp securing the diesel particulate filter/catalytic converter to the turbocharger, then undo the bolts/nuts securing the brackets to the cylinder block/head and lay the filter/converter to one side.

21 Undo the nuts and multi-spline bolts securing the EGR pipe to the right-hand end of the exhaust manifold and EGR cooler (see illustration). Remove the pipe and recover the gaskets.

22 Trace the exhaust manifold gas temperature sensor wiring back, releasing it from any retaining clips, disconnect its wiring plug at the bulkhead, and slide it from the retaining bracket. Unclip the wiring loom from the top of the turbocharger heat shield.

23 Undo the bolt securing the support

bracket/oil return pipe to the underside of the turbocharger, and then undo the bolt securing the top of the support bracket to the underside of the turbocharger. Now pull and twist the support bracket to disconnect it from the oil

11.19 EGR pipe-to-cooler bolts (arrowed)

return pipe at the top. Remove the pipe/bracket (see illustrations). Note the O-ring and copper sealing washer on the lower banjo bolt, and the two O-rings fitted to the base of the oil return pipe still fitted to the turbocharger.

11.21 Remove the EGR pipe between the manifold and cooler

11.23a Undo the banjo bolt at the base of the turbocharger support bracket/oil return pipe and the bolt at the top

11.23b Note the 2 O-ring seals (arrowed) at the base of the oil return pipe

11.26 Undo the bolt (arrowed) securing the timing belt guard

11.27 Undo the boost pressure solenoid valve nuts (arrowed)

11.28 Undo the cylinder head bolts using a M12 multi-splined (12-pointed star) tool

24 Note their fitted locations, then release the clamps and disconnect the various coolant hoses from the cylinder head.

25 Undo the bolt securing the turbocharger oil supply pipe bracket at the left-hand end of the cylinder head, the nut securing the bracket on the rear of the head, then undo the union bolts and remove the pipe. Renew any seals.

26 Undo the bolt securing the timing belt guard adjacent to the timing belt tensioner, and the bolt securing the camshaft position sensor, then remove the tensioner retaining nut **(see illustration)**.

27 Disconnect the turbocharger wastegate position sensor wiring plug, and the intake manifold changeover valve wiring plug. Note their fitted positions and disconnect the vacuum hoses from the EGR cooler (where the plastic pipe joins the metal pipe at the back of the cylinder head) and the turbocharger wastegate actuator. Undo the nuts securing the boost pressure solenoid valve to the bulkhead. Release the loom wiring plug, lay the wiring loom and vacuum hoses over the front of the engine, clear of the cylinder head **(see illustration)**. Make a final check to ensure all relevant wiring and vacuum hoses have been disconnected. Note the loom/hose routing to aid refitting.

28 Using an M12 multi-splined tool (12-pointed star), undo the cylinder head bolts, working from the outside-in, evenly and gradually **(see illustration)**. Remove the bolts and recover the washers. Check that nothing remains connected, and starting at the gearbox side, lift the cylinder head from

the engine block, sliding the belt tensioner from the mounting stud as the cylinder head is removed. Seek assistance if possible, as it is a heavy assembly, especially as it is being removed complete with the manifolds.

29 Remove the gasket from the top of the block, noting the locating dowels. If the dowels are a loose fit, remove them and store them with the head for safekeeping. Do not discard the gasket yet – it will be needed for identification purposes. If desired, the manifolds can be removed from the cylinder head with reference to Chapter 4B, Section 5 (inlet manifold) or Chapter 4D, Section 5 (turbocharger/exhaust manifold).

Inspection

30 Dismantling and inspection of the cylinder head is covered in Chapter 2E, Section 6.

Cylinder head gasket selection

Note: *A dial test indicator (DTI) will be required for this operation.*

31 Examine the old cylinder head gasket for manufacturer's identification markings **(see illustration)**. These will be in the form of holes, and a part number on the edge of the gasket. Unless new pistons have been fitted, the new cylinder head gasket must be of the same type as the old one.

32 If new piston assemblies have been fitted as part of an engine overhaul, or if a new short engine is to be fitted, the projection of the piston crowns above the cylinder head mating face of the cylinder block at TDC must be measured. This measurement is used to determine the thickness of the new cylinder head gasket required.

33 Anchor a dial test indicator (DTI) to the

top face (cylinder head gasket mating face) of the cylinder block, and zero the gauge on the gasket mating face.

34 Rest the gauge probe on No 1 piston crown, and turn the crankshaft slowly by hand until the piston reaches TDC. Measure and record the maximum piston projection at TDC **(see illustration)**.

35 Repeat the measurement for the remaining pistons, and record the results.

36 If the measurements differ from piston-to-piston, take the highest figure, and use this to determine the thickness of the head gasket required as follows:

Piston projection	Gasket identification (number of holes)
0.91 to 1.00 mm	1
1.01 to 1.10 mm	2
1.11 to 1.20 mm	3

37 Purchase a new gasket according to the results of the measurements.

Refitting

38 The mating faces of the cylinder head and block must be perfectly clean before refitting the head. Use a scraper to remove all traces of gasket and carbon, also clean the tops of the pistons. Take particular care with the aluminium surfaces, as the soft metal is easily damaged.

39 Make sure that debris is not allowed to enter the oil and water passages – this is particularly important for the oil circuit, as carbon could block the oil supply to the camshaft and crankshaft bearings. Using adhesive tape and paper, seal the water, oil and bolt holes in the cylinder block.

40 To prevent carbon entering the gap between the pistons and bores, smear a little grease in the gap. After cleaning a piston, rotate the crankshaft to that the piston moves down the bore, and then wipe out the grease and carbon with a cloth rag. Clean the other piston crowns in the same way.

41 Check the head and block for nicks, deep scratches and other damage. If slight, they may be removed carefully with a file. More serious damage may be repaired by machining, but this is a specialist job.

42 If warpage of the cylinder head is suspected, use a straight-edge to check it for distortion, as described in Chapter 2E, Section 7.

43 Ensure that the cylinder head bolt holes in

11.31 The holes (arrowed) identify the thickness of the cylinder head gasket

11.34 Measure the piston protrusion using a DTI guage

the crankcase are clean and free of oil. Syringe or soak up any oil left in the bolt holes. This is most important in order that the correct bolt tightening torque can be applied, and to prevent the possibility of the block being cracked by hydraulic pressure when the bolts are tightened.

44 Turn the crankshaft anti-clockwise all the pistons at an equal height, approximately halfway down their bores from the TDC position (see Section 3). This will eliminate any risk of piston-to-valve contact as the cylinder head is refitted.

45 Where applicable, refit the manifolds with reference to Chapter 4B, Section 5 (inlet manifold) or Chapter 4D, Section 5 (turbocharger/exhaust manifold).

46 Ensure that the cylinder head locating dowels are in place in the cylinder block, and then fit the new cylinder head gasket over the dowels, ensuring that the part number is uppermost **(see illustration)**. Note that VW recommend that the gasket is only removed from its packaging immediately prior to fitting.

47 Lower the cylinder head into position on the gasket, ensuring that it engages correctly over the dowels. Refit the timing belt tensioner as the cylinder head is refitted.

48 Fit the washers in place then fit the new cylinder head bolts to the locations, and bolt them in as far as possible by hand. Do not oil the bolt threads.

49 Working progressively, in sequence, tighten all the cylinder head bolts to the specified Stage 1 torque **(see illustrations)**.

50 Again working progressively, in sequence, tighten all the cylinder head bolts to the specified Stage 2 torque.

51 Tighten all the cylinder head bolts, in sequence, through the specified Stage 3 angle **(see illustration)**.

52 Finally, tighten all the cylinder head bolts, in sequence, through the specified Stage 4 angle.

53 The remainder of the refitting procedure is a reversal of the removal procedure, noting the following points:

a) *Tighten all fasteners to their specified torque where given.*

b) *Renew all seals and gaskets.*

c) *Refill the cooling system, as described in Chapter 1B, Section 31.*

d) *Refill the engine oil, as described in Chapter 1B, Section 3.*

e) *Ensure all wiring is correctly routed.*

11.46 Ensure the dowels are in place, then fit the new gasket with the part number uppermost (arrowed)

11.49b Tighten the cylinder head bolts to the Stage 1 torque

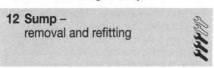

12 Sump –
removal and refitting

Removal

1 Apply the handbrake, then jack up the front of the vehicle and support securely on axle stands (see *Jacking and vehicle support*).

2 Remove the securing bolts and withdraw the engine undershield(s).

3 Drain the engine oil as described in Chapter 1B, Section 3.

4 Release the clamp, raise the retaining clip and remove the air duct from the intercooler outlet **(see illustration)**.

5 Undo the retaining bolts, release the clamp and remove the charge air pipe from the front of the cylinder block **(see illustration**

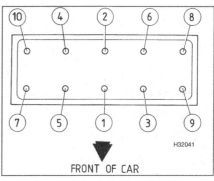

11.49a Cylinder head bolt tightening sequence

11.51 Use an angle-tightening gauge

11.11a and 11.11b). Disconnect the charge air pressure sensor wiring plug as the pipe is withdrawn.

6 Undo the retaining bolt and move the electric coolant circulation pump to one side **(see illustration)**.

7 Undo the bolt securing the turbo-to-intercooler air pipe to the sump.

8 Disconnect the wiring connector from the oil level/temperature sender in the sump.

9 Pull the sump insulation cover downwards at the rear to release the retaining clips, then prise down the centre clip and pull the clip on the front side of the cover downwards (where fitted) **(see illustrations)**.

10 Unscrew and remove the bolts securing the sump to the cylinder block, and the bolts securing the sump to the transmission casing, then withdraw the sump. If necessary, release the sump by tapping with a soft-faced hammer.

12.4 Raise the clip (arrowed) and disconnect the air duct from the intercooler

12.6 Electric coolant circulation pump retaining bolt (arrowed)

12.9a Pull the insulation down at the rear to release the clips (arrowed)

12.9b At the front, prise down the centre pin and pull the clip downwards (arrowed)

Refitting

11 Begin refitting by thoroughly cleaning the mating faces of the sump and cylinder block. Ensure that all traces of old sealant are removed.
12 Ensure that the cylinder block mating face of the sump is free from all traces of old sealant, oil and grease, and then apply a 2.0 to 3.0 mm thick bead of silicone sealant (VW D 176 404 A2 or equivalent) to the sump (**see illustration**). Note that the sealant should be run around the inside of the bolt holes in the sump. The sump must be fitted within 5 minutes of applying the sealant.
13 Offer the sump up to the cylinder block, then refit the sump-to-cylinder block bolts, and lightly tighten them by hand, working progressively in a diagonal sequence. **Note:** *If the sump is being refitted with the engine and transmission separated, make sure that the sump is flush with the flywheel end of the cylinder block.*

H46180

12.12 Apply a bead of sealant around the inside of the bolt holes

14 Refit the sump-to-transmission casing bolts, and tighten them lightly, using a socket.
15 Again working in a diagonal sequence, lightly tighten the sump-to-cylinder block bolts, using a socket.
16 Tighten the sump-to-transmission casing bolts to the specified torque.

17 Working in a diagonal sequence, progressively tighten the sump-to-cylinder block bolts to the specified torque.
18 The remainder of refitting is a reversal of removal, noting to allow at least 30 minutes from the time of refitting the sump for the sealant to dry, then refill the engine with oil, with reference to Chapter 1B, Section 3.

13 Oil pump and balance shaft assembly – removal, inspection and refitting

Removal

1 Remove the sump as described in Section 12.

Oil pump

2 Remove the retaining circlip, then pull the oil pump shaft out using an M3 bolt (**see illustrations**).
3 Undo the retaining bolts, and then detach the pick-up pipe from the pump (**see illustration**).
4 Undo the bolts and detach the oil pump from the balance shaft assembly (**see illustration**).

Balance shaft assembly

5 Lock the camshafts and crankshaft at TDC on No 1 cylinder as described in Section 3.
6 Working gradually and evenly, undo the retaining bolts and detach the balance shaft assembly from the base of the cylinder block.

Inspection

7 At the time of writing, it would appear that no parts are available for the oil pump or balance shaft assembly. If defective, the oil pump or balance shaft assembly must be renewed. Consult a VW dealer or parts specialist.

Refitting

Oil pump

8 Refit the pump to the balance shaft assembly and tighten the retaining bolts to the specified torque.
9 Refit the oil pick-up pipe using a new O-ring, then tighten the retaining bolts to the specified torque (**see illustration**).
10 Push the driveshaft into place, and secure it with the circlip.
11 The remainder of refitting is a reversal of removal.

13.2a Remove the circlip . . .

13.2b . . . and pull out the oil pump shaft using an M3 bolt

13.3 Oil pump pick-up pipe bolts (arrowed)

13.4 Oil pump mounting bolts (arrowed)

13.9 Renew the pick-up pipe O-ring seal

13.12a Rotate the balance shaft until the groove (arrowed) on the end of the rear shaft is vertical . . .

13.12b . . . and tool No T10255 . . .

13.12c . . . can be fitted

Balance shaft assembly

Note: *If the original balance shaft assembly is being refitted, it's essential that neither the drivegear on the crankshaft or the crankshaft itself has been renewed, or the idler gear bolt has been slackened. If they have, proceed under the heading for the installation of a new balance shaft assembly.*

Refitting the original assembly

12 Rotate the balance shaft until VW tool No T10255 can be fitted into the groove on the left-hand end of the rear shaft **(see illustrations)**.
13 Ensure the engine is still locked at TDC for No 1 cylinder, and then position the balance shaft assembly over the locating dowels on the base of the cylinder block. The idler gear must engage with the drivegear of the crankshaft, and there must be noticeable backlash.
14 Fit the new balance shaft assembly retaining bolts, and working from the centre outwards, tighten them to the specified torque. Remove the VW tool.
15 The remainder of refitting is a reversal of removal.

Fitting a new balance shaft assembly

16 New balance shaft assemblies are supplied with an idler gear with a special coating. Once fitted, the coating wears down to give the correct backlash between the gears.
17 Ensure the engine is still locked at TDC for No 1 cylinder as described in Section 3.
18 Slacken the idler gear retaining bolt 90°.
19 Position the balance shaft assembly over the locating dowels on the base of the cylinder block, ensuring the white mark on the idler gear is centrally aligned with the crankshaft drivegear. Idler gears not marked with a white mark can be installed in any position.
20 Fit the new balance shaft assembly retaining bolts, and working from the centre outwards, tighten them to the specified torque.
21 Rotate the balance shaft until VW tool No T10255 can be fitted into the groove on the left-hand end of the rear shaft **(see illustration 13.12a, 13.12b and 13.12c)**.
22 Fit the balance shaft drivegear onto the shaft so the holes in the gear align with the holes in the shaft. Tighten the retaining bolts to the specified torque.

23 Have an assistant push the idler gear between the two gears to remove any backlash. At the same time, rotate the balance shaft anti-clockwise slightly, and tighten the idler gear retaining bolt to the specified torque. Remove the balance shaft locking tool.
24 The remainder of refitting is a reversal of removal.

14 Flywheel – removal, inspection and refitting

Removal

1 On manual transmission models, remove the transmission (see Chapter 7A, Section 3) and clutch (see Chapter 6, Section 6).
2 On automatic transmission models, remove the semi-automatic (DSG) transmission as described in Chapter 7B, Section 2.
3 Manual models are fitted with a dual-mass flywheel, which can only be fitted in one position due to the offset of the mounting bolt holes in the end of the crankshaft.
4 Rotate the outside of the dual-mass flywheel so that the bolts align with the holes (if necessary).
5 Unscrew the bolts and remove the flywheel. Use a locking tool to counterhold the flywheel **(see illustration)**. Discard the bolts, as new ones must be fitted. **Note:** *In order not to damage the flywheel, do not allow the bolt heads to make contact with the flywheel during the unscrewing procedure.*

14.5 Use a locking tool to counterhold the flywheel

Inspection

6 Check the flywheel for wear and damage. Examine the starter ring gear for excessive wear to the teeth. If the driveplate or its ring gear is damaged, the complete driveplate must be renewed. The flywheel ring gear, however, may be renewed separately from the flywheel, but the work should be entrusted to a VW dealer. If the clutch friction face is discoloured or scored excessively, it may be possible to regrind it, but this work should also be entrusted to a VW dealer.
7 The following are *guidelines* only, but should indicate whether professional inspection is necessary. The dual-mass flywheel should be checked as follows:
   There should be no cracks in the drive surface of the flywheel. If cracks are evident, the flywheel may need renewing.

Warpage
   Place a straightedge across the face of the drive surface, and check by trying to insert a feeler gauge between the straightedge and the drive surface **(see illustration)**. The flywheel will normally warp like a bowl – i.e. higher on the outer edge. If the warpage is more than 0.40 mm, the flywheel may need renewing.

Free rotational movement
   This is the distance the drive surface of the flywheel can be turned independently of the flywheel primary element, using finger effort alone. Move the drive surface in one direction and make a mark where the locating pin aligns with the flywheel edge. Move the drive surface

14.7a Flywheel warpage check – see text

14.7b Flywheel free rotational movement check alignment marks – see text

14.7c Flywheel lateral movement check marks – see text

in the other direction (finger pressure only) and make another mark **(see illustration)**. The total of free movement should not exceed 20.0 mm. If it's more, the flywheel may need renewing.

Total rotational movement

This is the total distance the drive surface can be turned independently of the flywheel primary element. Insert two bolts into the clutch pressure plate/damper unit mounting holes, and with the crankshaft/flywheel held stationary, use a lever/pry bar between the bolts and use some effort to move the drive surface fully in one direction – make a mark where the locating pin aligns with the flywheel edge. Now force the drive surface fully in the opposite direction, and make another mark. The total rotational movement should not exceed 44.0 mm. If it does, have the flywheel professionally inspected.

Lateral movement

The lateral movement (up and down) of the drive surface in relation to the primary element of the flywheel should not exceed 2.0 mm. If it does, the flywheel may need renewing. This can be checked by pressing the drive surface down on one side into the flywheel (flywheel horizontal) and making an alignment mark between the drive surface and the inner edge of the primary element. Now press down on the opposite side of the drive surface, and make another mark above the original one. The difference between the two marks is the lateral movement **(see illustration)**.

Refitting

8 Refitting is a reversal of removal. Use new bolts when refitting the flywheel or driveplate, and coat the threads of the bolts with locking fluid before inserting them. Tighten them to the specified torque.

---

15 Crankshaft oil seals – renewal

Note: *The oil seals are a PTFE (Teflon) type and are fitted dry, without using any grease or oil. These have a wider sealing lip and have been introduced instead of the coil spring type oil seal.*

Timing belt end oil seal

1 Remove the timing belt as described in Section 7, and the crankshaft sprocket with reference to Section 8.

2 To remove the seal without removing the housing, drill two small holes diagonally opposite each other, insert self-tapping screws, and pull on the heads of the screws with pliers **(see illustration)**.

3 Alternatively, to remove the oil seal complete with its housing, proceed as follows.

a) *Remove the sump as described in Section 12. This is necessary to ensure a satisfactory seal between the sump and oil seal housing on refitting.*

b) *Unscrew and remove the oil seal housing.*

c) *Working on the bench, lever the oil seal from the housing using a suitable*

screwdriver. Take care not to damage the seal seating in the housing **(see illustration)**.

4 Thoroughly clean the oil seal seating in the housing.

5 Wind a length of tape around the end of the crankshaft to protect the oil seal lips as the seal (and housing, where applicable) is fitted.

6 Fit a new oil seal to the housing, pressing or driving it into position using a socket or tube of suitable diameter. Ensure that the socket or tube bears only on the hard outer ring of the seal, and take care not to damage the seal lips. Press or drive the seal into position until it is seated on the shoulder in the housing. Make sure that the closed end of the seal is facing outwards.

7 If the oil seal housing has been removed, proceed as follows, otherwise proceed to paragraph 11.

8 Clean all traces of old sealant from the crankshaft oil seal housing and the cylinder block, then coat the cylinder block mating faces of the oil seal housing with a 2.0 to 3.0 mm thick bead of silicone sealant (VW D 176 404 A2, or equivalent). Note that the seal housing must be refitted within 5 minutes of applying the sealant.

Caution: DO NOT put excessive amounts of sealant onto the housing as it may get into the sump and block the oil pick-up pipe.

9 Refit the oil seal housing, and tighten the bolts progressively to the specified torque **(see illustration)**.

10 Refit the sump as described in Section 12.

11 Refit the crankshaft sprocket with reference to Section 8, and the timing belt as described in Section 7.

Flywheel end oil seal

Note: *In these engines, the seal, sealing flange and sender wheel are a complete unit. Special tools are required to refit the sealing flange, and press the sender wheel onto the end of the crankshaft. It is not possible to accurately fit these parts without the tools, which may be available from VW (part No T10134) and are available from aftermarket automotive tool specialists.*

12 Remove the flywheel as described in Section 14, then prise the intermediate plate from the locating dowels on the cylinder block.

15.2 Pull the screw and seal from place using pliers

15.3 Prise the oil seal from the crankshaft oil seal housing

15.9 Slide the oil seal housing over the end of the crankshaft

13 Undo the bolts securing the sealing flange to the cylinder block **(see illustration)**.

14 Insert three 6 x 35 mm bolts into the threaded holes in the sealing flange. Tighten the bolts gradually and evenly, and press the sealing flange and sender wheel from the crankshaft/cylinder block **(see illustration)**. The seal, sender wheel and sealing flange are supplied as a complete unit.

15 Ensure the mating face of the cylinder block is clean and free from debris. The new sealing flange/seal/sender wheel assembly is supplied with a sealing lip support ring, which serves as a fitting sleeve, and must not be removed prior to installation. Equally, the sender wheel must not be separated from the assembly.

16 If using the VW tool, proceed as follows. If using an aftermarket tool specialist's product, follow the instructions supplied with the tool. Rotate the large spindle nut until it's level with the end of the clamping surface of the spindle, then clamp the spindle in a vice **(see illustrations)**.

17 Press the tool housing downwards until it rests on the nut and washer. Rotate the nut until the inner part of the tool is at the same height as the housing **(see illustration)**.

18 Remove the seal securing clip. The hole on the sender wheel must align with the marking on the sealing flange **(see illustrations)**.

19 Place the flange outer side down on a clean, flat surface, then press the seal guide fitting sleeve (supplied ready fitted), housing, and sender wheel downwards until all the

15.13 Sealing flange bolts (arrowed)

15.16a Rotate the nut until it is level with the end of the clamping surface (arrowed) . . .

components are flat on the surface. In this position the upper edge of the sender wheel should be level with the edge of the sealing flange **(see illustrations)**.

20 Place the sealing flange on the assembly tool, so the pin locates in the hole in the sender wheel **(see illustration)**.

21 Push the sealing flange and guide fitting

15.14 Bolt in three 6 x 35 mm bolts (arrowed) and draw the sealing flange and sender wheel from place

15.16b . . . then clamp it in a vice

15.17 Rotate the nut until the inner part of the tool is flush with the housing (arrowed)

15.18a Remove the securing clip . . .

15.18b . . . the hole in the sender wheel should align with the marking on the flange (arrowed)

15.19a Press the assembly downwards on a clean, flat surface . . .

15.19b . . . so the upper edge of the sender wheel is level with the edge of the flange (arrowed)

15.20 Fit the flange to the tool, ensuring the pin locates in the hole (arrowed)

15.21 With the pin engaged in the hole, tighten the 3 knurled bolts to secure the flange to the tool

15.23 Unscrew the nut to the end of the thread, and push the spindle in as far as possible

15.24 Hand-tighten the Allen bolts to secure the tool to the crankshaft (arrowed)

sleeve against the tool whilst tightening the 3 knurled bolts. Ensure the pin is still located in the sender wheel **(see illustration)**.

22 Ensure the end of the crankshaft is clean, and is locked at TDC on No 1 cylinder as described in Section 3.

23 Unscrew the large nut to the end of the spindle threads, then press the spindle inwards as far as possible **(see illustration)**.

24 Align the flat side of the assembly with the sump flange, then secure the tool to the crankshaft using the integral Allen bolts **(see illustration)**. Only hand-tighten the bolts.

25 Insert two M7 x 35 mm bolts to guide the sealing flange to the cylinder block **(see illustration)**.

26 Using hand-pressure alone, push the tool assembly onto the crankshaft until the seal guide fitting sleeve contacts the crankshaft flange, then push the guide pin (black knob)

into the hole in the crankshaft. This is to ensure the sender wheel reaches its correct installation position **(see illustration)**.

27 Rotate the large nut until it makes contact with the tool housing, then tighten it to 35 Nm (26 lbf ft). After tightening this nut, a small air gap must still be present between the sealing flange and cylinder block **(see illustration)**.

28 Unscrew the large nut; the two M7 x 35 mm bolts, the three knurled bolts and the Allen bolts securing the tool to the crankshaft. Remove the tool, and pull the seal guide fitting sleeve from place (if it didn't come out with the tool).

29 Use a vernier caliper or feeler gauge to measure the fitted depth of the sender wheel in relation to the crankshaft flange **(see illustration)**. The correct depth is 0.5 mm.

30 If the gap is correct, fit the sealing flange bolts and tighten them to the specified torque.

31 If the gap is too small, re-attach the tool to the sealing flange and crankshaft, then refit the two M7 x 35 mm guide bolts to the flange. Tighten the large spindle nut to 40 Nm (30 lbf ft), remove the tool and measure the air gap. If the gap is still too small, re-attach the tool and tighten the spindle nut to 45 Nm (33 lbf ft). Measure the gap again. When the gap is correct, refit the flange retaining bolts, and tighten them to the specified torque.

32 The remainder of refitting is a reversal of removal.

16 Engine/transmission mountings – inspection and renewal

Inspection

1 If improved access is required, jack up the front of the vehicle, and support it securely on axle stands (see *Jacking and vehicle support*). Remove the engine top cover, which also incorporates the air filter, and then remove the engine undershield(s).

2 Check the mounting rubbers to see if they are cracked, hardened or separated from the metal at any point; renew the mounting if any such damage or deterioration is evident.

3 Check that all the mountings are securely tightened; use a torque wrench to check if possible.

4 Using a large screwdriver or a crowbar, check for wear in the mounting by carefully levering against it to check for free play. Where this is not possible, enlist the aid of an assistant to move the engine/transmission back-and-forth, or from side-to-side, whilst you observe the mounting. While some free play is to be expected, even from new components, excessive wear should be obvious. If excessive free play is found, check first that the fasteners are correctly secured, and then renew any worn components as described in the following paragraphs.

Renewal

Note: *New mounting securing bolts will be required on refitting.*

Right-hand mounting

5 Attach a hoist and lifting tackle to the engine lifting brackets on the cylinder head, and raise

15.25 Use 2 M7 x 35 mm bolts (arrowed) to guide the sealing flange

15.26 Push the black knob (arrowed) into the hole in the crankshaft

15.27 After tightening the spindle nut there should be an air gap between the sealing flange and the cylinder block (arrowed)

15.29 Measure the fitted depth of the sender wheel in relation to the end of the crankshaft

16.7 Unbolt the supplementary fuel pump from the top of the mounting

16.8 Undo the filter retaining bolts/nut - arrowed

16.9 Right-hand engine mounting

the hoist to just take the weight of the engine. Alternatively the engine can be supported on a trolley jack under the engine. Use a block of wood between the sump and the head of the jack, to prevent any damage to the sump.

6 For improved access, unscrew the coolant reservoir and move it to one side, leaving the coolant hoses connected.

7 Where fitted, undo the retaining bolts and move the supplementary fuel pump to one side (see illustration). For further information see Chapter 4B, Section 9.

8 Undo the retaining bolts and move the fuel filter to one side (see illustration). Where applicable, move any wiring harnesses, pipes or hoses to one side to enable removal of the engine mounting.

9 Unscrew the bolts securing the mounting to the engine bracket, and then unscrew the bolts securing it to the body. Also, unscrew the movement limiter. Withdraw the mounting from the engine compartment (see illustration).

10 Refitting is a reversal of removal, bearing in mind the following points.
a) Use new securing bolts.
b) There must be at least 10 mm between the engine mounting bracket and the right-hand side chassis member (see illustration).
c) The side of the mounting support arm

must be parallel to the side of the engine mounting bracket.
d) Tighten all fixings to the specified torque.

Left-hand mounting

11 Remove the engine top cover.

12 Attach a hoist and lifting tackle to the engine lifting brackets on the cylinder head, and raise the hoist to just take the weight of the engine and transmission. Alternatively the engine can be supported on a trolley jack under the transmission. Use a block of wood between the transmission and the head of the jack, to prevent any damage to the transmission.

13 Remove the battery and battery tray, as described in Chapter 5A, Section 3.

14 Unscrew the bolts securing the mounting to the transmission, and the remaining bolts securing the mounting to the body, then lift the mounting from the engine compartment.

15 Refitting is a reversal of removal, bearing in mind the following points:
a) Use new mounting bolts.
b) The edges of the mounting support arm must be parallel to the edge of the mounting.
c) Tighten all fixings to the specified torque.

Rear mounting (torque arm)

16 Apply the handbrake, then jack up the

front of the vehicle and support securely on axle stands (see Jacking and vehicle support). Remove the engine undershield(s) for access to the rear mounting (torque arm).

17 Support the rear of the transmission beneath the final drive housing. To do this, use a trolley jack and block of wood, or alternatively wedge a block of wood between the transmission and the subframe.

18 Working under the vehicle, unscrew and remove the bolt securing the mounting to the subframe.

19 Unscrew the two bolts securing the mounting to the transmission, then withdraw the mounting from under the vehicle (see illustration).

20 Refitting is a reversal of removal, but use new mounting securing bolts, and tighten all fixings to the specified torque.

17 Engine oil cooler/ filter housing – removal and refitting

Removal

Engine codes CFFA, CFFB & CFGB

1 The oil cooler is mounted on the lower part of the oil filter housing on the front of

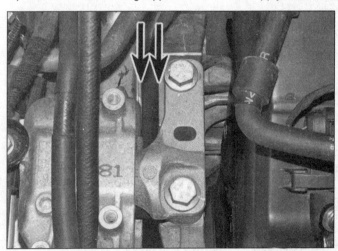

16.10 There must be at least 10 mm between the bracket and the chassis member (arrowed)

16.19 Rear lower mounting arm-to-transmission bolts (arrowed)

17.5 Oil filter/cooler mounting details

1 Oil cooler securing plate	9 Oil pressure relief valve piston (not on all models)	15 Oil supply pipe to turbo
2 O-ring		16 Banjo bolt – turbo (or sealing plug – non-turbo models)
3 Oil cooler	10 Oil pressure warning light switch	
4 O-ring	11 Gasket	17 Oil filter cover
5 Washer	12 Mounting bolt	18 O-ring
6 Sealing plug	13 Oil filter housing	19 Oil filter
7 Sealing plug	14 Seal	
8 Oil pressure relief valve spring (not on all models)		

18.1 Oil pressure warning light switch on filter housing

18 Oil pressure warning light switch – removal and refitting

Removal

Engine codes CBAA, CBAB & CBBB

1 The oil pressure warning light switch is fitted to the oil filter housing **(see illustration)**. Remove the engine top cover to gain access to the switch (see Section 4).

2 Disconnect the wiring connector and wipe clean the area around the switch.

3 Unscrew the switch from the filter housing and remove it, along with its sealing washer. If the switch is to be left removed from the engine for any length of time, plug the oil filter housing aperture.

Engine codes CFFA, CFFB & CFGB

4 The oil pressure warning light switch is fitted to the left-hand rear of the cylinder head, which is the same as the 1.6 litre diesel engine. Refer to Chapter 2C, Section 18, for the removal refitting procedure.

Refitting

5 Examine the sealing washer for signs of damage or deterioration and if necessary renew.

6 Refit the switch, complete with washer, and tighten it to the specified torque.

7 Securely reconnect the wiring connector then check and, if necessary, top-up the engine oil as described in *Weekly checks*. On completion, refit the engine top cover(s).

the cylinder block, which is the same as the 1.6 litre diesel engine. Refer to Chapter 2C, Section 17, for the removal refitting procedure

Engine codes CBAA, CBAB & CBBB

2 The oil cooler is mounted on the lower part of the oil filter housing on the front of the cylinder block.

3 Position a container beneath the oil filter housing to catch escaping oil and coolant.

4 Clamp the oil cooler coolant hoses to minimise coolant spillage, and disconnect them from the top of the cooler. If required, drain the cooling system as described in Chapter 1B, Section 31.

5 Unscrew the oil cooler centre bolt and

lower the oil cooler from oil filter housing **(see illustration)**. Recover the O-rings from between the cooler and the oil filter housing, new ones will be required for refitting.

6 If required, undo the retaining bolts and remove the oil filter housing from the cylinder block.

Refitting

7 Refitting is a reversal of removal, bearing in mind the following points:
  a) *Use new oil cooler and housing O-rings.*
  b) *Tighten the oil cooler and filter housing bolts to the correct torque.*
  c) *On completion, check and if necessary top-up the oil and coolant levels.*

19 Oil level/temperature sender – removal and refitting

The oil level/temperature sender is fitted to bottom of the sump, which is the same as the 1.6 litre diesel engine. Refer to Chapter 2C, Section 19, for the removal refitting procedure

Chapter 2 Part E:
Engine removal and overhaul procedures

Contents

Degrees of difficulty

Easy, suitable for novice with little experience	**Fairly easy,** suitable for beginner with some experience	**Fairly difficult,** suitable for competent DIY mechanic	**Difficult,** suitable for experienced DIY mechanic	**Very difficult,** suitable for expert DIY or professional

Specifications

Engine codes*

1.4 litre petrol engines:

Non-turbocharged engines	CGGA & BUD
Turbo-charged engines	CAXA
1.6 litre diesel engines	CAYB and CAYC
2.0 litre diesel engines	CBAA, CBAB, CBBB, CFFA, CFFB and CFGB

* Note: *See 'Vehicle identification' at the end of this manual for the location of engine code markings.*

Piston rings

	New	Wear limit
End gaps:		
Petrol engines:		
1.4 litre CGGA & BUD:		
Top compression ring	0.20 to 0.50 mm	1.0 mm
Lower compression ring	0.40 to 0.70 mm	1.0 mm
Oil scraper ring	0.40 to 1.40 mm	N/A
1.4 litre CAXA:		
Top compression ring	0.20 to 0.40 mm	1.0 mm
Lower compression ring	0.40 to 0.60 mm	1.0 mm
Oil scraper ring	0.20 to 0.80 mm	N/A
Diesel engines:		
1.6 litre:		
Compression rings	0.20 to 0.40 mm	1.0 mm
Oil scraper ring	0.25 to 0.50 mm	1.0 mm
2.0 litre:		
Compression rings	0.25 to 0.50 mm	1.0 mm
Oil scraper ring	0.25 to 0.50 mm	1.0 mm
Ring-to-groove clearance:		
Petrol engines:		
1.4 litre CGGA & BUD:		
Top compression ring	0.04 to 0.08 mm	0.15 mm
Lower compression ring	0.04 to 0.08 mm	0.15 mm
Oil scraper ring	N/A	N/A
1.4 litre CAXA:		
Top compression ring	0.04 to 0.08 mm	0.15 mm
Lower compression ring	0.02 to 0.06 mm	0.15 mm
Oil scraper ring	N/A	N/A
Diesel engines		
1st compression ring	0.06 to 0.09 mm	0.25 mm
2nd compression ring	0.05 to 0.08 mm	0.25 mm
Oil scraper ring	0.03 to 0.06 mm	0.15 mm

Crankshaft

Endfloat	**New**	**Wear limit**
Petrol engines	See Note in Section 2	
Diesel engines:		
1.6 litre engines	0.07 to 0.17 mm	0.37 mm
2.0 litre engines	0.07 to 0.23 mm	0.30 mm

Spigot bearing

Fitted depth in end of crankshaft:	
Petrol engines	Flush
Diesel engines:	
1.6 litre engines	1.5 to 1.8 mm
2.0 litre engines	2.0 mm

Cylinder head

Minimum permissible dimension between top of valve stem and top surface of cylinder head:	
Petrol engines	7.6 mm
Diesel engines	No reworking permitted
Minimum cylinder head height:	
Petrol engines	No reworking permitted
Diesel engines	No reworking permitted
Maximum cylinder head gasket face distortion:	
Petrol engines	0.05 mm
Diesel engines	0.1 mm

Valves

	Inlet valves	**Exhaust valves**
Valve stem diameter:		
Petrol engines	5.973 mm	5.953 mm
Diesel engines	5.968 to 5.982 mm	5.958 to 5.972 mm
Valve seat angle (all engines)	45°	45°

Torque wrench settings

Refer to Chapter 2A, 2B, 2C or 2D, as applicable.

1 General information

How to use this Chapter

Included in this Part of Chapter 2 are details of removing the engine from the car and general overhaul procedures for the cylinder head, cylinder block and all other engine internal components.

The information given ranges from advice concerning preparation for an overhaul and the purchase of new parts, to detailed step-by-step procedures covering removal, inspection, renovation and refitting of engine internal components.

After Section 8, all instructions are based on the assumption that the engine has been removed from the car. For information concerning in-car engine repair, as well as the removal and refitting of those external components necessary for full overhaul, refer to the relevant in-car repair procedure section (Chapters 2A, 2B, 2C or 2D) and to Section 5 of this Chapter. Ignore any preliminary dismantling operations described in the relevant in-car repair sections that are no longer relevant once the engine has been removed from the car.

Apart from torque wrench settings, which are given at the beginning of the relevant in-car repair procedure in Chapters 2A, 2B, 2C or 2D, all specifications relating to engine overhaul are given at the beginning of this Part of Chapter 2.

2 Engine overhaul – general information

Note: *On 1.4 litre (CGGA & BUD) engines, the crankshaft must not be removed. Just loosening the main bearing cap bolts will cause deformation of the cylinder block. On these engines, if the crankshaft or main bearing surfaces are worn or damaged, the complete crankshaft/cylinder block assembly must be renewed.*

1 It is not always easy to determine when, or if, an engine should be completely overhauled, as a number of factors must be considered.

2 High mileage is not necessarily an indication that an overhaul is needed, while low mileage does not preclude the need for an overhaul. Frequency of servicing is probably the most important consideration. An engine, which has had regular and frequent oil and filter changes, as well as other required maintenance, should give many thousands of miles of reliable service. Conversely, a neglected engine may require an overhaul very early in its life.

3 Excessive oil consumption is an indication that piston rings, valve seals and/or valve guides are in need of attention. Make sure that oil leaks are not responsible before deciding that the rings and/or guides are worn. Perform a compression (or leakdown) test, as described in Part A, B, C or D of this Chapter (as applicable), to determine the likely cause of the problem.

4 Check the oil pressure with a gauge fitted in place of the oil pressure switch, and then compare it with that specified (see Specifications in Part A, B, C or D of this Chapter). If it is extremely low, the main and big-end bearings, and/or the oil pump, are probably worn.

5 Loss of power, rough running, knocking or metallic engine noises, excessive valve gear noise, and high fuel consumption may also point to the need for an overhaul, especially if they are all present at the same time. If a complete service does not remedy the situation, major mechanical work is the only solution.

6 An engine overhaul involves restoring all internal parts to the specification of a new engine. During an overhaul, the pistons and the piston rings are renewed. New main and big-end bearings are generally fitted (where possible); if necessary, the crankshaft may be renewed to restore the journals. The valves are also serviced as well, since they are usually in less-than-perfect condition at this point. While the engine is being overhauled, other components, such as the starter and alternator, can be overhauled as well. The end result should be an as-new engine that will give many trouble-free miles. **Note:** *Critical cooling system components such as the hoses, thermostat and coolant pump should be renewed when an engine is overhauled. The radiator should be checked carefully, to ensure that it is not clogged or leaking. Also, it is a good idea to renew the oil pump whenever the engine is overhauled.*

7 Before beginning the engine overhaul, read through the entire procedure, to familiarise yourself with the scope and requirements of the job. Overhauling an engine is not difficult if you follow carefully all of the instructions, have the necessary tools and equipment, and pay close attention to all specifications. It can, however, be time-consuming. Plan on the car being off the road for a minimum of two weeks, especially if parts must be taken to an engineering works for repair or reconditioning. Check on the availability of parts and make sure that any necessary special tools and equipment are obtained in advance. Most work can be done with typical hand tools, although a number of precision measuring tools are required for inspecting parts to determine if they must be renewed. Often the engineering works will handle the inspection of parts and offer advice concerning reconditioning and renewal. **Note:** *Always wait until the engine has been completely dismantled, and until all components (especially the cylinder block and the crankshaft) have been inspected, before deciding what service and repair operations must be performed by an engineering works. The condition of these components will be the major factor to consider when determining whether to overhaul the original engine, or to*

buy a reconditioned unit. Do not, therefore, purchase parts or have overhaul work done on other components until they have been thoroughly inspected. As a general rule, time is the primary cost of an overhaul, so it does not pay to fit worn or sub-standard parts.

8 As a final note, to ensure maximum life and minimum trouble from a reconditioned engine, everything must be assembled with care, in a spotlessly clean environment.

3 Engine/transmission removal – preparation and precautions

If you have decided that the engine must be removed for overhaul or major repair work, several preliminary steps should be taken.

Locating a suitable place to work is extremely important. Adequate workspace, along with storage space for the vehicle, will be needed. If a workshop or garage is not available, at the very least a solid, level, clean work surface is required.

If possible, clear some shelving close to the work area and use it to store the engine components and ancillaries as they are removed and dismantled. In this manner, the components stand a better chance of staying clean and undamaged during the overhaul. Laying out components in groups together with their fixings bolts, screws, etc, will save time and avoid confusion when the engine is refitted.

Clean the engine compartment and engine before beginning the removal procedure; this will help visibility and help to keep tools clean.

The help of an assistant is essential; there are certain instances when one person cannot safely perform all of the operations required to remove the engine from the vehicle. Safety is of primary importance, considering the potential hazards involved in this kind of operation. A second person should always be in attendance to offer help in an emergency. If this is the first time you have removed an engine, advice and aid from someone more experienced would also be beneficial.

Plan the operation ahead of time. Before starting work, obtain (or arrange for the hire of) all of the tools and equipment you will need. Access to the following items will allow the task of removing and refitting the engine to be completed safely and with relative ease: a hoist and lifting tackle – rated in excess of the weight of the engine, complete sets of spanners and sockets as described at the rear of this manual, wooden blocks, and plenty of rags and cleaning solvent for mopping-up spilled oil, coolant and fuel. A selection of different-sized plastic storage bins will also prove useful for keeping dismantled components grouped together. If any of the equipment must be hired, make sure that you arrange for it in advance, and perform all of the operations possible without it beforehand; this may save you time and money.

4.4 Remove the battery and tray

Plan on the vehicle being out of use for quite a while, especially if you intend to carry out an engine overhaul. Read through the whole of this Section and work out a strategy based on your own experience, and the tools, time and workspace available to you. Some of the overhaul processes may have to be carried out by a VW dealer or an engineering works – these establishments often have busy schedules, so it would be prudent to consult them before removing or dismantling the engine, to get an idea of the amount of time required to carry out the work.

When removing the engine from the vehicle, be methodical about the disconnection of external components. Labelling cables and hoses as they are removed will greatly assist the refitting process.

Always be extremely careful when lifting the engine from the engine compartment. Serious injury can result from careless actions. If help

is required, it is better to wait until it is available rather than risk personal injury and/or damage components by continuing alone. By planning ahead and taking your time, a job of this nature, although major, can be accomplished successfully and without incident.

4 Engine and transmission – removal and refitting

Removal

1 On 1.4-litre petrol engines, the engine and transmission are lifted from the engine compartment. On diesel models, access to the front of the engine is gained by moving the lock carrier assembly to its Service position, or alternatively removing it completely after evacuating the air conditioning system (by an air conditioning specialist).

2 Switch off the ignition and all electrical consumers, and remove the ignition key.

3 Remove the engine top cover and air filter assembly (Chapter 4A or Chapter 4B, Section 2) and all associated air ducting.

4 Remove the battery as described in Chapter 5A, Section 3, and then remove the battery tray **(see illustration)**.

5 Apply the handbrake, then jack up the front of the vehicle and support it on axle stands (see *Jacking and vehicle support*). Remove both front roadwheels.

6 Move the lock carrier, located at the front of the engine compartment, to its Service position as follows:

a) Remove the front bumper (Chapter 11, Section 6).

b) Disconnect the bonnet release cable over the right-hand headlight **(see illustration)**.

c) On models with a turbocharger, remove the charge air ducts, see Chapter 4D.

d) Support the lock carrier, then unscrew the mounting bolts and substitute them with a threaded rod on each side of the car **(see illustration)**.

e) Carefully pull the lock carrier forwards approximately 10 cm to provide access to the front of the engine **(see illustration)**.

Alternatively, the air conditioning system may be evacuated by a specialist, and the lock carrier removed completely from the front of the car to provide additional working space.

⚠ **Warning: Have the air conditioning system discharged by a suitably qualified specialist before attempting to remove the compressor.**

7 Drain the cooling system as described in Chapter 1A, Section 30 (petrol) or Chapter 1B, Section 31 (diesel). On 1.4 litre petrol engines the temperature sensor may be removed from the bottom hose to drain the system **(see illustration)**.

8 Noting their locations, disconnect all wiring, coolant hoses, vacuum hoses and fuel lines from the engine/transmission, with reference to the relevant Chapters of this Manual. Alternatively, the engine wiring loom may remain on the engine by disconnecting it from the left-hand side of the engine compartment, and removing the engine management ECU (Chapter 4A, Section 3 or Chapter 4B, Section 3) located on the bulkhead **(see illustrations)**. Tape over or plug fuel lines to prevent entry of dust and dirt.

4.6a Disconnect the bonnet release cable...

4.6b ...and unscrew the crossmember mounting bolts (arrowed) ...

4.6c ...and fit the threaded rods (arrowed)

4.7 Remove the electric cooling fan switch from the bottom hose to drain the cooling system

4.8a Remove the wiring from the supports on the front of the engine

4.8b Engine wiring loom support on exhaust manifold

4.10 Remove the rear engine support/ torque arm

4.11 Disconnect the gearchange cables

4.14 Suspend the driveshafts cleasr of the transmission

9 Remove the front exhaust pipe with reference to Chapter 4C, Section 7 or Chapter 4D, Section 9.

10 Unbolt the rear engine support/torque arm from the transmission **(see illustration)**.

11 Disconnect the gearchange mechanism with reference to Chapter 7A, Section 2 (manual transmission) or Chapter 7B, Section 4 (DSG transmission) **(see illustration)**.

12 On manual transmission models, remove the clutch slave cylinder. **Note:** *Do not depress the clutch pedal once the slave cylinder has been removed.*

13 Refer to Chapter 3, Section 10, and unbolt the air conditioning compressor from the front of the engine, without disconnecting the refrigerant lines. Suspend the compressor to one side of the engine compartment.

14 Refer to Chapter 8, Section 2, and disconnect the driveshafts from the transmission drive flanges. Suspend them from the underbody **(see illustration)**.

15 Unbolt the washer fluid reservoir for access to the right-engine mounting. Also unbolt the coolant expansion tank and place to one side.

16 Connect a hoist and lifting tackle to the engine lifting brackets on the cylinder head, and raise the hoist to just take the weight of the engine/transmission **(see illustration)**.

17 Unbolt the right- and left-hand engine mountings with reference to Chapter 2A, 2B, 2C or 2D.

18 Make a final check to ensure that all relevant wiring, hoses and pipes have been disconnected, then carefully swivel the engine/transmission assembly away from the sides of the engine compartment, lift it upwards or lower it (see paragraph 1), and withdraw forwards from the front of the car.

Separation

Engine and manual transmission

19 Remove the starter motor (Chapter 5A, Section 8).

20 Where applicable, unscrew the bolt securing the small engine-to-transmission plate to the transmission.

21 Ensure that both engine and transmission are adequately supported, and then unscrew the remaining engine-to-transmission bolts, noting the location of each bolt, and the

locations of any brackets secured by the bolts.

22 Carefully withdraw the transmission from the engine, ensuring that the weight of the transmission is not allowed to hang on the input shaft while it is engaged with the clutch friction disc. Recover the engine-to-transmission plate.

Engine and DSG (dual clutch) transmission

23 Remove the starter motor (Chapter 5A, Section 8).

24 Disconnect the coolant hoses from the gearbox oil cooler. Plug the openings to prevent contamination.

25 Disconnect the wiring harness between the engine and gearbox, and move to one side.

26 Ensure that both engine and transmission are adequately supported, and then unscrew the engine-to-transmission bolts, noting the location of each bolt, and the locations of any brackets secured by the bolts.

27 Carefully withdraw the transmission from the engine (take care – the transmission is heavy).

Reconnection and refitting

Engine and manual transmission

28 Reconnection and refitting are a reversal of removal, bearing in mind the following points:

a) Smear the splines of the transmission input shaft with a little high melting-point grease.

b) Ensure that any brackets noted before removal are in place on the engine-to-transmission bolts.

4.16 Lift the engine/transmission with a hoist

c) Tighten all fixings to the specified torque, where given.

d) Where applicable, have the air conditioning system recharged with refrigerant by a suitably qualified professional.

e) Ensure that all wiring, hoses and pipes are correctly reconnected and routed as noted before removal.

f) Ensure that the fuel lines are correctly reconnected.

g) On completion, refill the cooling system as described in Chapter 1A, Section 30 or Chapter 1B, Section 31.

Engine and DSG (dual clutch) transmission

29 Reconnection and refitting are a reversal of removal, bearing in mind the following points:

a) When fitting the torque converter (where applicable), make sure that both the drive pins engage with the transmission fluid pump.

b) On completion, check and if necessary top-up the transmission fluid level as described in Chapter 1A, Section 27 or Chapter 1B, Section 25.

---

5 Engine overhaul – preliminary information

1 It is much easier to dismantle and work on the engine if it is mounted on a portable engine stand. These stands can often be hired from a tool hire shop. Before the engine is mounted on a stand, the flywheel should be removed, so that the stand bolts can be tightened into the end of the cylinder block/crankcase. **Note:** *Do not measure cylinder bore dimensions with the engine mounted on this type of stand.*

2 If a stand is not available, it is possible to dismantle the engine with it blocked up on a sturdy workbench, or on the floor. Be very careful not to tip or drop the engine when working without a stand.

3 If you intend to obtain a reconditioned engine, all ancillaries must be removed first, to be transferred to the new engine (just as they will if you are doing a complete engine overhaul yourself). These components include the following (it may be necessary to transfer

6.6a Compress a valve spring with a compressor tool

6.6b Remove the spring cap...

6.6c ...and valve spring

additional components, such as the oil level dipstick/tube assembly, oil filter housing, etc, depending on which components are supplied with the reconditioned engine:

Petrol engines

a) Alternator (including mounting brackets) and starter motor (Chapter 5A).
b) The ignition system components including all sensors and spark plugs (Chapters 1A and 5B).
c) The fuel injection system components (Chapter 4A).
d) All electrical switches, actuators and sensors, and the engine wiring harness (Chapters 3, 4A and 5B).
e) Inlet and exhaust manifolds, and turbocharger (where applicable) (Chapters 4A and 4C).
f) Engine mountings (Chapter 2A or 2B).
g) Clutch components (Chapter 6).
h) Oil separator (where applicable).

Diesel engines

a) Alternator (including mounting brackets) and starter motor (Chapter 5A).
b) The glow plug/preheating system components (Chapter 5C).
c) All fuel system components, including fuel injectors, all sensors and actuators (Chapter 4B).
d) The brake vacuum pump (Chapter 9).
e) All electrical switches, actuators and sensors, and the engine wiring harness (Chapter 3, 4B and 5C).
f) Inlet and exhaust manifolds/turbocharger (where applicable) (Chapters 4B and 4D).

g) Engine mountings (see Chapter 2C or 2D).
h) Clutch components (Chapter 6).

All engines

Note: When removing the external components from the engine, pay close attention to details that may be helpful or important during refitting. Note the fitted position of gaskets, seals, spacers, pins, washers, bolts, and other small components.

4 If you are obtaining a short engine (the engine cylinder block/crankcase, crankshaft, pistons and connecting rods, all fully assembled), then the cylinder head, sump, oil pump, timing belt(s) and chain (as applicable – together with tensioner(s) and covers), auxiliary drivebelt (together with its tensioner), coolant pump, thermostat housing, coolant outlet elbows, oil filter housing and where applicable oil cooler will also have to be removed.

5 If you are planning a full overhaul, the engine can be dismantled in the order given below:

a) Inlet and exhaust manifolds (see the relevant part of Chapter 4).
b) Timing belt or timing chain (as applicable), sprockets and tensioner (see the relevant part of Chapter 2).
c) Cylinder head (see the relevant part of Chapter 2).
d) Flywheel/driveplate (see the relevant part of Chapter 2).
e) Sump (see the relevant part of Chapter 2).
f) Oil pump (see the relevant part of Chapter 2).
g) Piston/connecting rod assemblies (see Section 9).
h) Crankshaft (see Section 10).

6 Cylinder head – dismantling

Note: A valve spring compressor tool will be required for this operation.

Petrol engines

1 With the cylinder head removed, proceed as follows.
2 Remove the inlet and exhaust manifolds as described in Chapter 4A, Section 8 and Chapter 4C, Section 6 respectively.
3 On non-turbo engines, unscrew the securing bolt and remove the secondary timing belt tensioner from the timing belt end of the cylinder head.
4 Unbolt any remaining auxiliary brackets and/or engine lifting brackets from the cylinder head as necessary, noting their locations to aid refitting.
5 Turn the cylinder head over, and rest it on one side.
6 Using a valve spring compressor, compress each valve spring in turn until the split collets can be removed. Release the compressor, and lift off the spring cap and spring. If, when the valve spring compressor is screwed down, the spring cap refuses to free and expose the split collets, gently tap the top of the tool, directly over the spring cap, with a light hammer. This will free the retainer **(see illustrations)**.
7 Using a pair of pliers, or a removal tool, carefully extract the valve stem oil seal from the top of the valve guide **(see illustrations)**.
8 Withdraw the valve from the gasket side of the cylinder head **(see illustration)**.

6.7a Use a removal tool...

6.7b ...to remove the valve stem oil seals

6.8 Removing a valve

9 It is essential that each valve is stored together with its collets, cap, spring and spring seat. The valves should be kept in their correct sequences, unless they are so badly worn that they are to be renewed.

Diesel engines

10 With the cylinder head removed, proceed as follows.

11 Remove the inlet and exhaust manifolds (and turbocharger, where applicable) as described in Chapter 4B, Section 5 and Chapter 4D, Section 5.

12 Remove the camshaft and hydraulic tappets, as described in Chapter 2C, Section 9 or Chapter 2D, Section 9.

13 Remove the glow plugs, with reference to Chapter 5C, Section 2.

14 Remove the fuel injectors, with reference to Chapter 4B, Section 4.

15 Unscrew the nut and remove the timing belt tensioner pulley from the stud on the timing belt end of the cylinder head.

16 Unbolt any remaining auxiliary brackets and/or engine lifting brackets from the cylinder head as necessary, noting their locations to aid refitting.

17 Proceed as described in paragraphs 5 to 9.

---

7 Cylinder head and valves – cleaning and inspection

---

1 Thorough cleaning of the cylinder head and valve components, followed by a detailed inspection, will enable you to decide how much valve service work must be carried out during engine overhaul. **Note:** *If the engine has been severely overheated, it is best to assume that the cylinder head is warped ñ check carefully for signs of this.*

Cleaning

2 Using a suitable degreasing agent, remove all traces of oil deposits from the cylinder head, paying particular attention to the camshaft bearing surfaces, hydraulic tappet bores, valve guides and oil ways. Scrape off any traces of old gasket from the mating surfaces, taking care not to score or gouge them. If using emery paper, do not use a grade of less than 100. Turn the head over and, using a blunt blade, scrape any carbon deposits from the combustion chambers and ports. Finally, wash the entire head casting with a suitable solvent to remove the remaining debris.

3 Clean the valve heads and stems using a fine wire brush (or a power-operated wire brush). If the valve is covered with heavy carbon deposits, scrape off the majority of the deposits with a blunt blade first, then use the wire brush.

4 Thoroughly clean the remainder of the components using solvent and allow them to dry completely. Discard the oil seals, as new ones must be fitted when the cylinder head is reassembled.

Inspection

Cylinder head

Note: *If the valve seats are to be re-cut, ensure that the maximum permissible reworking dimension (where applicable) is not exceeded (the maximum dimension will only allow minimal reworking to produce a perfect seal between valve and seat). If the maximum dimension is exceeded, the function of the hydraulic tappets cannot be guaranteed, and the cylinder head must be renewed. Refer to paragraph 6 for details of how to calculate the maximum permissible reworking dimension. Reworking is **not** permitted on diesel engines.*

5 Examine the head casting closely to identify any damage or cracks that may have developed. Cracks can often be identified from evidence of coolant or oil leakage. Pay particular attention to the areas around the valve seats and spark plug/fuel injector holes. If cracking is discovered in this area, VW state that on diesel engines, the cylinder head may be re-used, provided the cracks are no larger than 0.5 mm wide. More serious damage will mean the renewal of the cylinder head casting.

6 Moderately pitted and scorched valve seats can be repaired by lapping the valves in during reassembly, as described later in this Chapter. Badly worn or damaged valve seats may be restored by re-cutting where permitted, however, the maximum permissible reworking dimension **must** not be exceeded, only minimal reworking being possible (see note at beginning of paragraph 5). To calculate the maximum permissible reworking dimension, proceed as follows **(see illustration):**

 a) *If a new valve is to be fitted, use the new valve for the following calculation.*
 b) *Insert the valve into its guide in the cylinder head, and push the valve firmly on to its seat.*
 c) *Using a flat edge placed across the top surface of the cylinder head, measure the distance between the top face of the valve stem, and the top surface of the cylinder head. Record the measurement obtained.*
 d) *Consult the Specifications, and look up the value for the minimum permissible dimension between the top face of the*

7.6 Measure the distance (A) between the top face of the valve stem and the top surface of the cylinder head

 valve stem and the top surface of the cylinder head.
 e) *Now take the measured distance and subtract the minimum permissible dimension, to give the maximum permissible reworking dimension; e.g. Measured distance (34.4 mm) Minus Minimum permissible dimension (34.0 mm) = Maximum permissible reworking dimension (0.4 mm).*

7 Measure any distortion of the gasket surfaces using a straight-edge and a set of feeler blades. Take one measurement longitudinally on the manifold mating surface(s). Take several measurements across the head gasket surface, to assess the level of distortion in all planes **(see illustration)**. Compare the measurements with the figures in the Specifications.

8 If the head is distorted beyond the specified limit, the head must be renewed.

Camshaft

9 Inspection of the camshaft is covered in Chapters 2A, 2B, 2C or 2D, as applicable.

Valves and associated components

10 Examine each valve closely for signs of wear. Inspect the valve stems for wear ridges, scoring or variations in diameter; measure their diameters at several points along their lengths with a micrometer, and compare with the figures given in the Specifications **(see illustration)**.

7.7 Measure the distortion of the cylinder head gasket surface

7.10 Measure the diameter of the valve stems using a micrometer

7.13 Measure the free length of each valve spring

11 The valve heads should not be cracked, badly pitted or charred. Note that light pitting of the valve head can be rectified by lapping-in the valves during reassembly, as described in Section 8.

12 Check that the valve stem end face is free from excessive pitting or indentation; this could be caused by defective hydraulic tappets.

13 Using vernier calipers, measure the free length of each of the valve springs. As a manufacturer's figure is not quoted, the only way to check the length of the springs is by comparison with a new component. Note that valve springs are usually renewed during a major engine overhaul **(see illustration)**.

14 Stand each spring on its end on a flat surface, against an engineer's square **(see illustration)**. Check the squareness of the spring visually, and renew it if it appears distorted.

15 Renew the valve stem oil seals regardless of their apparent condition.

8.2 Grinding-in a valve

8.8b Fit a protective sleeve over the valve stem before fitting the stem seal

7.14 Check the squareness of a valve spring

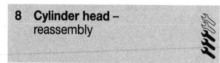

8 Cylinder head – reassembly

Note: *A valve spring compressor tool will be required for this operation.*

Petrol engines

1 To achieve a gas-tight seal between the valves and their seats, it will be necessary to lap-in (or grind-in) the valves. To complete this process you will need a quantity of fine/coarse grinding paste and a grinding tool – this can either be of the rubber sucker type, or the automatic type which is driven by a rotary power tool.

2 Smear a small quantity of *fine* grinding paste on the sealing face of the valve head. Turn the cylinder head over so that the combustion chambers are facing upwards

8.8a Lubricate the valve stem with clean engine oil

8.9 Use a long-reach socket to fit a valve stem oil seal

and insert the valve into the correct guide. Attach the grinding tool to the valve head and using a backward/forward rotary action, grind the valve head into its seat. Periodically lift the valve and rotate it to redistribute the grinding paste **(see illustration)**.

3 Continue this process until the contact between valve and seat produces an unbroken, matt grey ring of uniform width, on both faces. Repeat the operation on the remaining valves.

4 If the valves and seats are so badly pitted that coarse grinding paste must be used, bear in that there is a maximum permissible reworking dimension for the valves and seats. Refer to the Specifications at the beginning of this Chapter for the minimum dimension from the end of the valve stem to the top face of the cylinder head (see Section 7, paragraph 6). If this minimum dimension is exceeded due to excessive lapping-in, the hydraulic tappets may not operate correctly, and the cylinder head must be renewed.

5 Assuming the repair is feasible, work as described previously, but use coarse grinding paste initially, to achieve a dull finish on the valve face and seat. Wash off the coarse paste with solvent and repeat the process using fine grinding paste to obtain the correct finish.

6 When all the valves have been ground in, remove all traces of grinding paste from the cylinder head and valves using solvent, and allow the head and valves to dry completely.

7 Turn the cylinder head on its side.

8 Working on one valve at a time, lubricate the valve stem with clean engine oil, and insert the valve into its guide. Fit one of the protective plastic sleeves (where supplied) to fit over the end of the valve stem – this will protect the oil seal as it is being fitted **(see illustrations)**.

9 Dip a new valve stem seal in clean engine oil, and carefully push it over the valve stem and onto the top of the valve guide – take care not to damage the stem seal as it is fitted. Use a suitable long-reach socket or a valve stem seal fitting tool to press the seal firmly into position **(see illustration)**. Remove the protective sleeve from the valve stem.

10 Locate the valve spring over the valve stem, ensuring that the lower end of the spring seats correctly on the cylinder head **(see illustration)**.

8.10 Fit a valve spring...

8.11a ...and upper spring seat ...

8.11b ... then compress a valve spring using a compressor tool

8.11c Use grease to hold the split collets in the groove

11 Fit the upper spring seat over the top of the spring, then using a valve spring compressor, compress the spring until the upper seat is pushed beyond the collet grooves in the valve stem. Refit the split collets. Gradually release the spring compressor, checking that the collets remain correctly seated as the spring extends. When correctly seated, the upper spring seat should force the collets securely into the grooves in the end of the valve stem (see illustrations).

12 Repeat this process for the remaining sets of valve components, ensuring that all components are refitted to their original locations. To settle the components after installation, strike the end of each valve stem with a mallet, using a block of wood to protect the stem from damage. Check before progressing any further that the split collets remain firmly seated in the grooves in the end of the valve stem.

13 Refit any auxiliary brackets and/or engine lifting brackets to their original locations, as noted before removal.

14 On 1.4 litre non-turbo engines, refit the secondary timing belt tensioner, and then refit the securing bolt.

15 Refit the inlet and exhaust manifolds as described in Chapter 4A, Section 8 and Chapter 4C, Section 6.

Diesel engines

16 Proceed as described in paragraphs 1 to 13.

17 Refit the timing belt tensioner pulley to the stud on the cylinder head, and refit the securing nut.

18 Refit the fuel injectors, with reference to Chapter 4B, Section 4.

19 Refit the glow plugs, with reference to Chapter 5C, Section 2.

20 Refit the hydraulic tappets and camshaft, as described in Chapter 2C, Section 9 or Chapter 2D, Section 9.

21 Refit the inlet and exhaust manifolds (and turbocharger, where applicable), as described in Chapter 4B, Section 5 and Chapter 4D, Section 5.

9 Piston/connecting rod assemblies – removal

1 Proceed as follows according to engine type:

a) On 1.4 litre petrol engines, remove the cylinder head, sump, and oil pick-up pipe, as described in Chapter 2A or 2B.

b) On 1.6 litre diesel engines, remove the cylinder head, sump and oil baffle plate, oil pump and pick-up pipe, and the balancer shaft assembly as described in Chapter 2C.

c) On 2.0 litre diesel engines, remove the cylinder head, sump and oil baffle plate, and oil pump and pick-up pipe, as described in Chapter 2D.

2 Inspect the tops of the cylinder bores for ridges at the point where the pistons reach top dead centre. These must be removed otherwise the pistons may be damaged when they are pushed out of their bores. Use a scraper or ridge reamer to remove the ridges.

Such a ridge indicates excessive wear of the cylinder bore.

3 Check the connecting rods and big-end caps for identification markings. Both connecting rods and caps should be marked with the cylinder number on one side of each assembly. Note that No 1 cylinder is at the timing belt end of the engine. If no marks are present, using a hammer and centre-punch, paint or similar, mark each connecting rod and big-end bearing cap with its respective cylinder number – note on which side of the connecting rods and caps the marks are made (see illustration).

4 Similarly, check the piston crowns for direction markings. An arrow on each piston crown should point towards the timing belt end of the engine. On some engines, this mark may be obscured by carbon build-up, in which case the piston crown should be cleaned to check for a mark. In some cases, the direction arrow may have worn off, in which case a suitable mark should be made on the piston crown using a scriber – do not deeply score the piston crown, but ensure that the mark is easily visible.

5 Turn the crankshaft to bring No's 1 and 4 pistons to bottom dead centre.

6 Unscrew the bolts or nuts, as applicable, from No 1 piston big-end bearing cap. Lift off the cap, and recover the bottom half bearing shell. If the bearing shells are to be re-used, tape the cap and bearing shell together. Note that if the bearing shells are to be re-used, they must be fitted to the original connecting rod and cap (see illustrations).

7 Where the bearing caps are secured with

9.3 Mark the big-end caps and connecting rods with their cylinder numbers (arrowed)

9.6a Unscrew the big-end bearing cap bolts...

9.6b ...and remove the cap

9.7 Wrap the threaded ends of the bolts with tape

9.12a Remove the securing bolts...

9.12b ...and withdraw the piston cooling oil spray jets

9.12c Piston cooling spray jet and retainer

nuts, wrap the threaded ends of the bolts with insulating tape to prevent them scratching the crankpins and bores when the pistons are removed **(see illustration)**.

8 Using a hammer handle, push the piston up through the bore, and remove it from the top of the cylinder block. Where applicable, take care not to damage the piston cooling oil spray jets in the cylinder block as the piston/connecting rod assembly is removed. Recover the upper bearing shell, and tape it to the connecting rod for safe-keeping.

9 Loosely refit the big-end cap to the connecting rod, and secure with the bolts or nuts, as applicable – this will help to keep the components in their correct order.

10 Remove No.4 piston assembly in the same way.

11 Turn the crankshaft as necessary to bring No's 2 and 3 pistons to bottom dead centre, and remove them in the same way.

12 Where applicable, remove the securing bolts, and withdraw the piston cooling oil spray jets from the bottom of the cylinder block **(see illustrations)**.

10 Crankshaft – removal

> **Warning: On 1.4 litre (CGGA & BUD) petrol engines, the crankshaft must not be removed. Just loosening the main bearing cap bolts on these engines will cause deformation of the cylinder block. If the crankshaft or main bearing surfaces are worn or damaged, the complete crankshaft/cylinder block assembly must be renewed. The following procedure applies to all other engines.**

Note: If no work is to be done on the pistons

10.5 Slacken and remove the main bearing cap bolts

11.1 EGR cooler located on the rear of the engine

and connecting rods, there is no need to push the pistons out of the cylinder bores. The pistons should just be pushed far enough up the bores so that they are positioned clear of the crankshaft journals.

1 Proceed as follows according to engine type:
  a) On 1.4 litre petrol engines (engine codes CAXA), remove the timing belt/chain, sump, oil pump and pick-up pipe, flywheel/driveplate, and the crankshaft oil seal housing, as described in Chapter 2B.
  b) On diesel engines, remove the timing belt and crankshaft sprocket, sump and oil baffle plate, oil pump and pick-up pipe, flywheel/driveplate, and the crankshaft oil seal housings, as described in Chapter 2C or 2D.

2 Remove the pistons and connecting rods, or disconnect them from the crankshaft, as described in Section 9 (see Note at the beginning of this Section).

3 Check the crankshaft endfloat as described in Section 13, then proceed as follows.

4 The main bearing caps should be numbered 1 to 5 from the timing belt end of the engine. If the bearing caps are not marked, mark them accordingly using a centre-punch. Note the orientation of the markings to ensure correct refitting.

5 Slacken and remove the main bearing cap bolts, and lift off each cap. If the caps appear to be stuck, tap them with a soft-faced mallet to free them from the cylinder block **(see illustration)**. Recover the lower bearing shells, and tape them to their caps for safekeeping.

6 Recover the lower crankshaft endfloat control thrustwasher halves from either side of the No 3 main bearing cap, noting their orientation.

7 Lift the crankshaft from the cylinder block. Take care, as the crankshaft is heavy. On engines with a crankshaft speed/position sensor fitted, lay the crankshaft on wooden blocks – **do not** rest the crankshaft on the sensor wheel.

8 Recover the upper bearing shells from the cylinder block, and tape them to their respective caps for safekeeping. Similarly, recover the upper crankshaft endfloat control thrustwasher halves, noting their orientation.

9 On engines with a crankshaft speed/position sensor wheel, unscrew the securing bolts, and remove the sensor wheel, noting which way round it is fitted.

11 Cylinder block/crankcase – cleaning and inspection

Cleaning

1 Remove all external components and electrical switches/sensors from the block, including mounting brackets, coolant pump, oil filter housing, oil cooler and EGR cooler **(see illustration)**, etc. For complete cleaning,

the core plugs should ideally be removed. Drill a small hole in the plugs, and then insert a self-tapping screw into the hole. Extract the plugs by pulling on the screw with a pair of grips, or by using a slide hammer.

2 Scrape all traces of gasket and sealant from the cylinder block/crankcase, taking care not to damage the sealing surfaces.

3 Remove all oil gallery plugs (where fitted). The plugs are usually very tight – they may have to be drilled out, and the holes re-tapped. Use new plugs when the engine is reassembled.

4 If the casting is extremely dirty, it should be steam-cleaned. After this, clean all oil holes and galleries one more time. Flush all internal passages with warm water until the water runs clear. Dry thoroughly, and apply a light film of oil to all mating surfaces and cylinder bores, to prevent rusting. If you have access to compressed air, use it to speed up the drying process, and to blow out all the oil holes and galleries.

 Warning: Wear eye protection when using compressed air.

5 If the castings are not very dirty, you can do an adequate cleaning job with hot, soapy water and a stiff brush. Take plenty of time, and do a thorough job. Regardless of the cleaning method used, be sure to clean all oil holes and galleries very thoroughly, and to dry all components well. Protect the cylinder bores as described above, to prevent rusting.

6 Where applicable, check the piston cooling oil spray jets for damage, and renew if necessary. Check the oil spray hole and the oil passages for blockage.

7 All threaded holes must be clean, to ensure accurate torque readings during reassembly. To clean the threads, run the correct-size tap into each of the holes to remove rust, corrosion, thread sealant or sludge, and to restore damaged threads **(see illustration)**. If possible, use compressed air to clear the holes free of debris produced by this operation. **Note:** *Take extra care to exclude all cleaning liquid from blind tapped holes, as the casting may be cracked by hydraulic action if a bolt is threaded into a hole containing liquid.*

8 After coating the mating surfaces of the new core plugs with suitable sealant, fit them to the cylinder block. Make sure that they are driven in straight and seated correctly, or leakage could result.

9 Apply suitable sealant to the new oil gallery plugs, and insert them into the holes in the block. Tighten them securely.

10 If the engine is not going to be reassembled immediately, cover it with a large plastic bag to keep it clean; protect all mating surfaces and the cylinder bores, to prevent rusting.

Inspection

11 Visually check the castings for cracks and corrosion. Look for stripped threads in the threaded holes. If there has been any history of internal coolant leakage, it may

be worthwhile having an engine overhaul specialist check the cylinder block/crankcase for cracks with special equipment. If defects are found, have them repaired, if possible, or renew the assembly.

12 Check each cylinder bore for scuffing and scoring.

13 If in any doubt as the condition of the cylinder block have the block/bores inspected and measured by an engine reconditioning specialist. They will be able to advise on whether the block is serviceable, whether a re-bore is necessary, and supply the appropriate pistons and rings.

14 If the bores are in reasonably good condition and not excessively worn, then it may only be necessary to renew the piston rings.

15 If this is the case, the bores should be honed, to allow the new rings to bed-in correctly and provide the best possible seal. Consult an engine reconditioning specialist

16 On diesel engines, if the oil/water pump housing was removed, it can be refitted at this stage if wished. Use a new gasket, and before fully tightening the bolts, align the housing faces with those of the engine block.

17 The cylinder block/crankcase should now be completely clean and dry, with all components checked for wear or damage, and repaired or overhauled as necessary.

18 Apply a light coating of engine oil to the mating surfaces and cylinder bores to prevent rust forming.

19 Refit as many ancillary components as possible, for safekeeping. If reassembly is not to start immediately, cover the block with a large plastic bag to keep it clean, and protect the machined surfaces as described above to prevent rusting.

---

12 Piston/connecting rod assemblies – cleaning and inspection

Cleaning

1 Before the inspection process can begin, the piston/connecting rod assemblies must be cleaned, and the original piston rings removed from the pistons.

2 The rings should have smooth, polished working surfaces, with no dull or carbon-coated sections (showing that the ring is not sealing correctly against the bore wall, so allowing combustion gases to blow by) and no traces of wear on their top and bottom surfaces. The end gaps should be clear of carbon, but not polished (indicating a too-small end gap), and all the rings (including the elements of the oil control ring) should be free to rotate in their grooves, but without excessive up-and-down movement. If the rings appear to be in good condition, they are probably fit for further use; check the end gaps (in an unworn part of the bore) as described in Section 16.

3 If any of the rings appears to be worn or

11.7 To clean the cylinder block threads, run a correct-size tap into the holes

damaged, or has an end gap significantly different from the specified value, the usual course of action is to renew all of them as a set. **Note:** *While it is usual to renew piston rings when an engine is overhauled, they may be re-used if in acceptable condition. If re-using the rings, make sure that each ring is marked during removal to ensure that it is refitted correctly.*

4 Carefully expand the old rings over the top of the pistons. The use of two or three old feeler blades will be helpful in preventing the rings dropping into empty grooves **(see illustration)**. Be careful not to scratch the piston with the ends of the ring. The rings are brittle, and will snap if they are spread too far. They are also very sharp – protect your hands and fingers. Note that the third ring incorporates an expander. Keep each set of rings with its piston if the old rings are to be re-used. Note which way up each ring is fitted to ensure correct refitting.

5 Scrape away all traces of carbon from the top of the piston. A hand-held wire brush (or a piece of fine emery cloth) can be used, once the majority of the deposits have been scraped away.

6 Remove the carbon from the ring grooves in the piston, using an old ring. Break the ring in half to do this (be careful not to cut your fingers – piston rings are sharp). Be careful to remove only the carbon deposits – do not remove any metal, and do not nick or scratch the sides of the ring grooves.

7 Once the deposits have been removed, clean the piston/connecting rod assembly

12.4 Old feeler blades can be used to prevent piston rings from dropping into empty grooves

12.17 Measure the piston ring-to-groove clearance using a feeler blade

12.20a Use a small flat-bladed screwdriver to prise out the circlip...

12.20b ...then push out the gudgeon pin and separate the piston and connecting rod

with paraffin or a suitable solvent, and dry thoroughly. Make sure that the oil return holes in the ring grooves are clear.

Inspection

8 If the pistons and cylinder bores are not damaged or worn excessively, and if the cylinder block does not need to be re-bored, the original pistons can be refitted.

9 Have the pistons and cylinder bore measure by an engine reconditioning specialist. They will be able to advise on possible repairs, and supply the correct replacement parts. **Note:** *If the cylinder block was re-bored during a previous overhaul, oversize pistons may already have been fitted.*

10 Normal piston wear shows up as even vertical wear on the piston thrust surfaces, and slight looseness of the top ring in its groove. New piston rings should always be used when the engine is reassembled.

11 Carefully inspect each piston for cracks around the skirt, around the gudgeon pin holes, and at the piston ring 'lands' (between the ring grooves).

12 Look for scoring and scuffing on the piston skirt, holes in the piston crown, and burned areas at the edge of the crown. If the skirt is scored or scuffed, the engine may have been suffering from overheating, and/or abnormal combustion, which caused excessively high operating temperatures. The cooling and lubrication systems should be checked thoroughly.

13 Scorch marks on the sides of the pistons show that blow-by has occurred.

14 A hole in the piston crown, or burned areas

at the edge of the piston crown, indicates that abnormal combustion (pre-ignition, knocking, or detonation) has been occurring.

15 If any of the above problems exist, the causes must be investigated and corrected, or the damage will occur again. The causes may include incorrect ignition/injection pump timing, inlet air leaks or incorrect air/fuel mixture (petrol engines), or a faulty fuel injector (diesel engines).

16 Corrosion of the piston, in the form of pitting, indicates that coolant has been leaking into the combustion chamber and/or the crankcase. Again, the cause must be corrected, or the problem may persist in the rebuilt engine.

17 Locate a new piston ring in the appropriate groove and measure the ring-to-groove clearance using a feeler blade **(see illustration)**. Note that the rings are of different widths, so use the correct ring for the groove. Compare the measurements with those listed; if the clearances are outside of the tolerance band, then the piston must be renewed. Confirm this by checking the width of the piston ring with a micrometer.

18 Examine each connecting rod carefully for signs of damage, such as cracks around the big-end and small-end bearings. Check that the rod is not bent or distorted. Damage is highly unlikely, unless the engine has been seized or badly overheated. Detailed checking of the connecting rod assembly can only be carried out by a VW dealer or engine repair specialist with the necessary equipment.

19 The gudgeon pins are of the floating

type, secured in position by two circlips. The pistons and connecting rods can be separated as follows.

20 Using a small flat-bladed screwdriver, prise out the circlips, and push out the gudgeon pin **(see illustrations)**. Hand pressure should be sufficient to remove the pin. Identify the piston and rod to ensure correct reassembly. Discard the circlips – new ones *must* be used on refitting. If the gudgeon pin proves difficult to remove, heat the piston to 60°C with hot water – the resulting expansion will then allow the two components to be separated.

21 Examine the gudgeon pin and connecting rod small-end bearing for signs of wear or damage. It should be possible to push the gudgeon pin through the connecting rod bush by hand, without noticeable play. Wear can be cured by renewing both the pin and bush. Bush renewal, however, is a specialist job – press facilities are required, and the new bush must be reamed accurately.

22 Examine all components, and obtain any new parts from your VW dealer or engine reconditioning specialist. If new pistons are purchased, they will be supplied complete with gudgeon pins and circlips. Circlips can also be purchased individually.

23 The orientation of the piston with respect to the connecting rod must be correct when the two are reassembled. The piston crown is marked with an arrow (which may be obscured by carbon deposits); this must point towards the timing belt/chain end of the engine when the piston is installed. The connecting rod and its bearing cap both have recesses machined into them on one side, close to their mating surfaces – these recesses must both face the same way as the arrow on the piston crown (ie, towards the timing belt/chain end of the engine) when correctly installed. Reassemble the two components to satisfy this requirement **(see illustrations)**.

24 Apply a smear of clean engine oil to the gudgeon pin. Slide it into the piston and through the connecting rod small-end. Check that the piston pivots freely on the rod, then secure the gudgeon pin in position with two new circlips. Ensure that each circlip is correctly located in its groove in the piston.

25 Repeat the cleaning and inspection process for the remaining pistons and connecting rods.

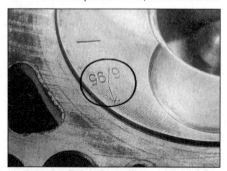

12.23a The piston crown is marked with an arrow which must point towards the timing belt/chain end of the engine

12.23b The recesses (arrowed) in the connecting rod and bearing cap must face the timing belt/chain end of the engine

13 Crankshaft –
checking endfloat,
spigot bearing, and inspection

Checking endfloat

1 If the crankshaft endfloat is to be checked, this must be done when the crankshaft is still installed in the cylinder block/crankcase, but is free to move (see Section 10).

2 Check the endfloat using a dial gauge in contact with the end of the crankshaft. Push the crankshaft fully one way, and then zero the gauge. Push the crankshaft fully the other way, and check the endfloat. The result can be compared with the specified amount, and will give an indication as to whether new thrustwasher halves are required **(see illustration)**. Note that all thrustwashers must be of the same thickness.

3 If a dial gauge is not available, feeler blades can be used. First push the crankshaft fully towards the flywheel end of the engine, and then use feeler blades to measure the gap between the web of No 3 crankpin and the thrustwasher halves **(see illustration)**.

Spigot bearing

Note: *On 7-speed DSG semi-automatic transmissions, the spigot needle roller bearing needs to be renewed; every time the transmission is removed from the engine.*

4 On some models, there is a bearing positioned in the end of the crankshaft, which supports the transmission shaft.

5 Remove the transmission as described in Chapter 7A, Section 3 (manual transmission) or Chapter 7B, Section 2 (DSG transmissions)

6 On manual models, remove the clutch assembly as described in Chapter 6, Section 6.

7 Before removing the bearing, check the fitted depth of the bearing inside the end of the crankshaft **(see illustration)**. See specifications at the beginning of this Chapter to find the relevant depth for each engine.

8 Using an internal puller, slide the bearing out from the centre of the crankshaft **(see illustrations)**.

9 Using a drift, drive the bearing into the end of the crankshaft **(see illustration)**, taking care not to drive it in to far, as noted on removal. Also see specifications at the beginning of Chapter for depth of bearing.

⚠️ *Warning: If the new bearing is driven into the end of the crankshaft to far, then it will need to be completely removed and another new one fitted.*

Inspection

10 Clean the crankshaft using paraffin or a suitable solvent, and dry it, preferably with compressed air if available. Be sure to clean the oil holes with a pipe cleaner or similar probe, to ensure that they are not obstructed.

⚠️ *Warning: Wear eye protection when using compressed air.*

13.2 Measure crankshaft endfloat using a dial gauge

13.3 Measure crankshaft endfloat using feeler blades

11 Check the main and big-end bearing journals for uneven wear, scoring, pitting and cracking.

12 Big-end bearing wear is accompanied by distinct metallic knocking when the engine is running (particularly noticeable when the engine is pulling from low speed) and some loss of oil pressure.

13 Main bearing wear is accompanied by severe engine vibration and rumble – getting progressively worse as engine speed increases – and again by loss of oil pressure.

14 Check the bearing journal for roughness by running a finger lightly over the bearing surface. Any roughness (which will be accompanied by obvious bearing wear) indicates that the crankshaft requires regrinding (where possible) or renewal.

15 If the crankshaft has been reground, check for burrs around the crankshaft oil holes (the holes are usually chamfered, so burrs should not be a problem unless regrinding has been

carried out carelessly). Remove any burrs with a fine file or scraper, and thoroughly clean the oil holes as described previously.

16 Have the crankshaft measured and inspected by an engine reconditioning specialist. They will be able to advise any possible repairs and supply the correct parts.

17 Check the oil seal contact surfaces at each end of the crankshaft for wear and damage. If the seal has worn a deep groove in the surface of the crankshaft, consult an engine overhaul specialist; repair may be possible, but otherwise a new crankshaft will be required.

18 If the crankshaft journals have not already been reground, it may be possible to have the crankshaft reconditioned, and to fit undersize shells (see Section 17). If no undersize shells are available and the crankshaft has worn beyond the specified limits, it will have to be renewed. Consult your VW dealer or engine specialist for further information on parts availability.

13.7 Check the depth of the bearing using a vernier gauge

13.8a Using an internal bearing puller ...

13.8b ... to withdraw the bearing

13.9 Using a drift to carefully tap the bearing back into position

14.1 Typical bearing failures

Labels in illustration:
FATIGUE FAILURE — CRATERS OR POCKETS
IMPROPER SEATING — BRIGHT (POLISHED) SECTIONS
SCRATCHED BY DIRT — DIRT EMBEDDED INTO BEARING MATERIAL
LACK OF OIL — OVERLAY WIPED OUT
EXCESSIVE WEAR — OVERLAY WIPED OUT
TAPERED JOURNAL — RADIUS RIDE

14 Main and big-end bearings – inspection and selection

Inspection

1 Even though the main and big-end bearings should be renewed during the engine overhaul, the old bearings should be retained for close examination, as they may reveal valuable information about the condition of the engine **(see illustration)**.

2 Bearing failure can occur due to lack of lubrication, the presence of dirt or other foreign particles, overloading the engine, or corrosion. Regardless of the cause of bearing failure, the cause must be corrected before the engine is reassembled, to prevent it from happening again.

3 When examining the bearing shells, remove them from the cylinder block/crankcase, the main bearing caps, the connecting rods and the connecting rod big-end bearing caps. Lay them out on a clean surface in the same general position as their location in the engine. This will enable you to match any bearing problems with the corresponding crankshaft journal. Do not touch any shell's internal bearing surface with your fingers while checking it, or the delicate surface may be scratched.

4 Dirt and other foreign matter get into the engine in a variety of ways. It may be left in the engine during assembly, or it may pass through filters or the crankcase ventilation system. It may get into the oil, and from there into the bearings. Metal chips from machining operations and normal engine wear are often present. Abrasives are sometimes left in engine components after reconditioning, especially when parts are not thoroughly cleaned using the proper cleaning methods. Whatever the

source, these foreign objects often end up embedded in the soft bearing material, and are easily recognised. Large particles will not embed in the bearing, but will score or gouge the bearing and journal. The best prevention for this cause of bearing failure is to clean all parts thoroughly, and keep everything spotlessly clean during engine assembly. Frequent and regular engine oil and filter changes are also recommended.

5 Lack of lubrication (or lubrication breakdown) has a number of interrelated causes. Excessive heat (which thins the oil), overloading (which squeezes the oil from the bearing face) and oil leakage (from excessive bearing clearances, worn oil pump or high engine speeds) all contribute to lubrication breakdown. Blocked oil passages, which usually are the result of misaligned oil holes in a bearing shell, will also oil-starve a bearing, and destroy it. When lack of lubrication is the cause of bearing failure, the bearing material is wiped or extruded from the steel backing of the bearing. Temperatures may increase to the point where the steel backing turns blue from overheating.

6 Driving habits can have a definite effect on bearing life. Full-throttle, low-speed operation (labouring the engine) puts very high loads on bearings, tending to squeeze out the oil film. These loads cause the bearings to flex, which produces fine cracks in the bearing face (fatigue failure). Eventually, the bearing material will loosen in pieces, and tear away from the steel backing.

7 Short-distance driving leads to corrosion of bearings, because insufficient engine heat is produced to drive off the condensed water and corrosive gases. These products collect in the engine oil, forming acid and sludge. As the oil is carried to the engine bearings, the acid attacks and corrodes the bearing material.

8 Incorrect bearing installation during engine assembly will lead to bearing failure as well. Tight-fitting bearings leave insufficient bearing running clearance, and will result in oil starvation. Dirt or foreign particles trapped behind a bearing shell result in high spots on the bearing, which lead to failure.

9 *Do not* touch any shell's internal bearing surface with your fingers during re-assembly, as there is a risk of scratching the delicate surface, or of depositing particles of dirt on it.

10 As mentioned at the beginning of this Section, the bearing shells should be renewed as a matter of course during engine overhaul. To do otherwise is false economy.

Selection

11 Main and big-end bearings for the engines described in this Chapter are available in standard sizes and a range of undersizes to suit reground crankshafts.

12 Have the crankshaft measured by an engine reconditioning specialist. They will be able to supply the correctly sized bearings.

15 Engine overhaul – reassembly sequence

1 Before reassembly begins, ensure that all new parts have been obtained, and that all necessary tools are available. Read through the entire procedure to familiarise yourself with the work involved, and to ensure that all items necessary for reassembly of the engine are at hand. In addition to all normal tools and materials, thread-locking compound will be needed. A suitable tube of liquid sealant will also be required for the joint faces that are fitted without gaskets.

2 In order to save time and avoid problems, engine reassembly can be carried out in the following order, referring to Part A, B, C or D of this Chapter unless otherwise stated. Where applicable, use new gaskets and seals when refitting the various components.
   a) *Crankshaft (Section 17).*
   b) *Piston/connecting rod assemblies (Section 18).*
   c) *Oil pump.*
   d) *Sump.*
   e) *Flywheel/driveplate.*
   f) *Cylinder head.*
   g) *Timing belt/chain, tensioner and sprockets.*
   h) *Engine external components.*

3 At this stage, all engine components should be absolutely clean and dry, with all faults repaired. The components should be laid out (or in individual containers) on a completely clean work surface.

16 Piston rings – refitting

1 Before fitting new piston rings, the ring end gaps must be checked as follows.

2 Lay out the piston/connecting rod assemblies and the new piston ring sets, so that the ring sets will be matched with the same piston and cylinder during the end gap measurement and subsequent engine reassembly.

3 Insert the top ring into the first cylinder, and push it down the bore using the top of the piston. This will ensure that the ring remains square with the cylinder walls. Position the ring approximately 15.0 mm the bottom of the cylinder bore, at the lower limit of ring travel. Note that the top and second compression rings are different.

4 Measure the end gap using feeler blades, and compare the measurements with the figures given in the Specifications **(see illustration)**.

5 If the gap is too small (unlikely if genuine VW parts are used), it must be enlarged, or the ring ends may contact each other during engine operation, causing serious damage. Ideally, new piston rings providing

the correct end gap should be fitted. As a last resort, the end gap can be increased by filing the ring ends very carefully with a fine file. Mount the file in a vice equipped with soft jaws, slip the ring over the file with the ends contacting the file face, and slowly move the ring to remove material from the ends. Take care, as piston rings are sharp, and are easily broken.

6 With new piston rings, it is unlikely that the end gap will be too large. If the gaps are too large, check that you have the correct rings for your engine and for the particular cylinder bore size.

7 Repeat the checking procedure for each ring in the first cylinder, and then for the rings in the remaining cylinders. Remember to keep rings, pistons and cylinders matched up.

8 Once the ring end gaps have been checked and if necessary corrected, the rings can be fitted to the pistons.

9 Fit the piston rings using the same technique as for removal. Fit the bottom (oil control) ring first, and work up. Note that a two- or three-section oil control ring may be fitted; where a two-section ring is fitted, first insert the wire expander, then fit the ring. Ensure that the rings are fitted the correct way up – the top surface of the rings is normally marked TOP **(see illustration)**. Offset the piston ring gaps by 120° from each other. **Note:** *Always follow any instructions supplied with the new piston ring sets – different manufacturers may specify different procedures. Do not mix up the top and second compression rings, as they have different cross-sections.*

17 Crankshaft – refitting

1 Wipe off the surfaces of the bearing shells in the crankcase and bearing caps.

16.4 Check a piston ring end gap using a feeler blade

2 Press the bearing shells into their locations, ensuring that the tab on each shell engages in the notch in the cylinder block or bearing cap, and that the oil holes In the cylinder block and bearing shell are aligned **(see illustration)**. Take care not to touch any shells bearing surface with your fingers.

3 Where applicable, refit the crankshaft speed/position sensor wheel, and tighten the securing bolts to the specified torque. Make sure that the sensor wheel is correctly orientated as noted before removal.

4 Liberally coat the bearing shells in the crankcase with clean engine oil of the appropriate grade **(see illustration)**. Make sure that the bearing shells are still correctly seated in their locations.

5 Lower the crankshaft into position so that No 1 cylinder crankpin is at BDC, ready for fitting No 1 piston. Ensure that the crankshaft endfloat control thrustwasher halves, either side of the No 3 main bearing location, remain in position. Where applicable, take care not to damage the crankshaft speed/position

16.9 Piston ring TOP marking

sensor wheel as the crankshaft is lowered into position.

6 Lubricate the lower bearing shells in the main bearing caps with clean engine oil. Make sure that the crankshaft endfloat control thrustwasher halves are still correctly seated either side of No 3 bearing cap **(see illustrations)**.

7 Fit the main bearing caps in the correct order and orientation – No 1 bearing cap must be at the timing belt end of the engine and the bearing shell tab locating recesses in the crankcase and bearing caps must be adjacent to each other **(see illustration)**. Insert the bearing cap bolts (using new bolts where necessary), and hand-tighten them only.

8 Working from the centre bearing cap outwards, tighten the bearing cap bolts to their specified torque. On engines where two Stages are given for the torque, tighten all bolts to the Stage 1 torque, then go round again, and tighten all bolts through the Stage 2 angle **(see illustrations)**.

9 Check that the crankshaft rotates freely by turning it by hand. If resistance is felt, recheck the bearing running clearances, as described previously.

10 Check the crankshaft endfloat as described at the beginning of Section 13. If

17.2 Bearing shell correctly refitted

A Recess in cylinder block
B Lug on bearing shell
C Oil hole

17.4 Lubricate the upper bearing shells

17.6a Lubricate the lower bearing shells...

17.6b ...and make sure that the thrustwashers are correctly seated

17.7 Fitting No 1 main bearing cap

17.8a Tighten the main bearing cap bolts to the specified torque...

17.8b ...then through the specified angle

the thrust surfaces of the crankshaft have been checked and new thrustwashers have been fitted, then the endfloat should be within specification.

11 Refit the pistons and connecting rods or reconnect them to the crankshaft as described in Section 20.

12 Proceed as follows according to engine type:

a) On 1.4 litre petrol engines (engine code CAXA), refit the crankshaft oil seal housing, flywheel/driveplate, oil pump and pick-up pipe, sump, and main timing chain, as described in Chapter 2B.

b) On diesel engines, refit the crankshaft oil seal housings, flywheel/driveplate, oil pump and pick-up pipe, sump and oil baffle plate, and the crankshaft sprocket and timing belt, as described in Chapter 2C or 2D.

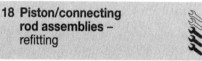

18 Piston/connecting rod assemblies – refitting

Note: A piston ring compressor tool will be required for this operation.

1 Note that the following procedure assumes that the crankshaft main bearing caps are in place.

2 Where applicable, refit the piston cooling oil spray jets to the bottom of the cylinder block, and tighten the securing bolts to the specified torque.

3 On engines where the big-end bearing caps are secured by nuts, fit new bolts to the connecting rods. Tap the old bolts out of the connecting rods using a soft-faced mallet, and tap the new bolts into position.

4 Ensure that the bearing shells are correctly

fitted, as described at the beginning of this Section. If new shells are being fitted, ensure that all traces of the protective grease are cleaned off using paraffin. Wipe dry the shells and connecting rods with a lint-free cloth.

5 Lubricate the cylinder bores, the pistons, piston rings and upper bearing shells with clean engine oil **(see illustrations)**. Lay out each piston/connecting rod assembly in order on a clean work surface. Where the bearing caps are secured with nuts, pad the threaded ends of the bolts with insulating tape to prevent them scratching the crankpins and bores when the pistons are refitted.

6 Start with piston/connecting rod assembly No 1. Make sure that the piston rings are still spaced as described in Section 16, then clamp them in position with a piston ring compressor tool.

7 Insert the piston/connecting rod assembly into the top of cylinder No 1. Lower the big-end in first, guiding it to protect the cylinder bores. Where oil jets are located at the bottoms of the bores, take particular care not to damage them when guiding the connecting rods onto the crankpins.

8 Ensure that the orientation of the piston in its cylinder is correct – the piston crown, connecting rod and big-end bearing cap have markings, which must point towards the timing belt end of the engine when the piston is installed in the bore **(see illustration)** – refer to Section 12 for details.

9 Using a block of wood or hammer handle against the piston crown, tap the assembly into the cylinder until the piston crown

18.5a Lubricate the pistons...

18.5b ...and big-end upper bearing shells with clean engine oil

18.8 Piston orientation and coding on diesel engines

18.9 Using a hammer handle to tap the piston into its bore

18.13a Tighten the big-end bearing cap bolts/nuts to the specified torque...

18.13b ...then through the specified angle

is flush with the top of the cylinder **(see illustration)**.

10 Ensure that the bearing shell is still correctly installed in the connecting rod, and then liberally lubricate the crankpin and both bearing shells with clean engine oil.

11 Taking care not to mark the cylinder bores; tap the piston/connecting rod assembly down the bore and onto the crankpin. On engines where the big-end caps are secured by nuts, remove the insulating tape from the threaded ends of the connecting rod bolts. Oil the bolt threads, and on engines where the big-end caps are secured by bolts, oil the undersides of the bolt heads.

12 Fit the big-end bearing cap, tightening its retaining nuts or bolts (as applicable) finger-tight at first. The connecting rod and its bearing cap both have recesses machined into them on one side, close to their mating surfaces – these recesses must both face the same way as the arrow on the piston crown (i.e. towards the timing end of the engine) when correctly installed. Reassemble the two components to satisfy this requirement.

13 Tighten the retaining bolts or nuts (as applicable) to the specified torque and angle, in the two stages given in the Specifications **(see illustrations)**.

14 Refit the other three remaining piston/connecting rod assemblies in the same way.

15 Rotate the crankshaft by hand. Check that it turns freely; some stiffness is to be expected if new parts have been fitted, but there should be no binding or tight spots.

16 On diesel engines, if new pistons have been fitted, or if a new short engine has been fitted, the projection of the piston crowns above the cylinder head mating face of the cylinder block at TDC must be measured. This measurement is used to determine the thickness of the new cylinder head gasket required. This procedure is described as part of the Cylinder head – removal, inspection and refitting procedure in Chapter 2C or 2D.

17 Proceed as follows according to engine type:

a) On 1.4 litre petrol engines, refit the oil

pick-up pipe, sump, and cylinder head, as described in Chapter 2A or 2B.
b) On 1.6 litre diesel engines, refit the oil pump and pick-up pipe, sump and oil baffle plate, cylinder head, as described in Chapter 2C.
c) On 2.0 litre diesel engines, refit the oil pump and pick-up pipe, sump and oil baffle plate, the balancer shaft assembly and cylinder head, as described in Chapter 2D.

19 Engine – initial start-up after overhaul and reassembly

1 Refit the remainder of the engine components in the order listed in Section 5 of this Chapter. Refit the engine to the vehicle as described in the relevant Section of this Chapter. Double-check the engine oil and coolant levels, and make a final check that everything has been reconnected. Make sure that there are no tools or rags left in the engine compartment.

2 Where necessary, reconnect the battery leads with reference to *'Disconnecting the battery'* at the rear of this manual.

Petrol models

3 Remove the spark plugs, referring to Chapter 1A, Section 25, for details.

4 The engine must be immobilised such that it can be turned over using the starter motor without starting – disable the fuel pump by unplugging the fuel pump power relay from the relay board with reference to Chapter 12, and also disable the ignition system by disconnecting the wiring from the DIS module or coils, as applicable.

Caution: To prevent damage to the catalytic converter, it is important to disable the fuel system.

5 Turn the engine using the starter motor until the oil pressure warning lamp goes out. If the lamp fails to extinguish after several seconds of cranking, check the engine oil level and oil filter security. Assuming these are correct,

check the security of the oil pressure switch wiring – do not progress any further until you are satisfied that oil is being pumped around the engine at sufficient pressure.

6 Refit the spark plugs, and reconnect the wiring to the fuel pump relay and DIS module or coils, as applicable.

Diesel models

7 Disconnect the injector harness wiring plug at the end of the cylinder head – refer to Chapter 4B, Section 4, for details.

8 Turn the engine using the starter motor until the oil pressure warning lamp goes out.

9 If the lamp fails to extinguish after several seconds of cranking, check the engine oil level and oil filter security. Assuming these are correct, check the security of the oil pressure switch cabling – do not progress any further until you are satisfied that oil is being pumped around the engine at sufficient pressure.

10 Reconnect the injector wiring plug.

All models

11 Start the engine, but be aware that as fuel system components have been disturbed, the cranking time may be a little longer than usual.

12 While the engine is idling, check for fuel, water and oil leaks. Don't be alarmed if there are some odd smells and the occasional plume of smoke as components heat up and burn off oil deposits.

13 Assuming all is well; keep the engine idling until hot water is felt circulating through the top hose.

14 After a few minutes, recheck the oil and coolant levels, and top-up as necessary.

15 There is no need to retighten the cylinder head bolts once the engine has been run following reassembly.

16 If new pistons, rings or crankshaft bearings have been fitted, the engine must be treated as new, and run-in for the first 600 miles. *Do not* operate the engine at full-throttle, or allow it to labour at low engine speeds in any gear. It is recommended that the engine oil and filter be changed at the end of this period.

Notes

Chapter 3
Cooling, heating and air conditioning systems

Contents

Degrees of difficulty

Easy, suitable for novice with little experience	Fairly easy, suitable for beginner with some experience	Fairly difficult, suitable for competent DIY mechanic	Difficult, suitable for experienced DIY mechanic	Very difficult, suitable for expert DIY or professional

Specifications

Engine codes*

1.4 litre:
  Non turbo engine . . . . CGGA and BUD
  Turbo charged engine. . . . . CAXA
Diesel engine:
  1.6 litre engine . . . . CAYB and CAYC
  2.0 litre engine . . . . CBAA, CBAB, CBBB, CFFA, CFFB and CFGB
* Note: *See 'Vehicle identification' at the end of this manual for the location of engine code markings.*

Cooling system pressure cap

Opening pressure. . . . . 1.4 to 1.6 bar

Radiator thermal switch

	Fan On	Fan Off
1.4 litre (Non turbo engine - CGGA and BUD):		
First level	92°C to 97°C	84°C to 91°C
Second level	99°C to 105°C	91°C to 98°C

Thermostat

	Begins to open	Fully open
Petrol engines:		
1.4 litre engine code CGGA and BUD	84°C	98°C
1.4 litre engine code CAXA:		
Thermostat 1 (lower element)	83°C	97°C
Thermostat 2 (upper element)	105°C	121°C
Diesel engines:		
2.0 litre engines	85°C	105°C
1.6 litre engine	92°C	107°C

Air-conditioning

Refrigerant:
    Capacity . . . . 525 ± 25g
    Type R134a
Compressor make/type:
    Delphi 6CVC 140
    Denso . . . . 6SEU14C, 7SEU17C or ES34
    Sanden . . . . 6PXE14 or PXE16
Refrigerant oil type:
    Delphi . . . . G 052 300 A2 or G 052 154 A2
    Denso . . . . G 052 300 A2
    Sanden . . . . G 052 154 A2
Refrigerant oil capacity for replacement compressor:
    Delphi 6CVC 140 . . . . 110cm³ ± 10cm³
    Denso 6SEU14C . . . . 90cm³ ± 10cm³
    Denso 7SEU17C . . . . 140cm³ ± 10cm³
    Denso ES34 . . . . 150cm³ ± 10cm³
    Sanden 6PXE14 . . . . 110cm³ ± 10cm³
    Sanden PXE16 . . . . 110cm³ ± 10cm³

Torque wrench settings

	Nm	lbf ft
Coolant pump:		
1.4 litre petrol engine code CGGA and BUD	20	15
Diesel engines:		
Common rail engines	9	6
Coolant pump pulley	20	15
Radiator	5	4
Radiator cooling fan shroud bolts	5	4
Thermostat cover bolts:		
1.4 litre petrol engine code CGGA and BUD	7	5
1.4 litre petrol engine code CAXA	5	4
All diesel engines	15	11
Thermostat housing-to-cylinder head bolts:		
1.4 litre petrol engine code CGGA and BUD	10	7
1.4 litre petrol engine code CAXA	11	7
All diesel engines	Not applicable	

1 General information and precautions

A pressurised cooling system is used, with a pump, an aluminium crossflow radiator, one or two electric cooling fans, a thermostat and a heater matrix, electric coolant circulation pump (turbo models), engine cooler as well as the interconnecting hoses. On automatic (DSG) transmission models, there is also a separate transmission oil cooler. On 1.4 litre non-turbo petrol engines, the thermostat is located on the top left-hand end of the cylinder head, in the coolant supply to the top of the radiator. On 1.4 litre turbocharged petrol engines, there are two thermostats located in the same housing, each having a different temperature control range. On all diesel engines, the thermostat is located in the front, right-hand side of the cylinder block, in the coolant return from the radiator.

The system functions as follows. Coolant is circulated through the cylinder block and head passages by the coolant pump which is driven by the auxiliary drivebelt on 1.4 litre turbocharged petrol engines, or by the timing belt on all other petrol and diesel engines. On diesel engines, an electrically operated coolant pump is also fitted. The coolant cools the cylinder bores, combustion surfaces and valve seats of the engine.

When the engine is cold, the thermostat is closed and the coolant only circulates around the engine and the heater matrix in the passenger compartment, however, when the engine reaches a predetermined temperature, the thermostat opens and the coolant passes through the radiator for additional cooling. The coolant enters the top of the radiator and is cooled, as it circulates down through the cooling tubes, by the inrush of air when the car is in forward motion. Airflow is supplemented by the action of the electric cooling fans when necessary. Upon leaving the bottom of radiator, the coolant returns to the engine and the cycle is repeated. As described earlier, the thermostat is located according to engine type, either in the coolant supply to the top of the radiator, or in the coolant return from the bottom of the radiator. The effect is identical in both cases – when it is closed, there is no circulation through the radiator, and when it is open, there is circulation. On some engines, the action of the thermostat is determined in conjunction with the engine management ECU.

Refer to Section 11 for information on the air conditioning system.

Precautions

Warning: Do not attempt to remove the expansion tank filler cap or disturb any part of the cooling system while the engine is hot, as there is a high risk of scalding. If the expansion tank filler cap must be removed before the engine and radiator have fully cooled (even though this is not recommended) the pressure in the cooling system must first be relieved. Cover the cap with a thick layer of cloth, to avoid scalding, and slowly unscrew the filler cap until a hissing sound can be heard. When the hissing has stopped, indicating that the pressure has reduced, slowly unscrew the filler cap until it can be removed; if more hissing sounds are heard, wait until they have stopped before unscrewing the cap completely. At all times keep well away from the filler cap opening.
• Do not allow antifreeze to come into contact with skin or painted surfaces of the vehicle. Rinse off spills immediately with plenty of water. Never leave antifreeze lying around in an open container or in a puddle in the driveway or on the garage floor. Children and pets are attracted by its sweet smell. Antifreeze can be fatal if ingested.

2.3 Using grips to release the hose clip

2.4a Pull out the retaining clip to release the radiator hoses ...

2.4b ... and the heater hoses

• *If the engine is hot, the electric cooling fan may start rotating even if the engine is not running, so be careful to keep hands, hair and loose clothing well clear when working in the engine compartment.*
• *Refer to Section 11 for additional precautions to be observed when working on models with air conditioning.*

2 Cooling system hoses – disconnection and renewal

Note: *Refer to the warnings given in Section 1 of this Chapter before proceeding.*
1 If the checks described in the relevant part of Chapter 1 reveal a faulty hose, it must be renewed as follows.
2 First drain the cooling system as described in Chapter1A, Section 30 (petrol engines) or Chapter 1B, Section 31 (diesel engines). If the coolant is not due for renewal, it may be re-used if it is collected in a clean container.
3 To disconnect a hose, release its retaining clips **(see illustration)**, then move them along the hose, clear of the relevant inlet/outlet union. Carefully work the hose free.
4 In order to disconnect the radiator inlet and outlet hoses (or heater hoses), apply pressure to hold the hose on to the relevant union, pull out the spring clip and pull the hose from the union **(see illustrations)**. Note that the radiator inlet and outlet unions are fragile; do not use excessive force when attempting to remove the hoses. If a hose proves to be difficult to remove, try to release it by rotating the hose ends before attempting to free it.
5 When fitting a hose, first slide the clips onto the hose, and then work the hose into position. If clamp type clips were originally fitted, it is a good idea to use screw type clips when refitting the hose. If the hose is stiff, use a little soapy water as a lubricant, or soften the hose by soaking it in hot water.
6 Work the hose into position, checking that it is correctly routed, and then slide each clip along the hose until it passes over the flared end of the relevant union, before securing it in position with the retaining clip.
7 Prior to refitting a radiator inlet or outlet

hose, renew the connection O-ring regardless of condition. The connections are a push-fit over the radiator unions.
8 Refill the cooling system as described in Chapter1A, Section 30 (petrol engines) or Chapter 1B, Section 31 (diesel engines).
9 Check thoroughly for leaks as soon as possible after disturbing any part of the cooling system.

3 Radiator – removal, inspection and refitting

Removal

1 Switch off the ignition and all electrical consumers.
2 Remove the air cleaner assembly as described in Chapter 4A, Section 2 (petrol

3.3a Undo the two retaining screws (arrowed) ...

3.5 Slacken the intercooler hose retaining clips - arrowed

engines) or Chapter 4B, Section 2 (diesel engines).
3 On all diesels and turbocharged petrol models, undo the two retaining screws and remove the air ducting from the front crossmember **(see illustrations)**.
4 Remove the engine undershield and drain the cooling system as described in Chapter 1A, Section 30 (petrol engines) or Chapter 1B, Section 31 (diesel engines). If the coolant is not due for renewal, it may be re-used if it is collected in a clean container.

Diesel Models

5 Slacken the retaining clips and remove the charge air intake hose from the left-hand side of the intercooler **(see illustration)**.
6 Release the locking clip and disconnect the cooling fan wiring block connector from the lower left-hand side of the radiator cowling **(see illustration)**.

3.3b ... and remove the air ducting

3.6 Disconnect the cooling fan wiring connector

3.7 Disconnect the radiator lower coolant hose

3.8a Undo the cowling lower retaining screws (arrowed) ...

3.8b ... then upper retaining screws (one side shown) ...

3.8c ... and withdraw the fan and cowling from under the vehicle

3.9 Disconnect the radiator upper coolant hose

hose to disconnect it from the upper left-hand side of the radiator **(see illustration)**.

10 Undo the two retaining bolts (one at each side of the radiator) and withdraw the radiator out through the top of the engine compartment **(see illustrations)**.

Petrol Models

11 Remove the front bumper as described in Chapter 11, Section 6.

12 Disconnect the wiring from the cooling fan connector at the bottom left-hand side of the radiator **(see illustration 3.6)**.

13 Unscrew the mounting bolts and remove the fans together with the cowling from the rear of the radiator.

14 Disconnect the coolant hoses from the radiator by pulling out the clips and easing off the hoses **(see illustration)**.

15 Working from the front of the vehicle, undo the two retaining screws (one at each side) to release the radiator side mountings **(see illustration)**.

16 Tilt the radiator and air-conditioning condenser backwards slightly, taking care not to damage the refrigerant pipes. **Do not** disconnect the refrigerant lines.

> ⚠ **Warning: Refer to the precautions given in Chapter 3, Section 11, before working on the air-conditioning system.**

17 With the radiator tilted back, undo the screw at the right-hand lower side of the radiator to release the refrigerant pipe mounting bracket.

18 Working at the front of the vehicle, undo the four retaining screws (two at each side) and

3.10a Undo the radiator securing nuts (one side shown) ...

3.10b ... and withdraw the radiator

7 Release the spring clip and pull the coolant hose to disconnect it from the lower right-hand side of the radiator **(see illustration)**.

8 Undo the cooling fan cowling retaining screws (two at each side), and then lower the

cooling fan and cowling out from under the vehicle **(see illustrations)**. As the cowling is removed, make sure that it does not damage the radiator or hoses as it is withdrawn.

9 Release the spring clip and pull the coolant

3.14 Disconnect the radiator upper coolant hose

3.15 Undo the retaining screws to release the mountings

3.18 Condenser to radiator securing screws – arrowed

3.23 Check the radiator side mountings

pull the radiator upwards to release it from the lower crossmember, then withdraw it from out of the engine compartment **(see illustration)**. Make sure the condenser is secured safely to the front crossmember, to prevent any damage to the fins or the refrigerant pipes.

Inspection

19 If the radiator has been removed due to suspected blockage, reverse flush it as described in the relevant part of Chapter 1.
20 Clean dirt and debris from the radiator fins, using an airline (in which case, wear eye protection) or a soft brush. Be careful, as the fins are sharp and easily damaged.
21 If necessary, a radiator specialist can perform a 'flow test' on the radiator, to establish whether an internal blockage exists.
22 A leaking radiator must be referred to a specialist for permanent repair. Do not attempt

to weld or solder a leaking radiator, as damage may result.
23 Check the radiator mounting rubbers, and renew if necessary **(see illustration)**.

Refitting

24 Refitting is a reversal of removal. On completion, refill the cooling system using the correct type of antifreeze as described in Chapter1A, Section 30 (petrol engines) or Chapter 1B, Section 31 (diesel engines).

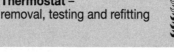

4 Thermostat –
removal, testing and refitting

Petrol engines

Removal

1 The thermostat is located in a housing at the left-hand end of the cylinder head. First, remove the engine top cover. Note, on turbocharged engines there are two thermostats in the coolant housing on the left-hand end of the cylinder head **(see illustration)**.
2 Remove the air cleaner assembly as described in Chapter 4A, Section 2.
3 Drain the cooling system as described in Chapter 1A, Section 30. If the coolant is not due for renewal, it may be re-used if it is collected in a clean container.
4 Disconnect the coolant hose(s) from the thermostat cover(s).
5 Undo the retaining screws, and remove the

thermostat cover, noting the locations of any brackets secured by the screws, then lift out the thermostat **(see illustrations)**. Recover the O-ring if it is loose.
6 On turbocharged engines, remove the spring and plunger for access to the thermostat element **(see illustrations)**.

Testing

Note: *If there is any question about the operation of the thermostat, it's best to renew it – they are not usually expensive items. Testing involves heating in, or over, an open pan of boiling water, which carries with it the risk of scalding. A thermostat that has seen more than five years' service may well be past its best already.*
7 A rough test of the thermostat, may be made by suspending it with a piece of string in a container full of water, but not touching the container. Heat the water to bring it to the boil – the thermostat must open by the time the water boils. If not, renew it.
8 If a thermometer is available, the precise opening temperature of the thermostat may be determined, and compared with the figures given in the Specifications. The opening temperature is also marked on the thermostat. On engine codes CAXA (1.4 litre turbocharged petrol engine), accurate testing will be difficult with the elements removed, but some indication may be obtained by testing with the thermostat assembled inside the housing.
9 A thermostat which fails to close as the water cools must also be renewed.

4.1 Location of thermostat - arrowed

4.5a Undo the screws...

4.5b ...remove the thermostat cover...

4.6a ...followed by the spring...

4.6b ...and plunger...

4.6c ...for access to the thermostat element - arrowed

4.11 Location of thermostat - arrowed

Refitting

10 Refitting is a reversal of removal, bearing in mind the following points.
a) Refit the thermostat using a new O-ring.
b) Refill the cooling system with the correct

type and quantity of coolant as described in Chapter 1A, Section 30.

Diesel engines

Removal

11 The thermostat is located behind the alternator at the front right-hand side of the engine cylinder block (see illustration). There are two types of thermostat fitted to diesel models:
1) Single hose to the thermostat cover, and the thermostat can be renewed separately.
2) Three hoses to the thermostat housing, the thermostat is part of the housing and can only be renewed as a complete assembly.

12 Drain the cooling system as described in Chapter 1B, Section 31. If the coolant is not due for renewal, it may be re-used if it is collected in a clean container.

13 Slacken the retaining clips and remove the rubber hose from the intercooler and

charge air ducting to the throttle housing/inlet manifold (see illustration).

14 Undo the bolt on the right-hand end of the sump, and disconnect the wiring connector from the charge pressure/temperature sensor on the charge air ducting (see illustrations).

15 Slacken the clip securing the charge air ducting to the throttle housing/inlet manifold, then undo the bolt at the rear of the air-conditioning compressor and withdraw the ducting out from the front of the engine (see illustrations).

16 To make access easier, remove the alternator as described in Chapter 5A, Section 5.

17 Release the securing clip(s) and disconnect the coolant hose(s) from the thermostat cover/housing (see illustration).

18 Unscrew the two securing bolts, and remove the thermostat cover/housing complete with the thermostat. Note the locations of any brackets secured by the bolts. Recover the O-ring if it is loose (see illustrations).

4.13 Remove the intercooler lower hose

4.14a Undo the charge air pipe retaining bolt -arrowed

4.14b Disconnect the charge air pressure sensor wiring connector

4.15a Slacken the hose retaining clip (arrowed) ...

4.15b ... undo the retaining bolt - arrowed ...

4.15c ... and remove the charge air pipe

4.17 Release the retaining clip - arrowed

4.18a Remove the thermostat housing ...

4.18b ... and renew the seal

5.7a Twin cooling fan set-up

5.7b Single cooling fan set-up

5.7c Release the wiring connector from the cowling

19 On models with one hose connections to the thermostat cover, remove the thermostat by twisting the thermostat 90° anti-clockwise, and then pull it from the cover.

20 On models with three hose connections to the thermostat housing, the thermostat cannot be removed, renew the complete unit.

Testing

21 Proceed as described in paragraphs 7 to 9.

Refitting

22 Refitting is a reversal of removal, bearing in mind the following points.
  a) *Refit the thermostat using a new O-ring.*
  b) *Insert the thermostat into the cover and twist 90° clockwise (where applicable). The thermostat should be fitted with the brace almost vertical.*
  c) *Ensure that any brackets are in place on the thermostat cover bolts as noted before removal.*
  d) *Refit the alternator (where applicable) with reference to Chapter 5A, Section 5.*
  e) *Refill the cooling system with the correct type and quantity of coolant as described in Chapter 1B, Section 31.*

5 Electric cooling fans – testing, removal and refitting

Testing

1 Depending on model, there may be one or two electric cooling fans fitted. The cooling fans are supplied with current through the ignition switch, cooling fan control unit (located on the motor), temperature sensor(s), the relays and fuses/fusible link (see Chapter 12). On 1.4 litre non-turbo petrol engines, the circuit is activated by a thermal switch, which is mounted in the outlet elbow at the bottom, left-hand side of the radiator. On all other engines, the engine management ECU activates the fan(s) according to the engine coolant temperature sensor(s). Testing of the cooling fan circuit is as follows.

2 If a fan does not appear to work, first check the fuses and fusible links. If they are

5.7d Undo the fan mounting nuts - arrowed ...

good, run the engine until normal operating temperature is reached, then allow it to idle. If the fan does not cut-in within a few minutes, the cause may be the temperature sender (where applicable), which can be checked by a VW dealer using specialist diagnostic equipment.

3 The motors can be checked, by disconnecting the motor wiring connector and connecting a 12-volt supply directly to the motor terminals. If the motor is faulty, it must be renewed, as no spares are available.

4 If the fan still fails to operate, check the cooling fan circuit wiring (Chapter 12). Check each wire for continuity and ensure that all connections are clean and free of corrosion.

5 On models with a cooling fan control unit, if no fault can be found, then it is likely that the cooling fan control unit is faulty. Testing of the unit should be entrusted to a VW dealer or specialist; if the unit is faulty it must be renewed.

Removal

6 Remove the cooling fan(s) complete with cowling from the rear of the radiator, as described in Section 3.

7 To remove the fan(s) and motor(s) from the shroud, first disconnect and release the wiring plugs, then unscrew the nuts and remove the units **(see illustrations)**.

Refitting

8 Refitting is a reversal of removal.

5.7e ... or retaining screws - arrowed

6 Cooling system electrical sensors – testing, removal and refitting

Testing

1 The switch/sensor contains a thermistor, which consists of an electronic component whose electrical resistance decreases at a predetermined rate as its temperature rises. When the coolant is cold, the switch/sensor resistance is high, current flow through the gauge is reduced, and the gauge needle points towards the 'cold' end of the scale. No resistance-to-temperature values are available. Therefore the only method of accurately checking the switch/sensor is with dedicated diagnostic equipment, and should be entrusted to a VW dealer or specialist. If the switch/sensor is faulty, it must be renewed.

Cooling fan thermal switch – 1.4 litre engine code CGGA and BUD

2 On 1.4 litre non-turbo petrol engines (with only one cooling fan fitted to the radiator), the fan thermal switch is located in the outlet elbow at the bottom left-hand side of the radiator.

3 The engine and radiator should be cold before removing the switch. Switch off the ignition and all electrical consumers.

4 Either drain the cooling system (as described in Chapter 1A, Section 30), or have ready a suitable plug that can be used to plug the switch aperture whilst it is removed.

6.6a Pull out the clip...

6.6b ... and remove the sensor with O-ring

6.12a Salcken the retaining clip (arrowed) ...

6.12b ... and undo the two retaining bolts (arrowed)

6.14a Disconnect the wiring connector - petrol engines

6.14b Disconnect the wiring connector (arrowed) - diesel engines

6.15a Pull out the clip...

6.15b ... and remove the sensor with O-ring - petrol engines

6.15c Pull out the clip and remove the sensor...

5 Disconnect the wiring plug from the switch.
6 Pull out the clip and remove the switch from the elbow. Recover the O-ring seals from the elbow and switch **(see illustrations)**.
7 Refitting is a reversal of removal, making sure that the switch is located securely in the

hose, using a new O-ring seal. On completion, refill the cooling system with the correct type and quantity of coolant as described in Chapter 1A, Section 30), or top-up as described in *Weekly checks*.
8 Start the engine and run it until it reaches

normal operating temperature, then continue to run the engine and check that the cooling fan cuts in and functions correctly. Check for any leaks around the hose and thermal switch.

Coolant temperature sensors – All models

9 The sensors are located in the different engines as follows:
 a) *On 1.4 litre non-turbocharged engines (with two cooling fans fitted) - one in thermostat housing on left-hand side of cylinder head.*
 b) *On 1.4 litre turbocharged engines – one in the bottom hose at left-hand side of the radiator, and one in thermostat housing on left-hand side of cylinder head.*
 c) *On all diesel engines – one in the upper hose at the right-hand side of the engine, and one in coolant housing on left-hand side of cylinder head.*

Sensors fitted to coolant housing

10 Where fitted, remove the upper trim cover from the top of the engine.
11 To access the temperature sensor fitted at the left-hand end of the cylinder head, remove the air cleaner assembly as described in Chapter 4A, Section 2 (petrol) or Chapter 4B, Section 2 (diesel).
12 On diesel engines, slacken the retaining clip, undo the two retaining bolts and move the charge air ducting away from the coolant housing **(see illustrations)**.
13 Either drain the cooling system, as described in Chapter 1A, Section 30 (petrol) or Chapter 1B, Section 31 (diesel), or have ready a suitable plug that can be used to plug the switch aperture whilst it is removed.
14 Disconnect the wiring connector from the sensor **(see illustrations)**.
15 Pull out the retaining clip and withdraw the sensor from the housing. Recover the O-ring **(see illustrations)**.
16 Refitting is a reversal of removal. Bearing in mind the following points.
 a) *Refit the sensor with a new O-ring.*
 b) *Refill the cooling system as described in Chapter 1A, Section 30 (petrol) or*

Chapter 1B, Section 31. Otherwise top-up as described in 'Weekly checks'.

Sensors fitted to coolant hoses

17 On 1.4 litre turbocharged engines, remove the sensor as described in paragraphs 3 to 8.

18 On diesel engines, the sensor is located in the hose positioned to the right-hand side of the engine **(see illustration)**. Remove the sensor from the hose as described in paragraphs 12 to 15.

19 Refitting is a reversal of removal.

7 Coolant pump – removal and refitting

1.4 litre petrol engine - codes CAXA

Note: *New coolant pumps are supplied with an integrated seal.*

Auxilliary belt-driven pump

1 Drain the cooling system as described in Chapter 1A, Section 30.

2 Before removing the auxiliary drivebelt, loosen the coolant pump pulley bolts **(see illustration)**, then remove the drivebelt as described in Chapter 1A, Section 26.

3 Unscrew the bolts and remove the pulley from the coolant pump **(see illustration)**.

4 Unscrew the mounting bolts and remove the coolant pump from the cylinder block **(see illustrations)**.

6.15d ...recover the O-ring from the housing - diesel engines

5 Refitting is a reversal of removal, bearing in mind the following points.
  a) *Clean the mating surfaces thoroughly before fitting the pump. If the original pump is being refitted, use a suitable sealant.*
  b) *Refill the cooling system as described in Chapter 1A, Section 30.*

Electric circulation pump

Note: *Only fitted to 1.4 litre turbocharged engines (code CAXA)*

6 On these models, the intercooler and turbocharger are cooled by a separate system, incorporating an auxiliary radiator, and an electrically operated coolant circulation pump. Begin by raising the front of the vehicle (see *Jacking and vehicle support*), and then remove the engine undershield. The pump is located under the inlet manifold **(see illustration)**. Access is limited.

7 Disconnect the wiring plug from the pump.

6.18 Coolant hose sensor - diesel engines

8 Clamp the coolant hoses to prevent loss, then release the clamps and disconnect the hoses from the pump **(see illustration)**.

9 Undo the retaining bolt and remove the pump.

10 Refitting is a reversal of removal. Top up the coolant, as described in Chapter 1A, Section 30.

1.4 litre petrol engine - code CGGA and BUD

Note: *New coolant pumps are supplied with an integrated seal.*

11 Drain the cooling system as described in Chapter 1A, Section 30.

12 Remove the camshaft timing belt as described in Chapter 2A, Section 6. If the belt is to be re-used, note the direction of rotation.

13 Remove the camshaft timing belt idler roller, and the upper bolt from the rear timing belt cover.

14 Unscrew the coolant pump retaining

7.2 Loosen the coolant pump pulley bolts before removing the auxiliary drivebelt

7.3 Removing the pulley from the coolant pump

7.4a Removing the coolant pump from the cylinder block – engine codes BKG, BLN, BAG, BLP, BLF and CAXA

7.4b Coolant pump removed from the engine

7.6 The electric circulation pump is located on the rear of the cylinder block (arrowed)

7.8 Disconnect the coolant hoses - arrowed

7.14 Coolant pump removal – engine codes CGGA and BUD

7.18a Undo the coolant pump bolts ...

7.18b ... remove it from the cylinder block ...

7.18c ... and renew the O-ring seal – diesel engines

bolts, and withdraw the pump from the engine block together with the rear timing belt cover. Recover the O-ring seal from the groove in the pump. If faulty, the pump must be renewed **(see illustration)**.

15 Refitting is a reversal of removal, bearing in mind the following points.

a) Clean the mating surfaces thoroughly before fitting the pump. If the original pump is being refitted, use a suitable sealant.

b) Refill the cooling system as described in Chapter 1A, Section 30.

All diesel engines

Belt driven coolant pump

16 Drain the cooling system as described in Chapter 1B, Section 31.

17 Remove the camshaft timing belt as described in Chapter 2C, Section 7 or Chapter 2D, Section 7.

18 Unscrew the coolant pump retaining bolts,

and remove the pump from the engine block. Recover the O-ring seal from the groove in the pump. If the pump is faulty, it must be renewed **(see illustrations)**.

19 Refitting is a reversal of removal, bearing in mind the following points.

a) Fit the coolant pump with a new O-ring.

b) Lubricate the O-ring with coolant.

c) Refill the cooling system as described in Chapter 1B, Section 31.

Electric circulation pump

20 Raise the front of the vehicle and support is securely on axle stands (see *Jacking and vehicle support*).

21 Undo the fasteners and remove the engine undertray.

22 Disconnect the wiring plug connector to the pump **(see illustration)**.

23 Fit hose clamps to the coolant hoses connected to the pump, and release the clips and disconnect the hoses from the pump **(see**

illustration). Be prepared for some loss of coolant.

24 Undo the retaining bolt and remove the pump **(see illustration)**.

25 Refitting is a reversal of removal. Top up the coolant, as described in Chapter 1B, Section 31.

8 Heating and ventilation system – general information

1 The heating/ventilation system consists of a four-speed blower motor (housed in the passenger compartment), face-level vents in the centre and at each end of the facia, and air ducts to the front and rear footwells.

2 The control unit is located in the facia, and the controls operate flap valves to deflect and mix the air flowing through the various parts of the heating/ventilation system. The flap valves are contained in the air distribution housing, which acts as a central distribution unit, passing air to the various ducts and vents.

3 Cold air enters the system through the grille at the rear of the engine compartment. A pollen filter is fitted to filter out dust, soot, pollen and spores from the air entering the vehicle.

4 The airflow, which can be boosted by the blower, flows through the various ducts, according to the settings of the controls. Stale air is expelled through ducts beneath the rear bumper. If warm air is required, the cold air is passed through the heater matrix, which is heated by the engine coolant.

5 If necessary, the outside air supply can be closed off, allowing the air inside the vehicle to be re-circulated. This can be useful to prevent unpleasant odours entering from outside the vehicle, but should only be used briefly, as the recirculated air quality inside the vehicle will soon deteriorate.

9 Heating and ventilation system components – removal and refitting

Heater/ventilation control unit

1 Switch off the ignition and all electrical consumers.

7.22 Disconnect the wiring connector - arrowed

7.23 Disconnect the coolant hoses - arrowed

7.24 Undo the pump bracket retaining bolt - arrowed

2 Carefully lever the trim panel from around the heater control panel, releasing the securing clips. Disconnect the wiring connector from the airbag warning light in the lower part of the trim panel **(see illustrations)**.

3 Undo the retaining screws and manouvre the control panel out from the facia **(see illustration)**.

4 As the panel is withdrawn, release the locking clips and disconnect the wiring connectors from the rear of the unit **(see illustration)**.

Heater matrix

5 At the rear of the engine compartment, remove the bulkhead trim from the plenum chamber, as described in Chapter 12, Section 18. This will make access to the coolant hoses on the bulkhead easier.

6 Using hose clamps, clamp the heater matrix inlet and return hoses located on the bulkhead at the rear of the engine compartment. Place a container beneath the hoses, then release the retaining clips and disconnect them **(see illustration)**. Note the location of the hoses for correct refitting.

7 With the hoses disconnected, remove the coolant from the matrix by blowing air into the upper tube, preferably using an airline, then the coolant can be caught coming out of the lower tube using a container.

Caution: Always use eye protection when using an airline.

8 Loosen (but do not remove) the bolt located between the matrix upper and lower tubes **(see illustration)**. This will make removal of the matrix easier.

9.2a Carefully lever the trim ...

9.2c ... then disconnect the wiring connector

9 Working in the passenger side foot well, undo the retaining screw and unclip the panel from the front of the centre console **(see illustrations)**.

10 Remove the passenger side glovebox

9.2b ... to release the retaining clips (arrowed) ...

9.3 Undo the heater control retaining screws (arrowed)

from the facia, as described in Chapter 11, Section 25.

11 Release the two retaining clips and remove the insulation trim from under the left-hand side of the facia **(see illustrations)**.

9.4 Release the locking clips and disconnect the wiring connectors

9.9a Undo the retaining screw ...

9.6 Disconnect the heater hoses from the bulkhead

9.9b ... and remove the console side trim panel

9.8 Slacken the securing bolt (arrowed)

9.11a Undo the two fasteners (arrowed) ...

9.11b ... and remove the trim panel

9.12 Undo the retaining screw and remove the heater ducting

9.13a Disconnect the wiring connector ...

9.13b ... undo the retaining bolt (arrowed) ...

9.13c ... and release the operating lever

15 Place cloth rags or similar on the floor beneath the heater matrix, then release the pipe clamps and pull the coolant pipes from the matrix (see illustrations). Take care not to damage the pipes as they are removed.

16 Withdraw the heater matrix out from the heater unit (see illustration).

17 Refitting is a reversal of removal, noting the following.

a) Fit the coolant pipe new seals to the heater matrix.

b) Make sure the foam seal is fitted correctly around the perimeter of the matrix.

c) When reconnecting the coolant pipes to the heater matrix, moisten the seals with coolant.

d) Make sure the conical ends of the pipes, locate in the matrix and the clamps must turn easily before tightening them securely.

e) Check that the rubber grommet in the bulkhead is correctly located in its hole.

f) Refill the cooling system and top-up the coolant level with reference to 'Weekly Checks' at the beginning of this Manual.

Heater housing

⚠ Warning: Refer to the precautions given in Section 11.

18 It is not possible to remove the housing without opening the refrigerant circuit to the air-conditioning evaporator; therefore this task must be entrusted to a VW dealer or an air conditioning specialist, before removal of the heater housing.

12 Undo the retaining screw and remove the passenger side footwell vent (see illustration).

13 Disconnect the wiring connector, then undo the retaining bolt and remove the flap motor from the side of the heater unit. As the

motor is withdrawn, unclip the operating arm from the flap lever (see illustrations).

14 Release the wiring loom from the lower part of the cover, then undo the retaining screws and remove the cover from the heater matrix (see illustrations).

9.14a Unclip the wiring loom ...

9.14b ...then undo the bolts and remove the plastic cover

9.15a Release the pipe clamps...

9.15b ...and pull the coolant pipes from the matrix

9.16 Withdraw the matrix from the heater unit

9.20 Heater housing unit retaining bolt - arrowed

9.21a Release the retaining clips (arrowed) …

9.21b … and disconnect the heater hoses from the bulkhead

Caution: The air conditioning compressor is driven permanently by the auxiliary drivebelt, and is not fitted with a magnetic clutch. It is not recommended that the engine is started without refrigerant being present in the system, as the compressor may overheat causing internal damage. Note also that if the refrigerant circuit is not opened within 10 minutes of evacuation, slight pressure may develop due to re-evaporation.

19 Remove the facia panel, as described in Chapter 11, Section 27.

20 At the rear of the engine compartment, remove the bulkhead trim from the plenum chamber, as described in Chapter 12, Section 18. Undo the heater housing securing bolt, behind the wiper motor at the rear of the bulkhead **(see illustration)**.

21 Using hose clamps, clamp the heater matrix inlet and return hoses located on the bulkhead at the rear of the engine compartment. Place a container beneath the hoses, then pull out the clips and disconnect them **(see illustrations)**. Note the location of the hoses for correct refitting.

22 With the hoses disconnected, remove the coolant from the matrix by blowing air into the upper tube; preferably using an airline, then the coolant can be caught coming out of the lower tube using a container.

 Warning: Always use eye protection when using an airline.

23 Where fitted, remove the cover from over the expansion valve on the bulkhead, by unscrewing the nut and releasing the retaining clips.

24 With the refrigerant evacuated, unscrew the bolts securing the refrigerant lines to the evaporator on the bulkhead at the rear of the engine compartment, and detach them. Recover the seals and plug the lines and evaporator openings to prevent entry of foreign matter and water vapour. Discard the seals, as new ones must be used on refitting **(see illustrations)**.

25 Working inside the vehicle, remove the footrest and condensation water drainage hose from the driver's side of the heater unit **(see illustrations)**.

9.24a Unscrew the bolts and remove the refrigerant lines from the evaporator

9.24b Plug the lines and evaporator while they are disconnected

26 Remove the right- and left-hand rear footwell ducts from the heater unit. It is recommended that the complete floor carpet be removed first, as the ducts are located below the carpets **(see illustrations)**. Also remove the centre console air duct.

27 Inside the car, place cloth rags or similar on the floor beneath the heater unit.

9.25a Remove the footrest...

9.25b ...and condensation water drainage hose from the heater unit

9.26a Remove the carpet …

9.26b ...then remove the right- and left-hand rear footwell ducts from the heater unit

9.28 Unclip the wiring loom retaining clips

9.29 Remove the central support legs

9.30a Remove the upper air inlet duct...

9.30b ... and lower air inlet duct

9.31 Undo the side support mounting bracket bolts (arrowed)

9.35 Heater control flap servo-motors (arrowed)

28 Note the location and routing of all wiring then disconnect it from the heater unit and metal support frame **(see illustration)**. Also note the location of plastic cable ties to ensure correct refitting.

29 Unbolt and remove the two central support legs located over the heater unit **(see illustration)**.

30 Remove the two air inlet ducts from the top of the heater **(see illustrations)**.

31 Undo the two retaining bolts from the mounting bracket on the right-hand side of the heater housing **(see illustration)**.

32 Carefully pull the heater unit from the bulkhead, taking care not to damage or bend the matrix tubes on the bulkhead. The help of an assistant may be required. Be prepared for coolant spillage as the assembly is removed from inside the car. As the heater unit assembly is removed, undo the fastener and release the wiring loom from the left-hand rear of the heater blower unit.

33 If necessary, the heater may be further dismantled on the bench.

34 Refitting is a reversal of removal, but refill the cooling system and top-up the coolant with reference to *Weekly Checks* at the beginning of this Manual. Have the air-conditioning system refilled by a VW dealer or an air conditioning specialist, when finished.

Fresh air/recirculating/ temperature/ flap positioning servomotors

Note: *Depending on model, there may be up to five air flap servomotors fitted. When there are five motors fitted, there are usually two each side of the heater housing and one by the blower motor housing.*

35 On the model being worked on, there are three air flap motors to the left-hand side of the heater housing **(see illustration)**, depending on which one is going to be worked

on, remove the passenger side glovebox and relevant facia trim panels, with reference to Chapter 11, Section 25.

36 Disconnect the wiring, undo the motor retaining bolt(s), then remove it from its mountings and separate it from the air flap lever **(see illustrations 9.13a, 9.13b & 9.13c)**.

37 Refitting is a reversal of removal. Note that if the motor is renewed, its basic settings must be reprogrammed by a VW dealer using specialist equipment.

Heater blower motor

38 Switch off the ignition and all electrical consumers.

39 Undo the screws and remove the cover from under the heater blower motor **(see illustrations 9.11a & 9.11b)**.

40 Disconnect the wiring connector from the blower motor, and where fitted undo the single securing screw **(see illustration)**.

9.40 Remove the retaining screw (arrowed) - where fitted

9.41a Release the locking peg ...

9.41b ... and remove the heater blower

9.45a Disconnect the wiring connector ...

9.45b ... and unclip the heater blower resistor

9.49a Disconnect the wiring connector ...

41 Release the catch and turn the blower motor clockwise to remove it from the heater housing **(see illustrations)**.
42 Refitting is a reversal of removal. Turn the blower motor anti-clockwise, in the direction of the arrow on the housing to lock the catch in position, if required fit screw to housing to secure the motor.

Heater blower motor series resistor

43 Switch off the ignition and all electrical consumers.
44 Undo the screws and remove the cover from under the heater blower motor **(see illustrations 9.11a & 9.11b)**.
45 Disconnect the wiring from the blower series resistor, then remove the resistor by pressing the catch upwards **(see illustrations)**.
Caution: The resistor may be very hot if the heater has recently been in use.
46 Refitting is the reverse of removal.

Footwell air temperature sensor

47 There are two sensors, one fitted to each side of the heater housing in the front footwell air ducting.
48 Remove the passenger side glovebox from the facia, to access the left-hand sesor. Remove the driver's side lower facia trim panels to access the right-hand sensor. Refer to Chapter 11, Section 25, for further information.
49 Reaching up behind the facia, disconnect the wiring plug connector, then turn the sensor

9.49b ... and remove the air temperature sensor

90° and pull it from the heater ducting **(see illustrations)**.
50 Refitting is a reversal of the removal procedure.

Side vent temperature sender

51 Switch off the ignition and all electrical consumers.
52 Unclip the trim panel from the relevant end of the facia.
53 Disconnect the wiring plug from the sender **(see illustration)**.
54 Turn the sender through 90°, and withdraw it from the housing.
55 Refitting is a reversal of removal.

Ambient temperature sender

56 Reach up behind the bumper, at the front, left-hand side of the radiator to locate the sensor. If required, remove the front bumper as described in Chapter 11, Section 6.

9.53 Right-hand side air vent temperature sensor (arrowed)

57 Disconnect the wiring connector, and then unclip the sender from its mounting bracket **(see illustrations)**.
58 Refitting is a reversal of removal. Make sure the wiring is fully connected to prevent entry of water.

Auxiliary heater

59 Some models are equipped with an auxiliary electrically powered heating element within the heating unit, next to the heater matrix. In order to remove the element, the glovebox must first be removed as described in Chapter 11, Section 25.
60 Undo the retaining nut, release the securing clip and disconnect the wiring block from the heater **(see illustrations)**.
61 Undo the retaining screw and remove the passenger side footwell vent **(see illustration 9.12)**.
62 Disconnect the wiring connector, then

9.57a Disconnect the wiring connector ...

9.57b ... and release the securing clip

9.60a Undo the wiring securing nut (arrowed) ...

9.60b ...release the securing clips ...

9.60c ...and disconnect the wiring block connector

9.64a Undo the retaining bolt (arrowed) ...

9.64b ... and withdraw the heating element

undo the retaining bolt and remove the flap motor from the side of the heater unit. As the motor is withdrawn, unclip the operating arm from the flap lever **(see illustrations 9.13a, 9.13b & 9.13c)**.

63 Release the wiring loom from the lower part of the cover, then undo the retaining screws and remove the cover from the heater matrix **(see illustrations 9.14a & 9.14b)**.
64 Undo the retaining bolt and withdraw

the heating element from the housing **(see illustrations)**.
65 Refitting is a reversal of removal.

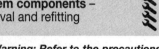

10 Air conditioning system components – removal and refitting

⚠ *Warning: Refer to the precautions given in Section 11, before working on the air-conditioning system.*

1 Before working on any components in the air-conditioning system, have the refrigerant evacuated from the air conditioning system by a VW dealer or refrigeration specialist.
Caution: The air conditioning compressor is driven permanently by the auxiliary drivebelt, and is not fitted with a magnetic clutch. It is not recommended that the engine be started without refrigerant being present in the system, as the compressor may overheat causing internal damage. Note also that if the refrigerant circuit is not opened within 10 minutes of evacuation, slight pressure may develop due to re-evaporation.

Evaporator

2 Remove the heater matrix and heater housing, as described earlier in Section 9.
3 Remove the rubber gaiter and foam cushion from around the coolant and refrigerant pipes **(see illustration)**.
4 Release any retaining clips and remove the coolant pipes from the housing **(see illustration)**.
5 Noting the routing and their fitted connections remove the wiring loom from around the heater housing **(see illustrations)**.
6 Working your way around the housing, undo the retaining bolts and split the housing into two parts **(see illustration)**.
7 To remove the evaporator, undo the retaining bolts and split the upper and lower halves of the housing, then withdraw the evaporator from the housing together with the refrigerant lines and rubber grommet **(see illustrations)**.
8 Refitting is a reversal of removal, fit new seals and have the system recharged by a VW dealer or refrigeration specialist.

10.3 Remove the rubber grommet from the pipes

10.4 Remove the heater pipes from the housing

10.5a Release the wiring loom from the retaining clips ...

10.5b ... and locating pegs on the heater housing

10.6 Unscrew the bolts securing the two section of the heater housing

10.7a Unscrew the bolts and separate the evaporator housing ...

10.7b ...then withdraw the evaporator

10.11 The condenser is bolted to the intercooler - diesel models

10.12 Disconnect the refrigerant lines from the condenser

10.17 Undo the refrigerant line securing bolts (arrowed) on the compressor

10.18 Disconnect the wiring connector

Condenser

9 Have the refrigerant evacuated from the air conditioning system by a VW dealer or refrigeration specialist.

10 Remove the radiator as described in Section 3 of this Chapter. On petrol engines, the condenser is attached to the front of the radiator.

11 On diesel engines, remove the intercooler as described in Chapter 4D, Section 7. The condenser is bolted to the front of the intercooler (see illustration).

12 Undo the screws and disconnect the refrigerant lines from the condenser (see illustration). Recover the seals and plug the lines and condenser openings to prevent entry of foreign matter and water vapour.

13 Carefully remove the condenser from the front of the engine compartment, taking care not to damage its fins.

14 Refitting is a reversal of removal, but fit new seals, and have the system recharged by a VW dealer or refrigeration specialist.

Compressor

15 Have the refrigerant evacuated from the air conditioning system by a VW dealer or refrigeration specialist.

16 Remove the auxiliary drivebelt as described in Chapter 1A, Section 26 (petrol) or Chapter 1B, Section 28 (diesel).

17 Unscrew the retaining bolts and disconnect the refrigeant lines from the compressor (see illustration). Remove the O-ring seals and renew them if necessary. Plug the open pipes and ports to prevent the ingress of moisture.

18 Disconnect the wiring plug connector from the rear of the compressor (see illustration).

19 Undo the retaining bolts (see illustration), and withdraw the compressor from the mounting bracket.

20 Refitting is a reversal of the removal procedure, ensure that all the fixings are tightened to the specified torque settings, where given. On completion, have new O-rings fitted to the refrigerant lines, and then have the system recharged by a VW dealer or refrigeration specialist.

Receiver/drier

Note: Check for the availability of parts before removal, there are different makes of receiver/drier and some cannot be renewed separately from the condenser.

21 The receiver/drier is attached to the left-hand side of the condenser.

10.19 Air conditioning compressor securing bolts - arrowed

22 Remove the condenser, as described in paragraphs 9 to 14.

Modine type

23 Unscrew the cap (with a T50 torx socket) from the top of the receiver/drier (see illustration). Peel back the warning label, where fitted.

Caution: DO NOT remove this cap if the system has not bee evacuated, as it will be under high pressure.

24 Insert a bolt into the receiver/drier sealing cover, push downwards slightly and extract the retaining circlip. Pull the receiver/drier element from place.

Showa type

25 The receiver/drier is bolted to the side of the condenser, undo the retaining bolt(s) and withdraw it from the condenser.

26 Refitting is a reversal of the removal

10.23 Unscrew cap (arrowed) to access receiver/drier

10.27 Evaporator temperature sensor

10.29 Disconnect the wiring connector from the sensor

procedure, ensure that all the fixings are tightened to the specified torque settings, where given. On completion, fit new O-rings and then have the system recharged by a VW dealer or refrigeration specialist.

Evaporator temperature sensor

27 The sensor is located to the right-hand side of the heater housing, behind the evaporator **(see illustration)**, to the left of the clutch pedal.

28 Working in the driver's side foot well, undo the retaining screw and unclip the panel from the front of the centre console.

29 Disconnect the wiring plug connector, then rotate the sensor 90° and pull it from the housing **(see illustration)**.

30 Refitting is a reversal of the removal procedure.

11 Air conditioning system – general information and precautions

General information

Air conditioning is fitted as standard to most models, and is available as manually

operated (Climatic) or automatically-operated (Climatronic). The Climatronic system works in conjunction with the heating and air conditioning systems to maintain a selected vehicle interior temperature fully automatically.

The air conditioning system enables the temperature of incoming air to be lowered, and dehumidifies the air, which makes for rapid demisting and increased comfort. The cooling side of the system works in the same way as a domestic refrigerator. Refrigerant gas is drawn into a belt-driven compressor and passes into a condenser mounted in front of the radiator, where it loses heat and becomes liquid. The liquid passes through an expansion valve to an evaporator, where it changes from liquid under high pressure to gas under low pressure. This change is accompanied by a drop in temperature, which in turn cools the evaporator. The refrigerant returns to the compressor and the cycle begins again.

Air blown through the evaporator passes to the air distribution unit, where it is mixed with hot air blown through the heater matrix to achieve the desired temperature in the passenger compartment.

The operation of the system is controlled

electronically by coolant temperature switches, and pressure switches which are screwed into the compressor high-pressure line. Any problems with the system should be referred to a VW dealer or an air conditioning specialist.

The only operation that can be carried out easily without discharging the refrigerant is the renewal of the compressor drivebelt, which is covered in the relevant part of Chapter 1. Removal of the evaporator and condenser requires the evacuation of the refrigerant. If necessary the compressor can be unbolted and moved aside, without disconnecting its flexible hoses, after removing the drivebelt **(see illustration)**.

Precautions

• *When an air conditioning system is fitted, it is necessary to observe special precautions whenever dealing with any part of the system, its associated components and any items which require disconnection of the system. If for any reason the system must be disconnected, entrust this task to your VW dealer or an air conditioning specialist.*

⚠️ *Warning: The refrigeration circuit contains a refrigerant and it is therefore dangerous to disconnect any part of the system without specialised knowledge and equipment. The refrigerant is potentially dangerous and should only be handled by qualified persons. If it is splashed onto the skin it can cause frostbite. It is not itself poisonous, but in the presence of a naked flame (including a cigarette) it forms a poisonous gas. Uncontrolled discharging of the refrigerant is dangerous and potentially damaging to the environment.*

• *Do not operate the air conditioning system if it is known to be short of refrigerant, as this may damage the compressor.*

Chapter 4 Part A:
Petrol engine fuel systems

Contents

Degrees of difficulty

Easy, suitable for novice with little experience	Fairly easy, suitable for beginner with some experience	Fairly difficult, suitable for competent DIY mechanic	Difficult, suitable for experienced DIY mechanic	Very difficult, suitable for expert DIY or professional

Specifications

Engine codes*
Indirect injection petrol engine .... BUD and CGGA
Direct injection turbocharged petrol engine (TSI)................ CAXA
* Note: *See 'Vehicle identification' at the end of this manual for the location of engine code markings.*

System type
Engine codes BUD and CGGA........................... Magneti-Marelli 4HV (indirect injection)
Engine code CAXA................................... Bosch Motronic MED17 (direct injection)
* Note: *See 'Vehicle identification' at the end of this manual for the location of engine code markings.*

Fuel system data
Fuel pump type .... Electric, immersed in fuel tank
Fuel pump delivery rate:
  Engine codes BUD and CGGA........................... 400 cc/min (battery voltage of 12.5 V)
  Engine code CAXA................................... 1450 cc/min (battery voltage of 12.5 V)
Regulated fuel pressure:
  Engine codes BUD and CGGA .... 2.5 bar
  Engine code CAXA................................... 4.0 to 7.0 bars
Engine idle speed.. non-adjustable, electronically controlled
Idle CO content (non-adjustable, electronically-controlled)......... 0.5% max
Injector electrical resistance (typical) .... 12 to 17 ohms

Torque wrench settings

	Nm	lbf ft
Accelerator pedal to bulkhead...............................	10	7
Fuel lift pump/gauge sender retaining ring.....................	110	81
Fuel tank retaining bolt:		
BUD and CGGA engines	20	15
CAXA engine...	25	18
Knock sensor	20	15
Oxygen (Lambda probe) sensors:		
BUD and CGGA engines	55	41
CAXA engine...	50	37
Camshaft position sensor	10	7
Fuel pressure sensor (engine code CAXA).....................	22	16
Fuel rail bolts (engine code BUD and CGGA)	7	5
High-pressure fuel line to pump (engine code CAXA)	18	13
High-pressure fuel pump (engine code CAXA)...................	20	15
Inlet manifold to cylinder head.............................	20	15
Throttle housing/module mounting bolts......................	7	5

* Do not re-use

1 General information and precautions

General information

The systems described in this Chapter are all self-contained engine management systems, which control both the fuel injection and ignition. This Chapter deals with the fuel system components only – see Chapter 4C for information on the turbocharger, exhaust and emission control systems, and to Chapter 5B for details of the ignition system.

The fuel injection system consists of a fuel tank, an electric fuel lift pump/level sender unit, a fuel filter, fuel supply and return lines, a throttle housing/module, four electronic fuel injectors, and an Electronic Control Unit (ECU) together with its associated sensors, actuators and wiring. Two basic fuel injection systems are fitted – an indirect (low pressure) injection system where the injectors inject fuel into the inlet manifold upstream of the inlet valves, and a direct (high pressure) injection system where the injectors inject fuel directly into the combustion chambers.

The indirect injection system uses a low pressure fuel rail and injectors fitted to the inlet manifold.

The direct injection system fitted to FSi (Fuel Stratified injection) and TSi (Turbocharged Stratified injection) engines) uses a high-pressure fuel pump mounted on top of the camshaft housing, actuated by a plunger in contact with the inlet camshaft. Fuel under high pressure is fed into a fuel rail incorporated into the lower inlet manifold. The injectors are located between the lower inlet manifold and cylinder head, and inject fuel directly into the combustion chambers.

The two basic fuel systems function in a very similar way, but there are significant detail differences, particularly in the sensors used and in the inlet manifold arrangements.

The fuel lift pump is immersed in the fuel inside the tank, and delivers a constant supply of fuel through a cartridge filter to the fuel rail or high-pressure fuel pump (according to engine). The fuel pressure regulator maintains a constant fuel pressure to the fuel injectors, and returns excess fuel to the tank through the return line. This constant flow system also helps to reduce fuel temperature, and prevents vaporisation. The pressure regulator is located on the fuel rail or high-pressure pump.

The fuel injectors are opened and closed by an Electronic Control Unit (ECU), which calculates the injection timing and duration according to engine speed, crankshaft/ camshaft position, throttle position and rate of opening, inlet manifold depression, inlet air temperature, coolant temperature, roadspeed and exhaust gas oxygen content information, received from sensors mounted on and around the engine.

Inlet air is drawn into the engine through the air cleaner, which contains a renewable paper filter element. On some non-turbo models, the inlet air temperature is regulated by a valve mounted in the air cleaner inlet trunking, which blends air at ambient temperature with hot air, drawn from over the exhaust manifold.

The temperature and pressure of the air entering the throttle housing is measured by a sensor mounted on the inlet manifold. This information is used by the ECU to fine-tune the fuelling requirements for different operating conditions. Turbocharged engines have an additional air temperature sensor mounted downstream of the throttle housing, which monitors the (compressed) air temperature after it has been through the turbocharger and intercooler.

Idle speed control is achieved partly by an electronic throttle valve positioning module, which is part of the throttle housing, and partly by the ignition system, which gives fine control of the idle speed by altering the ignition timing. As a result, manual adjustment of the engine idle speed is not necessary or possible.

The exhaust gas oxygen content is constantly monitored by the ECU by oxygen sensors (also known as lambda sensors), one before the catalytic converter, and one after – this improves sensor response time and accuracy, and the ECU compares the signals from each sensor to confirm that the converter is working correctly. The ECU uses the information from the sensors to modify the injection timing and duration to maintain the optimum air/fuel ratio. All models are fitted with one, two or three catalytic converters according to engine type – see Chapter 4C.

The ECU also controls the operation of the activated charcoal filter evaporative loss system – refer to Chapter 4C for further details.

It should be noted that fault diagnosis of all the engine management systems described in this Chapter is only possible with dedicated electronic test equipment. Problems with the systems operation should therefore be referred to a VW dealer for assessment. Once the fault has been identified, the removal/refitting sequences detailed in the following Sections will then allow the appropriate component(s) to be renewed as required.

Precautions

 Warning: Petrol is extremely flammable – great care must be taken when working on any part of the fuel system.

• *Do not smoke, or allow any naked flames or uncovered light bulbs near the work area. Note that gas-powered domestic appliances with pilot flames, such as heaters boilers and tumble-dryers, also present a fire hazard – bear this in mind if you are working in an area where such appliances are present. Always keep a suitable fire extinguisher close to the work area, and familiarise yourself with its operation before starting work. Wear eye protection when working on fuel systems, and wash off any fuel spilt on bare skin immediately with soap and water. Note that fuel vapour is just as dangerous as liquid fuel – possibly more so; a vessel that has been emptied of liquid fuel will still contain vapour, and can be potentially explosive.*

• *Many of the operations described in this Chapter involve the disconnection of fuel lines, which may cause an amount of fuel spillage. Before commencing work, refer to the above 'Warning' and the information in 'Safety first!' at the beginning of this manual.*

• *Residual fuel pressure always remains in the fuel system long after the engine has been switched off. This pressure must be relieved in a controlled manner before work can commence on any component in the fuel system – refer to Section 7.*

• *When working with fuel system components, pay particular attention to cleanliness – dirt entering the fuel system may cause blockages, which will lead to poor running.*

• *In the interests of personal safety and equipment protection, many of the procedures in this Chapter suggest that the negative lead be removed from the battery terminal. This firstly eliminates the possibility of accidental short-circuits being caused as the vehicle is being worked upon, and secondly prevents damage to electronic components (e.g. sensors, actuators, ECU's) which are particularly sensitive to the power surges caused by disconnection or reconnection of the wiring harness whilst they are still 'live'. Refer to 'Disconnecting the battery' at the rear of this manual.*

2 Air cleaner and inlet system
– removal and refitting

Removal

Engine code BUD and CGGA

1 The air cleaner is located on the inlet manifold at the rear of the engine. First, press down the clips and release the air inlet duct from the engine compartment front crossmember.
2 At the front left-hand corner, disconnect the small hose from the non-return valve.
3 Release the right-hand rear and left-hand front corners of the filter housing from the rubber grommets, by pulling sharply upwards and removing the air cleaner housing from the engine compartment.
4 With the assembly on the bench, if necessary, undo the screws and remove the cover, then remove the air filter element.

Engine code CAXA

5 The air cleaner is located in front of the battery on the left-hand side of the engine compartment.
6 Disconnect the vacuum hose from the filter housing (**see illustration**).

2.6 Disconnect the vacuum hose (arrowed)

2.7a Unclip the air ducting cover ...

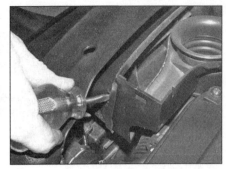

2.7b ... then release the retaining clips

2.8 Release the clamp and disconnect the hose from the turbocharger

2.9a Undo the retaining bolt (arrowed)...

2.9b ...and manoeuvre the air cleaner housing from place

7 Unclip the plastic cover from the air intake ducting, then release the two securing clips (one at each side) and remove the ducting from the front crossmember **(see illustrations)**.

8 Release the securing clip and disconnect the air intake hose from the turbo housing **(see illustration)**.

9 Undo the retaining bolt and pull the air cleaner housing upwards from the rubber mountings **(see illustrations)**.

Refitting

10 Refitting is a reversal of removal, noting the following points:

a) *Where applicable, ensure that the air filter element is correctly refitted, referring to Chapter 1A, Section 24, if necessary.*

b) *It is most important that an airtight seal is made between the air cleaner and the throttle housing/module.*

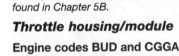

3 Fuel system components – removal and refitting

Note: *Observe the precautions in Section 1 before working on any component in the fuel system. Information on the engine management system sensors which are more directly related to the ignition system will be found in Chapter 5B.*

Throttle housing/module

Engine codes BUD and CGGA

1 On some models, the throttle housing is coolant-heated, so removing it entails disconnecting two coolant pipes. Even if the cooling system is drained as described in Chapter 1A, Section 30, it is likely that the throttle housing supply pipes will not be

drained, and spillage will result. If the coolant is not due for renewal, it may be preferable not to drain the system, but be prepared to plug the pipes once they have been disconnected.

2 As required, remove the air cleaner/air ducting as described in Section 2.

3 Disconnect the hose for the charcoal canister from the port on the throttle housing. Also disconnect the brake servo vacuum supply hose, where applicable.

4 Disconnect the wiring from the throttle housing/module **(see illustration)**.

5 Where applicable, disconnect the coolant pipes from the throttle housing/module, noting their positions for refitting. Be prepared for coolant spillage, and plug the pipe ends to prevent too much coolant loss.

6 Unscrew and remove the through-bolts, then lift the throttle housing/module away from the inlet manifold. Recover the O-ring seal **(see illustrations)**.

3.4 Throttle housing/module – (CAXA engine)

3.6a Remove the throttle housing/ module...

3.6b ...and recover the O-ring seal

3.8 Undo the bolts (arrowed) and remove the engine top cover

3.9a Unclip the hoses (arrowed) ...

3.9b ... from the air intake ducting

3.10 Disconnect the charge pressure sensor wiring connector

illustration). Pull out the engine oil level dipstick, and unclip the coolant hoses, as the cover is withdrawn.

9 Unclip the pressure/vacuum hoses from under the charge air pipe **(see illustrations).**

10 Disconnect the wiring plug connector from the charge pressure/intake air temperature sensor **(see illustration).**

11 Undo the two retaining screws, remove the securing clamp and release the charge air pipe from the turbocharger **(see illustrations).**

12 Release the two securing clips by spreading the retaining clips outwards, and release the charge air pipe from the throttle valve **(see illustrations).** Remove the charge air pipe from the engine compartment, making sure that there are no hoses or wiring still attached.

13 Disconnect the wiring plug **(see illustration),** then undo the retaining bolts and remove the throttle housing/module from the inlet manifold.

14 Refitting is a reversal of removal, noting the following:

  a) *Use a new throttle housing-to-inlet manifold seal.*

  b) *Tighten the throttle housing through-bolts evenly to the specified torque.*

  c) *Ensure that all hoses and electrical connectors are refitted securely.*

  d) *Apply a light coat of engine oil to the O-ring seal on the turbocharger prior to refitting the charge air pipe.*

Fuel injectors (and fuel rail where applicable)

Note: *Observe the precautions in Section 1 before working on any component in the fuel*

7 Refitting is a reversal of removal, noting the following:

  a) *Use a new throttle housing-to-inlet manifold seal.*

  b) *Tighten the throttle housing through-bolts evenly to the specified torque.*

  c) *Ensure that all hoses and electrical connectors are refitted securely.*

Engine code CAXA

8 Undo the retaining bolts and remove the cylinder head cover from the engine **(see**

3.11a Undo the screws (arrowed)...

3.11b ...recover the collar...

3.11c ...and remove the charge air pipe from the throttle housing

3.12a Press out the clip at each side...

3.12b ...and remove the charge air pipe from the turbocharger

3.13 Disconnect the throttle housing wiring connector

3.16 Disconnect the fuel lines

3.22 Renew the O-ring seal and spring element (arrowed)

3.23 Removing the fuel injectors from the cylinder head

system. If a faulty injector is suspected, before removing the injectors, it is worth trying the effect of one of the proprietary injector-cleaning treatments. These can be added to the petrol in the tank, and are intended to clean the injectors as you drive. Note that VW technicians use tool T10133 to remove the injectors and fit the new injector seals – although the tool may not be required to remove the injectors, it will be required to fit the new seals.

15 Refer to the wiring diagrams in Chapter 12, and then remove the fuel pump fuse, to ensure it is switched off. This is necessary, as opening the driver's door would otherwise start the pump.

Caution: Residual fuel pressure always remains in the fuel system long after the engine has been switched off; refer to Section 1.

16 On the right-hand side of the engine compartment, near the coolant expansion tank, disconnect the fuel supply line **(see illustration)**. Plug the end of the line to prevent entry of dust and dirt.

Engine code BUD and CGGA

17 Disconnect the wiring from the injectors located on the top of the inlet manifold.

18 Release the retaining clips and then remove the wiring loom guide, pull the fuel rail complete with injectors upwards and out from the inlet manifold.

19 Pull out the clips and remove the injectors from the fuel rail.

Engine code CAXA

20 Disconnect the wiring from the charcoal canister solenoid valve.

21 Remove the upper and lower parts of the inlet manifold as described in Section 8.

22 Remove the spring element and O-ring seal from the top of the injector **(see illustration)**. **Note:** *Both the spring element and O-ring seal must be renewed.*

23 At this stage VW technicians use the special slide-hammer tool to remove the injectors, however, if the injectors are not tight, they may have remained with the inlet manifold lower part when it was removed in paragraph 21 **(see illustration)**.

All engine codes

24 Refitting is a reversal of removal, but

thoroughly clean the cylinder head seatings, and fit new injector seals **(see illustrations)**. On CAXA, the seals are made of Teflon, and the special VW tool will be required to compress the seals before fitting the injectors to the cylinder head. **Do not** grease or oil the seals on these engines. On engine codes BUD and CGGA (i.e. low-pressure injection system), lightly moisten the O-ring seals with clean engine oil.

Charge air pressure/ temperature sender (engine code CAXA)

25 The air temperature/charge air pressure sensor is located on charge air pipe; disconnect the wiring connector **(see illustration 3.10)**.

26 Undo the screws and remove the sensor from the charge air pipe **(see illustration)**. Renew the O-ring seal.

27 Refitting is a reversal of removal.

3.24a Thoroughly clean the injector seatings in the cylinder head

3.26 Undo the charge air pressure sensor retaining screws - CAXA engine

Inlet manifold pressure sender (engine code CAXA)

28 The inlet manifold pressure sensor is located on the top of the inlet manifold **(see illustration)**. Disconnect the wiring connector, and then undo the screws and remove the sensor. Renew the O-ring seal.

29 Refitting is a reversal of removal.

Inlet manifold pressure/ temperature sender (engine codes BUD and CGGA)

30 The air pressure/temperature sender is located on the right-hand side of the inlet manifold. Note that access is limited.

31 Disconnect the wiring from the sender, release the retaining clips and withdraw the sender from the inlet manifold. Recover the seal and discard, as a new one must be used on refitting.

3.24b Fitting new injector seals

3.28 Inlet manifold air pressure sensor (arrowed) - CAXA engine

3.33 High pressure fuel pump (arrowed) - CAXA engine

3.35 Disconnect the fuel lines from the pump

Fuel pressure sensor (engine code CAXA)

43 The fuel pressure sensor is located on the left-hand side of the lower inlet manifold, below the throttle housing.

44 Depressurise the fuel injection system as described in Section 7.

45 Disconnect the wiring from the sensor, then unscrew and remove it. Be prepared for some loss of fuel by positioning a suitable container beneath the sensor.

46 Refitting is a reversal of removal, but tighten the sensor to the specified torque.

Coolant temperature sensor

47 Refer to Chapter 3, Section 6.

Camshaft position sensor

48 The camshaft position sensor is located on the top, left-hand rear of the camshaft housing (see illustration).

49 Undo the retaining bolts and remove the cylinder head cover from the engine (see illustration). Pull out the engine oil level dipstick, and unclip the coolant hoses, as the cover is withdrawn.

50 Disconnect the wiring, and then undo the retaining screw and withdraw the sensor from the camshaft housing. Recover the O-ring seal and check for any damage.

51 Refitting is a reversal of removal, but tighten the bolt to the specified torque setting and fit a new O-ring seal if required.

Engine speed sensor

52 The engine speed sensor is mounted at the left-hand rear of the cylinder block, next to the transmission bellhousing, and access is very difficult. Prise out the rubber bung for access to the sensor (see illustration).

53 Trace the wiring back from the sensor, and unplug the harness connector.

54 Unscrew the retaining bolt and withdraw the sensor from the cylinder block.

55 Refitting is a reversal of removal.

Oxygen (lambda probe) sensors

⚠️ *Warning: Working on the sensors is only advisable with the engine (and therefore the exhaust system) completely cold. The catalytic converter in particular will be very hot for some time after the engine has been switched off.*

56 All models have one sensor threaded into the exhaust manifold or at the top of the exhaust downpipe, ahead of the catalytic converter, and a second sensor mounted in the exhaust front pipe or intermediate pipe, downstream of the converter.

57 Working from the sensor, trace the wiring harness from the oxygen sensor back to the connector, and disconnect it (see illustration). Typically, the wiring plug is coloured black for the upstream sensor, and brown/purple for the downstream sensor. Unclip the sensor wiring from any retaining clips, noting how it is routed.

32 Refitting is a reversal of removal, but fit a new seal.

High-pressure fuel pump (engine code CAXA)

33 The high-pressure fuel pump is located on top of the camshaft housing (see illustration).

34 Depressurise the fuel injection system as described in Section 7.

35 Position cloth rags around the high-pressure fuel pump, then disconnect the fuel lines; release the clips and disconnect the low-pressure fuel line from the high-pressure pump. Unscrew the union nuts and disconnect the high-pressure fuel line, using an open-ended spanner to counter hold the pipe union (see illustration).

36 Disconnect the wiring connector from the side of the fuel pump.

37 Unscrew the mounting bolts, then remove the high-pressure fuel pump from the top of the camshaft housing. Recover the O-ring seal and discard it, as a new one must used on refitting.

38 Extract the roller bucket tappet from the camshaft cover housing.

39 Clean the mating faces of the pump and camshaft housing.

40 Lubricate the roller bucket tappet with clean engine oil, then insert it in the camshaft housing.

41 Smear clean engine oil on the new O-ring seal, then refit the fuel pump together with the O-ring seal. Insert the mounting bolts and tighten to the specified torque.

42 Reconnect the wiring, then reconnect the fuel lines and tighten the union nuts to the specified torque. To ensure correct seating, the nut(s) and bolts must be progressively tightened to their specified torque.

3.48 Camshaft position sensor (arrowed)

3.49 Remove cylinder head cover

3.52 Prise out the rubber bung for access to the speed sensor

3.57 Unclip the wiring from the bracket and disconnect the connector (arrowed)

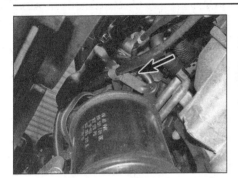

3.58a Upper oxygen sensor (arrowed)

3.58b Lower oxygen sensor (arrowed)

3.62 Release the wiring connector locking clip (arrowed)

58 Access to the upstream sensor is possible on some models from above, while the downstream sensor (where fitted) is only accessible from below **(see illustrations)**.

59 Unscrew and remove the sensor, taking care to avoid damaging the sensor probe as it is removed. **Note:** *As a flying lead remains connected to the sensor after it has been disconnected, if the correct-size spanner is not available, a slotted socket will be required to remove the sensor.*

60 Apply a little high-temperature anti-seize grease to the sensor threads – avoid contaminating the probe tip.

61 Refit the sensor, tightening it to the correct torque. Reconnect the wiring, making sure that the wiring loom is secured in its retaining clips.

Throttle pedal/position sensor

62 Release the securing clip and disconnect the wiring connector from the top of the accelerator pedal **(see illustration)**.

63 Prise off the cap, and undo the screw securing the throttle pedal to the bulkhead **(see illustration)**.

64 The throttle pedal is clipped to two metal pegs in the floor panel, using a lever and thin screwdriver, release the securing clips **(see illustration)**.

65 The outer clip can be released by pressing the screwdriver inwards to release the securing clip, whilst levering the pedal upwards. Then insert the screwdriver into the inner slot and push it to the left to release the securing clip **(see illustrations)**. Withdraw the throttle pedal from the floor panel and out from the vehicle.

66 Refitting is a reversal of removal.

Clutch pedal switch

67 The clutch pedal switch is clipped to the clutch master cylinder on the pedal bracket. Remove the master cylinder as described in Chapter 6, Section 4.

68 Unclip the pedal switch from the bottom of the master cylinder.

69 Refitting is a reversal of removal.

Electronic control unit (ECU)

Caution: Always wait at least 30 seconds after switching off the ignition before disconnecting the wiring from the ECU. When the wiring is disconnected, all the

3.63 Undo the pedal retaining bolt (arrowed)

learned values are erased, although any contents of the fault memory are retained. After reconnecting the wiring, the basic settings must be reinstated by a VW dealer using a special test instrument. Note also that if the ECU is renewed, the

3.65a Release the outer clip by pressing the screwdriver forwards

3.65c Direction (arrowed) to release the two securing clips

3.64 Throttle pedal securing pegs in the floor panel

identification of the new ECU must be transferred to the immobiliser control unit by a VW dealer.

70 The ECU is located centrally behind the engine compartment bulkhead **(see illustration)**, under one of the windscreen cowl

3.65b Release the inner clip by pushing the screwdriver inwards, and then to the left to release the clip

3.70 Electronic control unit located in scuttle panel

3.71 Unclip the control unit from the mounting bracket

3.72a Cut a slot in the end of the shear bolts (arrowed) …

3.72b … and use a screwdriver to remove them

3.73a Pull the clamp upwards …

3.73b … and remove it from around the control unit

3.74 Pull out the locking slides at each side to disconnect the wiring

panels. Remove the wiper arms and cowl panel as for windscreen wiper motor removal and refitting, described in Chapter 12, Section 18.

71 Release the ECU from the lower tray and withdraw it from inside the bulkhead **(see illustration)**. Disconnect the battery negative lead and position it away from the terminal. **Note:** *Refer to 'Disconnecting the battery' at the rear of this manual first.*

72 Place a piece of cardboard under the ECU and either drill out the shear bolts that are holding the wiring connector security cover together, or cut a slot in them and unscrew them with a screwdriver **(see illustrations)**. New shear bolts will be required for refitting.

73 Lever the top part upwards and remove the security cover from around the ECU **(see illustrations)**.

74 Disconnect the wiring plugs from the ECU by sliding the locking levers outwards,

to release them from the top of the ECU **(see illustration)**. Remove the ECU from the vehicle.

75 Refitting is a reversal of removal, using new shear bolts to secure the wiring cover. Bear in mind the comments made in the Caution above – the ECU will not work correctly until it has been electronically coded.

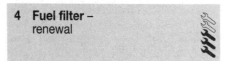

4 Fuel filter –
renewal

Note: *Observe the precautions in Section 1 before working on any component in the fuel system.*

1 The fuel filter is located in front of the fuel tank, on the right-hand underside of the car **(see illustration)**.

2 Jack up the right-hand rear of the car, and support it on an axle stand (see *Jacking and vehicle support*). When positioning the axle stand, ensure that it will not inhibit access to the filter.

Caution: Residual fuel pressure always remains in the fuel system long after the engine has been switched off; refer to Section 1.

3 Disconnect the fuel hoses at each end of the filter, noting their locations for refitting. There are two hoses fitted to the rear of the filter and one hose at the front.

4 The connections are of quick-release type, disconnected by pressing the catch on each connector **(see illustrations)**. It may be necessary to release the hoses from the clips on the underside of the car, to allow greater movement.

5 The filter is held in position by a large

4.1 Fuel filter location (arrowed)

4.4a Release the locking clips …

4.4b … and disconnect the fuel lines

retaining screw (see illustration). Before removing the filter, look for an arrow marking, which points in the direction of fuel flow – in this case, towards the front of the car. The new filter must be fitted the same way round.

6 Slide the filter out of position (see illustration). Try to keep it as level as possible, to reduce fuel spillage. Dispose of the old filter carefully – even if the fuel inside is tipped out, the filter element will still be soaked in fuel, and will be highly flammable.

7 Offer the new filter into position, ensuring that the direction-of-flow arrow is pointing towards the front of the car and the peg on the rear of the filter is located correctly (see illustrations). Tighten the securing screw on the filter retaining bracket.

8 Connect the fuel hoses to each end of the filter, in the same positions as noted on removal. Push the hoses fully onto the filter stubs, and if necessary, clip them back to the underside of the car.

9 Lower the car to the ground, then start the engine and check for signs of fuel leakage at both ends of the filter.

4.5 Slacken the retaining screw ...

4.6 ... and slide the filter out of the bracket

4.7a Make sure the arrow is facing forwards ...

4.7b ...and the peg on the filter (arrowed) locates in the bracket

5 Fuel lift pump and gauge sender unit – removal and refitting

Note: Observe the precautions in Section 1 before working on any component in the fuel system.

⚠ Warning: Avoid direct skin contact with fuel – wear protective clothing and gloves when handling fuel system components. Ensure that the work area is well ventilated to prevent the build-up of fuel vapour.

General information

1 The fuel lift pump and gauge sender unit are combined in one assembly, which is mounted in the top of the fuel tank. Access is beneath a cover in the load space floor. The unit protrudes into the fuel tank, and its removal involves exposing the contents of the tank to the atmosphere.

Removal

2 Ensure that the vehicle is parked on a level surface, then disconnect the battery negative lead and position it away from the terminal. Note: Refer to 'Disconnecting the battery' at the rear of this manual first.

3 Remove the rear seat cushion (Chapter 11, Section 22), and lift the carpet from the load space floor.

4 Where applicable, unclip the fuel pump control unit from the plastic cover and disconnect the wiring connector (see illustration).

5 Prise up the plastic cover and disconnect the wiring from the top of the lift pump/gauge sender unit (see illustration).

6 Pad the area around the supply and return fuel hoses with rags to absorb any spilt fuel from the fuel lines, and then squeeze

the catches to release the hose clips and disconnect them (see illustration). Observe the supply and return arrow markings on the ports – label the fuel hoses accordingly to ensure correct refitting later. The supply pipe is black, and may have white markings,

while the return pipe is blue, or has blue markings.

7 Note the position of the alignment marks, then unscrew and remove the securing ring. Use a pair of water pump pliers (or home-made tool) to grip and rotate the securing ring (see illustrations).

5.4 Disconnect the wiring connector block

5.5 Prise up the cover and disconnect the wiring from the pump/gauge unit

5.6 Fuel supply and return hoses

5.7a Note the alignment marks...

5.7b ...then use a suitable tool to unscrew...

5.7c ...and remove the securing ring

5.8 Removing the lift pump/gauge sender unit from the fuel tank

5.9 Lift pump/gauge sender unit removed from the car

5.11 If not removed with the unit, recover the rubber seal and check its condition

10 The fuel pick-up incorporated in the assembly is spring-loaded to ensure that it always draws fuel from the lowest part of the tank. Check that the pick-up is free to move under spring tension with respect to the sender unit body.

11 Inspect the rubber seal from the fuel tank aperture for signs of fatigue – renew it if necessary **(see illustration)**.

12 Inspect the sender unit wiper and track; clean off any dirt and debris that may have accumulated, and look for breaks in the track.

Engine code BUD and CGGA

13 If required, the sender unit can be separated from the assembly, as follows. Disconnect the two small wires (note their positions), then remove the four screws and slide the unit downwards to remove **(see illustrations)**.

14 The unit top plate can be removed by releasing the plastic tags at either side; recover the large spring that fits onto a peg on the plate underside **(see illustrations)**.

Engine code CAXA

15 Gently pull the sender unit to the side and upwards at the same time. If the sender unit is reluctant to release, gently push the retaining tabs outwards at the same time as pull the sender unit upwards **(see illustrations)**.

16 Note their fitted positions, release the clips and disconnect the sender unit wiring plugs **(see illustration)**. Note: *On later sender units, the plugs are released by depressing the clips on the front **and** rear of the plastic housing.*

8 Lift out the lift pump/gauge sender unit, holding it above the level of the fuel in the tank until the excess fuel has drained out. Recover the flange and seal **(see illustration)**.

9 With the pump/sender unit removed from

the car, lay it on an absorbent card or rag **(see illustration)**. Inspect the float at the end of the sender unit swinging arm for punctures and fuel ingress – renew the unit if it appears damaged.

5.13a Disconnect the small wires...

5.13b ...then undo the screws and slide out the sender unit

5.14a Prise up the retaining tags . . .

5.14b ...and recover the spring fitted under the top plate

5.15a Press the clips (arrowed) to the outside...

Refitting

17 Refit the lift pump/sender unit by following the removal procedure in reverse, noting the following points:

a) *Take care not to bend the float arm as the unit is refitted.*

b) *Smear the outside of tank aperture rubber seal with clean fuel or lubricating spray, to ease fitting. Locate the seal in the tank aperture before fitting the lift pump/ sender unit* (see illustrations).

c) *Tighten the securing ring to the specified torque setting.*

d) *Reconnect the fuel hoses to the correct ports – observe the direction-of-flow arrow markings, and refer to paragraph 6. Ensure that the fuel hose fittings click fully into place.*

e) *On completion, check that all associated pipes are securely clipped to the tank, then run the engine and check for fuel leaks.*

6 Fuel tank – removal and refitting

Note: *Observe the precautions in Section 1 before working on any component in the fuel system.*

Removal

1 Before the tank can be removed, it must be drained of as much fuel as possible. As no drain plug is provided, it is preferable to carry out this operation with the tank almost empty.

2 Open the fuel filler flap, and unscrew the fuel filler cap – leave the cap loosely in place.

3 Disconnect the battery negative lead and position it away from the terminal. **Note:** *Refer to 'Disconnecting the battery' at the rear of this manual first.* Using a hand pump or syphon, remove any remaining fuel from the bottom of the tank.

4 Loosen the right-hand rear wheel bolts, then jack up the rear of the car and remove the right-hand rear wheel.

5 Undo the retaining screws, release the retaining clips and remove the right-hand rear wheel arch liner.

6 Gain access to the top of the fuel pump/ sender unit and disconnect the wiring harness plug and fuel pipes from the top of the pump/ sender unit, refer to Section 5.

7 Open the fuel filler flap, and unscrew the fuel cap from the top of the filler neck. Unscrew the fuel filler flap unit retaining screw (on the side opposite the flap hinge), and then ease the flap unit out of position. Recover the rubber seal that fits around the filler neck.

8 Working under the wheel arch, unbolt the fuel filler pipe from the body.

9 Release the mounting rubbers and support the rear of the exhaust system to allow removal of the fuel tank.

Caution: Residual fuel pressure always remains in the fuel system long after the engine has been switched off; refer to Section 1.

5.15b ...and slide the sender unit upwards

5.17a Locate the seal in the tank aperture...

10 Disconnect the fuel feed pipe (black) and fuel breather pipe (white) from the connections at the front right-hand side of the fuel tank **(see illustration)**. Note the fuel filter can be removed with the fuel tank.

11 Position a trolley jack under the centre of the tank. Insert a block of wood between the jack head and the tank to prevent damage to the tank surface. Raise the jack until it just takes the weight of the tank.

12 Unscrew the mounting bolts and detach the tank strap **(see illustration)**.

13 Lower the jack and tank away from the underside of the vehicle. If necessary, unscrew the nuts and remove the heat shield from the tank.

14 If the tank is contaminated with sediment or water, remove the fuel pump/sender unit (see Section 5) and swill the tank out with clean fuel. The tank is injection-moulded from a synthetic material, and if damaged, it should be renewed.

6.10 Disconnect the fuel lines from the fuel filter

5.16 Depress the clips (arrowed) and pull the wiring plugs from the sender

5.17b ...then fit the lift pump/sender unit

However, in certain cases it may be possible to have small leaks or minor damage repaired. Seek the advice of a suitable specialist before attempting to repair the fuel tank.

Refitting

15 Refitting is the reverse of the removal procedure, noting the following points:

a) *When lifting the tank back into position, make sure the mounting rubbers are correctly positioned, and take care to ensure none of the hoses get trapped between the tank and vehicle body.*

b) *Ensure that all pipes and hoses are correctly routed, are not kinked, and are securely held in position with their retaining clips.*

c) *Tighten the tank strap retaining bolts to the specified torque.*

d) *On completion, refill the tank with fuel, and exhaustively check for signs of leakage prior to taking the vehicle out on the road.*

6.12 Fuel tank strap retaining bolts (arrowed)

8.8 Removing the inlet manifold from the cylinder head

7 Fuel injection system – depressurisation

Note: Observe the precautions in Section 1 before working on any component in the fuel system.

⚠ *Warning: The following procedure will merely relieve the pressure in the fuel system – remember that fuel will still be present in the system components and take precautions accordingly before disconnecting any of them.*

1 The fuel system referred to in this Section is defined as the tank-mounted fuel pump, the fuel filter, the fuel injectors, the fuel pressure regulator, and the metal pipes and flexible hoses of the fuel lines between these components. All these contain fuel, which will be under pressure while the engine is running and/or while the ignition is switched on. The pressure will remain for some time after the ignition has been switched off, and must be relieved before any of these components are disturbed for servicing work. Ideally, the engine should be allowed to cool completely before work commences.

2 On turbo engines with the high-pressure system, disconnect the wiring from the fuel pressure regulating valve on the high-pressure pump, then run the engine at idling speed for 10 seconds. *Note: With the engine switched off, disconnect the fuel lines as quickly as possible, as the internal fuel pressure may rise due to heat from the engine.*

3 On non-turbo engines, refer to Chapter 12 and remove the fuel pump relay. Alternatively, identify and remove tne fuel pump fuse from the fusebox. With the fuel pump disabled; crank the engine for about ten seconds. The engine may fire and run for a while, but let it continue running until it stops. The fuel injectors should have opened enough times during cranking to considerably reduce the line fuel pressure, and reduce the risk of fuel spraying out when a fuel line is disturbed.

4 Disconnect the battery negative lead and position it away from the terminal. **Note:** *Refer to 'Disconnecting the battery' at the rear of this manual first.*

5 Place a suitable container beneath the relevant connection/union to be disconnected, and have a large rag ready to soak up any escaping fuel not being caught by the container. Note the position of the fuel line for refitting, there is either a coloured dot on the connector or the release button is coloured.

The colour codes for push-on couplings are:

a) Fuel Supply	Black
b) Fuel return	Blue
c) Breather	White or Beige
d) Vacuum	Green

6 Slowly open the connection to avoid a sudden release of pressure, and position the rag around the connection to catch any fuel spray that may be expelled. Once the pressure has been released, disconnect the fuel line. Insert plugs to minimise fuel loss and prevent the entry of dirt into the fuel system.

7 After working on the fuel system, reconnect the wiring/fuse/relay as applicable. Have the engine management fault code memory checked by a VW dealer for codes inserted when disconnecting the wiring.

8 Inlet manifold and associated components – removal and refitting

Note: Observe the precautions in Section 1 before working on any component in the fuel system.

Removal

Engine codes BUD and CGGA

1 These engine are fitted with a one-piece inlet manifold, on these engines, the fuel rail is attached to and injects into the inlet manifold.

2 Disconnect the battery negative lead and position it away from the terminal. **Note:** *Refer to 'Disconnecting the battery' at the rear of this manual first.*

3 With reference to Section 3, remove the throttle housing/module from the inlet manifold.

4 Disconnect the vacuum hoses for the fuel pressure regulator, and (if not already removed) for the brake servo. Note how the hoses are routed, for use when refitting.

5 On low-pressure injection systems only, remove the fuel rail and injectors as described in Section 3. However, if the manifold is being removed as part of another procedure (such as cylinder head or engine removal), the fuel rail can be left in place.

6 Disconnect the wiring plug from the inlet air pressure/temperature sensor, referring if necessary to Section 3 for more details.

7 Where fitted, unbolt and remove the manifold support bracket from the engine block, then unbolt the mounting bracket for the secondary air inlet valve from the front of the manifold.

8 Progressively loosen the bolts/nuts and withdraw the manifold from the cylinder head **(see illustration)**. Recover the gasket or the four seals as applicable – all should be renewed when refitting the manifold.

Engine code CAXA

9 This engine is fitted with a two-piece inlet manifold, on this engine, the lower manifold is effectively the fuel rail, and the upper manifold is bolted to it.

Upper part

10 Disconnect the battery negative lead and position it away from the terminal. **Note:** *Refer to 'Disconnecting the battery' at the rear of this manual first.*

11 With reference to Section 3, remove the throttle housing/module from the inlet manifold. If preferred, the housing need not be unbolted from the manifold, and can be removed with it, but all the services to the housing must be disconnected.

12 Release the hose clip and disconnect the brake servo vacuum hose from the manifold.

13 Disconnect and unclip all wiring, coolant and vacuum hoses from the manifold (as applicable), noting their location for correct refitting **(see illustrations)**. Use clamps on the coolant hoses to minimise spillage.

14 As applicable, unbolt the support brackets from the manifold.

15 Remove the screws securing the upper part of the manifold to the lower part. Where necessary, prise out the plastic flanges.

16 Lift the upper part of the manifold off the lower part, and remove it from the engine compartment. Recover the four seals, single gasket or plastic air ducts **(see illustrations)**.

8.13a Disconnecting the hoses from the inlet manifold

8.13b On engine code CAXA, two coolant hoses are attached to the intercooler at the rear of the manifold (arrowed)

8.16a Removing the upper part of the inlet manifold

8.16b Renew the four manifold seals

8.20 Remove the lower part of the inlet manifold (complete with injectors)...

8.21 ...and recover the gasket

Lower part

17 Remove the upper part of the manifold as described previously in this Section.

18 Disconnect the wiring plug from the fuel pressure sender on the end of the lower manifold.

19 Check around the manifold, and unclip any hoses or wiring which may still be attached.

20 Progressively loosen the nuts and bolts and withdraw the manifold from the cylinder head **(see illustration)**. Recover the seals/gasket(s) – all should be renewed when refitting the manifold.

Refitting

21 Refitting is a reversal of removal **(see illustration)**. Use new seals or gaskets as necessary, and tighten the manifold-to-head nuts and bolts to the specified torque. It is most important that there are no air leaks at the joint.

9 Fuel injection system – testing and adjustment

1 If a fault appears in the fuel injection system, first ensure that all the system wiring connectors are securely connected and free of corrosion. Then ensure that the fault is not due to poor maintenance; i.e. check that the air cleaner filter element is clean, the spark plugs are in good condition and correctly gapped, the cylinder compression pressures are correct, the ignition system wiring is in good condition and securely connected, and the engine breather hoses are clear and undamaged, referring to Chapter 1A, Chapter 2A, 2B or 2E and Chapter 5B.

2 If these checks fail to reveal the cause of the problem, the vehicle should be taken to a suitably equipped VW dealer for testing. A diagnostic connector is located under the right-hand side of the driver's facia, above the throttle pedal. It is incorporated in the engine management system wiring harness, into which dedicated electronic test equipment can be plugged. The test equipment is capable of 'interrogating' the engine management system ECU electronically and accessing its internal fault log (reading fault codes).

3 Fault codes can only be extracted from the ECU using a dedicated fault code reader. A VW dealer will obviously have such a reader, but they are also available from other suppliers. It is unlikely to be cost-effective for the private owner to purchase a fault code reader, but a well-equipped local garage or auto-electrical specialist will have one.

4 Using this equipment, faults can be pin-pointed quickly and simply, even if their occurrence is intermittent. Testing all the system components individually in an attempt to locate the fault by elimination is a time-consuming operation that is unlikely to be fruitful (particularly if the fault occurs dynamically), and carries a high risk of damage to the ECU's internal components.

5 Experienced home mechanics equipped with an accurate tachometer and a carefully-calibrated exhaust gas analyser may be able to check the exhaust gas CO content and the engine idle speed; if these are found to be out of specification, then the vehicle must be taken to a suitably-equipped VW dealer for assessment. Neither the air/fuel mixture (exhaust gas CO content) nor the engine idle speed is manually adjustable; incorrect test results indicate the need for maintenance (possibly, injector cleaning) or a fault within the fuel injection system.

10 Cruise control system – general information

1 Certain models may be equipped with a cruise control system, in which the driver can set a chosen speed, which the system will then try to maintain regardless of gradients, etc.

2 Once the desired speed has been set, the system is entirely under the control of the engine management ECU, which regulates the speed with the throttle housing.

3 The system is deactivated if the clutch or brake pedals are pressed, signalled by the clutch pedal switch (Section 3) or the brake stoplight switch.

4 The cruise control switch is part of the steering column turn signal combination switch, which can be removed as described in Chapter 12, Section 4.

5 Any problems with the system, which are not caused by wiring faults or failure of the components mentioned in this Section, should be referred to a VW dealer. In the event of a problem occurring, it is advisable to first take the car to a suitably equipped dealer for electronic fault diagnosis, using a fault code reader – refer to Section 9.

Notes

Chapter 4 Part B:
Diesel engine fuel systems

Contents

Degrees of difficulty

Easy, suitable for novice with little experience		Fairly easy, suitable for beginner with some experience		Fairly difficult, suitable for competent DIY mechanic		Difficult, suitable for experienced DIY mechanic		Very difficult, suitable for expert DIY or professional	

Specifications

Engine codes*

1.6 litre	CAYB and CAYC
2.0 litre	CBAA, CBAB, CBBB, CFFA, CFFB and CFGB

* Note: *See 'Vehicle identification' at the end of this manual for the location of engine code markings.*

General

Fuel injection system	Electronic, direct, common rail injection
Firing order	1-3-4-2
Maximum engine speed.	N/A (ECU controlled)
Engine fast idle speed	N/A (ECU controlled)
Turbocharger type	Garrett or KKK

Torque wrench settings

	Nm	lbf ft
Camshaft position sensor (Hall sender)	10	7
EGR pipe flange-to-inlet manifold bolts.	8	6
Engine speed/TDC sender	5	4
Flap motor housing	10	7
Fuel pressure regulating valve (left-hand end of fuel rail).	80	59
Fuel pressure sender (right-hand end of fuel rail).	100	74
Fuel pump bolts*:		
Two lower bolts (long):		
Stage 1	20	15
Stage 2	Angle-tighten a further 180°	
One upper bolt (short):		
Stage 1	20	15
Stage 2	Angle-tighten a further 45°	
Fuel rail	22	16
High-pressure fuel pipe unions	28	20
Injector clamp/cover mounting:		
1.6 litre engines		
Clamp bolt*:		
Stage 1	8	6
Stage 2	Angle-tighten a further 180°	
2.0 litre engines (CFFA, CFFB and CFGB):		
Clamp bolt*:		
Stage 1	8	6
Stage 2	Angle-tighten a further 180°	
2.0 litre engines (CBAA, CBAB and CBBB):		
Clamp nut.	10	7
Cover bolt.	5	4
Inlet manifold to cylinder head.	8	6
Oxygen (Lambda probe) sensor.	50	37
Toothed belt pulley on high-pressure pump bolts*	20	15

* Do not re-use

1.1 The EOBD diagnostic connector (arrowed) is located under the driver's side of the facia

1 General information and precautions

General information

All engines covered by this Manual are fitted with a direct-injection fuelling system, incorporating a fuel tank, an engine-bay mounted fuel filter with an integral water separator, fuel supply and return lines and four fuel injectors.

The fuel system is the familiar Common Rail system, where fuel is supplied from a timing belt-driven high-pressure pump to a common fuel rail (or reservoir). The four injectors are fitted into the cylinder head and are connected to the fuel rail by rigid metal pipes. The precise timing of the pre-, main, and post-injections are controlled by the engine management ECM and an electrically operated Piezo crystal incorporated into the injector design. All engines are fitted with a turbocharger.

The direct-injection fuelling system is controlled electronically by a diesel engine management system, comprising an Electronic Control Module (ECM) and its associated sensors, actuators and wiring. In addition, the ECM manages the operation of the Exhaust Gas Recirculation (EGR) emission control system (Chapter 4D), the turbocharger boost pressure control system and the glow plug control system (Chapter 5C).

A flap valve/throttle valve module fitted to the intake manifold is closed by the ECM for 3 seconds as the engine is switched off, to minimise the air intake as the engine shuts down. This minimises the vibration felt as the pistons come up against the volume of highly compressed air present in the combustion chambers.

It should be noted that fault diagnosis of the diesel engine management system is only possible with dedicated electronic test equipment. Problems with the system's operation should therefore be referred to a VW dealer or suitably equipped specialist for assessment. Once the fault has been identified, the removal/refitting sequences detailed in the following Sections will then allow the appropriate component(s) to be renewed as required.

The Electronic On-Board Diagnostic (EOBD) connector is located under the driver's side of the facia **(see illustration)**.

2.1a Unclip the cover from the air intake

2.1c ...and remove the air ducting

2.1b Release the securing clips ...

2.2 Disconnect the air mass meter wiring plug

Precautions

Many of the operations described in this Chapter involve the disconnection of fuel lines, which may cause an amount of fuel spillage. Before commencing work, refer to the warnings below and the information in *Safety first!* at the beginning of this manual.

 Warning: When working on any part of the fuel system, avoid direct contact skin contact with diesel fuel – wear protective clothing and gloves when handling fuel system components. Ensure that the work area is well ventilated to prevent the build-up of diesel fuel vapour.

• *Fuel injectors operate at extremely high pressures and the jet of fuel produced at the nozzle is capable of piercing skin, with potentially fatal results. When working with pressurised injectors, take care to avoid exposing any part of the body to the fuel spray. It is recommended that a diesel fuel systems specialist should carry out any pressure testing of the fuel system components.*

• *Under no circumstances should diesel fuel be allowed to come into contact with coolant hoses – wipe off accidental spillage immediately. Hoses that have been contaminated with fuel for an extended period should be renewed.*

• *Diesel fuel systems are particularly sensitive to contamination from dirt, air and water. Pay particular attention to cleanliness when working on any part of the fuel system, to prevent the ingress of dirt. Thoroughly clean the area around fuel unions before disconnecting them. Only use lint-free cloths and clean fuel for component cleansing.*

• *Store dismantled components in sealed containers to prevent contamination and the formation of condensation.*

2 Air cleaner assembly – removal and refitting

Removal

1 Unclip the plastic cover from the air intake ducting, then release the two securing clips (one at each side) and remove the ducting from the front crossmember **(see illustrations)**. Note, on some models there may be a retaining screw securing the inner part of the lower ducting to the crossmember.

2 Disconnect the wiring plug from the air mass meter **(see illustration)**.

3 Disconnect the vacuum pipe from the air intake hose **(see illustration)**.

4 Loosen the clip and disconnect the air duct from the air mass meter **(see illustration)**.

5 Undo the retaining bolt and lift the air cleaner assembly upwards to release it from

2.3 Disconnect the vacuum pipe

2.4 Disconnect the air intake hose

2.5a Undo the retaining screw ...

2.5b ... and remove the air cleaner assembly out of the engine compartment

2.5c Release the drain tube as it is removed

2.6 Make sure the assembly is located correctly on the mounting pegs (arrowed)

the locating pegs **(see illustrations)**. As the air cleaner is removed, withdraw the water drain hose, under the air cleaner assembly out from the inner wing panel.

Refitting

6 Refit the air cleaner by following the removal procedure in reverse. Make sure the assembly is located correctly on the lower mounting pegs **(see illustration)**.

3	Diesel engine management system – component removal and refitting

Throttle valve housing/module

1 Remove the engine upper trim cover **(see illustrations)**.
2 Slacken the retaining clips and remove the air intake rubber hose from the throttle

housing **(see illustration)**. If required, undo the bolts securing the air intake plastic hose from the intercooler to the throttle housing, this will allow easier removal of the intake rubber hose.

3.1a Remove the engine upper trim cover ...

3 Disconnect the wiring plug connector, from the throttle housing/module **(see illustration)**.
4 Undo the retaining bolt and disconnect the dipstick guide tube from the throttle housing **(see illustration)**.

3.1b ... and the insulation cover (arrowed), where fitted

3.2 Slacken the two retaining clips (arrowed)

3.3 Disconnect the wiring connector

3.4 Undo the dipstick tube retaining bolt

3.5a Undo the three retaining bolts ...

3.5b ... and remove the throttle housing module

3.6 Fit new seal to housing on refitting

3.8 Disconnect the wiring connector

3.9 Undo the three retaining bolts (arrowed)

5 Unscrew and remove the retaining bolts, then lift the throttle housing/module away from the inlet manifold (see illustrations). Recover the O-ring seal; a new one will be required for refitting.
6 Refitting is a reversal of removal, noting the following:
 a) Use a new throttle housing-to-inlet manifold seal (see illustration).
 b) Tighten the throttle housing bolts evenly to the specified torque.
 c) Ensure that all hoses and electrical connectors are refitted securely.

Inlet manifold flap motor

Note: On some engines there is an electrically operated flap motor located on the inlet manifold, this is not fitted to all models.
7 Remove the engine upper trim cover (see illustrations 3.1a & 3.1b).
8 Disconnect the flap control motor wiring

plug from the lower part of the housing (see illustration).
9 Unscrew the bolts securing the flap motor housing to the manifold (see illustration), remove the flap housing and recover the O-ring seal.
10 Refitting is a reversal of removal. Renew the O-ring seal if it appears damaged.

Air mass meter

11 The air mass meter is located in the outlet from the air cleaner assembly on the left-hand side of the engine compartment.
12 Disconnect the wiring plug connector from the air mass meter (see illustration).
13 Slacken the retaining clip and disconnect the air intake ducting from the air mass meter (see illustration).
14 Undo the retaining screws securing the meter to the air cleaner. Withdraw the meter and recover the O-ring seal.

Caution: Handle the air mass meter carefully – its internal components are easily damaged.
15 Refitting is a reversal of removal. Renew the O-ring seal if it appears damaged.

Charge air pressure/ temperature sensor

16 The charge air pressure/temperature sensor is fitted in the air ducting from the intercooler to the throttle housing/inlet manifold, just below the air-conditioning compressor (see illustration). Jack up the front of the vehicle and support it on axle stands (see Jacking and vehicle support), and then remove the engine undertray.
17 Disconnect the wiring then undo the two retaining screws and remove the sensor from the intake ducting.
18 Refit the sensor by reversing the removal procedure, using a new O-ring seal.

Fuel pressure regulating valve

19 The fuel pressure regulating valve is fitted to the left-hand end of the fuel rail (see illustration). If the valve is removed from the fuel rail, then it will need to be renewed, as it has a deformable sealing lip as part of the valve.
20 To check the operation of the regulating valve, first disconnect the fuel return hose from the fuel rail and plug the end (see illustration). Then fit a piece of hose to the fuel rail and the other end into a container. There are three checks that can be made, the first two with the engine running and the third if the vehicle will not start:

3.12 Disconnect the air mass meter wiring plug

3.13 Disconnect the air intake hose

3.16 Charge air pressure sensor location (arrowed)

3.19 Fuel pressure regulator valve (arrowed)

3.20 Disconnect the fuel hose (arrowed)

3.22 Pressure regulator valve fitted to the left-hand end of the fuel rail

3.25 Disconnect the wiring connector from the fuel pressure sender

3.26 The fuel pressure sender is fitted to the right-hand end of the fuel rail

3.28 Fuel temperature sensor (arrowed)

1) *Start the engine and run at idle for 30 seconds, there should be approx. 75ml of fuel (1.6 litre engines) or 100ml of fuel (2.0 litre engines) in the container.*
2) *Start engine and increase engine speed to 2000rpm, there should be 0ml of fuel in the container (allow for a few droplets of fuel).*
3) *On vehicles that will not run, turn the ignition key and crank the engine, there should be 0ml of fuel in the container (allow for a few droplets of fuel).*

If any of these readings are not attained, renew the regulating valve.

21 To renew the valve, remove the fuel rail as described in Section 11.

22 Clean around the valve, then slacken the valve from the end of the fuel rail **(see illustration)**; counterhold the fuel rail using the flats on the housing. Plug the end of the rail to prevent dirt from entering.

23 Fit the new valve by reversing the removal procedure, making sure that the threads are all clean before fitting. Check the deformable seal on the new valve, before fitting, to check it is not damaged. Apply a small amount of Molybdenum grease to seal and threads.

Fuel pressure sender

24 The fuel pressure sender is fitted to the right-hand end of the fuel rail. If the engine will not start, disconnect the fuel pressure sender wiring connector and see if the engine will start. If the engine starts, the fuel pressure sender is faulty. With the connector removed a value is taken from the control

unit, so that the engine will start, in this mode the maximum engine speed is limited to 3000rpm.

25 To renew the sender, first disconnect the wiring plug connector **(see illustration)**.

26 Clean around the sender, then slacken it from the end of the fuel rail **(see illustration)**; plug the end of the rail to prevent dirt from entering.

27 Refit the pressure sender by reversing the removal procedure, making sure that the threads are all clean before refitting. The sender has a deformable seal, check for damage. Keep the threads free of oil and grease.

Fuel temperature sensor

28 The fuel temperature sensor is located in the fuel supply line at the top of the high-pressure fuel pump **(see illustration)**, on some 2.0 litre engines.

3.32 Camshaft position sensor (arrowed)

29 First, disconnect the wiring connector, then release the securing clips and disconnect the hoses from the sensor assembly.

30 Refit the fuel temperature sensor by reversing the removal procedure.

Coolant temperature sensors

31 Refer to Chapter 3, Section 6.

Camshaft position sensor

32 The camshaft position sensor (Hall sender) is located behind the timing belt cover, below the camshaft sprocket **(see illustration)**.

33 Remove the timing belt, as described in Chapter 2C (1.6 litre engine) or Chapter 2D (2.0 litre engine).

34 Disconnect the sensor wiring plug connector, located at the rear of the oil filter housing against the cylinder block **(see illustration)**.

35 To make access easier undo the retaining

3.34 Disconnect the sensor wiring connector (arrowed)

3.35 Unbolt the Idler pulley

3.36 Prise up the aperture cover (arrowed)

3.39 Crankshaft position speed sensor (arrowed)

3.41a Undo the retaining bolt ...

3.41b ... and withdraw the sensor

bolt and remove the timing belt idler pulley **(see illustration)**.

36 Using a screwdriver prise out the aperture cover in the rear plastic cover, then withdraw the wiring plug through the cover, unhooking it from the rear cover **(see illustration)**.

37 Undo the retaining bolt and remove the camshaft sensor from the cylinder head.

38 Refitting is a reversal of removal, but tighten the bolt to the specified torque setting and fit rubber plugs to the aperture for the wiring in the rear plastic cover.

Engine speed/TDC sensor

39 The engine speed/TDC sensor is mounted on the front cylinder block, adjacent to the mating surface of the block and transmission bellhousing **(see illustration)**.

40 Access is from beneath the engine compartment. Apply the handbrake, and then jack up the front of the vehicle and support

it on axle stands (see *Jacking and vehicle support*). Remove the engine undertray.

41 Remove the retaining screw and withdraw the sensor from the cylinder block **(see illustrations)**.

42 Refit the sensor by reversing the removal procedure.

Oxygen (lambda probe) sensor

⚠️ *Warning: Working on the sensors is only advisable with the engine (and therefore the exhaust system) completely cold. The catalytic converter in particular will be very hot for some time after the engine has been switched off.*

43 All models have a sensor threaded into the top of the catalytic converter/particulate filter **(see illustration)**. Note, on some models there may be a second sensor in the front pipe after the catalytic converter/particulate filter.

Do not confuse exhaust gas sensors fitted to the exhaust system.

44 Working from the sensor, trace the wiring harness from the oxygen sensor back to the connector, and disconnect it **(see illustration)**. Unclip the sensor wiring from any retaining clips, noting how it is routed.

45 Access to the upstream sensor is possible on some models from above, while the downstream sensor (where fitted) is only accessible from below.

46 Unscrew and remove the sensor, taking care to avoid damaging the sensor probe as it is removed. **Note:** *As a flying lead remains connected to the sensor after it has been disconnected, if the correct-size spanner is not available, a slotted socket will be required to remove the sensor.*

47 Apply a little high-temperature anti-seize grease to the sensor threads – avoid contaminating the probe tip.

48 Refit the sensor, tightening it to the correct torque. Reconnect the wiring; making sure that the wiring loom is secured in its retaining clips.

Throttle pedal/position sensor

49 Release the securing clip and disconnect the wiring connector from the top of the accelerator pedal **(see illustration)**.

50 Prise off the cap, and undo the screw securing the throttle pedal to the bulkhead **(see illustration)**.

51 The throttle pedal is clipped to two metal pegs in the floor panel, using a lever and thin screwdriver, release the securing clips **(see illustration)**.

3.43 Oxygen sensor (arrowed)

3.44 Disconnect the wiring connector on the bulkhead

3.49 Release the wiring connector locking clip (arrowed)

3.50 Undo the pedal retaining bolt (arrowed)

3.51 Throttle pedal securing pegs in the floor panel

3.52a Release the outer clip by pressing the screwdriver forwards

3.52b Release the inner clip by pushing the screwdriver inwards, and then to the left to release the clip

3.52c Direction (arrowed) to release the two securing clips

3.57 Electronic control unit located in scuttle panel

52 The outer clip can be released by pressing the screwdriver inwards to release the securing clip, whilst levering the pedal upwards. Then insert the screwdriver into the inner slot and push it to the left to release the securing clip (see illustrations). Withdraw the throttle pedal from the floor panel and out from the vehicle.
53 Refitting is a reversal of removal.

Clutch pedal switch

54 The clutch pedal switch is clipped to the clutch master cylinder on the pedal bracket. Remove the master cylinder as described in Chapter 6, Section 4.
55 Unclip the pedal switch from the bottom of the master cylinder.
56 Refitting is a reversal of removal.

Electronic control unit (ECU)

Caution: Always wait at least 30 seconds after switching off the ignition before disconnecting the wiring from the ECU. When the wiring is disconnected, all the learned values are erased, although any contents of the fault memory are retained. After reconnecting the wiring, the basic settings must be reinstated by a VW dealer using a special test instrument. Note also that if the ECU is renewed, the identification of the new ECU must be transferred to the immobiliser control unit by a VW dealer.

57 The ECU is located centrally behind the engine compartment bulkhead (see illustration), under one of the windscreen cowl panels. Remove the wiper arms and cowl panel as for windscreen wiper motor removal and refitting, described in Chapter 12, Section 18.
58 Release the ECU from the lower tray and withdraw it from inside the bulkhead (see illustration). Disconnect the battery negative lead and position it away from the terminal. Note: Refer to 'Disconnecting the battery' at the rear of this manual first.
59 Place a piece of cardboard under the ECU and either drill out the shear bolts that are holding the wiring connector security cover together, or cut a slot in them and unscrew them with a screwdriver (see illustrations). New shear bolts will be required for refitting.

3.58 Unclip the control unit from the mounting bracket

3.59a Cut a slot in the end of the shear bolts (arrowed) ...

3.59b ... and use a screwdriver to remove them

3.60a Pull the clamp upwards ...

3.60b ... and remove it from around the control unit

3.61 Pull out the locking slides at each side to disconnect the wiring

60 Lever the top part upwards and remove the security cover from around the ECU **(see illustrations)**.

61 Disconnect the wiring plugs from the ECU by sliding the locking levers outwards, to release them from the top of the ECU **(see illustration)**. Remove the ECU from the vehicle.

62 Refitting is a reversal of removal, using new shear bolts to secure the wiring cover. Bear in mind the comments made in the Caution above – the ECU will not work correctly until it has been electronically coded.

---

4   Injectors –
general information,
removal and refitting

⚠ *Warning: Exercise extreme caution when working on the fuel injectors. Never expose the hands or any part of the body to injector spray, as the high pressure can cause the fuel to penetrate the skin, with possibly fatal results. You are strongly advised to have any work which involves testing the injectors under pressure carried out by a dealer or fuel injection specialist. Refer to the precautions given in Section 1 of this Chapter before proceeding.*

General information

1 Injectors do deteriorate with prolonged use, and it is reasonable to expect them to need reconditioning or renewal after 60,000 miles (100,000 km) or so. Accurate testing, overhaul and calibration of the injectors must be left to a specialist.

Removal

Note: *Take care not to allow dirt into the injectors or fuel pipes during this procedure. Do* not drop the injectors or allow the needles at their tips to become damaged. The injectors are precision-made to fine limits, and must not be handled roughly. Keep the injectors identified for position to ensure correct refitting.

2 Pull the plastic cover over the engine upwards from its mountings. Where fitted, remove the foam insulation over the injectors **(see illustrations 3.1a & 3.1b)**.

3 Ensure the area around the injectors and the pipes/return hoses is clean and free from debris. The use of a vacuum cleaner is recommended. Plug all fuel lines when they have been disconnected to prevent any dirt ingress **(see illustration)**.

1.6 litre engine

4 Disconnect the injector wiring plug connectors **(see illustration)**.

5 Using a pair of long-nose pliers, withdraw the retaining clip from the side of the injector and remove the fuel return hose **(see illustrations)**. Discard the o-ring seals, as new ones will be required for refitting.

6 Counterhold the injector with an open-ended spanner when releasing the pipe union. Undo the unions and remove the high-pressure pipes from between the fuel rail and the injectors **(see illustrations)**. Plug the openings to prevent contamination.

7 Undo the bolt securing the injector clamp **(see illustration)**, note that one clamp secures two injectors in place.

8 VW technicians use a slide hammer (tool T10055) and adapter (T10402) to pull the injector from the cylinder head. If this tool is not available, it may be possible to fabricate

4.3 Fit sealing caps to prevent dirt ingress

4.4 Disconnect the wiring plugs from the injectors

4.5a Remove the retaining clips ...

4.5b ... and disconnect the fuel return pipes

4.6a Use two spanners to counterhold the fuel pipe to the injector ...

4.6b ...and remove the high pressure fuel pipes

4.7 Remove the injector clamp retaining bolts

4.9 Remove two injectors at a time with retaining clamp

4.11a Hold down the outer tabs, and prise up the centre piece (arrowed)...

4.11b ...then pull the return hose connector upwards from the injector

4.16 Lever up the clip (arrowed) and disconnect the injector wiring plugs

an equivalent tool to pull the injector out of the cylinder head.
9 Two injectors will need to be removed together, as the clamping piece is slotted into both injectors. Recover the copper seal and O-rings and discard. New ones must be used for refitting (see illustration). Note: *The injectors can only be refitted to their original positions. Mark the injectors to avoid confusion if refitting the original injectors.*

2.0 litre engines (CFFA, CFFB and CFGB)

10 Disconnect the injector wiring plug connectors.
11 Push the return hose connector downwards at its outer tabs, then pull up the centre piece and disconnect them from the top of the injectors (see illustrations). Plug the openings to prevent contamination.
12 Undo the unions and remove the high-pressure pipes from between the fuel

rail and the injectors. Counterhold the injector with an open-ended spanner when releasing the pipe union (see illustrations 4.6a & 4.6b). Plug the openings to prevent contamination.
13 Undo the bolt securing the injector clamp between the two injectors, note that one clamp secures two injectors in place.
14 VW technicians use a slide hammer (tool T10055) and adapter (T10415) to pull the injector from the cylinder head. If this tool is not available, it may be possible to fabricate an equivalent tool to pull the injector out of the cylinder head.
15 Two injectors will need to be removed together, as the clamping piece is slotted into both injectors. Recover the copper seal and O-rings and discard. New ones must be used for refitting. Note: *The injectors can only be refitted to their original positions. Mark the injectors to avoid confusion if refitting the original injectors.*

2.0 litre engines (CBAA, CBAB and CBBB)

16 Disconnect the injector wiring plugs (see illustration).
17 Ensure the area around the injectors and the pipes/return hoses is clean and free from debris. The use of a vacuum cleaner is recommended. Push the return hose connector downwards at its tabs, then pull up the centre piece and disconnect them from the injectors (see illustrations 4.11a & 4.11b). Plug the openings to prevent contamination.
18 Undo the unions remove the high-pressure pipes between the common fuel rail and the injectors (see illustration). Plug the openings to prevent contamination.
19 Undo the bolts securing the injector clamp cover, the slightly lift the cover and rotate it 90° for access to the injector retaining nuts (see illustrations).
20 Unscrew the injector retaining nuts.

4.18 Undo the unions and remove the high-pressure pipes between the common rail and the injectors

4.19a Undo the injector clamp cover bolts (arrowed)...

4.19b ...then lift and rotate it 90°

4.21a We attached an old injector pipe union onto the end of the slide hammer...

4.21b ...screwed it onto the top of the injector...

4.21c ...and pulled it from the cylinder head

21 VW technicians use a slide hammer (tool T10055) and adapter (T10055/1) to pull the injector from the cylinder head. This is a slide hammer with an adapter that screws onto the top of the injector. If this tool is not available, it is possible to fabricate an equivalent using slide hammer with the union from an old injector pipe brazed/welded onto the end. Screw the tool onto the top of the injector, and pull the injector out using a few gently taps. Recover the clamping piece, copper seal and O-rings and discard. New ones must be used for refitting **(see illustrations)**. **Note:** *The injectors can only be refitted to their original positions. Mark the injectors to avoid confusion if refitting the original injectors.*

Refitting

22 If required, renew the injector seals in the top of the camshaft cover. Using a screwdriver, prise the seal out from the cover; the new seal can then be pressed firmly into the cover **(see illustrations)**. There are different size seals depending on engine code, make sure the correct seals are supplied. Also make sure the spring on the inside lip of the seal does not drop into the camshaft cover.

23 Ensure the area around the injector locations in the cylinder head are clean and free from debris. Use a vacuum cleaner if available. Clean any carbon deposits from the injector and sealing surfaces with a cloth soaked in clean engine oil or rust-releasing spray.

24 On 2.0 litre engines (CBAA, CBAB and CBBB), if new cover plates are to be fitted, slide them on now **(see illustration)**.

25 To remove the copper sealing washer, spray rust-releasing spray around the injector nozzle, then clamp the seal in a vice, and use a twisting motion to pull the injector from the seal. Push the new copper seal into place **(see illustrations)**. Do not touch the very end of the injector, or you could block up the nozzle.

26 On 1.6 litre engines, apply a little clean engine oil to the return pipe connection, and fit the new O-ring **(see illustration)**.

27 On 2.0 litre engines, apply a little clean engine oil to the return pipe connection on the injector, and fit the new O-ring **(see illustration)**.

28 To renew the main injector O-ring seal, VW specify the use of tool no. T10377. This tool allows the O-ring to slide over the end of the injector without twisting. With care,

4.22a Carefully prise out the seal ...

4.22b ...making sure the spring does not fall into the cover

4.24 Slide the new cover plate onto the injector

4.25a Clean off the carbon around the end of the injector ...

4.25b ... and fit a new sealing washer

4.26 Fit new O-ring seals to the fuel return lines

4.27 Fit the new return pipe O-ring (arrowed) to the top of the injector

4.28 Fit a new main O-ring seal without twisting it

4.29 Slide the new clamping piece (arrowed) onto the injector

4.30a Lubricate the seal with some clean oil …

4.30b …then slide the injectors down into the cylinder head

4.33 Fit new clips to secure the fuel return lines

the seals can be fitted without the tool **(see illustrations)**.
29 On 2.0 litre engines (CBAA, CBAB and CBBB), slide the new clamping piece onto injector as shown **(see illustration)**.
30 Apply a smear of clean engine oil to the main O-ring seal, and insert the injector into place in the cylinder head **(see illustrations)**. Note that if the original injectors are being refitted, they must go into their original positions. Tighten the injector clamping bolt/ nut to the specified torque.
31 On 2.0 litre engines (CBAA, CBAB and CBBB), rotate the cover back to position and tighten the retaining bolt to the specified torque.
32 Refit the high-pressure fuel pipes and tighten the unions to the specified torque. Note that the pipes may be re-used providing the tapered seats are undamaged

and the pipes are not deformed, constricted or corroded. Counterhold the injector with an open-ended spanner when tightening the pipe union.
33 On 1.6 litre engines, when fitting the return hoses to the sides of the injector, use new securing clips **(see illustration)**.
34 The remainder of refitting is a reversal of removal, noting the following:
a) If one or more injectors have been renewed, the 'injector delivery calibration values' and 'injector voltage calibration values' must be entered into the ECM using VW diagnostic equipment. Entrust this task to a VW dealer or suitably equipped specialist.
b) After completion of the work, the fuel system must be bled as described in Section 10.

5 Inlet manifold – removal and refitting

Removal

Plastic manifold

1 Remove the throttle housing, as described in Section 3 of this Chapter.
2 Remove the fuel rail from the top of the inlet manifold, as described in Section 11 of this Chapter.
3 Undo the two retaining screws and move the coolant return pipe to one side **(see illustration)**.
4 Undo the two retaining screws and move the fuel return pipe to one side **(see illustration)**.
5 Where fitted, disconnect the wiring plug connector from the manifold flap motor **(see illustration)**.

5.3 Undo the coolant pipe retaining screws (arrowed)

5.4 Undo the fuel line retaining screws (arrowed)

5.5 Disconnect the wiring connector (arrowed)

5.6 Undo the solenoid valve mounting bracket securing bolt (arrowed)

5.7 Slacken the EGR pipe retaining clamp (arrowed)

5.8a Undo the retaining bolts (arrowed) ...

5.8b ...and remove the inlet manifold

5.8c Cover the inlet manifold recess with tape

Remember to renew any self-locking nuts. Tighten the manifold retaining bolts to the specified torque setting, starting from the inside and working outwards in a diagonal sequence.

6 Fuel filter – renewal

Note: *Observe the precautions in Section 1 before working on any component in the fuel system.*
 Refer to Chapter 1B, Section 8.

7 Fuel gauge sender unit – removal and refitting

Note: *Observe the precautions in Section 1 before working on any component in the fuel system.*

⚠️ *Warning: Avoid direct skin contact with fuel – wear protective clothing and gloves when handling fuel system components. Ensure that the work area is well ventilated to prevent the build-up of fuel vapour.*

1 The fuel gauge sender unit is mounted in the top of the fuel tank. Access is beneath a cover in the load space floor. The unit protrudes into the fuel tank, and its removal involves exposing the contents of the tank to the atmosphere.
2 Refer to the procedures in Chapter 4A, Section 5, for removal and refitting procedures.

6 Undo the retaining screw and remove the EGR cooler changeover valve from the manifold **(see illustration)**.
7 Slacken the retaining clamp and disconnect the EGR pipe **(see illustration)**.
8 Undo the manifold retaining bolts, starting from the outside and working inwards in a diagonal sequence **(see illustrations)**. Lift the manifold from the cylinder head and retrieve the gasket seals; discard, as new ones will be required for refitting.

Aluminium manifold

9 Remove the throttle housing and manifold flap motor (where fitted), as described in Section 3 of this Chapter.
10 Using thin, long-nosed pliers, carefully pull the wiring plugs from the top of the glow plugs **(see illustration)**.
11 With reference to Section 4, disconnect

the fuel return pipes from the injectors, fuel rail, and high-pressure pump.
12 Undo the retaining nut and remove the fuel return pipe **(see illustration)**.
13 Undo the unions and disconnect the high-pressure fuel pipe between the pump and fuel rail.
14 Disconnect the wiring plug from the manifold change-over motor.
15 Where applicable, undo the 2 retaining bolts and pull the engine oil level dipstick guide tube upwards from place.
16 Undo the retaining bolts, starting from the outside and working inwards in a diagonal sequence, then manoeuvre the manifold from position.

Refitting

17 Refitting is a reversal of removal, using new seals and gaskets **(see illustration)**.

5.10 Pull the wiring plugs from the glow plugs

5.12 Fuel return pipe nut (arrowed)

5.17 Renew the inlet manifold seals

8 Fuel tank – removal and refitting

Note: *Observe the precautions in Section 1 before working on any component in the fuel system.*

1 Refer to the procedures in Chapter 4A, Section 6. There is no fuel filter fitted to the front of the fuel tank on diesel models **(see illustration)**, other than this the procedure will be the same as petrol models.

9 Fuel pump – removal and refitting

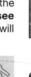

Removal

1.6 litre engines

1 Remove the timing belt and pump sprocket as described in Chapter 2C, Section 7.
2 Disconnect the wiring connector from the fuel metering valve on top of the fuel pump **(see illustration)**.
3 Undo the two retaining screws and move the coolant return pipe to one side **(see illustration 5.3)**.
4 Undo the two retaining screws and move the fuel return pipe to one side **(see illustration 5.4)**.
5 Undo the pipe retaining bracket screw and the two retaining bolts, then remove the lifting eye from the front of the engine **(see illustrations)**.

8.1 Fuel tank position

6 Slacken the fuel pipe unions and remove the high-pressure pipe from the pump to the fuel rail **(see illustration)**.
7 Release the retaining clips and disconnect the two fuel hoses from the top of the fuel pump **(see illustration)**.
8 Counterhold the pump hub using VW tool No. T10051, and undo the pump hub nut. In the absence of this special tool, counterhold the hub using something to lock the sprocket, whilst the centre nut is slackened **(see illustration)**.
9 Using a suitable two-legged puller (VW tool No. T40064) and two bolts, remove the hub complete with sprocket from the pump shaft.
10 Undo the 3 retaining bolts and remove the pump **(see illustration)**.

2.0 litre engines

11 Remove the timing belt and pump sprocket as described in Chapter 2D, Section 7.

9.2 Disconnect the pump wiring connector

12 Disconnect the fuel supply hose from the pump **(see illustration)**. Plug all openings to prevent contamination.
13 Disconnect the wiring plug from the sensor on the pump.
14 Slacken the unions and disconnect the high-pressure fuel pipe between the pump and common fuel rail. Undo the retaining screws to release the fuel pipe from the support brackets.
15 On some models it may be necessary to disconnect he wiring connectors from the glow plugs. Pulling only under the ridge at the top of the connectors, disconnect the wiring connectors. **Note:** *Take care not to damage the connectors or wiring, as the glow plug wiring loom/connectors are only available as a complete assembly.*
16 Undo the bolts securing the coolant pipe to the intake manifold, and position the pipe to one side.

9.5 Remove the lifting bracket from above the fuel pump

9.6 Remove the high pressure fuel line from the pump

9.7 Disconnect the fuel hoses (arrowed) from the pump

9.8 Remove the fuel pump centre hub nut

9.10 Fuel pump mounting bolts (arrowed)

9.12 Release the clip (arrowed) and disconnect the fuel supply hose

9.17 Fuel pump return hose (arrowed)

9.18 Counterhold the pump hub with a C-spanner, and undo the nut

9.19a Use a two-legged puller and 8 mm bolts to pull the hub from the pump shaft

9.19b Note the locating peg (arrowed) in the pump shaft

9.21 The triangles adjacent to the pump apertures indicate fuel flow (arrowed)

9.22 Supplementary fuel pump location (arrowed)

17 Disconnect the fuel return pipes from the pump and the common fuel rail **(see illustration)**.

18 Counterhold the pump hub using VW tool No. T10051, and undo the pump hub nut. In the absence of this special tool, counterhold the hub using a suitable C-spanner **(see illustration)**.

19 Using a suitable two-legged puller and two 8 mm bolts, remove the hub from the pump shaft **(see illustrations)**.

20 Undo the 3 retaining bolts and remove the pump.

Refitting

21 Refitting is a reversal of removal, noting the following points:
 a) *Ensure all fuel pipes/hose connections are clean and free from debris.*
 b) *The high-pressure fuel pipe from the pump to the common rail maybe re-used providing it's not been damaged.*

 c) *Tighten all fasteners to their specified torque where given.*
 d) *Fill the pump with clean fuel through the fuel supply pipe aperture prior to starting* **(see illustration)**.
 e) *Bleed the fuel system as described in Section 10.*

Supplementary fuel pump

Removal

22 The supplementary fuel pump is not fitted to all models, where fitted, it is located on a bracket bolted to the top of the right-hand engine mounting **(see illustration)**.

23 Disconnect the wiring plug from the exhaust gas pressure sensor, then undo the retaining bolt and move the sensor and bracket to one side **(see illustration)**.

24 Undo the retaining bolts and lift the supplementary fuel pump upwards to access the fuel pipes and wiring plug **(see illustration)**.

25 Release the fuel hoses from the retaining clips, and disconnect the fuel pump wiring plug.

26 Release the clamps and disconnect the fuel supply pipe from the fuel filter. Plug/cover the openings to prevent contamination.

27 Disconnect the fuel temperature sensor wiring plug, release the clamp and disconnect the fuel supply pipe from the high-pressure fuel pump. Plug/cover the openings to prevent contamination.

Refitting

28 Refitting is a reversal of removal, noting the following points:
 a) *Ensure the hoses are not kinked.*
 b) *Ensure all connections are clean and free from debris.*
 c) *Note the hose connections: The return hose is blue (or blue markings), and the supply hose is white.*
 d) *Bleed the system as described in Section 10.*

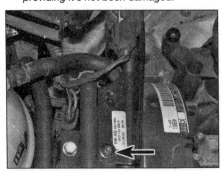

9.23 Undo the retaining screw (arrowed)

9.24 Undo the bolts and remove the pump bracket

10 Fuel system bleeding

1 Prime the high pressure fuel pump by filling it with clean diesel through the fuel supply aperture **(see illustration 9.20)**, then operate the starter for shorts bursts (no more than 10 seconds at a time) until the engine starts. Operate the engine at a fast idle (approx 2000 rpm) for several minutes before allowing it to return to its normal idle speed.

11.3a Remove the high pressure pipes from the rail and injectors ...

11.3b ...and fit sealing caps to prevent dirt ingress

11.4a Disconnect the hose from the return pipe ...

2 If the engine fails to start, it must be filled/bled using VW diagnostic equipment (VAS5051 etc.). Using this equipment operates the electric fuel pumps for 3 minutes.

3 Once the engine has been started, test drive the vehicle over a distance of at least 15 miles with at least one period of full acceleration. If there is any air left in the fuel system, the engine management ECU may switch to 'limp home' mode, and store a fault code. Have the fault code cleared and road test the vehicle again.

11.4b ...and the return pipe from the fuel rail

11.7 Lift the wiring loom over and place to one side

11 Fuel rail – removal and refitting

Note: *Observe the precautions in Section 1 before working on any component in the fuel system.*

Removal

1 Pull the plastic cover on the top of the engine upwards from its' mountings and remove the foam insulation (where fitted) **(see illustrations 3.1a and 3.1b)** Ensure the area around the fuel rail and pipes is clean and free from debris. If available, use a vacuum cleaner.

2 Disconnect the wiring connectors from the fuel injectors.

3 Counterhend the injector with an open-ended spanner when releasing the pipe union. Undo the unions and remove the high-pressure pipes from between the fuel rail and the injectors **(see illustrations)**. Plug the openings to prevent contamination.

4 Release the retaining clips and disconnect the fuel return hose from the fuel rail **(see illustrations)**

5 Undo the retaining bolts, disconnect the coolant return hose from the expansion tank, and move the coolant pipe/hose to one side **(see illustration 5.3)**.

11.8a Undo the fuel rail mounting bolts (arrowed) - CAYB & CAYC engines

6 Slacken the fuel pipe unions and remove the high-pressure pipe from the pump to the fuel rail **(see illustration 9.6)**.

7 Disconnect the wiring plugs from the glow plugs, fuel pressure regulating valve, and the fuel pressure sensor at each end of the fuel rail. Unclip the wiring loom retaining bracket from the top of the fuel rail and move it to one side **(see illustration)**.

8 Undo the multi-spline retaining bolts and remove the fuel rail **(see illustrations)**.

9 If required, note their fitted positions, then unscrew the fuel pressure sensor and pressure regulating valve from the fuel rail, as described in Section 3. **Note:** *VW insist that once removed, the pressure regulating valve cannot be re-used.*

11.8b Undo the fuel rail mounting bolts (arrowed) - CBAA, CBAB & CBBB engines

Refitting

10 Where applicable, refit the fuel pressure sensor and the new regulating valve to the fuel rail, and tighten them to the specified torque. Note that the threads of the sensors must be clean and free from oil and grease.

11 The remainder of refitting is a reversal of removal, noting the following points:

a) Refit the high-pressure fuel pipes and tighten the unions to the specified torque. Note that the high-pressure fuel pipes may be re-used providing the tapered seats are undamaged and the pipes are not deformed, constricted or corroded.

b) After completion of the work, the fuel system must be bled as described in Section 10.

Notes

Chapter 4 Part C:
Emission control and exhaust systems – petrol engines

Contents

Degrees of difficulty

Easy, suitable for novice with little experience	**Fairly easy,** suitable for beginner with some experience	**Fairly difficult,** suitable for competent DIY mechanic	**Difficult,** suitable for experienced DIY mechanic	**Very difficult,** suitable for expert DIY or professional

Specifications

Engine codes*

1.4 litre:
   Indirect injection petrol engine . . . . BUD and CGGA
   Direct injection turbocharged engine (TSi) . . . . CAXA
* Note: *See 'Vehicle identification' at the end of this manual for the location of engine code markings.*

Emission control applications

1.4 litre engine code BUD and CGGA . . . . One catalytic converter in exhaust manifold, one in intermediate pipe, pre-cat oxygen sensor in exhaust manifold, after-cat sensor behind cat in intermediate pipe, no EGR system

1.4 litre engine codes CAXA. . . . . One catalytic converter in exhaust front pipe. Pre-cat oxygen sensor in top of exhaust front pipe, after-cat sensor in the front of the intermediate/flexible pipe. No EGR system.

Torque wrench settings

	Nm	lbf ft
Catalytic converter support bracket to engine bolt (CAXA engine)* . . .	25	18
Coolant pipe-to-turbo bolts	8	6
Exhaust manifold nuts (BUD and CGGA engines)*	25	18
Exhaust manifold/turbo nuts (CAXA engine)*.	25	18
Exhaust front flexible pipe-to-catalytic converter:		
BUD and CGGA engines:		
Bolts.	20	15
Nut*.	40	30
CAXA engine:		
Nuts*.	25	18
Exhaust front pipe-to-middle pipe flange nuts*	25	18
Exhaust pipe clamp bolts.	25	18
Exhaust mounting bracket bolts	25	18
Intercooler mounting bolts (engine code CAXA)	7	3
Oil supply pipe:		
Banjo bolt-to-engine block*	30	22
Banjo bolt-to-oil filter/timing chain housing*	20	15
Supply pipe-to-turbo bolt.	8	6
Oil return pipe bolts	8	6
Oxygen (Lambda probe) sensors:		
BUD and CGGA engines	55	41
CAXA engine.	50	37
Turbocharger-to-catalytic converter/downpipe nuts*.	23	17
Turbocharger air recirculation valve bolts.	11	7

* Do not re-use

1.12 Exhaust pipe mounting rubbers

1 General information

Emission control systems

All petrol models are designed to use unleaded petrol, and are controlled by engine management systems that are programmed to give the best compromise between driveability, fuel consumption and exhaust emission production. In addition, a number of systems are fitted that help to minimise other harmful emissions. A crankcase emission control system is fitted, which reduces the release of pollutants from the engine's lubrication system, and a catalytic converter is fitted which reduces exhaust gas pollutant. An evaporative loss emission control system is fitted which reduces the release of gaseous hydrocarbons from the fuel tank.

Crankcase emission control

To reduce the emission of unburned hydrocarbons from the crankcase into the atmosphere, the engine is sealed and the blow-by gases and oil vapour are drawn from inside the crankcase, through a wire-mesh oil separator, into the inlet tract to be burned by the engine during normal combustion.

Under conditions of high manifold depression, the gases will be sucked positively out of the crankcase. Under conditions of low manifold depression, the gases are forced out of the crankcase by the (relatively) higher crankcase pressure. If the engine is worn, the raised crankcase pressure (due to increased blow-by) will cause some of the flow to return under all manifold conditions.

Exhaust emission control

To minimise the amount of pollutants that escape into the atmosphere, all petrol models are fitted with one or two catalytic converters in the exhaust system. The fuelling system is of the closed-loop type, in which an oxygen (lambda) sensor in the exhaust system provides the engine management system ECU with constant feedback, enabling the ECU to adjust the air/fuel mixture to optimise combustion.

The oxygen sensor has a built-in heating element, controlled by the ECU through the oxygen sensor relay, to quickly bring the sensor's tip to its optimum operating temperature. The sensor's tip is sensitive to oxygen, and sends a voltage signal to the ECU that varies according to the amount of oxygen in the exhaust gas. If the inlet air/fuel mixture is too rich, the exhaust gases are low in oxygen so the sensor sends a low-voltage signal, the voltage rising as the mixture weakens and the amount of oxygen rises in the exhaust gases. Peak conversion efficiency of all major pollutants occurs if the inlet air/fuel mixture is maintained at the chemically correct ratio for the complete combustion of petrol of 14.7 parts (by weight) of air to 1 part of fuel (the stoichiometric ratio). The sensor output voltage alters in a large step at this point, the ECU using the signal change as a reference point and correcting the inlet air/fuel mixture accordingly by altering the fuel injector pulse width.

All models covered in this manual have two oxygen (lambda probe) sensors, one before and one after the catalytic converter(s). This enables more efficient monitoring of the exhaust gas, allowing a faster response time. The overall efficiency of the converter itself can also be checked. Details of the oxygen (lambda probe) sensor removal and refitting are given in Chapter 4A, Section 3.

Evaporative emission control

To minimise the escape of unburned hydrocarbons into the atmosphere, an evaporative loss emission control system is fitted to all petrol models. The fuel tank filler cap is sealed and a charcoal canister is mounted behind the right-hand headlight unit to collect the petrol vapours released from the fuel contained in the fuel tank. It stores them until they can be drawn from the canister (under the control of the fuel injection/ignition system ECU) via the purge valve(s) into the inlet tract, where the engine then burns them during normal combustion.

To ensure that the engine runs correctly when it is cold and/or idling and to protect the catalytic converter from the effects of an over-rich mixture, the purge control valve(s) are not opened by the ECU until the engine has warmed-up, and the engine is under load; the valve solenoid is then modulated on and off to allow the stored vapour to pass into the inlet tract.

Exhaust systems

On most models, the exhaust system is the exhaust manifold, front pipe(s), intermediate pipe and silencer, and tailpipe and silencer. The systems fitted differ in detail depending on the engine fitted – for example, in how the catalytic converter is incorporated into the system. On turbo models the catalytic converter is incorporated in the exhaust front down pipe. On non-turbo models there are two catalytic converters, one is part of the exhaust manifold and the second one is part of the middle section of exhaust, fitted behind the front flexible pipe. On turbocharged models, the turbocharger is integral with the exhaust manifold, and is driven by the exhaust gases.

The system is supported by various metal brackets screwed to the vehicle floor, with rubber vibration dampers fitted to suppress noise, refer to Section 7¦ of this Chapter **(see illustration)**.

2 Evaporative loss emission control system – information and component renewal

1 The evaporative loss emission control system consists of the solenoid valve, the activated charcoal filter canister and a series of connecting vacuum hoses. The following procedure removes the charcoal canister and solenoid valve together, complete with hoses.
2 The purge valve and canister are located on the right-hand side of the engine compartment, in front of the windscreen washer reservoir filler **(see illustration)**.
3 Trace the smooth hose (return to fuel tank) back towards the rear of the engine compartment, to the side of the coolant reservoir, then release the securing clip and disconnect the hose connection **(see illustration)**.
4 Working at the rear of the engine compartment, disconnect the wiring plug connector, the hose to the inlet manifold, and then unclip the solenoid valve from the rear of the inlet manifold **(see illustrations)**.
5 Unscrew the mounting bolts, then lift the

2.2 Charcoal canister location on right-hand inner wing

2.3 Disconnect the fuel lines

charcoal canister out of its lower mounting, noting how it is fitted, and remove it from the engine compartment **(see illustrations)**. Withdraw canister complete with hoses from inside the engine compartment, releasing them from any retaining clips.

6 Refitting is a reversal of removal.

2.4a Disconnect the wiring connector …

2.4b … and pull the hose from the purge valve

3 Crankcase emission system – general information

1 The crankcase emission control system consists of hoses connecting the crankcase to the air cleaner or inlet manifold. Oil separator units are fitted to some petrol engines, usually at the back of the engine.

2 The system requires no attention other than to check at regular intervals that the hoses, valve and oil separator are free of blockages and in good condition.

4 Turbocharger – general information, precautions, removal and refitting

Note: A turbocharger is only fitted to 1.4 litre engine code CAXA.

2.5a Undo the two bolts and one nut …

2.5b … then remove the charcoal canister

General information

1 The turbocharger is integral with the exhaust manifold and cannot be removed separately. Lubrication is provided by an oil supply pipe that runs from the oil filter/timing chain housing or cylinder block, depending on engine. Oil is returned to the sump through a return pipe that connects to the cylinder block. A water-cooled turbocharger is fitted, and the charge pressure is controlled by an electrically operated air recirculation valve.

2 The turbocharger's internal components rotate at a very high speed, and as such are sensitive to contamination; a great deal of damage can be caused by small particles of dirt, particularly if they strike the delicate turbine blades.

Precautions

3 The turbocharger operates at extremely high speeds and temperatures. Certain precautions must be observed to avoid premature failure

of the turbo, or injury to the operator.

• **Do not operate the turbo with any parts exposed. Foreign objects falling onto the rotating vanes could cause excessive damage and (if ejected) personal injury.**

• **Cover the turbocharger air inlet ducts to prevent debris entering, and clean using lint-free cloths only.**

• **Do not race the engine immediately after start-up, especially if it is cold. Give the oil a few seconds to circulate.**

• **Observe the recommended intervals for oil and filter changing, and use a reputable oil of the specified quality. Neglect of oil changing, or use of inferior oil, can cause carbon formation on the turbo shaft and subsequent failure. Thoroughly clean the area around all oil pipe unions before disconnecting them, to prevent the ingress of dirt. Store dismantled components in a sealed container to prevent contamination.**

Caution: Thoroughly clean the area around all oil pipe unions before disconnecting them, to prevent the ingress of dirt. Store dismantled components in a sealed container to prevent contamination. Cover the turbocharger air inlet ducts to prevent debris entering, and clean using lint-free cloths only.

Removal

4 Disconnect the battery negative lead as described in Chapter 5A, Section 3.

5 Undo the bolts and remove the cover from the top of the engine **(see illustration)**. Unclip the coolant hoses, from the end of the cover as it is removed.

6 Use hose clamps to block-off the coolant hoses to and from the turbocharger **(see illustration)**.

7 Unclip the pressure/vacuum hoses from the charge air pipe, and disconnect the charge pressure sensor wiring plug **(see illustration)**.

4.5 Remove the cylinder head cover

4.6 Clamp the coolant hoses (arrowed) to and from the turbocharger

4.7 Disconnect the charge air pressure sensor wiring plug (arrowed)

4.8a Undo the bolts (arrowed)...

4.8b ...recover the collar...

4.8c ...push out the clip each side (arrowed)...

4.8d ...and remove the charge air pipe

4.9a Release the clamp (arrowed) and disconnect the air inlet hose ...

4.9b ... and the vacuum hose (arrowed)

8 The charge air pipe from the turbocharger to the throttle valve is secured by bolts at the turbo end, and clips at the valve end. Undo the bolts and remove the retaining clamp, then spread the retaining clips outwards slightly at the throttle housing end and remove the charge air pipe from the engine compartment **(see illustrations)**.

9 Release the securing clamps and disconnect the air inlet hose and vacuum hose from the turbocharger **(see illustrations)**.
10 Disconnect the wiring plug from the turbocharger air recirculation valve **(see illustration)**.
11 Undo the retaining bolts and remove the turbocharger heat shield **(see illustration)**.
12 Release the clamps and disconnect the turbocharger coolant hoses from the coolant pipes. Note, if the coolant has not been drained, be prepared for coolant loss.
13 Undo the retaining bolt and remove the bracket above the exhaust manifold **(see illustration)**.
14 Undo the retaining bolts and remove the metal coolant pipes from the turbocharger **(see illustration)**.
15 Remove the auxiliary drivebelt as described in Chapter 1A, Section 26.
16 With reference to Chapter 3, Section 9, unbolt the air conditioning compressor, and secure it to the front crossmember/lock carrier. **Note:** *There's no need to disconnect the refrigerant pipes, making sure they do not get damaged/kinked.*
17 Undo the retaining nuts and remove the catalytic converter from between the turbocharger and exhaust front flexible pipe, as described in Section 7.
18 Undo the retaining bolts and withdraw the exhaust manifold heat shield from the top of the manifold **(see illustration)**.
19 The turbocharger oil supply pipe is secured to the oil filter/timing chain housing by a banjo bolt and to the turbocharger by

4.10 Disconnect the wiring connector

4.11 Turbocharger heat shield bolts (arrowed)

4.13 Remove the mounting plate

4.14 Undo the coolant pipe retaining bolts (arrowed)

a bolt securing a flange. Undo the bolts and remove the oil supply pipe **(see illustrations)**. Discard the seals and banjo bolt – new ones must be fitted.

20 Working on the underside of the turbocharger **(see illustration)**, undo the bolts securing the oil return pipe to the turbocharger and cylinder block, and then remove the pipe. New gaskets will be needed.

21 If the alternator is secured by nuts with inner drive splines, slacken the nuts.

22 Undo the retaining nuts and remove the turbocharger/exhaust manifold from the front of the ngine compartment.

Refitting

23 Refit the turbocharger by following the removal procedure in reverse, noting the following points:

a) *Renew all gaskets, sealing washers and O-rings.*

b) *Top up the coolant if necessary.*

c) *Before reconnecting the oil supply pipe, fill the turbocharger with fresh oil using an oil can.*

d) *Tighten all nuts and bolts to the specified torque, where given.*

e) *Ensure that the air hose clips are securely tightened, to prevent air leaks.*

f) *When the engine is started after refitting, allow it to idle for approximately one minute to give the oil time to circulate around the turbine shaft bearings. Check for signs of oil or coolant leakage from the relevant unions.*

---

5 Intercooler – general information, removal and refitting

Note: *An intercooler is only fitted to turbo-charged engines (engine code CAXA).*

1 The intercooler is effectively an 'air radiator', used to cool the pressurised inlet air before it enters the engine.

2 When the turbocharger compresses the inlet air, one side effect is that the air is heated, causing the air to expand. If the inlet air can be cooled, a greater effective volume of air will be inducted, and the engine will produce more power.

3 On these models, the intercooler is fitted into the inlet manifold, and the temperature of the intake air is controlled by engine coolant flowing through the intercooler galleries.

Removal

4 Remove the lower part of the inlet manifold as described in Chapter 4A, Section 8.

5 Working from the ends of the intercooler towards the middle, gradually, evenly, slacken the retaining bolts and pull the intercooler squarely from the manifold **(see illustration)**.

Refitting

6 Check the condition of the sealing gasket and renew if necessary.

7 Ensure the sealing strip is fitted to the edge

4.18 Remove the manifold upper heat shield

4.19b ...and retaining bolt (arrowed) to turbocharger

of the intercooler, and the sealing gasket is fitted correctly on the inlet manifold.

8 Push the intercooler squarely into the manifold, then gradually and evenly, tighten the retaining bolts to the specified torque.

9 Refit the inlet manifold as described in Chapter 4A, Section 8.

---

6 Exhaust manifold – removal and refitting

Note: *This Section only covers the removal of the exhaust manifold on non-turbo models (engine codes BUD and CGGA). On turbo models (engine code CAXA), the exhaust manifold is integral with the turbocharger. Refer to Section 4.*

Removal

1 Apply the handbrake, then jack up the front

5.5 Intercooler retaining bolts (arrowed) – engine code CAXA

4.19a Undo the oil supply pipe banjo bolt (arrowed) ...

4.20 Undo the oil return pipe bolts (arrowed)

of the vehicle and support it on axle stands (see *Jacking and vehicle support*).

2 The exhaust manifold/catalytic converter is located on the front of the engine. To make access easier, first move the lock carrier to its Service position as follows, leaving the air conditioning refrigerant lines connected to the compressor:

a) *Remove the front bumper (Chapter 11, Section 6).*

b) *Support the front crossmember/lock carrier, then unscrew the mounting bolts and substitute them with VW special tools (or threaded rod) on both sides of the car* **(see illustration)**.

c) *If required, disconnect the bonnet release cable over the right-hand headlight (Chapter 11, Section 9).*

d) *Carefully pull the lock carrier forwards approximately 10 cm to provide easier access to the front of the engine.*

6.2 Using special tool to slide out the front crossmember

6.3 Cable guide bracket on the shroud lower mounting bolts

6.6a Unbolt and remove the exhaust manifold...

6.6b ...and recover the gasket

3 Undo the retaining bolts and remove the hot-air shroud from over the exhaust manifold, noting the cable guide bracket on the lower bolts **(see illustration)**.

4 Working under the vehicle, unbolt the exhaust front pipe/catalytic converter to front flexible flange bolts and nut. Lower the front pipe and recover the gasket; a new one will be required on refitting.

Caution: Handle the flexible, braided section of the front pipe carefully, and do not bend it excessively, if it is bent more than 10° it could get damaged.

5 Trace the wiring back from the oxygen sensor, located above the catalytic converter on the manifold, and then disconnect the wiring plug connector. Release the wiring from its retaining clips, noting its routing and fitted position.

6 Unscrew the nuts and withdraw the exhaust manifold from the cylinder head. Discard the nuts, as new ones must be used on refitting.

Also, recover the gasket and discard **(see illustrations)**.

Refitting

7 Refitting is a reversal of the removal procedure, but fit new gaskets and tighten all nuts and bolts to the specified torque where given.

7 Exhaust system – component renewal

⚠️ *Warning: Allow ample time for the exhaust system to cool before starting work. In particular, note that the catalytic converter runs at very high temperatures. If there is any chance that the system may still be hot, wear suitable gloves. When removing the exhaust sections, take care not to damage the oxygen sensors if they are not removed from their locations.*

Removal

1 The original VW system fitted in the factory is in three sections on non-turbo engines: the front flexible pipe section, the centre pipe/main catalytic converter section, and the rear section with two silencers. Also on non-turbo models, there is a second starter catalytic converter, which is part of the exhaust manifold, see Section 6. On turbo engines, there are four sections, front down pipe/catalytic converter, the front flexible pipe section, the centre pipe section, and the rear section with two silencers. The rear section has two silencers (a front and rear silencer), however each silencer may be renewed separately by cutting the middle of the pipe and fitting a joining clamp. See paragraph 16, in this Section.

2 To remove part of the system, first jack up the front or rear of the car and support it on axle stands (see *Jacking and vehicle support*). Alternatively, position the car over an inspection pit or on car ramps.

Front down pipe/catalytic converter (turbo engines)

Note: *Handle the flexible, braided section of the front pipe carefully, and do not bend it excessively.*

3 Undo the retaining bolts and remove the turbocharger upper heat shield **(see illustration)**.

4 Trace the wiring back from the upper sensor, which is positioned in the top of the catalytic converter and disconnect the wiring connector. The sensor can then come away with the front pipe/catalytic converter.

5 Unscrew and remove the nuts securing the front flange to the exhaust manifold/turbocharger **(see illustration)**.

6 Working under the vehicle, undo the exhaust front pipe/catalytic converter to front flexible flange nuts **(see illustration)**. Lower the front pipe and recover the gasket; a new one will be required on refitting.

Caution: Handle the flexible, braided section of the front pipe carefully, and do not bend it excessively, if it is bent more than 10° it could get damaged.

7 Unscrew the bolts securing the lower mounting bracket to the cylinder block **(see illustration)**. Unclip the wiring to the lower oxygen sensor from the retaining clips on the mounting bracket.

7.3 Remove the heat shield

7.5 Undo the four retaining nuts to turbocharger

7.6 Undo the two retaining nuts to catalytic converter

7.7 Undo the two mounting bracket retaining bolts (arrowed)

7.10 Undo the two retaining nuts to the front pipe

7.13 Exhaust system centre section

7.14 Slacken the securing clamp retaining bolts

7.16 Check for markings in the area of the arrows

7.18a Exhaust rubber mountings ...

7.18b ... at each side of the rear silencer

8 With the front flexible pipe supported, to prevent it from getting damaged, detach the front pipe/catalytic converter from the studs on the manifold/turbocharger. When it is free, lower it to the ground and remove it from under the car.

Front flexible pipe

Note: *Handle the flexible, braided section of the front pipe carefully, and do not bend it more than 10°, as it may get damaged.*

9 On turbo engine models, trace the wiring back from the oxygen sensor, which is fitted at the front of the flexible section **(see illustration 7.7)**. Trace the wiring back from the sensor and disconnect the wiring connector. Unclip the oxygen sensor wiring from any clips or brackets, noting how it is routed for refitting. If a new front flexible section is being fitted, unscrew the oxygen sensors from the pipe, as applicable.

10 Unscrew the nuts and release the rear of the pipe from the centre section **(see illustration)**.

11 Unscrew and remove the nuts securing the front flange to the lower part of the catalytic converter **(see illustration 7.6)**. On some models, the shield over the right-hand driveshaft inner CV joint must be removed to improve access. Separate the front joint, and move it down sufficiently to clear the mounting studs.

12 Support the front of the pipe, and then detach the rear of the pipe from the centre section and mounting bracket. When the pipe

is free, withdraw it forwards and remove it from under the car. Recover the gaskets from each end of the pipe, as new ones will be required on refitting.

Centre pipe/catalytic converter/ silencer

13 To remove the centre pipe, first unbolt the flange from the front flexible pipe **(see illustration)**.

14 At the rear of the centre pipe, slacken the two bolts on the securing clamp **(see illustration)**. Slide the clamp along the pipe to disengage, twisting it from side to side, to help slide it along the exhaust pipe.

15 Disengage the front part of the pipe and withdraw the centre pipe from under the vehicle.

Rear pipe and silencers

16 If the factory-fitted VW rear section is being worked on, examine the pipe between the two silencers for three pairs of punch marks, or three line markings **(see illustration)**. The centre marking indicates the point at which to cut the pipe, while the outer marks indicate the position for the ends of the new clamp required when refitting. Cut through the pipe using the centre mark as a guide, making the cut as square to the pipe as possible if either section is to be re-used.

17 If the factory-fitted rear section has already been renewed, loosen the nuts securing the clamp between the silencers so that the clamp can be moved.

Rear silencers

18 The rear silencers are supported by rubber mountings that locate on mounting brackets, which are bolted to the underside of the car **(see illustrations)**.

19 Undo the clamp bolts at the front of the rear silencers and slide it along the pipe to release it from the centre section. Lower the silencers out of position and release the mounting(s) from the underside of the car.

Refitting

20 Each section is refitted by a reversal of the removal sequence, noting the following points:

  a) *Ensure that all traces of corrosion have been removed from the flanges or pipe ends, and renew all necessary gaskets.*

  b) *If necessary, renew the clamps, and use the markings on the pipes as a guide to the clamp's correct fitted position.*

  c) *Inspect the mountings for signs of damage or deterioration, and renew as necessary.*

  d) *If using exhaust assembly paste, make sure this is only applied to joints downstream of the catalyst.*

  e) *Prior to tightening the exhaust system mountings and clamps, ensure that all rubber mountings are correctly located and that there is adequate clearance between the exhaust system and vehicle underbody. Try to ensure that no unnecessary twisting stresses are applied to the pipes – move the pipes relative to each other at the clamps to relieve this.*

8 Catalytic converter – general information and precautions

1 The catalytic converter is a reliable and simple device which needs no maintenance in itself, but there are some facts of which an owner should be aware if the converter is to function properly for its full service life:

a) *DO NOT use leaded or lead-replacement petrol in a car equipped with a catalytic converter – the lead (or other additives) will coat the precious metals, reducing their converting efficiency and will eventually destroy the converter.*

b) *Always keep the ignition and fuel systems well maintained in accordance with the manufacturer's schedule (see Chapter 1A).*

c) *If the engine develops a misfire, do not drive the car at all (or at least as little as possible) until the fault is cured.*

d) *DO NOT push- or tow-start the car – this will soak the catalytic converter in unburned fuel, causing it to overheat when the engine does start.*

e) *DO NOT switch off the ignition at high engine speeds – i.e. do not 'blip' the throttle immediately before switching off the engine.*

f) *DO NOT use fuel or engine oil additives – these may contain substances harmful to the catalytic converter.*

g) *DO NOT continue to use the car if the engine burns oil to the extent of leaving a visible trail of blue smoke.*

h) *Remember that the catalytic converter operates at very high temperatures. DO NOT, therefore, park the car in dry undergrowth, over long grass or piles of dead leaves after a long run.*

i) *Remember that the catalytic converter is FRAGILE – do not strike it with tools during servicing work, and take care handling it when removing it from the car for any reason.*

j) *In some cases, a sulphurous smell (like that of rotten eggs) may be noticed from the exhaust. This is common to many catalytic converter-equipped cars, and has more to do with the sulphur content of the brand of fuel being used than the converter itself.*

k) *The catalytic converter, used on a well-maintained and well-driven car, should last for between 50,000 and 100,000 miles – if the converter is no longer effective, it must be renewed.*

Chapter 4 Part D:
Emission control and exhaust systems – diesel engines

Contents

Degrees of difficulty

Easy, suitable for novice with little experience		Fairly easy, suitable for beginner with some experience		Fairly difficult, suitable for competent DIY mechanic		Difficult, suitable for experienced DIY mechanic		Very difficult, suitable for expert DIY or professional	

Specifications

Engine codes*

1.6 litre - common rail injection	CAYB, CAYA
2.0 litre - common rail injection	CBAA, CBAB, CBBB, CFFA, CFFB and CFGB

* **Note:** *See 'Vehicle identification' at the end of this manual for the location of engine code markings.*

Emission control applications

All engines	Particulate filter in the front downpipe with catalytic converter and oxygen (lambda probe) sensor. EGR system fitted, with exhaust gas temperature sensors and exhaust gas pressure sensor.

Torque wrench settings

	Nm	lbf ft
Catalytic converter/particulate filter mounting bracket nuts/bolts.	25	18
EGR cooler mounting bolts	9	6
EGR recirculation metal pipes (all engines except CBAA, CBAB and CBBB):		
to-cooler bolts	9	6
to-cylinder head bolts.	9	6
to-exhaust manifold nuts	24	18
to-inlet manifold clamp bolt	5	4
EGR recirculation metal pipes (CBAA, CBAB and CBBB):		
to-EGR valve bolts	20	15
to-cooler bolts	20	15
to-exhaust manifold nuts	20	15
EGR valve bolts (CBAA, CBAB and CBBB)	8	6
Exhaust clamp nuts	25	18
Exhaust gas temperature senders:		
to-exhaust manifiold.	45	33
to-top of catalytic converter/particulate filter	60	45
to-front pipe after catalytic converter/particulate filter.	60	45
Exhaust/turbo manifold to cylinder head:		
CBAA, CBAB and CBBB	20	15
All except CBAA, CBAB and CBBB	24	18
Turbocharger pulsation damper bolts	10	7
Turbocharger oil return pipe flange bolts*:		
CBAA, CBAB and CBBB	15	11
All except CBAA, CBAB and CBBB	17	13
Turbocharger oil return banjo bolt*.	40	30
Turbocharger oil supply banjo bolt (All except CBAA, CBAB and CBBB).	30	22
Turbocharger oil supply union nut (CBAA, CBAB and CBBB)	22	16
Turbocharger-to-downpipe/catalytic converter clamp.	7	5

* *Do not re-use*

2.1 Disconnecting the breather hose

1 General information

Emission control systems

All diesel-engined models have a crankcase emission control system, and in addition, are fitted with a catalytic converter. All diesel engines are fitted with an Exhaust Gas Recirculation (EGR) system to reduce exhaust emissions.

Crankcase emission control

To reduce the emission of unburned hydrocarbons from the crankcase into the atmosphere, the engine is sealed and the blow-by gases and oil vapour are drawn from inside the crankcase, through a wire mesh oil separator, into the inlet tract to be burned by the engine during normal combustion.

Under conditions of high manifold depression, the gases will be sucked positively out of the crankcase. Under conditions of low manifold depression, the gases are forced out of the crankcase by the (relatively) higher crankcase pressure. If the engine is worn, the raised crankcase pressure (due to increased blow-by) will cause some of the flow to return under all manifold conditions.

Exhaust emission control

An oxidation catalyst is fitted in the exhaust system of all diesel-engined models. This has the effect of removing a large proportion of the gaseous hydrocarbons, carbon monoxide and particulates present in the exhaust gas. Models covered in this manual, have a particulate filter, which is fitted behind the catalytic converter in order to filter out soot particles.

An Exhaust Gas Recirculation (EGR) system is fitted to all diesel-engined models. This reduces the level of nitrogen oxides produced during combustion by introducing a proportion of the exhaust gas back into the inlet manifold under certain engine operating conditions. The system is controlled electronically by the diesel engine management ECU.

Exhaust systems

The exhaust system consists of the exhaust manifold, front flexible pipe with catalytic converter/particulate filter and rear pipe section including silencer. The turbocharger is integral with the exhaust manifold, and is driven by the exhaust gases.

The system is supported by various metal brackets screwed to the vehicle floor, with rubber vibration dampers fitted to suppress noise.

3.1 Vacuum hose layout - diesel engines

1 EGR cooler changeover vacuum unit
2 Cylinder head cover
3 EGR cooler changeover valve
4 Non-return valve
5 Vacuum pump connection
6 To brake servo
7 Air filter
8 Silencer
9 Charge pressure control solenoid valve
10 Vacuum unit on turbocharger (with position sensor)

2 Crankcase emission system – general information

1 The crankcase emission control system consists of hoses connecting the crankcase to the air cleaner, cylinder head cover and/or inlet manifold **(see illustration)**.
2 The system requires no attention other than to check at regular intervals that the hoses and pressure-regulating valve are free of blockages and in good condition.

3 Exhaust Gas Recirculation (EGR) system – component removal

1 The EGR system consists of the EGR valve, which directs exhaust gas from the exhaust manifold to the inlet manifold, and a control (changeover) valve that actuates the system

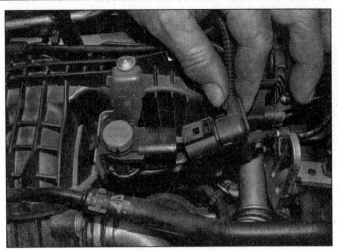

3.4 EGR cooler solenoid valve (arrowed)

3.5 Disconnect the wiring connector ...

according to engine load and speed **(see illustration)**. There is a vacuum-operated changeover unit, which is fitted on the EGR cooler for recirculating the exhaust gas. All this is connected by a series of vacuum hoses, and metal corrugated cooler pipes. There is also a recirculation potentiometer fitted to the EGR valve, this is controlled directly from the engine management ECU, which then activates the control motor.

2 On 2.0 litre (CBAA, CBAB and CBBB engines), the EGR valve is mounted between the throttle valve module and the inlet manifold. On the side of the EGR valve is a metal connecting pipe that goes to the exhaust gas cooler, which is bolted to the rear of the cylinder block. The gas cooler uses coolant from the engine cooling system to cool the exhaust gases before passing them to the inlet manifold. The system is activated by a solenoid valve mounted at the front of the inlet manifold, which is controlled by the ECU.

3 On all other engines the EGR valve is integral with the exhaust gas cooler, which is bolted to the rear of the cylinder block. It is joined to the exhaust manifold and cylinder head, by flanged corrugated metal pipes. The system is activated by a solenoid valve mounted at the front of the inlet manifold, which is controlled by the ECU.

EGR cooler 'change-over' solenoid valve

4 The EGR vacuum-solenoid valve is mounted on the front of the inlet manifold **(see illustration)**. Do not confuse the EGR solenoid with the turbo charge pressure control solenoid, which is mounted on the bulkhead.
5 Disconnect the wiring plug from the solenoid valve **(see illustration)**.
6 Unclip the valve from the mounting bracket **(see illustration)**, then identify the vacuum hoses for refitting and disconnect them from the valve.
7 Refitting is a reversal of removal. Ensure that

the hoses and wiring plug are reconnected securely and correctly.

EGR valve

Engine codes CBAA, CBAB and CBBB

8 Remove the throttle valve housing from the inlet manifold, as described in Chapter 4B, Section 3.
9 Undo the bolts securing the pipe to the left-hand side of the EGR valve **(see illustration)**.
10 Disconnect the wiring plug connector from the right-hand side of the EGR valve.
11 Undo the bolts and detach the valve from the inlet manifold. Discard the O-ring seal – a new one must be fitted.
12 Refitting is a reversal of removal, using a new EGR valve O-ring seal, and tightening the retaining bolts to the specified torque.

All other engine codes

13 The EGR valve is incorporated into the EGR cooler, remove the cooler as described in paragraphs 20 to 26. At the time of writing, it was not possible to separate the EGR valve from the cooler.

EGR cooler

14 Remove the exhaust front pipe/catalytic

converter/ particulate filter as described in Section 9.
15 Drain the cooling system as described in Chapter 1B, Section 31. If required the coolant hoses can be clamped before removal, to save draining the complete system.

Engine codes CBAA, CBAB and CBBB

16 Release the retaining clips and disconnect the coolant hoses from the EGR cooler. Be prepared for coolant spillage.
17 Undo the retaining bolts and disconnect the EGR metal connecting pipes from each end of the cooler.
18 Undo the upper bolts and lower banjo bolt and remove the turbocharger oil return pipe/ support from the rear of the engine.
19 Disconnect the vacuum hose from vacuum unit on the lower part of the cooler, then undo the retaining bolts, and remove the cooler from the rear of the engine **(see illustration)**.

All other engine codes

20 Release the retaining clips and disconnect the coolant hoses from each end of the EGR cooler **(see illustrations)**. Be prepared for coolant spillage.

3.6 ...then unclip the valve from the bracket

3.9 EGR pipe-to-valve bolts (arrowed)

3.20a Disconnect the coolant hose from the cooler

3.20b Release the retaining clips arrowed and remove hose

3.19 EGR cooler system – CBAA, CBAB and CBBB engines

1 EGR cooler	3 Vacuum unit	5 Gaskets
2 Connecting pipes	4 Vacuum pipe	6 Heat shield

3.21 Remove the EGR pipe from the cooler to the manifold

21 Undo the two retaining screws from the cooler, the two retaining nuts from the exhaust manifold and remove the EGR metal connecting pipe **(see illustration)**.

22 Undo the two retaining screws from the cooler, the two retaining screws from the cylinder head and remove the EGR metal connecting pipe **(see illustrations)**.

23 Undo the upper bolts and lower banjo bolt and remove the turbocharger oil return pipe/support from the rear of the engine **(see illustrations)**.

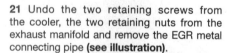

3.22a Undo the EGR pipe bolts (arrowed) to the cooler

3.22b Undo the EGR pipe bolts (arrowed) to the cylinder head

3.23a Undo the upper bolts (arrowed) ...

3.23b ...and lower banjo bolts ...

3.23c ...then remove the pipes and support bracket

3.24 Disconnect the wiring connector from the EGR valve

24 Disconnect the wiring plug connector from the EGR valve **(see illustration)**.
25 Disconnect the vacuum hose from vacuum unit on the lower part of the cooler **(see illustration)**, then undo the four retaining bolts, and remove the cooler from the rear of the engine.
26 Refitting is a reversal of removal, using new gaskets **(see illustration)**, and tightening the retaining bolts to the specified torque.

3.25 EGR cooler securing bolts (arrowed)

3.26 Fit new gaskets to the EGR pipes

4 Turbocharger – general information and precautions

General information

A turbocharger is fitted to all engines, and is integral with the exhaust manifold.

The turbocharger increases engine efficiency by raising the pressure in the inlet manifold above atmospheric pressure. Instead of the air simply being sucked into the cylinders, it is forced in.

Energy for the operation of the turbocharger comes from the exhaust gas. The gas flows through a specially shaped housing (the turbine housing) and in so doing, spins the turbine wheel. The turbine wheel is attached to a shaft, at the end of which is another vaned wheel, known as the compressor wheel. The compressor wheel spins in its own housing, and compresses the inducted air on the way to the inlet manifold.

Between the turbocharger and the inlet manifold, the compressed air passes through an intercooler (see Section 7 for details). The purpose of the intercooler is to remove from the inducted air some of the heat gained in being compressed. Because cooler air is denser, removal of this heat further increases engine efficiency.

Boost pressure (the pressure in the inlet manifold) is limited by a wastegate, which diverts the exhaust gas away from the turbine wheel in response to a pressure-sensitive actuator.

The turbo shaft is pressure-lubricated by an oil feed pipe from the engine oil filter mounting. The shaft 'floats' on a cushion of oil. Oil is returned to the sump through a return

pipe that connects to the rear of the cylinder block.

Precautions

The turbocharger operates at extremely high speeds and temperatures. Certain precautions must be observed to avoid premature failure of the turbo, or injury to the operator.

• *Do not operate the turbo with any parts exposed – foreign objects falling onto the rotating vanes could cause excessive damage and (if ejected) personal injury.*
• *Cover the turbocharger air inlet ducts to prevent debris entering, and clean using lint-free cloths only.*
• *Do not race the engine immediately after start-up, especially if it is cold. Give the oil a few seconds to circulate.*
• *Observe the recommended intervals for oil and filter changing, and use a reputable oil of the specified quality. Neglect of oil*

5.5a Disconnecting the breather hose ...

changing, or use of inferior oil, can cause carbon formation on the turbo shaft and subsequent failure. Thoroughly clean the area around all oil pipe unions before disconnecting them, to prevent the ingress of dirt. Store dismantled components in a sealed container to prevent contamination.

5 Turbocharger and exhaust manifold – removal and refitting

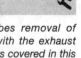

Note: *This Section describes removal of the turbocharger together with the exhaust manifold. On all diesel engines covered in this manual, the turbocharger cannot be removed from the exhaust manifold.*

Removal

1 Apply the handbrake, then jack up the front of the vehicle and support it on axle stands (see *Jacking and vehicle support*). Remove the engine compartment undertray and the engine top cover.
2 Remove the bulkhead panel from the rear of the engine compartment, as described in Chapter 12, Section 18.
3 Remove the air cleaner assembly and ducting as described in Chapter 4B, Section 2.
4 Remove the exhaust front pipe/catalytic converter/ particulate filter as described in Section 9.
5 Undo the retaining bolt, unclip the breather pipe and disconnect the air intake hose from the turbocharger **(see illustrations)**.
6 Disconnect the wiring connector and

5.5b ...undo the retaining screw ...

5.5c ...and disconnect the air intake hose

5.6a Disconnect the wiring connector ...

**5.6b ... and the vacuum hose from the
vacuum pump**

**5.7a Locate the exhaust gas temperature
sensor (arrowed) ...**

**5.7b ... and disconnect the wiring
connector on the bulkhead**

vacuum pipe from the vacuum unit on top of the turbocharger **(see illustrations)**.
7 Located at the engine compartment bulkhead, disconnect the exhaust gas

temperature sensor wiring plugs, and detach the connector from the bulkhead bracket **(see illustrations)**. Note that there is one wiring connector behind the mounting plate

on the bulkhead, trace the wiring back from the relevant sensor, noting its routing and releasing it from any retaining clips.
8 Slacken the retaining clips, undo the two retaining bolts and withdraw the pulsation damper from the charge air ducting to the turbo **(see illustration)**.
9 Undo the retaining screws and remove the EGR metal connecting pipes, with reference to Section 3.
10 Undo the two upper securing bolts and the lower banjo bolts for the oil supply and return for the turbocharger. Then remove the oil return pipe/support from the rear of the engine **(see illustrations 3.23a, 3.23b & 3.23c)**. On 2.0 litre (CBAA, CBAB and CBBB engines), undo the supply pipe union nut and disengage the supply pipe from the turbocharger.
11 Undo the two retaining screws and remove the heat shield from the manifold **(see illustration)**.
12 Check around the turbocharger/exhaust manifold and unclip any wiring or hoses still connected, noting their fitted position and the routing of all cables.
13 Undo the retaining nuts and manoeuvre the exhaust manifold/turbocharger assembly out from the engine compartment **(see illustration)**.

Refitting

14 Refit the turbocharger by following the removal procedure in reverse, noting the following points:
*a) Renew exhaust maniflold gaskets, sealing washers and O-rings **(see illustration)**.*

**5.8 Disconnect the charge air pipe/
pulsation damper from the turbo**

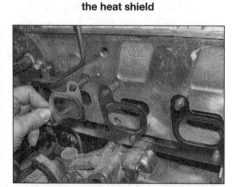

**5.11 Undo the two retaining screws from
the heat shield**

**5.13 Remove the turbocharger/manifold
from the engine compartment**

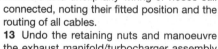

5.14a Fit new exhaust manifold gasket ...

5.14b ... oil return/supply pipe gasket ...

5.14c ...oil return banjo bolt ...

5.14d ...and oil supply sealing washers

b) *Fit a new gasket to the oil return pipe upper flange* **(see illustration).**

c) *Fit a new banjo bolt to the oil return pipe* **(see illustration).**

d) *Fit new sealing washers to the oil supply pipe* **(see illustration).**

e) *Before reconnecting the oil supply pipe, fill the turbocharger with fresh oil using an oil can.*

f) *Tighten all nuts and bolts to the specified torque, where given.*

g) *Ensure that the air hose clips are securely tightened, to prevent air leaks.*

h) *When the engine is started after refitting, allow it to idle for approximately one minute to give the oil time to circulate around the turbine shaft bearings. Check for signs of oil or coolant leakage from the relevant unions.*

6 Turbocharger charge control system components – description, removal and refitting

Description

1 The turbocharger pressure valve is operated by vacuum supplied by the brake vacuum pump mounted on the left-hand end of the cylinder head. The vacuum supply is controlled by an electrically operated solenoid valve activated by the engine management ECU. The solenoid valve is mounted on the bulkhead at the rear of the engine compartment. The valve has three hoses connecting it to the air cleaner, turbocharger and vacuum pump. It is important that the hoses are connected correctly to the solenoid valve **(see illustration 3.1).**

Charge pressure control solenoid valve

2 The charge pressure solenoid valve is mounted at the rear of the engine compartment **(see illustration)**, at the rear of the battery, on the bulkhead.

3 Disconnect the wiring from the valve **(see illustration).**

4 Undo the two retaining nuts and withdraw the solenoid valve away from the bulkhead, unclipping the vacuum hoses from their retaining clips **(see illustration).**

5 Remove the vacuum hoses from the ports on the control solenoid valve **(see illustration)**, noting their order of connection carefully to aid correct refitting.

6 Refitting is a reversal of removal.

Charge pressure valve (wastegate)

7 The charge pressure valve is an integral part of the turbocharger, and cannot be renewed separately.

7 Intercooler – general information, removal and refitting

General information

1 The intercooler is effectively an 'air radiator', used to cool the pressurised inlet air before it enters the engine.

6.2 Charge pressure solenoid valve (arrowed)

6.4 ... unclip the vacuum pipes ...

2 When the turbocharger compresses the inlet air, one side-effect is that the air is heated, causing it to expand. If the inlet air can be cooled, a greater effective volume of air will be inducted, and the engine will produce more power.

3 The compressed air from the turbocharger, which would normally be fed straight into the inlet manifold, is instead ducted around the engine to the base of the intercooler. The intercooler is mounted at the front of the car, in the airflow. The heated air entering the base of the unit rises upwards, and is cooled by the airflow over the intercooler fins, much as with the radiator. When it reaches the top of the intercooler, the cooled air is then ducted into the throttle housing.

4 There is a charge air pressure/temperature sensor fitted to the air inlet ducting from the intercooler to the inlet manifold. See Chapter 4B, Section 3, for removal and refitting procedure.

6.3 Disconnect the wiring connector ...

6.5 ... and disconnect them from the solenoid valve

7.6a Remove the charge air hoses ...

7.6b ...from both sides of the intercooler

7.7a Undo the retaining screws ...

7.7b ...to release the intercooler mountings (arrowed)

7.9 Undo the retaining screw (arrowed)

Removal

5 The intercooler is located in front of the radiator on the lock carrier (the crossmember incorporating the headlights and radiator grille). Remove the radiator as described in Chapter 3, Section 3, for access to the intercooler. This procedure may include moving the lock carrier to its Service position, See Chapter 2E, Section 4.

6 Slacken the retaining clips and release the air ducts from the inlet and outlet elbows at the bottom of the intercooler (see illustrations).

7 Working from the front of the vehicle, undo the two retaining screws (one at each side) to release the intercooler side mountings (see illustrations).

8 Tilt the intercooler and air-conditioning condenser backwards slightly, taking care not to damage the refrigerant pipes.

Warning: Refer to the precautions given in Chapter 3, Section 11, before working on the air-conditioning system.

9 With the intercooler tilted back, undo the screw at the right-hand lower side of the intercooler to release the refrigerant pipe mounting bracket (see illustration).

10 Working at the front of the vehicle, undo the four retaining screws (two at each side) and pull the intercooler upwards to release it from the lower crossmember, then withdraw it from out of the engine compartment (see illustrations). Make sure the condenser is secured safely to the front crossmember, to prevent any damage to the fins or the refrigerant pipes.

Refitting

11 Refitting is a reversal of removal, noting the following points:
  a) Make sure the mountings on the side of the intercooler are not damaged (see illustration).
  b) Check the rubber grommets are still located in the lower crossmember (see illustration).
  c) Refer to Chapter 3, Section 3, when refitting the radiator.
  d) Ensure that the air hose clips are securely refitted, to prevent air leaks.

7.10a Undo the two retaining screws (arrowed) ...

7.11a Check the condition of the mounting ...

7.10b ...and the two (arrowed) from the other side of the condenser

7.11b ...and the rubber grommets in the crossmember

8 Catalytic converter/ particulate filter – removal and refitting

Warning: Allow ample time for the exhaust system to cool before starting work. In particular, note that the catalytic converter runs at very high temperatures. If there is any chance that the system may still be hot, wear suitable gloves.

8.3 Unclip the wiring loom

8.4 Undo the exhaust/turbo securing clamp (arrowed)

8.5 Unclip the hoses from the retaining clips on the timing cover

8.6 Undo the retaining bolt (arrowed)

8.10 Support the flexible pipe with flat metal bar and securing clips

8.11 Slide the exhaust clamp along the exhaust

Note: *This Section describes removal of the exhaust front flexible pipe/catalytic converter/particulate filter, which is one complete assembly. The subframe will need to be removed, to allow enough room for the assembly to be lowered out from under the rear of the engine.*

1 Disconnect the battery negative lead and position it away from the terminal. **Note:** *Refer to 'Disconnecting the battery' at the rear of this manual first.*

2 Working at the engine compartment bulkhead, disconnect the wiring plugs for the oxygen sensor and exhaust gas temperature sensors **(see illustration 6.2)**.

3 Trace the wiring back from the sensors, noting their routing and release the wiring harness from the retaining clips **(see illustration)**. Note the sensors can stay fitted to the exhaust at this point, if a new catalytic

converter/particulate is fitted, then the sensors can be swapped over with the system of the vehicle.

4 Slacken the retaining bolt to release the clamp between the turbocharger and the catalytic converter/particulate filter **(see illustration)**.

5 Release the hoses from the timing cover **(see illustration)**, release the retaining clip and disconnect the pressure hose from the exhaust to the differential pressure sender.

6 Working at the right-hand rear corner of the cylinder head, slacken and remove the upper mounting bolt **(see illustration)**.

7 Apply the handbrake, then jack up the front of the vehicle and support it on axle stands (see *Jacking and vehicle support*). Remove the engine compartment undertray.

8 Remove the front subframe, as described in Chapter 10, Section 23.

9 Where fitted, undo the two retaining bolts and remove the heat shield from above the right-hand drive shaft.

10 To prevent any damage to the front flexible pipe use a couple of pieces of metal bar and some retaining clips to prevent the flexible pipe from bending to far and getting damaged **(see illustration)**.

Caution: Handle the flexible, braided section of the front pipe carefully, and do not bend it excessively, if it is bent more than 10° it could get damaged.

11 Slacken the retaining bolts and slide the exhaust clamp to the rear of the vehicle, to disengage the exhaust front pipe from the rear section **(see illustration)**.

12 Undo the nuts securing the catalytic converter/particulate filter lower support bracket to the cylinder block **(see illustrations)**.

8.12a Undo the upper securing nuts ...

8.12b ...and lower securing nuts ...

8.12c ...then remove the lower mounting bracket

13 Carefully manoeuvre the catalytic converter/particulate filter downwards from place. Take care not to damage any wiring, making sure that all wiring has been disconnected and release from their retaining clips. Also take care not to bend the flexible section of the exhaust pipe at an angle of more than 10°.

Refitting

14 Refit the exhaust catalytic converter/particulate filter assembly by following the removal procedure in reverse, but renew all gaskets **(see illustration)** and tighten all nuts and bolts to the specified torque, where given.

8.14 Renew the gasket between the particulate filter and the turbo

9 Exhaust system – component renewal

⚠️ **Warning: Allow ample time for the exhaust system to cool before starting work. In particular, note that the catalytic converter runs at very high temperatures. If there is any chance that the system may still be hot, wear suitable gloves.**

Removal

1 The original VW system fitted in the factory is in two sections. The front section includes the catalytic converter (or 'catalyst'), and particulate filter. The rear section, which connects to the front section under the centre of the vehicle has a silencer fitted. On 1.6 litre engines the silencer is alongside the fuel tank, on 2.0 litre engines the silencer is at the rear of the vehicle **(see illustrations)**.

2 To remove part of the system, first jack up the front or rear of the car and support it on axle stands (see *Jacking and vehicle support*). Alternatively, position the car over an inspection pit or on car ramps.

Front pipe (catalytic converter/particulate filter)

Caution: Handle the flexible, braided section of the front pipe carefully, and do not bend it excessively, if it is bent more than 10° it could get damaged.

3 The front flexible pipe section is part of the catalytic converter/particulate filter, remove the front pipe assembly as described in Section 8.

Rear pipe and single silencer

4 Unscrew the clamp bolt securing the rear section of exhaust to the front section **(see illustration)**.

5 Release the silencer from the rubber mountings, then twist it from the centre section and withdraw it from under the car **(see illustrations)**.

6 If required, undo the retaining bolts and remove the mounting brackets from across the exhaust tunnel, to make removal easier **(see illustration)**.

Rear pipe with two silencers

7 If the factory-fitted VW rear section is being worked on, examine the pipe between the two silencers for three pairs of punch marks, or three line markings. The centre marking indicates the point at which to cut the pipe, while the outer marks indicate the position for the ends of the new clamp required when refitting. Cut through the pipe using the centre mark as a guide, making the cut as square to the pipe as possible if either resulting section is to be re-used.

8 If the factory-fitted rear section has already been renewed, unscrew the clamp bolts between the two sections, to remove individual silencers.

Refitting

9 Each section is refitted by a reversal of the removal sequence, noting the following points:
a) Ensure that all traces of corrosion have been removed from the flanges or pipe ends, and renew all necessary gaskets.
b) The design of the clamps used between the exhaust sections means that they play

9.1a Rear exhaust system - 1.6 litre engines

9.1b Rear exhaust system - 2.0 litre engines

9.4 Slacken the bolts on the exhaust pipe clamp

9.5a Rear silencer exhaust rubber mounting

9.5b Rubber mounting on centre section of exhaust

9.6 Mounting bracket across exhaust tunnel

a greater role in ensuring a gas-tight seal
– fit new clamps if they are in less than
perfect condition.

c) When fitting the clamps, use the markings
on the pipes as a guide to the clamp's
correct fitted position.

d) Inspect the mountings for signs of
damage or deterioration, and renew as
necessary.

e) If using exhaust assembly paste,
make sure this is only applied to joints
downstream of the catalyst.

f) Prior to tightening the exhaust system
mountings and clamps, ensure that all
rubber mountings are correctly located
and that there is adequate clearance
between the exhaust system and vehicle
underbody.

10 Catalytic converter – general information and precautions

1 The catalytic converter fitted to diesel models
is simpler than that fitted to petrol models, but
it still needs to be treated with respect to avoid
problems. The converter is a reliable and simple
device which needs no maintenance in itself,
but there are some facts of which an owner
should be aware if the converter is to function
properly for its full service life:

a) DO NOT use fuel or engine oil additives –
these may contain substances harmful to
the catalytic converter.

b) DO NOT continue to use the car if the
engine burns (engine) oil to the extent of
leaving a visible trail of blue smoke.

c) Remember that the catalytic converter
is FRAGILE – do not strike it with tools
during servicing work, and take care
handling it when removing it from the car
for any reason.

d) The catalytic converter, used on a well-
maintained and well-driven car, should last
for between 50,000 and 100,000 miles – if
the converter is no longer effective, it must
be renewed.

Notes

Chapter 5 Part A:
Starting and charging systems

Contents

Degrees of difficulty

| Easy, suitable for novice with little experience 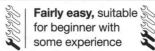 | Fairly easy, suitable for beginner with some experience | Fairly difficult, suitable for competent DIY mechanic | Difficult, suitable for experienced DIY mechanic | Very difficult, suitable for expert DIY or professional |

Specifications

General
System type . . . .   12 volt, negative earth

Starter motor
Rating:
  Petrol engines. . . . .   12V, 1.1 kW
  Diesel engines . . . .   12V, 2.0 kW

Battery
Ratings . . . .   36 to 72 Ah (depending on model and market)

Alternator
Rating. . . . .   55, 60, 70 or 90 amp
Minimum brush length . . . .   5.0 mm

Torque wrench settings	Nm	lbf ft
Alternator mounting bolts		
1.4 litre petrol:		
Non-turbo models (M8 x 90).	20	15
Turbo (TSI) models (M8 x 90)	23	17
1.6 litre diesel engine	20	15
2.0 litre diesel (81kW and 103kW) engines.	20	15
2.0 litre diesel (125kW) engines	25	18
1.4 litre - Non-turbo petrol engine		
Alternator mounting bracket bolts	40	30
Alternator drivebelt tensioner centre bolt (M8 x 45).	20	15
Tensioner roller centre bolt (M10 x 22)	60	44
1.4 litre - turbo (TSI) petrol engine		
Auxiliary drivebelt idler roller centre bolt	40	30
Auxiliary drivebelt tensioner:		
Centre bolt (M10 x 50):		
Stage 1	20	15
Stage 2	Angle-tighten a further 90°	
Mounting bracket bolts (M8 x 50)	25	18
Battery clamping plate bolt	35	26
Battery-to-starter positive cable retaining nut	20	15
Starter wiring bracket retaining nut	23	16
Starter mounting bolts:		
M10	40	30
M12	75	55

1 General information and precautions

General information

The engine electrical system consists of the charging and starting systems. Because of their engine-related functions, these are covered separately from the body electrical devices such as the lights, instruments, etc (which are covered in Chapter 12). On petrol engine models refer to Part B of this Chapter for information on the ignition system, and on diesel models refer to Part C for the preheating system.

The electrical system is of the 12-volt negative earth type.

The battery is of the low maintenance or maintenance-free (sealed for life) type and is charged by the alternator, which is belt-driven from the crankshaft pulley.

The starter motor is of the pre-engaged type, with an integral solenoid. On starting, the solenoid moves the drive pinion into engagement with the flywheel ring gear before the starter motor is energised. Once the engine has started, a one-way clutch prevents the motor armature being driven by the engine until the pinion disengages from the flywheel.

Further details of the various systems are given in the relevant Sections of this Chapter. While some repair procedures are given, the usual course of action is to renew the component concerned. The owner whose interest extends beyond mere component renewal should obtain a copy of the *Automotive Electrical & Electronic Systems Manual*, available from the publishers of this manual.

Precautions

⚠ **Warning: It is necessary to take extra care when working on the electrical system to avoid damage to semi-conductor devices (diodes and transistors), and to avoid the risk of personal injury. In addition to the precautions given in 'Safety first!' observe the following when working on the system:**
• *Always remove rings, watches, etc, before working on the electrical system.* Even with the battery disconnected, capacitive discharge could occur if a component's live terminal is earthed to a metal object. This could cause a shock or nasty burn.
• *Do not reverse the battery connections.* Components such as the alternator, electronic control units, or any other components having semi-conductor circuitry could be irreparably damaged.
• **Never disconnect the battery terminals, the alternator, any electrical wiring or any test instruments when the engine is running.**
• **Do not allow the engine to turn the alternator when the alternator is not connected.**

• **Never test for alternator output by flashing the output lead to earth.**
• **Always ensure that the battery negative lead is disconnected when working on the electrical system.**
• If the engine is being started using jump leads and a slave battery, connect the batteries *positive-to-positive* and *negative-to-negative* (see *Jump starting* at the beginning of the manual). This also applies when connecting a battery charger.
• Before using electric-arc welding equipment on the car, *disconnect the battery, alternator and components such as the electronic control units* (where applicable) to protect them from the risk of damage.
Caution: Certain audio units fitted as standard equipment by VW have a built-in security code to deter thieves. If the power source to the unit is cut, the anti-theft system will activate. Even if the power source is immediately reconnected, the unit will not function until the correct security code has been entered. Therefore, if you do not know the correct security code for the unit, do not disconnect the battery negative terminal or remove the radio/cassette unit from the vehicle. Refer to your VW dealer for further information on whether the unit fitted to your car has a security code. Refer to 'Disconnecting the battery' in the Reference section at the rear of this manual.

2 Battery – testing and charging

Testing

Standard and low-maintenance battery

1 If the vehicle covers a small annual mileage, it is worthwhile checking the specific gravity of the electrolyte every three months to determine the state of charge of the battery. Remove the battery (see Section 3) then remove the cell caps/cover (as applicable) and use a hydrometer to make the check, comparing the results with the following table. Note that the specific gravity readings assume an electrolyte temperature of 15°C; for every 10°C below 15°C subtract 0.007. For every 10°C above 15°C add 0.007. If the electrolyte level of any cell is low, top it up to the MAX level mark with distilled water.

	Above 25°C	Below 25°C
Fully-charged	1.210 to 1.230	1.270 to 1.290
70% charged	1.170 to 1.190	1.230 to 1.250
Discharged	1.050 to 1.070	1.110 to 1.130

2 If the battery condition is suspect, first check the specific gravity of electrolyte in each cell. A variation of 0.040 or more between any cells indicates loss of electrolyte or deterioration of the internal plates.
3 If the specific gravity variation is 0.040 or more, the battery should be renewed. If the cell variation is satisfactory but the battery

is discharged, it should be recharged as described later in this Section.

Maintenance-free battery

4 In cases where a sealed for life maintenance-free battery is fitted, topping-up and testing of the electrolyte in each cell is not possible. The condition of the battery can therefore only be tested using a battery condition indicator or a voltmeter.
5 Certain models may be fitted with a maintenance-free battery with a built-in charge condition indicator. The indicator is located in the top of the battery casing, and indicates the condition of the battery from its colour. If the indicator shows green, then the battery is in a good state of charge. If the indicator turns darker, eventually to black, then the battery requires charging, as described later in this Section. If the indicator shows clear/yellow, then the electrolyte level in the battery is too low to allow further use, and the battery should be renewed. **Do not** attempt to charge, load or jump-start a battery when the indicator shows clear/yellow.

All battery types

6 If testing the battery using a voltmeter, connect the voltmeter across the battery and note the voltage. The test is only accurate if the battery has not been subjected to any kind of charge for the previous six hours. If this is not the case, switch on the headlights for 30 seconds, then wait four to five minutes before testing the battery after switching off the headlights. All other electrical circuits must be switched off, so check that the doors and tailgate are fully shut when making the test.
7 If the voltage reading is less than 12.2 volts, then the battery is discharged, whilst a reading of 12.2 to 12.4 volts indicates a partially discharged condition. The battery should be recharged as described later in this Section.

Charging

Note: *The following is intended as a guide only. Always refer to the manufacturer's recommendations (often printed on a label attached to the battery) before charging a battery.*

8 If the battery is to be recharged, we recommend that you use a low current battery charger. Note that it is not necessary to disconnect the battery leads when using a low current battery charger. If the battery is disconnected (e.g. if it is to be removed and recharged on the bench), note that certain 'learned' values will be lost from the engine management ECU memory, requiring the car to be driven over a short distance after refitting the battery. Also, when the battery is reconnected, the warning lights for the ESP and electro-mechanical steering will light up and stay on. They will extinguish if you drive briefly in a straight line at a speed of 9 to 13 mph.

Standard and low maintenance battery

9 Charge the battery at a rate equivalent to 10% of the battery capacity (e.g. for a 45 Ah

battery charge at 4.5 A) and continue to charge the battery at this rate until no further rise in specific gravity is noted over a four-hour period.

10 Alternatively, a trickle charger charging at the rate of 1.5 amps can safely be used overnight.

11 Specially rapid boost charges, which are claimed to restore the power of the battery in 1 to 2 hours are not recommended, as they can cause serious damage to the battery plates through overheating.

12 While charging the battery, note that the temperature of the electrolyte should never exceed 38°C.

Maintenance-free battery

13 This battery type takes considerably longer to fully recharge than the standard type, the time taken being dependent on the extent of discharge, but it can take anything up to three days.

14 The battery should be removed from the car, and a constant voltage type charger is required, to be set, when connected, to 13.9 to 14.9 volts with a charger current below 25 amps. Using this method, the battery should be useable within three hours, giving a voltage reading of 12.5 volts, but this is for a partially discharged battery and, as mentioned, full charging can take far longer.

15 If the battery is to be charged from a fully discharged state (condition reading less than 12.2 volts), have it recharged by your local automotive electrician, as the charge rate is higher and constant supervision during charging is necessary.

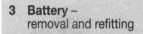

3 Battery – removal and refitting

Note: *If the vehicle has a security-coded audio unit, make sure that you have the code number before disconnecting the battery; refer to cautions in Section 1.*

Removal

1 The battery is located on the left-hand side of the engine compartment. Where an insulator cover is fitted, open the cover to gain access to the battery **(see illustration)**.

2 Loosen the clamp nut and disconnect the battery negative (-) then positive (+) leads from the terminals **(see illustrations)**.

3 With the battery terminals disconnected, withdraw the insulator cover from over the battery **(see illustration)**.

4 Unscrew the retaining clamp bolt **(see illustration)**, then lift the battery from the engine compartment.

5 If necessary, unbolt and remove the battery tray **(see illustration)**.

Refitting

6 Refit the battery by following the removal procedure in reverse, ensuring the following points:

3.1 Battery located under insulation cover

3.2b ... and battery positive terminal

a) Tighten the battery clamp bolt to the torque setting specified.

b) Re-connect the battery positive lead first, then negative terminal.

c) If the battery has been disconnected prior to airbag removal, ensure that no one is inside the vehicle, and the ignition is switched off before connecting terminals.

d) Re-activate the audio unit by inserting the security code (where applicable)

e) The ESP, TCS and PS warning lights on the facia panel may stay illuminated. Drive the vehicle in a straight line at 15 to 20 km/h, and then the lights should go out automatically. This will reactivate the steering angle sensor.

f) Fully open and close all electric windows to the limit stops, then hold the switch until the relay audibly switches (clicking noise from relay).

g) To restore the electric window automatic

3.4 Battery retaining clamp bolt (arrowed)

3.2a Disconnecting the battery negative terminal ...

3.3 Slide the insulation cover from over the battery

opening/closing function, ensure all windows and doors are closed, and then lock the vehicle via the driver's door. Now unlock the driver's door, and then lock it again – hold the key in the locking position for at least one second.

4 Alternator/charging system – testing in vehicle

Note: *Refer to Section 1 of this Chapter before starting work.*

1 If the charge warning light fails to illuminate when the ignition is switched on, first check the alternator wiring connections for security. If the light still fails to illuminate, check the continuity of the warning light feed wire from the alternator to the bulbholder. If all is satisfactory, the alternator is at fault and

3.5 Battery tray and retaining bolts (arrowed)

5.2 Unclip and remove the plastic upper trim cover

5.4 Remove the air intake hose (arrowed)

5.5 Move the fuel filter to one side

should be renewed or taken to an auto-electrician for testing and repair.

2 Similarly, if the charge warning light comes on with the ignition, but is then slow to go out when the engine is started, this may indicate an impending alternator problem. Check all the items listed in the preceding paragraph, and refer to an auto-electrical specialist if no obvious faults are found.

3 If the charge warning light illuminates when the engine is running, stop the engine and check that the auxiliary drivebelt is not broken (see Chapter 1A or 1B) and that the alternator connections are secure. If all is so far satisfactory, check the alternator brushes and slip-rings as described in Section 6. If the fault persists, the alternator should be renewed, or taken to an auto-electrician for testing and repair.

4 If the alternator output is suspect even though the warning light functions correctly, the regulated voltage may be checked as follows.

5 Connect a voltmeter across the battery terminals, and start the engine.

6 Increase the engine speed until the voltmeter reading remains steady; the reading should be approximately 12 to 13 volts, and no more than 14 volts.

7 Switch on as many electrical accessories (e.g. the headlights, heated rear window and heater blower) as possible, and check that the alternator maintains the regulated voltage at around 13 to 14 volts.

8 If the regulated voltage is not as stated, this may be due to worn brushes, weak brush springs, a faulty voltage regulator, a faulty

diode, a severed phase winding or worn or damaged slip-rings. The brushes and slip rings may be checked (see Section 6), but if the fault persists, the alternator should be renewed or taken to an auto-electrician.

5 Alternator – removal and refitting

Removal

1 Disconnect the battery negative lead and position it away from the terminal, refer to Section 3.

2 Pull the engine trim cover upward to release it from the top of the engine **(see illustration)**. On petrol (TSI models), unclip the vacuum hose from the side of the cover, as it is removed.

Diesel models

3 Remove the radiator cooling fans from the rear of the radiator as described in Chapter 3, Section 5.

4 Slacken the retaining clips and remove the air intake hose from the throttle housing **(see illustration)**. To give more access to the alternator, also undo the retaining bolts and lower the plastic air ducting away from the rear of the alternator.

5 Undo the retaining bolts, and then move the fuel filter to one side **(see illustration)**. The fuel pipes do not need to be disconnected from the filter.

6 Remove the auxiliary drivebelt as described in Chapter 1B, Section 28. Mark the drivebelt

for direction to ensure it is refitted in the same position.

Petrol models

7 Release the securing clips (or undo the retaining bolts) and move the charcoal canister to one side (turbo TSI engines only). The pipes do not need to be disconnected from the canister, just move the canister to one side.

8 Remove the auxiliary drivebelt as described in Chapter 1A, Section 26. Mark the drivebelt for direction to ensure it is refitted in the same position.

All models

9 Remove the air conditioning compressor from below the alternator, as described in Chapter 3, Section 9. The air-conditioning pipes do not need to be disconnected from the compressor, move the compressor to one side and secure it in place under the vehicle with cable-tie or similar.

10 Release the retaining clip and disconnect the wiring connector from the alternator **(see illustration)**.

11 Remove the protective plastic cap, unscrew and remove the nut (washer), then disconnect the battery positive cable from the alternator terminal. Where applicable, unscrew the nut and remove the cable guide **(see illustration)**.

12 Unscrew and remove the lower, then upper bolts, then lift the alternator away from its bracket **(see illustrations)**.

Refitting

13 Refitting is a reversal of removal. Refer to Chapter 1A, Section 26 or Chapter 1B,

5.10 Disconnecting the alternator wiring plug connector

5.11 Pull the plastic cover off and undo the retaining nut

5.12a Alternator mounting bolts (arrowed) - petrol engines

Section 28, as applicable for details of refitting and tensioning the auxiliary drivebelt. Tighten the alternator mounting bolts to the specified torque. Before fitting the alternator, it may be necessary to tap the sliding sleeve in the alternator housing back a couple of millimeters **(see illustration)**, so that it can be refitted to the mounting bracket eassier.

6 Alternator – brush holder/regulator module renewal

Removal

1 Remove the alternator, as described in Section 5.
2 Place the alternator on a clean work surface, with the pulley facing down.

Bosch

3 Undo the screw and the two retaining nuts, and lift away the outer plastic cover **(see illustration)**.
4 Unscrew the three securing screws, and remove the voltage regulator **(see illustrations)**.

Valeo

5 Prise off the spring clips, and remove the outer plastic cover **(see illustration)**.
6 Undo the two screws and single nut, and remove the voltage regulator **(see illustrations)**.
7 Slide off the brush cover by depressing the lugs on each side.

5.12b Alternator mounting bolts (arrowed) - diesel engines

Inspection

8 Measure the free length of the brush contacts **(see illustration)**. Check the measurement with the Specifications; renew the module if the brushes are worn below the minimum limit.

6.3 On the Bosch type, remove the outer cover...

6.4b ...and remove the brush holder/ regulator

6.5 On the Valeo type, remove the outer plastic cover...

6.6b ...and remove the voltage regulator

6.8 Measure the brush length

5.13 Tap the spacer (arrowed) down slightly to aid refitting

9 Clean and inspect the surfaces of the slip-rings **(see illustration)**, at the end of the alternator shaft. If they are excessively worn, or damaged, the alternator must be renewed.

6.4a ...undo the screws...

6.6a ...undo the two bolts and single nut...

6.9 Clean and inspect the surfaces of the slip-rings

8.5 Disconnecting the starter wiring plug connector

8.6a Remove the plastic cap, undo the nut ...

8.6b ...and disconnect the wiring from the starter motor

Refitting

Bosch

10 Refit the voltage regulator using a reversal of the removal procedure, tightening the screws securely. On completion, refer to Section 5 and refit the alternator.

Valeo

11 Depress the carbon brushes into the housing, then refit the voltage regulator and tighten the screws and nut securely. Slide on the brush cover until it is heard to engage. On completion, refer to Section 5 and refit the alternator.

7 Starting system – testing

Note: *Refer to Section 1 of this Chapter before starting work.*

1 If the starter motor fails to operate when the ignition key is turned to the appropriate position, the following possible causes may be to blame:

a) *The battery is faulty.*
b) *The electrical connections between the switch, solenoid, battery and starter motor are somewhere failing to pass the necessary current from the battery through the starter to earth.*
c) *The solenoid is faulty.*
d) *The starter motor is mechanically or electrically defective.*

2 To check the battery, switch on the headlights. If they dim after a few seconds,

8.7 Disconnect the earth cable - where fitted

this indicates that the battery is discharged – recharge (see Section 2) or renew the battery. If the headlights glow brightly, operate the ignition switch and observe the lights. If they dim, then this indicates that current is reaching the starter motor; therefore the fault must lie in the starter motor. If the lights continue to glow brightly (and no clicking sound can be heard from the starter motor solenoid), this indicates that there is a fault in the circuit or solenoid – see following paragraphs. If the starter motor turns slowly when operated, but the battery is in good condition, then this indicates that either the starter motor is faulty, or there is considerable resistance somewhere in the circuit.

3 If a fault in the circuit is suspected, disconnect the battery leads (including the earth connection to the body), the starter/solenoid wiring and the engine/transmission earth strap. **Note:** *Before disconnecting the battery, refer to 'Disconnecting the battery' in the Reference section at the rear of this manual.* Thoroughly clean the connections, and reconnect the leads and wiring, then use a voltmeter or test light to check that full battery voltage is available at the battery positive lead connection to the solenoid, and that the earth is sound.

4 If the battery and all connections are in good condition, check the circuit by disconnecting the wire from the solenoid blade terminal. Connect a voltmeter or test light between the wire end and a good earth (such as the battery negative terminal), and check that the wire is live when the ignition switch is turned to the start position. If it is, then the circuit is sound

8.8 Removing the wiring loom support bracket

– if not the circuit wiring can be checked as described in Chapter 12.

5 The solenoid contacts can be checked by connecting a voltmeter or test light between the battery positive feed connection on the starter side of the solenoid, and earth. When the ignition switch is turned to the start position, there should be a reading or lighted bulb, as applicable. If there is no reading or lighted bulb, the solenoid is faulty and should be renewed.

6 If the circuit and solenoid are proved sound, the fault must lie in the starter motor. It may be possible to have the starter motor overhauled by a specialist, but check on the availability and cost of spares before proceeding, as it may prove more economical to obtain a new or exchange motor.

8 Starter motor – removal and refitting

Removal

1 Disconnect the battery negative lead **Note:** *Before disconnecting the battery, refer to 'Disconnecting the battery' in the Reference section at the rear of this manual.*

2 Apply the handbrake, then jack up the front of the vehicle and support it on axle stands (see *Jacking and vehicle support*). Remove the engine undertray.

3 Pull the engine trim cover upward to release it from the top of the engine **(see illustration 5.2)**. On petrol (TSI models), unclip the vacuum hose from the side of the cover, as it is removed.

4 Remove the air cleaner housing as described in Chapter 4A (petrol) or Chapter 4B (diesel).

5 Release the securing clip and disconnect the wiring connector from the solenoid **(see illustration)**.

6 Unclip the plastic cover from the wiring connector and unscrew the nut to disconnect the battery positive lead from the starter motor **(see illustrations)**.

7 Where applicable, unscrew the nut from the upper starter bolt and disconnect the earth cable **(see illustration)**.

8 On petrol models, unscrew the nut from the lower starter mounting bolt, and then remove the wiring loom support bracket **(see illustration)**.

8.9a Starter motor mounting bolts (arrowed)

8.9b The upper bolt also secures the transmission - DSG transmissions

8.9c Guide the starter motor out of the bellhousing - petrol engine

9 Unscrew the mounting bolts noting there fitted position, then guide the starter motor out of the bellhousing aperture and out of the engine compartment (see illustrations). Note: *On vehicle with DSG transmissions, the starter motor upper bolt is also one of the transmission securing bolts.*

Refitting

10 Refit the starter motor by following the removal procedure in reverse. Tighten the mounting bolts to the specified torque.

9 Starter motor – testing and overhaul

If the starter motor is thought to be defective, it should be removed from the vehicle and taken to an auto-electrician for assessment. In the majority of cases, new starter motor brushes can be fitted at a reasonable cost. However, check the cost of repairs first as it may prove more economical to purchase a new or exchange motor.

Chapter 5 Part B:
Ignition system – petrol engines

Contents

Degrees of difficulty

Easy, suitable for novice with little experience	Fairly easy, suitable for beginner with some experience	Fairly difficult, suitable for competent DIY mechanic	Difficult, suitable for experienced DIY mechanic	Very difficult, suitable for expert DIY or professional

Specifications

System type*
1.4 litre engines:
    Engine codes CGGA & BUD. . . . . Magneti-Marelli 4HV
    Engine code CAXA . . . . Bosch Motronic MED17
Refer to Chapters 2A to 2B for engine code listings.

Ignition coil
Type . . . . One coil per spark plug

Spark plugs
See Chapter 1A Specifications

Torque wrench settings

	Nm	lbf ft
Knock sensor mounting bolt	20	15
Spark plugs	25	18

1 General information

The Bosch Motronic and Magneti-Marelli systems are self-contained engine management systems, which control both the fuel injection and ignition. This Chapter deals with the ignition system components only – refer to Chapter 4A for details of the fuel system components.

The ignition system is fitted with a 'static' type system; each spark plug has its own dedicated 'plug-top' HT coil that fits directly onto the spark plug, a spark is only generated at each plug once every engine cycle.

The ignition timing cannot be adjusted by conventional means, and the advance and retard functions are carried out by the Electronic Control Unit (ECU).

The ignition system consists of the spark plugs, four separate coils, camshaft position sensor, and the ECU together with its associated sensors and wiring.

The component layout varies slightly, but the basic operation is the same for all models: the ECU supplies a voltage to the input stage of the ignition coil, which causes the primary windings in the coil to be energised. The supply voltage is periodically interrupted by the ECU and this results in the collapse of primary magnetic field, which then induces a much larger voltage in the secondary coil, called the HT voltage. This voltage is directed to the spark plug in the cylinder currently on its ignition stroke. The spark plug electrodes form a gap small enough for the HT voltage to arc across, and the resulting spark ignites the fuel/air mixture in the cylinder. The timing of this sequence of events is critical, and is regulated solely by the ECU.

The ECU calculates and controls the ignition timing primarily according to engine speed, crankshaft position, camshaft position, and inlet airflow rate information, received from sensors mounted on and around the engine. Other parameters that affect ignition timing are throttle position and rate of opening, inlet air temperature, coolant temperature and engine knock, monitored by sensors mounted on the engine. Note that most of these sensors have a dual role, in that the information they provide is equally useful in determining the fuelling requirements as in deciding the optimum ignition or firing point – therefore, removal of some of the sensors mentioned below is described in Chapter 4A.

The ECU computes engine speed and crankshaft position from toothed impulse ring attached to the engine crankshaft, with an engine speed sensor whose inductive head runs just above ring. As the crankshaft rotates, the ring 'teeth' pass the engine speed sensor, which transmits a pulse to the ECU every time a tooth passes it. At the top dead centre (TDC) position, there is one missing tooth in the ring periphery, which results in a longer pause between signals from the sensor. The ECU recognises the absence of a pulse from the engine speed sensor at this point, and uses it to establish the TDC position for No 1 piston. The time interval between pulses, and the location of the missing pulse, allow the ECU to accurately determine the position of the crankshaft and its speed. The camshaft position sensor enhances this information by detecting whether a particular piston is on an inlet or an exhaust cycle.

Information on engine load is supplied to the ECU by the inlet manifold pressure sensor, and from the throttle position sensor. The engine load is determined by computation based on the quantity of air being drawn into the engine. Further engine load information is sent to the ECU from the knock sensor(s). These sensors are sensitive to vibration, and detect

3.1 Four ignition coils - one coil per spark plug

the knocking, which occurs when the engine starts to 'pink' (pre-ignite). If pre-ignition occurs, the ECU retards the ignition timing of the cylinder that is pre-igniting in steps until the pre-ignition ceases. The ECU then advances the ignition timing of that cylinder in steps until it is restored to normal, or until pre-ignition occurs again.

Sensors monitoring coolant temperature, throttle position, camshaft position, roadspeed, and (where applicable) automatic transmission gear position and air conditioning system operation, provide additional input signals to the ECU on vehicle operating conditions. From all this constantly changing data, the ECU selects, and if necessary modifies, a particular ignition advance setting from a map of ignition characteristics stored in its memory.

The ECU also uses the ignition timing to finely adjust the engine idle speed, in response to signals from the air conditioning switch (to prevent stalling), or if the alternator output voltage falls too low.

In the event of a fault in the system due to loss of a signal from one of the sensors, the ECU reverts to an emergency ('limp-home') program. This will allow the car to be driven, although engine operation and performance will be limited. A warning light on the instrument panel will illuminate if the fault is likely to cause an increase in harmful exhaust emissions.

It should be noted that comprehensive fault diagnosis of all the engine management systems described in this Chapter is only possible with dedicated electronic test equipment. In the event of a sensor failing or other fault occurring, a fault code will be stored in the ECU's fault log, which can only be extracted from the ECU using a dedicated fault code reader. A VW dealer will obviously have such a reader, but they are also available from other suppliers. It is unlikely to be cost-effective for the private owner to purchase a fault code reader, but a well-equipped local garage or auto-electrical specialist will have one. Once the fault has been identified,

5.4 Knock sensor and mounting bolt (arrowed)

the removal/refitting sequences detailed in the following Sections will then allow the appropriate component(s) to be renewed as required.

2 Ignition system – testing

> ⚠️ *Warning: Extreme care must be taken when working on the system with the ignition switched on; it is possible to get a substantial electric shock from a vehicle's ignition system. Persons with cardiac pacemaker devices should keep well clear of the ignition circuits, components and test equipment. Always switch off the ignition before disconnecting or connecting any component and when using a multimeter to check resistances.*

Engines with one coil per plug

1 If a fault appears in the engine management (fuel injection/ignition) system which is thought to ignition related, first ensure that the fault is not due to a poor electrical connection or poor maintenance; i.e. check that the air cleaner filter element is clean, the spark plugs are in good condition and correctly gapped, that the engine breather hoses are clear and undamaged, referring to Chapter 1A for further information. If the engine is running very roughly, check the compression pressures as described in Chapters 2A to 2D (as applicable).

2 If these checks fail to reveal the cause of the problem, the vehicle should be taken to a VW dealer for testing. A diagnostic connector is incorporated in the engine management circuit into which a special electronic diagnostic tester can be plugged. The tester will locate the fault quickly and simply, alleviating the need to test all the system components individually, which is a time-consuming operation that carries a high risk of damaging the ECU.

3 The only ignition system checks which can be carried out by the home mechanic are those described in Chapter 1A, relating

to the spark plugs. If necessary, the system wiring and wiring connectors can be checked as described in Chapter 12, ensuring that the ECU wiring connector(s) have first been disconnected.

3 HT coil(s) – removal and refitting

Removal of the ignition coils is covered in the spark plug renewal procedure in Chapter 1A, Section 25, since the coils must be removed for access to the plugs (see illustration).

4 Ignition timing – checking and adjusting

The ignition timing is under the control of the engine management system ECU and is not manually adjustable without access to dedicated electronic test equipment. A basic setting cannot be quoted because the ignition timing is constantly being altered to control engine idle speed (see Section 1 for details).

5 Knock sensor – removal and refitting

Removal

1 The knock sensor is located on the inlet manifold side of the cylinder block.

2 Remove the engine top covers to gain access to the sensor from above. If access from above is not sufficient, firmly apply the handbrake then jack up the front of the vehicle and support it on axle stands (see *Jacking and vehicle support*). Undo the retaining screws and remove the engine undertray(s) so access to the knock sensor can be gained from underneath. Access to the knock sensor is very awkward but it can only be improved by removing the inlet manifold (see Chapter 4A, Section 8).

3 Disconnect the wiring connector from the sensor or trace the wiring back from the sensor and disconnect its wiring connector (as applicable).

4 Unscrew the mounting bolt and remove the sensor from the cylinder block (see illustration).

Refitting

5 Refitting is the reverse of removal. Ensure the mating surfaces of the sensor and cylinder block are clean and dry and ensure the mounting bolt is tightened to the specified torque to ensure correct operation.

Chapter 5 Part C:
Preheating system – diesel engines

Contents

Section number

Degrees of difficulty

Easy, suitable for novice with little experience	**Fairly easy,** suitable for beginner with some experience	**Fairly difficult,** suitable for competent DIY mechanic	**Difficult,** suitable for experienced DIY mechanic	**Very difficult,** suitable for expert DIY or professional

Specifications

Glow plugs
Electrical resistance	1.0 ohm
Current consumption (typical – no value quoted by VW)	8 amps (per plug)

Torque wrench setting
	Nm	lbf ft
Glow plug to cylinder head	18	13

---

1 General information

To assist cold starting, diesel engine models are fitted with a preheating system, which consists of four glow plugs, a glow plug control unit, a facia-mounted warning light and the associated electrical wiring. The glow plug control unit on some models, is incorporated in the ECU, other models have a control unit/relay located under the fusebox in the engine compartment (see Section 3).

The glow plugs are miniature electric heating elements, encapsulated in a metal case with a probe at one end and electrical connection at the other. Each inlet tract has a glow plug threaded into it, which is positioned directly in line with the incoming spray of fuel. When the glow plug is energised, the fuel passing over it is heated, allowing its optimum combustion temperature to be achieved more readily in the combustion chamber.

The duration of the preheating period is governed by the ECU, which monitors the temperature of the engine through the coolant temperature sensor and alters the preheating time to suit the conditions. Pre-heating only takes place at coolant temperature below 9°C.

A facia-mounted warning light informs the driver that preheating is taking place. The light extinguishes when sufficient preheating has taken place to allow the engine to be started, but power will still be supplied to the glow plugs for a further period until the engine is started. If no attempt is made to start the engine, the power supply to the glow plugs is switched off to prevent battery drain and glow plug burn-out. If the warning light flashes, or comes on during normal driving, this indicates a fault with the diesel engine management system, which should be investigated by a VW dealer as soon as possible.

After the engine has been started, the glow plugs continue to operate for a further period of time. This helps to improve fuel combustion whilst the engine is warming-up, resulting in quieter, smoother running and reduced exhaust emissions.

2 Glow plugs – testing, removal and refitting

⚠️ *Warning: A correctly functioning glow plug will become red-hot in a very short time. This should be in mind when removing the glow plugs, if they have recently been in use. If a glow plug is dropped, it may be damaged internally, which could result in ceramic fragments entering the engine causing extensive damage. Do not fit a glow plug that has been dropped.*

Testing

1 If the system malfunctions, testing is ultimately by substitution of known good units, but some preliminary checks may be made as described in the following paragraphs.

2 Before testing the system, use a multi-meter to check that the battery voltage is at least 11.5. Switch off the ignition.

3 Pull the engine upper trim cover upwards to remove it from the top of the engine.

4 Disconnect the wiring plug from the coolant temperature sender at the left-hand end of the engine (left as seen from the driver's seat) – refer to Chapter 3 **(see illustration)**. Disconnecting the sender in this way simulates a cold engine, which is a requirement for the glow plug system to activate.

5 Disconnect the wiring connector from the most convenient glow plug, and connect a suitable multimeter between the wiring connector and a good earth.

6 Have an assistant switch on the ignition for approximately 20 seconds.

7 Battery voltage should be displayed – note that the voltage will drop to zero when the preheating period ends.

8 If no supply voltage can be detected at the glow plug, then either the glow plug relay (where applicable) or the supply wiring must be faulty. Also check that the glow plug fuse or fusible link has not blown – if it has, this may indicate a serious wiring fault; consult a VW dealer for advice.

9 To locate a faulty glow plug, first disconnect

2.4 Temperature sensor location (arrowed)

2.10 Testing the glow plugs using a multimeter

2.15 Disconnect the wiring plugs from the injectors

2.17 Disconnect the return hose from the fuel rail

2.19a Using long nose pliers ...

2.19b ... pull the connectors from the top of the glow plugs

the battery negative cable and position it away from the terminal.

10 Disconnect the wiring plug from the glow plug terminal. Measure the electrical resistance between the glow plug terminal and the engine earth **(see illustration)**. At the time of writing, this information is not available – as a guide, a resistance of more than a few ohms indicates that the plug is defective.

11 If a suitable ammeter is available, connect it between the glow plug and its wiring connector, and measure the steady-state current consumption (ignore the initial current surge, which will be about 50% higher). As a guide, high current consumption (or no current draw at all) indicates a faulty glow plug.

12 As a final check, remove the glow plugs and inspect them visually, as described in the next sub-Section. A badly burned or charred stem may be an indication of a faulty fuel injector.

Removal

Note: *Refer to the Warning at the start of this Section before proceeding.*

13 Pull the plastic cover on the top of the engine upwards from its mountings.

14 Where fitted, remove the noise insulation from above the injectors.

15 To make access easier, disconnect the wiring plugs from the injectors, exhaust gas pressure sensor, and fuel rail pressure sensor **(see illustration)**.

16 Undo the retaining bolts and detach the coolant pipe from the intake manifold. Move the pipe to the front of the manifold.

17 Release the retaining clip and disconnect the fuel return hose from the fuel rail **(see illustration)**. Be prepared for fuel spillage.

18 Release the retaining clips and disconnect the fuel return pipe connectors from the top of the fuel rail. Plug the openings to prevent

contamination. Move the entire fuel return pipe assembly to the one side.

19 Pull the connectors from the top of the glow plugs and move the wiring loom to one side. Be sure to only pull on the underside of the ridge at the top of the connectors **(see illustrations)**.

20 Clean the area around the glow plugs; use a vacuum cleaner if possible. Spray brake cleaner (or similar) around the glow plug opening, letting it penetrate briefly, and then blow out with compressed air.

Caution: Always wear protective goggles to protect your eyes, when using compressed air.

21 Using a universal joint, extension and a deep 10 mm socket, unscrew and remove the glow plug(s) from the cylinder head. Note that the plug must be kept 'straight' when being removed, as it can be easily damaged.

Refitting

22 Refitting is a reversal of removal, but tighten the glow plugs to the specified torque.

---

3 Glow plug control unit – removal and refitting

Note: *The glow plug control unit may be incorporated inside the engine management ECU. Follow the procedure below for models with separate glow plug control unit.*

Removal

1 The glow plug control unit (where applicable) is located under the fuse box in the engine compartment **(see illustration)**.

2 To gain access to the control unit, remove the battery and battery tray, as described in Chapter 5A, Section 3.

3 Release the retaining clip and slide the control unit mounting bracket from the underside of the fusebox housing **(see illustration)**.

4 Disconnect the wiring connector and remove the control unit

Refitting

5 Refitting is a reversal of removal.

3.1 Glow plug control unit location (arrowed)

3.3 Slide the control unit out and disconnect the wiring connector

Chapter 6
Clutch

Contents

Degrees of difficulty

Easy, suitable for novice with little experience   **Fairly easy,** suitable for beginner with some experience   **Fairly difficult,** suitable for competent DIY mechanic   **Difficult,** suitable for experienced DIY mechanic   **Very difficult,** suitable for expert DIY or professional

Specifications

General

Type:	
Luk clutch	Single dry friction disc, diaphragm spring with spring-loaded hub, self-adjusting pressure plate (SAC)
Sachs clutch	Single dry friction disc, diaphragm spring with spring-loaded hub
Clutch operation	Hydraulic with master and slave cylinders
Application:	
Petrol models:	
1.4 litre engine:	
5-speed transmission	0AF
6-speed transmission	02S or 0AJ
Diesel models:	
1.6 litre engine:	
5-speed transmission	0A4
2.0 litre engine:	
5-speed transmission	0A4
6-speed transmission	02Q

Torque wrench settings	Nm	lbf ft
Clutch pedal crash bar bolts*:		
1 bolt fitment	20	15
2 bolt fitment	10	7
Clutch pedal mounting bracket nuts*	25	18
Clutch pedal pivot nut*	25	18
Clutch pressure plate-to-flywheel bolts*:		
M7 bolt	20	15
M6 bolt	13	10
Clutch release bearing guide sleeve bolts:		
0AF and 0AJ transmissions*:		
Stage 1	5	4
Stage 2	Angle-tighten a further 90°	
0A4 and 02S transmissions	20	15
Clutch slave cylinder bolts	20	15

* Use new bolts/nuts.

2.3a Clutch slave cylinder bleed screw (arrowed) - 0AF, 0AJ, 0A4 and 02S transmissions

2.3b Clutch bleed screw (arrowed) - 02Q transmissions

1 General information

The clutch is of single dry plate type, incorporating a diaphragm spring pressure plate, and is hydraulically operated.

The pressure plate is bolted to the rear face of the flywheel, and the friction disc is located between the pressure plate and the flywheel friction surface. The friction disc hub is splined to the transmission input shaft and is free to slide along the splines. Friction lining material is riveted to each side of the disc, and the disc hub incorporates cushioning springs to absorb transmission shocks and ensure a smooth take-up of drive.

On all transmissions except 02Q, when the clutch pedal is depressed, the slave cylinder pushrod moves the release lever forwards. On 02Q transmissions, the slave cylinder is fitted concentrically around the transmission input shaft within the bellhousing. The release bearing is forced onto the pressure plate diaphragm spring fingers. As the centre of the diaphragm spring is pushed in, the outer part of the spring moves out and releases the pressure plate from the friction disc. Drive then ceases to be transmitted to the transmission.

When the clutch pedal is released, the diaphragm spring forces the pressure plate into contact with the linings on the friction disc, and at the same time pushes the disc slightly forward along the input shaft splines into engagement with the flywheel. The friction disc is now firmly sandwiched between the pressure plate and flywheel. This causes drive to be taken up.

As the linings wear on the friction disc, the pressure plate rest position moves closer to the flywheel resulting in the 'rest' position of the diaphragm spring fingers being raised. The hydraulic system requires no adjustment since the quantity of hydraulic fluid in the circuit automatically compensates for wear every time the clutch pedal is operated.

2 Hydraulic system – bleeding

Warning: Hydraulic fluid is poisonous, thoroughly wash off spills from bare skin without delay. Seek immediate medical advice if any fluid is swallowed or gets into the eyes. Certain types of hydraulic fluid are inflammable and may ignite when brought into contact with hot components. Hydraulic fluid is also an effective paint stripper. If spillage occurs onto painted bodywork or fittings, it should be washed off immediately, using copious quantities of cold water. It is also hygroscopic (i.e. it can absorb moisture from the air) which then renders it useless. Old fluid may have suffered contamination, and should never be re-used.

Note: *Suitable pressure-bleeding equipment will be required for this operation.*

1 If any part of the hydraulic system is dismantled, or if air has accidentally entered the system, the system will need to be bled. The presence of air is characterised by the pedal having a spongy feel and it results in difficulty in changing gear.

2 The design of the clutch hydraulic system does not allow bleeding to be carried out using the conventional method of pumping the clutch pedal. In order to remove all air present in the system, it is necessary to use pressure bleeding equipment. This is available from auto accessory shops at relatively low cost.

3 The pressure bleeding equipment should be connected to the brake/clutch hydraulic fluid reservoir in accordance with the manufacturer's instructions. The system is bled through the bleed screw of the clutch slave cylinder (all transmissions except 02Q), which is located on the top of the transmission housing. On 02Q transmissions, the slave cylinder bleed screw is located at the front of

the transmission, above the starter motor (see illustrations).

4 Bleed the system until the fluid being ejected is free from air bubbles. Close the bleed screw, then disconnect and remove the bleeding equipment.

5 Check the operation of the clutch to see that it is satisfactory. If air still remains in the system, repeat the bleeding operation.

6 Discard any fluid that is bled from the system, even if it looks clean. Hydraulic fluid absorbs water and its re-use can cause internal corrosion of the master and slave cylinders, leading to excessive wear and failure of the seals.

3 Clutch pedal – removal and refitting

Removal

1 Move the driver's seat fully to the rear, and adjust the steering column to its highest position.

2 Disconnect the battery negative lead and position it away from the terminal. **Note:** *Before disconnecting the battery, refer to 'Disconnecting the battery' in the reference section at the rear of this manual.*

3 Remove the driver's side lower facia trim panel, with reference to Chapter 11, Section 27.

4 Remove the driver's knee airbag, as described in Chapter 12, Section 26.

5 Release the retaining clip and unclip the wiring loom guide from under the steering column **(see illustration)**.

6 Undo the retaining bolt(s) and remove the crash bar from above the clutch pedal. There are two types of crash bar fitted; depending on vehicle, there could be either one or two bolts securing the crash bar.

7 Where fitted, release the securing clips and remove the insulation padding from around the clutch pedal mounting bracket.

3.5 Unclip the wiring bracket from the steering column

8 Undo the retaining nut and remove the pedal pivot bolt, move the pedal downwards and withdraw the over-centre spring from inside the top of the mounting bracket **(see illustration). Note:** *The clutch pedal will still be attached to the master cylinder pushrod.*

9 Working at each side of the clutch pedal, release the retaining clip to disengage the master cylinder pushrod from the pedal **(see illustration)**. The pedal can now be removed from the mounting bracket.

10 If required, undo the three mounting nuts and remove the mounting bracket from the bulkhead. Discard the self-locking nuts, as new ones will be required for refitting

Refitting

11 Refitting is a reversal of removal, bearing in mind the following points:
  a) *Press the pushrod retaining clip firmly into the pedal until it is heard to engage.*
  b) *Tighten all fixings to the specified torque, where given.*
  c) *On completion, check the brake/clutch fluid level, and top-up if necessary.*

4 Master cylinder –
removal, overhaul and refitting

Note: *Refer to the warning at the beginning of Section 2 regarding the hazards of working with hydraulic fluid.*

Removal

1 The clutch master cylinder is located through the bulkhead and is attached to the clutch pedal mounting bracket **(see illustration)**. Hydraulic fluid for the unit is supplied from the brake master cylinder reservoir.

2 Before proceeding, place cloth rags on the carpet inside the car to prevent damage from spilt hydraulic fluid.

3 Remove the engine top cover/air filter assembly. Additionally, on LHD models remove the battery and battery tray with reference to Chapter 5A, Section 3.

4 Working down the back of the engine compartment, clamp the hydraulic fluid hose (if it's rubber) leading from the brake fluid reservoir to the clutch master cylinder using a

H48710

3.8 Clutch pedal assembly

1 Clutch pedal	4 Over centre	7 Master cylinder
2 Pivot pin	spring	8 Seal
3 Bearing	5 Mounting bracket	9 Pivot bolt
bushes	6 Seal	10 Pedal securing clip

brake hose clamp. If the hose is plastic, then the end will need to be plugged to prevent fluid loss.

H48707

3.9 Master cylinder pushrod to pedal securing clip

1 Master cylinder	2 Securing clip	
pushrod	3 Clutch pedal	

5 Similarly (where possible), clamp the rubber section of the hydraulic hose leading from the master cylinder to the slave cylinder using a brake hose clamp, to prevent loss of hydraulic fluid. The rubber section of pipe may be further down towards the slave cylinder.

4.1 Location of master cylinder on bulkhead

4.6 Disconnect the fluid supply hose (arrowed)

6 Position a suitable container, or a wad of clean cloth, beneath the master cylinder to catch escaping hydraulic fluid. Release the clip and disconnect the fluid supply hose from the master cylinder – be prepared for fluid spillage **(see illustration)**.

7 Pull the fluid outlet hose retaining clip from the union on the master cylinder, then pull the pipe from the union **(see illustration)**. Again, be prepared for fluid spillage.

8 Disconnect the wiring from the clutch position sender on the side of the master cylinder.

9 Working inside the vehicle, remove the clutch pedal and mounting bracket as described in Section 3.

10 Release the clip and withdraw the master cylinder from the mounting bracket by twisting it anti-clockwise.

Overhaul

11 No spare parts are available from VW for the master cylinder. If the master cylinder is faulty or worn, the complete assembly must be renewed.

Refitting

12 Refitting is a reversal of removal, but bleed the clutch hydraulic system as described in Section 2.

5 Slave cylinder – removal, overhaul and refitting

Removal

All transmissions (except 02Q)

Note: *The hydraulic components fitted to transmissions 0AF and 0AJ are identical, however, those fitted to transmissions 02S and 0A4 differ slightly.*

1 The slave cylinder is located on the top of the transmission casing **(see illustrations)**.

2 Remove the battery and battery tray with reference to Chapter 5A, Section 3.

3 Remove the air cleaner housing, as described in Chapter 4A (petrol) or Chapter 4B (diesel).

4 Disconnect the gear selector cables from the gear selector levers, as described in Chapter 7A, Section 2. Withdraw the retaining clips and remove the outer cables from the mounting bracket, then unbolt the mounting bracket from the top of the transmission.

H48708

4.7 Master cylinder hose connection

1 Fluid pipe connection	3 Securing clip
2 Seal	4 Master cylinder

5 On 02S and 0A4 transmissions, undo the bolts and remove the gearbox support bracket from above the slave cylinder **(see illustration)**.

Caution: Refer to the warning at the beginning of Section 2 regarding the hazards of working with hydraulic fluid.

6 Place a wad of clean rag beneath the fluid line connection on the slave cylinder to catch escaping fluid.

7 Release the fluid pipe retaining clip from the union on the slave cylinder, then pull the pipe from the union. Position the fluid pipe clear of the slave cylinder, and plug the end. Be prepared for some fluid spillage.

8 Unscrew the two bolts securing the slave cylinder to the transmission casing, and withdraw the slave cylinder from the transmission **(see illustration)**.

02Q transmission

9 Remove the transmission as described in Chapter 7A.

10 Release the retaining clip and pull the fluid bleeder connection from the outside of the transmission casing **(see illustration)**.

5.1a Clutch slave cylinder - 0AF and 0AJ transmissions

5.1b Clutch slave cylinder- 0A4 and 02S transmissions

5.5 Remove the support bracket - 0A4 and 02S transmissions

5.8 Removing the clutch slave cylinder from the transmission

5.10 Prise up the clip (arrowed) and pull the connection from place- 02Q transmissions

11 Undo the bolts and remove the slave cylinder/release bearing assembly **(see illustration)**.

Overhaul

12 No spare parts are available from VW for the slave cylinder. If the slave cylinder is faulty or worn, the complete assembly must be renewed.

Refitting

13 Refitting is a reversal of removal, bearing in mind the following points:
a) *Tighten all fixings to the specified torque where given.*
b) *On completion, bleed the clutch hydraulic system as described in Section 2.*

---

6 Clutch friction disc and pressure plate – removal, inspection and refitting

---

⚠ *Warning: Dust created by clutch wear and deposited on the clutch components may contain asbestos, which is a health hazard. DO NOT blow it out with compressed air or inhale any of it. DO NOT use petrol or petroleum-based solvents to clean off the dust. Brake system cleaner or methylated spirit should be used to flush the dust into a suitable receptacle. After the clutch components are wiped clean with clean rags, dispose of the contaminated rags and cleaner in a sealed container.*

Note: *New clutch pressure plate securing bolts will be required on refitting. It is recommended that a friction disc centralising tool be used when refitting the clutch.*

Removal

1 Access to the clutch is obtained by removing the transmission as described in Chapter 7A Section 3.

5.11 Slave cylinder/release bearing retaining bolts - 02Q transmissions

2 Mark the clutch pressure plate and flywheel in relation to each other.
3 Hold the flywheel stationary, and then unscrew the clutch pressure plate bolts ¼ of a turn at a time **(see illustration)**. With the bolts unscrewed two or three turns, check that the pressure plate is not binding on the dowel pins. If necessary, use a screwdriver to release the pressure plate. On models with the Sachs clutch, as the bolts are removed the stop pin must slacken. If it doesn't, press the pin towards the flywheel **(see illustration)**.
4 Remove all the bolts, then lift the clutch pressure plate and friction disc from the flywheel.

Inspection

Note: *Due to the amount of work necessary to remove and refit clutch components, it is usually considered good practice to renew the clutch friction disc, pressure plate assembly and release bearing as a matched set, even if only one of these is actually worn enough to require renewal. It is also worth considering the renewal of the clutch components on a preventative basis if the engine and/or transmission have been removed for some other reason.*
5 Clean the pressure plate friction surface,

clutch friction disc and flywheel. Do not inhale the dust, as it may contain asbestos which is dangerous to health.
6 Examine the fingers of the diaphragm spring for wear or scoring. If the depth of wear exceeds half the thickness of the fingers, a new pressure plate assembly must be fitted.
7 Examine the pressure plate for scoring, cracking, distortion and discoloration. Light scoring is acceptable, but if excessive, a new pressure plate assembly must be fitted. If the distortion of the friction surface exceeds 1.0 mm, renew it.
8 Examine the friction disc linings for wear and cracking, and for contamination with oil or grease. The linings are worn excessively if they are worn down to, or near, the rivets. Check the disc hub and splines for wear by temporarily fitting it on the transmission input shaft. Renew the friction disc as necessary.
9 Examine the flywheel friction surface for scoring, cracking and discoloration (caused by overheating). If excessive, it may be possible to have the flywheel machined by an engineering works, otherwise it should be renewed.
10 Ensure that all parts are clean, and free of oil or grease, before reassembling. Apply just a small amount of lithium-based grease (VW No. G000100) to the splines of the friction disc hub. **Do not** use copper-based grease. Note that new pressure plates and clutch covers may be coated with protective grease. It is only permissible to clean the grease away from the friction disc lining contact area. Removal of the grease from other areas will shorten the service life of the clutch.

Refitting

11 Commence reassembly by locating the friction disc on the flywheel, with the raised side of the hub facing outwards (normally marked 'Getriebeseite' or 'Gearbox side'). If possible, the centralising tool (see paragraph 20) should

6.3a Undo the pressure plate retaining screws (arrowed)

6.3b Ensure the stop pin is free to move

6.11 The friction disc should be marked 'Getriebeseite' or 'Gearbox side'

be used to hold the disc on the flywheel at this stage **(see illustration)**.

Models with self-adjusting clutch (SAC)

12 On models with a Self-adjusting clutch (SAC), where a new friction disc is fitted, but the pressure plate is to be re-used, it is necessary to reset the pressure plate adjusting ring prior to assembly as follows.

13 Insert three 8 mm bolts into the pressure plate mounting holes at intervals of 120°. The bolts should be inserted from the flywheel side, and retained by nuts **(see illustration)**.

14 Place the pressure plate face down on the bed of an hydraulic press so that only the heads of the bolts make contact with the press bed, then place a circular spacer over the ends of the diaphragm springs fingers.

15 Use 2 screwdrivers to attempt to rotate the adjuster ring anti-clockwise. Apply just enough pressure with the hydraulic press until it's just possible to move the adjuster ring **(see illustration)**.

16 Once the adjuster ring edges are between the notches, relieve the pressure. The ring is now reset. **Note:** *New pressure plates are supplied in this reset position.*

All models

17 Locate the clutch pressure plate on the disc, and fit it onto the location dowels **(see illustration)**. If refitting the original pressure plate, make sure that the previously-made marks are aligned.

18 Insert the bolts finger-tight to hold the pressure plate in position.

19 The friction disc must now be centralised, to ensure correct alignment of the transmission input shaft with the disc centre. To do this, a proprietary tool may be used, or alternatively, use a wooden mandrel made to fit inside the friction disc and the hole in the centre of the

6.13 Insert three 8 mm bolts from the flywheel side, and secure with nuts

crankshaft. Insert the tool through the friction disc into the crankshaft, and make sure that it is central.

20 Tighten the pressure plate bolts progressively and in diagonal sequence, until the specified torque setting is achieved, then remove the centralising tool **(see illustration)**.

21 Check the release bearing in the

6.15 The edges of the adjuster ring (B) must be between the notches (A)

6.17 Fit the pressure plate over the locating dowel pins (arrowed)

6.20 With the pressure plate screws tightened, remove the centralising tool

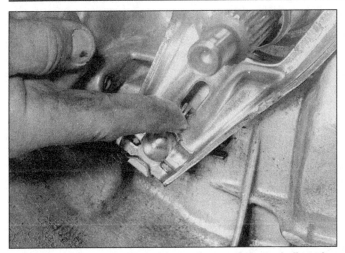

7.2 Push the spring clip to release the arm from the ball-stud

7.4a Use a screwdriver to depress the retaining tags...

transmission bellhousing for smooth operation, and if necessary renew it with reference to Section 7.

22 Refit the transmission with reference to Chapter 7A, Section 3.

7 Release bearing and lever – removal, inspection and refitting

Removal

Note: *On 02Q transmissions, the release bearing is part of the clutch slave cylinder (see Section 5).*

1 Remove the transmission as described in Chapter 7A, Section 3.

2 Using a screwdriver, prise the release lever from the ball-stud on the transmission housing. If this proves difficult, push the retaining spring from the release lever first **(see illustration)**. Where applicable, remove the plastic pad from the stud.

3 Slide the release bearing, together with the lever, from the guide sleeve, and withdraw it over the transmission input shaft.

4 Separate the release bearing from the lever **(see illustrations)**.

5 If the guide sleeve is worn excessively, unbolt it and remove the O-ring seal **(see illustration)**.

Inspection

6 Spin the release bearing by hand, and check it for smooth running. Any tendency to seize or run rough will necessitate renewal of the bearing. If the bearing is to be re-used, wipe it clean with a dry cloth; the bearing should not be washed in a liquid solvent, as this will remove the internal grease.

7 Clean the release lever, ball-stud and guide sleeve.

Refitting

8 If the guide sleeve was removed, locate a new O-ring seal over the input shaft, then fit

7.4b ...then remove the release bearing from the arm

the guide sleeve and tighten the bolts to the specified torque. If preferred, the guide sleeve may be assembled to the release bearing and lever, and the components fitted over the input shaft as one unit **(see illustration)**.

9 Lubricate the ball-stud in the transmission bellhousing with molybdenum sulphide-based

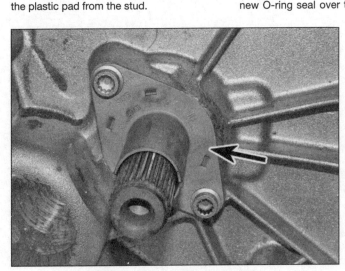

7.5 Guide sleeve on the transmission

7.8 Fitting the guide sleeve with assembled release bearing and lever

7.9 Lubricate the ball-stud with a little grease

7.11a Locate the spring over the end of the release lever...

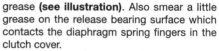

grease **(see illustration)**. Also smear a little grease on the release bearing surface which contacts the diaphragm spring fingers in the clutch cover.

10 Push the release bearing into position on the release lever.

11 Fit the retaining spring onto the release lever, then press the release lever onto the ball-stud until the retaining spring holds it in position **(see illustrations)**.

12 Refit the transmission as described in Chapter 7A, Section 3.

7.11b ...and press the spring into the hole...

7.11c ...then press the release lever onto the ball-stud until the spring clip holds it in position

Chapter 7 Part A:
Manual transmission

Contents

Degrees of difficulty

Easy, suitable for novice with little experience 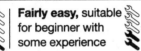	**Fairly easy,** suitable for beginner with some experience	**Fairly difficult,** suitable for competent DIY mechanic	**Difficult,** suitable for experienced DIY mechanic	**Very difficult,** suitable for expert DIY or professional

Specifications

General

Type . . . . Transversely-mounted, front-wheel-drive layout with integral transaxle differential/final drive, 5 or 6 forward speeds and 1 reverse

Application:
  Petrol models:
    1.4 litre engine:
      5-speed transmission 0AF
      6-speed transmission . . . . 02S or 0AJ
  Diesel models:
    1.6 litre engine:
      5-speed transmission 0A4
    2.0 litre engine:
      5-speed transmission 0A4
      6-speed transmission 02Q

Torque wrench settings

	Nm	lbf ft
Driveshaft flange bolt	30	22
Flywheel cover plate (where fitted)	10	7
Gearchange cable support bracket	20	15
Gear lever housing to body:		
M6 nuts	8	6
M8 nuts	25	18
Reversing light switch	20	15
Left-hand mounting bracket bolts: *		
To transmission (0AJ, 0AF, 02S & 0A4 transmissions):		
Stage 1	40	30
Stage 2	Angle-tighten a further 90°	
To transmission (02Q transmissions):		
Stage 1	60	45
Stage 2	Angle-tighten a further 90°	
To body (all transmissions):		
Stage 1	60	45
Stage 2	Angle-tighten a further 90°	
Transmission upper support bracket bolts (02S & 0A4 transmissions): *		
Stage 1	20	15
Stage 2	Angle-tighten a further 90°	
Transmission to engine:		
M12 bolts	80	59
M10 bolt	40	30

Do not re-use

2.3a Release the gearchange inner cable retaining clips ...

2.3b ...and slide out the outer cable securing clips

2.5 Remove the insulation from around the gearchange

1 General information

The manual transmission is bolted directly to the left-hand end of the engine. This layout has the advantage of providing the shortest possible drive path to the front wheels, as well as locating the transmission in the airflow through engine bay, optimising cooling. The unit is cased in aluminium alloy.

Drive from the crankshaft is transmitted through the clutch to the gearbox input shaft, which is splined to accept the clutch friction disc.

All forward gears are fitted with synchromesh. The floor-mounted gear lever is connected to the gearbox by shift cables.

Levers on the transmission actuate internal selector forks, which are connected to the synchromesh sleeves. The sleeves are locked to the gearbox shafts but can slide axially by means of splined hubs, and they press baulk rings into contact with the respective gear/pinion. The coned surfaces between the baulk rings and the pinion/gear act as a friction clutch, that progressively matches the speed of the synchromesh sleeve (and hence the gearbox shaft) with that of the gear/pinion. This allows gearchanges to be carried out smoothly.

Drive is transmitted to the differential crownwheel, which rotates the differential case and planetary gears, thus driving the sun gears and driveshafts. The rotation of the differential planetary gears on their shaft allows the inner roadwheel to rotate at a slower speed than the outer roadwheel during cornering.

2 Gear change housing and cable – removal, refitting and adjustment

Removal

1 Remove the battery and battery tray as described in Chapter 5A, Section 3.

2 Remove the air cleaner housing as described in Chapter 4A (petrol) or Chapter 4B (diesel).

3 Prise out the clips securing the inner cable to the lever on the transmission, and the outer cable to the support bracket **(see illustrations)**. Withdraw the cable from the support bracket and discard the clips – new ones must be fitted.

4 Working inside the vehicle, remove the centre console, as described in Chapter 11, Section 26.

5 Remove the insulation around the base of the gear change housing to access the mounting nuts **(see illustration)**.

6 Raise the front of the vehicle and support it securely on axle stands (see *Jacking and vehicle support*).

7 Remove the centre tunnel front heat shield from the underside of the vehicle to gain access to the base of the selector lever housing and cables **(see illustration)**. It

may be necessary to separate the exhaust downpipe from the intermediate pipe with reference to Chapter 4C (petrol) or Chapter 4D (diesel).

8 Working back inside the vehicle, undo the retaining nuts, then remove the bracket and lower the gear change housing downwards. Withdraw it complete with selector cables out from under the vehicle. It may be useful having the aid of an assistant at this point, to be under the vehicle when lowering the gear change housing.

9 To remove the cables from the gear change housing, prise out the clips securing the inner cable to the lower part of the gear lever, and then withdraw the securing clips from the outer cable to the gear change housing. Withdraw the cables and discard the clips – new ones must be fitted.

Refitting

10 Refitting is the reversal of the removal procedure, noting the following points:

a) *Ensure that the cables are correctly routed and secured, as noted on removal.*

b) *Take care not to bend or kink the cables.*

c) *Carry out the cable adjustment procedure described below before reconnecting the cable at the transmission end.*

d) *When refitting the cables, use new clips.*

Adjustment

11 Remove the engine top cover, air cleaner housing, and air ducting for access to the top of the transmission. If required remove the battery and battery tray, as described in Chapter 5A, Section 3.

12 With the gearchange set in the neutral position, push the two locking collars (one on each cable) forwards to compress the springs, turn them clockwise (looking from the driver's seat) to lock into position **(see illustration)**.

13 Press down on the selector shaft on the top of the transmission, and push the locking pin into the transmission while turning it clockwise, until it engages and the selector shaft cannot move **(see illustration)**.

14 Working inside the vehicle, unclip the gear lever gaiter from the centre console and lift out the insulator. Still in the neutral position, move the gear lever as far to the left as possible and

2.7 Lower section of gearchange assembly under vehicle

2.12 Push the collar down and lock in position

insert the locking pin (or drill bit) through the hole in the base of the gear lever and into the hole in the housing (see illustrations).

15 Working back in the engine bay, turn the two locking collars on the cables anti-clockwise so that the springs will release them back into position and lock the cables (see illustration).

16 With the cable adjustment set, the locking pin in the transmission housing, can now be turned anti-clockwise to its original position pointing upwards.

17 Inside the vehicle, remove the locking pin from the gear lever, and then check the operation of the selector mechanism. When the gear lever is at rest in neutral, it should be central, ready to select 3rd or 4th. The gear lever gaiter and insulator can now be refitted to the centre console.

18 Refit the air ducting, engine top cover/air filter and battery/tray as described in Chapter 5A, Section 3.

3 Transmission – removal and refitting

Removal

1 Select a solid, level surface to park the vehicle upon. Give yourself enough space to move around it easily. Apply the handbrake and chock the rear wheels.

2 Raise the front of the vehicle and support it securely on axle stands (see *Jacking and vehicle support*). Where fitted, remove the engine/transmission undertray sections. Position a suitable container beneath the transmission, then unscrew the drain plug and drain the transmission oil.

3 Remove the engine top cover/air filter. Remove the air cleaner housing as described in Chapter 4A or Chapter 4B.

4 Remove the battery and battery tray with reference to Chapter 5A, Section 3.

5 Release the retaining clips and disconnect the gear selector cables from the gear selector levers, as described in Section 2. Also, unbolt and remove the cable mounting bracket from the top of the transmission (see illustration).

6 Undo the retaining bolts, and then remove the support bracket (see illustration), from the top of the transmission (02S and 04A transmissions).

7 On models with the clutch slave cylinder on the top of the transmission (all except 02Q transmissions), undo the retaining bolts and place the cylinder to one side, with reference to Chapter 6, Section 5.

8 On 02Q transmissions, seal the slave cylinder flexible hose using a hose clamp, then prise out the clip and pull the fluid pipe from the bleeder connection on the slave cylinder supply pipe (see illustration). Refer to Chapter 6, Section 5.

9 Unbolt the earth cable from the engine/transmission or subframe.

2.13 Press down on (A), then push in locking pin (B)

2.14b Locking the gear lever in position using a drill bit

10 Unscrew and remove the upper bolts securing the transmission to the engine.

11 With reference to Chapter 5A, Section 8, remove the starter motor.

12 Remove the lower left-hand wheel arch liner.

3.5 Mounting bracket securing bolts (arrowed)

3.8 Prise up the clip a little and pull the hose from the connection - 02Q transmissions

2.14a Lift out the foam insulation

2.15 Release the two locking collars back into position

13 Disconnect the wiring from the reversing light switch (see illustrations), and where fitted, the neutral position switch on vehicles with a start/stop system.

14 Where fitted unbolt the metal shield from around the right-hand driveshaft.

3.6 Remove the support bracket (arrowed) - 0A4 and 02S transmissions

3.13a Reversing light switch (arrowed) ...

3.13b ...or neutral switch (arrowed) - depending on transmission

3.15a Slacken the exhaust clamp ...

3.15b ...and undo the exhaust mounting bracket bolts (arrowed)

15 Slacken the clamp securing the exhaust intermediate pipe to the rear section and undo the front mounting bracket bolts **(see illustrations)**. This will allow the engine to be moved forwards and backwards during the transmission removal and alignment procedures. Consequently, there is no need to completely separate the exhaust pipe sections.

16 With reference to the Chapter 8, Section 2, unscrew and remove the bolts securing the driveshafts to the transmission output flanges. Tie the right-hand driveshaft to one side, and then tie the left-hand driveshaft to the suspension strut, so that the shaft is as high as possible **(see illustration)**. Alternatively, completely remove the driveshaft as described in Chapter 8, Section 2.

17 On diesel models, remove the radiator cooling fans, as described in Chapter 3, Section 5. Cover the rear of the radiator to

prevent it from getting damaged as the engine/transmission is moved forward.

18 Unbolt the engine rear mounting torque arm from the bottom of the transmission **(see illustration)**.

19 Where applicable, unbolt the flywheel cover plate from the transmission bellhousing.

20 Using a suitable hoist, support the weight of the engine.

21 Unscrew the bolts securing the transmission mounting to the body. Also, unbolt the mounting bracket from the transmission **(see illustration)**.

22 Lower the engine/transmission assembly slightly and, using a trolley jack, support the transmission. Position the jack so that it can be withdrawn from the left-hand side of the car. As the engine/transmission is moved, make sure any wiring or hoses are not damaged.

23 Unscrew and remove the remaining lower transmission-to-engine mounting bolts,

including the bolt located on the left-hand rear of the engine **(see illustration)**.

24 Carefully pull the transmission directly away from the engine, taking care not to allow its weight to rest on the clutch friction disc hub. A second person is helpful to pull the engine as far forwards as possible.

25 On models with driveshafts that have a bolted flange, it will be necessary to manouvre the right-hand driveshaft flange, from around the flywheel on removal. If required, hold the drive flange in position and undo the centre securing bolt, then the drive flange can be removed **(see illustrations)**, make removal of the transmission easier.

⚠️ *Warning: Support the transmission to ensure that it remains steady on the jack head. Keep the transmission level until the input shaft is fully withdrawn from the clutch friction disc.*

3.16 Support the driveshafts

3.18 Unbolt the engine rear mounting torque arm

3.21 Transmission end mounting bracket

3.23 Undo the rear mounting bolt (arrowed)

3.25a Hold the drive flange in position ...

3.25b ...whilst removing the centre bolt ...

26 When the transmission is clear of the locating dowels and clutch components, lower the transmission to the ground and withdraw from under the car.

Refitting

27 Refitting the transmission is essentially a reversal of the removal procedure, but note the following points:

a) *Apply a smear of high melting-point grease to the clutch friction disc hub splines; take care to avoid contaminating the friction surfaces.*

b) *In order to align the transmission with the flywheel, gently pull the engine forward as the transmission is manoeuvred into place.*

c) *Tighten the transmission-to-engine bolts to the specified torque.*

d) *Refer to the relevant part of Chapter 2 and tighten the engine mounting bolts to the correct torque.*

e) *Refer to Chapter 8, Section 2, and then tighten the driveshaft bolts to the specified torque.*

f) *On completion, refer to Section 2 and check the gearchange linkage/cable adjustment.*

g) *Refill the transmission with the correct grade and quantity of oil. Refer to 'Lubricants and fluids' and Chapter 1A or 1B, as appropriate.*

4 Transmission overhaul – general information

The overhaul of a manual transmission is a complex (and often expensive) task for the DIY home mechanic to undertake, which requires access to specialist equipment. It involves dismantling and reassembly of many small

3.25c ...then slide the drive flange from the transmission

components, measuring clearances precisely and if necessary, adjusting them by selecting shims and spacers. Internal transmission components are also often difficult to obtain and in many instances, extremely expensive. Because of this, if the transmission develops a fault or becomes noisy, the best course of action is to have the unit overhauled by a specialist repairer or to obtain an exchange reconditioned unit.

Nevertheless, it is not impossible for the more experienced mechanic to overhaul the transmission if the special tools are available and the job is carried out in a deliberate step-by-step manner, to ensure nothing is overlooked.

The tools necessary for an overhaul include internal and external circlip pliers, bearing pullers, a slide hammer, a set of pin punches, a dial test indicator and possibly a hydraulic press. In addition, a large, sturdy workbench and a vice will be required.

During dismantling of the transmission, make careful notes of how each component is fitted to make reassembly easier and accurate.

Before dismantling the transmission, it will help if you have some idea of where the

problem lies. Certain problems can be closely related to specific areas in the transmission, which can make component examination and renewal easier. Refer to the *Fault finding* Section in this manual for more information.

5 Reversing light switch – testing, removal and refitting

Testing

1 Ensure that the ignition switch is turned to the OFF position.
2 Unplug the wiring harness from the reversing light switch at the connector. The switch is located on the front or top of the casing **(see illustrations 3.13a & 3.13b)**.
3 Connect the probes of a continuity tester, or multimeter set to the resistance measurement function, across the terminals of the reversing light switch.
4 The switch contacts are normally open, so with any gear other than reverse selected, the tester/meter should indicate an open circuit or infinite resistance. When reverse gear is selected, the switch contacts should close, causing the tester/meter to indicate continuity or zero resistance.
5 If the switch does not operate correctly, it should be renewed.

Removal

6 Ensure that the ignition switch is turned to the OFF position.
7 Unplug the wiring harness from the reversing light switch at the connector.
8 Unscrew the switch from the transmission casing, and recover the sealing ring.

Refitting

9 Refitting is a reversal of removal.

Chapter 7 Part B:
DSG semi-automatic transmission

Contents

Degrees of difficulty

| Easy, suitable for novice with little experience | | Fairly easy, suitable for beginner with some experience | | Fairly difficult, suitable for competent DIY mechanic | | Difficult, suitable for experienced DIY mechanic | | Very difficult, suitable for expert DIY or professional | |

Specifications

General

Description	DSG (Direct Shift Gearbox) semi-automatic 6- or 7-forward speeds and 1 reverse. Integral transaxle differential/final drive transmission with multi-plate clutch or dual-clutch.

Transmission type number:
  Petrol models:
    1.4 litre engine:
      7-speed. 0AM
  Diesel models:
    1.6 litre engine:
      7-speed. 0AM
    2.0 litre engine:
      6-speed. 02E
Transmission capacity:
  Type 02E – 6-speed transmission . . . .   5.2 litres
  Type 0AM – 7 speed transmission . . . .   1.7 litres
Clutch type:
  6-speed (02E) transmission . . . .   Multi-plate (wet clutch), 4 outer plates, 4 inner plates & 1 drive plate.
  7-speed (0AM) transmission . . . .   Two (Dual-clutch) dry friction discs, with spring loaded centre hub.
Clutch operation. . . . .   Mechatronic unit (mechanical and electronic).

Torque wrench settings

	Nm	lbf ft
Driveshaft flange bolt	30	22
Transmission-to-engine bolts:		
M10 bolts	40	30
M12 bolts	80	59
Transmission mounting bracket-to-casing bolts*:		
Stage 1	40	30
Stage 2	Angle-tighten a further 90°	
Transmission mounting-to-bracket bolts*:		
Stage 1	60	44
Stage 2	Angle-tighten a further 90°	
Drain plug (0AM transmission)	30	22
Drain/level plug (02E transmission)	45	31
Oil level tube (02E transmission)	3	2

Do not re-use

**1.2 Mechatronic unit -
0AM transmissions**

1 General information

The VW semi-automatic Direct Shift Gearbox (DSG) has six- or seven-forward speeds (and one reverse). In contrast to traditional automatic transmissions where a fluid flywheel (torque converter) transmits the power from the engine to the gearbox, the DSG has a multi-plate clutch in the six-speed transmission and a twin-clutch in the seven-speed transmission. The main advantages of the DSG transmission, is near-instant gear changes, with seamless, highly efficient drive, resulting in less exhaust emissions and improved fuel consumption.

On the front of the transmission housing is a mechatronic unit, this is made up of mechanical and electronic components. The electronic part of the unit uses information from sensors (e.g. engine speed, road speed, driving mode etc.) to determine the optimum gear and shift commands, the mechanical part then selects the correct gear required. On 6-speed (02E) transmissions, the unit is inside the transmission housing with a pressed steel cover, bolted to the front of the transmission casing. On 7-speed (0AM) transmissions, it is a sealed unit, and is bolted to the front of the transmission **(see illustration)**

On 6-speed (02E) transmissions, the clutch is of a multi-plate type, which runs in the transmission oil. It is made up of four outer plates, which have teeth on the outer edge to

locate in the clutch housing, four inner plates with teeth on the inner edge that locate on the clutch inner hub, and one drive plate that is located on the outside of the clutch plate assembly. The four larger outer plates (C1) operate 1st, 3rd, 5th and reverse gears, and then the four smaller inner plates (C2) operate 2nd, 4th and 6th gears. With this system whilst 'C1' has a gear engaged, then 'C2' will pre-select the next gear ready to change gear. The assembly requires special care, as all the components in the assembly are balanced together, during manufacture. The clutch assembly is sealed inside the bell housing by a clutch end cover, which also forms a seal, to prevent loss of oil. If the end cover is removed for any reason, it will need to be renewed.

On 7-speed (0AM) transmissions, the clutch is of a dual-clutch dry plate type, which has two friction discs and a spring loaded centre hub **(see illustration)**. The clutch friction disc nearest the engine is operated by the larger outer release lever (K1) and operates 1st, 3rd, 5th & 7th gears. The clutch friction disc nearest the transmission is operated by the smaller inner release lever (K2) and operates 2nd, 4th, 6th & Reverse gears. With this system whilst 'K1' has a gear engaged, then 'K2' will pre-select the next gear ready to change gear. The clutch assembly can only be purchased as a complete unit, and if renewed, new release levers will also need to be renewed.

A fault diagnosis system is integrated into the control unit, but analysis can only be undertaken with specialised equipment. It is important that any transmission fault be identified and rectified at the earliest possible opportunity. A VW dealer or suitable equipped specialist can 'interrogate' the ECM fault memory for stored fault codes, enabling him to pinpoint the fault quickly. Once the fault has been corrected and any fault codes have been cleared, normal transmission operation is restored.

Because of the need for special test equipment, the complexity of some of the parts, and the need for scrupulous cleanliness when these transmissions, the work which the owner can do is limited. Most major repairs and overhaul operations should be left to a

VW dealer or specialist, who will be equipped with the necessary equipment for fault diagnosis and repair. The information in this Chapter is therefore limited to a description of the removal and refitting of the transmission as a complete unit. The removal, refitting and adjustment of the selector cable is also described.

In the event of a transmission problem occurring, consult a VW dealer or transmission specialist before removing the transmission from the vehicle, since the majority of fault diagnosis is best carried out with the transmission still in the vehicle.

2 Transmission – removal and refitting

Note: *The mechatronic unit on the front of the 7-speed (0AM) transmission is a sealed unit. If any oil is lost from this mechatronic unit, it will need to be renewed, as it cannot be refilled. Remove the breather cap from the top of the unit and cover with blanking plug, to prevent any loss of oil (see illustration).*

Removal

1 The transmission is removed downwards from the engine compartment. First, select a solid, level surface to park the vehicle upon. Give yourself enough space to move around it easily. Select P, apply the handbrake, and chock the rear wheels.

2 Loosen the front wheel bolts, and the driveshaft hub bolts. Do not undo the hub bolt more than 90° at this point; otherwise the wheel bearing could be damaged, whilst the weight is still on the wheels.

3 Raise the front of the vehicle and rest it securely on axle stands (see *Jacking and vehicle support*). Remove the front wheels. Allow a suitable working clearance underneath for the eventual withdrawal of the transmission. Undo the fasteners and remove the engine/transmission undershield.

4 Drain the transmission oil, as described in Section 6.

⚠ *Warning: The mechatronic unit on the front of the 7-speed (0AM) transmission is a sealed unit. If any oil is lost from this unit, it will need to be renewed, as it cannot be refilled. Remove the breather cap from the top of the unit and cover with blanking plug, to prevent any loss of oil.*

5 Remove the air cleaner housing as described in Chapter 4A (petrol) or Chapter 4B (diesel).

6 On turbo models, undo the retaining clips and remove the turbocharger intake hose and charge air pipe to the intercooler.

7 Remove the engine front subframe, as described in Chapter 10, Section 23.

8 Remove the starter motor as described in Chapter 5A, section 8.

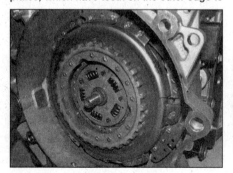

**1.4 Clutch assembly -
0AM transmissions**

**2.0 Breather cap on mechatronic unit -
0AM transmissions**

9 Disconnect the selector cable from the selector shaft lever on the top of the transmission, as described in Section 4. Position the cable to one side, noting that the retaining clip/circlip must be renewed.

10 On 6-speed (02E) transmissions there is a fluid cooler located on top of the transmission. Clamp off the cooler hoses with brake hose type clamps. Release the retaining clips and detach the hoses from the cooler **(see illustration)**. Take great care not to spill any coolant into the transmission unit, as this will cause damage.

11 Disconnect the wiring plug connectors from the front of the transmission **(see illustrations)**. If required, undo the nuts and detach the wiring loom retainer from the gearbox cover.

a) 6-speed 02E transmissions – rotate the collar anti-clockwise to disconnect.

b) 7-speed 0AM transmissions – slide the locking lever upwards to disconnect.

12 Disconnect the earth cable from either the transmission or the vehicle body **(see illustration)**.

13 Remove the upper engine-to-transmission mounting bolts.

14 Remove the radiator cooling fan assembly as described in Chapter 3, Section 5.

15 Undo the bolts and slide rearwards the exhaust pipe connecting piece between the front and rear sections of the exhaust system. Also undo the retaining bolts and remove the exhaust front mounting bracket **(see illustration)**.

16 Disconnect the wiring plug from the engine oil level/temperature sensor on the sump **(see illustration)**; this is to prevent it getting damaged when the engine moves forward.

17 With reference to Chapter 8, Section 2, unscrew and remove the bolts securing the driveshafts to the transmission output flanges. Tie the right-hand driveshaft to one side, and then tie the left-hand driveshaft to the suspension strut, so that the shaft is as high as possible **(see illustration)**. Alternatively, completely remove the driveshaft as described in Chapter 8, Section 2.

18 Support the engine with a hoist or support bar located on the front wing inner channels. Depending on the engine, temporarily remove components as necessary to attach the hoist.

19 Position a trolley jack underneath the transmission, and raise it to just take the weight of the unit.

20 Undo and remove the bolts securing the left-hand gearbox mounting. By controlling both the engine hoist/support bar and the trolley jack, lower the transmission slightly. To make removal easier undo the retaining bolts and remove the mounting bracket from the top of the transmission casing.

21 On 6-speed (02E) transmissions, undo the retaining bolt and remove the small cover plate located above the right-hand driveshaft flange.

22 Lower the engine/transmission until there

2.10 Clamp the transmission cooler hoses (arrowed) - 02E transmissions

2.11a Wiring plug and earth cable (arrowed) - 02E transmissions

2.11b Wiring plug connections ...

2.11c ...on the front of the transmission - 0AM transmissions

is sufficient clearance between the upper edge of the transmission and the left-hand chassis member.

23 Unscrew and remove the lower bolts

securing the transmission to the engine, noting the bolt locations, as they are of different sizes and lengths.

24 On models with driveshafts that have a

2.12 Undo the earth cable securing nut

2.15 Undo the exhaust mounting retaining bolts

2.16 Disconnect the oil level/temperature sensor wiring connector

2.17 Fasten the driveshaft to one side

2.24a Hold the drive flange in position ...

2.24b ...whilst removing the centre bolt ...

2.24c ...then slide the drive flange from the transmission

bolted flange, hold the flange in position and undo the flange securing bolt, then the flange can be removed **(see illustrations)**.

25 Check that all the fixings and attachments are clear of the transmission. Enlist the aid of an assistant to help in guiding and supporting the transmission during its removal.

26 The transmission is located on engine alignment dowels, and if stuck on them, it may be necessary to carefully tap and prise the transmission free of the dowels to allow separation. Once the transmission is disconnected from the location dowels, swivel the unit out and lower it out of the vehicle.

⚠️ **Warning: Support the transmission to ensure that it remains steady on the jack head.**

27 When the transmission is clear of the locating dowels and clutch components, lower the transmission to the ground and withdraw from under the car. Make sure that the transmission does not fall and lose any transmission oil. Also make sure that the clutch assembly comes away with the transmission, and stays inside the bell-housing.

Refitting

28 Refitting the transmission is essentially a reversal of the removal procedure, but note the following points:

a) On 7-speed (0AM) transmissions, renew the needle bearing in the end of the crankshaft (see Chapter 2E, Section 13).

b) When reconnecting the transmission to the engine, ensure that the location dowels are in position, and that the

4.4 Disconnect the wiring connector

transmission is correctly aligned with them before pushing it fully into engagement with the engine.

c) Tighten all retaining bolts to their specified torque wrench settings.

d) Be sure to guide the selector cable into the support bracket as the transmission is refitted – renew the retaining clips.

e) Adjust the selector cable, as described in Section 4.

f) Refer to Chapter 8, Section 2, and then tighten the driveshaft bolts to the specified torque.

g) On completion, check the coolant level.

h) If a new transmission unit has been fitted, it may be necessary to have the transmission ECM 'matched' to the engine management ECM electronically, to ensure correct operation – seek the advice of your VW dealer or suitably equipped specialist.

j) Refill the transmission with the correct grade and quantity of oil, as described in Section 6.

3 Transmission overhaul – general information

In the event of a fault occurring, it will be necessary to establish whether the fault is electrical, mechanical or hydraulic in nature, before repair work can be contemplated. Diagnosis requires detailed knowledge of the transmission's operation and construction, as

4.6 Selector cable clip and outer cable circlip (arrowed)

well as access to specialised test equipment, and so is deemed to be beyond the scope of this manual. It is therefore essential that problems with the automatic transmission be referred to a VW dealer or specialist for assessment.

Although it is possible to remove the clutch assembly from out of the bell housing, it is not possible to fit a new assembly without the use of special tools. When a new clutch is purchased, there are a number of shims and retaining clips of different thickness in the kit, therefore without the correct tools, it is not possible to correctly install the assembly back in place.

Note that a faulty transmission should not be removed before the vehicle has been assessed by a dealer or specialist, as fault diagnosis is best carried out with the transmission still in the vehicle.

4 Selector lever housing and cable – removal, refitting and adjustment

Note: *The selector lever housing and cable should not be separated, remove the housing and cable as a complete unit.*

Removal

1 Move the selector lever to the P position, and remove the battery and battery tray as described in Chapter 5A, Section 3.

2 Remove the air cleaner housing as described in Chapter 4A (petrol) or Chapter 4B (diesel).

3 Working inside the vehicle, remove the centre console and gear selector knob, as described in Chapter 11, Section 26.

4 Disconnect the wiring connector from the front of the gear selector housing **(see illustration)**.

6-speed (02E) transmission

5 Working inside the engine compartment, slacken the adjustment screw on the cable end fitting at the transmission end **(see illustration 4.16)**.

6 Prise out the clips securing the cable to the lever on the transmission, and the outer cable to the support bracket **(see illustration)**. Withdraw the cable from the support bracket and discard the clips – new ones must be fitted.

4.7 Prise the inner cable from the ball joint

4.8 Release the outer cable securing clip

4.11 Gearchange housing mounting nuts (arrowed)

4.16a Secure the outer cable in the bracket …

4.16b …and slacken the cable adjustment screw (arrowed)

4.18 Push the lever in the direction of the arrow

7-speed (0AM) transmission

7 Working inside the engine compartment, use a pair of long-nose pliers to release the cable end fitting from the ball head on the selector lever **(see illustration)**.

8 Prise out the clip securing the outer cable and withdraw the cable from the support bracket on the transmission **(see illustration)**. Discard the retaining clip – as a new one must be fitted.

All transmissions

9 Raise the front of the vehicle and support it securely on axle stands (see *Jacking and vehicle support*).

10 Remove the centre tunnel front heat shield from the underside of the vehicle to gain access to the base of the selector lever housing and cable. It may be necessary to separate the exhaust downpipe from the intermediate pipe with reference to Chapter 4C (petrol) or Chapter 4D (diesel).

11 Working inside the vehicle, undo the retaining nuts **(see illustration)**, then remove the bracket and lower the gear selector housing downwards. Withdraw it complete with selector cable out from under the vehicle. It may be useful having the aid of an assistant at this point, to be under the vehicle when lowering the selector housing.

Refitting

12 Refitting is the reversal of the removal procedure, noting the following points:
 a) *Do not grease the cable end fittings. This is stated by VW.*

 b) *Ensure that the cable is correctly routed and secured, as noted on removal.*
 c) *Take care not to bend or kink the cable.*
 d) *Carry out the cable adjustment procedure described below before reconnecting the cable at the transmission end.*
 e) *When refitting the outer cable to the support bracket, use new clips.*

Adjustment

13 Inside the car, move the selector lever to the P position.

14 If not already done, disconnect the cable from the selector lever on the transmission.

15 Move the selector lever inside the vehicle from 'P' to 'S' and back, repeatedly, to check that everything moves easily. VW recommend that you *do not* grease the cable.

16 Reconnect the cable to the lever at the transmission, and then slacken the cable adjusting bolt **(see illustrations)**.

17 Check that both the selector lever inside the car and the lever on the transmission are in their P positions. Gently rock the levers backwards and forwards to make sure the cable is settled. Do not move either lever out of the P position.

18 The transmission lever is in the P position when:
 a) *6-speed 02E transmissions - it's pushed all the way back towards the bulkhead*
 b) *7-speed 0AM transmissions – it's pushed*

back towards the selector cable mounting bracket **(see illustration)**.

19 When in position, tighten the cable adjusting bolt.

20 Verify the operation of the selector lever by shifting through all gear positions and checking that every gear can be selected smoothly and without delay.

5 Emergency release of selector lever

1 If the vehicles battery is disconnected or discharged, it is possible to release the selector lever from its locked position. First, ensure the handbrake is fully applied.

2 Carefully prise up the selector lever gaiter surround trim from the console and move it to one side **(see illustration)**.

5.2 Prise up the selector lever gaiter surround trim

5.3 Press down the yellow plastic peg

6.2 Transmission oil drain plug - 0AM transmissions

6.7 Breather cap on selector cover - 0AM transmissions

3 Press the yellow plastic wedge downwards **(see illustration)**. It should now be possible to move the selector lever to the desired position.

6 Transmission oil renewal

7-speed dual clutch 0AM transmission

Note: *This transmission is fitted to 1.4-litre petrol and 1.6-litre diesel engines. The transmission is filled for life, and does not have an oil level checking procedure. If there has been an oil leak from the transmission, after the leak has been rectified, renew the transmission oil as described in the following paragraphs.*

1 Take the vehicle on a short journey to warm the transmission oil, and then park the car on a level surface. For improved access to the drain plug, apply the handbrake, then jack up

6.13 Transmission fluid level check - 02E transmissions

1 Level plug   2 Level tube

the front of the vehicle and support it on axle stands (see *Jacking and vehicle support*), but note that the rear of the vehicle should also be raised to ensure all oil is drained.

2 Undo the retaining screws and remove the engine undertray. Wipe clean the area around the transmission drain plug, which is situated on the lower rear of the transmission **(see illustration)**.

3 Place a container under the transmission casing, then unscrew the drain plug from the base of the differential housing, and allow the oil to drain.

4 Remove the battery and battery tray as described in Chapter 5A, Section 3.

5 Remove the air cleaner housing as described in Chapter 4A, Section 2 (petrol) or Chapter 4B, Section 2, (diesel).

6 When the oil has finished draining, clean the surrounding area, refit the drain plug and tighten it to the specified torque.

7 Unclip the breather cap from the selector cover plate on the top of the transmission casing **(see illustration)**.

8 Using a length of hose, and funnel, add 1.7 litres of new oil to the transmission. Only use VW recommended oil, for 7-speed dual clutch 0AM transmission.

9 Refit the breather cap, making sure that it is secure. Renew if damaged.

10 The remainder of refitting is a reversal of removal.

6-speed dual clutch 02E transmission

Note: *An accurate fluid level check can only be made with the transmission fluid at a temperature of between 35°C and 45°C, and if it is not possible to ascertain this temperature, it is strongly recommended that the check be made by a VW dealer who will have the instrumentation to check the temperature and to check the transmission electronics for fault codes. Over-filling or under-filling adversely affects the function of the transmission.*

11 Take the vehicle on a short journey to warm the transmission oil. And then park the vehicle on level ground and engage P with the selector lever. Raise the front and rear of the vehicle and support it on axle stands (see *Jacking and vehicle support*), ensuring the vehicle is kept level. Undo the retaining screws and remove the engine undertray to gain access to the base of the transmission unit.

12 Start the engine and run it at idle speed until the transmission fluid temperature reaches 35°C.

13 Unscrew the fluid level plug from the bottom of the transmission sump **(see illustration)**.

14 If fluid **continually** drips from the level tube as the fluid temperature increases, the fluid level is correct and does not need to be topped-up. Note that there will be some fluid already present in the level tube, and it will be necessary to observe when this amount has drained before making the level check. Make sure that the check is made before the fluid temperature reaches 45°C.

15 If no fluid drips from the level tube, even when the fluid temperature has reached 45°C, it will be necessary to add fluid. VW technicians use an adapter which screws into the bottom of the transmission sump, however, a tube inserted up through the drain plug (into the space above the fluid); will allow fluid to be added. Ideally, the fluid should be allowed to cool before adding the fluid.

16 Check the condition of the seal on the level plug and renew it if necessary by cutting off the old seal and fitting a new one. Refit the plug and tighten to the specified torque.

17 Refit the engine undertray, tighten the retaining screws securely, and lower the vehicle to the ground.

18 Frequent need for topping-up indicates that there is a leak, which should be corrected as soon as possible.

Chapter 8
Driveshafts

Contents

Degrees of difficulty

Easy, suitable for novice with little experience	**Fairly easy,** suitable for beginner with some experience	**Fairly difficult,** suitable for competent DIY mechanic	**Difficult,** suitable for experienced DIY mechanic	**Very difficult,** suitable for expert DIY or professional

Specifications

General

Driveshaft type . . . . Steel shafts with outer constant velocity joints and inner tripod or constant velocity joints (according to type).

Type code differences:

VL 90 or VL 100 . . . . CV joints each end, inner joint diameter 90 mm or 100 mm bolted to transmission drive flanges on each side

VL 107 (bolt-on) . . . . CV joints each end, inner joint diameter 107 mm bolted to transmission drive flanges on each side

VL 107 (slip-on). . . . . CV joints each end, inner joint diameter 107 mm splined onto the transmission on each side

AAR 3300i. . . . . CV outer joint, tripod inner joint body bolted to transmission drive flanges on each side

Lubrication

Overhaul and repair . . . . Use only special grease supplied in sachets with gaiter/overhaul kits
Joint grease type . . . . Refer to VW dealer
Joint grease quantity:
Outer joint. . . . . 80 g
Inner joint . . . . 130 g

Torque wrench settings

	Nm	lbf ft
Driveshaft-to-transmission flange bolts:		
Stage 1	10	7
Stage 2:		
M8 x 48 bolts* - (VL90 & VL100 type joint)	40	30
M10 x 52 bolts* - (VL107 type joint)	70	52
M10 x 23 bolts - (AAR 3300i type joint)	70	52
Hub bolt (with ribbing under head): *		
Stage 1	70	52
Stage 2	Angle-tighten a further 90°	
Hub bolt (without ribbing under head): *		
Stage 1	200	148
Stage 2	Angle-tighten a further 180°	
Lower arm-to-balljoint nuts: *		
Cast steel lower arm	60	44
Forged aluminium lower arm	100	74
Lower rear mounting-to-transmission bolts: *		
Stage 1	50	37
Stage 2	Angle-tighten a further 90°	
Wheel bolts	120	89

* Use new bolt/nuts

2.0 Flange of bolt is ribbed

2.3 Remove the heat shield

2.4 Remove the driveshaft/hub bolt

1 General information

Drive is transmitted from the differential to the front wheels by means of two steel driveshafts of either solid or hollow construction (depending on model, and which side of the vehicle). Both driveshafts are splined at their outer ends, to accept the wheel hubs, and are secured to the hub by a large bolt. The inner end of each driveshaft is either bolted to a transmission drive flange or splined directly onto the differential splined shaft.

The outer ends of each driveshaft are fitted with ball-bearing type constant velocity (CV) joints, to ensure the smooth and efficient transmission of drive at all the angles possible, as the roadwheels move up-and-down with the suspension, and as they turn from side to side under steering.

The inner ends of each driveshaft (except for the AAR 3300i type joint) are fitted with ball and cage type constant velocity (CV) joint. The AAR 3300i driveshaft has a triple roller type (tripod) joint fitted to the inner end of the driveshaft.

Hytrel (thermoplastic elastomer) gaiters are fitted over the CV joints with steel clips. These gaiters combine the flexibility of rubber with the strength and durability of thermoplastics. The gaiters contain the grease that lubricates the joints, and also protect the joints from the entry of dirt and debris.

2 Driveshafts –
removal and refitting

Note: *A new hub bolt will be required on refitting. There are two different types of bolts fitted, one is ribbed (see illustration) under the face of the bolt head and one is smooth. The torque setting is different for each type of bolt (see Specifications), so it is important to make sure you check which is fitted.*

Removal

1 Remove the wheel trim/centre cap (as applicable) then apply the handbrake, and partially unscrew the relevant hub bolt with the vehicle resting on its wheels, by a maximum of 90° – note that the bolt is very tight, and a suitable extension bar will probably be required to aid unscrewing. Also slacken the road wheel securing bolts by half a turn. **Note:** *Do not loosen the bolt more than 90° with the vehicle standing on the ground, as the wheel bearings may be damaged.*

2 Apply the handbrake, then jack up the front of the vehicle and support it on axle stands (see *Jacking and vehicle support*). Remove the appropriate front roadwheel.

3 Remove the retaining screws and/or clips, and remove the undershields from beneath the engine/transmission unit to gain access to the driveshafts. Where necessary, also unbolt the heat shield from the transmission housing to improve access to the driveshaft inner joint **(see illustration)**.

4 Unscrew and remove the hub bolt **(see illustration). Note:** *Discard the bolt and obtain a new one, there are two types of bolt fitted, see note at the beginning of this Section.*

5 Unscrew the three nuts securing the front suspension lower arm balljoint to the lower arm **(see illustration)**. Discard the nuts, as new ones must be used on refitting.

6 Lever the lower arm downwards to release it from the balljoint studs, then pull the hub carrier outwards, and at the same time withdraw the driveshaft outer constant velocity joint from the hub **(see illustration)**. If the joint splines are a tight fit in the hub, tap the joint out of the hub using a soft-faced mallet and drift. If this fails to free the driveshaft from the hub, the joint will have to be pressed out using a suitable tool bolted to the hub.

7 On some models, in order to gain the necessary clearance required to withdraw the left-hand driveshaft, it may be necessary to unbolt the rear engine transmission mounting from the subframe **(see illustration)**, and move the engine slightly.

8 Proceed as follows according to driveshaft type.

Caution: Support the driveshaft by suspending it with wire or string – do not allow it to hang under its own weight, or the joint may be damaged.

Inner joint with drive flange – VL90, VL100 and VL107

9 Mark the inner joint in relation to the drive

2.5 Undo the lower ball joint retaining nuts

2.6 Slide the driveshaft out from the hub assembly

2.7 Unbolt the lower rear mounting bracket

flange for refitting. Using a multi-splined tool, unscrew and remove the six bolts securing the inner driveshaft joint to the transmission flange and, recover the retaining plates from underneath the bolts (see illustrations).

Inner joint splined to differential drive shaft – VL107

10 Position a container beneath the transmission to catch spilt oil, and then pull out the driveshaft. The internal driveshaft circlip may be tight in the transmission side gear, in which case careful use of a lever against the transmission casing will be required. Lever against a block of wood to prevent damage to the casing, and take care not to damage the oil seal as the driveshaft is being removed. **Note:** *Pull only on the inner joint body, not the driveshaft itself; otherwise the gaiter may be damaged.*

Inner joint triple roller (tripod) located in joint body – AAR 3300i

11 Mark the inner joint body and driveshaft in relation to each other, as the tripod joint will need to be refitted in the joint body in the same position. Loosen the larger retaining clip, ease off the rubber gaiter, and pull the triple roller out of the joint body.

All types

12 Manoeuvre the driveshaft out from underneath the vehicle and (where fitted) recover the gasket from the end of the inner constant velocity joint. **Note:** *Discard the gasket and obtain a new one.*
Caution: Do not allow the vehicle to rest on its wheels with one or both driveshaft(s) removed, as damage to the wheel bearings may result.
13 If moving the vehicle is unavoidable, temporarily insert the outer end of the driveshaft(s) in the hub(s), and tighten the driveshaft retaining bolt(s); in this case, the inner end(s) of the driveshaft(s) must be supported, for example by suspending with string from the vehicle underbody.

Refitting

14 Where applicable, check the condition of the circlip on the inner end of the driveshaft, and if necessary, renew it.
15 As applicable, clean the splines on each end of the driveshaft and in the hub and apply a little oil, and where applicable wipe clean the oil seal in the transmission casing. Check the oil seal and if necessary renew it as described in Chapter 7A or 7B. Smear a little oil on the lips of the oil seal before fitting the driveshaft.

Inner joint with bolted drive flange – VL90, VL100 and VL107

16 Ensure that the transmission flange and inner joint mating surfaces are clean and dry. Where necessary, fit a new gasket to the joint by peeling off its backing foil and sticking it in position (see illustration).
17 Manoeuvre the driveshaft into position, aligning the previously made marks (see

2.9a Make alignment marks (arrowed) ...

illustration), and then align the inner joint holes with those on the transmission flange. Refit the new retaining bolts and locking plates, and then tighten the retaining bolts to the specified torque.

Inner joint splined to differential drive shaft – VL107

18 Locate the inner end of the driveshaft into the transmission – turn the driveshaft as necessary to engage the splines. Press in the driveshaft until the internal circlip engages the groove. Check that the circlip is engaged by attempting to pull out the driveshaft with only moderate force.

Inner joint triple roller (tripod) located in joint body – AAR 3300i

19 Fill the inner joint with the specified quantity of grease, and then locate the driveshaft tripod into the joint body, aligning the previously made marks. Ease the gaiter onto the joint body, and secure the gaiter with a new retaining clip.

All types

20 With the lower arm levered downwards, engage the outer joint with the hub. Fit the new hub bolt and use it to draw the joint fully into position.
21 Align the balljoint studs with the holes in the lower arm, then release the arm and fit the three new nuts. Tighten the nuts to the specified torque.
22 Where applicable, refit the lower rear mounting-to-transmission bolts, and then tighten the new bolts to the specified torque.

2.16 Locate a new gasket on the inner joint

2.9b ...and remove the drive flange bolts and plates

23 Tighten the driveshaft bolt to the Stage 1 torque setting. **Note:** *The bolt must be tightened with the wheel clear of the ground. There are two different types of bolts fitted, one is ribbed (see illustration 2.0) under the face of the bolt head and one is smooth. See note at the beginning of this Section.*
24 Refit the roadwheel and lower the vehicle to the ground, then angle-tighten the driveshaft bolt through the Stage 2 angle (see Specifications).
25 Once the driveshaft bolt is correctly tightened, tighten the wheel bolts to the specified torque and refit the wheel trim/centre cap.

3 Driveshaft rubber gaiters – renewal

1 Remove the driveshaft from the car, as described in Section 2. Continue as described under the relevant sub-heading. Driveshafts with a tripod type inner joint can be identified by the shape of the inner CV joint; the driveshaft retaining bolt holes are in extensions from the joint, giving it a six-pointed star-shaped exterior, in contrast to the smooth, circular shape of the ball-and-cage joint (see illustrations).

Outer CV joint gaiter – All types of driveshafts

2 Secure the driveshaft in a vice equipped with soft jaws, and release the two outer

2.17 Align the markings made on removal when refitting

3.1a Driveshaft components – models with VL90 or VL100 CV joint

1   Hub bolt
2   Outer joint gaiter
3   Gaiter securing clip
4   Driveshaft
5   Inner joint
6   Flange bolts
7   Bolt retaining plate
8   Thrust washer
9   Circlip
10 Washer
11 Gasket
12 Inner joint gaiter
13 Outer joint

H48695

3.1b Driveshaft joint components – models with VL107 CV joint (bolt-on)

1   Outer joint
2   Hub bolt
3   Circlip
4   Thrust washer
5   Washer
6   Gaiter securing clip
7   Outer joint gaiter
8   Driveshaft
9   Inner joint gaiter
10 Flange bolts
11 Bolt retaining plate
12 Metal cover
13 Inner 'bolt-on' joint
14 Gasket
15 Circlip
16 Metal end cover

H48696

**3.1c Driveshaft joint components –
models with VL107 CV joint (slip-on)**

1 Outer joint
2 Hub bolt
3 Circlip
4 Thrust washer
5 Washer
6 Gaiter securing clip
7 Outer joint gaiter
8 Driveshaft
9 Inner joint gaiter
10 Inner 'slip-on' joint

H48697

**3.1d Driveshaft joint components –
models with AAR3300i triple roller joints**

1 Outer joint
2 Hub bolt
3 Circlip
4 Thrust washer
5 Washer
6 Gaiter securing clip
7 Outer joint gaiter
8 Driveshaft
9 Inner joint gaiter
10 Triple roller joint
11 Flange bolts
12 Inner joint housing

H48698

3.2 Release the outer joint gaiter clips...

3.3 ...and slide the gaiter away from the joint

3.4 Use a mallet to drive the outer joint from the driveshaft

3.5 Removing the circlip, thrustwasher and dished washer

3.6 Removing the outer gaiter

3.11 Temporarily tape over the splines to protect the new gaiter

joint gaiter retaining clips **(see illustration)**. If necessary, the retaining clips can be cut to release them.

3 Slide the rubber gaiter down the shaft to expose the constant velocity joint, and scoop out excess grease **(see illustration)**.

4 Using a soft-faced mallet, tap the joint off the end of the driveshaft **(see illustration)**.

5 Remove the circlip from the driveshaft groove, and slide off the thrustwasher and dished washer, noting which way around it is fitted **(see illustration)**.

6 Slide the rubber gaiter off the driveshaft and discard it **(see illustration)**.

7 Thoroughly clean the constant velocity joint(s) using paraffin, or a suitable solvent, and dry thoroughly. Carry out a visual inspection as follows.

8 Move the inner splined driving member from side-to-side to expose each ball in turn at the top of its track. Examine the balls for cracks, flat spots or signs of surface pitting.

9 Inspect the ball tracks on the inner and outer members. If the tracks have widened, the balls will no longer be a tight fit. At the same time, check the ball cage windows for wear or cracking between the windows.

10 If on inspection any of the constant velocity joint components are found to be worn or damaged, it will be necessary to renew the complete joint assembly. If the joint is in satisfactory condition, obtain a new gaiter and retaining clips, a constant velocity joint circlip and the correct type of grease. Grease is often supplied with the joint repair kit – if not, use good-quality molybdenum disulphide grease.

11 Tape over the splines on the end of the driveshaft, to protect the new gaiter as it is slid into place **(see illustration)**.

12 Slide the new gaiter onto the end of the driveshaft, then remove the protective tape from the driveshaft splines.

13 Slide on the dished washer, making sure its convex side is innermost, followed by the thrustwasher.

14 Pack the joint with half the quantity of the specified type of grease. Work the grease well into the bearing tracks whilst twisting the joint, and fill the rubber gaiter with the remaining half **(see illustrations)**.

15 Fit a new circlip to the driveshaft, then tap the joint onto the driveshaft until the circlip engages in its groove **(see illustrations)**. Make sure that the joint is securely retained by the circlip.

16 Ease the gaiter over the joint, and ensure that the gaiter lips are correctly located on both the driveshaft and constant velocity joint. Lift the outer sealing lip of the gaiter to

3.14a Pack half of the grease in the joint...

3.14b ...and the remaining half in the gaiter

3.15a Fit a new circlip...

equalise air pressure within the gaiter (see illustration).

17 Fit the large metal retaining clip to the gaiter. Pull the clip as tight as possible, and locate the hooks on the clip in their slots. Remove any slack in the gaiter retaining clip by carefully compressing the raised section of the clip. In the absence of the special tool, a pair of side-cutters may be used, taking care not to cut the clip (see illustrations). Secure the small retaining clip using the same procedure.

18 Check the constant velocity joint moves freely in all directions, then refit the driveshaft to the vehicle, as described in Section 2.

Inner gaiter with bolted drive flange – VL90, VL100 and VL107

19 Secure the driveshaft in a vice equipped with soft jaws, then release the gaiter small securing clip, securing the gaiter to the driveshaft (see illustration).

20 Using a hammer and a small drift, carefully drive the gaiter metal ring from the joint outer member (see illustration).

21 Slide the gaiter down the driveshaft to expose the constant velocity joint, and scoop out excess grease.

22 Remove the circlip from the end of the driveshaft using circlip pliers (see illustration).

23 Press or drive the driveshaft from the joint, taking great care not to damage the joint. Recover the dished washer fitted between the constant velocity joint and the gaiter (see illustrations).

3.15b ...then refit the outer joint

3.17a Fit the large metal retaining clip...

3.16 Seat the gaiter on the outer joint and driveshaft, then lift its inner lip to equalise the air pressure

3.17b ...and use a suitable tool to tighten it

24 Slide the gaiter from the end of the driveshaft (see illustration).

25 Proceed as described previously in paragraphs 7 to 12 (see illustrations).

26 Slide the dished washer onto the

driveshaft, making sure its convex side is innermost.

27 Fit the joint to the end of the driveshaft, noting that the chamfered edge of the internal splines on the joint should face towards

3.19 Release the gaiter small securing clip...

3.20 ...drive the metal ring from the joint outer member

3.22 Remove the circlip...

3.23a ...followed by the joint...

3.23b ...dished washer...

3.24 ...and gaiter

3.25a Tilt the splined hub and cage to remove the ball-bearings...

3.25b ...then separate the hub from the cage

3.25c Inner CV joint gaiter repair kit

3.29 Installation position of inner joint gaiter on left-hand driveshaft

A = 17.0 mm

3.30a Pack the inner joint with half of the grease...

the driveshaft. Drive or press the joint into position until it contacts the shoulder on the driveshaft.

28 Fit a new circlip to retain the joint on the end of the driveshaft.

29 If the left-hand driveshaft is being worked on, mark the final installation position of the gaiter outboard end on the driveshaft using tape or paint – do not scratch the surface of the driveshaft **(see illustration)**.

30 Pack the joint with the half the

recommended quantity of grease (see Specifications), and then pack the gaiter with the remaining half **(see illustrations)**.

31 Slide the gaiter up the driveshaft, and press or drive the gaiter metal ring onto the joint outer member. To ensure the bolt holes are correctly positioned, temporarily fit a couple of flange bolts **(see illustrations)**.

32 If the left-hand driveshaft is being worked on, slide the outboard end of the gaiter into position using the mark made previously (see

paragraph 29), then secure the outer gaiter securing clip in position as described in paragraph 17.

33 If the right-hand driveshaft is being worked on, slide the outboard end of the gaiter into position on the driveshaft, then secure the outer gaiter securing clip in position as described in paragraph 17 **(see illustration)**.

34 Check the driveshaft joint moves freely in all directions, then refit the driveshaft to the vehicle, as described in Section 2.

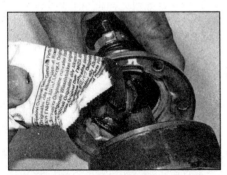

3.30b ...then pack the gaiter with the remaining half

3.31a Temporarily fit one of the flange bolts to ensure the bolt holes are correctly aligned...

3.31b ...then drive the metal ring onto the joint outer member

Inner gaiter with splined joint to transmission – VL107

35 Secure the driveshaft in a vice equipped with soft jaws, and release the two inner joint gaiter retaining clips. If necessary, the retaining clips can be cut to release them.

36 Slide the rubber gaiter down the shaft to expose the constant velocity joint, and scoop out excess grease.

37 Using a soft-faced mallet, tap the joint off the end of the driveshaft.

38 Remove the circlip from the end of the driveshaft groove, and then slide the rubber gaiter off the driveshaft and discard it.

39 Proceed as described previously in paragraphs 7 to 12.

40 Pack the joint with half the quantity of the specified type of grease. Work the grease well into the bearing tracks whilst twisting the joint, and fill the rubber gaiter with the remaining half.

41 Fit a new circlip to the driveshaft, then tap the joint onto the driveshaft until the circlip engages in its groove. Make sure that the joint is securely retained by the circlip.

42 Ease the gaiter over the joint, and ensure that the gaiter lips are correctly located on both the driveshaft and constant velocity joint. Lift the outer sealing lip of the gaiter to equalise air pressure within the gaiter.

43 Fit the large metal retaining clip to the gaiter, as described in paragraph 17. Secure the small retaining clip using the same procedure.

44 Check the constant velocity joint moves freely in all directions, then refit the driveshaft to the vehicle, as described in Section 2.

Inner gaiter with triple roller (tripod) joint – AAR 3300i

45 Secure the driveshaft in a vice equipped with soft jaws, and clean out the old grease from around the triple roller joint and inside the gaiter.

46 Remove the circlip from the end of the driveshaft.

47 Press or drive the driveshaft from the tripod, taking great care not to damage the surfaces of the roller locating arms.

48 Slide the outer member and the rubber gaiter from the end of the driveshaft.

49 Thoroughly clean the joint components using paraffin, or a suitable solvent, and dry thoroughly. Carry out a visual inspection as follows.

50 Inspect the tripod rollers and the joint

3.33 Installation position of inner joint gaiter on right-hand driveshaft

A Vent chamber in gaiter   B Vent hole

outer member for signs of wear, pitting or scuffing on their mating surfaces. Check that the joint rollers rotate smoothly, with no traces of roughness.

51 If the rollers or outer member shown signs of wear or damage, it will be necessary to renew the complete driveshaft, since the joint is not available separately. If the joint is in satisfactory condition, obtain a repair kit, consisting of a new gaiter, retaining clips, circlip, and the correct type and quantity of grease.

52 Tape over the splines on the end of the driveshaft, to protect the new gaiter as it is slid into place, and then slide the new gaiter over the end of the driveshaft and secure the smaller end in place with a new retaining clip. Remove the protective tape from the driveshaft splines.

53 Press or drive the tripod onto the end of the driveshaft until it contacts the stop, ensuring that the marks made on the end of the driveshaft and the tripod before dismantling are aligned. Note that the chamfered edge of the internal splines on the tripod should face towards the driveshaft.

54 Fit the new circlip to retain the tripod on the end of the driveshaft.

55 Check the triple roller joint moves freely, then refit the driveshaft to the vehicle, as described in Section 2.

4 Driveshaft overhaul – general information

If any of the checks described in Chapter 1A or 1B reveal wear in any driveshaft joint, first remove the roadwheel trim or centre cap (as applicable) and check that the hub bolt is tight. If the bolt is loose, obtain a new one, and tighten it to the specified torque (see Section 2). If the bolt is tight, refit the centre cap/trim, and repeat the check on the other hub bolt.

Road test the vehicle, and listen for a metallic clicking from the front of the vehicle as the vehicle is driven slowly in a circle on full-lock. If a clicking noise is heard, this indicates wear in the outer constant velocity joint; this means that the joint must be renewed.

If vibration consistent with roadspeed is felt through the car when accelerating, there is a possibility of wear in the inner constant velocity joints.

To check the joints for wear, remove the driveshafts, then dismantle them as described in Section 3. If any wear or free play is found, the affected joint must be renewed. Refer to a VW dealer for information on the availability of driveshaft components.

Chapter 9
Braking system

Contents

Degrees of difficulty

Easy, suitable for novice with little experience 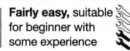	Fairly easy, suitable for beginner with some experience	Fairly difficult, suitable for competent DIY mechanic	Difficult, suitable for experienced DIY mechanic	Very difficult, suitable for expert DIY or professional

Specifications

Front brakes

Caliper type	FSIII or FN3 (according to model)
Disc diameter:	
FSIII.	280 mm
FN3:	
15" wheels	288 mm
16" wheels	312 mm
Disc thickness.	
New:	
FSIII.	22.0 mm
FN3	25.0 mm
Minimum permissible thickness:	
FSIII.	19.0 mm
FN3	22.0 mm
Maximum disc run-out	0.1 mm
Brake pad lining thickness (all models):	
New	14.0 mm
Minimum.	2.0 mm

Rear disc brakes

Caliper type:	
C 38	15" wheels
CII 38	16" wheels
Disc diameter:	
Type C 38	253 mm
Type CII 38	282 mm
Disc thickness:	
New:	
Type C 38	10.0 mm
Type CII 38	12.0 mm
Minimum thickness:	
Type C 38	8.0 mm
Type CII 38	10.0 mm
Maximum disc run-out	0.1 mm
Brake pad lining thickness (all models):	
New	11.0 mm
Minimum.	2.0 mm

Torque wrench settings

	Nm	lbf ft
ABS control unit retaining bolts	8	6
ABS control unit mounting bracket nuts	20	15
ABS wheel sensor retaining bolts	8	6
Brake pedal pivot shaft nut*	25	18
Brake light switch	5	4
Brake disc shield bolts	12	9
Front brake caliper:		
Guide pins	30	22
Mounting bracket bolts (FN3 calipers)	190	141
Hydraulic brake line to caliper banjo bolt	35	26
Hydraulic brake line union nuts	14	10
Master cylinder mounting nuts*	50	36
Rear brake caliper:		
Guide pin bolts*	35	26
Mounting bracket bolts (multi-point socket head): *		
Stage 1	90	66
Stage 2	Angle-tighten a further 90°	
Roadwheel bolts	120	89
Servo unit mechanical vacuum pump (diesel models)	10	8
Servo unit mounting bolts	25	18

* Use new bolts

1 General information and precautions

General information

The braking system is of servo-assisted, diagonal dual-circuit hydraulic type. The arrangement of the hydraulic system is such that each circuit operates one front and one rear brake from a tandem master cylinder. Under normal circumstances, both circuits operate in unison, but, if there is hydraulic failure in one circuit, full braking force will still be available at two wheels. On petrol engines, vacuum for the servo unit is supplied from the inlet manifold, however, on diesel engines a combined fuel lift pump and vacuum pump is driven off the end of the camshaft.

All models covered by this manual are equipped with disc brakes at the front and rear. ABS is fitted as standard to all models (refer to Section 19 for further information on ABS operation).

The front disc brakes are actuated by single-piston sliding type calipers, which ensure that equal pressure is applied to each disc pad.

The rear brakes are also actuated by single-piston sliding calipers, which incorporate independent mechanical handbrake mechanisms as well.

Precautions

● When servicing any part of the system, work carefully and methodically; also observe scrupulous cleanliness when overhauling any part of the hydraulic system. Always renew components in axle sets (where applicable) if in doubt about their condition, and use only genuine VW parts, or at least those of known good quality. Note the warnings given in Safety first! and at relevant points in this Chapter concerning the dangers of asbestos dust and hydraulic fluid.

2 Hydraulic system – bleeding

Warning: Hydraulic fluid is poisonous; wash off immediately and thoroughly in the case of skin contact, and seek immediate medical advice if any fluid is swallowed or gets into the eyes. Certain types of hydraulic fluid are flammable, and may ignite when allowed into contact with hot components; when servicing any hydraulic system, it is safest to assume that the fluid is flammable, and to take precautions against the risk of fire as though it is petrol that is being handled. Hydraulic fluid is also an effective paint stripper, and will attack plastics; if any is spilt, it should be washed off immediately, using copious quantities of fresh water. Finally, it is hygroscopic (it absorbs moisture from the air) – old fluid may be contaminated and unfit for further use. When topping-up or renewing the fluid, always use the recommended type, and ensure that it comes from a freshly opened sealed container.

Note: *VW specify that at least 0.25 litre of brake fluid should be expelled from each caliper.*

General

1 The correct operation of any hydraulic system is only possible after removing all air from the components and circuit; this is achieved by bleeding the system. Since the clutch hydraulic system also uses fluid from the brake system reservoir, it should also be bled at the same time by referring to Chapter 6, Section 2.

2 During the bleeding procedure, add only clean, unused hydraulic fluid of the recommended type; never re-use fluid that has already been bled from the system.

Ensure that sufficient fluid is available before starting work.

3 If there is any possibility of incorrect fluid being already in the system, the brake components and circuit must be flushed completely with uncontaminated, correct fluid, and new seals should be fitted to the various components.

4 If hydraulic fluid has been lost from the system, or air has entered because of a leak, ensure that the fault is cured before continuing further.

5 Park the vehicle on level ground, then chock the wheels and release the handbrake.

6 Check that all pipes and hoses are secure, unions tight and bleed screws closed. Clean any dirt from around the bleed screws.

7 Unscrew the master cylinder reservoir cap, and top the reservoir up to the MAX level line; refit the cap loosely, and remember to maintain the fluid level at least above the MIN level line throughout the procedure, or there is a risk of further air entering the system.

8 There is a number of one-man, do-it-yourself brake bleeding kits currently available from motor accessory shops. It is recommended that one of these kits is used whenever possible, as they greatly simplify the bleeding operation, and reduce the risk of expelled air and fluid being drawn back into the system. If such a kit is not available, the basic (two-man) method must be used, which is described in detail below.

9 If a kit is to be used, prepare the vehicle as described previously, and follow the kit manufacturer's instructions, as the procedure may vary slightly according to the type being used; generally, they are as outlined below in the relevant sub-section.

10 Whichever method is used, the same sequence must be followed (paragraph 12) to ensure the removal of all air from the system.

Bleeding sequence

11 If the system has been only partially

disconnected, and suitable precautions were taken to minimise fluid loss, it should be necessary only to bleed that part of the system.

12 If the complete system is to be bled, then it should be done working in the following sequence:

RHD models

a) *Right-hand front brake.*
b) *Left-hand front brake.*
c) *Right-hand rear brake.*
d) *Left-hand rear brake.*

LHD models

a) *Left-hand front brake.*
b) *Right-hand front brake.*
c) *Left-hand rear brake.*
d) *Right-hand rear brake.*

If the hydraulic fluid has run dry in either chamber of the reservoir, the system must be pre-bled as follows, before carrying out the bleeding sequence described above:

a) *Bleed the front left and right brakes simultaneously.*
b) *Bleed the rear left and right brakes simultaneously.*

Bleeding

Basic (two-man) method

13 Collect together a clean glass jar of reasonable size, a suitable length of plastic or rubber tubing which is a tight fit over the bleed screw, and a ring spanner to fit the screw. The help of an assistant will also be required.

14 Remove the dust cap from the first screw in the sequence **(see illustration)**. Fit the spanner and tube to the screw, place the other end of the tube in the jar, and pour in sufficient fluid to cover the end of the tube.

15 Ensure that the master cylinder reservoir fluid level is maintained at least above the MIN level line throughout the procedure.

16 Have the assistant fully depress the brake pedal several times to build-up pressure, and then maintain it on the final downstroke.

17 While pedal pressure is maintained, unscrew the bleed screw (approximately one turn) and allow the compressed fluid and air to flow into the jar. The assistant should maintain pedal pressure, following it down to the floor if necessary, and should not release it until instructed to do so. When the flow stops, tighten the bleed screw again, have the assistant release the pedal slowly, and recheck the reservoir fluid level.

18 Repeat the steps given in paragraphs 16 and 17 until the fluid emerging from the bleed screw is free from air bubbles. If the master cylinder has been drained and refilled, and air is being bled from the first screw in the sequence, allow approximately five seconds between cycles for the master cylinder passages to refill.

19 When no more air bubbles appear, tighten the bleed screw securely, remove the tube and spanner, and refit the dust cap. Do not overtighten the bleed screw.

20 Repeat the procedure on the remaining screws in the sequence, until all air is removed from the system and the brake pedal feels firm again.

Using a one-way valve kit

21 As their name implies, these kits consist of a length of tubing with a one-way valve fitted, to prevent expelled air and fluid being drawn back into the system; some kits include a translucent container, which can be positioned so that the air bubbles can be more easily seen flowing from the end of the tube.

22 The kit is connected to the bleed screw, which is then opened. The user returns to the driver's seat, depresses the brake pedal with a smooth, steady stroke, and slowly releases it; this is repeated until the expelled fluid is clear of air bubbles **(see illustration)**.

23 Note that these kits simplify work so much that it is easy to forget the master cylinder reservoir fluid level; ensure that this is maintained at least above the MIN level line at all times.

Using a pressure-bleeding kit

24 These kits are usually operated by the reservoir of pressurised air contained in the spare tyre. However, note that it will be probably necessary to reduce the pressure to less than 1.0 bar (14.5 psi); refer to the instructions supplied with the kit.

25 By connecting a pressurised, fluid-filled container to the master cylinder reservoir, bleeding can be carried out simply by opening each screw in turn (in the specified sequence), and allowing the fluid to flow out until no more air bubbles can be seen in the expelled fluid.

26 This method has the advantage that the large reservoir of fluid provides an additional safeguard against air being drawn into the system during bleeding.

27 Pressure-bleeding is particularly effective when bleeding 'difficult' systems, or when bleeding the complete system at the time of routine fluid renewal.

All methods

28 When bleeding is complete, and firm pedal feel is restored, wash off any spilt fluid, tighten the bleed screws securely, and refit their dust caps.

29 Check the hydraulic fluid level in the master cylinder reservoir, and top-up if necessary (see *Weekly checks*).

30 Discard any hydraulic fluid that has been bled from the system; it will not be fit for re-use.

31 Check the feel of the brake pedal. If it feels at all spongy, air must still be present in the system, and further bleeding is required. Failure to bleed satisfactorily after a reasonable repetition of the bleeding procedure may be due to worn master cylinder seals.

2.14 Remove the dust cap (arrowed) from the first bleed screw in the sequence

3 Hydraulic pipes and hoses – renewal

Note: *Refer to the note in Section 2 concerning the dangers of hydraulic fluid.*

1 If any pipe or hose is to be renewed, minimise fluid loss by first removing the master cylinder reservoir cap, then tightening it down onto a piece of polythene to obtain an airtight seal. Alternatively, flexible hoses can be sealed, if required, using a proprietary brake hose clamp; metal brake pipe unions can be plugged (if care is taken not to allow dirt into the system) or capped immediately they are disconnected. Place a wad of rag under any union that is to be disconnected, to catch any spilt fluid.

2 If a flexible hose is to be disconnected, where applicable unscrew the brake pipe union nut before removing the spring clip which secures the hose to its mounting bracket.

3 To unscrew the union nuts, it is preferable to obtain a brake pipe spanner of the correct size; these are available from most large motor accessory shops. Failing this, a close-fitting open-ended spanner will be required, though if the nuts are tight or corroded, their flats may be rounded-off if the spanner slips. In such a case, a self-locking wrench is often the only way to unscrew a stubborn union, but it follows that the pipe and the damaged nuts must be renewed on reassembly. Always clean a union and surrounding area before disconnecting it. If disconnecting a component with more

2.22 Bleeding a brake using a one-way valve kit

3.6a Brake hose retaining clip (arrowed)

3.6b Locating peg (arrowed) for brake hose end fitting

than one union, make a careful note of the connections before disturbing any of them.

4 If a brake pipe is to be renewed, it can be obtained, cut to length and with the union nuts and end flares in place, from VW dealers. All that is then necessary is to bend it to shape, following the line of the original, before fitting it to the car. Alternatively, most motor accessory shops can make up brake pipes from kits, but this requires very careful measurement of the original, to ensure that the new pipe is of the correct length. The safest answer is usually to take the original to the shop as a pattern.

5 On refitting, do not overtighten the union nuts. It is not necessary to exercise brute force to obtain a sound joint.

6 Ensure that the pipes and hoses are correctly routed, with no kinks, and that they are secured in the clips or brackets provided **(see illustrations)**. After fitting, remove the polythene from the reservoir, and bleed the

hydraulic system as described in Section 2. Wash off any spilt fluid, and check carefully for fluid leaks.

4 Front brake pads –
removal, inspection and refitting

⚠️ *Warning: Renew both sets of brake pads at the same time – never renew the pads on only one wheel, as uneven braking may result. Note that the dust created by wear of the pads may contain asbestos, which is a health hazard. Never blow it out with compressed air, and do not inhale any of it. An approved filtering mask should be worn when working on the brakes. DO NOT use petrol or petroleum-based solvents to clean brake parts; use brake cleaner or methylated spirit only.*

FSIII calipers

Removal

1 Apply the handbrake, then jack up the front of the vehicle and support it on axle stands (see *Jacking and vehicle support*). Remove the front roadwheels.

2 Trace the brake pad wear sensor wiring (where fitted) back from the pads, and disconnect it from the wiring connector. Note the routing of the wiring, and free it from any relevant retaining clips.

3 Where applicable, to improve access, undo the retaining bolts and remove the air deflector shield from the caliper.

4 Remove the two protective rubber caps and, using a suitable hexagon key, slacken and remove the two caliper guide pins from the caliper **(see illustrations)**. Then lift the caliper, together with pads, away from the hub carrier, and tie it to the suspension strut using a suitable piece of wire. Do not allow the caliper to hang unsupported on the flexible brake hose.

5 Remove the two brake pads from the caliper, noting that the inner pad is retained in the piston by a spring clip **(see illustrations)**. If the outer pad remains on the carrier, remove it. If the original pads are to be refitted, mark them so that they can be refitted in their original positions.

Inspection

6 First measure the thickness of each brake pad. If either pad is worn at any point to the specified minimum thickness or less, all four pads must be renewed. Also, the pads should

4.4a Remove the plastic caps ...

4.4b ...unscrew the caliper guide pins (arrowed) ...

4.4c ... and remove them

4.5a Removing the outer pad...

4.5b ...and inner pad from the caliper

4.5c Front brake pads

be renewed if any are fouled with oil or grease; there is no satisfactory way of degreasing friction material, once contaminated. If any of the brake pads are worn unevenly, or are fouled with oil or grease, trace and rectify the cause before reassembly. New brake pad kits are available from VW dealers.

7 If the brake pads are still serviceable, carefully clean them using a clean, fine wire brush or similar, paying particular attention to the sides and back of the metal backing. Clean out the grooves in the friction material (where applicable), and pick out any large embedded particles of dirt or debris. Carefully clean the pad locations in the caliper body/ mounting bracket.

8 Prior to fitting the pads, check that the guide pins are free to slide easily in the caliper body bushes, and are a reasonably tight fit. Brush the dust and dirt from the caliper and piston, but *do not* inhale it, as it is injurious to health. Inspect the dust seal around the piston for damage, and the piston for evidence of fluid leaks, corrosion or damage. If attention to any of these components is necessary, refer to Section 5.

Refitting

9 If new brake pads are to be fitted, the caliper piston must be pushed back into the cylinder to make room for them. Either use a G-clamp or similar tool, or use suitable pieces of wood as levers. To avoid any dirt entering the ABS solenoid valves, connect a pipe to the bleed nipple and, as the piston is pushed back, open the nipple and allow the displaced fluid to flow through the pipe into a suitable container **(see illustration)**.

10 Fit the new pads into the caliper. The inboard pad (piston side) is marked 'Piston side' **(see illustration)**.

11 Position the caliper and pads over the brake disc ensuring that the lug on the caliper engages correctly with the hub carrier **(see illustration)**. Pass the pad warning sensor wiring (where fitted) through the caliper aperture.

12 Position the caliper until it is possible to install the caliper guide pins. Apply a little copper grease to the pins before refitting them, and tighten them to the specified torque **(see illustration)**. **Note:** *Do not exert excess pressure on the caliper, as this will deform the pad springs, resulting in noisy operation of the brakes.*

13 Where applicable, reconnect the brake pad wear sensor wiring connectors, ensuring that the wiring is correctly routed. Where applicable, refit the air deflector shield to the caliper.

14 Depress the brake pedal repeatedly, until the pads are pressed into firm contact with the brake disc, and normal (non-assisted) pedal pressure is restored.

15 Repeat the above procedure on the remaining front brake caliper.

16 Refit the roadwheels, then lower the vehicle to the ground and tighten the roadwheel bolts to the specified torque.

4.9 Open the bleed nipple as the piston is pushed back into the caliper

4.11 Ensure the pads and caliper are correctly located on the carrier

17 New pads will not give full braking efficiency until they have bedded-in. Be prepared for this, and avoid hard braking as far as possible for the first hundred miles or so after pad renewal.

FN3 calipers

Removal

18 Proceed as described in paragraphs 1 and 2.

19 Using a screwdriver, lever the brake pad retaining spring from the caliper housing **(see illustration)**.

20 Remove the two protective rubber caps and using a suitable hexagon key, slacken and remove the two caliper guide pins from the caliper **(see illustration)**. Then lift the caliper away from the brake pads and hub, and tie it to the suspension strut using a suitable piece of wire. Do not allow the caliper to hang unsupported on the flexible brake hose.

4.19 Lever the spring from the caliper housing

4.10 The inboard pad is labelled 'Piston side'

4.12 Apply copper grease to the guide pins before inserting them

21 Withdraw the two brake pads from the caliper mounting bracket. If the original pads are to be refitted, identify them so that they can be refitted in their original locations. Where applicable, disconnect the pad wear sensor wiring connector.

Inspection

22 Examine the pads and caliper as described previously in paragraphs 6 to 8. If new pads are to be refitted, refer to paragraph 9 before attempting to push the piston back into the caliper.

Refitting

23 Where applicable, remove the protective foil from the outer pad backplate. Install the outer pad in the caliper mounting bracket, ensuring that the friction material of the pad is against the brake disc. Install the inner (piston side) pad into the caliper. If the original pads are being refitted, ensure that they are refitted to their original locations as noted before

4.20 Undo the caliper guide pins

4.23a Fit the outer pad to the caliper mounting bracket ...

4.23b ... and the inner pad to the caliper piston

4.24 Install the caliper guide pins

4.25 Refit the retaining spring securely

removal. The inner pad is fitted with a retaining clip, which engages with the recess in the piston. Where applicable, note that the pad with the wear sensor wiring should be installed as the inner pad. New pads are marked with an arrow on the backing plate, which identifies the direction of rotation. Consequently, the pads should be fitted with the arrows pointing to the ground (see illustrations).

24 Press the caliper into position. Install and tighten the guide pins to the specified torque (see illustration).

25 Refit the brake pad retaining spring to the caliper housing (see illustration).

26 Where applicable, reconnect the brake pad wear sensor wiring connectors, ensuring that the wiring is correctly routed.

27 Depress the brake pedal repeatedly, until the pads are pressed into firm contact with the brake disc, and normal (non-assisted) pedal pressure is restored.

5.8 Use a small screwdriver to extract the caliper piston hydraulic seal

28 Repeat the above procedure on the remaining front brake caliper.

29 Refit the roadwheels, then lower the vehicle to the ground and tighten the roadwheel bolts to the specified torque.

30 Check the hydraulic fluid level as described in *Weekly checks*.

31 New pads will not give full braking efficiency until they have bedded-in. Be prepared for this and avoid hard braking (where possible) in the first hundred miles or so after pad renewal.

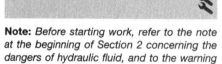

5 Front brake caliper – removal, overhaul and refitting

Note: *Before starting work, refer to the note at the beginning of Section 2 concerning the dangers of hydraulic fluid, and to the warning at the beginning of Section 4 concerning the dangers of asbestos dust.*

Removal

1 Apply the handbrake, then jack up the front of the vehicle and support it on axle stands (see *Jacking and vehicle support*). Remove the appropriate roadwheel.

2 Minimise fluid loss by first removing the master cylinder reservoir cap, and then tightening it down onto a piece of polythene, to obtain an airtight seal. Alternatively, use a brake hose clamp, a G-clamp or a similar tool to clamp the flexible hose.

3 Clean the area around the union, and then loosen the brake hose union nut.

4 Remove the brake pads as described in Section 4.

5 Unscrew the caliper from the end of the brake hose and remove it from the vehicle.

Overhaul

6 With the caliper on the bench, wipe away all traces of dust and dirt, but *avoid inhaling the dust, as it is injurious to health.*

7 Withdraw the partially ejected piston from the caliper body, and remove the dust seal.

8 Using a small screwdriver, extract the piston hydraulic seal, taking great care not to damage the caliper bore (see illustration).

9 Thoroughly clean all components, using only methylated spirit, isopropyl alcohol or clean hydraulic fluid as a cleaning medium. Never use mineral-based solvents such as petrol or paraffin, as they will attack the hydraulic system rubber components. Dry the components immediately, using compressed air or a clean, lint-free cloth. Use compressed air to blow clear the fluid passages.

10 Check all components, and renew any that are worn or damaged. Check particularly the cylinder bore and piston; these should be renewed if they are scratched, worn or corroded in any way (note that this means the renewal of the complete caliper body assembly). Similarly check the condition of the spacers/guide pins and their bushes/bores (as applicable); both spacers/pins should be undamaged and (when cleaned) a reasonably tight sliding fit in their bores. If there is any doubt about the condition of any component, renew it.

11 If the assembly is fit for further use, obtain the appropriate repair kit; the components are available from VW dealers in various combinations.

12 Renew all rubber seals, dust covers and caps disturbed on dismantling as a matter of course; these should never be re-used.

13 On reassembly, ensure that all components are clean and dry.

14 Thinly coat the piston and piston seal with brake fitting paste (VW part no G 052 150 A2). This should be included in the VW caliper overhaul/repair kit.

15 Fit the new piston (fluid) seal, using only your fingers (no tools) to manipulate it into the cylinder bore groove. Fit the new dust seal to the piston, and refit the piston to the cylinder bore using a twisting motion; ensure that the piston enters squarely into the bore. Press the piston fully into the bore, then press the dust seal into the caliper body.

Refitting

16 Screw the caliper fully onto the flexible hose union.

17 Refit the brake pads as described in Section 4.

18 Securely tighten the brake pipe union nut.

19 Remove the brake hose clamp or polythene, as applicable, and bleed the hydraulic system as described in Section 2. Note that, providing the precautions described

were taken to minimise brake fluid loss, it should only be necessary to bleed the relevant front brake.

20 Refit the roadwheel, then lower the vehicle to the ground and tighten the roadwheel bolts to the specified torque.

6 Brake disc – inspection, removal and refitting

Note: *Before starting work, refer to the note at the beginning of Section 4 concerning the dangers of asbestos dust.*
Note: *If either disc requires renewal, BOTH should be renewed at the same time, to ensure even and consistent braking. New brake pads should also be fitted.*

Front brake disc

Inspection

1 Apply the handbrake, then jack up the front of the car and support it on axle stands (see *Jacking and vehicle support*). Remove the appropriate front roadwheel.
2 Slowly rotate the brake disc so that the full area of both sides can be checked; remove the brake pads if better access is required to the inboard surface. Light scoring is normal in the area swept by the brake pads, but if heavy scoring or cracks are found, the disc must be renewed.
3 It is normal to find a lip of rust and brake dust around the perimeter of the disc; this can be scraped off if required. If, however, a lip has formed due to excessive wear of the brake pad swept area, then the disc thickness must be measured using a micrometer. Take measurements at several places around the disc, at the inside and outside of the pad swept area; if the disc has worn at any point to the specified minimum thickness or less, the disc must be renewed.
4 If the disc is thought to be warped, it can be checked for run-out. Either use a dial gauge mounted on any convenient fixed point, while the disc is slowly rotated, or use feeler blades to measure (at several points all around the disc) the clearance between the disc and a fixed point, such as the caliper mounting bracket. If the measurements obtained are at the specified maximum or beyond, the disc is excessively warped, and must be renewed; however, it is worth checking first that the hub bearings are in good condition. If the run-out is excessive, the disc must be renewed **(see illustration)**.
5 Check the disc for cracks, especially around the wheel bolt holes, and any other wear or damage, and renew if necessary.

Removal

6 Remove the brake pads as described in Section 4.
7 On models with FN3 front brake calipers, unscrew the two bolts securing the brake caliper mounting bracket to the hub carrier,

6.4 Using a DTI gauge to measure disc run-out

then slide the caliper assembly off the disc. Using a piece of wire or string, tie the caliper to the front suspension coil spring, to avoid placing any strain on the brake hose.
8 Use chalk or paint to mark the relationship of the disc to the hub, then remove the screw securing the brake disc to the hub, and remove the disc **(see illustrations)**. If it is tight, apply penetrating fluid, and tap its rear face gently with a hide or plastic mallet. The use of excessive force could cause the disc to be damaged.

Refitting

9 Refitting is the reverse of the removal procedure, noting the following points:
a) *Ensure that the mating surfaces of the disc and hub are clean and flat.*
b) *Align (if applicable) the marks made on removal, and securely tighten the disc retaining screw.*
c) *If a new disc has been fitted, use a suitable solvent to wipe any preservative coating from the disc, before refitting the caliper.*
d) *On models with FN3 brake calipers, slide the caliper into position over the disc, making sure the pads pass either side of the disc. Tighten the caliper bracket mounting bolts to the specified torque.*
e) *Fit the pads as described in Section 4.*
f) *Refit the roadwheel, then lower the vehicle to the ground and tighten the roadwheel bolts to the specified torque. On completion, repeatedly depress the*

6.8b ...and remove the front brake disc

brake pedal until normal (non-assisted) pedal pressure returns.

Rear brake disc

Inspection

10 Firmly chock the front wheels, then jack up the rear of the car and support it on axle stands. Remove the appropriate rear road-wheel.
11 Inspect the disc as described in paragraphs 1 to 5.

Removal

12 Unscrew the two bolts securing the brake caliper mounting bracket in position, then slide the caliper assembly off the disc. Using a piece of wire or string, tie the caliper to the rear suspension coil spring, to avoid placing any strain on the hydraulic brake hose.
13 Use chalk or paint to mark the relationship of the disc to the hub, then remove the screw securing the brake disc to the hub, and remove the disc **(see illustration)**. If it is tight, apply penetrating fluid, and tap its rear face gently with a hide or plastic mallet. The use of excessive force could cause the disc to be damaged.

Refitting

14 Refitting is a reversal of the removal procedure, noting the following points:
a) *Ensure that the mating surfaces of the disc and hub are clean and flat.*
b) *Align (if applicable) the marks made on removal, and securely tighten the disc retaining screw.*

6.8a Undo the retaining screw (arrowed)...

6.13 Remove the rear brake disc

8.3 Counterhold the guide pins

8.4 Remove the caliper

8.5a Remove the outer rear brake pad...

8.5b ...and inner rear brake pad

c) *If a new disc has been fitted, use a suitable solvent to wipe any preservative coating from the disc, before refitting the caliper.*

d) *Slide the caliper into position over the disc, making sure the pads pass either side of the disc. Tighten the caliper bracket mounting bolts to the specified torque. If new discs have been fitted and there is insufficient clearance between the pads to accommodate the new, thicker disc, it may be necessary to push the piston back into the caliper body as described in Section 8.*

e) *Refit the roadwheel, then lower the vehicle to the ground and tighten the roadwheel bolts to the specified torque. On completion, repeatedly depress the brake pedal until normal (non-assisted) pedal pressure returns.*

7 Front brake disc shield – removal and refitting

Removal

1 Remove the brake disc as described in Section 6.

2 Unscrew the securing bolts, and remove the brake disc shield.

Refitting

3 Refitting is a reversal of removal. Tighten the shield retaining bolts to the specified torque. Refit the brake disc with reference to Section 6.

8 Rear brake pads – removal, inspection and refitting

Note: *Before starting work, refer to the note at the beginning of Section 4 concerning the dangers of asbestos dust. New caliper mounting bolts will be required on refitting.*

Removal

1 Chock the front wheels, then jack up the rear of the vehicle and support it on axle stands (see *Jacking and vehicle support*). Remove the rear wheels.

2 Slacken the handbrake cable and detach it from the caliper as described in Section 16.

3 Slacken and remove the guide pin bolts, using a slim open-ended spanner to prevent

HAYNES HINT

In the absence of the special tool, the piston can be screwed back into the caliper using a pair of circlip pliers.

the guide pins from rotating **(see illustration)**. Discard the bolts – new ones must be used on refitting.

4 Lift the caliper away from the brake pads, and tie it to the suspension strut using a suitable piece of wire **(see illustration)**. Do not allow the caliper to hang unsupported on the flexible brake hose.

5 Withdraw the two brake pads from the caliper mounting bracket **(see illustrations)**, and on the CII38 type, recover the pad anti-rattle shims from the mounting bracket, noting their correct fitted locations. **Note:** *On the C38 type, the anti-rattle springs are attached to the pads themselves.*

Inspection

6 First measure the thickness of each brake pad. If either pad is worn at any point to the specified minimum thickness or less, **all four** pads must be renewed. Also, the pads should be renewed if any are fouled with oil or grease; there is no satisfactory way of degreasing friction material, once contaminated. If any of the brake pads are worn unevenly, or fouled with oil or grease, trace and rectify the cause before reassembly. New brake pads are available from VW dealers.

7 If the brake pads are still serviceable, carefully clean them using a clean, fine wire brush or similar, paying particular attention to the sides and back of the metal backing. Clean out the grooves in the friction material (where applicable), and pick out any large embedded particles of dirt or debris. Carefully clean the pad locations in the caliper body/ mounting bracket.

8 Prior to fitting the pads, check that the guide pins are free to slide easily in the caliper bracket, and check that the rubber guide pin gaiters are undamaged. Brush the dust and dirt from the caliper and piston, but **do not** inhale it, as it is injurious to health. Inspect the dust seal around the piston for damage, and the piston for evidence of fluid leaks, corrosion or damage. If attention to any of these components is necessary, refer to Section 9.

Refitting

9 If new brake pads are to be fitted, it will be necessary to retract the piston fully; by rotating it in a clockwise direction as it is pushed into the caliper bore **(see Haynes Hint)**. To avoid any dirt entering the ABS solenoid valves, connect a pipe to the bleed nipple, and as the piston is pushed back open the nipple and allow the displaced fluid to flow through the pipe into a suitable container.

10 On the CII38 type, fit the pad anti-rattle shims to the caliper mounting bracket, ensuring that they are correctly located (see note in paragraph 5). Install the pads in the mounting bracket, ensuring that each pad's friction material is against the brake disc. Remove the protective foil from the outer pad backing plate **(see illustrations)**.

8.10a Refit the anti-rattle shims ...

8.10b ...and install the brake pads

8.12 Hold the guide pin whilst tightening the guide pin bolt

11 Slide the caliper back into position over the pads.

12 Press the caliper into position, then install the new guide pin bolts, tightening them to the specified torque setting while retaining the guide pin with an open-ended spanner **(see illustration)**.

13 Depress the brake pedal repeatedly, until the pads are pressed into firm contact with the brake disc, and normal (non-assisted) pedal pressure is restored.

14 Repeat the above procedure on the remaining rear brake caliper.

15 Reconnect the handbrake cables to the calipers, and adjust the handbrake as described in Section 14.

16 Refit the roadwheels, then lower the vehicle to the ground and tighten the roadwheel bolts to the specified torque setting.

17 Check the hydraulic fluid level as described in *Weekly checks*.

18 New pads will not give full braking efficiency until they have bedded-in. Be prepared for this, and avoid hard braking as far as possible for the first hundred miles or so after pad renewal.

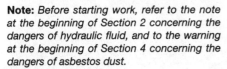

9 Rear brake caliper –
removal, overhaul and refitting

Note: *Before starting work, refer to the note at the beginning of Section 2 concerning the dangers of hydraulic fluid, and to the warning at the beginning of Section 4 concerning the dangers of asbestos dust.*

Removal

1 Chock the front wheels, then jack up the rear of the vehicle and support on axle stands (see *Jacking and vehicle support*). Remove the relevant rear wheel.

2 Minimise fluid loss by first removing the master cylinder reservoir cap, and then tightening it down onto a piece of polythene, to obtain an airtight seal. Alternatively, use a brake hose clamp, a G-clamp or a similar tool to clamp the flexible hose.

3 Clean the area around the union on the caliper, and then loosen the brake hose union nut.

4 Lift the caliper from the brake pads as described in Section 8.

5 Unscrew the caliper from the end of the flexible hose and remove it from the vehicle.

Overhaul

Note: *It is not possible to overhaul the brake caliper handbrake mechanism. If the mechanism is faulty, or fluid is leaking from the handbrake lever seal the caliper assembly must be renewed.*

6 With the caliper on the bench, wipe away all traces of dust and dirt, but avoid inhaling the dust, as it is injurious to health.

7 Using a small screwdriver, carefully prise out the dust seal from the caliper, taking care not to damage the piston.

8 Remove the piston from the caliper bore by rotating it in an anti-clockwise direction. This can be achieved using a suitable pair of circlip pliers engaged in the caliper piston slots. Once the piston turns freely but does not come out any further, the piston can be withdrawn by hand.

9 Using a small screwdriver, extract the piston hydraulic seal(s), taking care not to damage the caliper bore.

10 Withdraw the guide pins from the caliper, and remove the guide sleeve gaiters.

11 Thoroughly clean all components, using only methylated spirit, isopropyl alcohol or clean hydraulic fluid as a cleaning medium. Never use mineral-based solvents such as petrol or paraffin, as they will attack the hydraulic system rubber components. Dry the components immediately, using compressed air or a clean, lint-free cloth. Use compressed air to blow clear the fluid passages.

12 Check all components, and renew any that are worn or damaged. Check particularly the cylinder bore and piston; these should be renewed (note that this means the renewal of the complete caliper body assembly) if they are scratched, worn or corroded in any way. Similarly check the condition of the spacers/guide pins and their bushes/bores (as applicable); both spacers/pins should be undamaged and (when cleaned) a reasonably tight sliding fit in their bores. If there is any doubt about the condition of any component, renew it.

13 If the assembly is fit for further uses obtain the appropriate repair kit; the components

are available from VW dealers in various combinations.

14 Renew all rubber seals, dust covers and caps disturbed on dismantling as a matter of course; these should never be re-used.

15 On reassembly, ensure that all components are clean and dry.

16 Smear a thin coat of brake fitting paste (VW part no G 052 150 A2) on the piston, seal and caliper bore. This should be included in the overhaul/repair kit. Fit the new piston (fluid) seal, using only the fingers (no tools) to manipulate into the cylinder bore groove.

17 Fit the new dust seal to the piston groove, then refit the piston assembly. Turn the piston in a clockwise direction, using the method employed on dismantling, until it is fully retracted into the caliper bore.

18 Press the dust seal into position in the caliper housing.

19 Apply the grease supplied in the repair kit, or a copper-based brake grease or anti-seize compound, to the guide pins. Fit the new gaiters to the guide pins and fit the pins to the caliper ensuring that the gaiters are correctly located in the grooves on both the pins and caliper.

20 Prior to refitting, fill the caliper with fresh hydraulic fluid by slackening the bleed screw and pumping the fluid through the caliper until bubble-free fluid is expelled from the union hole.

Refitting

21 Screw the caliper fully onto the flexible hose union.

22 Refit the caliper over the brake pads as described in paragraphs 10 to 12 of Section 8.

23 Securely tighten the brake pipe union nut.

24 Remove the brake hose clamp or remove the polythene from the fluid reservoir, as applicable, and bleed the hydraulic system as described in Section 2. Note that, providing the precautions described were taken to minimise brake fluid loss, it should only be necessary to bleed the relevant rear brake.

25 Connect the handbrake cable to the caliper, and adjust the handbrake as described in Section 14.

26 Refit the roadwheel, then lower the vehicle to the ground and tighten the roadwheel bolts to the specified torque. On completion, check the hydraulic fluid level as described in *Weekly checks*.

10.4a Undo the retaining screw (arrowed) ...

10.4b ...and withdraw the footwell air ducting

10.5a Undo the retaining screws (arrowed) ...

10.5b ...and release the diagnostic socket

10.6 Removing the mounting bracket

10.7 Undo the crash bar mounting bolt (arrowed)

10 Brake pedal –
removal and refitting

Removal

1 Disconnect the battery negative lead. **Note:** *Before disconnecting the battery, refer to 'Disconnecting the battery' in the reference section at the rear of this manual.*
2 With reference to Chapter 11, Section 27, remove the driver's side lower facia trim panels, and the trim panel below the dash.

3 With reference to Chapter 12, Section 26, remove the driver's knee airbag.
4 Undo the retaining screw and remove the footwell air vent from above the pedal assembly **(see illustrations)**.
5 Undo the retaining screws and remove the diagnostic plug connector from the right-hand side of the mounting bracket **(see illustrations)**.
6 Undo the five retaining bolts, and then remove the knee airbag mounting bracket from around the steering column **(see illustration)**.
7 Undo the mounting bolt, and then remove the crash bar from above the brake pedal **(see illustration)**.

8 Where fitted, remove the noise insulation from the top of the brake pedal assembly **(see illustration)**.
9 It is now necessary to release the brake pedal from the ball on the vacuum servo pushrod. To do this, a VW special tool is available, but a suitable alternative can be improvised **(see illustration)**. Note that the plastic lugs in the pedal are very stiff, and it will not be possible to release them by hand. Depress and hold down the pedal, then, using the tool, release the securing lugs, and pull the pedal from the servo pushrod **(see illustrations)**.

10.8 Remove the insulation pad

10.9a Improvised special tool constructed from a modified exhaust clamp, used to release the brake pedal from the servo pushrod

10 Release the retaining clip, then undo and remove the pivot shaft nut **(see illustration)**.
11 Slide the pivot shaft bolt out, until the pedal is free, and then remove the pedal **(see illustration)**.
12 Carefully clean all components, and renew any that are worn or damaged.

Refitting

13 Prior to refitting, apply a smear of multi-purpose grease to the pivot shaft and pedal bearing surfaces.
14 Pull the servo unit pushrod down, and at the same time manoeuvre the pedal into position, ensuring that the pivot bush is correctly located.
15 Hold the servo unit pushrod, and push the pedal back onto the pushrod ball. Make sure the pedal is securely fastened to the pushrod.
16 Insert the pedal pivot bolt and tighten the retaining nut to the specified torque.
17 The remainder of the refitting procedure is the opposite of the removal; refer to the relevant Chapters where applicable.

11 Servo unit –
testing, removal and refitting

Testing

1 To test the operation of the servo unit, depress the footbrake several times to exhaust the vacuum, then start the engine whilst keeping the pedal firmly depressed. As the engine starts, there should be a noticeable 'give' in the brake pedal as the vacuum builds-up. Allow the engine to run for at least two minutes, and then switch it off. If the brake pedal is now depressed, it should feel normal, but further applications should result in the pedal feeling firmer, with the pedal stroke decreasing with each application.
2 If the servo does not operate as described, first inspect the servo unit non-return valve as described in Section 12. On diesel models, also check the operation of the vacuum pump as described in Section 21 or 22.
3 If the servo unit still fails to operate satisfactorily, the fault lies within the unit itself. Repairs to the unit are not possible – if faulty, the servo unit must be renewed.

Removal

4 Remove the master cylinder as described in Section 13.
5 Where applicable remove the heat shield from the servo, then carefully ease the vacuum hose out from the sealing grommet in the front of the servo. Where applicable, also disconnect the wiring from the servo vacuum sensor, then extract the retaining circlip with a screwdriver, and withdraw the sensor from the servo.
6 On LHD models with manual transmission, refer to Chapter 7A and disconnect the gearchange cables from the levers on the

10.9b Using the tool to release the brake pedal from the servo pushrod

transmission, then unbolt the gearchange support bracket and tie it to one side.
7 With reference to Chapter 11, remove the driver's side lower facia trim panels, and the trim panel below the dash.
8 Where fitted, unscrew the two retaining screws and remove the connecting plate between the clutch and brake pedals (manual transmission models only). Also, where fitted, remove the air duct and cover for access to the servo mounting nuts.
8 It is now necessary to release the brake pedal from the ball on the vacuum servo pushrod. To do this, a VW special tool is available, but a suitable alternative can be improvised. Note that the plastic lugs in the pedal are very stiff, and it will not be possible to release them by hand. Using the tool, release the securing lugs, and pull the pedal from the servo pushrod.
10 Again working in the footwell, undo the nuts securing the servo unit to the bulkhead, then return to the engine compartment and manoeuvre the servo unit out of position, and recover the gasket where fitted. Note that, on some RHD models, it may be necessary to remove the inlet manifold to give sufficient clearance to withdraw the servo.

Refitting

11 Check the servo unit vacuum hose sealing grommet for signs of damage or deterioration, and renew if necessary.
12 Where applicable, fit a new gasket to the rear of the servo unit, and then reposition the unit in the engine compartment.

10.10 Remove the securing clip/washer (arrowed)

10.9c Rear view of the brake pedal showing plastic lugs (arrowed) securing pedal to servo pushrod

13 From inside the vehicle, ensure that the servo unit pushrod is correctly engaged with the brake pedal, and push the pedal onto the pushrod ball. Check the pushrod ball is securely engaged, then refit the servo unit mounting nuts and tighten them to the specified torque.
14 As applicable, refit the connecting plate, air duct and cover.
15 Refit the facia trim panels.
16 On LHD models with manual transmission, refit the gearchange cables and support bracket.
17 Carefully ease the vacuum hose back into position in the servo, taking great care not to displace the sealing grommet. Refit the heat shield to the servo and, where applicable, refit the vacuum sensor and wiring.
18 Refit the master cylinder as described in Section 13 of this Chapter.
19 Where applicable on RHD models, refit the inlet manifold.
20 On completion, start the engine and check for air leaks at the vacuum hose-to-servo unit connection; check the operation of the braking system.

12 Servo non-return valve –
testing, removal and refitting

1 The non-return valve is located in the vacuum hose leading from the inlet manifold or vacuum pump to the brake servo **(see illustration)**.

10.11 Undo the upper pivot bolt (arrowed)

12.1 Non-return valve (arrowed) in vacuum pipe

Removal

2 Ease the vacuum hose out of the servo unit, taking care not to displace the grommet.

3 Note the routing of the hose, then slacken the retaining clip(s) and disconnect the opposite end of the hose assembly from the manifold/vacuum pump **(see illustration)**, and remove it from the car.

Testing

4 Examine the check valve and vacuum hose for signs of damage, and renew if necessary.

5 The valve may be tested by blowing through it in both directions; air should flow through the valve in one direction only; when blown through from the servo unit end of the valve. Renew the valve if this is not the case.

6 Examine the servo unit rubber sealing grommet for signs of damage or deterioration, and renew as necessary.

13.3 Filler cap incorporating brake fluid level warning switch

13.5 Reservoir retaining clip (arrowed)

12.3 Disconnect the hose from the vacuum pump

Refitting

7 Ensure that the sealing grommet is correctly fitted to the servo unit.

8 Ease the hose union into position in the servo, taking great care not to displace or damage the grommet.

9 Ensure that the hose is correctly routed, and connect it to the inlet manifold/vacuum pump, ensuring the hose is secured in the retaining clips.

10 On completion, start the engine and check the valve-to-servo unit connection for signs of air leaks.

---

13 Master cylinder – removal, overhaul and refitting

Note: *Before starting work, refer to the warning at the beginning of Section 2 concerning*

13.4 Clutch fluid supply hose and union

13.7 Master cylinder securing nuts (one side shown)

the dangers of hydraulic fluid. A new master cylinder O-ring will be required on refitting.

Removal

1 Disconnect the battery negative lead. **Note:** *Before disconnecting the battery, refer to 'Disconnecting the battery' in the Reference section at the rear of this manual.* Remove the engine top cover and air inlet trunking.

2 On LHD models, remove the battery and carrier with reference to Chapter 5A, Section 3.

3 Remove the master cylinder reservoir cap, disconnecting the wiring plug from the brake fluid level warning switch **(see illustration)**, and then syphon the hydraulic fluid from the reservoir. **Note:** *Do not syphon the fluid by mouth, as it is poisonous; use a syringe or an old antifreeze tester.* Also, disconnect the wiring connector from the brake light switch, at the lower part of the master cylinder.

4 On manual transmission models, disconnect and plug the clutch master cylinder supply hose from the side of the brake fluid reservoir **(see illustration)**.

5 Remove the hydraulic fluid reservoir from the top of the master cylinder. To do this, press the locking tabs outwards **(see illustration)**, and at the same time, pull the reservoir upwards from the rubber grommets.

6 Wipe clean the area around the brake pipe unions on the side of the master cylinder, and place absorbent rags beneath the pipe unions to catch any leaking fluid. Make a note of the correct fitted positions of the unions, then unscrew the union nuts and carefully withdraw the pipes. Plug or tape over the pipe ends and master cylinder orifices, to minimise the loss of brake fluid, and to prevent the entry of dirt into the system. Wash off any spilt fluid immediately with cold water.

7 Unscrew and remove the two nuts and washers securing the master cylinder to the vacuum servo unit, remove the heat shield (where fitted), then withdraw the unit from the engine compartment **(see illustration)**. Remove the O-ring from the rear of the master cylinder, and check it for damage, renew if required.

Overhaul

8 If the master cylinder is faulty, it must be renewed. Repair kits are not available from VW dealer, so the cylinder must be treated as a sealed unit.

9 The only items that can be renewed are the mounting seals for the fluid reservoir; if these show signs of deterioration, prise them out with a screwdriver. Lubricate the new seals with clean brake fluid, and press them into the master cylinder ports.

Refitting

10 Remove all traces of dirt from the master cylinder and servo unit mating surfaces, and fit a new O-ring to the groove on the master cylinder body.

11 Fit the master cylinder to the servo unit, ensuring that the servo unit pushrod enters

14.3 Removing the centre arm rest to access the adjuster (arrowed)

14.5 Slacken the adjuster nut

H32014

14.6 Turn the nuts until a gap (A) of between 1.0 and 1.5 mm can be seen

the master cylinder bore centrally. Refit the heat shield (where applicable), and the master cylinder mounting nuts, then tighten them to the specified torque.
12 Wipe clean the brake pipe unions, then refit them to the master cylinder ports and tighten them securely.
13 Refit the hydraulic fluid reservoir; making sure it is entered correctly in the rubber grommets.
14 On manual transmission models, reconnect the clutch master cylinder supply hose to the reservoir.
15 Refill the master cylinder reservoir with new fluid, and bleed the complete hydraulic system as described in Section 2.
16 Reconnect the wiring to the brake level sender unit and brake light switch as applicable.
17 On LHD models, refit the battery and carrier, with reference to Chapter 5A, Section 3.
18 Refit the engine cover and air trunking where necessary, and then reconnect the battery negative lead.

14 Handbrake – adjustment

1 To check the handbrake adjustment, first apply the footbrake firmly several times to establish correct pad-to-disc clearance, then apply and release the handbrake several times.
2 Applying normal moderate pressure, pull the handbrake lever to the fully applied position, counting the number of clicks from the handbrake ratchet mechanism. If adjustment is correct, there should be approximately 4 to 7 clicks before the handbrake is fully applied. If this is not the case, adjust as follows.
3 Depending on specification, it will be necessary to either remove the rear trim from the rear of the centre console or remove the complete centre armrest **(see illustration)**. See Chapter 11, Section 26, as applicable, to gain access to the handbrake lever.
4 Chock the front wheels, then jack up the rear of the vehicle and support it on axle stands.
5 With the handbrake fully released, slacken the handbrake adjuster nut until both the rear caliper handbrake levers are back against their stops **(see illustration)**.
6 From this point, tighten the adjusting nuts until both handbrake levers just move off the caliper stops. Ensure that the gap between each caliper handbrake lever and its stop is between 1.0 and 1.5 mm, and ensure both the right- and left-hand gaps are equal **(see illustration)**. Check that both wheels/discs rotate freely, and then check the adjustment by applying the handbrake fully and counting the clicks from the handbrake ratchet (see paragraph 2). If necessary, re-adjust.
7 Once adjustment is correct, refit the handbrake cover or centre console (as applicable).

15 Handbrake lever – removal and refitting

Removal

1 Remove the centre console as described in Chapter 11, Section 26.
2 If desired, remove the handbrake lever cover sleeve by depressing the locating tag with a screwdriver, then sliding the sleeve from the lever.
3 Disconnect the wiring plug from the handbrake 'on' warning light switch **(see illustration)**.
4 Slacken the handbrake cable adjuster nut sufficiently to allow the ends of the cables to be disengaged from the equaliser plate **(see illustrations)**.
5 Unscrew the retaining nuts, and withdraw the lever and bracket assembly from the floor **(see illustration)**.

15.3 Handbrake warning light switch (arrowed)

15.4a Handbrake cables and equaliser plate

15.4b Disengage the inner cables

15.5 Handbrake lever and bracket mounting nuts (arrowed)

16.5 Release the cable inner from its lever and withdraw the cable from the caliper

Refitting

6 Refitting is a reversal of removal, bearing in mind the following points.
a) *Prior to refitting the handbrake cover, adjust the handbrake as described in Section 14.*
b) *Check the operation of the handbrake 'on' warning switch prior to refitting the centre console.*

16 Handbrake cables – removal and refitting

Removal

1 Remove the centre console as described in Chapter 11, Section 26, to gain access to the handbrake lever. The handbrake cable consists of two sections, a right- and a left-hand section, which are linked to the lever by an equaliser plate. Each section can be removed individually.
2 Chock the front wheels, then jack up the rear of the car and support it on axle stands.
3 Slacken the handbrake cable adjuster nut sufficiently to allow the ends of the cables to be disengaged from the equaliser plate, see Section 15.
4 Working back along the length of the cable, note its correct routing, and free it from all the relevant guides and retaining clips.
5 Disengage the inner cable from the caliper handbrake lever, then remove the outer cable retaining clip and detach the cable from the caliper **(see illustration)**. Withdraw the cable from underneath the vehicle.

17.4 Unclip the handbrake warning light switch

Refitting

6 Refitting is a reversal of removal, bearing in mind the following points.
a) *When locating the handbrake cable sheath in the guide on the rear trailing arm, the cable clamping ring must lie in the middle of the clip.*
b) *Before refitting the centre console, adjust the handbrake as described in Section 14.*

17 Handbrake 'on' warning light switch – removal and refitting

Removal

1 Disconnect the battery negative lead. **Note:** *Before disconnecting the battery, refer to 'Disconnecting the battery' in the reference section at the rear of this manual.*
2 Remove the centre console, with reference to Chapter 11, Section 26 if necessary.
3 Disconnect the wiring plug from the switch.
4 Release the securing lugs, and remove the switch from the handbrake lever assembly **(see illustration)**.

Refitting

5 Refitting is a reversal of removal.

18 Brake light switch – removal and refitting

Removal

1 The brake light switch is located on the lower part of the master cylinder **(see illustration)**. Remove the engine top cover, and where applicable, remove the air inlet trunking to improve access.
2 Disconnect the wiring from the switch.
3 Unscrew the mounting bolt, then pull the switch from the bottom of the master cylinder, and remove it from the locking lug at the top.

Refitting

4 Refitting is a reversal of removal, but tighten the mounting bolt to the specified torque.

18.1 Brake light switch (arrowed)

19 Anti-lock braking system (ABS) – general information and precautions

The anti-lock braking system (ABS) fitted as standard to all models, prevents wheel lock-up under heavy braking, and not only optimises stopping distances, but also improves steering control. By electronically monitoring the speed of each roadwheel in relation to the other wheels, the system can detect when a wheel is about to lock-up, before control is actually lost. The brake fluid pressure applied to that wheel's brake caliper is then decreased and restored ('modulated') several times a second until control is regained. The system components are: four wheel-speed sensors, a hydraulic unit with integral Electronic Control Unit (ECU), brake lines and a dashboard-mounted warning light. The four wheel-speed sensors are mounted on the wheel hub carriers. Each wheel has a rotating toothed hub mounted on the driveshaft (front) or on the hub (rear). The wheel speed sensors are mounted in close proximity to these hubs. The teeth produce a voltage waveform whose frequency varies with the speed of the hubs. These waveforms are transmitted to the ECU, and used to calculate the rotational speed of each wheel. The ECU has a self-diagnostic facility, to inhibit the operation of the ABS if a fault is detected, lighting the dashboard-mounted warning light. The braking system will then revert to conventional, non-ABS operation. If the nature of the fault is not immediately obvious upon inspection, the vehicle *must* be taken to a VW dealer, who will have the diagnostic equipment required to interrogate the ABS ECU electronically and pin-point the problem.

There are two ABS systems fitted to the models covered in this Manual.

The Mark 70 version includes a traction control system (TCS), which uses the basic ABS system, with an additional pump and valves fitted to the hydraulic actuator. If wheelspin is detected at a speed below 30 mph, one of the valves opens, to allow the pump to pressurise the relevant brake, until the spinning wheel slows to a rotational speed corresponding to the speed of the vehicle. This has the effect of transferring torque to the wheel with most traction. At the same time, the throttle plate is closed slightly, to reduce the torque from the engine.

The Mark 60 version includes electronic differential locking (EDL) and an electronic stability programme (ESP). The EDL system applies the brake of the spinning wheel in order to transfer torque to the wheel with the better grip. On models with ESP, the system recognises critical driving conditions and stabilises the vehicle by individual wheel braking and by intervention in the engine control, which occurs independently of the position of the brake and accelerator pedals.

20.1 ABS hydraulic unit

20.4 Disconnect the wiring connector...

20.5 ...and unbolt the front wheel sensor

The operation of the ABS system is entirely dependent on electrical signals. To prevent the system responding to any inaccurate signals, a built-in safety circuit monitors all signals received by the ECU. If an inaccurate signal or low battery voltage is detected, the ABS system is automatically shut down, and the warning light on the instrument panel is illuminated, to inform the driver that the ABS system is not operational. Normal braking will still be available, however.

If a fault does develop in the ABS system, the car must be taken to a VW dealer for fault diagnosis and repair.

20 Anti-lock braking system (ABS) components – removal and refitting

Hydraulic unit

1 Removal and refitting of the hydraulic unit is best entrusted to a VW dealer. It is positioned in the left-hand rear corner of the engine compartment, behind the battery (see illustration). If the fluid is lost from the hydraulic unit, there is guarantee that the unit can be sufficiently filled or the fluid bled through the unit. Also a fault diagnosis check must be performed on completion using specialist equipment.

Electronic control module (ECM)

2 The ECM is mounted at the rear of the hydraulic unit, secured by three Torx screws. Although it can be separated from the hydraulic unit, due to the delicacy of the components and the need for absolute cleanliness, it is recommended that the work be entrusted to a VW dealer. See hydraulic unit information in paragraph 1.

Front wheel sensor

Removal

3 Chock the rear wheels, then firmly apply the handbrake, jack up the front of the car and support on axle stands (see *Jacking and vehicle support*). Remove the appropriate front roadwheel.
4 Disconnect the electrical connector from the sensor by carefully lifting up the retaining

tag, and pulling the connector from the sensor (see illustration).
5 Slacken and remove the hexagon socket-head bolt securing the sensor to the hub carrier, and remove the sensor from the car (see illustration).

Refitting

6 Ensure that the sensor and hub carrier sealing faces are clean.
7 Apply a thin coat of multi-purpose grease to the mounting hole inner surface, then fit the sensor to the hub carrier. Refit the retaining bolt and tighten it to the specified torque.
8 Ensure that the sensor wiring is correctly routed and retained by all the necessary clips, and reconnect the wiring connector.
9 Refit the roadwheel, then lower the car to the ground and tighten the roadwheel bolts to the specified torque.

Rear wheel sensor

Removal

10 Chock the front wheels, then jack up the rear of the car and support it on axle stands (see *Jacking and vehicle support*). Remove the appropriate roadwheel.
11 Remove the sensor as described in paragraphs 4 and 5, for front wheel speed sensor.

Refitting

12 Refit the sensor as described above in paragraphs 6 to 9.

21.5 Disconnect the small vacuum pipe

Reluctor rings

13 The reluctor rings are integral with the wheel bearings (front and rear), and can only be inspected after removal of the hub assembly. If faulty, the bearings must be renewed as described in Chapter 10, Section 3 (front) and Section 10 (rear).

21 Servo unit vacuum pump (diesel models) – testing, removal and refitting

Testing

1 The operation of the braking system vacuum pump can be checked using a vacuum gauge. First, remove the engine top cover to access the vacuum hose.
2 Disconnect the vacuum hose from the pump, and connect the gauge to the pump union using a suitable length of hose.
3 Start the engine and allow it to idle, and then measure the vacuum created by the pump. As a guide, after one minute, a minimum of approximately 500 mm Hg should be recorded. If the vacuum registered is significantly less than this, it is likely that the pump is faulty. However, seek the advice of a VW dealer before condemning the pump.
4 Reconnect the vacuum hose. Overhaul of the vacuum pump is not possible, since no major components are available separately for it. If faulty, the complete pump assembly must be renewed.

Removal

Note: *A new pump O-ring will be required on refitting.*
5 Disconnect the small vacuum pipe from the vacuum hose connector on the top of the vacuum pump (see illustration).
6 Release the securing clips and remove the air intake hose from across the end of the cylinder head, to access the vacuum pump.
7 Pull the vacuum hose from the top of the pump, noting the rubber seal may stay on the vacuum pump outlet pipe (see illustration).
8 Unscrew the four mounting bolts and withdraw the vacuum pump from the cylinder

21.7 Remove the vacuum hose and rubber seal

21.8 Vacuum pump securing bolts (arrowed)

head **(see illustration)**. Recover the O-ring seal and discard, as a new one will be required for refitting.

Refitting

9 Fit the new O-ring seal to the vacuum pump, and apply a smear of oil to aid installation.
10 Manoeuvre the vacuum pump into position, making sure that the slot in the pump drive gear aligns with the slot on the pump driveshaft.
11 Refit the pump retaining bolts, and tighten to the specified torque.
12 Reconnect the vacuum hoses and secure with the retaining clip (where fitted). If the vacuum hose seal is still fitted to the outlet pipe on the vacuum pump, remove it and fit it inside the end of the vacuum hose before refitting.
13 Refit the air intake pipe and engine top cover.

22 Servo unit electric vacuum pump – testing, removal and refitting

Note: *The electric vacuum pump is only fitted to petrol models with dual clutch (automatic) transmission.*

Testing

1 With the engine stopped, depress the brake pedal several times to exhaust the vacuum in the servo unit. The pedal will become firm.
2 Start the engine, and then slowly depress the brake pedal. An audible 'click' must be heard as the electric vacuum pump is activated, and the pedal will be easier to depress. Confirmation that the pump is running can be made by an assistant touching the pump as the pedal is depressed.
3 Overhaul of the electric vacuum pump is not possible, therefore, if faulty, the pump must be renewed.

Removal

4 The electric brake vacuum pump is located on a bracket on the front of the transmission. Apply the handbrake, and then jack up the front of the vehicle and support it on axle stands (see *Jacking and vehicle support*). Remove the left-hand front roadwheel.
5 Disconnect the vacuum hose from the pump.
6 Disconnect the wiring from the vacuum pump and release it from the clip.
7 Unscrew the bolts securing the bracket to the transmission and withdraw the assembly from the transmission.
8 Unbolt the bracket from the vacuum pump.

Refitting

9 Refitting is a reversal of removal, but tighten the mounting bolts to the specified torque.

Chapter 10
Suspension and steering systems

Contents

Degrees of difficulty

Easy, suitable for novice with little experience	**Fairly easy,** suitable for beginner with some experience	**Fairly difficult,** suitable for competent DIY mechanic	**Difficult,** suitable for experienced DIY mechanic	**Very difficult,** suitable for expert DIY or professional

Specifications

Front suspension

Type . . . .   Independent, with MacPherson struts incorporating coil springs, telescopic shock absorbers and anti-roll bar

Rear suspension

Type . . . .   Trailing arm with Multi-link transverse arms, separate gas-filled telescopic shock absorbers, coil springs and anti-roll bar

Steering

Type . . . .   Rack-and-pinion. Electro-mechanical power assistance standard

Wheel alignment and steering angles*

Front wheel:
  Camber angle:
    Standard suspension (2UA) .... -30' ± 30'
    Heavy duty suspension (2UB) .... -14' ± 30'
    Sports suspension (2UC) .... -41' ± 30'
    Maximum difference between sides (all models) .... 30'
  Castor angle:
    Standard suspension (2UA) .... 7° 34' ± 30'
    Heavy duty suspension (2UB) .... 7° 17' ± 30'
    Sports suspension (2UC) .... 7° 47' ± 30'
    Maximum difference between sides (all models) .... 30'
  Toe setting .... 10' ± 10'
  Toe-out on turns (20° left or right):
    Standard suspension (2UA) .... 1° 38' ± 20'
    Heavy duty suspension (2UB) .... 1° 38' ± 20'
    Sports suspension (2UC) .... 1° 40' ± 20'
Rear wheel:
  Camber angle... -1°20' ± 30'
  Maximum difference between sides......................... 30'
  Toe setting .... +10' ± 12.5'
  Maximum difference between sides......................... 20'
* Refer to a VW dealer for the latest recommendations.

Roadwheels

Type .... Aluminium alloy

Tyres

Size... 195/65R15, 205/60R15, 205/55R16, 225/45R17 and 225/40ZR18
Pressures .... See Lubricants, fluids and tyre pressures

Torque wrench settings	Nm	lbf ft
Front suspension		
Anti-roll bar link nuts*.....................................	65	48
Anti-roll bar to subframe:		
Stage 1..	20	15
Stage 2..	Angle-tighten a further 90°	
Hub bolt*..	See Chapter 8	
Hub to wheel bearing housing:		
Stage 1..	70	52
Stage 2..	Angle-tighten a further 90°	
Lower arm:		
To bracket*:		
Stage 1..	70	52
Stage 2..	Angle-tighten a further 180°	
To lower balljoint nuts: *		
Cast steel lower arm......................................	60	44
Forged aluminium lower arm	100	74
Mounting bracket to body:		
Stage 1..	70	52
Stage 2..	Angle-tighten a further 90°	
Mounting bracket to bracket:		
Stage 1..	50	37
Stage 2..	Angle-tighten a further 90°	
Rear engine mounting bolts: *		
To subframe:		
Stage 1..	100	74
Stage 2..	Angle-tighten a further 90°	
To transmission:		
Stage 1..	50	37
Stage 2..	Angle-tighten a further 90°	
Subframe-to-underbody/bracket bolts*:		
Stage 1..	70	52
Stage 2..	Angle-tighten a further 90°	

Torque wrench settings (continued)

	Nm	lbf ft
Splash plate to wheel bearing housing	10	7
Suspension strut:		
Bottom clamp*:		
Stage 1	70	52
Stage 2	Angle-tighten a further 90°	
Upper mounting*:		
Stage 1	15	11
Stage 2	Angle-tighten a further 90°	
Upper piston rod nut*	60	44
Vehicle level sender to subframe and lower arm	9	7

Rear suspension

	Nm	lbf ft
ABS speed sensor	8	6
Anti-roll bar:		
To subframe bolts*:		
Stage 1	20	15
Stage 2	Angle-tighten a further 90°	
Anti-roll bar link nut *	45	33
Hub to wheel bearing housing bolt: *		
Stage 1	200	148
Stage 2	Angle-tighten a further 180°	
Lower transverse link to wheel bearing housing bolt & nut: *		
Stage 1	70	52
Stage 2	Angle-tighten a further 180°	
Radius rods:		
To body:		
Stage 1	40	30
Stage 2	Angle-tighten a further 90°	
To subframe:		
Stage 1	90	66
Stage 2	Angle-tighten a further 45°	
Shock absorber:		
To wheel bearing housing	180	134
To body*:		
Stage 1	50	37
Stage 2	Angle-tighten a further 45°	
Piston rod nut*	25	18
Splash shield to wheel bearing housing	12	9
Stone deflector to transverse link	8	6
Subframe to body bolts: *		
Stage 1	70	66
Stage 2	Angle-tighten a further 180°	
Track control rod to subframe bolt & nut: *		
Stage 1	70	66
Stage 2	Angle-tighten a further 180°	
Track control rod to wheel bearing housing bolt & nut: *		
Stage 1	130	96
Stage 2	Angle-tighten a further 180°	
Trailing arm bolts: *		
To wheel bearing housing		
Stage 1	90	66
Stage 2	Angle-tighten a further 45°	
To mounting bracket:		
Stage 1	90	66
Stage 2	Angle-tighten a further 90°	
Mounting bracket to underbody:		
Stage 1	50	37
Stage 2	Angle-tighten a further 45°	
Transverse links to subframe	95	70
Upper transverse link to wheel bearing housing bolt & nut: *		
Stage 1	130	96
Stage 2	Angle-tighten a further 180°	
Vehicle level sender	5	4

Torque wrench settings (continued)

	Nm	lbf ft
Steering		
Crash bar (above brake/clutch pedal) bolt	20	15
Steering column:		
To mounting bracket bolts	20	15
Mounting bracket to body	20	15
Strut to mounting bracket/body............................	20	15
Universal joint to steering gear bolt*	30	22
Steering gear:		
To subframe*:		
Stage 1..	50	37
Stage 2..	Angle-tighten a further 90°	
Shield (Torx bolts)......................................	6	4
Steering wheel to column*:		
Stage 1..	30	22
Stage 2..	Angle-tighten a further 90°	
Track rod end to track rod	70	66
Track rod end to wheel bearing housing nut: *		
Stage 1..	20	15
Stage 2..	Angle-tighten a further 90°	
Track rod to steering gear rack	100	74
Roadwheels		
Roadwheel bolts..	120	89

Renew the nut/bolt every time it is removed

---

1 General information

The independent front suspension is of the MacPherson strut type, incorporating coil springs and integral telescopic shock absorbers. The struts are located by transverse lower suspension arms, which use rubber inner mounting bushes, and incorporate a balljoint at the outer ends. The front wheel bearing housings, which carry the wheel bearings, brake calipers and the hub/disc assemblies, are attached to the MacPherson struts by clamp bolts, and connected to the lower arms through the balljoints. A front anti-roll bar is fitted to all models. The anti-roll bar is rubber-mounted, and is connected to both lower suspension arms by short links.

The rear suspension consists of a trailing arm, rubber-mounted at its front end to the underbody, a wheel bearing housing, lower main transverse link and coil spring, track control rod, upper transverse link, and separate shock absorber. A rear anti-roll bar is fitted to all models. The anti-roll bar is rubber-mounted on the rear subframe, and is connected to the wheel bearing housings on each side by a short connecting link.

The safety steering column incorporates an intermediate shaft at its lower end. The intermediate shaft is connected to both the steering column and steering gear by universal joints, although the shaft is supplied as part of the column assembly and cannot be separated. Both the inner steering column and intermediate shaft have splined sections that collapse during a major frontal impact. The outer column is also telescopic with two sections, to facilitate reach adjustment.

The steering gear is mounted onto the front subframe, and is connected by two track rods, with balljoints at their inner and outer ends, to the steering arms projecting rearwards from the wheel bearing housings. The track rod ends are threaded to the track rods in order to allow adjustment of the front wheel toe setting. The steering gear has electro-mechanical assistance, and incorporates an integral control unit. It is only functional when the engine is running. There are no hydraulic components, and steering assistance is automatically matched to the vehicle speed, steering wheel torque and steering wheel angle.

All models are fitted with an Anti-lock Brake System (ABS), and can also be fitted with a Traction Control System (TCS), an Electronic Differential Lock (EDL) system and an Electronic Stability Program (ESP). The ABS may also be referred to as including EBD (Electronic Brake Distribution), which means it adjusts the front and rear braking forces according to the weight being carried. The TCS may also be referred to as ASR (Anti Slip Regulation).

The TCS system prevents the front wheels from losing traction during acceleration by reducing the engine output. The system is switched on automatically when the engine is started, and it utilises the ABS system sensors to monitor the rotational speeds of the front wheels.

The ESP system extends the ABS, TCS and EDL functions to reduce wheel spin in difficult driving conditions. It does this by using highly sensitive sensors that monitor the speed of the vehicle, lateral movement of the vehicle, the brake pressure, and the steering angle of the front wheels. If, for example, the vehicle is tending to oversteer, the brake will be applied to the front outer wheel to correct the situation. If the vehicle is tending to understeer, the brake will be applied to the rear inside wheel. The steering angle of the front wheels is monitored by an angle sensor on the top of the steering column.

The TCS/ESP systems should always be switched on, except when driving with snow chains, driving in snow or driving on loose surfaces, when some wheel spin may be advantageous. The ESP switch is located in the centre of the facia.

Some models are also fitted with an Electronic Differential Lock (EDL), which reduces unequal traction from the front wheels. If one front wheel spins 100 rpm or more faster than the other, the faster wheel is slowed down by applying the brake to that wheel. The system is not the same as the traditional differential lock, where the actual differential gears are locked. Because the system applies a front brake, in the event of a brake disc overheating the system will shut down until the disc has cooled. No warning light is displayed if the system shuts down. As is the case with the TCS system, the EDL system uses the ABS sensors to monitor front wheel speeds.

2 Front wheel bearing housing – removal and refitting

Note: *Renewal of the hub bearings does not require removal of the wheel bearing housing (see Section 3). This Section describes removal of the wheel bearing housing leaving the suspension strut in situ, however, if necessary it can be removed together with the suspension strut, and then separated on the bench. All self-locking nuts and bolts disturbed on removal must be renewed as a matter of course.*

Removal

1 Remove the wheel trim/hub cap (as applicable) and loosen the driveshaft retaining bolt (hub bolt) by 90° with the vehicle resting on its wheels. Also loosen the wheel bolts. **Note:** *Do not loosen the hub bolt more than 90° at this stage, or the wheel bearing may be damaged.*

2 Apply the handbrake, then jack up the front of the vehicle and support it on axle stands (see *Jacking and vehicle support*). Remove the front roadwheel.

3 Unscrew and remove the driveshaft retaining bolt.

4 Remove the ABS wheel sensor as described in Chapter 9, Section 20. Also, unbolt the brake hose/wiring bracket from the strut **(see illustration)**.

5 Remove the brake disc as described in Chapter 9, Section 6. This procedure includes removing the brake caliper; however **do not** disconnect the hydraulic brake hose from the caliper. Using a piece of wire or string, tie the caliper to the front suspension coil spring, to avoid placing any strain on the hydraulic brake hose.

6 Unbolt the splash plate from the wheel bearing housing.

7 Loosen the nut securing the steering track rod balljoint to the wheel bearing housing. To do this, fit a ring spanner to the nut, and then hold the balljoint pin stationary using an Allen key. With the nut removed, it may be possible to release the balljoint from the wheel bearing housing by turning the balljoint pin with an Allen key. If not, leave the nut on by a few turns to protect the threads, then use a universal balljoint separator to release the balljoint. Remove the nut completely once the taper has been released.

H32015

2.10a Tool used by VW technicians to open up the split wheel bearing housing

2.4 Removing the brake hose/wiring bracket

8 Unscrew the front suspension lower balljoint-to-lower arm retaining nuts **(see illustration)**, then lever the lower arm down to release the balljoint studs from the arm. Now use a soft-faced mallet to tap the driveshaft from the hub splines while pulling out the bottom end of the wheel bearing housing. If the driveshaft is tight on the splines, it may be necessary to use a puller bolted to the hub to remove it. Tie the driveshaft to one side.

9 Note which way round it is fitted, then unscrew the nut and remove the clamp bolt securing the wheel bearing housing to the bottom of the strut.

10 The wheel bearing housing must now be released from the strut. To do this, VW technicians insert a special tool into the split wheel bearing housing, and turn it through 90° to open up the clamp. A similar tool can be made out of an old screwdriver, or alternatively a suitable cold chisel can be driven into the split as a wedge. Slightly press inwards the top of the wheel bearing housing, and then push it downwards from the bottom of the strut **(see illustrations)**.

Refitting

11 Ensure that the driveshaft outer joint and hub splines are clean and dry, and then lubricate the splines with fresh engine oil. Also lubricate the threads and contact surface of the hub nut/bolt with oil.

12 Lift the wheel bearing assembly into position, and engage the hub with the splines on the outer end of the driveshaft. Fit the new hub bolt, tightening it by hand only at this stage.

2.10b Using a cold chisel to open up the wheel bearing housing and release the suspension strut

2.8 Lower ball joint securing nuts (arrowed)

13 Engage the wheel bearing housing with the bottom of the suspension strut; making sure that the hole in the side plate aligns with the holes in the split housing. Remove the tool used to open the split.

14 Insert the strut-to-wheel bearing housing clamp bolt from the front, and fit the new retaining nut. Tighten the nut to the specified torque.

15 Refit the lower arm balljoint to the lower arm, and tighten the nuts to the specified torque.

16 Refit the track rod balljoint to the wheel bearing housing, then fit a new retaining nut and tighten it to the specified torque. If necessary, hold the balljoint pin with an Allen key while tightening the nut.

17 Refit the splash plate and tighten the bolts.

18 Refit the brake disc and caliper with reference to Chapter 9, Section 6.

19 Refit the ABS wheel sensor as described in Chapter 9, Section 20.

20 Ensure that the outer joint is drawn fully into the hub, and then refit the roadwheel.

21 Have an assistant depress the brake pedal, and then tighten the driveshaft retaining bolt in the stages given in the Specifications. It is recommended that an angle gauge be used to ensure the correct tightening angle. **Note:** *The car must not be standing on its wheels when tightening the bolt, or the wheel bearing may be damaged.*

22 Lower the vehicle to the ground, tighten the roadwheel bolts, and refit the wheel trim/hub cap.

2.10c Withdrawing the wheel bearing housing from the bottom of the suspension strut

3.7a Removing the front hub/wheel bearing from the wheel bearing housing

3 Front hub bearings – renewal

Note: *The bearing is a sealed, pre-adjusted and pre-lubricated, double-row roller type, and requires no maintenance. It is bolted to the wheel bearing housing.*

1 Remove the wheel trim/hub cap (as applicable) and loosen the driveshaft retaining bolt (hub bolt) with the vehicle resting on its wheels. **Note:** *Do not loosen the hub bolt more than 90° at this stage, or the wheel bearing may be damaged.* Also loosen the wheel bolts.

2 Apply the handbrake, then jack up the front of the vehicle and support it on axle stands (see *Jacking and vehicle support*). Remove the front roadwheel.

3 Unscrew and remove the driveshaft retaining bolt.

4.3 Disconnect the anti-roll bar from the strut

4.6a Unscrew the securing nuts...

3.7b Front hub/wheel bearing

4 Remove the ABS wheel sensor as described in Chapter 9, Section 20.

5 Remove the brake disc as described in Chapter 9, Section 6. This procedure includes removing the brake caliper; however **do not** disconnect the hydraulic brake hose from the caliper. Using a piece of wire or string, tie the caliper to the front suspension coil spring, to avoid placing any strain on the hydraulic brake hose.

6 Press the driveshaft outer stub towards the transmission as far as possible, then unscrew and remove the wheel bearing retaining bolts from the rear of the housing.

7 Remove the hub/wheel bearing complete with hub from the outside of the housing while sliding it from the driveshaft splines **(see illustrations)**.

8 Fit the new wheel bearing to the housing and engage the hub splines with the driveshaft outer stub.

9 Refit the brake disc and caliper with reference to Chapter 9, Section 6.

4.5 Unscrew and remove the driveshaft retaining bolt

4.6b ...detach the lower arm from the balljoint studs...

10 Refit the ABS wheel sensor with reference to Chapter 9, Section 20.

11 Pull the driveshaft outer stub fully into the hub and fit a new hub bolt, hand-tight at this stage.

12 Ensure that the outer joint is drawn fully into the hub, and then refit the roadwheel.

13 Tighten the driveshaft retaining bolt in the stages given in the Specifications. It is recommended that an angle gauge be used to ensure the correct tightening angle. **Note:** *The car must not be standing on its wheels when tightening the bolt, or the wheel bearing will be damaged.*

14 Lower the vehicle to the ground and tighten the roadwheel bolts.

4 Front suspension strut – removal, overhaul and refitting

Note: *This section describes removal of the suspension strut leaving the wheel bearing housing in situ, however, if necessary it can be removed together with the wheel bearing housing, then separated on the bench. All self-locking nuts and bolts disturbed on removal must be renewed as a matter of course.*

Removal

1 Remove the wheel trim/hub cap (as applicable) and loosen the driveshaft retaining bolt (hub bolt) with the vehicle resting on its wheels. **Note:** *Do not loosen the hub bolt more than 90° at this stage, or the wheel bearing may be damaged.* Also loosen the wheel bolts.

2 Apply the handbrake, then jack up the front of the vehicle and support it on axle stands (see *Jacking and vehicle support*). Remove the appropriate roadwheel.

3 Unscrew the nut and disconnect the anti-roll bar link from the strut **(see illustration)**.

4 Release the ABS sensor wiring from the strut.

5 Unscrew and remove the driveshaft retaining bolt **(see illustration)**.

6 Unscrew the front suspension lower balljoint-to-lower arm retaining nuts, then lever the lower arm down to release the balljoint studs. Now use a soft-faced mallet to tap the driveshaft from the hub splines while pulling out the bottom end of the wheel bearing housing **(see illustrations)**. If the driveshaft

4.6c ...and withdraw the driveshaft from the hub splines

is tight on the splines, it may be necessary to use a puller bolted to the hub to remove it. Tie the driveshaft to one side, then refit the lower balljoint to the lower arm and secure with the nuts, hand-tightened.

7 Note which way round it is fitted, then unscrew the nut and remove the clamp bolt securing the wheel bearing housing to the bottom of the strut **(see illustration)**.

8 The wheel bearing housing must now be released from the strut. To do this, VW technicians insert a special tool into the split wheel bearing housing, and turn it through 90° to open up the clamp. A similar tool such as an Allen key can be used, or alternatively a suitable cold chisel can be driven into the split as a wedge. Slightly press inwards the top of the wheel bearing housing, and then push it downwards from the bottom of the strut **(see illustration)**. Support the wheel bearing housing to one side without straining the hydraulic brake hose.

9 Remove the wiper arms and the plenum chamber cover (Chapter 12, Section 17 & 18).

10 To ensure correct refitting, mark the strut upper mounting in relation to the body. If the reason for removing the strut is overhaul, loosen the upper mounting centre nut one turn, while holding the piston rod with an Allen key.

11 Support the strut, then unscrew the upper mounting bolts and lower the strut from under the wheel arch **(see illustrations)**.

Overhaul

⚠️ *Warning: Before attempting to dismantle the suspension strut, a suitable tool to hold the coil spring in compression must be obtained. Adjustable coil spring compressors are readily available, and are recommended for this operation. Any attempt to dismantle the strut without such a tool is likely to result in damage or personal injury.*

12 With the strut removed from the car, clean away all external dirt. If necessary, mount it upright in a vice during the dismantling procedure.

13 Fit the spring compressor, and compress the coil spring until all tension is relieved from the upper spring seat **(see illustration)**.

4.7 Remove the clamp bolt...

4.11a Unscrew the upper mounting bolts...

4.13 Compress the coil spring with the compressor tool

4.14b ...then remove the mounting, thrust bearing and coil spring

4.8 ...then use a suitable tool to expand the split, so that the strut can be pulled from the wheel bearing housing

4.11b ...and lower the strut from under the wheel arch

14 Unscrew and remove the upper centre retaining nut, whilst retaining the strut piston with a suitable Allen key, then remove the mounting, thrust bearing, and coil spring **(see illustrations)**.

15 Remove the protective sleeve and upper bearing race, and then remove the bump stop from the upper mounting **(see illustrations)**.

16 With the strut assembly now completely

4.14a Unscrew the upper centre nut...

4.15a Remove the protective sleeve...

4.15b ...and upper bearing race...

4.15c ...then remove the bump stop from the upper mounting

dismantled, examine all the components for wear, damage or deformation, and check the bearing for smoothness of operation. Renew any of the components as necessary.

17 Examine the strut for signs of fluid leakage. Check the strut piston for signs of pitting along its entire length, and check the strut body for signs of damage. While holding it in an upright position, test the operation of the strut by moving the piston through a full stroke, and then through short strokes of 50 to 100 mm. In both cases, the resistance felt should be smooth and continuous. If the resistance is jerky, or uneven, or if there is any visible sign of wear or damage to the strut, renewal is necessary.

18 If any doubt exists about the condition of the coil spring, carefully remove the spring compressors, and check the spring for distortion and signs of cracking. Renew the spring if it is damaged or distorted, or if there is any doubt as to its condition.

19 Inspect all other components for signs of damage or deterioration, and renew as necessary.

20 Assemble the bump stop to the upper mounting, and then refit the upper bearing race and protective sleeve to the mounting. The larger diameter of the bump stop must be against the upper mounting.

21 Fit the coil spring (together with the compressor tool) onto the strut, making sure its lower (larger diameter) end is correctly located against the spring seat stop.

22 Refit the thrust bearing and upper mounting, then screw on a new retaining nut.

Tighten the nut to the specified torque while holding the piston rod with an Allen key.

Refitting

23 Manoeuvre the strut into position under the wheel arch, and locate in the suspension strut turret in the previously noted position. If a new strut is being fitted, locate it so that one of the two arrows marked on the upper mounting point's forwards, and the bolt holes are aligned. Insert the bolts and tighten to the specified torque.

24 Refit the plenum chamber cover and wiper arms.

25 Engage the wheel bearing housing with the bottom of the suspension strut; making sure that the hole in the side plate aligns with the holes in the split housing. Raise the housing, while pressing it inwards to assist entry. Use a trolley jack if necessary. When fully entered, remove the tool used to open the split.

26 Insert the new strut-to-wheel bearing housing bolt from the front, and fit the new retaining nut. Tighten the nut to the specified torque.

27 Unscrew the nuts from the lower balljoint and lever down the lower arm to release it from the wheel bearing housing. Insert the outer end of the driveshaft through the hub and engage it with the splines. Fit the new hub bolt, tightening it by hand only at this stage.

28 Refit the lower arm balljoint to the lower arm, and tighten the nuts to the specified torque. Where applicable, refit the headlight range control sensor arm to the lower arm and tighten the nut.

29 Refit the ABS wheel sensor as described in Chapter 9, Section 20.

30 Ensure that the outer joint is drawn fully into the hub, and then refit the roadwheel.

31 Have an assistant depress the brake pedal, and then tighten the driveshaft retaining bolt in the stages given in the Specifications. It is recommended that an angle gauge be used to ensure the correct tightening angle. **Note:** *The car must not be standing on its wheels when tightening the bolt, or the wheel bearing may be damaged.*

32 Lower the vehicle to the ground and tighten the roadwheel bolts.

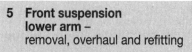

5 Front suspension lower arm – removal, overhaul and refitting

Note: *The lower arm is available in either cast steel or sheet steel ñ when renewing the arm, make sure the correct type is fitted according to model. VW subframe locating pins (T10096) or similar are required for the work in this Section, to ensure correct front wheel alignment. All self-locking nuts and bolts disturbed on removal must be renewed as a matter of course.*

Removal

1 Apply the handbrake, then jack up the front of the vehicle and support it on axle stands (see *Jacking and vehicle support*). Remove the appropriate front roadwheel and the engine compartment undertray.

2 Unscrew the front suspension lower balljoint-to-lower arm retaining nuts, then lever down the lower arm to release the arm from the balljoint studs (see illustration 4.6a and 4.6b).

3 At this stage, VW technicians use locating pins T10096 in place of the rear outer subframe mounting bolts to ensure correct front wheel alignment. If these pins are not available, only remove and refit one lower arm at a time, and mark the position of the subframe accurately with dabs of paint.

4 Unscrew and remove the rear outer mounting bolt (see illustration) and, where available, substitute it with a locating pin tightened to 20 Nm (15 lbf ft).

5 Unscrew and remove the front mounting bolt, then support the lower arm and unscrew the two rear inner mounting bolts (see illustrations). Remove the lower arm from beneath the car.

Overhaul

6 Thoroughly clean the lower arm, then check carefully for cracks or any other signs of wear or damage, paying particular attention to the rubber mounting bushes. If either bush requires renewal, take the lower arm to a VW dealer or suitably equipped garage. Alternatively, a hydraulic press and suitable spacers may be used to press the bushes out

5.4 Remove the outer mounting bolt (arrowed)

5.5a Undo the inner front mounting bolt ...

5.5b ...and the inner rear mounting bolts (arrowed)

of the arm and rear bracket, and to install the new ones. Dip the bushes in a mild solution of washing-up liquid and water. Note the following:

a) *When fitting a new front mounting bush, it must be initially tilted with one lip in the bore. As the bush is inserted, it will straighten up. Make sure the bush is centred in its bore.*

b) *After pressing a new rear mounting bush into the rear mounting bracket, press the bracket and bush fully onto the lower arm rear pivot.*

Refitting

7 Locate the lower arm on the subframe and insert the front mounting bolt loosely.

8 Insert the two rear outer mounting bolts loosely, then position the inner bolt hole in the exact position noted during removal. If a VW location pin was used on removal, the bracket will be correctly positioned on the pin. Tighten the two outer bolts to the specified torque, then remove the pin and refit the inner bolt, and tighten to the specified torque.

9 Tighten the front mounting bolt to the specified torque.

10 Lever down the lower arm and locate the balljoint studs in their holes. Fit the new nuts and tighten to the specified torque.

11 Refit the roadwheel and undertray, and lower the car to the ground.

---

6 Front suspension lower arm balljoint – removal, inspection and refitting

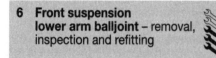

Note: *All self-locking nuts and bolts disturbed on removal must be renewed as a matter of course.*

Removal

Method 1

1 Remove the wheel bearing housing as described in Section 2.

2 Unscrew and remove the balljoint retaining nut **(see illustration)**, then release the balljoint from the wheel bearing housing using a universal balljoint separator. Withdraw the balljoint.

Method 2

3 Remove the wheel trim/hub cap (as applicable) and loosen the driveshaft retaining bolt (hub bolt) with the vehicle resting on its wheels. **Note:** *Do not loosen the hub bolt more than 90° at this stage, or the wheel bearing may be damaged.* Also loosen the wheel bolts.

4 Apply the handbrake, then jack up the front of the vehicle and support it on axle stands (see *Jacking and vehicle support*). Remove the appropriate roadwheel.

5 Unscrew and remove the driveshaft retaining bolt.

6 Unscrew the front suspension lower balljoint-to-lower arm retaining nuts, then lever

6.2 Front suspension lower arm balljoint retaining nut

the lower arm down to release the balljoint studs. Now use a soft-faced mallet to tap the driveshaft from the hub splines while pulling out the bottom end of the wheel bearing housing. If the driveshaft is tight on the splines, it may be necessary to use a puller bolted to the hub to remove it. It is not necessary to remove the driveshaft completely from the hub. Retain the wheel bearing housing away from the lower arm by inserting a block of wood between the strut and the inner body panel.

7 Unscrew and remove the balljoint retaining nut, then release the balljoint from the wheel bearing housing using a universal balljoint separator. Withdraw the balljoint.

Inspection

8 With the balljoint removed, check that it moves freely, without any sign of roughness. Check also that the balljoint rubber gaiter shows no sign of deterioration, and is free from cracks and splits. Renew as necessary.

Refitting

Method 1

9 Fit the balljoint to the wheel bearing housing and fit the new retaining nut. Tighten the nut to the specified torque, noting that the balljoint shank can be retained with an Allen key if necessary to prevent it from rotating.

10 Refit the wheel bearing housing with reference to Section 2.

Method 2

11 Fit the balljoint to the wheel bearing housing and fit the new retaining nut. Tighten the nut to the specified torque setting, noting that the

7.3 Disconnect the drop link from the anti-roll bar

balljoint shank can be retained with an Allen key if necessary to prevent it from rotating.

12 Remove the wooden block and move the strut inwards, then refit the balljoint to the lower arm using new nuts, and tighten them to the specified torque.

13 Refit the driveshaft retaining bolt and tighten it sufficiently to draw the driveshaft fully into the hub, then refit the roadwheel.

14 Have an assistant depress the brake pedal, and then tighten the driveshaft retaining bolt in the stages given in the Specifications. It is recommended that an angle gauge be used to ensure the correct tightening angle. **Note:** *The car must not be standing on its wheels when tightening the bolt, or the wheel bearing may be damaged.*

15 Lower the vehicle to the ground and tighten the roadwheel bolts.

---

7 Front anti-roll bar – removal and refitting

Note: *As the subframe must be lowered during this procedure, VW subframe locating pins (T10096) or similar are required ensuring correct front wheel alignment. All self-locking nuts and bolts disturbed on removal must be renewed as a matter of course.*

Removal

1 Apply the handbrake, then jack up the front of the vehicle and support it on axle stands (see *Jacking and vehicle support*). Remove both front roadwheels and the engine compartment undertray.

2 Inside the car, undo the nuts and remove the trim beneath the foot pedals for access to the steering column universal joint. Unscrew the clamp bolt and pull the universal joint from the steering gear pinion.

3 The anti-roll bar may be removed with or without the side links. Unscrew the nuts securing the links to the struts or anti-roll bar as required **(see illustration)**.

4 Working on each side in turn, unscrew the front suspension lower balljoint-to-lower arm retaining nuts, then disconnect the track rod ends with reference to Section 25.

5 Unscrew the bolts securing the anti-roll bar clamps to the subframe **(see illustrations)**.

7.5a Undo the two mounting bolts (arrowed) ...

7.5b ...to release the anti-roll bar clamp (arrowed) on the subframe

Mark the anti-roll bar to indicate which way round it is fitted, and the position of the rubber mounting bushes; this will aid refitting.

6 Unscrew and remove the engine/ transmission rear mounting bolts from the transmission.

7 Support the subframe with a trolley jack and block of wood. If not using the special VW locating pins T10096, accurately mark the position of the subframe to ensure correct wheel alignment.

8 Unscrew the mounting bolts and slightly lower the subframe, taking care not to damage the electrical wiring. Where available, fit the VW locating pins to facilitate refitting.

9 Lift the anti-roll bar forwards over the bracket, and lower it to the floor.

10 Carefully examine the anti-roll bar components for signs of wear, damage or deterioration, paying particular attention to the rubber mounting bushes. Renew worn components as necessary.

Refitting

11 Refitting is a reversal of removal but tighten all nuts and bolts to the specified torque where given. When refitting the subframe, align it with the marks made on removal, or use the special VW location pins before tightening the mounting bolts. To assist entry of the steering gear gaiter through the bulkhead, apply a soapy solution to it. Have the front wheel alignment checked at the earliest opportunity.

8 Front anti-roll bar connecting link – removal and refitting

Note: *All self-locking nuts and bolts disturbed on removal must be renewed as a matter of course.*

Removal

1 Apply the handbrake, then jack up the front of the vehicle and support it on axle stands (see *Jacking and vehicle support*). Remove the relevant front roadwheel.

2 Unscrew and remove the nuts securing the link to the strut and anti-roll bar.

3 Inspect the link rubbers for signs of damage or deterioration. If evident, renew the link complete.

Refitting

4 Refitting is a reversal of removal, but tighten the nuts to the specified torque.

9 Rear wheel bearing housing – removal and refitting

Removal

1 Chock the front wheels, then jack up the rear of the vehicle and support it on axle stands (see *Jacking and vehicle support*).

2 Remove the rear coil spring as described in Section 15.

3 Remove the rear hub as described in Section 10.

4 Unbolt the splash plate from the rear wheel bearing housing.

5 Disconnect the wiring, then unscrew the mounting bolt and remove the ABS sensor from the rear wheel bearing housing.

6 Unscrew the bolt securing the rear shock absorber to the rear wheel bearing housing.

7 Unscrew the bolts securing the upper transverse link and lower transverse links to the rear wheel bearing housing.

8 Unscrew the bolt securing the rear track control rod to the rear wheel bearing housing.

9 Support the rear wheel bearing housing, and then unscrew the mounting bolts from the trailing arm. Also, undo the nut and disconnect the anti-roll bar link from the trailing arm.

10 Withdraw the rear wheel bearing housing from the car.

Refitting

Note: *Do not fully tighten the rear wheel bearing housing mounting bolts until the coil spring and shock absorber have been fitted, and the suspension is fully extended.*

11 Attach the rear wheel bearing housing to the rear track control rod, and the upper and lower transverse links, and hand-tighten the bolts.

12 Fit the wheel bearing housing to the trailing arm and insert the rear, upper bolt loosely.

13 Insert the two remaining bolts securing the trailing arm to the rear wheel bearing housing, and tighten them to the specified torque.

14 Refit the splash plate and tighten the bolts to the specified torque.

9.16 Code for suspension (arrowed)

15 Refit the rear hub with reference to Section 10.

16 Position the centre of the rear hub to the following ride-height distance from the top/ centre of the wheel arch, using the trolley jack to adjust the position:

Front suspension:

a) *Standard running gear (2UA) = 382 ± 10 mm*
b) *Heavy duty running gear (2UB) = 402 ± 10 mm*
c) *Sports running gear (2UC) = 367 ± 10 mm*

Rear suspension:

a) *Standard running gear (2UA) = 380 ± 10 mm*
b) *Heavy duty running gear (2UB) = 400 ± 10 mm*
c) *Sports running gear (2UC) = 365 ± 10 mm*

The type of running gear (and all other vehicle information) can be found on a label, which is stuck to the floor panel in the luggage compartment **(see illustration)**.

17 Tighten the following bolts to their specified torque, in the order given:

a) *Track control rod.*
b) *Lower transverse link.*
c) *Upper transverse link. Position the washer so that it clears the splash plate.*

18 Refit the shock absorber lower mounting bolt and tighten to the specified torque.

19 Remove the trolley jack, then refit the rear coil spring with reference to Section 15.

20 Refit the ABS sensor and tighten the mounting bolt. Reconnect the wiring.

21 Refit the roadwheel, then lower the vehicle to the ground, tighten the roadwheel bolts, and refit the wheel trim/hub cap. Have the rear wheel alignment checked and if necessary adjusted by a VW dealer.

10 Rear hub/wheel bearings – checking and renewal

Note: *The rear wheel bearings cannot be renewed independently of the rear hub, because the outer races are formed in the hub itself. If excessive wear is evident, the rear hub must be renewed complete. The rear hub bolt must always be renewed after removal.*

Removal

1 Chock the front roadwheels, then jack up the rear of the vehicle and support on axle stands (see *Jacking and vehicle support*). Release the handbrake and remove the relevant rear roadwheel.

2 Remove the rear brake caliper and mounting bracket with reference to Chapter 9, Section 9. **Do not** disconnect the hydraulic brake pipe. Move the caliper just clear of the brake disc, without bending the hydraulic pipe excessively, and support it with welding rod or on an axle stand.

3 Undo the crosshead screw then withdraw the brake disc from the hub.

4 Remove the dust cap from the centre of the hub using a screwdriver or cold chisel **(see illustration)**.

5 Unscrew and remove the hub bolt, using a multi-spline tool. Note that it is tightened to a high torque and a socket extension bar may be required to loosen it. The bolt must be renewed whenever removed.

6 Using a suitable puller, pull the hub and bearings from the stub axle. The bearing inner race will remain on the stub axle, and a puller will be required to remove it; use a sharp cold chisel to move the race away from the stub axle base so that the puller legs can fully engage the race.

7 Examine the hub and bearings for wear, pitting and damage. If any damage is evident, renew the hub complete.

Refitting

8 Wipe clean the stub axle, then check that the bearing races are adequately lubricated with suitable grease. Check that the inner bearing race is located correctly in the hub. Also make sure that the ABS rotor is pressed firmly onto the inner end of the hub.

9 Locate the hub as far as possible on the stub axle.

10 Screw on the new bolt and tighten it to the specified torque.

11 Check the dust cap for damage and renew it if necessary. Use a hammer to carefully tap the cap into the hub. **Note:** *A badly fitting dust cap will allow moisture to enter the bearing, reducing its service life.*

12 Refit the brake disc and tighten the crosshead screw.

13 Refit the rear brake mounting bracket and caliper with reference to Chapter 9, Section 9.

14 Refit the roadwheel and lower the vehicle to the ground.

| 11 Rear radius rods – removal and refitting |

Removal

1 The rear radius rods (where fitted) extend from the front of the rear subframe to the underbody, just in front of the trailing arms. The bolts on the subframe must only be loosened or tightened with the vehicle resting on its wheels. First, mark the position of the radius rods on the underbody and subframe, using marking pens or dabs of paint, and then loosen the bolts securing the radius rod to the subframe.

2 Chock the front roadwheels, then jack up the rear of the vehicle and support on axle stands (see *Jacking and vehicle support*).

3 Unscrew the mounting bolts and remove the radius rod from under the vehicle.

Refitting

4 Locate the radius rod on the underbody and subframe and insert the mounting bolts loosely.

10.4 Removing the dust cap

5 Align the radius rod with the marks made on removal, then tighten the two underbody bolts to the specified torque.

6 Lower the vehicle to the ground, and then tighten the bolts securing the radius rod to the subframe to the specified torque. Have the rear wheel alignment checked and if necessary adjusted by a VW dealer.

| 12 Rear track control rod – removal and refitting |

Removal

1 Chock the front roadwheels, then jack up the rear of the vehicle and support on axle stands (see *Jacking and vehicle support*). Remove the relevant rear roadwheel.

2 Remove the rear coil spring as described in Section 15.

3 Undo the retaining nut and disconnect the link rod from the end of the anti-roll bar. Undo the anti-roll bar mounting bracket bolts and move the anti-roll bar to access the inner mounting bolt for the track control arm. See Section 17 for further information.

4 Note the fitted position of the rear track control rod, with either the 'closed' side facing forwards or the 'open' side facing downwards. Also, note which way round the mounting bolts are fitted.

5 To make access easier for the inner track control securing bolts, undo the retaining nuts and securing clips and remove the plastic shield from below the track control rod **(see illustration)**.

12.5 Remove the plastic undershield (arrowed)

6 Unscrew and remove the mounting bolts and nuts, and withdraw the track control rod from under the vehicle. Note the location of the special 'star' washer beneath the head of the bolt securing the outer end of the rod to the wheel bearing housing.

Refitting

7 Refitting is a reversal of removal, but tighten the bolts to the specified torque and position the rod and bolts as previously noted. Check that a clearance exists between the special 'star' washer and the track control rod. Have the rear wheel alignment checked and if necessary adjusted by a VW dealer.

| 13 Rear transverse links – removal and refitting |

Upper link

Removal

1 Chock the front roadwheels, then jack up the rear of the vehicle and support on axle stands (see *Jacking and vehicle support*). Remove the roadwheel.

2 Remove the rear coil spring as described in Section 15.

3 Release the ABS speed sensor wiring from the upper link, and then unscrew the bolt securing the link to the wheel bearing housing.

4 At the inner end of the upper link, mark the position of the eccentric bolt and subframe in relation to each other. This alignment determines the camber setting of the rear wheels.

5 Note which way round the eccentric bolt is fitted, then unscrew and remove it and withdraw the upper link.

Refitting

6 Refitting is a reversal of removal, but delay fully-tightening the mounting bolts until the rear suspension is set to the correct ride-height given in Section 9. Make sure the eccentric bolt is correctly aligned as previously noted, and also position the 'star' washer to provide a clearance between one of its points and the splash plate. Have the rear wheel alignment checked and if necessary adjusted by a VW dealer.

Lower transverse link

Removal

7 Chock the front roadwheels, then jack up the rear of the vehicle and support on axle stands (see *Jacking and vehicle support*). Remove the roadwheel.

8 Remove the rear coil spring as described in Section 15.

9 Unscrew the bolt securing the lower transverse link to the wheel bearing housing.

10 On models with headlight range control, unscrew the nut and disconnect the sensor arm from the link.

13.11 Eccentric bolts (arrowed) for adjustment of rear suspension

11 At the inner end of the lower link, mark the position of the eccentric bolt and subframe in relation to each other **(see illustration)**. This alignment determines the camber setting of the rear wheels.

12 Unscrew and remove the inner bolt and withdraw the lower transverse link from under the car.

Refitting

13 Refitting is a reversal of removal, but delay fully-tightening the mounting bolts until the rear suspension is set to the correct ride-height given in Section 9. Make sure the eccentric bolt is correctly aligned as previously noted, and also position the 'star' washer to provide a clearance between one of its points and the splash plate. Have the rear wheel alignment checked and if necessary adjusted by a VW dealer.

14 Rear trailing arm and bracket –
removal, overhaul and refitting

Removal

1 Chock the front roadwheels, then jack up the rear of the vehicle and support on axle stands (see *Jacking and vehicle support*). Remove the roadwheel.

2 Remove the rear coil spring as described in Section 15.

3 Unscrew the bolt securing the handbrake cable support to the trailing arm.

14.9a Make a vertical line along holes (1) and (2) on the arm as shown...
angle (A) = 90°

14.6 Rear trailing arm mounting bracket

4 Unscrew the nut and detach the anti-roll bar link.

5 Unscrew the bolts securing the trailing arm to the rear wheel bearing housing.

6 Mark the position of the trailing arm front mounting bracket in relation to the underbody **(see illustration)**.

7 Support the front mounting bracket on a trolley jack, then unscrew the bolts, lower the assembly and withdraw the rear trailing arm and bracket from under the vehicle.

Overhaul

8 Thoroughly clean the trailing arm and bracket, then unscrew the front pivot bolt and separate the arm from the bracket. Check carefully for cracks or any other signs of wear or damage, paying particular attention to the rubber mounting bush.

9 If the bush requires renewal, take the arm to a VW dealer or suitably equipped garage. Alternatively, a hydraulic press and suitable spacers may be used to press the bush out of the arm, and to install the new one. Dip the bush in a mild solution of washing-up liquid and water. When fitting the new bush to the front of the trailing arm, it is important to position it correctly. Make a vertical line on the arm as shown in the accompanying illustration, and then press in the new bush so that the line is between the two projections shown **(see illustrations)**.

10 With the new bush in position, locate the front of the arm in the bracket, and insert the

14.9b ...then press in the new bush so that the centre line is as shown

bolt. Position the arm in relation to the bracket as shown **(see illustration)** then tighten the bolt/nut to the specified torque. There are two types of bush.

Refitting

11 Fit the trailing arm to the wheel bearing housing and insert the bolts loosely.

12 Fit the anti-roll bar link and screw on the nut loosely.

13 Raise the front mounting bracket and locate it on the underbody in its previously noted position. Insert the new bolts and tighten to the specified torque.

14 Lower the jack then tighten the arm-to-housing bolts to the specified torque.

15 Tighten the anti-roll bar link nut.

16 Refit the handbrake cable support and tighten the bolt.

17 Refit the rear coil spring with reference to Section 15.

18 Refit the roadwheel and lower the vehicle to the ground. Have the rear wheel alignment checked and if necessary adjusted by a VW dealer.

15 Rear coil spring –
removal and refitting

⚠ *Warning: Adjustable coil spring compressors are readily available, and are recommended for this operation. Any attempt to remove the coil spring without such a tool is likely to result in damage or personal injury.*

Removal

1 Chock the front roadwheels, then jack up the rear of the vehicle and support on axle stands (see *Jacking and vehicle support*). Remove the relevant rear roadwheel.

2 Fit the tool to the coil spring and compress it until it can be removed from the trailing arm and underbody **(see illustrations)**. With the coil spring on the bench, carefully release the tension of the tool and remove it.

3 With the coil spring removed, recover the upper and lower spring seats and check them

14.10 Mounting bracket assembly to trailing arm

1 Mounting bracket	2 Trailing arm
	a = 34.0 mm

15.2a Rear coil spring

15.2b Compress the rear coil spring with the special tool...

15.2c ...then remove it from the trailing arm and underbody

for damage. Obtain new ones if necessary, but note that they are different, the lower one having a location pin that enters a hole in the lower transverse link. Also clean thoroughly the spring locations on the underbody and trailing arm.

Refitting

4 Refitting is a reversal of removal, but make sure that the lug on the lower spring seat engages in the hole in the lower transverse link and the lower end of the coil spring abuts the stop on the seat. Also make sure the upper seat is correctly engaged with the lug on the underbody **(see illustrations)**. Note: *To ensure even rear suspension, both rear coil springs should be renewed at the same time.*

15.4a Rear coil spring seat (arrowed) located in the lower transverse link...

15.4b ...and underbody

16 Rear shock absorber – removal and refitting

Note: *All self-locking nuts and bolts disturbed on removal must be renewed as a matter of course.*

Removal

1 Before removing the shock absorber, an idea of how effective it is can be gained by depressing the rear corner of the car. If the shock absorber is in good condition, the body should rise then settle in its normal position. If the body oscillates more than this, the shock absorber is defective. **Note:** *To ensure even rear suspension, both rear shock absorbers should be renewed at the same time.*
2 Chock the front roadwheels, then jack up the rear of the vehicle and support on axle stands (see *Jacking and vehicle support*). Remove the relevant rear roadwheel.
3 Remove the wheel arch liner **(see illustration)**.
4 Position a trolley jack and block of wood beneath the coil spring position on the trailing arm, and raise the arm so that the shock absorber is slightly compressed. Note on some models, it may be necessary to remove the plastic stone protection guard first. If preferred, the rear coil spring may be removed completely at this stage.
5 Unscrew the lower mounting bolt, then unscrew the upper mounting bolts

and withdraw the shock absorber **(see illustrations)**.
6 With the shock absorber on the bench, remove the cap, then unscrew the nut from

the top of the piston rod and remove the upper mounting bracket, followed by the bump stop, support ring (where fitted), protective tube, and protective cap **(see illustrations)**. **Note:** *Two*

16.3 Removing the rear wheel arch liner

16.5a Unscrew the rear shock absorber lower mounting bolt...

16.5b ...and upper mounting bolts

16.6a Remove the cap...

16.6b ...unscrew the nut while holding the piston...

16.6c ...remove the upper mounting bracket...

16.6d ...and bump stop

types of bump stop are supplied; a short version with a support ring, and a long version without a support ring.

7 If necessary, the action of the shock absorber can be checked by mounting it upright in a vice. Fully depress the rod, and then pull it up fully. The piston rod must move smoothly over its complete length.

Refitting

8 Locate the components removed from the top of the shock absorber in their correct order, and screw on a new nut. Tighten the nut and fit the cap.
9 Locate the shock absorber in the rear wheel arch, then insert the upper mounting bolts and tighten to the specified torque.
10 Extend the shock absorber if necessary, and insert the lower mounting bolt loosely.
11 Raise the trailing arm until the rear suspension is set to the correct ride-height given in Section 9, then fully tighten the shock absorber lower mounting bolt.
12 Refit the rear coil spring with reference to Section 15.
13 Refit the wheel arch liner.
14 Refit the roadwheel and lower the vehicle to the ground.

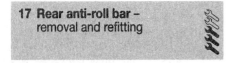

17 Rear anti-roll bar –
removal and refitting

Removal

1 Chock the front roadwheels, then jack up

17.5 Rear anti-roll bar mounting clamp bolts (arrowed)

the rear of the vehicle and support on axle stands (see *Jacking and vehicle support*). Remove both rear roadwheels.
2 Working on each side in turn, unscrew the nut and detach the connecting links from the anti-roll bar, see Section 18.
3 To make access easier, undo the retaining nuts and securing clips and remove the plastic shield from below the anti-roll bar **(see illustration 12.5)**.
4 Mark the anti-roll bar to indicate which way round it is fitted, and the position of the rubber mounting bushes; this will aid refitting.
5 Unscrew the bolts securing the anti-roll bar clamps to the rear subframe, and recover the clamps **(see illustration)**.

Refitting

6 Refitting is a reversal of removal but tighten all nuts and bolts to the specified torque.

18 Rear anti-roll bar connecting link –
removal and refitting

Removal

1 Chock the front roadwheels, then jack up the rear of the vehicle and support on axle stands (see *Jacking and vehicle support*). Remove the relevant rear roadwheel.
2 Note that upper part of the connecting link to the trailing arm has a balljoint, and the lower part of the connecting link to the end of the anti-roll bar, is fitted with a rubber bush **(see illustration)**.

18.2 Rear anti-roll bar drop link joints

3 Unscrew the nut securing the ball joint to the trailing arm, then undo the bolt and nut from the end of the anti-roll bar to withdraw the link from under the vehicle.
4 Inspect the link rubber/balljoint for signs of damage or deterioration. If evident, renew the link complete.

Refitting

5 Refitting is a reversal of removal, but renew the retaining nuts and tighten to the specified torque.

19 Vehicle level sender –
removal and refitting

Removal

1 The front sender for the headlight range control system is located on the left-hand side of the front subframe, and incorporates an arm and link attached to the left-hand front lower suspension arm. The rear sender is bolted to the left-hand side of the rear subframe, and an arm and link is attached to a bracket on the lower transverse link.
2 To remove the front sender, apply the handbrake then jack up the front of the vehicle and support it on axle stands (see *Jacking and vehicle support*). Remove the front roadwheel, and then note the position of the sender on the lower arm. Unscrew the nut and disconnect the link and bracket from the lower arm. Disconnect the wiring then unscrew the bolt and remove the sender from the front subframe.
3 To remove the rear sender, chock the front roadwheels and then jack up the rear of the vehicle and support on axle stands (see *Jacking and vehicle support*). Disconnect the wiring from the sender. Unscrew the bolts securing the link and bracket to the lower transverse link, then unscrew the bolts and remove the sender from the rear subframe.

Refitting

4 Refitting is a reversal of removal, but tighten the mounting bolts to the specified torque. If necessary, have the sender outputs checked by a VW dealer. This work requires the use of special equipment not available to the home mechanic.

20 Steering wheel –
removed and refitting

Warning: During the airbag removal and refitting procedures, avoid sitting in the front seats.

Removal

1 Set the front wheels in the straight-ahead position, and release the steering lock by inserting the ignition key.
2 Disconnect the battery negative (earth) lead and position it away from the terminal.
3 Adjust the steering column to its highest position, then extend it into the passenger compartment as far as possible, and lock it in this position.
Caution: To prevent any discharge of static electricity into the airbag circuit, temporarily touch the vehicle bodywork before disconnecting the wiring.
4 Remove the driver's airbag as described in Chapter 12, Section 26.

Warning: Position the airbag in a safe and secure place, away from the work area.

5 Using a multi-spline socket, unscrew and remove the retaining bolt, while holding the steering wheel stationary **(see illustrations)**. Discard the retaining bolt – a new one must be fitted.
6 Check if the steering wheel is marked in relation to the column. If not, use a dab of paint to mark them, and then ease the steering wheel from the column splines by firmly rocking it side-to-side **(see illustrations)**.

Refitting

7 Locate the steering wheel on the column splines making sure that the previously made marks are correctly aligned.
8 Refit the retaining bolt and tighten to the specified torque while holding the steering wheel stationary.
9 Refit the driver's airbag with reference to Chapter 12, Section 26.
10 Reconnect the battery negative (earth) lead.

20.5a using a splined tool ...

20.5b ...unscrew and remove the bolt

20.6a The steering wheel should be marked for its central position

20.6b Removing the steering wheel

21 Steering column –
removal, inspection and refitting

Removal

1 Disconnect the battery negative lead (see *Reference* at end of Manual), and position it away from the terminal.
2 Remove the steering wheel as described in Section 20.
3 Return the steering to the straight-ahead position. Adjust the steering column to its lowest position and extend it into the passenger compartment as far as possible, and then lock it in this position.
4 Unclip and remove the upper shroud from the steering column, then undo the two upper

screws and single lower screw and remove the lower shroud from the steering column, as described in Chapter 11, Section 25.
5 Remove the lower facia panels located around the steering column as described in Chapter 11, Section 27.
6 Und othe retaining screw and remove the footwell heater ducting from above the pedals **(see illustration)**.
7 Remove the switch assembly from the top of the steering column as described in Chapter 12, Section 4.
8 Disconnect the wiring connector from the transponder around the ignition switch, and then release the wiring retaining clips from the steering column **(see illustrations)**.
9 Follow the wiring loom down the length of the steering column, undo the earth cable retaining nut, release the retaining clips

21.6 Remove the footwell air ducting

21.8a Disconnect the wiring connector ...

21.8b ...and release the wiring loom securing clips

21.9a Undo the earth wire securing nut ...

21.9b ...release the retaining clips ...

21.9c ...and remove the wiring loom bracket

21.10a Remove the retaining clip ...

21.10b ...and remove the footrest trim

and remove the wiring loom from under the steering column, noting its fitted position **(see illustrations)**.

10 Working in the footwell, release the retaining clips and remove the plastic footrest trim panel **(see illustrations)**.

21.11 Recess (arrowed) for securing bolt

21.13b ...and withdraw the steering column ...

21.13a Undo the mounting bolts (one side sown) ...

21.13c ...unhooking it from the lug on the mounting bracket (arrowed)

11 Undo the clamp bolt from the steering column lower universal joint. Unscrew the clamp bolt and pull the universal joint from the steering gear pinion. Note that the pinion shaft has a cut-out to enable fitting of the clamp bolt, and the splined pinion shaft incorporates a flat making it impossible to assemble the joint to the shaft in the wrong position **(see illustration)**. Discard the clamp bolt; a new one should be used on refitting.

12 Note that the inner and outer columns, and the intermediate shaft, are telescopic, to facilitate the reach adjustment. It is important to keep the splined sections of the inner steering column engaged with each other while the steering column is removed. If they become detached due to the outer column sections being separated, especially on a vehicle, which has completed a high mileage, it is possible that rattling noises may occur.

13 Support the steering column, then unscrew and remove the mounting bolts. Withdraw the steering column from inside the car **(see illustrations)**. Note that the mounting bracket on the bulkhead has locating lug, which aligns with a slot on the top of the steering column.

Caution: Do not carry the steering column by suspending it from the universal joint or intermediate shaft, as this will damage the universal joint and steering column bushes. Also, do not bend the joints by more than 90°.

14 If necessary, remove the ignition switch/ steering column lock with reference to Section 22.

Inspection

15 The steering column is designed to collapse in the event of a front-end crash, to prevent the steering wheel injuring the driver. Before refitting the steering column, examine the column and mountings for signs of damage and deformation.

16 Check the inner column sections for signs of free play in the column bushes. If any damage or wear is found on the steering column bushes, the column must be renewed as an assembly.

17 The intermediate shaft is permanently attached to the inner column and cannot be renewed separately. Inspect the universal joints for excessive wear. If evident, the complete steering column must be renewed.

Refitting

18 Where removed, refit the ignition switch/ steering column lock/switch carrier with reference to Section 22.

22.4 Disconnect the wiring connector

22.5 Peel back the label

22.6a Insert two thin screwdrivers in the recesses (arrowed) ...

19 Refit the steering column to the bulkhead bracket, making sure it located on the locating lug. Insert the mounting bolts, and tighten to the specified torque, starting with the upper bolts first and then the lower bolts.
20 Attach the universal joint on the steering gear pinion splines, making sure the road wheels and steering wheel are in the correct position. Insert the new clamp bolt, and tighten to the specified torque.
21 Reconnect the earth cable and tighten the retaining nut, then refit the wiring harness under the steering column.
22 Reconnect the wiring to the ignition switch transponder and secure the wiring in its retaining clips.
23 Refit the footrest trim and footwell vent under the steering column.
24 Refit the light switch assembly with reference to Chapter 12, Section 4.
25 Refit the lower facia panels, as described in Chapter 11, Section 27.
26 Refit the lower and upper shrouds, as described in Chapter 11, Section 25.
27 Refit the steering wheel with reference to Section 20.
28 Reconnect the battery negative lead.
29 On models with ESP, the steering angle sensor basic settings must be set by a VW dealer using specialist diagnostic equipment.

22 Ignition switch/lock cylinder – removal and refitting

Ignition switch

Removal

1 Disconnect the battery negative lead (see *Reference* at end of Manual), and position it away from the terminal.
2 Remove the steering wheel as described in Section 20.
3 Unclip and remove the upper shroud from the steering column, then undo the two upper screws and single lower screw and remove the lower shroud from the steering column, as described in Chapter 11, Section 25.
4 Release the retaining clip and disconnect the wiring plug from the rear of the ignition switch **(see illustration)**.

22.6b ...to release the two securing clips (arrowed)...

5 Pull back the label, then using a small screwdriver prise the plastic cover from the rear of the switch **(see illustration)**.
6 Using two small screwdrivers in the slots in the outer housing release the two retaining clips, and then withdraw the ignition electrical switch **(see illustrations)**.

Refitting

7 Refit the switch to the steering lock housing and press in until the two retaining clips engage. Making sure the slot in the rear of the switch is aligned correctly.
8 Refit the plastic cover to the rear of the switch and stick down the label.
9 Reconnect the wiring plug to the ignition switch.
10 Refit the upper and lower shrouds, and tighten the screws.
11 Refit the steering wheel with reference to Section 20.
12 Reconnect the battery negative lead.

22.16a Hole provided in the ignition switch

22.6c ...and withdraw the electrical switch

Lock cylinder

Removal

13 Carry out the procedures as described in paragraphs 1 to 3.
14 Disconnect the wiring connector from the transponder around the ignition switch **(see illustration 21.8a)**.
15 Insert the ignition key and turn the lock cylinder to the drive position (which is 90° from off position).
16 Insert a piece of wire 1.2 mm in diameter in the drilling next to the ignition key, slide it in to release the locking lever, then withdraw the lock cylinder from the housing **(see illustrations)**. To make the piece of wire locate in the locking lever easier, file an angle on the end of the wire.

Refitting

17 Refit the lock cylinder with the ignition key in the Drive position, then remove the wire.

22.16b insert a thin rod through the hole ...

22.16c ...to release the locking lever (arrowed)

18 Reconnect the wiring connector to the transponder.
19 Refit the upper and lower shrouds, and tighten the screws.
20 Refit the steering wheel with reference to Section 20.
21 Reconnect the battery negative lead.

Ignition switch/lock cylinder housing

Removal

22 The ignition switch/lock housing is integral with the switch assembly carrier, which is secured to the steering column with shear-head bolts (see illustration).
23 To remove the housing first remove the steering column as described in Section 21.
24 The switch/lock carrier is secured by shear-head bolts, and the heads are broken off in the tightening procedure. To remove the old bolts, either drill them out, or use a sharp

23.5a Unclip the wiring cover ...

23.5c ...disconnect the earth cable ...

22.22 Steering lock housing shear bolts (arrowed)

cold chisel to cut off their heads or turn them anti-clockwise. Withdraw the carrier from the steering column.
25 When refitting locate the switch/lock carrier on the steering column, and insert the new shear-head bolts. Tighten the bolts until their heads break off.
26 The remaining procedure is a reversal of removal.

23 Steering gear assembly – removal, overhaul and refitting

Note: As the subframe must be lowered during this procedure, VW subframe locating pins (T10096) or similar are required to ensure correct front wheel alignment. New subframe mounting bolts, track rod balljoint nuts, steering gear retaining bolts, and an

23.5b ...disconnect the wiring from the fusebox...

23.5d ...disconnect the wiring plug connector ...

intermediate shaft universal joint clamp bolt will be required on refitting.

Removal

1 Disconnect the battery negative lead (refer to Disconnecting the battery in the Reference Chapter at the end of this manual).
2 Apply the handbrake, then jack up the front of the vehicle and support it on axle stands positioned on the underbody, leaving the subframe free (see Jacking and vehicle support). Position the steering straight-ahead, and then remove both front roadwheels. Also remove the engine compartment undertray.
3 Inside the vehicle, undo the screws and remove the plastic cover for access to the universal joint connecting the steering inner column to the steering gear pinion (see Section 21). Unscrew and remove the clamp bolt, and pull the universal joint from the pinion splines. Note: The steering gear pinion incorporates a cut-out for the clamp bolt, and therefore the joint can only be fitted in one position. Discard the clamp bolt; a new one should be used on refitting.
4 Remove the battery and carrier with reference to Chapter 5A, Section 3.
5 Unclip the plastic cover from the wiring loom, which runs along the left-hand chassis leg under the battery tray. Trace the wiring loom from the steering rack, undo the retaining nuts and disconnect the wiring connections so that the wiring loom can be removed with the steering rack assembly (see illustrations).
6 Disconnect the track rod ends from the steering arms on the front wheel bearing housings, as described in Section 25.
7 Working on each side in turn, disconnect the anti-roll bar links to the struts, as described in Section 8.
8 Working on each side in turn, unscrew the front suspension lower balljoint-to-lower arm retaining nuts, then lever the lower arms down to release the balljoint studs, as described in Section 6.
9 Unscrew and remove the engine/transmission rear mounting bolts from the transmission (see illustration).
10 Unbolt the exhaust system mounting from the subframe (see illustration). Where applicable unbolt the exhaust system heat shield from the subframe.

23.5e ...and lift the wiring loom out of position

23.9 Undo the lower rear mounting bracket bolts

23.10 Undo the exhaust mounting bracket bolts (arrowed)

23.11a Mark the position of the front (arrowed) ...

11 Support the subframe with a trolley jack and block of wood. If not using the special VW locating pins T10096, accurately mark the position of the subframe to ensure correct wheel alignment **(see illustrations)**.

12 Unscrew the mounting bolts and slightly lower the subframe **(see illustration)**, taking care not to damage the electrical wiring, as it is being lowered. Where available, fit the VW locating pins to facilitate refitting.

13 Lower the subframe together with the steering gear to the floor, then undo the retaining screws and remove the heat shield from over the steering gear.

14 Disconnect all wiring from the steering gear assembly **(see illustrations)**. Release the wiring loom from the clips along the steering rack and subframe, noting its fitted position.

Caution: Do not touch the wiring terminals on the electronic control unit, as a static electricity discharge may damage the internal components.

15 Unbolt the steering gear from the subframe **(see illustration)**, and carefully place it on the floor taking care not to damage the electronic control unit.

Overhaul

16 Examine the steering gear assembly for signs of wear or damage, and check that the rack moves freely throughout the full length of its travel, with no signs of roughness or excessive free play between the steering gear pinion and rack.

17 It is not possible to overhaul the steering gear assembly housing components, and if it is faulty, the assembly must be renewed. The only components that can be renewed individually are the steering gear gaiters, the track rod end balljoints and the track rods, as described later in this Chapter.

Refitting

18 Refitting is a reversal of removal, noting the following points:

a) Align the subframe with the marks made on removal, or use the special VW location pins before tightening the mounting bolts.

b) Make sure that all mounting bolts are tightened to the specified torque.

c) Make sure wiring connections are secure

23.11b ...and rear subframe mounting positions

and that the wiring loom is routed correctly.

d) Have the front wheel alignment checked at the earliest opportunity.

e) On models with ESP, the steering angle

23.14a Disconnect the wiring connector on the rear ...

23.14c ...then undo the wiring loom securing bolt (arrowed)

23.12 Subframe front and rear mounting bolts (one side shown)

sensor basic settings must be set by a VW dealer using specialist diagnostic equipment. If a new steering gear has been fitted, it must also be adapted to the vehicle by a VW dealer.

23.14b ...and the front of the steering electric motor ...

23.15 Steering rack mounting bolts (arrowed)

24.2 Steering rack gaiter securing clips (arrowed)

24 Steering gear rubber gaiters and track rods – renewal

Steering gear rubber gaiters

1 Remove the track rod end balljoint as described in Section 25. Also, unscrew the locking nut from the track rod arm, after noting its position.

2 Wipe clean the rubber gaiter to prevent entry of dirt or moisture. Note the fitted position of the gaiter on the track rod, then release the retaining clips and slide the gaiter off the steering gear housing and track rod (see illustration).

3 Wipe clean the track rod and the steering gear housing, and then apply a film of suitable grease to the surface of the rack. To do this, turn the steering wheel as necessary to fully extend the rack from the housing, then reposition it in its central position.

4 Carefully slide the new gaiter onto the track rod, and locate it on the steering gear housing. Position the gaiter as previously noted on removal, making sure that it is not twisted, then lift the outer sealing lip of the gaiter to equalise air pressure within the gaiter.

5 Secure the gaiter in position with new retaining clips. Where crimped-type clips are used, pull the clip as tight as possible, and locate the hooks in their slots. Remove any slack in the clip by carefully compressing the raised section. In the absence of the special crimping tool, a pair of side-cutters may be used, taking care not to cut the clip.

6 Screw on the locking nut, then refit the track rod end balljoint as described in Section 25.

Track rods

7 Remove the relevant steering gear rubber gaiter as described earlier. If there is insufficient working room with the steering gear mounted in the car, remove it as described in Section 23 and hold it in a vice while renewing the track rod.

8 Hold the steering rack stationary with one spanner on the flats provided, then loosen the balljoint nut with another spanner. Fully unscrew the nut and remove the track rod from the rack.

9 Locate the new track rod on the end of the steering rack and screw on the nut. Hold the rack stationary with one spanner and tighten the balljoint nut to the specified torque. A crow's foot adapter may be required since the track rod prevents access with a socket, and care must be taken to apply the correct torque in this situation.

10 Refit the steering gear or rubber gaiter with reference to the earlier paragraphs or Section 23. On completion check and, if necessary, adjust the front wheel alignment as described in Section 26.

25 Track rod end – removal and refitting

Note: *A new balljoint retaining nut will be required on refitting.*

Removal

1 Apply the handbrake, then jack up the front of the vehicle and support it on axle stands (see *Jacking and vehicle support*). Remove the relevant roadwheel.

2 If the track rod end is to be re-used, mark its position in relation to the track rod to facilitate refitting.

3 Unscrew the track rod end locknut by a quarter of a turn (see illustration). Do not move the locknut from this position, as it will serve as a handy reference mark on refitting.

4 Loosen and remove the nut securing the track rod end balljoint to the wheel bearing housing, and release the balljoint tapered shank using a universal balljoint separator. Note that the balljoint shank has a hexagon hole – hold the shank with an Allen key while loosening the nut (see illustrations).

5 Counting the exact number of turns necessary to do so, unscrew the track rod end from the track rod (see illustration).

6 Carefully clean the balljoint and the threads. Renew the balljoint if its movement is sloppy or too stiff, if excessively worn, or if damaged in any way; carefully check the stud taper and threads. If the balljoint gaiter is damaged, the complete balljoint assembly must be renewed; it is not possible to obtain the gaiter separately.

Refitting

7 Screw the track rod end onto the track rod by the number of turns noted on removal. This should bring the track rod end to within a quarter of a turn of the locknut, with the

25.3 Slacken the lock nut (arrowed)

25.4a Using an Allen key to hold the ball joint shank while loosening the nut

25.4b Release the track rod ball joint

25.4c Use a ball joint separator to release the track rod ball joint if it is a tight fit

25.5 Unscrewing the track rod end from the track rod

alignment marks that were made on removal (if applicable) lined up. Tighten the locknut.

8 Refit the balljoint shank to the steering arm on the wheel bearing housing, then fit a new retaining nut and tighten it to the specified torque. Hold the shank with an Allen key if necessary.

9 Refit the roadwheel, then lower the car to the ground and tighten the roadwheel bolts to the specified torque.

10 Check and, if necessary, adjust the front wheel toe setting as described in Section 26.

26 Wheel alignment and steering angles – general information

Definitions

1 A car's steering and suspension geometry is defined in three basic settings – all angles are expressed in degrees; the steering axis is defined as an imaginary line drawn through the axis of the suspension strut, extended where necessary to contact the ground **(see illustration)**.

2 Camber is the angle between each roadwheel and a vertical line drawn through its centre and tyre contact patch, when viewed from the front or rear of the car. Positive camber is when the roadwheels are tilted outwards from the vertical at the top; negative camber is when they are tilted inwards.

3 The front Camber angle is only adjustable by loosening the front suspension subframe mounting bolts and moving it slightly to one side. The camber angle can be checked using a camber checking gauge. This will also alter the Castor angle.

4 The rear Camber angle is only adjustable by loosening the upper transverse inner mounting nut, then turning the eccentric bolt (this can be turned left or right to a maximum range of 90º). The camber angle can be checked using a camber checking gauge. This will also alter the Castor angle.

5 Castor is the angle between the steering axis and a vertical line drawn through each roadwheel's centre and tyre contact patch, when viewed from the side of the car. Positive castor is when the steering axis is tilted so that it contacts the ground ahead of the vertical; negative castor is when it contacts the ground behind the vertical. Slight castor angle adjustment is possible by loosening the front suspension subframe bolts and moving it slightly to one side. This also alters the Camber angle.

6 Castor is not easily adjustable, and is given for reference only; while it can be checked using a castor checking gauge, if the figure obtained is significantly different from that specified, the car must be taken for careful checking by a professional, as the fault can only be caused by wear or damage to the body or suspension components.

7 Toe is the difference, viewed from above, between lines drawn through the roadwheel centres and the car's centre-line. Toe-in is when the roadwheels point inwards, towards each other at the front, while toe-out is when they splay outwards from each other at the front.

8 The front wheel toe setting is adjusted by screwing the track rod(s) in/out of the outer balljoint(s) to alter the effective length of the track rod assembly.

9 Rear wheel toe setting is adjusted by loosening the lower transverse inner mounting nut, and then turning the eccentric bolt (this can be turned left or right to a maximum range of 90º).

10 If the figures obtained are significantly different from that specified, the car must be taken for careful checking by a professional, as the fault can only be caused by wear or damage to the body or suspension components.

Checking and adjustment

11 Due to the special measuring equipment necessary to check the wheel alignment, and the skill required to use it properly, the checking and adjustment of these settings is best left to a VW dealer or similar expert. Note that most tyre-fitting centres now possess sophisticated checking equipment.

26.1 Front wheel geometry

Chapter 11
Bodywork and fittings

Contents

Degrees of difficulty

Easy, suitable for novice with little experience	Fairly easy, suitable for beginner with some experience	Fairly difficult, suitable for competent DIY mechanic	Difficult, suitable for experienced DIY mechanic	Very difficult, suitable for expert DIY or professional

Specifications

Torque wrench settings	Nm	lbf ft
Bonnet hinge nuts	22	16
Door hinges:		
To body*	50	37
To door*	38	28
Eccentric pin	28	21
Guide bolt	10	7
Door lock	20	15
Front window glass clamp bolts (left-hand thread)	8	6
Front seat belt adjuster bolt	20	15
Front seat belt lower mounting bolt (microencapsulated)*	40	30
Front seat belt stalk to seat frame bolt (microencapsulated)*	20	15
Front seat mounting retaining bolts	40	30
Inertia reel mounting bolts	40	30
Seat belt and stalk anchorage bolts	40	30
Tailgate hinge upper retaining bolts	10	7
Tailgate hinge lower retaining nut	24	18

Renew the bolts

1 General information

The body shell is made of pressed-steel sections, and is available in both three- and five-door Hatchback and five-door estate versions. Most components are welded together, and some use is made of structural adhesives; the front wings are bolted on.

The bonnet, door, and some other vulnerable panels are made of zinc-coated metal, and are further protected by being coated with an anti-chip primer before being sprayed.

Extensive use is made of plastic materials, mainly in the interior, but also in exterior components. The front and rear bumpers, and front grille, are injection-moulded from a synthetic material that is very strong and yet light. Plastic components such as wheel arch liners are fitted to the underside of the vehicle, to improve the body's resistance to corrosion.

2 Maintenance – bodywork and underframe

The general condition of a vehicle's bodywork is the one thing that significantly affects its value. Maintenance is easy, but needs to be regular. Neglect, particularly after minor damage, can lead quickly to further deterioration and costly repair bills. It is important also to keep watch on those parts of the vehicle not immediately visible, for instance the underside, inside all the wheel arches, and the lower part of the engine compartment.

The basic maintenance routine for the bodywork is washing – preferably with a lot of water, from a hose. This will remove all the loose solids, which may have stuck to the vehicle. It is important to flush these off in such a way as to prevent grit from scratching the finish. The wheel arches and underframe need washing in the same way, to remove any accumulated mud, which will retain moisture and tend to encourage rust. Paradoxically enough, the best time to clean the underframe and wheel arches is in wet weather, when the mud is thoroughly wet and soft. In very wet weather, the underframe is usually cleaned of large accumulations automatically, and this is a good time for inspection.

Periodically, except on vehicles with a wax-based underbody protective coating, it is a good idea to have the whole of the underframe of the vehicle steam-cleaned, engine compartment included, so that a thorough inspection can be carried out to see what minor repairs and renovations are necessary. Steam cleaning is available at many garages, and is necessary for the removal of the accumulation of oily grime, which sometimes is allowed to become thick in certain areas. If steam-cleaning facilities are not available, there are some excellent grease solvents available which can be brush-applied; the dirt can then be simply hosed off. Note that these methods should not be used on vehicles with wax-based underbody protective coating, or the coating will be removed. Such vehicles should be inspected annually, preferably just prior to Winter, when the underbody should be washed down, and any damage to the wax coating repaired. Ideally, a completely fresh coat should be applied. It would also be worth considering the use of such wax-based protection for injection into door panels, sills, box sections, etc, as an additional safeguard against rust damage, where such protection is not provided by the vehicle manufacturer.

After washing paintwork, wipe off with a chamois leather to give an unspotted clear finish. A coat of clear protective wax polish will give added protection against chemical pollutants in the air. If the paintwork sheen has dulled or oxidised, use a cleaner/polisher combination to restore the brilliance of the shine. This requires a little effort, but such dulling is usually caused because regular washing has been neglected. Care needs to be taken with metallic paintwork, as special non-abrasive cleaner/polisher is required to avoid damage to the finish. Always check that the door and ventilator opening drain holes and pipes are completely clear, so that water can be drained out. Brightwork should be treated in the same way as paintwork. Windscreens and windows can be kept clear of the smeary film that often appears, by the use of proprietary glass cleaner. Never use any form of wax or other body or chromium polish on glass.

3 Maintenance – upholstery and carpets

Mats and carpets should be brushed or vacuum-cleaned regularly, to keep them free of grit. If they are badly stained, remove them from the vehicle for scrubbing or sponging, and make quite sure they are dry before refitting. Seats and interior trim panels can be kept clean by wiping with a damp cloth. If they do become stained (which can be more apparent on light-coloured upholstery), use a little liquid detergent and a soft nail brush to scour the grime out of the grain of the material. Do not forget to keep the headlining clean in the same way as the upholstery. When using liquid cleaners inside the vehicle, do not over-wet the surfaces being cleaned. Excessive damp could get into the seams and padded interior, causing stains, offensive odours or even rot.

If the inside of the vehicle gets wet accidentally, it is worthwhile taking some trouble to dry it out properly, particularly where carpets are involved. Do not leave oil or electric heaters inside the vehicle for this purpose.

4 Minor body damage – repair

Scratches

If the scratch is very superficial, and does not penetrate to the metal of the bodywork, repair is very simple. Lightly rub the area of the scratch with a paintwork renovator, or a very fine cutting paste, to remove loose paint from the scratch, and to clear the surrounding bodywork of wax polish. Rinse the area with clean water.

Apply touch-up paint to the scratch using a fine paintbrush; continue to apply fine layers of paint until the surface of the paint in the scratch is level with the surrounding paintwork. Allow the new paint at least two weeks to harden, and then blend it into the surrounding paintwork by rubbing the scratch area with a paintwork renovator or a very fine cutting paste. Finally, apply wax polish.

Where the scratch has penetrated right through to the metal of the bodywork, causing the metal to rust, a different repair technique is required. Remove any loose rust from the bottom of the scratch with a penknife, and then apply rust-inhibiting paint to prevent the formation of rust in the future. Using a rubber or nylon applicator, fill the scratch with bodystopper paste. If required, this paste can be mixed with cellulose thinners to provide a very thin paste that is ideal for filling narrow scratches. Before the stopper-paste in the scratch hardens, wrap a piece of smooth cotton rag around the top of a finger. Dip the finger in cellulose thinners, and quickly sweep it across the surface of the stopper-paste in the scratch; this will ensure that the surface of the stopper-paste is slightly hollowed. The scratch can now be painted over as described earlier in this Section.

Dents

When deep denting of the vehicle's bodywork has taken place, the first task is to pull the dent out, until the affected bodywork almost attains its original shape. There is little point in trying to restore the original shape completely, as the metal in the damaged area will have stretched on impact, and cannot be reshaped fully to its original contour. It is better to bring the level of the dent up to a point, which is about 3 mm below the level of the surrounding bodywork. In cases where the dent is very shallow anyway, it is not worth trying to pull it out at all. If the underside of the dent is accessible, it can be hammered out gently from behind, using a mallet with a wooden or plastic head. Whilst doing this, hold a suitable block of wood firmly against the outside of the panel, to absorb the impact from the hammer blows and thus prevent a large area of the bodywork from being 'belled-out'.

Should the dent be in a section of the

bodywork that has a double skin, or some other factor making it inaccessible from behind, a different technique is called for. Drill several small holes through the metal inside the area – particularly in the deeper section. Then screw long self-tapping screws into the holes, just sufficiently for them to gain a good purchase in the metal. Now the dent can be pulled out by pulling on the protruding heads of the screws with a pair of pliers.

The next stage of the repair is the removal of the paint from the damaged area, and from an inch or so of the surrounding 'sound' bodywork. This is accomplished most easily by using a wire brush or abrasive pad on a power drill, although it can be done just as effectively by hand, using sheets of abrasive paper. To complete the preparation for filling, score the surface of the bare metal with a screwdriver or the tang of a file, or alternatively, drill small holes in the affected area. This will provide a really good 'key' for the filler paste.

To complete the repair, see the Section on filling and respraying.

Rust holes or gashes

Remove all paint from the affected area, and from an inch or so of the surrounding 'sound' bodywork, using an abrasive pad or a wire brush on a power drill. If these are not available, a few sheets of abrasive paper will do the job most effectively. With the paint removed, you will be able to judge the severity of the corrosion, and therefore decide whether to renew the whole panel (if this is possible) or to repair the affected area. New body panels are not as expensive as most people think, and it is often quicker and more satisfactory to fit a new panel than to attempt to repair large areas of corrosion.

Remove all fittings from the affected area, except those, which will act as a guide to the original shape of the damaged bodywork (e.g. headlight shells etc). Then, using tin snips or a hacksaw blade, remove all loose metal and any other metal badly affected by corrosion. Hammer the edges of the hole inwards, in order to create a slight depression for the filler paste.

Wire-brush the affected area to remove the powdery rust from the surface of the remaining metal. Paint the affected area with rust-inhibiting paint, if the back of the rusted area is accessible, treat this also.

Before filling can take place, it will be necessary to block the hole in some way. This can be achieved by the use of aluminium or plastic mesh, or aluminium tape.

Aluminium or plastic mesh, or glassfibre matting, is probably the best material to use for a large hole. Cut a piece to the approximate size and shape of the hole to be filled, then position it in the hole so that its edges are below the level of the surrounding bodywork. It can be retained in position by several blobs of filler paste around its periphery.

Aluminium tape should be used for small or very narrow holes. Pull a piece off the roll, trim it to the approximate size and shape required, then pull off the backing paper (if used) and stick the tape over the hole; it can be overlapped if the thickness of one piece is insufficient. Burnish down the edges of the tape with the handle of a screwdriver or similar, to ensure that the tape is securely attached to the metal underneath.

Filling and respraying

Before using this Section, see the Sections on dent, deep scratch, rust holes and gash repairs.

Many types of bodyfiller are available, but generally speaking, those proprietary kits, which contain a tin of filler paste and a tube of resin hardener, are best for this type of repair. A wide, flexible plastic or nylon applicator will be found invaluable for imparting a smooth and well-contoured finish to the surface of the filler.

Mix up a little filler on a clean piece of card or board – measure the hardener carefully (follow the maker's instructions on the pack), otherwise the filler will set too rapidly or too slowly. Using the applicator, apply the filler paste to the prepared area; draw the applicator across the surface of the filler to achieve the correct contour and to level the surface. As soon as a contour that approximates to the correct one is achieved, stop working the paste – if you carry on too long, the paste will become sticky and begin to 'pick-up' on the applicator. Continue to add thin layers of filler paste at 20-minute intervals, until the level of the filler is just proud of the surrounding bodywork.

Once the filler has hardened, the excess can be removed using a metal plane or file. From then on, progressively finer grades of abrasive paper should be used, starting with a 40-grade production paper, and finishing with a 400-grade wet-and-dry paper. Always wrap the abrasive paper around a flat rubber, cork, or wooden block – otherwise the surface of the filler will not be completely flat. During the smoothing of the filler surface, the wet-and-dry paper should be periodically rinsed in water. This will ensure that a very smooth finish is imparted to the filler at the final stage.

At this stage, the dent should be surrounded by a ring of bare metal, which in turn should be encircled by the finely 'feathered' edge of the good paintwork. Rinse the repair area with clean water, until all of the dust produced by the rubbing-down operation has gone.

Spray the whole area with a light coat of primer – this will show up any imperfections in the surface of the filler. Repair these imperfections with fresh filler paste or bodystopper, and once more smooth the surface with abrasive paper. Repeat this spray-and-repair procedure until you are satisfied that the surface of the filler, and the feathered edge of the paintwork, are perfect. Clean the repair area with clean water, and allow to dry fully.

The repair area is now ready for final spraying. Paint spraying must be carried out in a warm, dry, windless and dust-free atmosphere. This condition can be created artificially if you have access to a large indoor working area, but if you are forced to work in the open, you will have to pick your day very carefully. If you are working indoors, dousing the floor in the work area with water will help to settle the dust, which would otherwise be in the atmosphere. If the repair area is confined to one body panel, mask off the surrounding panels; this will help to minimise the effects of a slight mis-match in paint colours. Bodywork fittings (e.g. chrome strips, door handles etc) will also need to be masked off. Use genuine masking tape, and several thicknesses of newspaper, for the masking operations.

Before commencing to spray, agitate the aerosol can thoroughly, and then spray a test area (an old tin, or similar) until the technique is mastered. Cover the repair area with a thick coat of primer; the thickness should be built up using several thin layers of paint, rather than one thick one. Using 400-grade wet-and-dry paper, rub down the surface of the primer until it is really smooth. While doing this, the work area should be thoroughly doused with water, and the wet-and-dry paper periodically rinsed in water. Allow to dry before spraying on more paint.

Spray on the top coat, again building up the thickness by using several thin layers of paint. Start spraying at one edge of the repair area, and then, using a side-to-side motion, work until the whole repair area and about 2 inches of the surrounding original paintwork is covered. Remove all masking material 10 to 15 minutes after spraying on the final coat of paint.

Allow the new paint at least two weeks to harden, then, using a paintwork renovator, or a very fine cutting paste, blend the edges of the paint into the existing paintwork. Finally, apply wax polish.

Plastic components

With the use of more and more plastic body components by the vehicle manufacturers (e.g. bumpers. spoilers, and in some cases major body panels), rectification of more serious damage to such items has become a matter of either entrusting repair work to a specialist in this field, or renewing complete components. Repair of such damage by the DIY owner is not really feasible, owing to the cost of the equipment and materials required for effecting such repairs. The basic technique involves making a groove along the line of the crack in the plastic, using a rotary burr in a power drill. The damaged part is then welded back together, using a hot-air gun to heat up and fuse a plastic filler rod into the groove. Any excess plastic is then removed, and the area rubbed down to a smooth finish. It is important that a filler rod of the correct plastic is used, as body components can be made of a variety of different types (e.g. polycarbonate, ABS, polypropylene).

6.2 Undo the screws (arrowed)

6.3a Insert plastic too

...the securing clips (arrowed) ...

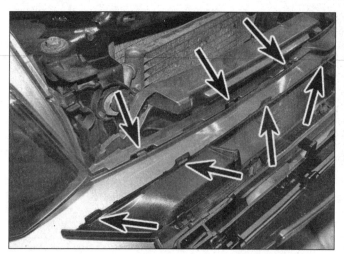

6.3c ...along the lower edge of the grille

6.4 Undo the two retaining screws (arrowed)

Damage of a less serious nature (abrasions, minor cracks etc) can be repaired by the DIY owner using a two-part epoxy filler repair material. Once mixed in equal proportions, this is used in similar fashion to the bodywork filler used on metal panels. The filler is usually cured in twenty to thirty minutes, ready for sanding and painting.

If the owner is renewing a complete component himself, or if he has repaired it with epoxy filler, he will be left with the problem of finding a suitable paint for finishing which is compatible with the type of plastic used. At one time, the use of a universal paint was not possible, owing to the complex range of plastics encountered in body component applications. Standard paints, generally speaking, will not bond to plastic or rubber satisfactorily. However, it is now possible to obtain a plastic body parts finishing kit, which consists of a pre-primer treatment, a primer and coloured top coat. Full instructions are normally supplied with a kit, but basically, the method of use is to first apply the pre-primer to the component concerned, and allow it to dry for up to 30 minutes. Then the primer is applied, and left to dry for about an hour before finally applying the special-coloured top coat. The result is a correctly coloured component, where the paint will flex with the plastic or rubber, a property that standard paint does not normally possess.

5 Major body damage – repair

Where serious damage has occurred, or large areas need renewal due to neglect, it means that complete new panels will need welding-in, and this is best left to professionals. If the damage is due to impact, it will also be necessary to check completely the alignment of the body shell, and this can only be carried out accurately by a VW dealer using special jigs. If the body is left misaligned, it is primarily dangerous, as the car will not handle properly, and secondly, uneven stresses will be imposed on the steering, suspension and possibly transmission, causing abnormal wear, or complete failure, particularly to such items as the tyres.

6 Front bumper – removal and refitting

Note: *Depending on the model, it is possible that slight changes to the removal and refitting procedures may be necessary.*

Removal

1 Apply the handbrake, then jack up the front of the vehicle and support it on axle stands (see *Jacking and vehicle support*).
2 Open the bonnet, and undo the screws securing the top of the grille trim panel to the engine compartment crossbar **(see illustration)**.
3 Using a lever, starting from the outer edges, carefully unclip the retaining clips along the lower part of the upper grille trim panel. Withdraw the grille forwards away from the top of the front bumper trim **(see illustrations)**.
4 Undo the 2 screws from the top of the bumper trim panel **(see illustration)**. These are located behind the upper grille panel, which is why it needs to be removed, as described in paragraph 3.
5 Undo the lower screws from under the front edge of the bumper **(see illustration)**.

6.5 Undo the lower retaining screws (arrowed)

6 Working at each side in turn, undo the screws securing the wheel arch liners to the ends of the bumper **(see illustrations)**.

7 Remove the front number plate from the bumper. Depending on where the screws for the number plate are fitted, they may be screwed through the front crossmember.

8 With the help of an assistant, unclip each end of the bumper from the edge of the front wing panels, and withdraw the front bumper from the vehicle until it is possible to disconnect the wiring from the foglights and parking sensors (where fitted) **(see illustration)**. Also, where applicable, release the headlamp washer hoses.

9 On models with headlamp washers, remove the washer jets as described in Chapter 12, Section 20.

Refitting

10 Refitting is a reverse of the removal procedure, ensuring that the bumper ends engage correctly with the locating clips on the edge of the front wing panels. Make sure all wiring plugs are reconnected.

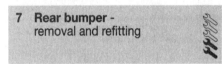

---

7 Rear bumper - removal and refitting

Note: *Depending on the model, it is possible that slight changes to the removal and refitting procedures may be necessary.*

Removal

1 To improve access, chock the front wheels, and then jack up the rear of the vehicle and support it on axle stands (see *Jacking and vehicle support*).

2 Remove the rear light clusters as described in Chapter 12, Section 7.

Hatchback

3 Remove the ten screws (five each side) securing the wheel arch liners to the bumper ends **(see illustrations)**. Note on GTD and GTi models there are six screws securing the bumper at each side.

4 Undo the two screws from under the lower edge of the bumper **(see illustration)**.

5 With the help of an assistant, release

6.6a Undo the upper retaining screw ...

6.6b ...and lower...

6.6c ...retaining screws (arrowed)

6.8 Unclip the sides of the bumper from the wing panel

the bumper from the rear wing panels at the left- and right-hand ends, and then withdraw the bumper from the rear of the vehicle until it is possible to disconnect the

7.3a Remove the upper screws (arrowed) ...

wiring from the number plate lights **(see illustration)**.

Estate

6 Remove the six screws (three each side)

7.3b ...and the lower screws - Hatchback

7.3c Remove the screw (arrowed) from under the bumper- Hatchback

7.4 Undo the two retaining screws (arrowed) - Hatchback

7.5 Release the two retaining clips (arrowed) - Hatchback

7.6 Remove the screws (arrowed) - Estate

7.7 Release the retaining clip - Estate

7.8 Undo the two retaining screws (arrowed) - Estate

7.9 Remove the screws (arrowed) from under the rear of the bumper - Estate

7.10 Undo the screws from inside the light aperture - Estate

7.11a Slide the bumper backwards...

securing the wheel arch liners to the bumper ends **(see illustration)**.
7 Pull back the top of the wheel arch liner and release the retaining clip that joins the bumper to the rear wing panel **(see illustration)**.

8 On the right-hand side of the vehicle, undo the two screws from under the lower edge of the bumper **(see illustration)**.
9 Undo the three screws securing the lower edge of the rear bumper **(see illustration)**.

10 Undo the four upper mounting screws (two each side), from inside the rear light unit recess **(see illustration)**.
11 With the help of an assistant, release the bumper from the rear wing panels at the left- and right-hand ends, and then withdraw the bumper from the rear of the vehicle until it is possible to disconnect the wiring from the number plate lights **(see illustrations)**.

Refitting

12 Refitting is a reverse of the removal procedure, ensuring that the bumper ends engage correctly with the rear wing panels, as the bumper is refitted. Where applicable, retrieve the centre pins for the plastic rivets from the plastic slides before refitting the bumper - renew if necessary.

7.11b ... to release the mounting bracket lugs (arrowed) - Estate

8.2a Unclip the washer jet...

8 Bonnet - removal, refitting and adjustment

Removal

1 Open the bonnet and using a pencil or felt tip pen, mark the outline of each bonnet hinge relative to the bonnet, to use as a guide on refitting.
2 Unclip the washer jets from under the rear edge of the bonnet and disconnect the washer hose **(see illustrations)**, release the rubber grommet from the bonnet and withdraw the washer hose from inside the bonnet. Where necessary, disconnect the wiring from the jet heating elements.

8.2b ...disconnect the washer hose...

8.2c ...then release the grommet from the bonnet

3 Before disconnecting the gas support strut, get help from an assistant to support the bonnet. Using a small screwdriver release the retaining clip, and then disconnect the gas support strut from the bonnet **(see illustration)**.

4 Undo the bonnet retaining nuts **(see illustration)**, and then carefully lift the bonnet clear. Store the bonnet out of the way in a safe place.

5 Inspect the bonnet hinges for signs of wear and free play at the pivots, and if necessary renew. Each hinge is secured to the body by two bolts **(see illustration)**, mark the position of the hinge on the body then undo the retaining bolts and remove it from the vehicle. On refitting, align the new hinge with the marks and tighten the retaining bolts.

Refitting and adjustment

6 With the aid of an assistant, offer up the bonnet and loosely fit the retaining bolts. Align the hinges with the marks made on removal, and then tighten the retaining bolts/nuts securely.

7 Refit the washer hose, wiring and gas strut in the reverse order of removal.

8 Close the bonnet, and check for alignment with the adjacent panels. If necessary, unscrew the hinge bolts and re-align the bonnet. Once the bonnet is correctly aligned **(see illustration)**, tighten the hinge bolts. Check that the bonnet fastens and releases satisfactorily.

---

9 Bonnet release cable – removal and refitting

Removal

1 The bonnet release cable is in two sections, with a coupling located over the right-hand headlight. To remove the shorter front section cable, remove the bonnet lock as described in Section 10.

2 To remove the rear section, first release the coupling from over the right-hand headlight, as described in Section 10, paragraph 4

3 Working inside the vehicle, locate the release lever and pull it out slightly, then insert

a small screwdriver into the gap between the release lever and its securing clip. Let the lever return to its original position, then release the clip with a screwdriver (note that the clip may fall behind the trim) **(see illustrations)**.

4 Unscrew the plastic screws, and then unclip the trim at the centre and at the lower edge from sill trim to remove **(see illustrations)**.

5 Undo the two retaining screws and withdraw

8.3 Unclip the bonnet strut

8.4 Bonnet to hinge securing nuts

8.5 Hinge to inner wing panel securing bolts

8.8 Adjustment bolt (arrowed)

9.3a Insert a screwdriver...

9.3b ...to release the securing clip

9.4a Undo the retaining nut...

9.4b ...and screw/clip...

9.4c ...then remove the trim panel

9.5 Unscrew the release handle mounting bracket screws

9.6 Unclip the release cable from the lever

9.11 Slide the securing clip into the handle before refitting

the bonnet release lever from the bottom of the A-pillar **(see illustration)**.

6 Release the outer cable from the mounting bracket, and then detach the inner cable from the lever **(see illustration)**.

7 Working along the length of the cable and noting its correct routing, free it from any retaining clips/ties and release the cable sealing grommet from the bulkhead.

8 Tie a length of string to the end of the cable inside the vehicle, and then withdraw the cable through into the engine compartment.

9 Once the cable is free, untie the string and leave it in position in the vehicle; the string can then be used to draw the new cable back into position.

Refitting

10 Tie the inner end of the string to the end of the cable, and then use the string to draw the bonnet release cable back from the engine

compartment. Once the cable is through, untie the string.

11 Refitting is a reversal of removal. **Note:** *Before refitting the bonnet release lever, fit the securing clip back into the lever (see illustration), and then push the lever back into place.*

12 Ensure the rubber grommet in the bulkhead is fitted correctly, and the cable is correctly routed and secured to all the relevant retaining clips.

13 Before closing the bonnet, check the operation of the release lever and cable.

10 Bonnet lock – removal and refitting

Removal

1 Open the bonnet then remove the radiator grille, as described in Section 6.

2 Disconnect the wiring for the contact micro switch at the connector located by the left-hand headlight **(see illustration)**.

3 If required, to access the bonnet release cable join adapter, undo the retaining bolts and remove the mounting bracket from across the top of the headlight.

4 Disconnect the bonnet cable at the join adapter located above the right-hand headlight, unclip the outer cable and release the two parts of the release cable **(see illustrations)**. This will allow the cable to be disconnected from the bonnet lock.

5 Note the location of the three mounting bolts in their slots to ease refitting, then unscrew and remove them **(see illustration)**.

6 Prise the lock from the crossmember, and withdraw the cable and wiring from the front panel, release them from any retaining clips. If required lift the cover and unhook the release cable end fitting from the lock lever **(see illustrations)**.

10.2 Disconnecting the bonnet lock wiring connector (arrowed) next to the radiator top hose

10.4a Unclip the cable joiner from under the panel...

10.4b ...and disconnect the two parts of the cable

10.5 Unscrew the mounting bolts...

10.6a ...prise the lock from the crossmember...

10.6b ...and disconnect the cable

11.1a Release the rubber bellows for wiring protection

11.1b Release the locking lever

11.2 Door hinge guide bolt (arrowed)

Refitting

7 Refitting is a reversal of removal. Check that the bonnet fastens and releases satisfactorily before refitting the radiator grille. If adjustment is necessary, loosen the bonnet lock retaining bolts, and adjust the position of the lock to suit. Finally, tighten the bolts.

11 Door –
removal, refitting and adjustment

Note: *The hinge bolts must always be renewed if loosened.*

Removal

1 Open the door then disconnect the wiring at the A- or B-pillar as applicable. To do this, first release the rubber bellows by pressing the small tab at the top. Pull down the locking lever and disconnect the wiring plug **(see illustrations)**.
2 Each hinge has a guide bolt screwed into it, although, the bolt is not threaded into the pillar, but acts purely as a guide. **Do not** remove these bolts **(see illustration)**.
3 Unscrew and remove the upper and lower bolts from the lower hinge, then support the door and unscrew the upper bolt from the upper hinge **(see illustrations)**. Withdraw the door from the A- or B-pillar.
4 Examine the hinges for signs of wear or damage. If renewal is necessary, the upper hinge can be unbolted from the A- or B-pillar from the outside, however, one of the lower hinge retaining bolts is fitted from inside the vehicle making it necessary to remove the A- or B-pillar trim for access to them. Before

11.3a Front door lower hinge bolts...

removing them, accurately mark their position to ensure correct refitting.

Refitting

5 Where renewed, fit the hinges and tighten the bolts to the specified torque. Refit the trim.
6 With the aid of an assistant, offer up the door to the vehicle and locate it on the guide bolts. Fit the new hinge bolts and tighten to the specified torque.
7 Reconnect the wiring plug and secure with the locking lever, then refit the rubber bellows.

Adjustment

8 Close the door and check the door alignment with the surrounding body panels. There must be an even gap all around, and the door must be level with the surrounding body panels.
9 Slight adjustment can be made with the eccentric pin of the upper hinge **(see illustration)**, loosen the lock nut, and then turn the pin as necessary, retighten the lock-nut when completed.

11.3b ...and upper hinge bolt

10 Check that the striker enters the door lock centrally as the door is closed, and if necessary adjust the position of the striker by loosening its mounting bolts **(see illustration)**.

12 Door inner trim panel –
removal and refitting

Note: *As the trim panel is removed, the retaining studs/clips may be damaged; it may be necessary to get new retaining studs/clips before proceeding.*

Removal

1 Switch off the ignition, before disconnecting any wiring connectors.

Front door

2 Using a lever, unclip the trim cover from the door grab handle and remove it **(see illustration)**.

11.9 Slacken lock nut (arrowed)

11.10 Door lock striker mounted on the B-pillar

12.2 Prise out the grip inner trim panel...

12.3 ...and undo the retaining screws (arrowed)

12.4 Undo the door trim lower screw (arrowed)

12.5 Unclip the door trim panel

12.6a Disconnect the LED wiring connector

12.6b Disconnect the door lock switch wiring connector

window slot. Support the panel away from the door **(see illustration)**.

6 On the driver's door panel, disconnect the wiring connectors from the door locking switch and the red LED warning light on the top of the trim panel **(see illustrations)**.

7 Disconnect the wiring connectors from the door switch panel/control unit **(see illustrations)**.

8 Release the retaining clip and unhook the cable from the inner door handle **(see illustration)**, and then remove the trim panel from the vehicle.

9 If required the trim from the inside of the door mirror can now be unclipped from the door frame, disconnect the wiring from the 'tweeter' loudspeaker, as the trim is removed. Refer to Chapter 12, Section 22.

Rear doors

10 Using a lever, carefully unclip the trim cover from the door grab handle and remove it **(see illustration)**.

11 Undo the two trim panel screws located in the door trim panel, behind the trim cover **(see illustration)**.

12 Undo the retaining screw from the lower edge of the trim panel **(see illustration)**.

13 On models with manually operated windows, note the closed position of the handle, then press the spacer/clip located under the handle towards the front of the car, and slide the handle from the splines **(see illustrations)**.

14 Release the door trim panel studs, carefully levering between the panel and door with a flat-bladed lever. Work around the outside of the panel, and when all the studs

3 Undo the three trim panel screws located in the door trim panel, behind the trim cover **(see illustration)**.

4 Undo the retaining screw from the lower edge of the trim panel **(see illustration)**.

5 Release the door trim panel studs, carefully levering between the panel and door with a flat-bladed lever. Work around the outside of the panel, and when all the studs are released, lift the door trim panel upwards and off the

12.7a Disconnect the switch panel...

12.7b ...wiring connectors

12.8 Unclip the operating cable from the handle

12.10 Prise out the grip inner trim panel...

12.11 ...and undo the retaining screws (arrowed)

12.12 Undo the door trim lower screw (arrowed)

12.13a Press the spacer/clip...

12.13b ...and slide the handle from the splines

12.14 Release the door panel from the studs...

12.15 ...and disconnect the wiring from the switch...

12.16 ...and the speaker

are released, lift the door trim panel upwards and off the window slot. Support the panel away from the door **(see illustration)**.

15 On models with electrically operated windows, disconnect the wiring connector from the switch **(see illustration)**.

16 Disconnect the wiring from the 'tweeter' loudspeaker, as the trim is removed **(see illustration)**.

17 Release the retaining clip and unhook the cable from the inner door handle **(see illustration)**, and then remove the trim panel from the vehicle.

Refitting

18 Before refitting, check whether any of the trim panel retaining studs where broken on removal, and renew them as necessary. If the retaining clip part of the stud has been pressed down onto the stud, then it will need to be withdraw back into position to the end of the centre stud **(see illustration)**. The Refitting of the trim panel is then a reversal of removal. Check the operation of the door electrical equipment.

---

13 Door handle and lock components – removal and refitting

Removal

Front door lock cylinder/ door handle end cap

1 If working on the right-hand door handle,

using a small screwdriver in the slot provided **(see illustrations)**, carefully release the trim cover from the door lock cylinder.

2 Open the door, then remove the plastic cap

in the rear edge of the door to locate the two retaining screws **(see illustration)**.

3 Unscrew both of the retaining screws until they stop, and then push the inner screw

12.17 Unclip the operating cable from the handle

13.1a Insert a small screwdriver...

12.18 Clip on the left shows how it should be, before refitting the trim panel

13.1b ...and remove the plastic cap

13.2 Unclip the cover from the lock securing screws

13.3a Slacken the two retaining screws...

13.3b ...and push on the inner one...

13.3c ...to release the locking clamp - in the direction of the arrow

inwards to release the locking clamp **(see illustrations)**.

4 Pull out the door handle, and hold it in this position whilst withdrawing the lock cylinder/end cap out of the door handle, then release the handle to its original position **(see illustration)**.

13.4 Pull out the door handle, and remove the door lock cylinder

Rear door handle end cap

5 Open the door, then remove the rubber cap at the rear edge of the door **(see illustration)**.
6 VW technicians use a special tool (T10389) to release the locking clamp. A tool can be made

out of a length of metal rod, put a small hook on the end, and then wrap a piece of insulation tape 60mm up from the end **(see illustration)**.
7 Insert the special tool approx 60mm (up to the insulation tape) through the hole in the door. With the hook facing to the inside of the vehicle, hook the locking clamp and pull, to release the clamp **(see illustration)**.
8 Pull out the door handle, and hold it in this position whilst withdrawing the end cap out of the door handle, then release the handle to its original position **(see illustration)**.

Exterior door handle

9 Depending on door being worked on, either remove the door lock cylinder or door handle end cap, as described previously in this Section.
10 Slide the handle to the rear edge of the door, to release it from the door handle mounting plate, and then pull it outwards and disengage it from the door **(see illustrations)**.

13.5 Remove the rubber grommet (arrowed)

13.6 Insert hooked rod...

13.7 ...to pull the locking clip - in the direction of the arrow

13.8 Pull out the door handle, and remove the end cap

13.10a Slide the door handle to the rear of the door...

13.10b ...then pull it out to remove

13.11 Unclip the seal from the door panel

13.14 Undo the retaining screw (arrowed)

13.16a Unclip the outer cable...

11 If required recover the gasket from the handle aperture (see illustration).

Exterior door handle mounting plate

12 Remove the exterior door handle as described in paragraphs 9 and 10.
13 Remove the window regulator as described in Section 14.
14 On the outside of the door, undo the retaining screw from the front of the door handle aperture (see illustration).
15 Reaching up inside the door, slide the mounting plate to the rear edge of the door, and then disengage it from the outer panel.
16 Unhook the operating cable from the mounting bracket, unclip the end of the outer cable and release the inner cable from the mechanism (see illustrations).

Door lock

17 Remove the window regulator as described in Section 14.
18 Undo the two lock retaining screws, on the rear edge of the door (see illustration).
19 Reaching up inside the door, remove the door lock assembly, releasing the grommet for the wiring connector, as it is removed (see illustration).
20 To remove the operating cables, release the locking pegs, twist the outer cable and then unhook the inner cable from the operating lever (see illustrations).

Refitting

Front door lock cylinder/ door handle end cap

21 Pull out the door handle and insert the

13.16b ...hinge the outer cable upwards...

13.16c...and unhook the inner cable from the lever

lock cylinder housing/end cap into the door handle mounting-bracket.
22 Whilst keeping pressure on the lock cylinder/end cap, tighten both retaining screws in the rear edge of the door to 4Nm.

23 Where applicable, refit the plastic trim cover to the door lock cylinder.
24 Refit the plastic cap to cover the screws at the rear edge of the door.
25 Check the operation of the lock before

13.18 Undo the door lock retaining bolts...

13.19 ...and remove the lock assembly from inside the door panel

13.20a Using a small screwdriver...

13.20b ...release the outer cable locking pegs...

13.20c ...then disconnect the inner cable from the lever

13.27 Press the locking clamp back into position

14.2 Prise out the access caps

14.4 Loosen the window glass clamps clockwise (arrowed)

closing the door, by sliding a screwdriver into the lock to operate the mechanism.

Rear door handle end cap

26 Pull out the door handle and insert the end cap into the door handle mounting-bracket.

14.7 Remove the access cap...

14.9a Use a 5.0 mm bolt to pull out the plastic centre roll-pin...

14.5 Lift the window glass from the front door

27 Whilst keeping pressure on the handle end cap, use a screwdriver through the hole in the rear edge of the door to press the locking clamp back into position **(see illustration)**.
28 Refit the rubber grommet to cover the hole at the rear edge of the door.

14.8 ...to remove the roll pins (arrowed)

14.9b ...then use an 8.0 mm bolt to pull out the plastic outer roll-pin

29 Check the operation of the lock before closing the door, by sliding a screwdriver into the lock to operate the mechanism.

Exterior door handle

30 If removed, locate the gasket on the door handle aperture.
31 Insert the handle into the door at the front end first, and then pivot the handle back into position. Slide the handle towards the front of the door, to lock it back in position in the mounting bracket.
32 Refit the lock cylinder or handle end cap, as described previously in this Section and check that it functions correctly.

Exterior door handle mounting plate

33 Refitting is a reversal of removal, making sure the operating cable is attached to the mounting bracket securely. Tighten the securing screw securely. Refit the window regulator as described in Section 14.

Door lock

34 Refitting is a reversal of removal, making sure the operating cables are attached to the lock securely. Tighten the mounting bolts to the specified torque. Refit the window regulator as described in Section 14.

14 Door window glass and regulator – removal and refitting

Removal

Front door window glass

1 Remove the door inner trim panel as described in Section 12.
2 Prise out the access caps from the inner door panel **(see illustration)**.
3 Temporarily connect the wiring to the switches, then switch on the ignition, and lower the window glass until the bolts attaching it to the regulator are visible through the access holes. If there is a fault with the electric motor, remove the motor in order to lower the glass.
4 Loosen the bolts on the regulator to release the window glass clamps **(see illustration)**. Note that the bolts are fitted from the outside, so will have to be turned clockwise to loosen them (do not remove bolts completely).
5 Lift the rear of the window glass so that it is tilted, then remove it upwards from the door **(see illustration)**.

Rear door window glass

6 Remove the door inner trim panel as described in Section 12.
7 Prise out the access cap from the inner door panel **(see illustration)**.
8 Lower the window glass until the plastic roll-pins are visible through the access hole **(see illustration)**. On models with electric windows, temporarily reconnect the switch to operate the glass. If there is a fault with the electric motor, remove the motor in order to lower the glass.
9 Screw a 5.0 mm diameter bolt into the

14.10 Unclip the outer window seal

14.11a Pull out the window channel rubber moulding...

14.11b ...and undo the retaining screws (arrows)...

14.11c ...then remove the door frame trim panel

14.12 Lift the window glass from the rear door

14.14 Unclip the inner window seal

plastic centre roll-pin and pull it out, then screw an 8.0 mm diameter bolt into the outer part of the roll-pin and remove **(see illustrations)**. Do not apply too much pressure, as the roll-pin may drop inside the door, causing further dismantling of the window regulator to retrieve it. It is recommended that the roll-pin is renewed whenever removed.

10 Carefully unclip the outer window seal trim from the upper edge of the door panel **(see illustration)**.

11 Pull out the window channel rubber from the front of the door frame, undo the retaining screws and remove the trim panel from the front of the door frame by pulling it down slightly **(see illustrations)**.

12 Lift the window glass and withdraw it from the outside of the door **(see illustration)**.

Rear door fixed window

13 Remove the door inner trim panel as described in Section 12.

14 Carefully unclip the inner window seal trim from the upper edge of the door panel **(see illustration)**.

15 Working around the upper door frame, carefully remove the window channel rubber and outer door seal trim.

16 On the inside of the door, peel back the covers and undo the two retaining bolts securing the window channel **(see illustration)**.

17 Pushing the fixed window slightly, release the two upper retaining clips, in the upper part of the door frame. With the upper retaining clips released, withdraw the window complete with channel upwards and out from the door.

Window regulator assembly

18 Remove the door inner trim panel as described in Section 12.

19 Remove the door window glass as described earlier or disconnect the glass from

the regulator and slide it to the top of the frame, securing it in place with strong tape **(see illustration)**.

20 Open the door then disconnect the wiring at the A- or B-pillar as applicable. To do this, first release the rubber bellows by pressing the small tab at the top. Pull down the locking lever and disconnect the wiring plug **(see illustrations 11.1a & 11.1b)**.

21 On front doors, disconnect the wiring connector to the small speaker in the upper plastic trim panel. Release the retaining clip and disconnect the connector from the door panel **(see illustrations)**.

22 Also on front doors, trace the wiring down from the door mirror and release the retaining clip from the door assembly, then disconnect the wiring plug from the control unit **(see illustrations)**.

23 Disconnect the wiring connector to the door lock unit **(see illustration)**.

14.16 Peel back seals and undo the two retaining bolts

14.19 Tape the window glass in position to the frame

14.21a Disconnect the speaker wiring connector...

14.21b ...unclip the wiring connector from the door frame

14.22a Unclip the wiring loom from the inner panel...

14.22b ...and disconnect the wiring connectors from the control unit

24 Working your way around the window regulator assembly pull out the centre pins and remove the retaining clips (see illustrations). It may be necessary to drill out some metal rivets

which were used on assembly, if so replace these with plastic rivets on re-assembly
25 On front doors, peel back the covers and undo the retaining bolts securing the upper

part of the window regulator assembly (see illustration).
26 As the assembly is removed, withdraw the door lock operating cable through the panel, then reach inside the door to release the wiring loom retaining clip and rubber grommet from the front of the door (see illustrations).

Window regulator motor and control unit

27 Remove the door inner trim panel as described in Section 12.
28 With the window fully closed, use adhesive tape to hold the glass in position (see illustration 14.19).
29 Release the locking clips and disconnect the wiring plugs from the motor/control unit (see illustrations).
30 Undo the three mounting screws and remove the motor and control unit from the mounting plate (see illustrations).

14.23 Disconnect the door lock wiring connector

14.24a Pull out the centre pin...

14.24b ...and remove the inner panel securing clips

14.24c Drill out the rivets (arrowed) - where fitted

14.25 Peel back the seals (arrowed) to access the retaining bolts

14.26a Release the door operating cable from the inner panel...

14.26b ...and unclip the wiring loom retaining clip

14.29a Disconnect the wiring connectors (arrowed) - front door

14.29b Disconnect the wiring connector (arrowed) - rear door

14.30a Undo the three retaining screws...

14.30b ...and remove the window regulator

Refitting

Front door window glass

31 Carefully lower the tilted window glass into the door and engage it with the regulator clamps. Apply light downwards pressure to the glass to make sure it is correctly located in the channels, then tighten the regulator clamp bolts. Note that the bolts are fitted from the outside, so will have to be turned anti-clockwise to tighten them

32 If necessary, the window may be checked for correct operation at this stage by connecting the wiring to the switches.

33 Refit the access caps.

34 Refit the door inner trim panel with reference to Section 12.

Rear door window glass

35 Before fitting the window glass to the door, fit the new outer roll-pin so that it extends by equal amounts on each side of the glass, then secure with the new inner roll-pin.

36 Lower the window glass into the door and locate the roll-pin on the regulator clip. Press directly downwards until the roll-pin engages with the clip.

37 If necessary, the window may be checked for correct operation at this stage by connecting the wiring to the switches.

38 Refit the access cap.

39 Refit the door inner trim panel with reference to Section 12.

Rear door fixed window

40 Refitting is a reversal of removal, making sure that the door seals and window channels are fitted securely. Refit the door inner trim panel with reference to Section 12.

Window regulator

41 Refitting is a reversal of removal, noting the following points:

a) Make sure the wiring is routed correctly through the front of the door.

b) Feed the door lock operating cable through the rear of the panel.

c) On front doors, tighten the upper retaining bolts securely.

d) Secure the assembly with the plastic rivets, renewing any that are damaged.

e) Make sure the wiring connector is fitted securely to the A- or B-pillar connection.

f) Refit the window glass as described previously in this Section.

g) Refit the door inner trim panel with reference to Section 12.

Window regulator motor and control unit

42 Locate the motor and control unit on the mounting plate and insert the mounting bolts hand-tight.

43 Reconnect the wiring plug(s), then remove the adhesive tape and operate the window down and up a short distance to allow the splines between the motor and cable drum to engage.

44 Fully tighten the motor mounting bolts.

45 Operate the window twice to its upper and lower stops to normalise the window and activate the pinch/roll-back function.

46 Refit the door inner trim panel with reference to Section 12.

15.1a Undo the screws (arrowed) in the grab handle recesses - Hatchback

15.2 Unclip the access panels at each side - Hatchback

15 Tailgate and support struts – removal and refitting

Removal

Tailgate

1 With the tailgate open, undo the trim panel retaining screws inside the grab handles **(see illustrations)**.

2 On hatchback models, to give easier access to some of the securing clips, remove the small trim panels from each end of the tailgate trim **(see illustration)**.

3 Release the trim panel clips, carefully levering between the panel and tailgate with a flat-bladed lever. Work around the outside of the panel, and when all the clips are released, remove the panel **(see illustrations)**.

15.1b Remove the plastic covers to access the screws - Estate

15.3a Unclip the panel from the tailgate

15.3b Tailgate trim securing clips (arrowed) - Hatchback

15.3c Tailgate trim securing clips (arrowed) - Estate

15.4a Release the retaining clips (arrowed)...

15.4b ...and remove the upper trim panel

15.5a Disconnect the wiring connectors from the tailgate components...

15.5b ...including the light units on hatchback models

15.6 Disconnect the washer tube from the wiper motor on estate models

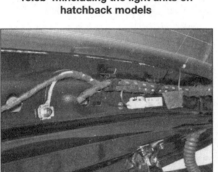

15.7 Disconnect the wiring connectors from the top of the tailgate

15.8 Release the wiring grommets from the tailgate

4 Unclip the upper trim from the tailgate starting from the outer ends and working towards the middle (see illustrations).

5 Disconnect all of the wiring connectors situated behind the trim panel (see illustrations).

6 On estate models, release the securing clip and disconnect the washer hose from the wiper motor (see illustration).

7 Working at the top of the tailgate, disconnect the wiring connectors from the heated rear screen terminals and on hatchback models, free the washer hose (see illustration).

8 Free the wiring grommets from the tailgate (see illustration), and then tie a piece of string to each end of the wiring then, noting the correct routing of the wiring harness, release the harness rubber grommets from the tailgate and withdraw the wiring. When the end of the wiring appears, untie the string and leave it in position in the tailgate; it can then be used on refitting to draw the wiring into position.

9 Using a suitable marker pen, draw around the outline of each hinge marking its correct position on the tailgate.

10 With the help of an assistant to support the tailgate, remove the support struts as described below.

11 Unscrew and remove the bolts securing the hinges to the tailgate (see illustration).

15.11 Tailgate hinge retaining bolts (arrowed)

15.14a Lift locking clip upwards, then pull strut off upper balljoint...

15.14b ...also remove the lower end of the strut

Where necessary, recover the gaskets that are fitted between the hinge and vehicle body.

12 Inspect the hinges for signs of wear or damage and renew if necessary. The hinges are secured to the vehicle by nuts or bolts (depending on model), which can be accessed once the headlining rear cover strip has been removed.

Support struts

 Warning: The support struts are filled with a gas and must be disposed of safely.

13 With the help of an assistant, support the tailgate in the open position.

14 Using a small flat-bladed screwdriver lift the locking clip, and pull the gas support strut off its balljoint mounting on the tailgate **(see illustrations)**. Repeat the procedure on the lower strut mounting and remove the strut from the vehicle body. **Note:** *If the gas strut is to be re-used, the locking clip must not be taken all the way out, or the clip will be damaged.*

Refitting

Tailgate

15 Refitting is the reverse of removal, aligning the hinges with the marks made before removal. Tighten retaining bolts to the specified torque.

16 On completion, close the tailgate and check its alignment with the surrounding panels. If necessary slight adjustment can be made by unscrewing the retaining bolts and

15.17a Slacken the centre screw to adjust the tailgate buffer...

repositioning the tailgate on its hinges. If the tailgate buffers are in need of adjustment, continue as follows.

17 Locate the adjustment buffers on the tailgate. Through the hole in the rubber cap, insert an Allen key and undo the screw until the centre notched slide will move freely in or out, in the housing. When the adjustment buffer has been set to the correct position tighten the centre screw. When renewing buffers the notched slide is preset at 12.5 mm from the housing **(see illustrations)**. To remove the adjustment buffer, turn anti-clockwise 90° with a spanner.

Support struts

18 Refitting is a reverse of the removal procedure, ensuring that the strut is securely retained by its retaining clips.

15.17b ...check the setting on each buffer to line up tailgate

16 Tailgate lock components – removal and refitting

Removal

Note: *If the lock is inoperative, the tailgate can be opened manually by inserting the key into the slot provided, in the lower part of the inner tailgate trim, and then sliding it to the left-hand side of the vehicle (see illustration).*

Tailgate lock

1 Open up the tailgate and remove the trim panel as described in Section 15.

2 Disconnect the wiring from the lock **(see illustration)**.

3 Undo the retaining bolts and remove the lock from the lower edge of the tailgate **(see illustration)**.

16.0 Slide the key in the slot in the trim panel, to operate the lever to open the tailgate

16.2 Disconnect the wiring from the tailgate lock

16.3 Undo the lock retaining screws (arrowed)

16.5 Disconnect the wiring connector...

16.6 ...and undo the tailgate handle/release unit bolts - Hatchback

16.7 Disconnect the wiring connector and undo the nuts (arrowed) - Estate

16.8 Remove the release handle cover - Estate

16.9 Withdraw the release handle from the tailgate

Tailgate handle/release unit

4 Open up the tailgate and remove the trim panel as described in Section 15.

Hatchback models

5 Disconnect the wiring from the handle/release unit (see illustration).

6 Undo the retaining screws holding the unit to the tailgate and locking brackets, and then turn it clockwise and remove (see illustration).

Estate models

7 Disconnect the wiring plug, from the rear of the handle (see illustration).

8 Undo the two retaining nuts, release the retaining clip at the centre of the shield, and then remove the shield from the rear of the handle (see illustration).

9 The handle/release unit can now be withdrawn from the outside of the tailgate (see illustration).

Refitting

10 Refitting is a reversal of removal, however, before refitting the trim panel, check the operation of the lock components.

17 Central locking components – description, removal and refitting

Description

1 The central locking system consists of the following main components. Note that the central locking and anti-theft alarm systems share some components (see Chapter 12):

a) Convenience system onboard supply control unit located behind the driver's side facia panel.

b) Door control units integrated in the window regulator motors.

c) Electric door lock actuators integrated in the door locks.

d) Fuel tank filler cap flap actuator located behind the luggage compartment trim.

e) Tailgate lock actuator located in the tailgate, together with the release button.

f) Anti-theft alarm horn located beneath the front wheel arch.

g) Bonnet contact switch located on the bonnet lock.

h) Remote control transmitter on the ignition key fob.

Removal

2 Before working on any electrical circuit, disconnect the battery negative lead (refer to *Disconnecting the battery* in the *Reference* Chapter at the end of this manual).

Convenience system onboard supply control unit

3 Remove the driver's side facia trim panel as described in Section 27.

4 Release the securing clip and remove the right-hand relay from the relay carrier below the control unit (see illustration).

5 Using a flat piece of metal, release the two retaining clips in the top edges of the relay carrier, and remove it from under the control unit (see illustrations).

6 Release the locking clips and disconnect the three wiring connectors from under the control unit (see illustration).

7 Release the two securing clips (one at each side), and then lower the front of the control unit and withdraw it from the relay carrier (see illustrations).

17.4 Remove the relay

17.5a Release the securing clips...

17.5b ...through the two slots (arrowed)...

17.5c ...then remove the lower relay mounting bracket

17.6 Disconnect the three wiring block connectors

17.7a Release the two securing clips (arrowed)...

17.7b ...and withdraw the control unit out from its mounting bracket

Door control unit

8 Remove the window regulator motor as described in Section 14.

Electric door lock actuator

9 Remove the door lock (see Section 13).

17.11 Disconnect the wiring connector...

Fuel tank filler cap flap actuator

10 Remove the right-hand trim from the luggage compartment with reference to Section 25.
11 Disconnect the wiring plug from the actuator (see illustration).
12 Slacken the mounting bolts, and then

slide the actuator upwards and release it from the inner body panel (see illustrations). Note that the bolts are fitted from the other side, so will have to be turned clockwise to loosen them (do not remove bolts completely).
13 Withdraw the actuator upward, complete with operating rod.

Tailgate/boot lid lock activator

14 Remove the tailgate handle/release unit as described in Section 16.

Bonnet contact switch

15 Remove the bonnet lock as described in Section 10. If necessary, the operating cable may remain attached to the lock.
16 On the lock, release the tab and push the switch from the slotted holes.

Remote control transmitter battery

17 Using a screwdriver inserted in the slot, separate the transmitter unit cover from the key (see illustrations).

17.12a ...slacken the retaining screws (arrowed)...

17.12b ...and slide the motor out from the panel

17.17a Using a small screwdriver, release the clip...

17.17b ...and open the battery cover

17.18a Remove the battery...

17.18b ...noting which way it is fitted

18.3 Release the wiring loom retaining clip

18.4 Undo the mirror retaining bolt (arrowed)

18.5 Remove the exterior mirror glass...

18.6 ...and disconnect the wiring (arrowed)

18.8a Undo the two screws and release the two securing clips (arrowed)...

18.8b ...then remove the inner housing

18 Carefully prise out the battery, noting which way round it is fitted (see illustrations).

Refitting

19 Refitting is a reversal of removal; on completion check the operation of the central locking system.

18 Mirrors and associated components – removal and refitting

Removal

Exterior mirror

1 Remove the door inner trim panel as described in Section 12.
2 If not already removed, unclip the small inner trim panel from the door frame and disconnect the speaker wiring connector.

3 Trace the wiring from the exterior mirror and disconnect the wiring plug at the window regulator motor/control unit. Also, release the wiring support clips from the door panel (see illustration).
4 Unscrew the mounting bolt while supporting the exterior mirror, then withdraw the exterior mirror from the door while guiding the wiring through the hole (see illustration).

Mirror glass

Note: The mirror glass is clipped into place. Removal of the glass without the VW special forked tool (number 80-200) may result in breakage of the glass. Wear protective gloves and glasses to prevent personal injury.

5 Press in the bottom of the mirror glass so that the top edge is furthest from the housing. If required, protect the edge of the housing with masking tape, then insert the special tool and lever the mirror glass from its mounting

clips. Take great care when removing the glass; do not use excessive force, as the glass is easily broken. If the VW special tool is not available, use a flat-bladed lever (see illustration).
6 Disconnect the wiring connectors from the mirror heating element (see illustration).

Mirror housing

7 Remove the mirror glass as described in paragraphs 5 and 6.
8 Undo the two retaining screws and then release the two upper retaining clips to remove the inner housing (see illustrations).
9 Release the securing clips along the lower edge of the upper outer trim and then remove (see illustration).
10 Release the securing clip at the inner edge of the lower outer trim, disconnect the wiring connector for the indicator side repeater and then remove (see illustrations).

18.9 Unclip the upper outer shell

18.10a Release the securing clips to remove the lower housing...

18.10b ...and disconnect the wiring connector

18.14a Unclip the sides of mirror housing…

18.14b …disconnect the wiring connector…

18.15 …and slide the mirror from its mounting bracket

Mirror switch

11 Refer to Chapter 12, Section 4.

Refitting

12 Refitting is the reverse of the relevant removal procedure. When refitting the mirror glass, press firmly at the centre taking care not to use excessive force, as the glass is easily broken.

Caution: Wear protective gloves and glasses to prevent personal injury.

Interior mirror

13 Switch off the ignition and all electrical consumers and remove the ignition key.
14 Separate the left and right mirror base covers, and disconnect the wiring plug **(see illustrations)**.
15 Slide the mirror downwards to release it from the mirror base **(see illustration)**. The mirror base is bonded to the windscreen. Whilst it is possible to remove the base, great care must be exercised to avoid damaging the windscreen. Due to the hazardous chemicals involved, it is recommended that the bonding of the mirror base to the windscreen be entrusted to a VW dealer or suitably equipped specialist.
16 With the base in place, refit the mirror to the base, reconnect the sensor wiring plugs and refit the two halves of the mirror base covers.

19 Windscreen and rear window glass – general information

These areas of glass are bonded in position with a special adhesive. Renewal of such fixed glass is a difficult, messy and time-consuming task, which is beyond the scope of the home mechanic. It is difficult, unless one has plenty of practice, to obtain a secure, waterproof fit. Furthermore, the task carries a high risk of breakage; this applies especially to the laminated glass windscreen. In view of this, owners are strongly advised to have this sort of work carried out by one of the many specialist windscreen fitters.

20 Sunroof – general information

Due to the complexity of the sunroof mechanism, considerable expertise is needed to repair, renew or adjust the sunroof components successfully. Removal of the roof first requires the headlining to be removed, which is a complex and tedious operation, and not a task to be undertaken lightly. Therefore, any problems with the sunroof should be referred to a VW dealer. On models with an electric sunroof, if the sunroof motor fails to operate, first check the relevant fuse. If the fault cannot be traced and rectified, the sunroof can be opened and closed manually using an Allen key to turn the motor spindle (a suitable key is supplied with the vehicle, and should be clipped onto the inside of the sunroof motor trim). To gain access to the motor, unclip the rear of the trim cover to open. Unclip the Allen key, and then insert it fully into the motor opening (against spring pressure). Rotate the key to move the sunroof to the required position.

21 Body exterior fittings – removal and refitting

Wheel arch liners and body under-panels

1 The various plastic covers fitted to the underside of the vehicle are secured in position by a mixture of screws, nuts and retaining clips and removal will be fairly obvious on inspection. Work methodically around the panel removing its retaining screws and releasing its retaining clips until the panel is free and can be removed from the underside of the vehicle. Most clips used on the vehicle are simply prised out of position. Remove the wheels to ease the removal of the wheel arch liners.
2 On refitting, renew any retaining clips that may have been broken on removal, and ensure that the panel is securely retained by all the relevant clips and screws.

Body trim strips and badges

3 The various body trim strips and badges are held in position with a special adhesive tape and locating lugs. Removal requires the trim/badge to be heated, to soften the adhesive, and then carefully lifted away from the surface. Due to the high risk of damage to the vehicle's paintwork during this operation, it is recommended that this task should be entrusted to a VW dealer.

22 Seats – removal and refitting

Note: *Refer to the warnings in Chapter 12, Section 25, on airbags.*

Removal

Front seats

Note: *The amount of wiring connectors under the seat may vary depending on the vehicle specification.*

1 Disconnect the battery negative lead (refer to *Disconnecting the battery* in the *Reference* Chapter at the end of this manual).
2 Slide the seat forwards as far as possible and unscrew the rear mounting bolts **(see illustration)**.
3 Slide the seat rearwards as far as possible and unscrew the front mounting bolts **(see illustration)**.

⚠️ *Warning: As a precaution against unintentional electrostatic discharge into the airbag, briefly*

22.2 Seat rear mounting bolts (arrowed)

22.3 Seat front mounting bolts (arrowed)

22.4 Open the flap in the carpet and disconnect the wiring connector

22.7 Unclip the plastic 'ISOFIX' seat anchorage covers

22.8a Pull the front of the seat base upwards to release

22.8b Unhook the sides of the seat cushion from the securing hooks (arrowed)

22.9 Release the seat belt stalks from the seat cushion

touch part of the vehicle body before disconnecting the wiring.

4 Tilt the seat back slightly and lift up the small section of carpet to access the wiring connectors **(see illustration)**, disconnect the wiring connectors. VW technicians fit an adapter to the airbag wiring connector as a safety precaution; however, wrap the wiring connectors with insulation tape or similar, to prevent any contact of the wiring.

5 Check that the wiring harness is released from any clips in the floor, and then remove

the headrests from the seat backs; this will give more room when removing the seat from the vehicle.

6 When removing the seat from the vehicle, do not lift the seat by the seat belt stalk or by the seat adjustment levers. If necessary, have an assistant help to remove the seat, as it is heavy, and surrounding trim panels may be otherwise damaged. Make sure that the seat runners; do not damage the paintwork as the seat is withdrawn.

Rear seat cushion

7 At the rear of the seat cushion, unclip the four guides from the child ISOFIX seat mountings **(see illustration)**.

8 Pull the front edge of the cushion upwards from the location sockets, then push the cushion to the rear to release the ends of the seat from the outer locating brackets **(see illustrations)**.

9 Lift the seat cushion upwards, releasing the seat belt stalks from the rear of the seat cushion **(see illustration)**.

Rear seat backrest

10 Remove the seat cushion as described in paragraphs 7 to 9.

11 On estate models lift up the covers, then undo the retaining screws and remove the rear panel from behind the rear seats **(see illustrations)**.

12 Fold the backrest forwards, then pull back the carpet and remove the trim (where fitted) from the centre mounting **(see illustration)**.

13 Unbolt the clamp, then remove the left backrest by lifting it from the centre mounting and sliding it off the outer mounting pin **(see illustrations)**.

22.11a Open the flaps and undo the retaining screws

22.11b Remove the panel from the luggage compartment

22.12 Unclip the trim cover

22.13a Unbolt the securing bracket

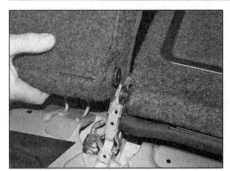

22.13b Lift the seat back at the centre...

22.13c ...and slide it out from base of the pillar

22.14 Removing the seat belt stalk

22.16 Undo the retaining nut

22.17a Lift the trim out from the bracket (arrowed)...

22.17b ...then pull it out from the upper locating slot (arrowed)

14 Before removing the right-hand seat back it will be necessary to unscrew the bolt and remove the centre stalk from the floor **(see illustration)**.

15 Remove the right backrest by lifting it from the centre mounting and sliding it off the outer mounting pin, as shown for the left seat back.

Rear seat backrest side pads - Estate models

16 Remove the seat cushion as described in paragraphs 7 to 9, then undo the retaining nut at the base of the side pad **(see illustration)**.

17 Fold the backrest forwards, then lift the side pad upwards to release it from the two locating points in the wheel arch panel **(see illustrations)**.

Refitting

18 Refitting is a reversal of removal, but tighten the mounting bolts to the specified torque where given.

23 Front seat belt tensioning mechanism – general information

All models covered in this manual are fitted with a front seat belt tensioner system incorporated in each of the inertia reels. Rear seat belt inertia reels with the tensioner system are only fitted to some models, other models having standard inertia reels.

The system is designed to instantaneously take up any slack in the seat belt in the case of a sudden frontal impact, therefore reducing

the possibility of injury to the front seat occupants. The seat belt tensioner is triggered by a frontal impact above a predetermined force. Lesser impacts, including impacts from behind, will not trigger the system.

When the system is triggered, the explosive gas in the tensioner mechanism retracts and locks the seat belt. This prevents the seat belt moving and keeps the occupant firmly in position in the seat. Once the tensioner has been triggered, the seat belt will be permanently locked and the assembly must be renewed.

There is a risk of personal injury if the system is triggered inadvertently when working on the vehicle, and it is therefore strongly recommended that any work involving the seat belt inertia reels be entrusted to a VW dealer. Note the following warnings before contemplating any work on the front seat belts.

> ⚠ *Warning: Do not expose the tensioner mechanism to temperatures in excess of 100°C.*
> • *Before removing any components, disconnect the battery negative lead (refer to Disconnecting the battery in the Reference Chapter at the end of this manual).*
> • *If the tensioner mechanism is dropped, it must be renewed, even it has suffered no apparent damage.*
> • *Do not allow any solvents to come into contact with the tensioner mechanism.*
> • *Do not attempt to open the tensioner mechanism as it contains explosive gas.*
> • *Tensioners must be discharged before*

they are disposed of, but this task should be entrusted to a VW dealer.
• *Some of the bolts securing the seat belts are microencapsulated and need to be heated with a hot air blower before they are slackened. Microencapsulated means that the threads of the bolts are coated with a locking compound from new. New bolts will be required for refitting.*

24 Seat belt components – removal and refitting

> ⚠ *Warning: Refer to Section 23 before proceeding.*

Front seat belt removal

5-door models

1 Disconnect the battery negative lead (refer to *Disconnecting the battery* in the *Reference* Chapter at the end of this manual).

2 Remove the upper and lower trim panels from the B-pillar with reference to Section 25.

3 Pull back the carpet, then unscrew and remove the seat belt lower anchor mounting bolt and remove the belt from the floor **(see illustration)**. Note that the bolt may be microencapsulated and must be heated with a hot air blower before being loosened. Protect the seat belt with a dampened cloth while heating the bolt. Discard the bolt and obtain a new one. Also, note that the threads of the corresponding nut must be cleaned with a tap before fitting the new bolt.

24.3 Seat belt lower anchorage bolt (arrowed)

24.4 Release the locking peg, to disconnect wiring connector

24.5 Front seat belt inertia reel mounting bolt

24.6 Front seat belt guide

24.7 Front seat belt upper anchor

⚠ *Warning: As a precaution against unintentional electrostatic discharge, briefly touch part of the vehicle body before disconnecting the wiring.*
4 Release the locking clip and disconnect the wiring connector from the inertia reel **(see illustration)**.
5 Unscrew the mounting bolt and remove the inertia reel from the bottom of the B-pillar **(see illustration)**.

6 Undo the screws and remove the belt guide from the B-pillar **(see illustration)**.
7 Unscrew and remove the bolt securing the seat belt upper anchor to the height adjuster on the B-pillar **(see illustration)**. The seat belt assembly can then be removed from the vehicle.
8 To remove the belt height adjustment, remove the securing bolt from the top of the adjuster and lift upwards to release from the pillar.

3-door models

9 Remove the relevant rear seat and backrest as described in Section 22.
10 Remove the upper trim panel from the B-pillar with reference to Section 25.
11 Remove the sill and side trim panels with reference to Section 25.
12 Unscrew the bolts securing the anchor rail to the sill, and slide the rail from the end of the seat belt **(see illustration)**.
13 On models without rear seat belt tensioners, unscrew the mounting bolt and withdraw the inertia reels.
14 On models with rear seat belt tensioners, disconnect the battery negative lead (refer to *'Disconnecting the battery'* in the *Reference* Chapter at the end of this manual), then unscrew the inertia reel mounting bolt, withdraw the reel and disconnect the wiring **(see illustrations)**.

⚠ *Warning: As a precaution against unintentional electrostatic discharge, briefly touch part of the vehicle body before disconnecting the wiring.*
15 Undo the screws and remove the belt guide from the B-pillar.
16 Unscrew and remove the bolt securing the seat belt upper anchor to the height adjuster on the B-pillar **(see illustration)**.
17 Remove the seat belt assembly from the vehicle.
18 To remove the belt height adjustment, remove the securing bolt from the top of the adjuster and lift upwards to release from the pillar.

Front seat belt stalk removal

19 Remove the front seat assembly as described in Section 22.
20 Slide the seat runners forward to access

24.12 Front seat belt anchor rail bolt on the sill - 3-door

24.14b Front seat belt inertia reel mounting bolt (arrowed)

24.14a Disconnecting the wiring connector

24.16 Front seat belt upper anchor

24.23 Undo the seat belt lower anchorage bolt

24.24a Rear side seat belt inertia reel mounting bolt (arrowed) - Hatchback

24.24b Rear side seat belt inertia reel mounting bolt - Estate

the seat belt stalk retaining bolt, under the seat frame. Unscrew and remove the bolt securing the stalk to the seat, and remove the stalk. On 3-door models, the stalk must be turned through 90° in order to remove it. Note that the bolt is microencapsulated and must be heated with a hot air blower before being loosened. Protect the seat with a dampened cloth while heating the bolt. Discard the bolt and obtain a new one. Also, note that the threads of the corresponding nut must be cleaned with a tap before fitting the new bolt.

Rear seat side belt removal

21 Remove the rear seat as described in Section 22.
22 Remove the side panel trim, luggage compartment side trim and C-pillar trim panel with reference to Section 25. **Note**: *Refer to Chapter 12 on models with rear side airbags.*

23 Unbolt the belt from the floor anchorage **(see illustration)**.
24 Unscrew the mounting bolt and withdraw the inertia reel, from the rear panel **(see illustrations)**
25 On models with rear seat belt tensioners, disconnect the battery negative lead (refer to *'Disconnecting the battery'* in the 'Reference' Chapter at the end of this manual), then disconnect the wiring, as shown in illustration 24.4.

⚠️ *Warning: As a precaution against unintentional electrostatic discharge, briefly touch part of the vehicle body before disconnecting the wiring.*

Rear seat centre belt and buckle removal

26 Remove the rear seat cushion and backrest as described in Section 22.

27 To remove the inertia reel, first prise the belt guide from the top of the backrest **(see illustrations)**.
28 Undo the screws and remove the hinge **(see illustration)**.
29 Press down the padding around the headrest guides, then use a screwdriver to release the locking lugs and pull out the headrest guides **(see illustration)**.
30 Carefully prise the moulding from the edge of the backrest **(see illustration)**.
31 Unbolt and remove the inertia reel **(see illustration)**.

Refitting

32 Refitting is a reversal of the removal procedure, ensuring that all the seat belt units are located correctly and mounting bolts are securely tightened to their specified torque. Check all the trim panels are securely retained by all the relevant retaining clips. When refitting

24.27a Prise out the trim panel...

24.27b ...and remove it from the seat belt

24.28 Undo the hinge retaining screws

24.29 Remove the headrest guides

24.30 Release the seat trim from the seat frame

24.31 Rear centre seat belt inertia reel mounting bolt

the B-pillar upper trim panels, ensure that the height adjustment peg engages correctly with the trim panel (see illustration).

25 Interior trim –
removal and refitting

Interior trim panels

1 The interior trim panels are secured using either screws or various types of trim fasteners, usually studs or clips.
2 Check that there are no other panels overlapping the one to be removed; usually there is a sequence that has to be followed, and this will only become obvious on close inspection.
3 Remove all obvious fasteners, such as screws. If the panel will not come free, it will

24.32 Align the upper trim panel with the upper seat belt height adjuster

be held by hidden clips or fasteners. These are usually situated around the edge of the panel and can be prised up to release them; note, however, that they can break quite easily so new ones should be available. The best way

of releasing such clips, without the correct type of tool, is to use a large flat-bladed screwdriver. Note in many cases that the adjacent sealing strip must be prised back to release a panel.
4 When removing a panel, **never** use excessive force or the panel may be damaged; always check carefully that all fasteners or other relevant components have been removed or released before attempting to withdraw a panel.
5 On models with side airbags, disconnect the battery negative lead (refer to 'Disconnecting the battery' in the 'Reference' Chapter at the end of this manual).
6 Refitting is the reverse of the removal procedure; secure the fasteners by pressing them firmly into place and ensure that all disturbed components are correctly secured to prevent rattles.

3-door models

7 Remove the upper trim from the B-pillar (see illustrations). Undo the lower seat belt mounting bracket and pass the seat belt through the panel to remove it completely.
8 Remove the rear seat cushion and backrest as described in Section 22.
9 Carefully lever the sill trim panel upwards to release the retaining clips and remove the trim panel (see illustration).
10 Working at the rear upper corner of the seat side trim panel, unclip the plastic cover. Undo the screw and remove the seat side trim panel, disconnect the wiring from the speaker as it is removed (see illustrations).
11 Remove the tailgate lock trim cover as described in paragraphs 43 to 46.
12 Undo the two retaining screws (one at the front edge and one at the rear) and remove the parcel shelf support from the side of the luggage compartment. Where applicable, depending on which side is removed, disconnect the wiring connectors from the luggage compartment light or 12-volt supply plug.
13 Release the retaining clips at the rear of the carpet, undo the two retaining screws from the luggage anchor, then remove the side trim carpet from the luggage compartment (see illustration).
14 Carefully unclip the trim from the rear of the roof panel (see illustration).

25.7a Carefully unclip the trim...

25.7b ...and undo the retaining screw...

25.7c ...then withdraw the seat belt from the trim panel

25.9 Unclip the sill trim panel

25.10a Unclip trim cover to access screws

25.10b Disconnect the speaker wiring connector

25.13 Remove the side trim from the luggage compartment

25.14 Unclip the rear plastic trim panel from the headlining

25.16a Undo the securing nut...

25.16b ...and remove the rear upper trim panel

15 Remove the airbag emblem and retaining screw from the C-pillar upper trim panel **(see illustrations 25.7a and 25.7b)**.
16 Undo the retaining nut at the rear of the trim panel, then carefully prise the trim from the rear pillar and out from the side of the luggage compartment **(see illustrations)**.
17 Refitting is the reverse of removal.

5-door models (except Estate)

18 Remove the rear seat cushion and backrest as described in Section 22.
19 Remove the upper trim from the B-pillar **(see illustrations)**. Undo the lower seat belt mounting bracket and pass the seat belt through the panel to remove it completely.
20 Working at the rear of the sill trim, undo the retaining nut and unclip the rear wheel arch trim from the sill trim panel **(see illustrations)**.

25.19a Carefully unclip the trim and undo the retaining screw

25.19b Pull the trim out at the bottom...

21 Unclip the plastic cover, undo the retaining screw and remove the rear wheel arch side trim panel **(see illustration)**.
22 Carefully lever the sill trim panel upwards

to release the retaining clips and remove the trim panel **(see illustrations)**.
23 Undo the two retaining screws and remove the middle trim from the B-pillar **(see**

25.19c ...then slide it down from the headlining

25.19d Unclip the seat belt from the sill trim panel

25.20a Undo the trim lower retaining nut (arrowed)

25.20b Unclip the lower part of the side trim from the sill trim

25.21 Undo the upper retaining screw

25.22a Unclip the rear of the sill trim panel...

25.22b ...and then unclip it at the centre

25.23a Undo the two retaining screws

25.23b Disconnect the wiring connector as the trim is removed

25.25a Undo the front retaining screw...

25.25b ...and the rear retaining screw...

25.25c ...then unclip the side trim

illustrations). Disconnect the wiring from the alarm interior sensor switch as the panel is removed.

24 Remove the tailgate lock trim cover as described in paragraphs 43 to 46.

25 Undo the two retaining screws (one at the front edge and one at the rear) and remove the parcel shelf support from the side of the luggage compartment (see illustrations). Where applicable, depending on which side

is removed, disconnect the wiring connectors from the luggage compartment light or 12-volt supply plug.

26 Release the retaining clips at the rear of the carpet, undo the two retaining screws from the luggage anchor, then remove the side trim carpet from the luggage compartment (see illustrations).

27 Carefully unclip the trim from the rear of the roof panel (see illustration).

28 Remove the airbag emblem and retaining screw from the C-pillar upper trim panel (see illustrations 25.7a and 25.7b).

29 Undo the retaining nut at the rear of the trim panel, then carefully prise the trim from the rear pillar and out from the side of the luggage compartment (see illustrations).

30 Refitting is the reverse of removal.

Estate models

31 Remove the rear seat backrest and side padding as described in Section 22.

25.26a Release the two securing clips (arrowed)...

25.26b ...then remove the side trim from the luggage compartment

25.27 Unclip the rear plastic trim panel from the headlining

25.29a Undo the securing nut...

25.29b ...and remove the rear upper trim panel...

25.29c ...releasing the locating peg (arrowed) from the rear panel

25.32 Undo the retaining screws (arrowed)

25.33 Undo the support strap retaining screw

25.34 Undo the three retaining screws (arrowed)

25.36a Undo the two screws at the front and the two nuts at the rear...

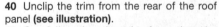

25.36b ...then slide the floor panel assembly upwards and forwards...

32 Lift the luggage compartment floor, undo the 4 bolts and manoeuvre it from place (see illustration).
33 Open the floor storage compartment, and undo the support strap lower bolt (see illustration).
34 Lift up the 3 plastic covers at the front edge, undo the retaining bolts and manoeuvre the storage compartment from place (see illustration).
35 Remove the cover from over the spare wheel.
36 Undo the 2 nuts, and 2 bolts, then pull up the front edge of the floor lining assembly, then slide it forwards and remove it (see illustrations).
37 Remove the tailgate lock trim cover as described in paragraphs 48 to 50.
38 Undo the retaining bolts and remove the luggage anchorages (see illustrations).
39 Remove the plastic 'scrivet' at the front, upper edge, then pull the luggage compartment

side panel inwards to release the retaining clips (see illustrations). Take care when unclipping the panel from the D-pillar trim panel. Where applicable, disconnect the power outlet socket wiring plug as the panel is withdrawn.

40 Unclip the trim from the rear of the roof panel (see illustration).
41 Carefully prise the trim from the rear pillar, releasing it from the retaining clips (see illustration).

25.36c ...to release it from the rear panel (arrowed)

25.38a Undo the 2 bolts securing the luggage anchor...

25.38b ...and the single bolt securing the hook

25.39a Undo the central screw, and pull out the 'scrivet' at the front, upper corner of the side panel...

25.39b ...then remove the side trim from the luggage compartment

25.40 Unclip the rear plastic trim panel from the headlining

25.41 Unclip the rear upper trim panel

25.44 Unclip the sides of the rear trim panel

42 Refitting is the reverse of removal.

Tailgate lock trim cover – Hatchback models

43 Open the tailgate and remove the carpet from the luggage compartment.

25.46a Pull the trim panel upwards...

25.49 Unscrew the plastic nuts (arrowed)

25.53a Carefully unclip the trim...

44 Working at each side of the trim panel, unclip it from the rear side pillars (see illustration).
45 Release the lower edge of the trim cover inside the luggage compartment, by pulling it forwards.

25.46b ...to release the retaining clips

25.50 Pull the trim panel upwards to release the retaining clips

25.53b ...and undo the retaining screw (arrowed)

46 Pull the trim cover upwards to release the retaining clips along the upper edge, and then remove from the vehicle (see illustrations).
47 Refitting is the reverse of removal.

Tailgate lock trim cover – Estate models

48 Open the tailgate and remove the carpet from the luggage compartment.
49 Release the two plastic retaining nuts on the inside lower edge of the trim (see illustration).
50 Pull the trim cover upwards to release the retaining clips along the upper edge, and then remove from the vehicle (see illustration).
51 Refitting is the reverse of removal.

A-pillar trim

52 Unclip the A-pillar middle trim panel (see illustration 25.64a).
53 Carefully prise out the plastic airbag logo from the top of the trim panel, and then undo the retaining screw (see illustrations).
54 Pull the trim panel out from the top of the pillar to release the three retaining clips along the length of the trim and then pull upwards to release from behind the facia panel (see illustration).
55 Refitting is the reverse of removal.

Steering column shrouds

56 Remove the steering wheel as described in Chapter 10, Section 20.
57 Unclip the upper shroud from the bottom of the instrument panel and the top of the steering column, then remove it from the vehicle (see illustrations).

25.54 Unclip the trim panel from the A-pillar

25.57a Unclip the upper shroud from the instrument panel...

25.57b ...and at the front from the lower shroud

25.58a Undo the lower screw (arrowed)...

58 Undo the retaining screw from under the steering column lower shroud and the top of the steering column, then remove it from the vehicle **(see illustrations)**.
59 Refitting is the reverse of removal.

Glovebox

60 Switch off the ignition.
61 Remove the upper trim from the front of the centre console, as described in Section 26
62 Undo the retaining screw at the inner edge of the glovebox **(see illustration)**.
63 Using a lever, unclip the end panel on the passenger side of the facia **(see illustration)**. Note on some models, it may be necessary to unbolt the headlight range control unit from inside the end of the facia, as it is bolted to the side of the glovebox.
64 Unclip the A-pillar middle trim panel and then remove the lower A-pillar sill trim kick panel **(see illustrations)**.

25.58b ...the two upper screws...

25.58c ...then lower the shroud from the steering column

65 Undo the three retaining screws from under the lower edge of the glovebox **(see illustration)**.
66 Open up the glovebox lid then unscrew

and remove the three retaining screws **(see illustration)**.
67 Slide the glovebox out of position, disconnecting the glovebox illumination light,

25.62 Undo the retaining screw (arrowed)

25.63 Unclip the side trim from the facia

25.64a Unclip the centre side trim...

25.64b ...and the lower kick panel trim

25.65 Undo the three lower retaining screws (arrowed)

25.66 Undo the three upper retaining screws (arrowed)

25.67a Slide the glovebox out slightly...

25.67b ...disconnect the glovebox light connector...

25.67c ...the footwell light connector...

25.67d ...the passenger airbag switch connector...

25.67e ...and disconnect the air cooler hose

the footwell illumination light, the passenger airbag isolation switch and the air conditioning cooling hose as they become accessible **(see illustrations)**.

68 Refitting is the reverse of removal.

Carpets

69 The passenger compartment floor carpet is in one piece and is secured at its edges by screws or clips, usually the same fasteners used to secure the various adjoining trim panels.

70 Carpet removal and refitting is reasonably straightforward but very time-consuming because all adjoining trim panels must be removed first, as must components such as the seats, the centre console and seat belt lower anchorages.

Headlining

71 The headlining is clipped to the roof and can be withdrawn only once all fittings such as the grab handles, sun visors, interior lights, sunroof (if fitted), and related upper trim panels have been removed. Also the door, tailgate and sunroof aperture sealing strips need to be prised clear of the headlining.

72 To remove the sun visors and grab handles, the plastic covers have to be unclipped first, to gain access to the securing screws **(see illustrations)**

73 Note that headlining removal requires considerable skill and experience if it is to be carried out without damage and is therefore best entrusted to an expert.

---

26 Centre console –
removal and refitting

Removal

Front upper trim

1 Switch off the ignition.

2 Unclip the trim panel from around the gear lever and undo the two retaining screws in front of the gear lever **(see illustrations)**.

3 Withdraw the ashtray/switch panel from the

25.72a Carefully unclip the cover...

25.72b ...and undo the retaining screws (arrowed)

25.72c Unclip the cover to access the screw for the sunvisor

25.72d Unclip the cover to access the screw for the sunvisor locating mount

26.2a Release the gaiter trim from the centre console...

26.2b ...then undo the screws (arrowed)

26.3 Remove the front switch panel

26.4a Carefully prise the trim surround...

26.4b ...to release the retaining clips

26.5a Unclip the heater control surround...

26.5b ...and disconnect the wiring connector (arrowed)

front of the centre console and disconnect the wiring connectors, as it is removed (see illustration).
4 Carefully unclip the trim panel from around the Radio/CD player (see illustrations).
5 Carefully unclip the trim panel from around the heater control panel and disconnect the wiring connector from the passenger airbag warning light (see illustrations).
6 Unclip the trim panel from under the heater control panel (see illustration).
7 Undo the two retaining screws and slide the front upper trim rearwards to unclip it from the centre console (see illustrations).

Low specification models

8 Remove the centre console front upper trim, as described in paragraphs 1 to 7.
9 Pull the trim forwards off the handbrake lever.

10 Remove the lining mats from the rear console oddments recesses, then undo the screws now visible (see illustration).
11 Lift the rear console and withdraw it

forwards over the handbrake lever (see illustration). Disconnect the wiring as applicable.
12 Prise out the covers and undo the lower

26.6 Unclip the lower cover

26.7a Undo the screws (arrowed)...

26.7b ...then unclip the front upper cover

26.10 Undo the screws (arrowed)...

26.11 ...then withdraw the rear console forwards over the handbrake lever

26.12a Prise out the covers and undo the lower side screws...

26.12b ...then unclip the lower covers

26.13 Prise out the side covers...

26.14a ...undo the front screws...

26.14b ...and rear screw...

26.14c ...and withdraw the centre console

side cover retaining screws. Unclip the lower covers from the centre console and remove **(see illustrations)**.

13 Prise out the small upper side covers from each side **(see illustration)**.

14 Undo the mounting screws and withdraw

the centre console from inside the vehicle **(see illustrations)**.

High specification models

15 Remove the centre console front upper trim, as described in paragraphs 1 to 7.

16 Working inside the front footwell, undo the lower side cover retaining screw, then unclip the trim from the centre console and remove **(see illustrations)**.

17 Remove the rubber mat from the storage compartment, then undo the mounting screw **(see illustration)**.

18 Open the top of the armrest, then using two flat pieces of metal (radio releasing keys), withdraw the storage unit out from inside the armrest housing **(see illustrations)**. Disconnect the wiring connector from the base as it is removed.

19 Open the drinks holder at the rear of the centre console and undo the two retaining screws **(see illustration)**.

20 Release the securing clips (one at each side) and withdraw the cup holder **(see illustrations)**.

21 Using a lever, carefully prise the trim

26.16a Undo the front screw

26.16b ...then unclip the lower covers

26.17 Undo the screw under the rubber mat

26.18a Using radio keys to release the locking clips

26.18b Disconnect the wiring connector on removal

26.19 Undo the two rear screws

26.20a Release the retaining clips...

26.20b ...and withdraw the rear cup holder

26.21a Unclip the rear cover...

26.21b ...and release it from the rear of the console

26.22a Undo the inner screw (arrowed)...

panel from the rear of the centre console **(see illustrations)**.
22 Undo the retaining screw inside the front of the armrest aperture and the two screws at the rear of the armrest housing **(see illustrations)**.
23 Unclip the switch/auxiliary plug from the

front of the armrest housing and disconnect the wiring connector; the housing can then be lifted upwards over the handbrake **(see illustrations)**.
24 On DSG semi-automatic transmissions, the gear selector knob will need to be removed. Pull out the button on the side

of the lever and slide a thin screwdriver to prevent it going back in, then from under the gaiter, press the black plastic collar upwards until the gear selector knob can be removed **(see illustrations)**. Disconnect the wiring connector from the base as it is removed

26.22b ...and the two rear side screws (one side shown)

26.23a Unclip the auxiliary switch...

26.23b ...and withdraw the rear armrest

26.24a Pull the side button outwards...

26.24b ...slide a thin screwdriver between the button and the gear lever...

26.24c ...then slide the collar upwards to release the gear knob/gaiter

26.24d Disconnect the wiring connector from the surround

26.25 Withdraw the centre console

27.4 Unclip the cover from the side of the facia

25 The centre console can now be removed from inside the vehicle **(see illustration)**.

Refitting

26 Refitting is a reversal of removal, but tighten the screws securing the centre console to the facia first, before tightening the rest.

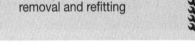

27 Facia panel assembly – removal and refitting

Note: *Refer to the warnings in Chapter 12 for airbags.*

Removal

1 Disconnect the battery negative lead (refer to *Disconnecting the battery* in the *Reference* Chapter at the end of this manual).

2 Remove the steering column shrouds as described in Section 25.
3 Remove the steering column control unit and switch assembly, as described in Chapter 12, Section 4.
4 Prise out the trim panels from each end of the facia **(see illustration)**.
5 Remove the A-pillar upper trim panels, as described in Section 25.
6 Remove the glovebox as described in Section 25.
7 Release the two plastic retaining clips and remove the trim from under the glovebox **(see illustration)**.
8 Working inside the glovebox aperture, undo the two screws from the passenger side airbag mounting bracket and disconnect the wiring connector from the end of the airbag unit **(see illustration)**.
Note: *The facia is removed together with the passenger airbag.*

9 Remove the centre console as described in Section 26.
10 Remove the radio/CD or navigation unit, as described in Chapter 12, Section 21.
11 Remove the Climatronic/heater controls, as described in Chapter 3, Section 9.
12 Undo the two retaining screws and then carefully prise out the central air vents from the top of the facia **(see illustrations)**. Disconnect the wiring connector from the hazard switch as the vents are removed.
13 Remove the facia trim panel located on the outside of the steering column as follows:
a) *Depress the light switch and turn it clockwise until vertical, then remove it and disconnect the wiring. See Chapter 12, Section 4.*
b) *Open the storage compartment and squeeze it in at the sides to remove it from the facia (see illustrations).*

27.7 Release the two clips (arrowed)

27.8 Undo the two screws (arrowed) and disconnect the wiring connector (arrowed)

27.12a Undo the screws (arrowed)...

27.12b ...and prise out the centre air vents

27.13a Press in at each side...

27.13b ...to remove the storage compartment

27.13c Undo the three screws (arrowed)...

27.13d ...the upper screw (arrowed)...

27.13e ...then remove the trim panel from the facia

27.14a Undo the inner screw (arrowed)...

27.14b ...the lower screw (arrowed)...

27.14c ...the upper screw (arrowed)...

c) *Undo the retaining screws, then withdraw the facia trim panel and disconnect the wiring from the headlight range control regulator (see illustrations).*

14 Undo the retaining screws, then remove the facia trim panel located on the inside of the steering column **(see illustrations)**.
15 Remove the driver's knee airbag, as described in Chapter 12, Section 26.

16 Undo the two screws from the driver's knee airbag mounting bracket **(see illustration)**.
17 Remove the bonnet release handle and sill trim kick panel as described in Section 9.
18 Unbolt the fusebox from the driver's side of the facia, and place to one side **(see illustrations)**.
19 Remove the instrument panel as described in Chapter 12, Section 10.
20 Unscrew the retaining screws from the facia assembly, then, with the help of an assistant, pull out from the bulkhead clips and remove from the vehicle **(see illustrations)**. As the facia is being removed, disconnect any wiring retaining clips, noting its routing to aid refitting.

Refitting

21 Refitting is a reversal of the removal procedure, noting the following points:
  a) *Ensure the facia guides engage correctly*

27.14d ...and the outer screw (arrowed)

27.16 Undo the two screws (arrowed)...

27.18a Undo the fusebox upper screw...

27.18b ...and lower screw (arrowed)

27.20a Undo the facia left-hand side retaining screws (arrowed)

27.20b Undo the retaining screw (arrowed)

27.20c Undo the centre retaining screw (arrowed)

27.20d Undo the facia right-hand side upper retaining screw (arrowed)...

27.20e ...and lower retaining screws (arrowed)

27.20f The facia can now be withdrawn out from the passenger compartment

with the clips on the bulkhead. As the facia is being fitted, check that all wiring is routed as noted during removal.

b) Insert all of the retaining screws hand-tight, then close both front doors and check that the facia is positioned centrally between the door trims. If it needs to be moved one way or another, place a wad of cloth between the facia and door trim, then close the door. This should move the facia as required. When central, fully tighten the securing screws.

c) On completion, reconnect the battery and check that all the electrical components and switches function correctly.

Chapter 12
Body electrical system

Contents

Degrees of difficulty

Easy, suitable for novice with little experience	Fairly easy, suitable for beginner with some experience	Fairly difficult, suitable for competent DIY mechanic	Difficult, suitable for experienced DIY mechanic	Very difficult, suitable for expert DIY or professional

Specifications

System type . . . . 12 volt negative earth

Fuses . . . . See *Wiring diagrams* on page 12•26

Bulbs
	Wattage/Type
Brake light (estate models)	21W - bayonet
Brake light (hatchback models)	16W - wedge
Brake light – High level	LEDs
Footwell light	5W - wedge
Front direction indicators	24W - PSY
Front foglight (all except GTi)	51W - HB4
Front foglight (Gti models)	35W - H8
Front sidelight	5W - wedge
Glovebox light	5W - wedge
Headlight:	
Halogen:	
Daytime running/Main beam	15W/55W – H15
Dipped beam	55W - H7
Gas discharge bulb	35W - D1S (high voltage)
Interior light (front and centre)	5W - wedge
Interior light (vanity mirror)	5W - festoon
Luggage compartment light	10W - festoon
Number plate light (secured by clip)	5W - wedge
Number plate light (secured by screws)	5W - festoon
Rear direction indicators (estate models)	21W - bayonet (amber)
Rear direction indicators (hatchback models)	21W - wedge (amber)
Rear side/brake light (estate models)	5/21W - bayonet
Rear sidelight (hatchback models)	16W - wedge
Reversing light (estate models)	21W - bayonet

Torque wrench settings
	Nm	lbf ft
Crash sensor mounting bolt	9	7
Driver's knee airbag mounting nuts	9	7
Passenger airbag and bracket retaining screws	9	7
Wiper arm securing nut:		
Front	20	15
Rear	12	9

1 General information and precautions

⚠️ **Warning: Before carrying out any work on the electrical system, read through the precautions given in 'Safety first!' at the beginning of this manual, and in Chapter 5A.**

The electrical system is of 12-volt negative earth type. Power for the lights and all electrical accessories is supplied by a lead-acid type battery, which is charged by the alternator.

This Chapter covers repair and service procedures for the various electrical components not associated with the engine. Information on the battery, alternator and starter motor can be found in Chapter 5A.

It should be noted that prior to working on any component in the electrical system, the ignition and all electrical consumers must be switched off. Additionally, where stated, the battery negative lead must be disconnected, however, note the information given in *Disconnecting the battery* in the *Reference* chapter at the end of this manual, as special procedures have to be carried out when reconnecting the battery.

Some models are fitted with gas discharge headlight systems, which include automatic range control to reduce the possibility of dazzling oncoming drivers. Note the special precautions which apply to these systems as given in Section 5.

2 Electrical fault finding – general information

Note: Refer to the precautions given in 'Safety first!' and in Chapter 5A before starting work. The following tests relate to testing of the main electrical circuits, and should not be used to test delicate electronic circuits (such as anti-lock braking systems), particularly where an electronic control module is used.

General

1 A typical electrical circuit consists of an electrical component; any switches, relays, motors, fuses, fusible links or circuit breakers related to that component, and the wiring and connectors which link the component to both the battery and the chassis. To help to pin-point a problem in an electrical circuit, wiring diagrams are included at the end of this Chapter. **Note:** *Many of the circuits are controlled by computerised systems (for instance, the windscreen wipers will only operate with the bonnet closed), so before assuming there are faults, it is worthwhile checking if specific conditions apply.*

2 Before attempting to diagnose an electrical fault, first study the appropriate wiring diagram to obtain a complete understanding of the components included in the particular circuit concerned. The possible sources of a fault can be narrowed down by noting if other components related to the circuit are operating properly. If several components or circuits fail at one time, the problem is likely to be related to a shared fuse or earth connection.

3 Electrical problems usually stem from simple causes, such as loose or corroded connections, a faulty earth connection, a blown fuse, a melted fusible link, or a faulty relay (refer to Section 3 for details of testing relays). Visually inspect the condition of all fuses, wires and connections in a problem circuit before testing the components. Use the wiring diagrams to determine which terminal connections will need to be checked in order to pin-point the trouble spot.

4 The basic tools required for electrical fault finding include a circuit tester or voltmeter (a 12-volt bulb with a set of test leads can also be used for certain tests); a self-powered test light (sometimes known as a continuity tester); an ohmmeter (to measure resistance); a battery and set of test leads; and a jumper wire, preferably with a circuit breaker or fuse incorporated, which can be used to bypass suspect wires or electrical components. Before attempting to locate a problem with test instruments, use the wiring diagram to determine where to make the connections.

5 To find the source of an intermittent wiring fault (usually due to a poor or dirty connection, or damaged wiring insulation), a wiggle test can be performed on the wiring. This involves wiggling the wiring by hand to see if the fault occurs as the wiring is moved. It should be possible to narrow down the source of the fault to a particular section of wiring. This method of testing can be used in conjunction with any of the tests described in the following sub-Sections.

6 Apart from problems due to poor connections, two basic types of fault can occur in an electrical circuit – open-circuit, or short-circuit.

7 Open-circuit faults are caused by a break somewhere in the circuit, which prevents current from flowing. An open-circuit fault will prevent a component from working, but will not cause the relevant circuit fuse to blow.

8 Short-circuit faults are caused by a short somewhere in the circuit, which allows the current flowing in the circuit to escape along an alternative route, usually to earth. Short-circuit faults are normally caused by a breakdown in wiring insulation, which allows a feed wire to touch either another wire, or an earthed component such as the bodyshell. A short-circuit fault will normally cause the relevant circuit fuse to blow.

Finding an open-circuit

9 To check for an open-circuit, connect one lead of a circuit tester or voltmeter to either the negative battery terminal or a known good earth.

10 Connect the other lead to a connector in the circuit being tested, preferably nearest to the battery or fuse.

11 Switch on the circuit, bearing in mind that some circuits are live only when the ignition switch is moved to a particular position.

12 If voltage is present (indicated either by the tester bulb lighting or a voltmeter reading, as applicable), this means that the section of the circuit between the relevant connector and the battery is problem-free.

13 Continue to check the remainder of the circuit in the same fashion.

14 When a point is reached at which no voltage is present, the problem must lie between that point and the previous test point with voltage. Most problems can be traced to a broken, corroded or loose connection.

Finding a short-circuit

15 To check for a short-circuit; first disconnect the load(s) from the circuit (loads are the components which draw current from a circuit, such as bulbs, motors, heating elements, etc).

16 Remove the relevant fuse from the circuit, and connect a circuit tester or voltmeter to the fuse connections.

17 Switch on the circuit, bearing in mind that some circuits are live only when the ignition switch is moved to a particular position.

18 If voltage is present (indicated either by the tester bulb lighting or a voltmeter reading, as applicable), this means that there is a short circuit.

19 If no voltage is present, but the fuse still blows with the load(s) connected, this indicates an internal fault in the load(s).

Finding an earth fault

20 The battery negative terminal is connected to earth – the metal of the engine/transmission and the car body – and most systems are wired so that they only receive a positive feed, the current returning through the metal of the car body. This means that the component mounting and the body form part of that circuit. Loose or corroded mountings can therefore cause a range of electrical faults, ranging from total failure of a circuit, to a puzzling partial fault. In particular, lights may shine dimly (especially when another circuit sharing the same earth point is in operation), motors (e.g. wiper motors or the radiator cooling fan motor) may run slowly, and the operation of one circuit may have an apparently unrelated effect on another. Note that on many vehicles, earth straps are used between certain components, such as the engine/transmission and the body, usually where there is no metal-to-metal contact between components due to flexible rubber mountings, etc.

21 To check whether a component is properly earthed, disconnect the battery (refer to the warnings given in the Reference section at the rear of the manual) and connect one lead of an ohmmeter to a known good earth point. Connect the other lead to the wire or earth connection being tested. The resistance reading should be zero; if not, check the connection as follows.

22 If an earth connection is thought to be

faulty, dismantle the connection and clean back to bare metal both the bodyshell and the wire terminal or the component earth connection mating surface. Be careful to remove all traces of dirt and corrosion, and then use a knife to trim away any paint, so that a clean metal-to-metal joint is made. On reassembly, tighten the joint fasteners securely; if a wire terminal is being refitted, use serrated washers between the terminal and the bodyshell to ensure a clean and secure connection. When the connection is remade, prevent the onset of corrosion in the future by applying a coat of petroleum jelly or silicone-based grease or by spraying on (at regular intervals) a proprietary ignition sealer or a water dispersant lubricant.

3.2 Fusebox on right-hand side of facia

3.3 Removing a fuse from the facia fusebox

3 Fuses and relays – general information

Fuses and fusible links

1 Fuses are designed to break a circuit when a predetermined current is reached, in order to protect the components and wiring, which could be damaged by excessive current flow. Any excessive current flow will be due to a fault in the circuit, usually a short-circuit (see Section 2).
2 On Golf models, the main fuses are located in the fusebox on the driver's side of the facia; open the driver's door and unclip the fusebox cover from the end of the facia to gain access to the fuses (see illustration). The fuse locations are marked onto the rear of the fusebox cover.
3 To remove a fuse, first switch off the circuit concerned (or the ignition), and then pull the fuse out of its terminals (see illustration).
4 The wire within the fuse should be visible; if the fuse has blown it will be broken or melted.
5 Always renew a fuse with one of the correct rating; never use a fuse with a different rating from that specified.
6 Refer to the wiring diagrams for details of the fuse ratings and the circuits protected. The fuse rating is stamped on the top of the fuse; the fuses are also colour-coded as follows.

Colour	Rating
Light brown	5A
Brown	7.5A
Red	10A
Blue	15A
Yellow	20A
White or clear	25A
Green	30A
Orange	40A

7 Never renew a fuse more than once without tracing the source of the trouble. If the new fuse blows immediately, find the cause before renewing it again; a short to earth as a result of faulty insulation is most likely. Where a fuse protects more than one circuit, try to isolate the fault by switching on each circuit in turn (where possible) until the fuse blows again.

3.8a Slide the locking tabs in the direction of the arrows...

Always carry a supply of spare fuses of each relevant rating on the vehicle.
8 Additional fuses and relays are located in the fusebox located on the left-hand side of the engine compartment. Release the two securing clips and withdraw the cover to gain access to the fuses and relays (see illustrations).
9 To renew a fusible link, first disconnect the battery negative terminal. Unscrew the retaining nuts then remove the blown link from the front of the engine compartment fusebox (see illustration). Fit the new link to its terminals and reconnect the leads. Ensure the link and leads are correctly seated then refit the retaining nuts and tighten securely. Clip the cover back into position then reconnect the battery.

Relays

10 A relay is an electrically operated switch, which is used for the following reasons:

3.9 Fusible link on the front of the fuse/ relay box

3.8b ...to access the fuse and relay box in the engine compartment

a) A relay can switch a heavy current remotely from the circuit in which the current is flowing, allowing the use of lighter-gauge wiring and switch contacts.
b) A relay can receive more than one control input, unlike a mechanical switch.
c) A relay can have a timer function – for example, the intermittent wiper relay.

11 Most of the relays are located on the relay plate behind the driver's side facia, however, additional relays are located in the engine compartment fusebox (see illustration 3.8).
12 Access to the relays can be obtained after removing the driver's side lower facia panel as described in Chapter 11, Section 27 (see illustration). Identification details of the relays are given at the start of the wiring diagrams.
13 If a circuit or system controlled by a relay develops a fault, and the relay is suspect, operate the system. If the relay is functioning, it should be possible to hear it click as it is

3.12 Relays located behind the facia

4.4 Disconnect the wiring connector

4.5a Undo the retaining screw (arrowed)

4.5b Insert a 2.5mm pin (arrowed) to release the front securing clip

4.5c Release the rear clip and remove control unit

4.5d Two securing clips (arrowed)

4.6a Release the two securing clips (arrowed)...

4.6b ...and remove the airbag clock spring/slip-ring unit

4.7a Slide a feeler blade down to release the securing clip...

4.7b ...then unclip and remove the switch

energised. If this is the case, the fault lies with the components or wiring of the system. If the relay is not being energised, then either the relay is not receiving a main supply or a switching voltage, or the relay itself is faulty. Testing is by the substitution of a known

good unit, but be careful – while some relays are identical in appearance and in operation, others look similar but perform different functions.

14 To remove a relay, first ensure that the relevant circuit is switched off. The relay can

then simply be pulled out from the socket, and pushed back into position.

15 The direction indicator/hazard flasher relay is integral with the hazard warning switch. Refer to Section 4 for the switch removal procedure.

4 Switches – removal and refitting

Note: *Before working on any electrical systems switch off the ignition and all electrical consumers and remove the ignition key.*

Ignition switch

1 Refer to Chapter 10, Section22.

Wiper and indicator/ cruise switches

2 Check that the front wheels are pointing straight-ahead and the steering wheel is in its centre position, then remove the steering wheel as described in Chapter 10, Section 20.

3 Remove the steering column shrouds, as described in Chapter 11, Section 25.

Models up to 05/2010

4 Disconnect the wiring connectors from the electronic control unit **(see illustration)**.

5 Remove the steering column electronics control unit, from below the steering column. To do this, undo the single retaining screw, then insert a 2.5 mm diameter rod (drill bit) through the hole provided (below the screw hole), and release the centre clip. Now use a screwdriver to release the rear clip. Pull down the control unit from the column switch carrier **(see illustrations)**.

6 The airbag clock spring/slip-ring must be held in its centre position while it is removed, to ensure correct refitting. Unclip the airbag clock spring/slip-ring from the combination switch carrier by lifting the retaining hooks **(see illustrations)**.

7 Remove the relevant switch by inserting a 1.0 mm feeler gauge through the slot provided to release the switch from the carrier. Release the securing clip at the rear of the switch and slide the switch forwards out from the housing **(see illustrations)**.

8 Refitting is a reversal of removal.

Models from 06/2010

Note: *On these models the lighting and wiper switch is one unit and cannot be renewed separately.*

9 Disconnect the wiring connectors from the airbag clock spring/electronic control unit. Note this is one unit and cannot be separated.

10 On switch assembly manufactured by VALEO, undo the three retaining screws and withdraw the airbag clock spring/electronic control unit from over the steering column. Then undo the three securing screws and remove the switch assembly.

11 On switch assembly manufactured by KOSTAL, undo the retaining screw at the lower part of the assembly, then release the two upper securing clips, then withdraw the airbag clock spring/electronic control unit from over the steering column. Undo the securing screw from the lower part of the assembly, and then remove the switch assembly.

12 Refitting is a reversal of removal. Note, as the switch assembly is being refitted, make sure the indicator switch is in the centre position; otherwise the reset lever if extended can break off as the switch is fitted.

Lighting switch

13 With the light switch in position O, press the switch centre inwards and turn it slightly to the right. Hold this position and pull the switch from the dash **(see illustration)**.

14 As the switch is withdrawn from the dash, disconnect the wiring plug.

15 To refit the switch, first reconnect the wiring plug, then hold the switch and press the rotary part inwards and slightly to the right. Insert the switch into the dash, turn the rotary part to position O and release. Check the switch for correct operation.

Headlamp range control and instrument illumination switch

16 Remove the lighting switch as described in paragraphs 13 to 15.

17 Remove the driver's side storage compartment **(see illustration)**.

18 Reach up behind the facia and release the clips and remove the switch **(see illustrations)**. Disconnect the wiring from the switch.

19 Refitting is a reversal of removal.

4.13 Press the switch centre inwards and turn it slightly to the right to remove

4.18a Reach inside and unclip the switch...

Air conditioning/rear window heating switches

20 The switches are integral with the heater control panel, and cannot be removed separately. Refer to Chapter 3 for details of heater control panel removal and refitting.

Heater blower motor switch

21 The switch is integral with the heater control panel, and cannot be removed separately. Refer to Chapter 3 for details of heater control panel removal and refitting.

Hazard warning

22 Using two feeler blades or similar, carefully unclip the switch from the facia, disconnect the wiring connector on removal **(see illustration)**. Refitting is a reversal of removal.

4.17 Unclip the storage compartment from the facia

4.18b ...then remove it from the facia

ESP/ASR(TCS)/Parking sensor switches etc.

23 Remove the ashtray/switch panel from the front of the centre console as described in Chapter 11, Section 26.

24 Release the retaining clips and withdraw the switch from the top of the switch panel **(see illustration)**.

25 Refitting is a reversal of removal.

Passenger air bag on/off switch

26 Remove the glovebox, as described in Chapter 11, Section 25.

27 Release the retaining clips and withdraw the switch from inside the glovebox **(see illustration)**.

28 Refitting is a reversal of removal.

Glovebox light switch

29 Remove the glovebox, as described in Chapter 11, Section 25.

4.22 Using feeler blades to release the switch from the facia

4.24 Unclip the switch from the trim panel

4.27 Unclip the switch from inside the glovebox

4.30 Release the clip and slide the switch down to remove

4.36a Release the securing clips...

30 Release the retaining lug and lide the switch downwards to remove it from the rear of the glovebox **(see illustration)**.
31 Refitting is a reversal of removal.

Driver's door locking switch

32 Remove the door inner trim panel, as described in Chapter 11, Section 12.
33 Release the securing clips and withdraw the switch from the inside of the door trim panel **(see illustration)**.
34 Refitting is a reversal of removal.

Electric window/mirror switch assembly

35 Remove the door inner trim panel, as described in Chapter 11, Section 12.
36 Release the securing clips and withdraw the switch panel from the outside of the door trim panel **(see illustrations)**.
37 Refitting is a reversal of removal.

4.43 Unclip the switch from the B-pillar trim panel

4.33 Unclip the switch from the rear of the door trim panel

4.36b ...and remove the switch panel from the outside of the door trim

Handbrake 'on' warning switch

38 Refer to Chapter 9, Section 17.

Brake light switch

39 Refer to Chapter 9, Section 18.

Reversing light switch

40 Refer to Chapter 7A, Section 5.

Courtesy light switches

41 The courtesy light switch is integrated into the door lock mechanism, and cannot be renewed independently. If the courtesy light switch is faulty, renew the door lock mechanism as described in Chapter 11, Section 13.

Luggage area light switch

42 The luggage compartment light switch is integrated into the tailgate/boot lid lock mechanism, and cannot be renewed independently. If the luggage compartment

4.47 Disconnect the wiring connector from the sensor

light switch is faulty, renew the tailgate/boot lid lock mechanism as described in Chapter 11, Section 16.

Interior monitoring deactivation switch

43 Carefully prise the switch from the B-pillar trim panel **(see illustration)**, and disconnect the wiring plug.
44 Refitting is a reversal of removal.

Rain and light sensor

45 The windscreen wipers/lights (depending on model) are automatically activated, when the sensor located in the interior mirror base detects droplets of water/darkness.
46 Remove the interior mirror, as described in Chapter 11, Section 18.
47 Remove the plastic trim/stay, and disconnect the wiring connector from the sensor **(see illustration)**.
48 The mirror base/sensor is bonded to the windscreen **(see illustration)**. Whilst it is possible to remove the base by means of a scraper, great care must be exercised to avoid damaging the windscreen.
49 Due to the hazardous chemicals involved, it is recommended that the bonding of the mirror base to the windscreen be entrusted to a VW dealer or suitably equipped specialist.
50 With the base/sensor in place, refit the mirror with reference to Chapter 11, Section 18

5 Bulbs (exterior lights) – renewal

General

1 Whenever a bulb is renewed, note the following points:
 a) *Switch off the ignition and all electrical consumers before commencing work.*
 b) *Remember that if the light has just been in use the bulb may be extremely hot.*
 c) *Always check the bulb contacts and holder, ensuring that there is clean metal-to-metal contact. Clean off any corrosion or dirt before fitting a new bulb.*
 d) *Wherever bayonet-type bulbs are fitted ensure that the spring-tensioned arms bear firmly against the bulb contacts.*

4.48 Sensor and mirror base fitted to windscreen

5.2 Remove the rubber cover

5.3 Turn the bulb anti-clockwise to remove

5.5 Make sure of good connections (arrowed)

e) *Always ensure that the new bulb is of the correct rating and that it is thoroughly clean before fitting it.*

Headlight main beam/ daytime running light

Note: *Do not touch the glass envelope of the bulb if it is to be re-used.*

2 Working in the engine compartment, remove the rubber cover from the rear of the headlight **(see illustration)**.

3 Turn the bulbholder anti-clockwise a quarter of a turn and remove it from the rear of the headlight unit **(see illustration)**. **Note:** *The bulb is integral with the bulbholder.*

4 When handling the new bulb, use a tissue or clean cloth to avoid touching the glass with the fingers; moisture and grease from the skin can cause blackening and rapid failure of this type of bulb. If the glass is accidentally touched, wipe it clean using methylated spirit.

5 Install the new bulb; ensuring that it is located correctly in the headlight unit, turn it clockwise to secure it in position with the electrical terminals **(see illustration)**.

6 Refit the headlight cover, making sure that it is secure.

Headlight dip beam

Halogen headlights

Note: *Do not touch the glass envelope of the bulb if it is to be re-used.*

7 Working in the engine compartment, remove the outermost rubber cover from the rear of the 'HELLA' headlight unit **(see illustrations)**. On VALEO make headlights, release the

securing clip to remove the rear plastic cover. If required, pull back the inner wheel arch liner and access the outer light bulb from under the front wing panel.

8 Turn the bulbholder anti-clockwise and remove it from the rear of the headlight unit **(see illustrations)**. The bulb can then be pulled out from the bulb holder.

9 When handling the new bulb, use a tissue or clean cloth to avoid touching the glass with the fingers; moisture and grease from the skin can cause blackening and rapid failure of this type of bulb. If the glass is accidentally touched, wipe it clean using methylated spirit.

10 Fit the new bulb to the bulbholder, ensuring that the location lugs are aligned, then fit the bulbholder to the headlight and turn clockwise to secure **(see illustration)**.

11 Refit the headlight cover, making sure that it is secure.

Gas discharge headlights

⚠️ **Warning: The headlight bulb contains gas at very high pressure, and it is recommended that gloves and eye protection be worn to prevent potential personal injury.**

Note: *Do not touch the glass envelope of the bulb if it is to be re-used.*

12 Remove the headlight as described in Section 7.

13 Remove the outermost cover from the rear of the headlight.

14 Disconnect the wiring connector, by releasing the securing clip and pulling the wiring connector from the lower part of the bulb.

15 Turn the gas discharge bulb and holder anti-clockwise and carefully withdraw it from the headlight. **Note:** *The gas discharge bulb is integral with the bulbholder.*

5.7a Remove the rubber cover

5.7b Reach up inside the inner wing to remove bulb (arrowed) on the left-hand side

5.8a Turn the bulb anti-clockwise to remove...

5.8b ...then pull the bulb from the holder

5.10 The bulb holder can only be fitted in one position

5.20a Pull the bulb holder from the light unit...

5.20b ...and withdraw the bulb

5.22 Remove the rubber cover...

5.23 ...turn the bulbholder anti-clockwise and remove it...

5.24 ...then unclip the bulb from the wiring plug

16 When handling the new bulb, use a tissue or clean cloth to avoid touching the glass with the fingers; moisture and grease from the skin can cause blackening and rapid failure of this type of bulb. If the glass is accidentally touched, wipe it clean using methylated spirit.
17 Fit the new gas discharge bulb and holder to the headlight and turn clockwise to secure. Reconnect the wiring connector to the lower part of the bulb.
18 Refit the headlight cover, making sure that it is secure.
Caution: After refitting a gas discharge headlamp, the basic setting of the Automatic Range Control system should be checked.

Front sidelight

19 Working in the engine compartment, remove the innermost small plastic cover from the rear of the headlight **(see illustration 5.2)**.
20 Carefully pull the sidelight bulbholder from

the headlight unit. The bulb is a push-fit in the holder and can be removed by grasping the end of the bulb and pulling it out **(see illustrations)**.
21 Refitting is a reversal of removal, making sure that the headlight cover is securely refitted.

Front direction indicator

22 Working in the engine compartment, remove the centre small rubber cover from the rear of the headlight **(see illustration)**.
23 Turn the bulbholder anti-clockwise and remove it from the headlight complete with bulb **(see illustration)**.
24 Disconnect the wiring connector, by releasing the securing clip and pulling the wiring connector from the bulb holder **(see illustration)**. Note: *The bulb is integral with the bulbholder.*
25 When handling the new bulb, use a tissue or clean cloth to avoid touching the glass with the fingers; moisture and grease from the skin

can cause blackening and rapid failure of this type of bulb. If the glass is accidentally touched, wipe it clean using methylated spirit.
26 Reconnect the wiring connector to the bulb and holder, then fit the bulbholder to the headlight and turn clockwise to secure.
27 Refit the headlight cover, making sure that it is secure.

Front foglight

28 Pull back the inner wheel arch liner to access the rear of the foglight unit and disconnect the wiring connector **(see illustration)**.
29 Turn the bulbholder anti-clockwise and remove it complete with bulb from the rear of the foglight **(see illustration)**. Note: *The bulb is integral with the bulbholder.*
30 Fit the new bulb using a reversal of the removal procedure.

Direction indicator in exterior mirror

31 There are no conventional bulbs in the exterior mirror, but LED's instead, therefore if the direction indicator is not working, the complete unit must be renewed as described in Chapter 11, Section 18.

Rear light cluster

Hatchback – indicator/stop/tail

32 Remove the rear light cluster as described in Section 7.
33 Release the retaining clips and remove the bulbholder from the rear of the cluster. The bulbs are a glass wedge type – pull the bulbs to remove **(see illustrations)**.

5.28 Disconnect the wiring connector...

5.29 ...then turn the bulbholder anti-clockwise to remove

5.33a Remove the rear light bulbholder...

5.33b ...and remove the relevant bulb - Hatchback

5.36a Remove the tailgate bulbholder...

5.36b ...and remove the relevant bulb - Hatchback

5.38 Remove the inner trim panel - Estate

5.39 Squeeze together the retaining clips to remove the bulbholder...

5.40 ...and twist the bayonet type bulb to remove - Estate

34 Fit the new bulb using a reversal of the removal procedure.

Hatchback – reversing/fog/tail

35 Open the tailgate and prise the cover from the tailgate trim cover.
36 Release the retaining clips and remove the bulbholder from the rear of the light unit. The bulbs are a glass wedge type – pull the bulbs to remove (see illustrations).
37 Fit the new bulb using a reversal of the removal procedure.

Estate

38 Open the access cover in the side panel trim (see illustration).
39 Squeeze together the retaining clips and remove the bulbholder assembly (see illustration).
40 The bulbs are a bayonet-fit in the bulbholder – depress and twist the relevant bulb to remove it (see illustration).
41 Fit the new bulb using a reversal of the removal procedure.

High-level brake light

Note: *The light is of LED design; therefore if faulty the complete unit must be renewed. Note that the LEDs are arranged in groups of four, and if just one group fails, the light still meets legal requirement. Failure of more than one group renders the light illegal.*
42 Remove the high-level light unit as described in Section 7.

Number plate light – secured with clip

43 Release the securing clip, and withdraw the light unit from the tailgate (see illustration).

44 Twist the bulb holder to remove from light unit, and then pull the bulb to remove it from the holder (see illustrations).
45 Fit the new bulb using a reversal of the removal procedure.

5.43 Unclip the light unit...

5.44b ...then pull the bulb from the holder

Number plate light – secured with screws

46 Undo the two securing screws and withdraw the light unit from the tailgate (see illustrations).

5.44a ...twist and remove bulb holder...

5.46a Undo the screws...

5.46b ...and remove the rear number plate light

6.3a Release the two securing clips (arrowed)...

6.3b ...and remove the storage compartment

47 Unclip the bulb from the light unit; the bulb is a festoon type.
48 Fit the new bulb using a reversal of the removal procedure.

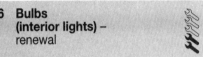
6 Bulbs (interior lights) – renewal

General

1 Whenever a bulb is renewed, note the following points:
  a) *Switch off the ignition and all electrical consumers before commencing work.*
  b) *Remember that if the light has just been in use the bulb may be extremely hot.*
  c) *Always check the bulb contacts and holder, ensuring that there is clean metal-to-metal contact between them. Clean off*

any corrosion or dirt before fitting a new bulb.
  d) *Wherever bayonet-type bulbs are fitted ensure that the live contact(s) bear firmly against the bulb contact.*
  e) *Always ensure that the new bulb is of the correct rating and that it is completely clean before fitting it.*

Front courtesy/reading light

2 For access to the light bulbs, the complete light unit will need to be removed.
3 Release the retaining clips and remove the compartment from the rear of the light console **(see illustrations)**.
4 Unclip the rear of the cover over the sensors and undo the two retaining screws **(see illustrations)**.
5 Withdraw the light unit from the roof panel and disconnect the wiring connectors **(see illustrations)**.

6 To remove the bulb, twist the bulbholder anti-clockwise and remove it from the rear of the light unit, then pull out the wedge-type bulb from the holder **(see illustration)**.
7 Fit the new bulb and light unit using a reversal of the removal procedure.

Front footwell illumination lights

8 Use a screwdriver to prise out the light, and then disconnect the wiring **(see illustration)**.
9 Unclip the lens from the metal heat shield, and pull out the wedge-type bulb **(see illustrations)**.
10 Refitting is a reverse of the removal procedure.

Rear courtesy/reading lights

11 Using a screwdriver, carefully release the locking lugs and remove the lens from the light unit **(see illustration)**.

6.4a Unclip and hinge the trim forwards...

6.4b ...then undo the two retaining screws (arrowed)

6.5a Unclip the switch/light panel...

6.5b ...and disconnect the wiring connectors

6.6 Remove the bulb from the light unit

6.8 Remove the light unit and disconnect the wiring

6.9a Unclip the metal shield...

6.9b ...then pull the bulb from the spring contacts

6.11 Unclip the light cover...

6.12 ...and pull out the wedge-type bulb

6.13a Unclip the rear light housing...

6.13b ...and disconnect the wiring connector

12 Pull the wedge-type bulb from the light **(see illustration)**.

13 If required remove the light unit by releaseing the two retaining clips and removing it from the headlining. Disconnect the wiring connector as it is removed **(see illustrations)**.

14 Fit the new bulb and light unit using a reversal of the removal procedure.

Vanity mirror lights

15 Carefully prise the light unit from its location in the headlining **(see illustrations)**. The festoon-type bulb is a push-fit in the spring contacts

16 No renewal procedure is recommended for the microswitch in the sun visor. If the switch is faulty, the visor must be renewed.

Glovebox illumination light

17 Open the glovebox, then use a screwdriver to prise out the lens **(see illustration)**. Disconnect the wiring.

18 Unclip the lens from the metal heat shield, and pull out the wedge-type bulb **(see illustrations 6.9a and 6.9b)**.

19 Fit the new bulb using a reversal of the removal procedure.

Luggage compartment light

20 Carefully prise the light unit from its location in the luggage compartment or boot lid, as applicable. The festoon-type bulb is a push-fit in the spring contacts **(see illustrations)**.

6.15a Prise out the vanity mirror light...

6.15b ...and remove the festoon-type bulb

6.17 Prise out the glovebox light unit

6.20a Prise out the luggage compartment light...

6.20b ...and remove the festoon-type bulb

21 Fit the new bulb using a reversal of the removal procedure.

Instrument panel illumination/ warning lights

22 The instrument panel illumination/warning lights are non-renewable LEDs.

Cigarette lighter/ ashtray illumination

23 Remove the centre console, as described in Chapter 11, Section 26.
24 Lift the retaining clip, and pull the bulbholder from the rear of the assembly and disconnect the wiring plug. The bulb is integral with the bulbholder (see illustration).
25 Fit the new bulb using a reversal of the removal procedure.

Heater/ventilation control panel illumination

26 The control panel is illuminated by LEDs built into the panel. Consequently, if a fault develops, renewal of the panel is necessary.

Switch illumination

27 The switch illumination bulbs are integral with the switches. If a bulb fails, the complete switch must be renewed.

7 Exterior light units – removal and refitting

1 Before removing any light units, switch off the ignition and all electrical consumers, and then remove the ignition key.

6.24 The bulb is integral with the holder

Headlight

2 Remove the front bumper cover, as described in Chapter 11, Section 6.
3 Mark the position of the headlight mountings to ensure correct alignment on refitting
4 Working at the rear of the light unit undo the lower retaining screw (see illustration).
5 Undo the three mounting bolts along the top of the headlight unit, and then pull the headlight unit forward slightly (see illustration).
6 Unplug the wiring multipin connector as the headlight is withdrawn (see illustration).
7 Refitting is a reversal of removal, but on completion, check that the headlight is aligned flush with the surrounding bodywork. If not, turn the eccentric adjustment bushing on the inside of the headlight as required (see illustration). Finally, have the headlight alignment checked at the earliest opportunity.

Caution: After refitting a gas discharge headlamp, the basic setting of the Automatic Range Control system should be checked. Because of the requirement for specialised equipment, this can only be carried out by a VW dealer or suitably equipped specialist. The headlight bulb contains gas at very high pressure, and it is recommended that gloves and eye protection be worn to prevent potential personal injury.

Gas discharge bulb control unit/ starter

Note: *There are two control units on the base of the headlight unit, one is the output module (three screws) and one is the starter (two screws).*
8 Remove the headlight as described above.
9 Undo the retaining screws, and remove the control unit from the base of the headlight. Note that the electrical connections are automatically separated when the unit is removed.
10 Refitting is a reversal of removal.

Direction indicator in mirror

11 Remove the exterior mirror housing as described in Chapter 11, Section 18.

Front foglight

12 Carefully unclip the trim from around the foglight (see illustrations).
13 Undo the retaining screw and then unclip the foglight from the front bumper (see illustrations), disconnect the wiring connector as the light unit is removed.

7.4 Undo the retaining screw (arrowed)

7.5 Undo the upper retaining screws (arrowed)

7.6 Disconnecting the wiring connector

7.7 Headlight adjustment bolt (arrowed)

7.12a Prise out the trim cover...

7.12b ...and unclip it from the bumper

7.13a Undo the retaining screw (arrowed)...

7.13b ...and unclip the inside from the bumper

7.15 Disconnecting the wiring connector...

7.16 ...and unscrew the securing bolt/ spring - Hatchback

7.17a Align the lugs/guides at the side (arrowed)...

7.17b ...and lower edge (arrowed) of the light unit

14 Refitting is a reversal of removal.

Rear light cluster

Hatchback – indicator/stop/tail

15 Inside the rear luggage compartment, fold back the carpet to access the light cluster wiring connector and securing bolt (see illustration).
16 Disconnect the wiring plug, and unscrew the securing bolt (see illustration). The light unit can then be withdrawn from the rear of the vehicle.
17 Refitting is a reversal of removal, making sure that the alignment lugs locate on refitting (see illustrations).

Hatchback – reversing/fog/tail

18 Open the tailgate, prise the cover from inside the tailgate trim and remove the bulb holder, as described in Section 5.
19 Undo the two retaining nuts and remove the light unit from the tailgate (see illustration).
20 Refitting is a reversal of removal.

Estate models

21 Open the tailgate, and remove the bulb holder from inside the rear light cluster, as described in Section 5.
22 Unscrew the mounting nuts and withdraw the rear light cluster from the rear of the vehicle (see illustration).
23 Disconnect the wiring plug, as the light unit is withdrawn (see illustration).
24 Refitting is a reversal of removal, making sure that the alignment lugs locate on refitting (see illustration).

High level brake light

All models except GTi

Note: The light is of LED design; therefore if faulty the complete unit must be renewed.

7.19 Tailgate light securing nuts - Hatchback

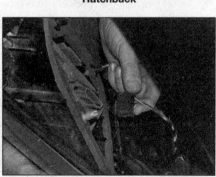

7.23 Disconnecting the wiring connector

Note that the LEDs are arranged in groups of four, and if just one group fails, the light still meets legal requirement. Failure of more than one group renders the light illegal.
25 The high-level brake light is removed from

7.22 Rear light securing nuts - Estate

7.24 Align the locating peg and grommet (arrowed)

7.26 Unclip the high-level brake light...

7.27 ...and disconnect the wiring connector

the outside of the tailgate. First, protect the surrounding paintwork with adhesive tape.

26 Insert a wedge tool between the upper edge of the light and the tailgate, taking care not to damage the seal, and then tap in the wedge to release the light unit **(see illustration)**.

27 Disconnect the wiring and remove the light unit **(see illustration)**.

28 Fit the new light unit using a reversal of the removal procedure.

GTi models

Note: *The high-level brake light is incorporated in the spoiler. Use of cutting thread is necessary to release the spoiler from the adhesive tape. Do not use cutting wire, as this will damage the paintwork.*

29 Use the cutting thread on each end of the spoiler to cut through the adhesive tape.

30 Carefully prise the spoiler from the tailgate retaining clips, and disconnect the wiring.

31 Undo the screws and remove the light unit from the spoiler.

32 Refitting is a reversal of removal.

Rear number plate light

33 The procedure is described as part of the rear number plate light bulb renewal procedure in Section 5.

8 Headlight beam adjustment components – removal and refitting

Headlight adjustment switch

1 The switch is integral with the instrument illumination switch.

8.14 Unclip the trim cover from the side of the facia

2 Removal and refitting of the switch assembly is covered in Section 4.

Headlight range adjustment motor

Halogen (Hella)

3 Remove the headlight (see Section 7).

4 Remove the outer cover from the rear of the headlight.

5 Disconnect the wiring from the range control motor, then turn it clockwise and pull it back slightly, then press the ball-head downwards out of the cup, and remove the motor.

6 Refitting is a reversal of removal, making sure the ball joint mounting is correctly located in the headlight reflector.

Halogen (Valeo)

7 Remove the headlight (see Section 7).

8 Release the securing clip and remove the plastic cover from the rear of the headlight unit.

9 On the upper part of the headlight unit, turn the manual adjuster screw for the vertical adjustment, fully clockwise (right-hand headlight) or fully anti-clockwise (left-hand headlight).

10 Working inside the rear of the light unit, disconnect the wiring connector from the range control motor.

11 Swivel the motor downwards to release it from the rear of the light unit. Tilt and pull it back slightly, then press the ball-head downwards out of the cup, and remove the motor.

12 Refitting is a reversal of removal, making sure the ball joint mounting is correctly located in the headlight reflector.

Gas discharge headlights

13 The range control motor cannot be

9.2 Headlight adjustment screws (arrowed)

removed from the headlight unit. If faulty renew the headlight unit as described in Section 7.

Automatic range control ECU

Note: *Although it is possible to remove and refit the ECU, the new unit will need to be coded before it will function correctly. This task can only be carried out by a VW dealer or suitably equipped specialist.*

14 The ECU is located behind the passenger end of the facia **(see illustration)**. First, prise off the end cover.

15 Release the locking lever and open the wiring connector so that it can be disconnected.

16 Undo the mounting screw and withdraw the ECU from the side of the glovebox.

17 Refitting is a reversal of removal, but make sure the ECU is correctly located in the bracket before reconnecting the wiring.

Vehicle level sender

18 Refer to Chapter 10, Section 19.

9 Headlight beam alignment – general information

1 Accurate adjustment of the headlight beam is only possible using optical beam setting equipment and this work should be carried out by a VW dealer or suitably-equipped workshop.

2 For reference, the headlights can be manually adjusted using the adjuster assemblies fitted to the top of each light unit **(see illustration)**. The inner adjuster alters the lateral position of the beam whilst the outer adjuster alters the height of the beam.

10 Instrument panel – removal and refitting

Removal

1 Switch off the ignition and all electrical consumers and remove the ignition key. Release the steering wheel adjustment handle, pull the wheel out as far as possible, and set it in the lowest position.

2 Carefully prise out the steering column upper gap cover, and then undo the two

10.2a Unclip the upper shroud from the instrument panel...

10.2b ...and undo the retaining screws (arrowed)

10.3a Release the upper part of the instrument panel and withdraw it from the facia...

screws at the lower part of the instrument panel **(see illustrations)**.

3 Release the upper retaining clips and carefully pull the instrument panel from the facia, release the locking lever and disconnect the wiring plug from the rear of the instrument panel **(see illustrations)**.

Refitting

4 Refitting is a reversal of removal.

11 Instrument panel components – removal and refitting

It is not possible to dismantle the instrument panel. If any of the gauges are faulty, the complete instrument panel must be renewed.

12 Service interval indicator – general information and resetting

1 All models are equipped with a service interval indicator. After all necessary maintenance work has been completed; the service interval display code must be reset. If more than one service schedule is carried out, note that the relevant display intervals must be reset individually.

2 The display is reset using the button on the left-hand side of the instrument panel (below the speedometer) and the clock setting button on the right-hand side of the panel (below the clock/tachometer). Resetting is described in the relevant part of Chapter 1.

13 Clock – removal and refitting

The clock is integral with the instrument panel, and cannot be removed separately. The instrument panel is a sealed unit, and if the clock, or any other components, are faulty, the complete instrument panel must be renewed. Refer to Section 10 to remove it.

14 Cigarette lighter – removal and refitting

Removal

1 Disconnect the battery negative lead (refer to *Disconnecting the battery* in the *Reference* Chapter at the end of this manual).

2 Remove the centre console as described in Chapter 11, Section 26.

3 Remove the bulbholder as described in Section 6.

4 Release the retaining clips and push the centre element of the lighter out of the outer plastic mounting.

Refitting

5 Refitting is a reversal of removal.

15 Horn – removal and refitting

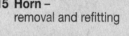

Removal

1 Switch off the ignition and all electrical consumers and remove the ignition key.

2 Remove the front bumper as described in Chapter 11, Section 6. It may be possible to release the front of the inner wheel arch liner and reach up behind the front bumper to access the horn. Note on some models there are two horns, one at each side of the vehicle.

3 Disconnect the wiring, then unscrew the mounting bolt and withdraw the horn together with the mounting bracket **(see illustrations)**.

4 If required, unscrew the nut on the top of the horn to remove the bracket.

Refitting

5 Refitting is a reversal of removal.

16 Speedometer sensor – general information

Unlike earlier models, no electronic speedometer sensor is fitted to the models covered in this manual. Vehicle speed is determined from the ABS wheel sensor signals, and processed by the engine management ECU.

10.3b ...then release locking clip (arrowed) to disconnect the wiring connector

15.3a Disconnect the wiring connector...

15.3b ...and undo the bolt (arrowed)

17.2 Make alignment marks with a piece of tape

17.3a Unscrew the spindle nut...

17.3b ...and remove the wiper arm

17.4a Prise up the cover and remove the nut (arrowed)...

17.4b ...then remove the tailgate wiper arm

17.5 Use a small puller to remove wiper arm, if required

17 Wiper arm – removal and refitting

Removal

1 Operate the wiper motor, then switch off so that the wiper arms return to the at-rest position. Alternatively, set the wiper blades to the Winter/Service (vertical) position by operating the wipers within 10 seconds of switching off the ignition. **Note:** *The wiper motor will only operate with the bonnet closed.*
2 Stick a piece of masking tape to the glass along the edge of the wiper blade to use as an alignment aid on refitting **(see illustration)**.
3 On front wiper arms, prise off the wiper arm spindle nut cover, then slacken but do not completely remove the spindle nut. Lift the blade off the glass and carefully rock the

wiper arm from side to side, until it releases from the spindle. Remove the spindle nut and the wiper arm **(see illustrations)**. **Note:** *If both windscreen wiper arms are to be removed at the same time mark them for identification; the arms are not interchangeable.*
4 On rear wiper arms, unclip the spindle nut cover, then slacken but do not completely remove the spindle nut. Lift the blade off the glass and carefully rock the wiper arm from side to side, until it releases from the spindle. Remove the spindle nut and wiper arm **(see illustrations)**.
5 If the arm is a tight fit on the spindle, the arm can be removed from the spindle using a small puller **(see illustration)**.

Refitting

6 Ensure that the wiper arm and spindle splines are clean and dry, and then refit the arm to the spindle, aligning the wiper blade with the tape fitted on removal. Refit the

spindle nut, tightening it securely, and clip the nut cover back in position.
Note: *Where the wipers were set to the Winter/Service position in paragraph 1, they will only resume their normal position after actuating the wipers twice, or after starting a journey when the speed of the car is greater than 1 mph.*

18 Windscreen wiper motor and linkage – removal and refitting

Removal

1 The wiper motor control unit is integrated into the wiper motor. Note that the windscreen wiper system has an APP (alternating park position) function. Every second time the wipers are switched off, the wiper arm is moved up slightly from its lowest position in order to maintain the efficiency of the wiper blades. If the motor crank is disconnected, it must be reset by first deactivating the APP function, however, this requires the use of diagnostic equipment not available to the home mechanic. It is therefore important to accurately mark the crank in relation to the motor spindle before removing it. Reactivation of the function occurs automatically after 100 cycles of the wiper movement, and this also applies to new motors.
2 Remove the wiper arms as described in Section 17.
3 Disconnect the battery negative lead (refer to *Disconnecting the battery* in the *Reference* Chapter at the end of this manual).
4 Pull off the rubber sealing strip from the

18.4a Peel back the rubber seal...

18.4b ...and remove the foam side pieces

18.5a Release the washer pipe...

18.5b ...then unclip the cowling from along the windscreen seal...

18.5c ...and remove it from the vehicle

18.6a Undo the retaining bolt (arrowed)...

18.6b ...and the retaining nut (arrowed)...

18.6c ...then remove the bulkhead panel

top of the bulkhead and remove the seal from around the bottom of the hinge (see illustrations).

5 Starting on the right-hand side, unclip the washer pipe from the end of the cover, and then carefully pull the plastic windscreen cowling from the windscreen seal (see illustrations).
Caution: Do not use a screwdriver to lever between the cowling and windscreen, as this is likely to result in the windscreen cracking.

6 Unscrew the mounting bolt (right-hand side) and nut (left-hand side) and remove the bulkhead panel from the rear of the engine compartment (see illustrations).

7 Disconnect the wiring plug from the wiper motor (see illustration).

8 Unscrew the mounting bolts and manoeuvre the windscreen wiper motor and linkage out from the scuttle (see illustrations).

9 Recover the washers and spacers from the motor mounting rubbers, noting their locations, then inspect the rubbers for signs of damage or deterioration, and renew if necessary.

10 To separate the motor from the linkage, proceed as follows.
 a) Make alignment marks between the motor spindle and the linkage to ensure correct alignment on refitting, and note the orientation of the linkage.
 b) Unscrew the nut securing the linkage crank to the motor spindle.
 c) Unscrew the three bolts securing the motor to the mounting plate (see illustration), and then remove the motor.

Refitting

11 Refitting is a reversal of removal, bearing in mind the following points.
 a) If the motor has been separated from the linkage, ensure that the marks made

on the motor spindle and linkage before removal are aligned, and ensure that the linkage is orientated as noted before removal.
 b) Ensure that the washers and spacers are

18.7 Disconnecting the wiring plug

18.8a Unscrew the right-hand mounting bolt (arrowed)...

18.8b ...and left-hand mounting bolt (arrowed)...

18.8c ...then remove the windscreen wiper motor and linkage

18.10 Wiper motor retaining screws

18.11 Align the locating peg and grommet (arrowed)

fitted to the motor mounting rubbers as noted before removal.
c) Make sure the locating peg aligns with the grommet in the bulkhead, when refitting **(see illustration)**.

d) Lubricate the windscreen cowling mounting slots with a silicone-based spray lubricant to ease installation. Do not strike the cowling to seat it in position as this could result in the windscreen cracking.

e) Refit the wiper arms as described in Section 17.

19 Rear wiper motor – removal and refitting

Removal

1 Remove the wiper arm as described in Section 17.
2 Recover the wiper motor shaft sealing ring.
3 Open the tailgate, then remove the trim panel as described in Chapter 11, Section 15.
4 Release the locking clip and unplug the wiring connector from the motor **(see illustration)**.
5 On estate models, disconnect the washer fluid hose from the washer nozzle connector on the motor assembly **(see illustration)**.
6 Unscrew the three nuts securing the motor, and then withdraw the assembly. Note the position of the rubber sealing ring, renew if necessary **(see illustrations)**.

Refitting

7 Refitting is a reversal of removal, but ensure that the motor shaft rubber sealing ring/ grommet is correctly refitted to prevent water leaks, and refit the wiper arm with reference to Section 17.

20 Washer system components – removal and refitting

Washer fluid reservoir and pumps

1 Switch off the ignition and all electrical consumers and remove the ignition key.
2 In the engine compartment, unscrew the mounting bolt and remove the top from the reservoir filler neck **(see illustrations)**.
3 Remove the front bumper as described in Chapter 11, Section 6.
4 Disconnect the wiring connector from the top of the washer pump **(see illustration)**.
5 Note the position of the hoses, and then disconnect them from the washer pump **(see**

19.4 Disconnect the wiring...

19.5 ...and washer fluid hose from the tailgate wiper motor - Estate

19.6a Tailgate wiper motor securing nuts - Hatchback

19.6b Tailgate wiper motor securing nuts - Estate

19.6c Removing the tailgate wiper motor

20.2a Undo the retaining bolt (arrowed)...

20.2b ...and remove the filler neck

illustration). Position a suitable container beneath the reservoir to catch spilt fluid. **Note:** *Depending on model, there may be more than one washer pump.*

6 To remove the washer pump, pull it upwards from the reservoir and out from its rubber grommet.

7 Where fitted, disconnect the wiring plug from the fluid level sender unit.

8 Release the retaining clips and disconnect the wiring loom from the side of the washer reservoir.

9 Unscrew the mounting bolt and two mounting nuts, then remove the reservoir from the vehicle (see illustration).

10 Refitting is a reversal of removal.

Windscreen washer jets

11 Open the bonnet, and pull the washer jet towards the front of the bonnet, and down to remove. Release the securing clip and disconnect the washer tube (and wiring where applicable), then remove the washer jet, See Chapter 11, Section 8.

12 Refitting is a reversal of removal. Note that the aim of the jet can be adjusted using a screwdriver and turning the eccentric shaft at the base of the washer jet.

Tailgate washer jet

13 Switch off the ignition and all electrical consumers and remove the ignition key.

14 On estate models, unclip the cover from the wiper arm spindle for access to the washer jet (see illustration), and pull the jet from the centre of the spindle.

15 On hatchback models, the washer jet is fitted to the high level brake light, remove the light as described in Section 7. Release the retaining clips and remove the washer jet from the brake light.

16 On GTi models, the washer jet is fitted to the rear spoiler, remove the spoiler, release the retaining clips and remove the washer jet.

17 On refitting, ensure that the jet is securely pushed into position. Check the operation of the jet. If necessary, adjust the nozzle, aiming the spray at a point slightly above the area of glass swept by the wiper blade.

Headlight pop-up washer jets

18 Switch off the ignition and all electrical consumers and remove the ignition key.

19 Carefully pull the washer jet out from the front bumper to its full extent, and hold it. Carefully prise the end cap from the washer jet.

20 Still holding the washer jet, lift the securing clip slightly, and pull the jet from the lift cylinder.

21 Refitting is a reversal of removal. Operate the washers several times to bleed any trapped air.

Headlight pop-up washer jet lift cylinder

22 Remove the washer jet end cap as described in paragraphs 19 and 20.

23 Remove the front bumper as described in Chapter 11, Section 6.

20.4 Disconnect the wiring connector

20.9 Washer fluid reservoir mounting bolt/nuts (arrowed)

24 Undo the two retaining screws, and withdraw the cylinder.

25 Clamp the hose, squeeze the retaining clip, and disconnect the hose.

26 Refitting is a reversal of removal. Operate the washers several times to bleed any trapped air.

21 Radio/CD player/changer – removal and refitting

Note: *This Section only applies to standard-fit audio equipment.*

Radio/CD player

Removal

1 The radio/CD player is equipped with an electronic anti-theft system linked to the instrument panel. If the voltage supply to

21.3a Carefully remove the surround...

20.5 Disconnect the washer fluid hoses

20.14 Rear washer jet (arrowed) - Estate

the radio is temporarily disconnected, the radio will function again when the supply is reconnected, without entering the safety code number, provided the radio is located in the original vehicle. Should the radio operation be blocked, normal operation can be restored by entering the correct anti-theft code.

2 Remove any CDs which may be in the unit. Switch off the ignition and all electrical consumers, and remove the ignition key.

3 Carefully unclip the trim panel from around the radio/CD player (see illustrations).

4 Undo the radio/CD player mounting screws, and pull out the unit until the wiring plugs can be disconnected (see illustrations). Release the locking clips and disconnect the wiring connectors from the rear of the unit.

5 Withdraw the radio/CD player unit from the facia.

Refitting

6 Refitting is a reversal of removal.

21.3b ...by releasing the retaining clips (arrowed)

21.4a Undo the screws (arrowed)...

21.4b ...then withdraw the radio/CD player and disconnect the wiring...

21.4c ...and aerial leads

21.10 Using radio keys to withdraw from the centre armrest

CD changer/media storage compartment

Removal

7 The CD changer (where fitted) is located in the storage compartment beneath the armrest located between the driver and passenger front seats. It is fitted with special mounting clips, requiring the use of special removal tools, which should be supplied with the vehicle, or may be obtained from an in-car entertainment specialist. Alternatively, two feeler blades can be used.

8 Switch off the ignition and all electrical consumers, and remove the ignition key.

9 Open the armrest and remove any CDs which may be in the unit.

10 Insert the tools into the slots on each side of the unit and push them until they snap into place **(see illustration)**. The CD changer/media storage compartment can then be pulled out of the armrest using the tools, and any wiring connectors disconnected.

Refitting

11 Refitting is a reversal of removal.

22 Loudspeakers – removal and refitting

Front treble speaker

1 Switch off the ignition and all electrical consumers, and remove the ignition key.

2 Remove the inner door trim as described in Chapter 11, Section 12.

3 Disconnect the speaker wiring plug, and unclip the triangular trim cover from the front of the door frame **(see illustration)**.

4 The loudspeaker is integral with the triangular mirror cover.

5 Refitting is a reversal of removal.

Rear treble speaker

6 The loudspeaker is located on the inner side trim panel (3-door models) and in the rear door inner trim panel (5-door models). First, switch off the ignition and all electrical consumers, and remove the ignition key.

7 On 3-door models, remove the rear inner trim, as described in Chapter 11, Section 25.

8 On 5-door models, remove the door inner trim, as described in Chapter 11, Section 12.

9 With the wiring disconnected from the loudspeaker, cut the trim plate plastic rivets **(see illustration)**, and remove the unit from the door trim.

10 Refitting is a reversal of removal, but use a soldering iron to 'weld' the trim plate plastic rivets in position.

Front and rear bass speakers

11 Switch off the ignition and all electrical consumers, and remove the ignition key.

12 On 3-door models, remove the rear inner trim, as described in Chapter 11, Section 25.

13 On 5-door models, remove the door inner trim, as described in Chapter 11, Section 12.

14 Disconnect the wiring plug from the loudspeaker **(see illustration)**.

15 Drill out the retaining rivets, and withdraw the speaker from the door **(see illustration)**. Recover the rubber sealing ring between the speaker and door trim. **Note:** *Where mid-range loudspeakers are fitted, they are secured with screws instead of rivets.*

16 Refitting is a reversal of removal. The

22.3 Unclip the triangle trim/speaker cover

22.9 Door speaker (arrowed) in door trim panel

22.14 Disconnect the wiring connector

22.15 Door-mounted loudspeaker secured with rivets

special-sized rivets should be available from VW dealers and in-car entertainment specialists.

23 Radio aerials, filters and modules – removal and refitting

Aerials

1 The radio aerial is integrated into the rear window that is bonded in position with a special adhesive. If the aerial is faulty, a new rear window must be fitted.

2 The navigation, telephone and auxiliary heater telestart aerial is fitted to the rear of the roof panel.

3 Carefully unclip the trim panel from across the rear of the headlining **(see illustration)**. If required remove the C-pillar trim panels as described in Chapter 11, Section 25. This will allow the rear of the headlining to be lowered further to gain better access.

4 Carefully lower the rear of the headlining, taking care not to damage it. Disconnect the wiring; note the fitted position of the wiring, as there may be more than one connector, depending on model.

5 Unscrew the securing nut and withdraw the aerial base from the roof. Hold the aerial base as the nut is being unscrewed to prevent the base from rotating and scratching the roof panel. Recover the rubber spacer.

6 Refitting is a reversal of removal, but make sure that the two guide lugs on the rubber spacer are correctly located in the aerial base.

Filters

7 The aerial that is integrated into the rear window has frequency filters, which are fitted behind the inner tailgate trim. There are three filters, two for Frequency Modulation (FM) and one for Amplitude Modulation (AM).

8 Remove the tailgate inner trim panel as described in Chapter 11, Section 15.

9 The two FM filters are clipped to the inside of the tailgate, one at each side of the rear window **(see illustration)**. Disconnect the wiring connector and unclip the filter from the tailgate. **Note:** *The filter to the left of the rear window is positioned in the negative wire, and the filter to the*

23.3 Unclip the trim from the rear edge of the roof panel

right of the rear window is positioned in the positive wire.

10 The AM filter is secured to the inside of the tailgate by three screws **(see illustrations)**. Release the locking clips and then disconnect the wiring connectors, undo the three retaining screws and remove the filter from the tailgate.

11 Refitting is a reversal of removal.

Modules

12 There are two aerial modules that are located behind the tailgate upper trim at the top of the rear window **(see illustration)**.

a) *The right-hand module is for FM/ AM reception, FM1, aerial amplifier/ impedance converter and optional DAB digital reception.*

b) *The left-hand module is for FM reception, FM2 and aerial amplifier/impedance converter.*

13 Remove the tailgate inner trim panel as described in Chapter 11, Section 15.

14 Disconnect the wiring connector, undo the retaining screw and move the module to the right to remove it from the tailgate.

15 Refitting is a reversal of removal.

24 Anti-theft alarm system and engine immobiliser – general information

Note: *This information is applicable only to the anti-theft alarm system fitted by VW as standard equipment.*

Models in the range are fitted with an anti-theft alarm system as standard equipment. The alarm

23.9 Unclip the trim from the inside edge of the tailgate

has switches on all the doors (including the tailgate/boot lid), the bonnet and the ignition switch. If the tailgate/boot lid, bonnet or any of the doors are opened whilst the alarm is set, the alarm horn will sound and the hazard warning lights will flash. Some models are equipped with an internal monitoring system, which will activate the alarm system if any movement in the cabin is detected.

The alarm is set using the key in the driver's or passenger's front door lock, and tailgate/ boot lid lock, or with the central locking remote control transmitter. The alarm system will then start to monitor its various switches approximately 30 seconds later.

With the alarm set, if the tailgate/boot lid is unlocked, the lock switch sensing will automatically be switched off but the door and bonnet switches will still be active. Once the tailgate/boot lid is shut and locked again, the switch sensing will be switched back on.

All models are fitted with an immobiliser system, which is activated by the ignition switch. A transponder reading coil on the ignition switch reads a code contained within the ignition key. The system sends a signal to the engine management electronic control unit (ECU), which allows the engine to start if the code is correct. If an incorrect ignition key is used, the engine will not start.

If a fault is suspected with the alarm or immobiliser systems, the vehicle should be taken to a VW dealer for examination. They will have access to a special diagnostic tester that will quickly trace any fault present in the system.

23.10a Radio AM filter secured to tailgate

23.10b Release the locking clips on the wiring connectors

23.12 Radio modules secured to upper part of tailgate

26.4a Insert screwdriver...

26.4b ...to release the airbag clips (arrowed)

25 Airbag system – general information and precautions

⚠ **Warning: Before carrying out any operations on the airbag system, disconnect the battery negative terminal (refer to 'Disconnecting the battery' in the Reference section at the rear of this manual). When operations are complete, make sure no one is inside the vehicle when the battery is reconnected.**
• *Note that the airbags must not be subjected to temperatures in excess of 90°C. When the airbag is removed, ensure that it is stored with the pad upwards to prevent possible inflation.*
• *Do not allow any solvents or cleaning agents to contact the airbag assemblies. They must be cleaned using only a damp cloth.*
• *The airbags and control unit are both sensitive to impact. If either is dropped or damaged they should be renewed.*

A driver's airbag, passenger's airbag and side airbags were fitted as standard to the Golf range. Certain models also have curtain airbags located behind the headlining on each side of the car. The airbag system consists of the airbag unit (complete with gas generator), which is fitted to the steering wheel (driver's side), facia (passenger's side), roof (where applicable) and front seats, an impact sensor, the control unit and a warning light in the instrument panel.

The airbag system is triggered in the event

of a heavy frontal or side impact above a predetermined force, depending on the point of impact. The airbag is inflated within milliseconds and forms a safety cushion between the driver and the steering wheel, the passenger and the facia, and in the case of side impact, between front seat occupants and the sides of the cabin. This prevents contact between the upper body and cabin interior, and therefore greatly reduces the risk of injury. The airbag then deflates almost immediately.

Every time the ignition is switched on, the airbag control unit performs a self-test. The self-test takes approximately 3 seconds and during this time the airbag warning light on the facia is illuminated. After the self-test has been completed the warning light should go out. If the warning light fails to come on, remains illuminated after the initial 3-second period or comes on at any time when the vehicle is being driven, there is a fault in the airbag system. The vehicle should then be taken to a VW dealer for examination at the earliest possible opportunity.

26 Airbag system components – removal and refitting

Note: *Refer to the warnings in Section 25 before carrying out the following operations.*
1 Disconnect the battery negative lead (refer to *Disconnecting the battery* in the *Reference* Chapter at the end of this manual), then continue as described under the relevant heading.

Caution: To prevent any discharge of static electricity into the airbag circuit, temporarily touch the vehicle bodywork before disconnecting the wiring from any airbag unit.

Driver's airbag

2 Set the front wheels to the straight-ahead position, and release the steering lock by inserting the ignition key.
3 Adjust the steering column to its highest position by releasing the adjustment handle, then extend the steering wheel as far as possible. Lock the column in this position.
4 With the spokes in the vertical position, insert a screwdriver approximately 8 mm into the hole in the upper rear of the steering wheel hub, then move it up to release the clip and free the airbag locking lug **(see illustrations)**. Now turn the steering wheel through 180° and release the remaining airbag locking lug.
5 Carefully withdraw the airbag module from the steering wheel, release the locking clip and disconnect the wiring connector **(see illustration)**.
6 Turn the steering wheel to its central, straight-ahead position.

⚠ *Warning: Position the airbag in a safe and secure place, away from the work area.*

7 When refitting make sure the steering wheel is in the straight-ahead position, then locate the airbag module in position and reconnect the wiring. Carefully press in the module until both locking lugs are heard to engage. Reconnect the battery negative lead, ensuring that nobody is inside the vehicle as the lead is connected.

Passenger's airbag

8 Remove the passenger side glovebox with reference to Chapter 11, Section 25.
9 Release the locking clip and disconnect the wiring from the passenger's airbag **(see illustration)**.
10 Undo the mounting screws, then remove the airbag and side brackets from under the facia **(see illustration)**.

⚠ *Warning: Position the airbag in a safe and secure place, away from the work area.*
Caution: Before fitting a new airbag, it will

26.5 Disconnect the wiring as it is removed

26.9 Disconnect the wiring connector (arrowed)

26.10 Passenger airbag securing screws (arrowed)

26.11 Unclip the front sill trim

26.12 Disconnect the wiring connector (arrowed)

26.13 Knee airbag module removal

need to be checked to see if an additional earth cable will be required. At the rear of the airbag unit, check to see if there is an earth wire going from the wiring block connector to one of the securing nuts on the airbag unit. If there is no earth cable, an earth wire will need to be connected to one of the mounting bracket retaining bolts and to the earth on the lower sill, behind the kick trim panel. The earth cable needs to have a cross section of 1mm and be 600mm in length.

11 Refitting is a reversal of removal, but tighten the mounting screws to the specified torque. If the airbag housing is made of plastic, use locking fluid on the screws before refitting. Reconnect the battery negative lead, ensuring that nobody is inside the vehicle as the lead is connected. If an additional earth cable needs to be fitted (see caution above), attach it to the earth point behind the sill trim panel (see illustration).

Driver's knee airbag

12 Working inside the drivers side footwell, release the locking clip and disconnect the wiring connector from the left-hand side of the airbag (see illustration).

13 Undo the four mounting nuts (two at each side), then remove the airbag from under the driver's side facia (see illustration).

 Warning: Position the airbag in a safe and secure place, away from the work area.

14 Refitting is a reversal of removal, but tighten the mounting nuts to the specified torque. Reconnect the battery negative lead, ensuring that nobody is inside the vehicle as the lead is connected.

Front seat side impact airbags

15 The side impact air bags are integral with the seats. As seat upholstery removal requires considerable skill and experience, if it is to be carried out without damage, it is best entrusted to an expert.

Roof curtain and rear side airbags

16 This work involves removing the headlining and major dismantling of interior trim panels, and is best entrusted to a VW dealer.

26.18 Lift the foot rest trim upwards to remove

Airbag control unit

17 The airbag control unit is located beneath the centre of the facia, under the heater housing.

18 Undo the retaining screw, slide the footrest upwards and remove it from inside the driver's footwell (see illustration).

19 Remove the trim from the driver's side of the centre console with reference to Chapter 11.

20 Pull back the carpet, undo the retaining nuts and remove the footrest mounting bracket from the floor panel (see illustration).

21 Release the locking lever and disconnect the wiring from the control unit (see illustration).

22 Unscrew the nuts and remove the control unit from the vehicle (see illustration).

23 Refitting is the reverse of removal making sure the wiring connector is securely

26.21 Disconnect the wiring connector

26.20 Undo the two securing nuts (arrowed)

reconnected. Reconnect the battery negative lead, ensuring that nobody is inside the vehicle as the lead is connected.

Airbag wiring contact unit

24 The airbag contact unit/clock spring is part of the steering column switch assembly, remove the contact unit as described in Section 4.

25 The airbag clock spring/slip-ring must be held in its central position while it is removed, to ensure correct refitting. Unclip the airbag clock spring/slip-ring from the combination switch carrier by lifting the retaining hooks.

26 Before refitting the airbag clock spring/slip-ring, check that it is in its central position as follows. There are two types fitted according to manufacturer as shown (see illustrations). With the first type, the black rectangles must

26.22 Airbag control unit securing nuts

26.26a Airbag wiring contact unit centre setting – type 1

26.26b Airbag wiring contact unit centre setting – type 2

be visible in the window. With the second type, the yellow strip must be visible as shown.

27 The remaining procedure is a reversal of removal. Reconnect the battery negative lead, ensuring that nobody is inside the vehicle as the lead is connected.

Passenger airbag on/ off switch

28 The switch is located inside the glovebox. Remove the switch with reference to Section 4.

Front door crash sensor

29 Remove the inner door trim as described in Chapter 11, Section 12.

26.30a Disconnect the wiring connector...

26.33 Undo the sensor retaining screw (arrowed)

30 Disconnect the wiring from the crash sensor, then release the securing clip and withdraw the sensor from the door panel **(see illustrations)**.

31 Refitting is a reversal of removal. Make sure that nobody is inside the vehicle when first switching on the ignition.

Rear wheel housing crash sensor

32 Remove the rear inner trim panels from the rear wheel arch as described in Chapter 11, Section 25.

33 Release the securing clip and disconnect the wiring from the crash sensor, undo the

26.30b ...and unclip the sensor from the door panel

27.4 Control unit in facia relay housing

retaining screw and remove the sensor from the floor panel **(see illustrations)**.

34 Refitting is a reversal of removal. Make sure that nobody is inside the vehicle when first switching on the ignition.

27 Parking aid components – general information, removal and refitting

General information

1 The parking aid system is available as a standard fitment on highline models, and optional on other models. Four ultrasound sensors are located in the front and rear bumper. These measure the distance to the closest object behind or in front of the car, and inform the driver using acoustic signals from a warning buzzer. The nearer the object, the more frequent the acoustic signals.

2 The system includes a control unit and self-diagnosis program, and therefore, in the event of a fault, the vehicle should be taken to a VW dealer.

3 Switch off the ignition and all electrical consumers and remove the ignition key, before removing any electrical components.

Control unit

4 The parking aid control unit is located above the convenience system onboard supply control unit and relay carrier, behind the facia on the driver's side of the vehicle **(see illustration)**. Refer to Chapter 11, Section 17.

5 Depress the locking lugs and disconnect the wiring plugs from the control unit.

6 Unclip the unit from the mounting bracket above the relays.

7 Refitting is a reversal of removal.

Range/distance sensor

8 Remove the bumper as described in Chapter 11, Section 6 (front bumper) or Section 7 (rear bumper).

9 Disconnect the wiring from the sensor **(see illustration)**.
10 Release the two retaining clips at each side and pull the sensor from the bumper **(see illustration)**.
11 Refitting is a reversal of removal. Press the sensor firmly into position until the retaining clips engage.

Warning buzzer

12 The warning buzzers are located behind the right-hand luggage compartment trim for the rear sensors, and inside the front scuttle panel for the front sensors.
13 To remove the rear warning buzzer, remove the right-hand inner trim, with reference to Chapter 11, Section 25. Disconnect the wiring, then release the two plastic rivets and remove the warning buzzer.

27.9 Disconnect the wiring connector...

27.10 ...and unclip the sensor from the bumper

14 To remove the front warning buzzer, remove the wiper motor assembly, with reference to Section 18. Undo the three retaining nuts and remove the cover. Disconnect the wiring, then release the two plastic rivets and remove the warning buzzer.
15 Refitting is a reversal of removal.

VW Golf wiring diagrams | **Diagram 1**

WARNING: *This vehicle is fitted with a supplemental restraint system (SRS) consisting of a combination of driver (and passenger) airbag(s), side impact protection airbags and seatbelt pre-tensioners. The use of electrical test equipment on any SRS wiring systems may cause the seatbelt pre-tensioners to abruptly retract and airbags to explosively deploy, resulting in potentially severe personal injury. Extreme care should be taken to correctly identify any circuits to be tested to avoid choosing any of the SRS wiring in error.*
For further information see airbag system precautions in body electrical systems chapter.
Note: The SRS wiring harness can normally be identified by yellow and/or orange harness or harness connectors.

Key to symbols

Solenoid actuator
Earth point and location
Wire colour (red with black tracer) — Rt/Sw
Dashed outline denotes part of a larger item, containing in this case an electronic or solid state device (pins 25 and 26 of a single connector designated 52c).

Bulb
Switch
Fuse/Fusible link F26
Resistor
Variable resistor
Variable resistor

Wire splice, soldered joint, or unspecified connector
Connecting wires
Diode
Light-emitting diode
Item number 12
Motor/pump M
Heating element

Battery fusebox

Alternative fitment

Note for fuse ratings see fusebox cover.

Engine fusebox

Alternative fitment

Passenger fusebox

Earth locations

E1   LH cross member
E2   LH cross member
E3   LH cross member
E4   On cylinder block
E5   Electric fan earth
E6   Engine to gearbox earth
E7   At LH headlight
E8   Front of left longitudinal member
E9   On LH suspension strut
E10 Earth strap, battery to body
E11 LH plenum chamber
E12 Lower LH 'A' pillar
E13 Front LH footwell
E14 On steering column
E15 Front of roof
E16 LH rear wing
E17 LH luggage compartment
E18 RH tailgate
E19 RH rear wing
E20 RH rear wing
E21 Centre underbody
E22 Behind centre console
E23 Front RH footwell
E24 Lower LH 'A' pillar
E25 RH plenum chamber
E26 On engine bulkhead
E27 Front of right longitudinal member
E28 At RH headlight
E29 RH cross member

H47698

Colour codes

Ws	White	**Or**	Orange
Bl	Blue	**Rt**	Red
Gr	Grey	**Rs**	Pink
Ge	Yellow	**Gn**	Green
Br	Brown	**Vi**	Purple
Sw	Black		

Key to items

1 Battery
2 Starter motor
3 Alternator
4 Battery fusebox
5 Engine fusebox
   a = engine management main relay
6 On-board power supply control unit
7 Terminal 50 relay
8 Terminal 15 relay

9 High tone horn
10 Low tone horn
11 Horn relay
12 Passenger fusebox
13 Steering column control unit
14 Steering wheel clock springs
15 Horn switch
16 Engine cooling fan 1/control unit
17 Engine cooling fan 2

18 Accessory socket
19 Blocking diode
20 Cigar lighter
21 X-contact relay

Diagram 2

H47699

Typical starting & charging

Typical engine cooling fan

Typical horn

Typical cigar lighter & accessory socket

Colour codes

Ws	White	Or	Orange
Bl	Blue	Rt	Red
Gr	Grey	Rs	Pink
Ge	Yellow	Gn	Green
Br	Brown	Vi	Purple
Sw	Black		

Key to items

1   Battery
4   Battery fusebox
5   Engine fusebox
6   On-board power supply control unit
8   Terminal 15 relay
12 Passenger fusebox
13 Steering column control unit
24 Stop light switch
25 Reversing light switch
26 High level stop light
27 LH outer light unit
    a = stop & tail light
28 RH outer light unit
    a = stop & tail light
29 LH inner light unit
    a = reversing light
    b = tail light
30 RH inner light unit
    b = tail light
31 LH number plate light
32 RH number plate light
33 Multifunction switch
    a = headlight dip/flash
34 LH sidelight
35 RH sideliight
36 LH headlight dip beam
37 RH headlight dip beam
38 LH headlight main beam
39 RH headlight main beam
40 Lighting switch
    a = side/headlight switch
    b = control unit
    c = switch illumination

Diagram 3

H47700

Typical stop & reversing lights

Typical headlights, side, tail & number plate lights

Colour codes

Ws	White	Or	Orange
Bl	Blue	Rt	Red
Gr	Grey	Rs	Pink
Ge	Yellow	Gn	Green
Br	Brown	Vi	Purple
Sw	Black		

Key to items

1 Battery
4 Battery fusebox
5 Engine fusebox
6 On-board power supply control unit
8 Terminal 15 relay
12 Passenger fusebox
13 Steering column control unit
27 LH outer light unit
  b = direction indicator
28 RH outer light unit
  b = direction indicator
30 RH inner light unit
  a = foglight

33 Multifunction switch
  b = direction indicator switch
40 Lighting switch
  b = control unit
  d = foglight switch
  e = foglight warning light
44 Hazard warning switch
45 LH front direction indicator
46 RH front direction indicator
47 Driver's mirror assembly
  a = direction indicator side repeater
48 Passenger's mirror assembly
  a = direction indicator side repeater

Diagram 4

49 Driver's door control unit
50 Passenger's door control unit
51 LH front foglight
52 RH front foglight
53 Headlight levelling switch/ interior lighting dimmer
54 LH headlight levelling motor
55 RH headlight levelling motor

H47701

Typical direction indicators & hazard warning lights

Typical front/rear foglights

Typical headlight levelling

Colour codes

Ws White   **Or** Orange
Bl Blue   **Rt** Red
Gr Grey   **Rs** Pink
Ge Yellow **Gn** Green
Br Brown   **Vi** Purple
Sw Black

Key to items

1 Battery
4 Battery fusebox
5 Engine fusebox
6 On-board power supply control unit
8 Terminal 15 relay
12 Passenger fusebox
13 Steering column control unit
21 X-contact relay
60 Rain and light sensor
61 Front wiper motor

62 Rear wiper motor
63 Washer pump
64 Wash/wipe switch
  a = front wash/wipe
  b = rear wash/wipe
  c = wiper delay
65 Instrument cluster
66 Oil level and temperature sensor
67 LH front pad wear sensor
68 Data bus interface

69 Handbrake switch
70 Low coolant level sensor
71 Air temperature sensor
72 Low washer fluid sensor
73 Immobiliser reader coil
74 Low brake fluid level sensor
75 Fuel gauge sensder unit/fuel pump
76 Low oil pressure switch

Diagram 5

H47702

Typical wash/wipe

Typical instrument cluster

Colour codes

Ws	White	**Or**	Orange
Bl	Blue	**Rt**	Red
Gr	Grey	**Rs**	Pink
Ge	Yellow	**Gn**	Green
Br	Brown	**Vi**	Purple
Sw	Black		

Key to items

6 On-board power supply control unit
47 Driver's mirror assembly
   b = entry light
48 Passenger's mirror assembly
   b = entry light
49 Driver's door control unit
50 Passenger's door control unit
53 Headlight levelling switch/
   interior lighting dimmer
80 Glovebox light switch
81 Glovebox light
82 Luggage compartment light
83 LH footwell light

84 RH footwell light
85 Front interior light
   a = front interior light/
      driver's map reading light
   b = passenger's map reading light
   c = switch illumination
86 Sunroof switch illumination
87 Rear interior light
88 Driver's vanity mirror light
89 Passenger's vanity mirror light
90 Driver's vanity mirror light switch
91 Passenger's vanity mirror light switch

Diagram 6

H47703

Typical interior lighting

Colour codes

Ws	White	**Or**	Orange
Bl	Blue	**Rt**	Red
Gr	Grey	**Rs**	Pink
Ge	Yellow	**Gn**	Green
Br	Brown	**Vi**	Purple
Sw	Black		

Key to items

1 Battery
4 Battery fusebox
5 Engine fusebox
6 On-board power supply control unit
8 Terminal 15 relay
12 Passenger fusebox
21 X-contact relay
94 High pressure sensor
95 Recirciulation flap motor
96 Centre vent temperature sensor

97 Air conditioning control unit
  a = heater blower switch
  b = passenger's heated seat regulator
  c = driver's heated seat regulator
  d = recirculation on warning light
  e = fresh air/recirculation flap switch
  f = switch illumination
  g = heated rear window warning light
  h = heated rear window switch
  i = temperature controller

98 Footwell vent temperature sensor
99 Evaporator temperature sensor
100 Temperature flap control motor
101 Air distribution flap motor
102 Air conditioning regulator valve
103 Heater blower resistors
104 Heater blower motor

Diagram 7

H47704

Typical air conditioning & heated rear window

Colour codes

Ws	White	**Or**	Orange
Bl	Blue	**Rt**	Red
Gr	Grey	**Rs**	Pink
Ge	Yellow	**Gn**	Green
Br	Brown	**Vi**	Purple
Sw	Black		

Key to items

1 Battery
4 Battery fusebox
12 Passenger fusebox
47 Driver's mirror assembly
   c = heated mirror element
   d = mirror fold motor
   e = vertical adjustment motor
   f = horizontal adjustment motor
   g = anti-dazzle mirror
48 Passenger's mirror assembly
   (c to g as above)

49 Driver's door control unit
50 Passenger's door control unit
107 Mirror adjustment switch
   a = mirror heater switch
   b = mirror fold switch
   c = change over switch
   d = adjustment switch
   e = switch illumination

Diagram 8

H47705

Typical electric mirrors

Colour codes

Ws	White	Or	Orange
Bl	Blue	Rt	Red
Gr	Grey	Rs	Pink
Ge	Yellow	Gn	Green
Br	Brown	Vi	Purple
Sw	Black		

Key to items

1 Battery
4 Battery fusebox
6 On-board power supply control unit
12 Passenger fusebox
49 Driver's door control unit
50 Passenger's door control unit
110 LH rear door control unit
111 RH rear door control unit
112 Driver's door lock unit
113 Passenger's door lock unit
114 LH rear door lock unit
115 RH rear door lock unit
116 Central locking interior switch
117 Deadlock function warning light
118 Fuel filler flap lock
119 Central locking antenna
120 Tailgate lock unit
121 Tailgate button

Diagram 9

H47706

Typical central locking

Colour codes

Ws	White	**Or**	Orange
Bl	Blue	**Rt**	Red
Gr	Grey	**Rs**	Pink
Ge	Yellow	**Gn**	Green
Br	Brown	**Vi**	Purple
Sw	Black		

Key to items

1	Battery
4	Battery fusebox
12	Passenger fusebox
49	Driver's door control unit
50	Passenger's door control unit
110	LH rear door control unit
111	RH rear door control unit
125	LH rear window switch
126	RH rear window switch

127	Driver's door window switch
	a = RH front window
	b = LH front window
	c = RH rear window
	d = LH rear window
	e = child lock warning light
	f = switch illumination
	g = child lock
128	Passenger's door window switch

Diagram 10

H47707

Typical electric windows

Reference

Dimensions and weights

Note: *All figures and dimensions are approximate and may vary according to model. Refer to manufacturer's data for exact figures.*

Overall length . . . .   4199 to 4308 mm

Overall width (all models) . . . .   1786 mm

Overall height (unladen) . . . .   1465 to 1500 mm

Wheelbase (all models) . . . .   2575 mm

Turning circle (all models) . . . .   10.9 m

Weights

Kerb weight

1.4 litre petrol models:
    Manual transmission . . . .   1217 to 1290 kg
    DSG transmission . . . .   1316 kg
1.6 litre diesel models:
    Manual transmission . . . .   1314 kg
    DSG transmission . . . .   1337 kg
2.0 litre diesel models:
    Manual transmission . . . .   1351 to 1387 kg
    DSG transmission . . . .   1372 to 1431 kg

Maximum gross vehicle weight

1.4 litre petrol models . . . .   1750 to 1850 kg
1.6 litre diesel models . . . .   1750 to 1890 kg
2.0 litre diesel models . . . .   1910 to 1940 kg

Maximum towing weights

	Unbraked trailer	Braked trailer
1.4 litre petrol models	600 to 650 kg	800 to 1300 kg
1.6 litre diesel models	650 to 660 kg	1400 kg
2.0 litre diesel models	660 to 730 kg	1500 to 1600 kg

REF•2 Conversion factors

Length (distance)

Inches (in)	x 25.4	= Millimetres (mm)	x 0.0394	= Inches (in)
Feet (ft)	x 0.305	= Metres (m)	x 3.281	= Feet (ft)
Miles	x 1.609	= Kilometres (km)	x 0.621	= Miles

Volume (capacity)

Cubic inches (cu in; in³)	x 16.387	= Cubic centimetres (cc; cm³)	x 0.061	= Cubic inches (cu in; in³)
Imperial pints (Imp pt)	x 0.568	= Litres (l)	x 1.76	= Imperial pints (Imp pt)
Imperial quarts (Imp qt)	x 1.137	= Litres (l)	x 0.88	= Imperial quarts (Imp qt)
Imperial quarts (Imp qt)	x 1.201	= US quarts (US qt)	x 0.833	= Imperial quarts (Imp qt)
US quarts (US qt)	x 0.946	= Litres (l)	x 1.057	= US quarts (US qt)
Imperial gallons (Imp gal)	x 4.546	= Litres (l)	x 0.22	= Imperial gallons (Imp gal)
Imperial gallons (Imp gal)	x 1.201	= US gallons (US gal)	x 0.833	= Imperial gallons (Imp gal)
US gallons (US gal)	x 3.785	= Litres (l)	x 0.264	= US gallons (US gal)

Mass (weight)

Ounces (oz)	x 28.35	= Grams (g)	x 0.035	= Ounces (oz)
Pounds (lb)	x 0.454	= Kilograms (kg)	x 2.205	= Pounds (lb)

Force

Ounces-force (ozf; oz)	x 0.278	= Newtons (N)	x 3.6	= Ounces-force (ozf; oz)
Pounds-force (lbf; lb)	x 4.448	= Newtons (N)	x 0.225	= Pounds-force (lbf; lb)
Newtons (N)	x 0.1	= Kilograms-force (kgf; kg)	x 9.81	= Newtons (N)

Pressure

Pounds-force per square inch (psi; lbf/in²; lb/in²)	x 0.070	= Kilograms-force per square centimetre (kgf/cm²; kg/cm²)	x 14.223	= Pounds-force per square inch (psi; lbf/in²; lb/in²)
Pounds-force per square inch (psi; lbf/in²; lb/in²)	x 0.068	= Atmospheres (atm)	x 14.696	= Pounds-force per square inch (psi; lbf/in²; lb/in²)
Pounds-force per square inch (psi; lbf/in²; lb/in²)	x 0.069	= Bars	x 14.5	= Pounds-force per square inch (psi; lbf/in²; lb/in²)
Pounds-force per square inch (psi; lbf/in²; lb/in²)	x 6.895	= Kilopascals (kPa)	x 0.145	= Pounds-force per square inch (psi; lbf/in²; lb/in²)
Kilopascals (kPa)	x 0.01	= Kilograms-force per square centimetre (kgf/cm²; kg/cm²)	x 98.1	= Kilopascals (kPa)
Millibar (mbar)	x 100	= Pascals (Pa)	x 0.01	= Millibar (mbar)
Millibar (mbar)	x 0.0145	= Pounds-force per square inch (psi; lbf/in²; lb/in²)	x 68.947	= Millibar (mbar)
Millibar (mbar)	x 0.75	= Millimetres of mercury (mmHg)	x 1.333	= Millibar (mbar)
Millibar (mbar)	x 0.401	= Inches of water (inH₂O)	x 2.491	= Millibar (mbar)
Millimetres of mercury (mmHg)	x 0.535	= Inches of water (inH₂O)	x 1.868	= Millimetres of mercury (mmHg)
Inches of water (inH₂O)	x 0.036	= Pounds-force per square inch (psi; lbf/in²; lb/in²)	x 27.68	= Inches of water (inH₂O)

Torque (moment of force)

Pounds-force inches (lbf in; lb in)	x 1.152	= Kilograms-force centimetre (kgf cm; kg cm)	x 0.868	= Pounds-force inches (lbf in; lb in)
Pounds-force inches (lbf in; lb in)	x 0.113	= Newton metres (Nm)	x 8.85	= Pounds-force inches (lbf in; lb in)
Pounds-force inches (lbf in; lb in)	x 0.083	= Pounds-force feet (lbf ft; lb ft)	x 12	= Pounds-force inches (lbf in; lb in)
Pounds-force feet (lbf ft; lb ft)	x 0.138	= Kilograms-force metres (kgf m; kg m)	x 7.233	= Pounds-force feet (lbf ft; lb ft)
Pounds-force feet (lbf ft; lb ft)	x 1.356	= Newton metres (Nm)	x 0.738	= Pounds-force feet (lbf ft; lb ft)
Newton metres (Nm)	x 0.102	= Kilograms-force metres (kgf m; kg m)	x 9.804	= Newton metres (Nm)

Power

Horsepower (hp)	x 745.7	= Watts (W)	x 0.0013	= Horsepower (hp)

Velocity (speed)

Miles per hour (miles/hr; mph)	x 1.609	= Kilometres per hour (km/hr; kph)	x 0.621	= Miles per hour (miles/hr; mph)

Fuel consumption*

Miles per gallon, Imperial (mpg)	x 0.354	= Kilometres per litre (km/l)	x 2.825	= Miles per gallon, Imperial (mpg)
Miles per gallon, US (mpg)	x 0.425	= Kilometres per litre (km/l)	x 2.352	= Miles per gallon, US (mpg)

Temperature

Degrees Fahrenheit = (°C x 1.8) + 32   Degrees Celsius (Degrees Centigrade; °C) = (°F - 32) x 0.56

It is common practice to convert from miles per gallon (mpg) to litres/100 kilometres (l/100km), where mpg x l/100 km = 282

Spare parts are available from many sources, including maker's appointed garages, accessory shops, and motor factors. To be sure of obtaining the correct parts, it will sometimes be necessary to quote the vehicle identification number. If possible, it can also be useful to take the old parts along for positive identification. Items such as starter motors and alternators may be available under a service exchange scheme – any parts returned should be clean.

Our advice regarding spare parts is as follows.

Officially appointed garages

This is the best source of parts which are peculiar to your car, and which are not otherwise generally available (eg, badges, interior trim, certain body panels, etc). It is also the only place at which you should buy parts if the car is still under warranty.

Accessory shops

These are very good places to buy materials and components needed for the maintenance of your car (oil, air and fuel filters, light bulbs, drivebelts, greases, brake pads, touch-up paint, etc). Components of this nature sold by a reputable shop are usually of the same standard as those used by the car manufacturer.

Besides components, these shops also sell tools and general accessories, usually have convenient opening hours, charge lower prices, and can often be found close to home. Some accessory shops have parts counters where components needed for almost any repair job can be purchased or ordered.

Motor factors

Good factors will stock all the more important components which wear out comparatively quickly, and can sometimes supply individual components needed for the overhaul of a larger assembly (eg, brake seals and hydraulic parts, bearing shells, pistons, valves). They may also handle work such as cylinder block reboring, crankshaft regrinding, etc.

Engine reconditioners

These specialise in engine overhaul and can also supply components. It is recommended that the establishment is a member of the Federation of Engine Re-Manufacturers, or a similar society.

Tyre and exhaust specialists

These outlets may be independent, or members of a local or national chain. They frequently offer competitive prices when compared with a main dealer or local garage, but it will pay to obtain several quotes before making a decision. When researching prices, also ask what extras may be added – for instance fitting a new valve, balancing the wheel and tyre disposal all both commonly charged on top of the price of a new tyre.

Other sources

Beware of parts or materials obtained from market stalls, car boot sales, on-line auctions or similar outlets. Such items are not invariably sub-standard, but there is little chance of compensation if they do prove unsatisfactory. In the case of safety-critical components such as brake pads, there is the risk not only of financial loss, but also of an accident causing injury or death.

Second-hand components or assemblies obtained from a car breaker can be a good buy in some circumstances, but this sort of purchase is best made by the experienced DIY mechanic.

Disconnecting the battery

Caution: After reconnecting the battery, the safety function of the electric windows will not be re-instated until the windows have been reprogrammed. This could potentially cause severe pinching injuries.
Several of the systems require battery power to be available at all times (permanent live). This is either to ensure their continued operation (such as the clock), or to maintain electronic memory settings which would otherwise be erased. Whenever the battery is to be disconnected, first note the following points, to ensure there are no unforeseen consequences:

a) *Firstly, on any vehicle with central door locking, it is a wise precaution to remove the key from the ignition, and to keep it with you. This avoids the possibility of the key being locked inside the car, should the central locking engage when the battery is reconnected.*
b) *If a security-coded audio unit is fitted, and the unit and/or the battery is disconnected, the unit will not function until the correct security code has been entered. Therefore, if you do not know the correct security code for the radio/CD unit, do not disconnect either of the battery terminals, or remove the radio/CD unit from the vehicle. The code appears on a code card supplied with the car when new. Details for entering the code appear in the vehicle handbook. Should the code have been misplaced or forgotten, on production of proof of ownership, a VW dealer or in-car entertainment specialist may be able to help.*
c) *The engine management system ECU is of the 'self-learning' type, meaning that, as it operates, it adapts to changes in operating conditions, and stores the optimum settings found (this is especially true for idle speed settings). When the battery is disconnected, these 'learned' settings are lost, and the ECU reverts to the base factory settings. When the engine is restarted, it may idle and run roughly until the ECU has 'relearned' the best settings. To further this 'learning' process, take the car for a road test of at least 15 minutes' duration, covering as many engine speeds and loads as possible, and concentrating on the 2000 to 4000 rpm range. On completion, let the engine idle for at least 10 minutes, turning the steering wheel occasionally and switching on high-current-draw equipment such as the heater fan or heated rear window. If the engine does not regain its normal performance, have the system checked for faults by a VW dealer.*
d) *On vehicles equipped with an original equipment anti-theft alarm system, before disconnecting the battery, de-activate the alarm system, otherwise the alarm will be triggered.*
e) *After the battery has been reconnected, the warning lights for the ESP and electro-mechanical steering will light up and stay on. They will extinguish if you drive briefly in a straight line at a speed of 9 to 13 mph.*

Devices known as 'memory-savers' or 'code-savers' can be used to avoid some of the above problems. Precise details of use vary according to the device used. Typically, it is plugged into the cigarette lighter socket, and is connected by its own wiring to a spare battery; the vehicle battery is then disconnected from the electrical system, leaving the memory-saver to pass sufficient current to maintain audio unit security codes, and other memory values, and also to run permanently-live circuits such as the clock.

⚠️ **Warning: Some of these devices allow a considerable amount of current to pass, which can mean that many of the vehicle's systems are still operational when the main battery is disconnected. If a memory-saver is used, ensure that the circuit concerned is actually 'dead' before carrying out any work on it.**

Whenever servicing, repair or overhaul work is carried out on the car or its components, observe the following procedures and instructions. This will assist in carrying out the operation efficiently and to a professional standard of workmanship.

Joint mating faces and gaskets

When separating components at their mating faces, never insert screwdrivers or similar implements into the joint between the faces in order to prise them apart. This can cause severe damage which results in oil leaks, coolant leaks, etc upon reassembly. Separation is usually achieved by tapping along the joint with a soft-faced hammer in order to break the seal. However, note that this method may not be suitable where dowels are used for component location.

Where a gasket is used between the mating faces of two components, a new one must be fitted on reassembly; fit it dry unless otherwise stated in the repair procedure. Make sure that the mating faces are clean and dry, with all traces of old gasket removed. When cleaning a joint face, use a tool which is unlikely to score or damage the face, and remove any burrs or nicks with an oilstone or fine file.

Make sure that tapped holes are cleaned with a pipe cleaner, and keep them free of jointing compound, if this is being used, unless specifically instructed otherwise.

Ensure that all orifices, channels or pipes are clear, and blow through them, preferably using compressed air.

Oil seals

Oil seals can be removed by levering them out with a wide flat-bladed screwdriver or similar implement. Alternatively, a number of self-tapping screws may be screwed into the seal, and these used as a purchase for pliers or some similar device in order to pull the seal free.

Whenever an oil seal is removed from its working location, either individually or as part of an assembly, it should be renewed.

The very fine sealing lip of the seal is easily damaged, and will not seal if the surface it contacts is not completely clean and free from scratches, nicks or grooves. If the original sealing surface of the component cannot be restored, and the manufacturer has not made provision for slight relocation of the seal relative to the sealing surface, the component should be renewed.

Protect the lips of the seal from any surface which may damage them in the course of fitting. Use tape or a conical sleeve where possible. Where indicated, lubricate the seal lips with oil before fitting and, on dual-lipped seals, fill the space between the lips with grease.

Unless otherwise stated, oil seals must be fitted with their sealing lips toward the lubricant to be sealed.

Use a tubular drift or block of wood of the appropriate size to install the seal and, if the seal housing is shouldered, drive the seal down to the shoulder. If the seal housing is unshouldered, the seal should be fitted with its face flush with the housing top face (unless otherwise instructed).

Screw threads and fastenings

Seized nuts, bolts and screws are quite a common occurrence where corrosion has set in, and the use of penetrating oil or releasing fluid will often overcome this problem if the offending item is soaked for a while before attempting to release it. The use of an impact driver may also provide a means of releasing such stubborn fastening devices, when used in conjunction with the appropriate screwdriver bit or socket. If none of these methods works, it may be necessary to resort to the careful application of heat, or the use of a hacksaw or nut splitter device. Before resorting to extreme methods, check that you are not dealing with a left-hand thread!

Studs are usually removed by locking two nuts together on the threaded part, and then using a spanner on the lower nut to unscrew the stud. Studs or bolts which have broken off below the surface of the component in which they are mounted can sometimes be removed using a stud extractor.

Always ensure that a blind tapped hole is completely free from oil, grease, water or other fluid before installing the bolt or stud. Failure to do this could cause the housing to crack due to the hydraulic action of the bolt or stud as it is screwed in.

For some screw fastenings, notably cylinder head bolts or nuts, torque wrench settings are no longer specified for the latter stages of tightening, "angle-tightening" being called up instead. Typically, a fairly low torque wrench setting will be applied to the bolts/nuts in the correct sequence, followed by one or more stages of tightening through specified angles.

When checking or retightening a nut or bolt to a specified torque setting, slacken the nut or bolt by a quarter of a turn, and then retighten to the specified setting. However, this should not be attempted where angular tightening has been used.

Locknuts, locktabs and washers

Any fastening which will rotate against a component or housing during tightening should always have a washer between it and the relevant component or housing.

Spring or split washers should always be renewed when they are used to lock a critical component such as a big-end bearing retaining bolt or nut. Locktabs which are folded over to retain a nut or bolt should always be renewed.

Self-locking nuts can be re-used in non-critical areas, providing resistance can be felt when the locking portion passes over the bolt or stud thread. However, it should be noted that self-locking stiffnuts tend to lose their effectiveness after long periods of use, and should then be renewed as a matter of course.

Split pins must always be replaced with new ones of the correct size for the hole.

When thread-locking compound is found on the threads of a fastener which is to be re-used, it should be cleaned off with a wire brush and solvent, and fresh compound applied on reassembly.

Special tools

Some repair procedures in this manual entail the use of special tools such as a press, two or three-legged pullers, spring compressors, etc. Wherever possible, suitable readily-available alternatives to the manufacturer's special tools are described, and are shown in use. In some instances, where no alternative is possible, it has been necessary to resort to the use of a manufacturer's tool, and this has been done for reasons of safety as well as the efficient completion of the repair operation. Unless you are highly-skilled and have a thorough understanding of the procedures described, never attempt to bypass the use of any special tool when the procedure described specifies its use. Not only is there a very great risk of personal injury, but expensive damage could be caused to the components involved.

Environmental considerations

When disposing of used engine oil, brake fluid, antifreeze, etc, give due consideration to any detrimental environmental effects. Do not, for instance, pour any of the above liquids down drains into the general sewage system, or onto the ground to soak away. Many local council refuse tips provide a facility for waste oil disposal, as do some garages. You can find your nearest disposal point by calling the Environment Agency on 08708 506 506 or by visiting www.oilbankline.org.uk.

Note: *It is illegal and anti-social to dump oil down the drain. To find the location of your local oil recycling bank, call 08708 506 506 or visit www.oilbankline.org.uk.*

Modifications are a continuing and unpubliclsed process in vehicle manufacture, quite apart from major model changes. Spare parts manuals and lists are compiled upon a numerical basis, the individual vehicle identification numbers being essential to correct identification of the component concerned.

When ordering spare parts, always give as much information as possible. Quote the car model, year of manufacture and registration, chassis and engine numbers as appropriate.

The *Vehicle Identification Number (VIN)* plate is visible from the outside of the vehicle, through the left-hand lower corner of the windscreen, and is also stamped on the top of the right-hand inner wing in the engine compartment **(see illustrations)**.

The *Vehicle Data Sticker* is located in the spare wheel well accessed through the luggage compartment **(see illustration)**. It contains the VIN, vehicle type, engine power, transmission type, engine and transmission codes, paint number, interior equipment, optional extras, and PR numbers (for maintenance schedule).

The *Type plate and factory plate* is located at the bottom of the front , left-hand door A-pillar, and is visible with the door open. It contains the gross vehicle weight, front axle weight and rear axle weight.

The Engine Number is stamped into the left-hand end of the cylinder block and on the right-hand end of the cylinder head on petrol engines. On diesel engines it is stamped into the front of the cylinder block, next to the engine-to-transmission joint. A barcode identification sticker is located on the top of the timing cover or on the right-hand end of the cylinder head **(see illustrations)**.

Vehicle Identification Number (VIN) located on the left-hand front edge of the windscreen

Vehicle Identification Number (VIN) located on the top of the right-hand inner wing

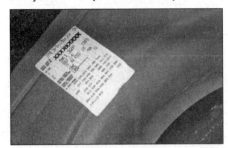

Vehicle Data Sticker located in the spare wheel well

VIN (A) and engine number (B) located on the left-hand B-pillar label

Engine code sticker on the right-hand end of the cylinder head on petrol engines

Engine code sticker on the top of the timing cover on diesel engines

Jacking and vehicle support

The jack supplied with the vehicle tool kit should only be used for changing the roadwheels – see *Wheel changing* at the front of this book. When carrying out any other kind of work, raise the vehicle using a hydraulic (or 'trolley') jack, and always supplement the jack with axle stands positioned under the vehicle jacking points.

When using a hydraulic jack or axle stands, always position the jack head or axle stand head under one of the relevant jacking points.

To raise the front and/or rear of the vehicle, use the jacking/support points at the front and rear ends of the door sills, indicated by the triangular depressions in the sill panel **(see illustration)**. Position a block of wood with a groove cut in it on the jack head to prevent the vehicle weight resting on the sill edge; align the sill edge with the groove in the wood so that the vehicle weight is spread evenly over the surface of the block. Supplement the jack with axle stands (also with slotted blocks of

wood) positioned as close as possible to the jacking points **(see illustrations)**.

Do not jack the vehicle under any other part of the sill, sump, floor pan, or any of the steering or suspension components. With the vehicle raised, an axle stand should be positioned beneath the vehicle jack location point on the sill.

⚠️ *Warning: Never work under, around, or near a raised car, unless it is supported in at least two places.*

Front and rear jacking points (arrowed)

The jacking points are indicated by an arrow on the sill

Use an axle stand with a suitable block of wood

Introduction

A selection of good tools is a fundamental requirement for anyone contemplating the maintenance and repair of a motor vehicle. For the owner who does not possess any, their purchase will prove a considerable expense, offsetting some of the savings made by doing-it-yourself. However, provided that the tools purchased meet the relevant national safety standards and are of good quality, they will last for many years and prove an extremely worthwhile investment.

To help the average owner to decide which tools are needed to carry out the various tasks detailed in this manual, we have compiled three lists of tools under the following headings: *Maintenance and minor repair, Repair and overhaul*, and *Special*. Newcomers to practical mechanics should start off with the *Maintenance and minor repair* tool kit, and confine themselves to the simpler jobs around the vehicle. Then, as confidence and experience grow, more difficult tasks can be undertaken, with extra tools being purchased as, and when, they are needed. In this way, a *Maintenance and minor repair* tool kit can be built up into a *Repair and overhaul* tool kit over a considerable period of time, without any major cash outlays. The experienced do-it-yourselfer will have a tool kit good enough for most repair and overhaul procedures, and will add tools from the *Special* category when it is felt that the expense is justified by the amount of use to which these tools will be put.

Maintenance and minor repair tool kit

The tools given in this list should be considered as a minimum requirement if routine maintenance, servicing and minor repair operations are to be undertaken. We recommend the purchase of combination spanners (ring one end, open-ended the other); although more expensive than open-ended ones, they do give the advantages of both types of spanner.

☐ *Combination spanners:*
  Metric - 8 to 19 mm inclusive
☐ *Adjustable spanner - 35 mm jaw (approx.)*
☐ *Spark plug spanner (with rubber insert) - petrol models*
☐ *Spark plug gap adjustment tool - petrol models*
☐ *Set of feeler gauges*
☐ *Brake bleed nipple spanner*
☐ *Screwdrivers:*
  Flat blade - 100 mm long x 6 mm dia
  Cross blade - 100 mm long x 6 mm dia
  Torx - various sizes (not all vehicles)
☐ *Combination pliers*
☐ *Hacksaw (junior)*
☐ *Tyre pump*
☐ *Tyre pressure gauge*
☐ *Oil can*
☐ *Oil filter removal tool (if applicable)*
☐ *Fine emery cloth*
☐ *Wire brush (small)*
☐ *Funnel (medium size)*
☐ *Sump drain plug key (not all vehicles)*

Repair and overhaul tool kit

These tools are virtually essential for anyone undertaking any major repairs to a motor vehicle, and are additional to those given in the *Maintenance and minor repair* list. Included in this list is a comprehensive set of sockets. Although these are expensive, they will be found invaluable as they are so versatile - particularly if various drives are included in the set. We recommend the half-inch square-drive type, as this can be used with most proprietary torque wrenches.

The tools in this list will sometimes need to be supplemented by tools from the *Special* list:

☐ *Sockets to cover range in previous list (including Torx sockets)*
☐ *Reversible ratchet drive (for use with sockets)*
☐ *Extension piece, 250 mm (for use with sockets)*
☐ *Universal joint (for use with sockets)*
☐ *Flexible handle or sliding T "breaker bar" (for use with sockets)*
☐ *Torque wrench (for use with sockets)*
☐ *Self-locking grips*
☐ *Ball pein hammer*
☐ *Soft-faced mallet (plastic or rubber)*
☐ *Screwdrivers:*
  Flat blade - long & sturdy, short (chubby), and narrow (electrician's) types
  Cross blade – long & sturdy, and short (chubby) types
☐ *Pliers:*
  Long-nosed
  Side cutters (electrician's)
  Circlip (internal and external)
☐ *Cold chisel - 25 mm*
☐ *Scriber*
☐ *Scraper*
☐ *Centre-punch*
☐ *Pin punch*
☐ *Hacksaw*
☐ *Brake hose clamp*
☐ *Brake/clutch bleeding kit*
☐ *Selection of twist drills*
☐ *Steel rule/straight-edge*
☐ *Allen keys (inc. splined/Torx type)*
☐ *Selection of files*
☐ *Wire brush*
☐ *Axle stands*
☐ *Jack (strong trolley or hydraulic type)*
☐ *Light with extension lead*
☐ *Universal electrical multi-meter*

Sockets and reversible ratchet drive

Brake bleeding kit

Torx key, socket and bit

Hose clamp

Angular-tightening gauge

Special tools

The tools in this list are those which are not used regularly, are expensive to buy, or which need to be used in accordance with their manufacturers' instructions. Unless relatively difficult mechanical jobs are undertaken frequently, it will not be economic to buy many of these tools. Where this is the case, you could consider clubbing together with friends (or joining a motorists' club) to make a joint purchase, or borrowing the tools against a deposit from a local garage or tool hire specialist.

The following list contains only those tools and instruments freely available to the public, and not those special tools produced by the vehicle manufacturer specifically for its dealer network. You will find occasional references to these manufacturers' special tools in the text of this manual. Generally, an alternative method of doing the job without the vehicle manufacturers' special tool is given. However, sometimes there is no alternative to using them. Where this is the case and the relevant tool cannot be bought or borrowed, you will have to entrust the work to a dealer.

- ☐ *Angular-tightening gauge*
- ☐ *Valve spring compressor*
- ☐ *Valve grinding tool*
- ☐ *Piston ring compressor*
- ☐ *Piston ring removal/installation tool*
- ☐ *Cylinder bore hone*
- ☐ *Balljoint separator*
- ☐ *Coil spring compressors (where applicable)*
- ☐ *Two/three-legged hub and bearing puller*
- ☐ *Impact screwdriver*
- ☐ *Micrometer and/or vernier calipers*
- ☐ *Dial gauge*
- ☐ *Tachometer*
- ☐ *Fault code reader*
- ☐ *Cylinder compression gauge*
- ☐ *Hand-operated vacuum pump and gauge*
- ☐ *Clutch plate alignment set*
- ☐ *Brake shoe steady spring cup removal tool*
- ☐ *Bush and bearing removal/installation set*
- ☐ *Stud extractors*
- ☐ *Tap and die set*
- ☐ *Lifting tackle*

Buying tools

Reputable motor accessory shops and superstores often offer excellent quality tools at discount prices, so it pays to shop around.

Remember, you don't have to buy the most expensive items on the shelf, but it is always advisable to steer clear of the very cheap tools. Beware of 'bargains' offered on market stalls, on-line or at car boot sales. There are plenty of good tools around at reasonable prices, but always aim to purchase items which meet the relevant national safety standards. If in doubt, ask the proprietor or manager of the shop for advice before making a purchase.

Care and maintenance of tools

Having purchased a reasonable tool kit, it is necessary to keep the tools in a clean and serviceable condition. After use, always wipe off any dirt, grease and metal particles using a clean, dry cloth, before putting the tools away. Never leave them lying around after they have been used. A simple tool rack on the garage or workshop wall for items such as screwdrivers and pliers is a good idea. Store all normal spanners and sockets in a metal box. Any measuring instruments, gauges, meters, etc, must be carefully stored where they cannot be damaged or become rusty.

Take a little care when tools are used. Hammer heads inevitably become marked, and screwdrivers lose the keen edge on their blades from time to time. A little timely attention with emery cloth or a file will soon restore items like this to a good finish.

Working facilities

Not to be forgotten when discussing tools is the workshop itself. If anything more than routine maintenance is to be carried out, a suitable working area becomes essential.

It is appreciated that many an owner-mechanic is forced by circumstances to remove an engine or similar item without the benefit of a garage or workshop. Having done this, any repairs should always be done under the cover of a roof.

Wherever possible, any dismantling should be done on a clean, flat workbench or table at a suitable working height.

Any workbench needs a vice; one with a jaw opening of 100 mm is suitable for most jobs. As mentioned previously, some clean dry storage space is also required for tools, as well as for any lubricants, cleaning fluids, touch-up paints etc, which become necessary.

Another item which may be required, and which has a much more general usage, is an electric drill with a chuck capacity of at least 8 mm. This, together with a good range of twist drills, is virtually essential for fitting accessories.

Last, but not least, always keep a supply of old newspapers and clean, lint-free rags available, and try to keep any working area as clean as possible.

Micrometers

Dial test indicator ("dial gauge")

Oil filter removal tool (strap wrench type)

Compression tester

Bearing puller

MOT test checks

This is a guide to getting your vehicle through the MOT test. Obviously it will not be possible to examine the vehicle to the same standard as the professional MOT tester. However, working through the following checks will enable you to identify any problem areas before submitting the vehicle for the test.

It has only been possible to summarise the test requirements here, based on the regulations in force at the time of printing. Test standards are becoming increasingly stringent, although there are some exemptions for older vehicles.

An assistant will be needed to help carry out some of these checks.

The checks have been sub-divided into four categories, as follows:

1 Checks carried out **FROM THE DRIVER'S SEAT**

2 Checks carried out **WITH THE VEHICLE ON THE GROUND**

3 Checks carried out **WITH THE VEHICLE RAISED AND THE WHEELS FREE TO TURN**

4 Checks carried out on **YOUR VEHICLE'S EXHAUST EMISSION SYSTEM**

---

1 Checks carried out **FROM THE DRIVER'S SEAT**

Handbrake (parking brake)

☐ Test the operation of the handbrake. Excessive travel (too many clicks) indicates incorrect brake or cable adjustment.
☐ Check that the handbrake cannot be released by tapping the lever sideways. Check the security of the lever mountings.

☐ If the parking brake is foot-operated, check that the pedal is secure and without excessive travel, and that the release mechanism operates correctly.
☐ Where applicable, test the operation of the electronic handbrake. The brake should engage and disengage without excessive delay. If the warning light does not extinguish when the brake is disengaged, this could indicate a fault which will need further investigation.

Footbrake

☐ Depress the brake pedal and check that it does not creep down to the floor, indicating a master cylinder fault. Release the pedal, wait a few seconds, then depress it again. If the pedal travels nearly to the floor before firm resistance is felt, brake adjustment or repair is necessary. If the pedal feels spongy, there is air in the hydraulic system which must be removed by bleeding.

☐ Check that the brake pedal is secure and in good condition. Check also for signs of fluid leaks on the pedal, floor or carpets, which would indicate failed seals in the brake master cylinder.
☐ Check the servo unit (when applicable) by operating the brake pedal several times, then keeping the pedal depressed and starting the engine. As the engine starts, the pedal will move down slightly. If not, the vacuum hose or the servo itself may be faulty.

Steering wheel and column

☐ Examine the steering wheel for fractures or looseness of the hub, spokes or rim.
☐ Move the steering wheel from side to side and then up and down. Check that the steering wheel is not loose on the column, indicating wear or a loose retaining nut. Continue moving the steering wheel as before, but also turn it slightly from left to right.

☐ Check that the steering wheel is not loose on the column, and that there is no abnormal movement of the steering wheel, indicating wear in the column support bearings or couplings.
☐ Check that the ignition lock (where fitted) engages and disengages correctly.
☐ Steering column adjustment mechanisms (where fitted) must be able to lock the column securely in place with no play evident.

Windscreen, mirrors and sunvisor

☐ The windscreen must be free of cracks or other significant damage within the driver's field of view. (Small stone chips are acceptable.) Rear view mirrors must be secure, intact, and capable of being adjusted.

☐ The driver's sunvisor must be capable of being stored in the "up" position.

Seat belts and seats

Note: *The following checks are applicable to all seat belts, front and rear.*

☐ Examine the webbing of all the belts (including rear belts if fitted) for cuts, serious fraying or deterioration. Fasten and unfasten each belt to check the buckles. If applicable, check the retracting mechanism. Check the security of all seat belt mountings accessible from inside the vehicle, ensuring any height adjustable mountings lock securely in place.

☐ Seat belts with pre-tensioners, once activated, have a "flag" or similar showing on the seat belt stalk. This, in itself, is not a reason for test failure.

☐ The front seats themselves must be securely attached and the backrests must lock in the upright position.

Doors

☐ Both front doors must be able to be opened and closed from outside and inside, and must latch securely when closed.

Bonnet and boot/tailgate

☐ The bonnet and boot/tailgate must latch securely when closed.

2 Checks carried out WITH THE VEHICLE ON THE GROUND

Vehicle identification

☐ Number plates must be in good condition, secure and legible, with letters and numbers correctly spaced – spacing at (A) should be 33 mm and at (B) 11 mm. At the front, digits must be black on a white background and at the rear black on a yellow background. Other background designs (such as honeycomb) are not permitted.

☐ The VIN plate and/or homologation plate must be permanently displayed and legible.

Electrical equipment

☐ Switch on the ignition and check the operation of the horn.

☐ Check the windscreen washers and wipers, examining the wiper blades; renew damaged or perished blades. Also check the operation of the stop-lights.

☐ Check the operation of the sidelights and number plate lights. The lenses and reflectors must be secure, clean and undamaged.

☐ Check the operation and alignment of the headlights. The headlight reflectors must not be tarnished and the lenses must be undamaged.

☐ Switch on the ignition and check the operation of the direction indicators (including the instrument panel tell-tale) and the hazard warning lights. Operation of the sidelights and stop-lights must not affect the indicators - if it does, the cause is usually a bad earth at the rear light cluster. Indicators should flash at a rate of between 60 and 120 times per minute – faster or slower than this could indicate a fault with the flasher unit or a bad earth at one of the light units.

☐ Check the operation of the rear foglight(s), including the warning light on the instrument panel or in the switch.

☐ The warning lights must illuminate in accordance with the manufacturer's design. For most vehicles, the ABS and other warning lights should illuminate when the ignition is switched on, and (if the system is operating properly) extinguish after a few seconds. Refer to the owner's handbook.

Footbrake

☐ Examine the master cylinder, brake pipes and servo unit for leaks, loose mountings, corrosion or other damage. If ABS is fitted, this unit should also be examined for signs of leaks or corrosion.

☐ The fluid reservoir must be secure and the fluid level must be between the upper (A) and lower (B) markings.

☐ Inspect both front brake flexible hoses for cracks or deterioration of the rubber. Turn the steering from lock to lock, and ensure that the hoses do not contact the wheel, tyre, or any part of the steering or suspension mechanism. With the brake pedal firmly depressed, check the hoses for bulges or leaks under pressure.

Steering and suspension

☐ Have your assistant turn the steering wheel from side to side slightly, up to the point where the steering gear just begins to transmit this movement to the roadwheels. Check for excessive free play between the steering wheel and the steering gear, indicating wear or insecurity of the steering column joints, the column-to-steering gear coupling, or the steering gear itself.

☐ Have your assistant turn the steering wheel more vigorously in each direction, so that the roadwheels just begin to turn. As this is done, examine all the steering joints, linkages, fittings and attachments. Renew any component that shows signs of wear or damage. On vehicles with power steering, check the security and condition of the steering pump, drivebelt and hoses.

☐ Check that the vehicle is standing level, and at approximately the correct ride height.

Shock absorbers

☐ Depress each corner of the vehicle in turn, then release it. The vehicle should rise and then settle in its normal position. If the vehicle continues to rise and fall, the shock absorber is defective. A shock absorber which has seized will also cause the vehicle to fail.

Exhaust system

☐ Start the engine. With your assistant holding a rag over the tailpipe, check the entire system for leaks. Repair or renew leaking sections.

3 Checks carried out
WITH THE VEHICLE RAISED AND THE WHEELS FREE TO TURN

Jack up the front and rear of the vehicle, and securely support it on axle stands. Position the stands clear of the suspension assemblies. Ensure that the wheels are clear of the ground and that the steering can be turned from lock to lock.

Steering mechanism

☐ Have your assistant turn the steering from lock to lock. Check that the steering turns smoothly, and that no part of the steering mechanism, including a wheel or tyre, fouls any brake hose or pipe or any part of the body structure.
☐ Examine the steering rack rubber gaiters for damage or insecurity of the retaining clips. If power steering is fitted, check for signs of damage or leakage of the fluid hoses, pipes or connections. Also check for excessive stiffness or binding of the steering, a missing split pin or locking device, or severe corrosion of the body structure within 30 cm of any steering component attachment point.

Front and rear suspension and wheel bearings

☐ Starting at the front right-hand side, grasp the roadwheel at the 3 o'clock and 9 o'clock positions and rock gently but firmly. Check for free play or insecurity at the wheel bearings, suspension balljoints, or suspension mount-ings, pivots and attachments.
☐ Now grasp the wheel at the 12 o'clock and 6 o'clock positions and repeat the previous inspection. Spin the wheel, and check for roughness or tightness of the front wheel bearing.

☐ If excess free play is suspected at a component pivot point, this can be confirmed by using a large screwdriver or similar tool and levering between the mounting and the component attachment. This will confirm whether the wear is in the pivot bush, its retaining bolt, or in the mounting itself (the bolt holes can often become elongated).

☐ Carry out all the above checks at the other front wheel, and then at both rear wheels.

Springs and shock absorbers

☐ Examine the suspension struts (when applicable) for serious fluid leakage, corrosion, or damage to the casing. Also check the security of the mounting points.
☐ If coil springs are fitted, check that the spring ends locate in their seats, and that the spring is not corroded, cracked or broken.
☐ If leaf springs are fitted, check that all leaves are intact, that the axle is securely attached to each spring, and that there is no deterioration of the spring eye mountings, bushes, and shackles.

☐ The same general checks apply to vehicles fitted with other suspension types, such as torsion bars, hydraulic displacer units, etc. Ensure that all mountings and attachments are secure, that there are no signs of excessive wear, corrosion or damage, and (on hydraulic types) that there are no fluid leaks or damaged pipes.
☐ Inspect the shock absorbers for signs of serious fluid leakage. Check for wear of the mounting bushes or attachments, or damage to the body of the unit.

Driveshafts (fwd vehicles only)

☐ Rotate each front wheel in turn and inspect the constant velocity joint gaiters for splits or damage. Also check that each driveshaft is straight and undamaged.

Braking system

☐ If possible without dismantling, check brake pad wear and disc condition. Ensure that the friction lining material has not worn excessively, (A) and that the discs are not fractured, pitted, scored or badly worn (B).

☐ Examine all the rigid brake pipes underneath the vehicle, and the flexible hose(s) at the rear. Look for corrosion, chafing or insecurity of the pipes, and for signs of bulging under pressure, chafing, splits or deterioration of the flexible hoses.
☐ Look for signs of fluid leaks at the brake calipers or on the brake backplates. Repair or renew leaking components.
☐ Slowly spin each wheel, while your assistant depresses and releases the footbrake. Ensure that each brake is operating and does not bind when the pedal is released.

□Examine the handbrake mechanism, checking for frayed or broken cables, excessive corrosion, or wear or insecurity of the linkage. Check that the mechanism works on each relevant wheel, and releases fully, without binding.

□It is not possible to test brake efficiency without special equipment, but a road test can be carried out later to check that the vehicle pulls up in a straight line.

Fuel and exhaust systems

□ Inspect the fuel tank (including the filler cap), fuel pipes, hoses and unions. All components must be secure and free from leaks. Locking fuel caps must lock securely and the key must be provided for the MOT test.

□Examine the exhaust system over its entire length, checking for any damaged, broken or missing mountings, security of the retaining clamps and rust or corrosion.

Wheels and tyres

□Examine the sidewalls and tread area of each tyre in turn. Check for cuts, tears, lumps, bulges, separation of the tread, and exposure of the ply or cord due to wear or damage. Check that the tyre bead is correctly seated on the wheel rim, that the valve is sound and properly seated, and that the wheel is not distorted or damaged.

□ Check that the tyres are of the correct size for the vehicle, that they are of the same size and type on each axle, and that the pressures are correct.

□Check the tyre tread depth. The legal minimum at the time of writing is 1.6 mm over the central three-quarters of the tread width. Abnormal tread wear may indicate incorrect front wheel alignment or wear in steering or suspension components.

□If the spare wheel is fitted externally or in a separate carrier beneath the vehicle, check that mountings are secure and free of excessive corrosion.

Body corrosion

□Check the condition of the entire vehicle structure for signs of corrosion in load-bearing areas. (These include chassis box sections, side sills, cross-members, pillars, and all suspension, steering, braking system and seat belt mountings and anchorages.) Any corrosion which has seriously reduced the thickness of a load-bearing area (or is within 30 cm of safety-related components such as steering or suspension) is likely to cause the vehicle to fail. In this case professional repairs are likely to be needed.

□Damage or corrosion which causes sharp or otherwise dangerous edges to be exposed will also cause the vehicle to fail.

Towbars

□Check the condition of mounting points (both beneath the vehicle and within boot/hatchback areas) for signs of corrosion, ensuring that all fixings are secure and not worn or damaged. There must be no excessive play in detachable tow ball arms or quick-release mechanisms.

4 Checks carried out on YOUR VEHICLE'S EXHAUST EMISSION SYSTEM

Petrol models

□The engine should be warmed up, and running well (ignition system in good order, air filter element clean, etc).

□Before testing, run the engine at around 2500 rpm for 20 seconds. Let the engine drop to idle, and watch for smoke from the exhaust. If the idle speed is too high, or if dense blue or black smoke emerges for more than 5 seconds, the vehicle will fail. Typically, blue smoke signifies oil burning (engine wear); black smoke means unburnt fuel (dirty air cleaner element, or other fuel system fault).

□An exhaust gas analyser for measuring carbon monoxide (CO) and hydrocarbons (HC) is now needed. If one cannot be hired or borrowed, have a local garage perform the check.

CO emissions (mixture)

□The MOT tester has access to the CO limits for all vehicles. The CO level is measured at idle speed, and at 'fast idle' (2500 to 3000 rpm). The following limits are given as a general guide:

At idle speed – Less than 0.5% CO
At 'fast idle' – Less than 0.3% CO
Lambda reading – 0.97 to 1.03

□If the CO level is too high, this may point to poor maintenance, a fuel injection system problem, faulty lambda (oxygen) sensor or catalytic converter. Try an injector cleaning treatment, and check the vehicle's ECU for fault codes.

HC emissions

□The MOT tester has access to HC limits for all vehicles. The HC level is measured at 'fast idle' (2500 to 3000 rpm). The following limits are given as a general guide:

At 'fast idle' – Less then 200 ppm

□Excessive HC emissions are typically caused by oil being burnt (worn engine), or by a blocked crankcase ventilation system ('breather'). If the engine oil is old and thin, an oil change may help. If the engine is running badly, check the vehicle's ECU for fault codes.

Diesel models

□The only emission test for diesel engines is measuring exhaust smoke density, using a calibrated smoke meter. The test involves accelerating the engine at least 3 times to its maximum unloaded speed.

Note: *On engines with a timing belt, it is VITAL that the belt is in good condition before the test is carried out.*

□With the engine warmed up, it is first purged by running at around 2500 rpm for 20 seconds. A governor check is then carried out, by slowly accelerating the engine to its maximum speed. After this, the smoke meter is connected, and the engine is accelerated quickly to maximum speed three times. If the smoke density is less than the limits given below, the vehicle will pass:

Non-turbo vehicles: 2.5m-1
Turbocharged vehicles: 3.0m-1

□If excess smoke is produced, try fitting a new air cleaner element, or using an injector cleaning treatment. If the engine is running badly, where applicable, check the vehicle's ECU for fault codes. Also check the vehicle's EGR system, where applicable. At high mileages, the injectors may require professional attention.

Engine

- ☐ Engine fails to rotate when attempting to start
- ☐ Engine rotates, but will not start
- ☐ Engine difficult to start when cold
- ☐ Engine difficult to start when hot
- ☐ Starter motor noisy or excessively-rough in engagement
- ☐ Engine starts, but stops immediately
- ☐ Engine idles erratically
- ☐ Engine misfires at idle speed
- ☐ Engine misfires throughout the driving speed range
- ☐ Engine hesitates on acceleration
- ☐ Engine stalls
- ☐ Engine lacks power
- ☐ Engine backfires
- ☐ Oil pressure warning light illuminated with engine running
- ☐ Engine runs-on after switching off
- ☐ Engine noises

Cooling system

- ☐ Overheating
- ☐ Overcooling
- ☐ External coolant leakage
- ☐ Internal coolant leakage
- ☐ Corrosion

Fuel and exhaust systems

- ☐ Excessive fuel consumption
- ☐ Fuel leakage and/or fuel odour

Clutch

- ☐ Pedal travels to floor – no pressure or very little resistance
- ☐ Clutch fails to disengage (unable to select gears).
- ☐ Clutch slips (engine speed increases, with no increase in vehicle speed).
- ☐ Judder as clutch is engaged
- ☐ Noise when depressing or releasing clutch pedal

Manual transmission

- ☐ Noisy in neutral with engine running
- ☐ Noisy in one particular gear
- ☐ Difficulty engaging gears
- ☐ Vibration
- ☐ Jumps out of gear
- ☐ Lubricant leaks

Automatic transmission

- ☐ Fluid leakage
- ☐ General gear selection problems
- ☐ Transmission fluid brown, or has burned smell
- ☐ Engine will not start in any gear, or starts in gears other than Park or Neutral
- ☐ Transmission slips, shifts roughly, is noisy, or has no drive in forward or reverse gears

Driveshafts

- ☐ Clicking or knocking noise on turns (at slow speed on full-lock)

Braking system

- ☐ Vehicle pulls to one side under braking
- ☐ Noise (grinding or high-pitched squeal) when brakes applied
- ☐ Brakes binding
- ☐ Excessive brake pedal travel
- ☐ Brake pedal feels spongy when depressed
- ☐ Excessive brake pedal effort required to stop vehicle
- ☐ Judder felt through brake pedal or steering wheel when braking
- ☐ Rear wheels locking under normal braking

Suspension and steering

- ☐ Vehicle pulls to one side
- ☐ Excessive pitching and/or rolling around corners, or during braking
- ☐ Lack of power assistance
- ☐ Wandering or general instability
- ☐ Excessively-stiff steering
- ☐ Excessive play in steering
- ☐ Wheel wobble and vibration
- ☐ Tyre wear excessive

Electrical system

- ☐ Battery will not hold a charge for more than a few days
- ☐ Ignition/no-charge warning light remains illuminated with engine running
- ☐ Ignition/no-charge warning light fails to come on
- ☐ Lights inoperative
- ☐ Instrument readings inaccurate or erratic
- ☐ Horn inoperative, or unsatisfactory in operation
- ☐ Windscreen wipers inoperative, or unsatisfactory in operation
- ☐ Windscreen washers inoperative, or unsatisfactory in operation
- ☐ Electric windows inoperative, or unsatisfactory in operation
- ☐ Central locking system inoperative, or unsatisfactory in operation

Introduction

The vehicle owner who does his or her own maintenance according to the recommended service schedules should not have to use this section of the manual very often. Modern component reliability is such that, provided those items subject to wear or deterioration are inspected or renewed at the specified intervals, sudden failure is comparatively rare. Faults do not usually just happen as a result of sudden failure, but develop over a period of time. Major mechanical failures in particular are usually preceded by characteristic symptoms over hundreds or even thousands of miles. Those components that do occasionally fail without warning are often small and easily carried in the vehicle.

With any fault-finding, the first step is to decide where to begin investigations. Sometimes this is obvious, but on other occasions, a little detective work will be necessary. The owner who makes half a dozen haphazard adjustments or component renewals may be successful in curing a fault (or its symptoms). However, will be none the wiser if the fault recurs, and ultimately may have spent more time and money than was necessary. A calm and logical approach will be found to be more satisfactory in the long run. Always take into account any warning signs or abnormalities that may have been noticed in the period preceding the fault – power loss, high or low gauge readings, unusual smells, etc. – and remember that failure of components such as fuses or spark plugs may only be pointers to some underlying fault.

The pages which follow provide an easy-reference guide to the more common problems which may occur during the operation of the vehicle. These problems and their possible causes are grouped under headings denoting various components or systems, such as Engine, Cooling system, etc. The general Chapter which deals with the problem is also shown in brackets; refer to the relevant part of that Chapter for system-specific information. Whatever the fault, certain basic principles apply. These are as follows:

Verify the fault. This is simply a matter of being sure that you know what the symptoms are before starting work. This is particularly important if you are investigating a fault for someone else, who may not have described it very accurately.

Do not overlook the obvious. For example, if the vehicle will not start, is there petrol in the tank? (Do not take anyone else's word on this particular point, and do not trust the fuel gauge either!) If an electrical fault is indicated, look for loose or broken wires before digging out the test gear.

Cure the disease, not the symptom. Substituting a flat battery with a fully-charged one will get you off the hard shoulder, but if the underlying cause is not attended to, the new battery will go the same way. Similarly, changing oil-fouled spark plugs for a new set will get you moving again, but remember that the reason for the fouling (if it was not simply an incorrect grade of plug) will have to be established and corrected.

Do not take anything for granted. Particularly, do not forget that a new component may itself be defective (especially if it's been rattling around in the boot for months). Also do not leave components out of a fault diagnosis sequence just because they are new or recently fitted. When you do finally diagnose a difficult fault, you will probably realise that all the evidence was there from the start.

Diesel fault diagnosis

The majority of starting problems on small diesel engines are electrical in origin. The mechanic who is familiar with petrol engines but less so with diesel may be inclined to view the diesel's injectors and pump in the same light as the spark plugs and distributor, but this is generally a mistake.

When investigating complaints of difficult starting for someone else, make sure that the correct starting procedure is understood and is being followed. Some drivers are unaware of the significance of the preheating warning light – many modern engines are sufficiently forgiving for this not to matter in mild weather, but with the onset of winter, problems begin.

As a rule of thumb, if the engine is difficult to start but runs well when it has finally got going, the problem is electrical (battery, starter motor or preheating system). If poor performance is combined with difficult starting, the problem is likely to be in the fuel system. The low-pressure (supply) side of the fuel system should be checked before suspecting the injectors and high-pressure pump. The most common fuel supply problem is air getting into the system, and any pipe from the fuel tank forwards must be scrutinised if air leakage is suspected. Normally the pump is the last item to suspect, since unless it has been tampered with, there is no reason for it to be at fault.

Engine

Engine fails to rotate when attempting to start

- ☐ Battery terminal connections loose or corroded (*Weekly checks*).
- ☐ Battery discharged or faulty (Chapter 5A).
- ☐ Broken, loose or disconnected wiring in the starting circuit (Chapter 5A).
- ☐ Defective starter solenoid or switch (Chapter 5A).
- ☐ Defective starter motor (Chapter 5A).
- ☐ Starter pinion or flywheel ring gear teeth loose or broken (Chapters 2A, 2B, 2C, 2D and 5A).
- ☐ Engine earth strap broken or disconnected (Chapter 5A).

Engine rotates, but will not start

- ☐ Fuel tank empty.
- ☐ Battery discharged (engine rotates slowly) (Chapter 5A).
- ☐ Battery terminal connections loose or corroded (*Weekly checks*).
- ☐ Ignition components damp or damaged – petrol models (Chapters 1A and 5B).
- ☐ Broken, loose or disconnected wiring in the ignition circuit – petrol models (Chapters 1A and 5B).
- ☐ Worn, faulty or incorrectly gapped spark plugs – petrol models (Chapter 1A).
- ☐ Fuel injection system fault (Chapter 4A and 4B).
- ☐ Air in fuel system – diesel models (Chapter 4B).
- ☐ Major mechanical failure (e.g. timing belt) (Chapter 2A, 2B, 2C or 2D).

Engine difficult to start when cold

- ☐ Battery discharged (Chapter 5A).
- ☐ Battery terminal connections loose or corroded (*Weekly checks*).
- ☐ Worn, faulty or incorrectly gapped spark plugs – petrol models (Chapter 1A).
- ☐ Fuel injection system fault (Chapter 4A and 4B).
- ☐ Other ignition system fault – petrol models (Chapters 1A and 5B).
- ☐ Preheating system fault – diesel models (Chapter 5C).
- ☐ Low cylinder compressions (Chapter 2A, 2B, 2C or 2D).

Engine difficult to start when hot

- ☐ Air filter element dirty or clogged (Chapter 1A or 1B).
- ☐ Fuel injection system fault (Chapter 4A and 4B).
- ☐ Low cylinder compressions (Chapter 2A, 2B, 2C or 2D).

Starter motor noisy or excessively rough in engagement

- ☐ Starter pinion or flywheel ring gear teeth loose or broken (Chapters 2A, 2B, 2C, 2D and 5A).
- ☐ Starter motor mounting bolts loose or missing (Chapter 5A).
- ☐ Starter motor internal components worn or damaged (Chapter 5A).

Engine starts, but stops immediately

- ☐ Loose or faulty electrical connections in the ignition circuit – petrol models (Chapters 1A and 5B).
- ☐ Vacuum leak at the throttle body or inlet manifold – petrol models (Chapter 4A).
- ☐ Blocked injector/fuel injection system fault (Chapter 4A or 4B).
- ☐ Faulty injector(s) – diesel models (Chapter 4B).
- ☐ Air in fuel system – diesel models (Chapter 4B).

Engine idles erratically

- ☐ Air filter element clogged (Chapter 1A or 1B).
- ☐ Vacuum leak at the throttle body, inlet manifold or associated hoses – petrol models (Chapter 4A).
- ☐ Worn, faulty or incorrectly gapped spark plugs – petrol models (Chapter 1A).
- ☐ Uneven or low cylinder compressions (Chapter 2A, 2B, 2C or 2D).
- ☐ Camshaft lobes worn (Chapter 2A, 2B, 2C or 2D).
- ☐ Timing belt incorrectly tensioned (Chapter 2A, 2B, 2C or 2D).
- ☐ Blocked injector/fuel injection system fault (Chapter 4A or 4B).
- ☐ Faulty injector(s) – diesel models (Chapter 4B).

Engine misfires at idle speed

- ☐ Worn, faulty or incorrectly gapped spark plugs – petrol models (Chapter 1A).
- ☐ Vacuum leak at the throttle body, inlet manifold or associated hoses (Chapter 4A or 4B).
- ☐ Blocked injector/fuel injection system fault (Chapter 4A and 4B).
- ☐ Faulty injector(s) – diesel models (Chapter 4B).
- ☐ Uneven or low cylinder compressions (Chapter 2A, 2B, 2C or 2D).
- ☐ Disconnected, leaking, or perished crankcase ventilation hoses (Chapter 4C and 4D).

Engine misfires throughout the driving speed range

- ☐ Fuel filter choked (Chapter 1A or 1B).
- ☐ Fuel pump faulty, or delivery pressure low (Chapter 4A or 4B).
- ☐ Fuel tank vent blocked, or fuel pipes restricted (Chapter 4A or 4B).
- ☐ Vacuum leak at the throttle body, inlet manifold or associated hoses – petrol models (Chapter 4A).
- ☐ Worn, faulty or incorrectly gapped spark plugs – petrol models (Chapter 1A).
- ☐ Faulty injector(s) – diesel models (Chapter 4B).
- ☐ Faulty ignition coil – petrol models (Chapter 5B).
- ☐ Uneven or low cylinder compressions (Chapter 2A, 2B, 2C or 2D).
- ☐ Blocked injector/fuel injection system fault (Chapter 4A or 4B).

Engine (continued)

Engine hesitates on acceleration

- [ ] Worn, faulty or incorrectly gapped spark plugs – petrol models (Chapter 1A)
- [ ] Vacuum leak at the throttle body, inlet manifold or associated hoses – petrol models (Chapter 4A)
- [ ] Blocked injector/fuel injection system fault (Chapter 4A or 4B)
- [ ] Faulty injector(s) – diesel models (Chapter 4B)
- [ ] Incorrect injection pump timing – diesel models (Chapter 4B)

Engine stalls

- [ ] Vacuum leak at the throttle body, inlet manifold or associated hoses – petrol models (Chapter 4A)
- [ ] Fuel filter choked (Chapter 1A or 1B)
- [ ] Fuel pump faulty, or delivery pressure low – petrol models (Chapter 4A)
- [ ] Fuel tank vent blocked, or fuel pipes restricted (Chapter 4A or 4B)
- [ ] Blocked injector/fuel injection system fault (Chapter 4A or 4B)
- [ ] Faulty injector(s) – diesel models (Chapter 4B)
- [ ] Air in fuel system – diesel models (Chapter 4B)

Engine lacks power

- [ ] Timing belt incorrectly fitted or tensioned (Chapter 2A, 2B, 2C or 2D)
- [ ] Fuel filter choked (Chapter 1A or 1B)
- [ ] Fuel pump faulty, or delivery pressure low – petrol models (Chapter 4A)
- [ ] Uneven or low cylinder compressions (Chapter 2A, 2B, 2C or 2D)
- [ ] Worn, faulty or incorrectly gapped spark plugs – petrol models (Chapter 1A)
- [ ] Vacuum leak at the throttle body, inlet manifold or associated hoses – petrol models (Chapter 4A)
- [ ] Blocked injector/fuel injection system fault (Chapter 4A or 4B)
- [ ] Brakes binding (Chapters 1A or 1B and 9)
- [ ] Clutch slipping (Chapter 6)

Engine backfires

- [ ] Timing belt incorrectly fitted or tensioned (Chapter 2A, 2B, 2C or 2D)
- [ ] Vacuum leak at the throttle body, inlet manifold or associated hoses – petrol models (Chapter 4A)
- [ ] Blocked injector/fuel injection system fault (Chapter 4A or 4B)

Oil pressure warning light illuminated with engine running

- [ ] Low oil level, or incorrect oil grade (Weekly checks)
- [ ] Faulty oil pressure warning light switch (Chapter 2A, 2B, 2C or 2D)

- [ ] Worn engine bearings and/or oil pump (Chapter 2A, 2B, 2C or 2D)
- [ ] High engine operating temperature (Chapter 3)
- [ ] Oil pressure relief valve defective (Chapter 2A, 2B, 2C or 2D)
- [ ] Oil pick-up strainer clogged (Chapter 2A, 2B, 2C or 2D)

Engine runs-on after switching off

- [ ] Excessive carbon build-up in engine (Chapter 2A, 2B, 2C or 2D)
- [ ] High engine operating temperature (Chapter 3)
- [ ] Fuel injection system fault – petrol models (Chapter 4A)
- [ ] Faulty stop solenoid – diesel models (Chapter 4B)

Engine noises

Pre-ignition (pinking) or knocking during acceleration or under load

- [ ] Ignition system fault – petrol models (Chapters 1A and 5B)
- [ ] Incorrect grade of spark plug – petrol models (Chapter 1A)
- [ ] Incorrect grade of fuel (Chapter 4A)
- [ ] Vacuum leak at the throttle body, inlet manifold or associated hoses – petrol models (Chapter 4A)
- [ ] Excessive carbon build-up in engine (Chapter 2A, 2B, 2C or 2D)
- [ ] Blocked injector/fuel injection system fault – petrol models (Chapter 4A)

Whistling or wheezing noises

- [ ] Leaking inlet manifold or throttle body gasket – petrol models (Chapter 4A)
- [ ] Leaking exhaust manifold gasket or pipe-to-manifold joint (Chapter 4C or 4D)
- [ ] Leaking vacuum hose (Chapters 4A, 4B, 4C, 4D and 9)
- [ ] Blowing cylinder head gasket (Chapter 2A, 2B, 2C or 2D)

Tapping or rattling noises

- [ ] Worn valve gear or camshaft (Chapter 2A, 2B, 2C or 2D)
- [ ] Ancillary component fault (coolant pump, alternator, etc.) - Chapters 3, 5A, etc.

Knocking or thumping noises

- [ ] Worn big-end bearings (regular heavy knocking, perhaps worsening under load) (Chapter 2E)
- [ ] Worn main bearings (rumbling and knocking, perhaps less under load) (Chapter 2E)
- [ ] Piston slap (most noticeable when cold) (Chapter 2E)
- [ ] Ancillary component fault (coolant pump, alternator, etc.) - Chapters 3, 5A, etc.

Cooling system

Overheating

- [ ] Insufficient coolant in system (Weekly checks)
- [ ] Thermostat faulty (Chapter 3)
- [ ] Radiator core blocked, or grille restricted (Chapter 3)
- [ ] Electric cooling fan or thermoswitch faulty (Chapter 3)
- [ ] Pressure cap faulty (Chapter 3)
- [ ] Ignition system fault – petrol engines (Chapters 1A and 5B)
- [ ] Inaccurate temperature gauge sender unit (Chapter 3)
- [ ] Airlock in cooling system

Overcooling

- [ ] Thermostat faulty (Chapter 3)
- [ ] Inaccurate temperature gauge sender unit (Chapter 3)

External coolant leakage

- [ ] Deteriorated or damaged hoses or hose clips (Chapter 1A or 1B)
- [ ] Radiator core or heater matrix leaking (Chapter 3)
- [ ] Pressure cap faulty (Chapter 3)
- [ ] Water pump seal leaking (Chapter 3)
- [ ] Boiling due to overheating (Chapter 3)
- [ ] Core plug leaking (Chapter 2E)

Internal coolant leakage

- [ ] Leaking cylinder head gasket (Chapter 2A, 2B, 2C or 2D)
- [ ] Cracked cylinder head or cylinder bore (Chapter 2E)

Corrosion

- [ ] Infrequent draining and flushing (Chapter 1A or 1B)
- [ ] Incorrect coolant mixture or inappropriate coolant type (Chapter 1A or 1B)

Fuel and exhaust systems

Excessive fuel consumption

- [ ] Air filter element dirty or clogged (Chapter 1A or 1B).
- [ ] Fuel injection system fault (Chapter 4A or 4B).
- [ ] Ignition system fault – petrol models (Chapters 1A and 5B).
- [ ] Faulty injector(s) – diesel models (Chapter 4B).
- [ ] Tyres under-inflated (*Weekly checks*).

Fuel leakage and/or fuel odour

- [ ] Damaged or corroded fuel tank, pipes or connections (Chapter 4A or 4B).
- [ ] Excessive noise or fumes from exhaust system (Chapters 4C or 4D)
- [ ] Leaking exhaust system or manifold joints (Chapters 1A, 1B, 4C or 4D).
- [ ] Leaking, corroded or damaged silencers or pipe (Chapters 1A, 1B, 4C or 4D).
- [ ] Broken mountings causing body or suspension contact (Chapter 1A or 1B).

Clutch

Pedal travels to floor – no pressure or very little resistance

- [ ] Hydraulic fluid level low/air in hydraulic system (Chapter 6).
- [ ] Broken clutch release bearing or fork (Chapter 6).
- [ ] Broken diaphragm spring in clutch pressure plate (Chapter 6).

Clutch fails to disengage (unable to select gears)

- [ ] Clutch disc sticking on transmission input shaft splines (Chapter 6).
- [ ] Clutch disc sticking to flywheel or pressure plate (Chapter 6).
- [ ] Faulty pressure plate assembly (Chapter 6).
- [ ] Clutch release mechanism worn or incorrectly assembled (Chapter 6).

Clutch slips (engine speed increases, with no increase in vehicle speed)

- [ ] Clutch disc linings excessively worn (Chapter 6).
- [ ] Clutch disc linings contaminated with oil or grease (Chapter 6).
- [ ] Faulty pressure plate or weak diaphragm spring (Chapter 6).

Judder as clutch is engaged

- [ ] Clutch disc linings contaminated with oil or grease (Chapter 6).
- [ ] Clutch disc linings excessively worn (Chapter 6).
- [ ] Faulty or distorted pressure plate or diaphragm spring (Chapter 6).
- [ ] Worn or loose engine or transmission mountings (Chapter 2A, 2B, 2C or 2D).
- [ ] Clutch disc hub or transmission input shaft splines worn (Chapter 6).

Noise when depressing or releasing clutch pedal

- [ ] Worn clutch release bearing (Chapter 6).
- [ ] Worn or dry clutch pedal bushes (Chapter 6).
- [ ] Faulty pressure plate assembly (Chapter 6).
- [ ] Pressure plate diaphragm spring broken (Chapter 6).
- [ ] Broken clutch disc cushioning springs (Chapter 6).

Manual transmission

Noisy in neutral with engine running

- [ ] Input shaft bearings worn (noise apparent with clutch pedal released, but not when depressed) (Chapter 7A).*
- [ ] Clutch release bearing worn (noise apparent with clutch pedal depressed, possibly less when released) (Chapter 6).

Noisy in one particular gear

- [ ] Worn, damaged or chipped gear teeth (Chapter 7A).*

Difficulty engaging gears

- [ ] Clutch fault (Chapter 6).
- [ ] Worn or damaged gear linkage (Chapter 7A).
- [ ] Incorrectly adjusted gear linkage (Chapter 7A).
- [ ] Worn synchroniser units (Chapter 7A).*

Vibration

- [ ] Lack of oil (Chapter 1A or 1B).
- [ ] Worn bearings (Chapter 7A).*

Jumps out of gear

- [ ] Worn or damaged gear linkage (Chapter 7A).
- [ ] Incorrectly adjusted gear linkage (Chapter 7A).
- [ ] Worn synchroniser units (Chapter 7A).*
- [ ] Worn selector forks (Chapter 7A).*

Lubricant leaks

- [ ] Leaking differential output oil seal (Chapter 7A).
- [ ] Leaking housing joint (Chapter 7A).*
- [ ] Leaking input shaft oil seal (Chapter 7A).*

* Although the corrective action necessary to remedy the symptoms described is beyond the scope of the home mechanic, the above information should be helpful in isolating the cause of the condition. This should enable the owner can communicate clearly with a professional mechanic.

Automatic/DSG transmission

Note: *Due to the complexity of the automatic transmission, it is difficult for the home mechanic to properly diagnose and service this unit. For problems other than the following, the vehicle should be taken to a dealer service department or automatic transmission specialist. Do not be too hasty in removing the transmission if a fault is suspected, as most of the testing is carried out with the unit still fitted.*

Fluid leakage

☐ Automatic transmission fluid is usually dark in colour. Fluid leaks should not be confused with engine oil, which can easily be blown onto the transmission by airflow.

☐ To determine the source of a leak, first remove all built-up dirt and grime from the transmission housing and surrounding areas using a degreasing agent, or by steam-cleaning. Drive the vehicle at low speed, so airflow will not blow the leak far from its source. Raise and support the vehicle, and determine where the leak is coming from.

General gear selection problems

☐ Chapter 7B deals with checking and adjusting the selector cable on automatic/DSG transmissions. The following are common problems which may be caused by a poorly-adjusted cable:

a) Engine starting in gears other than Park or Neutral.

b) Indicator panel indicating a gear other than the one actually being used.

c) Vehicle moves when in Park or Neutral.

d) Poor gear shift quality or erratic gearchanges.

Transmission fluid brown, or has burned smell

☐ Transmission fluid level low (Chapter 1A or 1B). If the fluid appears to have deteriorated badly it is recommended that it is renewed.

Engine will not start in any gear, or starts in gears other than Park or Neutral

☐ Incorrect selector cable adjustment (Chapter 7B).

Transmission slips, shifts roughly, is noisy, or has no drive in forward or reverse gears

☐ There are many probable causes for the above problems, but unless there is a very obvious reason (such as a loose or corroded wiring plug connection on or near the transmission), the car should be taken to a franchise dealer for the fault to be diagnosed. The transmission control unit incorporates a self-diagnosis facility, and any fault codes can quickly be read and interpreted by a dealer with the proper diagnostic equipment.

Driveshafts

Clicking or knocking noise on turns (at slow speed on full-lock)

☐ Lack of constant velocity joint lubricant, possibly due to damaged gaiter (Chapter 8).

☐ Worn outer constant velocity joint (Chapter 8).
☐ Vibration when accelerating or decelerating
☐ Worn inner constant velocity joint (Chapter 8).
☐ Bent or distorted driveshaft (Chapter 8).

Braking system

Note: *Before assuming that a brake problem exists, make sure that the tyres are in good condition and correctly inflated, that the front wheel alignment is correct, and that the vehicle is not loaded with weight in an unequal manner. Apart from checking the condition of all pipe and hose connections, any faults occurring on the anti-lock braking system should be referred to a VW dealer for diagnosis.*

Vehicle pulls to one side under braking

☐ Worn, defective, damaged or contaminated brake pads on one side (Chapters 1A or 1B and 9).
☐ Seized or partially seized brake caliper piston (Chapters 1A or 1B and 9).
☐ A mixture of brake pad lining materials fitted between sides (Chapters 1A or 1B and 9).
☐ Brake caliper mounting bolts loose (Chapter 9).
☐ Worn or damaged steering or suspension components (Chapters 1A or 1B and 10).

Noise (grinding or high-pitched squeal) when brakes applied)

☐ Brake pad friction lining material worn down to metal backing (Chapters 1A or 1B and 9).
☐ Excessive corrosion of brake disc. This may be apparent after the vehicle has been standing for some time (Chapters 1A or 1B and 9).
☐ Foreign object (stone chipping, etc.) trapped between brake disc and shield (Chapters 1A or 1B and 9).

Brakes binding

☐ Seized brake caliper piston(s) (Chapter 9).
☐ Incorrectly adjusted handbrake mechanism (Chapter 9).
☐ Faulty master cylinder (Chapter 9).

Excessive brake pedal travel

☐ Faulty master cylinder (Chapter 9).

☐ Air in hydraulic system (Chapters 1A or 1B and 9).
☐ Faulty vacuum servo unit (Chapter 9).

Brake pedal feels spongy when depressed

☐ Air in hydraulic system (Chapters 1A or 1B and 9).
☐ Deteriorated flexible rubber brake hoses (Chapters 1A or 1B and 9).
☐ Master cylinder mounting nuts loose (Chapter 9).
☐ Faulty master cylinder (Chapter 9).

Excessive brake pedal effort required to stop vehicle

☐ Faulty vacuum servo unit (Chapter 9).
☐ Faulty brake vacuum pump – diesel models (Chapter 9).
☐ Disconnected, damaged or insecure brake servo vacuum hose (Chapter 9).
☐ Primary or secondary hydraulic circuit failure (Chapter 9).
☐ Seized brake caliper piston(s) (Chapter 9).
☐ Brake pads incorrectly fitted (Chapters 1A or 1B and 9).
☐ Incorrect grade of brake pads fitted (Chapters 1A or 1B and 9).
☐ Brake pads contaminated (Chapters 1A or 1B and 9).

Judder felt through brake pedal or steering wheel when braking

☐ Excessive run-out or distortion of discs (Chapters 1A or 1B and 9).
☐ Brake pad worn (Chapters 1A or 1B and 9).
☐ Brake caliper mounting bolts loose (Chapter 9).
☐ Wear in suspension or steering components or mountings (Chapters 1A or 1B and 10).

Rear wheels locking under normal braking

☐ Rear brake pads contaminated (Chapters 1A or 1B and 9).
☐ ABS system fault (Chapter 9).

Suspension and steering

Note: *Before diagnosing suspension or steering faults, be sure that the trouble is not due to incorrect tyre pressures, mixtures of tyre types, or binding brakes.*

Vehicle pulls to one side

- [ ] Defective tyre (*Weekly checks*).
- [ ] Excessive wear in suspension or steering components (Chapters 1A or 1B and 10).
- [ ] Incorrect front wheel alignment (Chapter 10).
- [ ] Accident damage to steering or suspension components (Chapter 1A or 1B and 10).

Excessive pitching and/or rolling around corners, or during braking

- [ ] Defective shock absorbers (Chapters 1A or 1B and 10).
- [ ] Broken or weak spring and/or suspension component (Chapters 1A or 1B and 10).
- [ ] Worn or damaged anti-roll bar or mountings – where applicable (Chapter 10).

Lack of power assistance

- [ ] Faulty rack-and-pinion steering gear (Chapter 10).

Wandering or general instability

- [ ] Incorrect front wheel alignment (Chapter 10).
- [ ] Worn steering or suspension joints, bushes or components (Chapters 1A or 1B and 10).
- [ ] Roadwheels out of balance (Chapters 1A or 1B and 10).
- [ ] Faulty or damaged tyre (*Weekly checks*).
- [ ] Wheel bolts loose (refer to Chapters 1A or 1B and 10 for correct torque).
- [ ] Defective shock absorbers (Chapters 1A or 1B and 10).

Excessively stiff steering

- [ ] Lack of steering gear lubricant (Chapter 10).
- [ ] Seized track rod end balljoint or suspension balljoint Chapters 1A or 1B and 10).
- [ ] Incorrect front wheel alignment (Chapter 10).
- [ ] Steering rack or column bent or damaged (Chapter 10).

Excessive play in steering

- [ ] Worn steering column intermediate shaft universal joint (Chapter 10).
- [ ] Worn steering track rod end balljoints (Chapters 1A or 1B and 10).
- [ ] Worn rack-and-pinion steering gear (Chapter 10).
- [ ] Worn steering or suspension joints, bushes or components (Chapters 1A or 1B and 10).

Wheel wobble and vibration

- [ ] Front roadwheels out of balance (vibration felt mainly through the steering wheel) (Chapters 1A or 1B and 10).
- [ ] Rear roadwheels out of balance (vibration felt throughout the vehicle) (Chapters 1A or 1B and 10).
- [ ] Roadwheels damaged or distorted (Chapters 1A or 1B and 10).
- [ ] Faulty or damaged tyre (*Weekly checks*).
- [ ] Worn steering or suspension joints, bushes or components (Chapters 1A or 1B and 10).
- [ ] Wheel bolts loose (Chapter 10).

Tyre wear excessive

Tyres worn on inside or outside edges

- [ ] Tyres under-inflated (wear on both edges) (*Weekly checks*).
- [ ] Incorrect camber or castor angles (wear on one edge only) (Chapter 10).
- [ ] Worn steering or suspension joints, bushes or components (Chapters 1A or 1B and 10).
- [ ] Excessively hard cornering.
- [ ] Accident damage.

Tyre treads exhibit feathered edges

- [ ] Incorrect toe setting (Chapter 10).

Tyres worn in centre of tread

- [ ] Tyres over-inflated (*Weekly checks*).

Tyres worn on inside and outside edges

- [ ] Tyres under-inflated (*Weekly checks*).

Tyres worn unevenly

- [ ] Tyres/wheels out of balance (Chapter 1A, 1B or 10).
- [ ] Excessive wheel or tyre run-out (Chapter 1A, 1B or 10).
- [ ] Worn shock absorbers (Chapters 1A or 1B and 10).
- [ ] Faulty tyre (*Weekly checks*).

Electrical system

Note: *For problems associated with the starting system, refer to the faults listed under 'Engine' earlier in this Section.*

Battery will not hold a charge for more than a few days

- [ ] Battery defective internally (Chapter 5A).
- [ ] Battery terminal connections loose or corroded (*Weekly checks*).
- [ ] Auxiliary drivebelt worn or incorrectly adjusted (Chapter 1A or 1B).
- [ ] Alternator not charging at correct output (Chapter 5A).
- [ ] Alternator or voltage regulator faulty (Chapter 5A).
- [ ] Short-circuit causing continual battery drain (Chapters 5A and 12).

Ignition/no-charge warning light remains illuminated with engine running

- [ ] Auxiliary drivebelt broken, worn, or incorrectly adjusted (Chapter 1A or 1B).
- [ ] Alternator brushes worn, sticking, or dirty (Chapter 5A).
- [ ] Alternator brush springs weak or broken (Chapter 5A).
- [ ] Internal fault in alternator or voltage regulator (Chapter 5A).
- [ ] Broken, disconnected, or loose wiring in charging circuit (Chapter 5A).

Electrical system (continued)

Ignition/no-charge warning light fails to come on

- ☐ Warning light LED defective (Chapter 12).
- ☐ Broken, disconnected, or loose wiring in warning light circuit (Chapter 12).
- ☐ Alternator faulty (Chapter 5A).

Lights inoperative

- ☐ Bulb blown or LED unit faulty (Chapter 12).
- ☐ Corrosion of bulb or bulbholder contacts (Chapter 12).
- ☐ Blown fuse (Chapter 12).
- ☐ Faulty relay (Chapter 12).
- ☐ Broken, loose, or disconnected wiring (Chapter 12).
- ☐ Faulty switch (Chapter 12).

Instrument readings inaccurate or erratic

Fuel or temperature gauges give no reading

- ☐ Faulty gauge sender unit (Chapters 3, 4A or 4B).
- ☐ Wiring open-circuit (Chapter 12).
- ☐ Faulty gauge (Chapter 12).

Fuel or temperature gauges give continuous maximum reading

- ☐ Faulty gauge sender unit (Chapters 3, 4A or 4B).
- ☐ Wiring short-circuit (Chapter 12).
- ☐ Faulty gauge (Chapter 12).

Horn inoperative, or unsatisfactory in operation

Horn operates all the time

- ☐ Horn push either earthed or stuck down (Chapter 12).
- ☐ Horn cable-to-horn push earthed (Chapter 12).

Horn fails to operate

- ☐ Blown fuse (Chapter 12).
- ☐ Cable or cable connections loose, broken or disconnected (Chapter 12).
- ☐ Faulty horn (Chapter 12).

Horn emits intermittent or unsatisfactory sound

- ☐ Cable connections loose (Chapter 12).
- ☐ Horn mountings loose (Chapter 12).
- ☐ Faulty horn (Chapter 12).

Windscreen/tailgate wipers inoperative, or unsatisfactory in operation

Wipers fail to operate, or operate very slowly

- ☐ Bonnet not closed (built-into the electronic control system) (Chapter 12).
- ☐ Wiper blades stuck to screen, or linkage seized or binding (*Weekly checks* and Chapter 12).
- ☐ Blown fuse (Chapter 12).
- ☐ Cable or cable connections loose, broken or disconnected (Chapter 12).
- ☐ Faulty relay (Chapter 12).
- ☐ Faulty wiper motor (Chapter 12).

Wiper blades sweep over too large or too small an area of the glass

- ☐ Wiper arms incorrectly positioned on spindles (Chapter 12).
- ☐ Excessive wear of wiper linkage (Chapter 12).
- ☐ Wiper motor or linkage mountings loose or insecure (Chapter 12).

Wiper blades fail to clean the glass effectively

- ☐ Wiper blade rubbers worn or perished (*Weekly checks*).
- ☐ Wiper arm tension springs broken, or arm pivots seized (Chapter 12).
- ☐ Insufficient windscreen washer additive to adequately remove road film (*Weekly checks*).

Windscreen/tailgate washers inoperative, or unsatisfactory in operation

One or more washer jets inoperative

- ☐ Blocked washer jet (Chapter 1A or 1B).
- ☐ Disconnected, kinked or restricted fluid hose (Chapter 12).
- ☐ Insufficient fluid in washer reservoir (Chapter 1A or 1B).

Washer pump fails to operate

- ☐ Broken or disconnected wiring or connections (Chapter 12).
- ☐ Blown fuse (Chapter 12).
- ☐ Faulty washer switch (Chapter 12).
- ☐ Faulty washer pump (Chapter 12).

Electric windows inoperative, or unsatisfactory in operation

Window glass will only move in one direction

- ☐ Faulty switch (Chapter 12).

Window glass slow to move

- ☐ Regulator seized or damaged, or in need of lubrication (Chapter 11).
- ☐ Door internal components or trim fouling regulator (Chapter 11).
- ☐ Faulty motor (Chapter 11).

Window glass fails to move

- ☐ Blown fuse (Chapter 12).
- ☐ Faulty relay (Chapter 12).
- ☐ Broken or disconnected wiring or connections (Chapter 12).
- ☐ Faulty motor (Chapter 11).

Central locking system inoperative, or unsatisfactory in operation

Complete system failure

- ☐ Blown fuse (Chapter 12).
- ☐ Faulty relay (Chapter 12).
- ☐ Broken or disconnected wiring or connections (Chapter 12).
- ☐ Faulty control unit (Chapter 11).

Latch locks but will not unlock, or unlocks but will not lock

- ☐ Faulty control unit (Chapter 11).
- ☐ Broken or disconnected latch operating rods or levers (Chapter 11).
- ☐ Faulty relay (Chapter 12).

One actuator fails to operate

- ☐ Broken or disconnected wiring or connections (Chapter 12).
- ☐ Faulty actuator (Chapter 11).
- ☐ Broken, binding or disconnected latch operating rods or levers (Chapter 11).
- ☐ Fault in door lock (Chapter 11).

Note: *References throughout this index are in the form* **"Chapter number"** • **"Page number"**. *So, for example, 2C•15 refers to page 15 of Chapter 2C.*

*Note: References throughout this index are in the form "**Chapter number**" • "**Page number**". So, for example, 2C•15 refers to page 15 of Chapter 2C.*

Note: *References throughout this index are in the form* **"Chapter number"** • **"Page number".** *So, for example, 2C•15 refers to page 15 of Chapter 2C.*

Note: *References throughout this index are in the form* **"Chapter number"** • **"Page number"**. *So, for example, 2C•15 refers to page 15 of Chapter 2C.*

Haynes Manuals – The Complete UK Car List

Title	Book No.
ALFA ROMEO Alfasud/Sprint (74 - 88) up to F *	0292
Alfa Romeo Alfetta (73 – 87) up to E *	0531
AUDI 80, 90 & Coupe Petrol (79 – Nov 88) up to F	0605
Audi 80, 90 & Coupe Petrol (Oct 86 – 90) D to H	1491
Audi 100 & A6 Petrol & Diesel (May 91 – May 97) H to P	3504
Audi A3 Petrol & Diesel (96 – May 03) P to 03	4253
Audi A3 Petrol & Diesel (June 03 – Mar 08) 03 to 08	4884
Audi A4 Petrol & Diesel (95 – 00) M to X	3575
Audi A4 Petrol & Diesel (01 – 04) X to 54	4609
Audi A4 Petrol & Diesel (Jan 05 – Feb 08) 54 to 57	4885
AUSTIN A35 & A40 (56 – 67) up to F *	0118
Mini (59 – 69) up to H *	0527
Mini (69 – 01) up to X	0646
Austin Healey 100/6 & 3000 (56 – 68) up to G *	0049
BEDFORD/Vauxhall Rascal & Suzuki Supercarry (86 – Oct 94) C to M	3015
BMW 1-Series 4-cyl Petrol & Diesel (04 – Aug 11) 54 to 11	4918
BMW 316, 320 & 320i (4-cyl)(75 – Feb 83) up to Y *	0276
BMW 3- & 5- Series Petrol (81 – 91) up to J	1948
BMW 3-Series Petrol (Apr 91 – 99) H to V	3210
BMW 3-Series Petrol (Sept 98 – 06) S to 56	4067
BMW 3-Series Petrol & Diesel (05 – Sept 08) 54 to 58	4782
BMW 5-Series 6-cyl Petrol (April 96 – Aug 03) N to 03	4151
BMW 5-Series Diesel (Sept 03 – 10) 53 to 10	4901
BMW 1500, 1502, 1600, 1602, 2000 & 2002 (59 – 77) up to S *	0240
CHRYSLER PT Cruiser Petrol (00-09) W to 09	4058
CITROEN 2CV, Ami & Dyane (67 – 90) up to H	0196
Citroen AX Petrol & Diesel (87- 97) D to P	3014
Citroen Berlingo & Peugeot Partner Petrol & Diesel (96 – 10) P to 60	4281
Citroen C1 Petrol (05 – 11) 05 to 11	4922
Citroen C3 Petrol & Diesel (02 – 09) 51 to 59	4890
Citroen C4 Petrol & Diesel (04 – 10) 54 to 60	5576
Citroen C5 Petrol & Diesel (01 – 08) Y to 08	4745
Citroen C15 Van Petrol & Diesel (89 – Oct 98) F to S	3509
Citroen CX Petrol (75 – 88) up to F	0528
Citroen Saxo Petrol & Diesel (96 – 04) N to 54	3506
Citroen Visa Petrol (79 – 88) up to F	0620
Citroen Xantia Petrol & Diesel (93 – 01) K to Y	3082
Citroen XM Petrol & Diesel (89 – 00) G to X	3451
Citroen Xsara Petrol & Diesel (97 – Sept 00) R to W	3751
Citroen Xsara Picasso Petrol & Diesel (00 – 02) W to 52	3944
Citroen Xsara Picasso (Mar 04 – 08) 04 to 58	4784
Citroen ZX Diesel (91 – 98) J to S	1922
Citroen ZX Petrol (91 – 98) H to S	1881
FIAT 126 (73 – 87) up to E *	0305
Fiat 500 (57 – 73) up to M *	0090
Fiat 500 & Panda (04 – 12) 53 to 61	5558
Fiat Bravo & Brava Petrol (95 – 00) N to W	3572
Fiat Cinquecento (93 – 98) K to R	3501
Fiat Panda (81 – 95) up to M	0793
Fiat Punto Petrol & Diesel (94 – Oct 99) L to V	3251
Fiat Punto Petrol (Oct 99 – July 03) V to 03	4066
Fiat Punto Petrol (03 – 07) 03 to 07	4746

Title	Book No.
Fiat Punto Petrol (Oct 99 – 07) V to 07	5634
Fiat X1/9 (74 – 89) up to G *	0273
FORD Anglia (59 – 68) up to G *	0001
Ford Capri II (& III) 1.6 & 2.0 (74 – 87) up to E *	0283
Ford Capri II (& III) 2.8 & 3.0 V6 (74 – 87) up to E	1309
Ford C-Max Petrol & Diesel (03 – 10) 53 to 60	4900
Ford Escort Mk I 1100 & 1300 (68 – 74) up to N *	0171
Ford Escort Mk I Mexico, RS 1600 & RS 2000 (70 – 74) up to N *	0139
Ford Escort Mk II Mexico, RS 1800 & RS 2000 (75 – 80) up to W *	0735
Ford Escort (75 – Aug 80) up to V *	0280
Ford Escort Petrol (Sept 80 – Sept 90) up to H	0686
Ford Escort & Orion Petrol (Sept 90 – 00) H to X	1737
Ford Escort & Orion Diesel (Sept 90 – 00) H to X	4081
Ford Fiesta Petrol (Feb 89 – Oct 95) F to N	1595
Ford Fiesta Petrol & Diesel (Oct 95 – Mar 02) N to 02	3397
Ford Fiesta Petrol & Diesel (Apr 02 – 08) 02 to 58	4170
Ford Fiesta Petrol & Diesel (08 – 11) 58 to 11	4907
Ford Focus Petrol & Diesel (98 – 01) S to Y	3759
Ford Focus Petrol & Diesel (Oct 01 – 05) 51 to 05	4167
Ford Focus Petrol (05 – 09) 54 to 09	4785
Ford Focus Diesel (05 – 09) 54 to 09	4807
Ford Fusion Petrol & Diesel (02 – 11) 02 to 61	5566
Ford Galaxy Petrol & Diesel (95 – Aug 00) M to W	3984
Ford Galaxy Petrol & Diesel (00 – 06) X to 06	5556
Ford Granada Petrol (Sept 77 – Feb 85) up to B *	0481
Ford Ka (96 – 08) P to 58	5567
Ford Mondeo Petrol (93 – Sept 00) K to X	1923
Ford Mondeo Petrol & Diesel (Oct 00 – Jul 03) X to 03	3990
Ford Mondeo Petrol & Diesel (July 03 – 07) 03 to 56	4619
Ford Mondeo Petrol & Diesel (Apr 07 – 12) 07 to 61	5548
Ford Mondeo Diesel (93 – Sept 00) L to X	3465
Ford Sierra V6 Petrol (82 – 91) up to J	0904
Ford Transit Connect Diesel (02 – 11) 02 to 11	4903
Ford Transit Diesel (Feb 86 – 99) C to T	3019
Ford Transit Diesel (00 – Oct 06) X to 56	4775
Ford 1.6 & 1.8 litre Diesel Engine (84 – 96) A to N	1172
HILLMAN Imp (63 – 76) up to R *	0022
HONDA Civic (Feb 84 – Oct 87) A to E	1226
Honda Civic (Nov 91 – 96) J to N	3199
Honda Civic Petrol (Mar 95 – 00) M to X	4050
Honda Civic Petrol & Diesel (01 – 05) X to 55	4611
Honda CR-V Petrol & Diesel (02 – 06) 51 to 56	4747
Honda Jazz (02 to 08) 51 to 58	4735
JAGUAR E-Type (61 – 72) up to L *	0140
Jaguar Mk I & II, 240 & 340 (55 – 69) up to H *	0098
Jaguar XJ6, XJ & Sovereign, Daimler Sovereign (68 – Oct 86) up to D	0242
Jaguar XJ6 & Sovereign (Oct 86 – Sept 94) D to M	3261
Jaguar XJ12, XJS & Sovereign, Daimler Double Six (72 – 88) up to F	0478
JEEP Cherokee Petrol (93 – 96) K to N	1943
LAND ROVER 90, 110 & Defender Diesel (83 – 07) up to 56	3017
Land Rover Discovery Petrol & Diesel (89 – 98) G to S	3016

Title	Book No.
Land Rover Discovery Diesel (Nov 98 – Jul 04) S to 04	4606
Land Rover Discovery Diesel (Aug 04 – Apr 09) 04 to 09	5562
Land Rover Freelander Petrol & Diesel (97 – Sept 03) R to 53	3929
Land Rover Freelander (97 – Oct 06) R to 56	5571
Land Rover Series II, IIA & III 4-cyl Petrol (58 – 85) up to C	0314
Land Rover Series II, IIA & III Petrol & Diesel (58 – 85) up to C	5568
MAZDA 323 (Mar 81 – Oct 89) up to G	1608
Mazda 323 (Oct 89 – 98) G to R	3455
Mazda B1600, B1800 & B2000 Pick-up Petrol (72 – 88) up to F	0267
Mazda MX-5 (89 – 05) G to 05	5565
Mazda RX-7 (79 – 85) up to C *	0460
MERCEDES-BENZ 190, 190E & 190D Petrol & Diesel (83 – 93) A to L	3450
Mercedes-Benz 200D, 240D, 240TD, 300D & 300TD 123 Series Diesel (Oct 76 – 85) up to C	1114
Mercedes-Benz 250 & 280 (68 – 72) up to L *	0346
Mercedes-Benz 250 & 280 123 Series Petrol (Oct 76 – 84) up to B *	0677
Mercedes-Benz 124 Series Petrol & Diesel (85 – Aug 93) C to K	3253
Mercedes-Benz A-Class Petrol & Diesel (98 – 04) S to 54	4748
Mercedes-Benz C-Class Petrol & Diesel (93 – Aug 00) L to W	3511
Mercedes-Benz C-Class (00 – 07) X to 07	4780
Mercedes-Benz Sprinter Diesel (95 – Apr 06) M to 06	4902
MGA (55 – 62)	0475
MGB (62 – 80) up to W	0111
MGB 1962 to 1980 (special edition) *	4894
MG Midget & Austin-Healey Sprite (58 – 80) up to W *	0265
MINI Petrol (July 01 – 06) Y to 56	4273
MINI Petrol & Diesel (Nov 06 – 13) 56 to 13	4904
MITSUBISHI Shogun & L200 Pick-ups Petrol (83 – 94) up to M	1944
MORRIS Minor 100C (56 – 71) up to K	0024
NISSAN Almera Petrol (95 – Feb 00) N to V	4053
Nissan Almera & Tino Petrol (Feb 00 – 07) V to 56	4612
Nissan Micra (83 – Jan 93) up to K	0931
Nissan Micra (93 – 02) K to 52	3254
Nissan Micra Petrol (03 – Oct 10) 52 to 60	4734
Nissan Primera Petrol (90 – Aug 99) H to T	1851
Nissan Qashqai Petrol & Diesel (07 – 12) 56 to 62	5610
OPEL Ascona & Manta (B-Series) (Sept 75 – 88) up to F *	0316
Opel Ascona Petrol (81 – 88)	3215
Opel Ascona Petrol (Oct 91 – Feb 98)	3156
Opel Corsa Petrol (83 – Mar 93)	3160
Opel Corsa Petrol (Mar 93 – 97)	3159
Opel Kadett Petrol (Oct 84 – Oct 91)	3196
Opel Omega & Senator Petrol (Nov 86 – 94)	3157
Opel Vectra Petrol (Oct 88 – Oct 95)	3158
PEUGEOT 106 Petrol & Diesel (91 – 04) J to 53)	1882
Peugeot 107 Petrol (05 – 11) 05 to 11	4923
Peugeot 205 Petrol (83 – 97) A to P	0932
Peugeot 206 Petrol & Diesel (98 – 01) S to X	3757

* Classic reprint

Title	Book No.
Peugeot 206 Petrol & Diesel (02 – 06) 51 to 06	4613
Peugeot 207 Petrol & Diesel (06 – July 09) 06 to 09	4787
Peugeot 306 Petrol & Diesel (93 – 02) K to 02	3073
Peugeot 307 Petrol & Diesel (01 – 08) Y to 58	4147
Peugeot 308 Petrol & Diesel (07 – 12) 07 to 12	5561
Peugeot 405 Diesel (88 – 97) E to P	3198
Peugeot 406 Petrol & Diesel (96 – Mar 99) N to T	3394
Peugeot 406 Petrol & Diesel (Mar 99 – 02) T to 52	3982
Peugeot 407 Diesel (04 -11) 53 to 11	5550
PORSCHE 911 (65 – 85) up to C	0264
Porsche 924 & 924 Turbo (76 – 85) up to C	0397
RANGE ROVER V8 Petrol (70 – Oct 92) up to K	0606
RELIANT Robin & Kitten (73 – 83) up to A *	0436
RENAULT 4 (61 – 86) up to D *	0072
Renault 5 Petrol (Feb 85 – 96) B to N	1219
Renault 19 Petrol (89 – 96) F to N	1646
Renault Clio Petrol (91 – May 98) H to R	1853
Renault Clio Petrol & Diesel (May 98 – May 01) R to Y	3906
Renault Clio Petrol & Diesel (June 01 – 05) Y to 55	4168
Renault Clio Petrol & Diesel (Oct 05 – May 09) 55 to 09	4788
Renault Espace Petrol & Diesel (85 – 96) C to N	3197
Renault Laguna Petrol & Diesel (94 – 00) L to W	3252
Renault Laguna Petrol & Diesel (Feb 01 – May 07) X to 07	4283
Renault Megane & Scenic Petrol & Diesel (96 – 99) N to T	3395
Renault Megane & Scenic Petrol & Diesel (Apr 99 – 02) T to 52	3916
Renault Megane Petrol & Diesel (Oct 02 – 08) 52 to 58	4284
Renault Scenic Petrol & Diesel (Sept 03 – 06) 53 to 06	4297
Renault Trafic Diesel (01 – 11) Y to 11	5551
ROVER 216 & 416 Petrol (89 – 96) G to N	1830
Rover 211, 214, 216, 218 & 220 Petrol & Diesel (Dec 95 – 99) N to V	3399
Rover 25 & MG ZR Petrol & Diesel (Oct 99 – 06) V to 06	4145
Rover 414, 416 & 420 Petrol & Diesel (May 95 – 99) M to V	3453
Rover 45 / MG ZS Petrol & Diesel (99 – 05) V to 55	4384
Rover 618, 620 & 623 Petrol (93 – 97) K to P	3257
Rover 75 / MG ZT Petrol & Diesel (99 – 06) S to 06	4292
Rover 820, 825 & 827 Petrol (86 – 95) D to N	1380
Rover 3500 (76 – 87) up to E *	0365
Rover Metro, 111 & 114 Petrol (May 90 – 98) G to S	1711
SAAB 95 & 96 (66 – 76) up to R *	0198
Saab 90, 99 & 900 (79 – Oct 93) up to L	0765
Saab 900 (Oct 93 – 98) L to R	3512
Saab 9000 4-cyl (85 – 98) C to S	1686
Saab 9-3 Petrol & Diesel (98 – Aug 02) R to 02	4614
Saab 9-3 Petrol & Diesel (92 – 07) 52 to 57	4749
Saab 9-3 Petrol & Diesel (07-on) 57 on	5569
Saab 9-5 4-cyl Petrol (97 – 05) R to 55	4156
Saab 9-5 (Sep 05 – Jun 10) 55 to 10	4891
SEAT Ibiza & Cordoba Petrol & Diesel (Oct 93 – Oct 99) L to V	3571
Seat Ibiza & Malaga Petrol (85 – 92) B to K	1609
Seat Ibiza & Diesel (May 02 – Apr 08) 02 to 08	4889

Title	Book No.
SKODA Fabia Petrol & Diesel (00 – 06) W to 06	4376
Skoda Felicia Petrol & Diesel (95 – 01) M to X	3505
Skoda Octavia Petrol (98 – April 04) R to 04	4285
Skoda Octavia Diesel (May 04 – 12) 04 to 61	5549
SUBARU 1600 & 1800 (Nov 79 – 90) up to H *	0995
SUNBEAM Alpine, Rapier & H120 (68 – 74) up to N *	0051
SUZUKI SJ Series, Samurai & Vitara 4-cyl Petrol (82 – 97) up to P	1942
Suzuki Supercarry & Bedford/Vauxhall Rascal (86 – Oct 94) C to M	3015
TOYOTA Avensis Petrol (98 – Jan 03) R to 52	4264
Toyota Aygo Petrol (05 – 11) 05 to 11	4921
Toyota Carina E Petrol (May 92 – 97) J to P	3256
Toyota Corolla (80 – 85) up to C	0683
Toyota Corolla (Sept 83 – Sept 87) A to E	1024
Toyota Corolla (Sept 87 – Aug 92) E to K	1683
Toyota Corolla Petrol (Aug 92 – 97) K to P	3259
Toyota Corolla Petrol (July 97 0 Feb 02) P to 51	4286
Toyota Corolla Petrol & Diesel (02 – Jan 07) 51 to 56	4791
Toyota Hi-Ace & Hi-Lux Petrol (69 – Oct 83) up to A	0304
Toyota RAV4 Petrol & Diesel (94 – 06) L to 55	4750
Toyota Yaris Petrol (99 – 05) T to 05	4265
TRIUMPH GT6 & Vitesse (62 0 74) up to N *	0112
Triumph Herald (59 – 71) up to K *	0010
Triumph Spitfire (62 – 81) up to X	0113
Triumph Stag (70 – 78) up to T *	0441
Triumph TR2, TR3, TR3A, TR4 & TR4A (52 – 67) up to F *	0028
Triumph TR5 & TR6 (67 – 75) up to P *	0031
Triumph TR7 (75 – 82) up to Y *	0322
VAUXHALL Astra Petrol (Oct 91 – Feb 98) J to R	1832
Vauxhall/Opel Astra & Zafira Petrol (Feb 98 – Apr 04) R to 04	3758
Vauxhall/Opel Astra & Zafira Diesel (Feb 98 – Apr 04) R to 04	3797
Vauxhall/Opel Astra Petrol (04 – 08)	4732
Vauxhall/Opel Astra Diesel (04 – 08)	4733
Vauxhall/Opel Astra Petrol & Diesel (Dec 09 – 13) 59 to 13	5578
Vauxhall/Opel Calibra (90 – 98) G to S	3502
Vauxhall Cavalier Petrol (Oct 88 0 95) F to N	1570
Vauxhall/Opel Corsa Diesel (Mar 93 – Oct 00) K to X	4087
Vauxhall Corsa Petrol (Mar 93 – 97) K to R	1985
Vauxhall/Opel Corsa Petrol (Apr 97 – Oct 00) P to X	3921
Vauxhall/Opel Corsa Petrol & Diesel (Oct 03 – Aug 06) 53 to 06	4617
Vauxhall/Opel Corsa Petrol & Diesel (Sept 06 – 10) 56 to 10	4886
Vauxhall/Opel Corsa Petrol & Diesel (00 – Aug 06) X to 06	5577
Vauxhall/Opel Frontera Petrol & Diesel (91 – Sept 98) J to S	3454
Vauxhall/Opel Insignia Petrol & Diesel (08 – 12) 08 to 61	5563
Vauxhall/Opel Meriva Petrol & Diesel (03 – May 10) 03 to 10	4893
Vauxhall/Opel Omega Petrol (94 – 99) L to T	3510
Vauxhall/Opel Vectra Petrol & Diesel (95 – Feb 99) N to S	3396

Title	Book No.
Vauxhall/Opel Vectra Petrol & Diesel (Mar 99 – May 02) T to 02	3930
Vauxhall/Opel Vectra Petrol & Diesel (June 02 – Sept 05) 02 to 55	4618
Vauxhall/Opel Vectra Petrol & Diesel (Oct 05 – Oct 08) 55 to 58	4887
Vauxhall/Opel Vivaro Diesel (01 – 11) Y to 11	5552
Vauxhall/Opel Zafira Petrol & Diesel (05 -09) 05 to 09	4792
Vauxhall/Opel 1.5, 1.6 & 1.7 litre Diesel Engine (82 – 96) up to N	1222
VW Beetle 1200 (54 – 77) up to S	0036
VW Beetle 1300 & 1500 (65 – 75) up to P	0039
VW 1302 & 1302S (70 – 72) up to L *	0110
VW Beetle 1303, 1303S & GT (72 – 75) up to P	0159
VW Beetle Petrol & Diesel (Apr 99 – 07) T to 57	3798
VW Golf & Jetta Mk 1 Petrol 1.1 & 1.3 (74 – 84) up to A	0716
VW Golf, Jetta & Scirocco Mk 1 Petrol 1.5, 1.6 & 1.8 (74 – 84) up to A	0726
VW Golf & Jetta Mk 1 Diesel (78 – 84) up to A	0451
VW Golf & Jetta Mk 2 Petrol (Mar 84 – Feb 92) A to J	1081
VW Golf & Vento Petrol & Diesel (Feb 92 – Mar 98) J to R	3097
VW Golf & Bora Petrol & Diesel (Apr 98 – 00) R to X	3727
VW Golf & Bora 4-cyl Petrol & Diesel (01 – 03) X to 53	4169
VW Golf & Jetta Petrol & Diesel (04 – 09) 53 to 09	4610
VW LT Petrol Vans & Light Trucks (76 – 87) up to E	0637
VW Passat 4-cyl Petrol & Diesel (May 88 – 96) E to P	3498
VW Passat 4-cyl Petrol & Diesel (Dec 96 – Nov 00) P to X	3917
VW Passat Petrol & Diesel (Dec 00 – May 05) X to 05	4279
VW Passat Diesel (June 05 – 10) 05 to 60	4888
VW Polo Petrol (Nov 90 – Aug 94) H to L	3245
VW Polo Hatchback Petrol & Diesel (94 – 99) M to S	3500
VW Polo Hatchback Petrol (00 – Jan 02) V to 51	4150
VW Polo Petrol & Diesel (02 – May 05) 51 to 05	4608
VW Transporter 1600 (68 – 79) up to V	0082
VW Transporter 1700, 1800 & 2000 (72 – 79) up to V *	0226
VW Transporter (air cooled) Petrol (79 – 82) up to Y *	0638
VW Transporter (water cooled) Petrol (82 – 90) up to H	3452
VW Type 3 (63 – 73) up to M *	0084
VOLVO 120 & 130 Series (& P1800) (61 – 73) up to M *	0203
Volvo 142, 144 & 145 (66 – 74) up to N *	0129
Volvo 240 Series Petrol (74 – 93) up to K	0270
Volvo 440, 460 & 480 Petrol (87 – 97) D to P	1691
Volvo 740 & 760 Petrol (82 – 91) up to J	1258
Volvo 850 Petrol (92 – 96) J to P	3260
Volvo 940 Petrol (90 – 98) H to R	3249
Volvo S40 & V40 Petrol (96 – Mar 04) N to 04	3569
Volvo S40 & V50 Petrol & Diesel (Mar 04 – Jun 07) 04 to 07	4731
Volvo S60 Petrol & Diesel (01 – 08) X to 09	4793
Volvo S70, V70 & C70 Petrol (96 – 99) P to V	3573
Volvo V70 / S80 Petrol & Diesel (98 – 07) S to 07	4263
Volvo V70 Diesel (June 07 – 12) 07 to 61	5557
Volvo XV60 / 90 Diesel (03 – 12) 52 to 62	5630

* Classic reprint

CL 27.08.13

Preserving Our Motoring Heritage

< The Model J Duesenberg Derham Tourster. Only eight of these magnificent cars were ever built – this is the only example to be found outside the United States of America

Almost every car you've ever loved, loathed or desired is gathered under one roof at the Haynes Motor Museum. Over 300 immaculately presented cars and motorbikes represent every aspect of our motoring heritage, from elegant reminders of bygone days, such as the superb Model J Duesenberg to curiosities like the bug-eyed BMW Isetta. There are also many old friends and flames. Perhaps you remember the 1959 Ford Popular that you did your courting in? The magnificent 'Red Collection' is a spectacle of classic sports cars including AC, Alfa Romeo, Austin Healey, Ferrari, Lamborghini, Maserati, MG, Riley, Porsche and Triumph.

A Perfect Day Out

Each and every vehicle at the Haynes Motor Museum has played its part in the history and culture of Motoring. Today, they make a wonderful spectacle and a great day out for all the family. Bring the kids, bring Mum and Dad, but above all bring your camera to capture those golden memories for ever. You will also find an impressive array of motoring memorabilia, a comfortable 70 seat video cinema and one of the most extensive transport book shops in Britain. The Pit Stop Cafe serves everything from a cup of tea to wholesome, home-made meals or, if you prefer, you can enjoy the large picnic area nestled in the beautiful rural surroundings of Somerset.

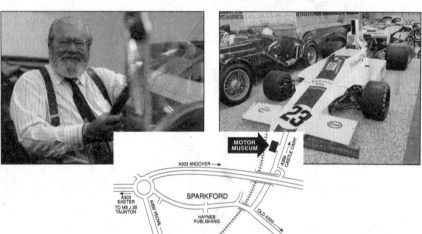

John Haynes O.B.E., > Founder and Chairman of the museum at the wheel of a Haynes Light 12.

< Graham Hill's Lola Cosworth Formula 1 car next to a 1934 Riley Sports.

The Museum is situated on the A359 Yeovil to Frome road at Sparkford, just off the A303 in Somerset. It is about 40 miles south of Bristol, and 25 minutes drive from the M5 intersection at Taunton.
Open 9.30am - 5.30pm (10.00am - 4.00pm Winter) 7 days a week, *except Christmas Day, Boxing Day and New Years Day*
Special rates available for schools, coach parties and outings Charitable Trust No. 292048